The Ultimate

SPANISH
Review and Practice

The *Ultimate*
SPANISH
Review and Practice

MASTERING SPANISH GRAMMAR
FOR CONFIDENT COMMUNICATION

Ronni L. Gordon, Ph.D.
David M. Stillman, Ph.D.

New York Chicago San Francisco Lisbon London Madrid Mexico City
Milan New Delhi San Juan Seoul Singapore Sydney Toronto

The **McGraw·Hill** Companies

Library of Congress Cataloging-in-Publication Data

Gordon, Ronni L.
      The ultimate Spanish review and practice : mastering Spanish grammar
  for confident communication / Ronni L. Gordon and David M. Stillman
        p.   cm. — (The ultimate grammar review and practice)
    Includes index.
    ISBN 0-658-00075-6
      1. Spanish language Textbooks for foreign speakers—English.
    2. Spanish language—Grammar.   I. Series.
    PC4129.E5U58   1999
    468.29421—dc21   99-41090
                                                  CIP

Acknowledgments are on page vi, which is to be considered
an extension of this copyright page.

18 19 20 21 22 23 24 25 26 27 28 29 30 31 32 33 34 35   QPD/QPD   0 9 8

ISBN 978-0-658-00075-1
MHID   0-658-00075-6

Cover design by Jeanette Wojtyla
Cover illustration copyright © Susy Pilgrim Waters

McGraw-Hill books are available at special quantity discounts to use as premiums and sales
promotions or for use in corporate training programs. To contact a representative, please visit the
Contact Us pages at www.mhprofessional.com.

This book is printed on acid-free paper.

PREFACE

The Ultimate Spanish Review and Practice is designed to provide intermediate through advanced learners of Spanish with a powerful tool for review and progress in the language. This book presents clear, concise, and well-organized **grammar explanations** with examples that reflect everyday usage, most often in the form of conversational exchanges. These presentations of structure are easy to understand, and the examples will encourage you to see the study of grammar as a stepping stone to communication.

The **exercises** provide extensive practice with all the grammar topics that learners of Spanish at this level should know. These engaging exercises are contextualized, and the instructions in Spanish help set the scene and prepare you for the task at hand. **Vocabulary boxes** provide a review of the vocabulary common to most first- and second-year Spanish textbooks, as well as additional vocabulary that enhances your ability to express yourself on a variety of topics. Vocabulary presentations are grouped by topic and are integrated with the exercises. Many self-expression exercises are also included to encourage you to use the grammar and vocabulary presented to express your own ideas. Generous verb charts and an index to help locate grammar topics complete the book.

Most chapters have an **Ejercicio oral,** which gives an additional opportunity for communicative expression in person, either with a Spanish-speaking friend or a fellow learner of Spanish. This oral exercise is followed in most chapters by a section called **Estructuras en acción,** a comprehension exercise based on the reading of authentic documents reproduced in the book that contain examples of the grammar topic of the chapter. You will greatly increase your oral and written mastery of structure and vocabulary as you work through these delightful and informative authentic materials taken from a variety of Spanish-language newspapers, periodicals, and advertisements.

Notas culturales are featured in every chapter. These cultural notes enhance the effectiveness of the grammar exercises by providing an authentic Hispanic context in which to practice. To further your progress, we have also included a chapter of **Idioms, expressions, & proverbs** (Chapter 26) and a chapter that aims at helping eliminate some of the most common errors made by English-speaking learners of Spanish, **¡Ojo! Common errors & pitfalls** (Chapter 28).

The Ultimate Spanish Review and Practice bridges grammar practice and communication by emphasizing culture and authentic language use along with structural exercises. It is a uniquely comprehensive, integrated, and engaging review book that will provide you with the solid knowledge needed to increase your confidence in using Spanish to express your own thoughts, to comprehend those of Spanish speakers, and to communicate in both speaking and writing in a wide variety of situations.

Acknowledgments

The publisher wishes to thank the following for permission to reproduce their material:

page 14: "Don Planchón" (*Cambio 16*, Madrid, España; 26 septiembre 1994, No. 1.192, pág. 42).

page 23: Consorcio Transportes, Madrid (España).

page 39: "Tiempos difíciles" (*Cambio 16*, Madrid, España; 23 enero 1995, No. 1.209, pág. 100). "Los jueves, la química del éxito" (*Cambio 16*, Madrid, España; 6 marzo 1995, No. 1.215).

page 55: "¿Dónde está mi violin?" (*Cambio 16*, Madrid, España; 23 enero 1995, No. 1.209, págs. 80–82).

page 73: "Piedra santa" (photo from *Spain 1993*, Ministerio del Portavoz del Gobierno, page 99).

page 85: "Matrimonio—Sí quiero pero menos" (*Cambio 16*, Madrid, España; 20 marzo 1995, No. 1.217, págs. 18, 22).

page 104: "México se asfixia" (*Semana*, Bogotá, Colombia; abril 4–11 de 1995, Edición No. 674, pág. 93).

page 112: "Cursos y conferencias" (*Los Andes*, Mendoza, Argentina; lunes, 3 de abril 1995, pág. 12; año CXIII, no. 38.095). "Universidades" (*Los Andes*, Mendoza, Argentina; lunes, 3 de abril 1995, pág. 8; año CXIII, No. 38.095).

page 125: "La crisis no perdona: Portugal espera menos turistas españoles" (*ABC*, Madrid, España; sábado, 8/IV/95, pág. 72).

page 137: "¡Basta ya de perder ...!" (*El País*, Madrid, España; martes, 18 de abril de 1995).

pages 168–169: "Exámenes: La prueba final" (*Cambio 16*, Madrid, España; 22 mayo 1995, No. 1.226, págs. 62, 64–65).

page 179: "Costa Cruceros" (*El País*, Madrid, España; miércoles, 7 de junio de 1995, pág. 54). "Tele ABC" (*ABC*, Madrid, España; jueves, 15/VI/95, pág. 22). "SEAT" (*El País*, Madrid, España; miércoles, 7 de junio de 1995, pág. 45). "Olivetti" (*El País*, Madrid, España; miércoles, 7 de junio de 1995, pág. 7). "Paradores" (*ABC*, Madrid, España; jueves, 15/VI/95, pág. 61).

page 194: "No permitas ..." (*ABC*, Madrid, España; jueves, 15/VI/95, pág. 102). "Bellsouth ..." (*El Mercurio*, Santiago de Chile; lunes, 3 de abril de 1995, C-3). "Acer ..." (*Excelsior*, México, D.F.; lunes, 3 de abril de 1995, pág. 18-A). "American Language ..." (*El diario/La prensa*, Nueva York; domingo, 9 de abril de 1995, pág. 9).

page 223: "Veladas literarias" (*ABC*, Madrid, España; domingo, 2/VII/95, pág. 68).

page 249: "El tiempo" (*ABC*, Madrid, España; 2/VII/95, pág. 66. *El País*, Madrid, España; domingo, 2 de julio de 1995, pág. 36).

page 284: "Con una casa ..." (*ABC*, Madrid, España; sábado, 15/VII/95, pág. 41).

page 321: "Un agente ..." (*ABC*, Madrid, España; viernes, 21/VII/95, pág. 11).

page 347: "Tierra Santa" (*Excelsior*, México, D.F.).

page 356: "Tren tierras del Cid" (*Pasa a la historia*; RENFE, Trenes turísticos).

CONTENTS

Part One: Verbs—Forms and Uses

Part Two: Nouns and Their Modifiers; Pronouns

Part Three: Other Elements of the Sentence

Part Four: Idiomatic Usage

Verbs—
Forms
and
Uses

CHAPTER 1
THE PRESENT TENSE

A The present tense of regular -ar, -er, and -ir verbs

- All Spanish verbs belong to one of three different classes, or conjugations, according to the ending of the infinitive, the verb form ending in **-ar, -er,** or **-ir**:
  - first conjugation (**-ar**) verbs like **hablar** (*to speak*)
  - second conjugation (**-er**) verbs like **aprender** (*to learn*)
  - third conjugation (**-ir**) verbs like **escribir** (*to write*)
- Each conjugation has its own set of endings that are added to the stem for the different persons of the verb. Verbs conjugated according to the patterns below are called *regular* verbs.
- Verbs of the first conjugation (**-ar** verbs) are conjugated like **hablar** (*to speak*):

	singular		*plural*	
first person	**yo**	habl**o**	**nosotros**	habl**amos**
second person	**tú**	habl**as**	**vosotros**	habl**áis**
third person	**él** **ella** **Ud.**	habl**a**	**ellos** **ellas** **Uds.**	habl**an**

- Verbs of the second conjugation (**-er** verbs) are conjugated like **aprender** (*to learn*):

	singular		*plural*	
first person	**yo**	aprend**o**	**nosotros**	aprend**emos**
second person	**tú**	aprend**es**	**vosotros**	aprend**éis**
third person	**él** **ella** **Ud.**	aprend**e**	**ellos** **ellas** **Uds.**	aprend**en**

- Verbs of the third conjugation (**-ir** verbs) are conjugated like **escribir** (*to write*):

	singular		*plural*	
first person	**yo**	escrib**o**	**nosotros**	escrib**imos**
second person	**tú**	escrib**es**	**vosotros**	escrib**ís**
third person	**él** **ella** **Ud.**	escrib**e**	**ellos** **ellas** **Uds.**	escrib**en**

Notes:

1. Verbs of the first conjugation (**-ar**) and the second conjugation (**-er**) are conjugated alike with the difference that **-ar** verbs have -a- in all endings except the *yo* form and **-er** verbs have **-e-** in all endings except the *yo* form.

2. Verbs of the third conjugation (**-ir**) have **-i-** in the endings for *nosotros* and *vosotros*. The other persons are the same as the second conjugation (**-er**).

 B *Uses of the present tense*

- The present tense forms of Spanish verbs express both the English simple present (*I walk*) and the English present progressive (*I'm walking*):

Tocas el piano.	{ *You play the piano.* { *You're playing the piano.*
¿**Comen** Uds. torta?	{ *Do you eat cake?* { *Are you eating cake?*

- Questions can be formed in Spanish by inverting the subject and the verb or by changing intonation:

¿**Trabajan** Uds. aquí? }
¿Uds. **trabajan** aquí? }   *Do you work here?*

- The present tense can be used to ask for instructions:

¿**Hablamos** del tema ahora?	***Shall we talk** about the topic now?*
¿**Entrego** el informe?	***Shall I hand in** the report?*

- The present tense can refer to the future if another element of the sentence expresses future time. English often uses the present progressive to indicate future time:

Mando la carta mañana.	*I'll **send** the letter tomorrow.*
Vera **cena** conmigo el viernes.	*Vera's **having dinner** with me on Friday.*

- The construction **hace** + *expression of time* + **que** + *verb in the present tense* is used to designate actions that began in the past but that continue into the present. The question form of this construction is ¿**Cuánto tiempo hace que ...?** The word **tiempo** is optional:

—¿**Cuánto (tiempo) hace que viven** en esta casa?	*How long have you been living in this house?*
—**Hace ocho años que vivimos** aquí.	*We've been living here for eight years.*

- **Hace** + *expression of time* may also appear at the end of the sentence; **que** is omitted in this case:

Vivimos aquí **hace ocho años.**   *We've been living here for eight years.*

- Another construction used to designate actions that began in the past and continue into the present is *verb in present tense* + **desde hace** + *expression of time.* To form a question, ¿**Desde cuándo ...?** is used:

—¿**Desde cuándo** buscas trabajo?   *How long have you been looking for a job?*
—Busco trabajo **desde hace un mes.**   *I've been looking for a job **for a month.***

Some common **-ar** verbs:

aceptar *to accept*
acompañar *to go with, accompany*
aconsejar *to advise*
ahorrar *to save*
alquilar *to rent*
apagar *to turn off, shut off*
arreglar *to arrange, fix up*
aumentar *to increase*
averiguar *to find out*
ayudar *to help*
bailar *to dance*
bajar *to go down, lower, turn down*
besar *to kiss*
borrar *to erase*
buscar *to look for*
cambiar *to change*
caminar *to walk*
cantar *to sing*
celebrar *to celebrate*
cenar *to have dinner*
cocinar *to cook*
colocar *to put, place*
comprar *to buy*
contestar *to answer*
cortar *to cut*
cruzar *to cross*
dejar *to let, leave*
desear *to want*

dibujar *to draw*
disfrutar *to enjoy*
doblar *to turn (change direction)*
durar *to last*
echar *to throw*
empujar *to push*
entrar *to go/come in, enter*
entregar *to hand in/over*
escuchar *to listen (to)*
esperar *to wait, hope, expect*
esquiar *to ski*
estacionar *to park*
estudiar *to study*
explicar *to explain*
felicitar *to congratulate*
firmar *to sign*
ganar *to earn, win*
gastar *to spend, waste*
grabar *to record*
gritar *to shout*
hablar *to speak*
invitar *to invite*
llamar *to call*
llegar *to arrive*
llevar *to carry, wear*
llorar *to cry*
mandar *to send, order*
manejar *to drive*
marcar *to dial, mark*

mirar *to look at*
nadar *to swim*
necesitar *to need*
pagar *to pay*
parar *to stop*
pasar *to spend (time), pass*
patinar *to skate*
pintar *to paint*
practicar *to practice*
preguntar *to ask (a question)*
preparar *to prepare*
presentar *to present, introduce*
quitar *to take away*
regresar *to come back, return*
repasar *to review*
sacar *to take out*
saludar *to greet*
tardar *to be late*
terminar *to finish, end*
tirar *to throw*
tocar *to play a musical instrument, touch*
tomar *to take, drink*
trabajar *to work*
trotar *to jog*
usar *to use, wear*
viajar *to travel*

Some common **-er** verbs:

aprender *to learn*
beber *to drink*
comer *to eat*
comprender *to understand*

correr *to run*
deber *ought, must, to be supposed to*
leer *to read*
meter *to put in*

prender *to turn on*
romper *to break*
toser *to cough*
vender *to sell*

Some common **-ir** verbs:

abrir *to open*
añadir *to add*
asistir *to attend*
describir *to describe*

discutir *to discuss, argue*
escribir *to write*
interrumpir *to interrupt*
ocurrir *to happen*

recibir *to receive*
subir *to go up, raise*
sufrir *to suffer*
vivir *to live*

A. **En la clase de español.** Escriba lo que pasa en la clase de español del profesor Sierra. Construya oraciones en presente siguiendo el modelo.

> MODELO   los estudiantes / hablar español
> → Los estudiantes hablan español.

En la clase de español

levantar la mano to raise one's hand	**el modismo** idiom
el libro de texto textbook	**tomar apuntes** to take notes

---

1. Daniel / pronunciar muy bien
2. nosotros / abrir el libro de texto
3. tú / levantar la mano
4. los chicos / comprender la lección
5. Ud. / tomar apuntes
6. yo / leer el diálogo
7. Isabel y tú / aprender los modismos
8. vosotros / escribir un ejercicio

Nota cultural

- En los países hispánicos, los estudiantes de los colegios particulares generalmente tienen que comprar sus libros. En la mayor parte de los colegios públicos los estudiantes tienen que comprarlos también. Los estudiantes reciben una lista de los libros que necesitan para cada clase.

- En Hispanoamérica la escuela secundaria se llama **colegio, liceo** o **instituto.** En los colegios de estos países y en España, las notas se calculan a base de diez como nota máxima.

B. **¿En esta clase? ¡Qué va!** Use el presente para escribir las cosas que *nunca* pasan en la clase de la profesora Reyes. Siga el modelo.

> MODELO   ¿los estudiantes? / ¿gritar?
> → Los estudiantes nunca gritan.

Lo que no se hace en la clase

empujar to push	**mascar chicle** to chew gum
faltar to be absent	**saltar** to jump
gritar to shout, scream	**tardar en llegar** to take long to arrive

1. ¿Uds.? / ¿correr?
2. ¿nosotros? / ¿faltar?
3. ¿Juan Carlos? / ¿mascar chicle?
4. ¿yo? / ¿saltar?
5. ¿Laura y Carmen? / ¿empujar?
6. ¿tú? / ¿interrumpir?
7. ¿las chicas? / ¿beber refrescos?
8. ¿Ud. y yo? / ¿tardar en llegar?

C. **¿Qué hacen sus profesores?** Diga lo que sus profesores hacen o no hacen en la sala de clase escogiendo frases de la columna B para completar las frases de la columna A. Siga el modelo.

MODELO   Mi profesor de inglés …   hablar en voz alta/fumar
→ Mi profesor de inglés **habla en voz alta.**
→ Mi profesor de inglés **no fuma.**

A
1. Mi profesor de historia …
2. Nuestra profesora de química …
3. Nuestros maestros de matemáticas …
4. Las profesoras de francés …
5. Los maestros de gimnasia …

B
a. enseñar bien
b. arreglar sus papeles
c. preparar exámenes
d. esperar mucho de nosotros
e. escribir en la pizarra
f. pasar lista
g. colocar sus libros en el escritorio
h. calcular las notas todos los días
i. hablar de muchos temas
j. saltar
k. trotar

D. **¡Las quince primaveras!** Cecilia celebra su cumpleaños con una fiesta en su casa. Para saber cómo es, escriba la forma correcta del presente de los verbos que aparecen entre paréntesis.

Los padres y los hermanos de Cecilia _____ (1. planear) la fiesta. La mamá _____ (2. cocinar) los platos favoritos de Cecilia y _____ (3. comprar) una torta de chocolate. El padre y los hermanos de Cecilia _____ (4. colocar) globos y una piñata en la sala. Cecilia _____ (5. invitar) a todos sus amigos. _____ (6. Llegar) la hora de la fiesta. Paula, la mejor amiga de Cecilia, _____ (7. vivir) al lado y _____ (8. llegar) primero. Durante la fiesta, todos _____ (9. comer), _____ (10. beber) y _____ (11. bailar). Juan Pedro _____ (12. tocar) el piano y los otros amigos _____ (13. cantar). Mientras Cecilia _____ (14. abrir) los regalos que _____ (15. recibir), su padre _____ (16. sacar) fotos. Los invitados _____ (17. felicitar) a la cumpleañera y _____ (18. brindar) por ella.

Nota cultural

Las chicas que viven en los países hispánicos suelen celebrar los quince años igual que las norteamericanas celebran los dieciséis. El cumpleaños de **las quince primaveras** es como el cumpleaños dieciséis que se llama *sweet sixteen* en los Estados Unidos.

E. **¡Un lío telefónico!** Mario necesita llamar a su novia para decirle que no puede llegar a su casa a las siete. Para saber lo que pasa, escoja los verbos correctos de la lista y escríbalos en la forma correcta del presente en los espacios en blanco.

marcar	contestar	meter	creer	dejar
deber	buscar	quedar	funcionar	tardar
decidir	esperar	desear	comunicar	

Mario (1) _____ llamar a su novia Isabel para decirle que (2) _____ para su cita.

Él (3) _____ una cabina telefónica. (4) _____ una en la esquina. Mario (5) _____ una

moneda y (6) _____ el número de teléfono. (Ellos) no (7) _____ en casa de Isabel.

Mario (8) _____ que (9) _____ dejar un recado y (10) _____ escuchar la contestadora.

Pero la contestadora no (11) _____. Mario (12) _____ otra moneda. Esta vez parece

que (ellos) (13) _____ o (14) _____ descolgado. ¡Por fin, Mario (15) _____ correr a

casa de Isabel!

C   The present tense of irregular verbs

- The following verbs have an irregular first person singular (*yo*) form in the present tense. All other forms are regular.

- **-G-** verbs, that is, verbs that have an unexpected **-g-** in the *yo* form:

infinitive	*yo* form	other forms of the present tense
caer *to fall*	caigo	caes, cae, caemos, caéis, caen
hacer *to make, do*	hago	haces, hace, hacemos, hacéis, hacen
poner *to put*	pongo	pones, pone, ponemos, ponéis, ponen
salir *to go out*	salgo	sales, sale, salimos, salís, salen
traer *to bring*	traigo	traes, trae, traemos, traéis, traen
valer *to be worth*	valgo	vales, vale, valemos, valéis, valen

Notes:

1. Verbs conjugated like **poner: componer** (*to compose*), **disponer** (*to dispose*), **imponer** (*to impose*), **proponer** (*to propose*), **reponerse** (*to get well*), **suponer** (*to suppose*), etc.

2. Verbs conjugated like **traer: atraer** (*to attract*), **contraer** (*to contract*), **distraer** (*to distract*), etc.

- The following **-g-** verbs are irregular in other persons also:

decir *to say, tell*		**oír** *to hear*	
digo	decimos	**oigo**	oímos
dices	decís	oyes	oís
dice	dicen	oye	oyen

tener *to have*	
tengo	tenemos
tienes	tenéis
tiene	tienen

venir *to come*	
vengo	venimos
vienes	venís
viene	vienen

Note: Verbs conjugated like **tener**: **contener** (*to contain*), **detener** (*to stop, detain*), **mantener** (*to maintain*), **obtener** (*to obtain*), **retener** (*to retain*), etc.

- **Ir** (*to go*) is conjugated like an **-ar** verb. The *yo* form ends in **-oy**: **voy.** The stem of the verb is the letter **v.** Note that the *vosotros* form has no accent because it has only one syllable: **vais.**

ir *to go*	
voy	vamos
vas	vais
va	van

- **Ir** + **a** + *infinitive* is used to refer to future time as is *to be going to* in English.

—Aquí está el cine. **Voy a estacionar** el coche. — *Here's the movie theater. **I'm going to park** the car.*

—Y **yo voy a comprar** las entradas. — *And **I'm going to buy** the tickets.*

- **Dar** (*to give*), like **ir,** is conjugated like an **-ar** verb. The *yo* form ends in **-oy**: **doy.** **Ver** (*to see*) is a regular **-er** verb except for the *yo* form: **veo.** The *vosotros* form has no accent because it has only one syllable: **veis.**

- **Saber** (*to know*) and **caber** (*to fit*) are irregular in the first person only.

infinitive	*yo form*	*other forms of the present tense*
saber *to know*	**sé**	sabes, sabe, sabemos, sabéis, saben
caber *to fit*	**quepo**	cabes, cabe, cabemos, cabéis, caben

- In most verbs that end in a vowel + **-cer** or **-cir, c** changes to **zc** before **o** and **a.** In the present tense, the change occurs only in the first-person singular (*yo* form).

conocer *to know*	
cono**zco**	conocemos
conoces	conocéis
conoce	conocen

Note: Verbs conjugated like **conocer**: **reconocer** (*to recognize*), **desconocer** (*to be ignorant of*)

- Most verbs with infinitives in **-ecer** have **-zco** in the *yo* form like **conozco.** The other persons of the present tense are regular:

    agradecer (agradezco) *to thank,* **aparecer** (aparezco) *to appear,* **crecer** (crezco) *to grow,* **desaparecer** (desaparezco) *to disappear,* **establecer** (establezco) *to establish,* **merecer** (merezco) *to deserve,* **obedecer** (obedezco) *to obey,* **ofrecer** (ofrezco) *to offer,* **parecer** (parezco) *to seem,* **permanecer** (permanezco) *to remain,* **pertenecer** (pertenezco) *to belong,* etc.

- Verbs in **-ucir** also have **-zco** in the *yo* form, but are regular in the other persons: **conducir** (conduzco) *to drive*, **lucir** (luzco) *to shine/show off*, **producir** (produzco) *to produce*, **reducir** (reduzco) *to reduce*, **traducir** (traduzco) *to translate*.

F. Un viaje de negocios. Usted es jefe de una gran compañía internacional. Su secretario le hace unas preguntas sobre su viaje de negocios a Europa. Conteste sus preguntas según el modelo.

MODELO —¿Hace Ud. un viaje en noviembre?
—Sí, hago un viaje en noviembre.

1. ¿Sale Ud. la semana próxima?

2. ¿Viene Ud. a la oficina el viernes?

3. ¿Va Ud. a Francia y España?

4. ¿Conoce Ud. Italia?

5. ¿Hace Ud. las maletas mañana?

6. ¿Sabe Ud. cuándo regresa?

G. ¡Cuánto trabajo tenemos! Los chicos reciben una invitación pero no saben si tienen tiempo para ir. Escriba lo que dicen, según el modelo.

MODELO Juan → **Viene** si **tiene** tiempo.

1. las chicas

2. Ud.

3. tú y yo

4. Sara

5. Uds.

6. yo

H. ¿Oyes lo que dicen? ¡Aunque se habla en voz baja todo se oye! Escriba en español que todos oyen lo que dicen otras personas, según el modelo.

MODELO Anita / Gustavo → Anita **oye** lo que Gustavo **dice.**

1. yo / Uds.

2. tú / nosotros

3. Guillermo / Teresa

4. Rosa y yo / Ud.

5. Ud. y su primo / yo

6. Carmen y Paco / tú

I. ¡Lo hago yo! Escriba que Ud. es quien hace las siguientes cosas. Siga el modelo.

MODELO —¿Quién hace una pregunta?
—Yo hago una pregunta.

1. ¿Quién pone la mesa?

2. ¿Quién trae las flores?

3. ¿Quién da un paseo?

4. ¿Quién ve televisión?

5. ¿Quién traduce el libro?

J. **¿Hablan en serio?** ¡Sus amigos tienen ideas geniales! ¿O es que le toman el pelo? Escriba lo que dicen.

> MODELO —Carlota, ¿qué propones? (un plan brillante)
> —Propongo un plan brillante.

1. Luz, ¿qué mereces? (recibir el premio Nobel)

2. Juan Diego, ¿qué compones? (una obra maestra mozartiana)

3. Chicos, ¿qué obtienen? (una beca de dos millones de dólares)

4. Eugenia, ¿qué traduces? (novelas del vasco al sánscrito)

5. José Luis, ¿qué conduces? (la limosina presidencial)

6. Norberto, ¿qué supones? (que yo tengo razón siempre)

K. **¿Cuánto tiempo hace?** Ud. le pregunta a su amigo cuánto tiempo hace que sus amigos se dedican a sus aficiones. Escriba cada pregunta dos veces usando las construcciones del modelo.

> MODELO María / escribir cuentos
> → **¿Cuánto tiempo hace que** María **escribe** cuentos?
> → **¿Desde cuándo escribe** María cuentos?

1. Uds. / cocinar a la francesa

2. Mario y Federico / nadar

3. Consuelo / tocar el violín

4. tú / hacer carpintería

5. Esteban / bailar flamenco

6. sus hermanos / coleccionar monedas

L. **Hace mucho tiempo que ...** Su amigo le contesta las preguntas del ejercicio K de dos modos, como en el modelo.

> MODELO María / escribir cuentos / seis meses
> → **Hace** *seis meses* **que** María **escribe** cuentos.
> → María **escribe** cuentos **desde hace** *seis meses*.

1. Uds. / cocinar a la francesa / un año

2. Mario y Federico / nadar / tres años

3. Consuelo / tocar el violín / seis años

4. tú / hacer carpintería / siete semanas

5. Esteban / bailar flamenco / ocho meses

6. sus hermanos / coleccionar monedas / dos años y medio

M. **¿Cómo son?** Nadie conoce a esta gente. Use el verbo **conocer** para decir eso, según el modelo. Recuerde que debe usar la **a** personal. (Si necesita repasar la **a** personal, vea el capítulo 19, sección C.)

> MODELO —¿Sabe Juan si Paula es argentina?
> —No, él no conoce a Paula.

1. ¿Sabes si esos muchachos son simpáticos?

2. ¿Saben tus padres si los señores Gorostiza son ricos?

3. ¿Saben Uds. si la profesora de economía es famosa?

4. ¿Sabemos tú y yo si aquel médico es competente?

5. ¿Sabe Ud. si Alfredo Parra es inteligente?

6. ¿Sabe Marta si Agustín es de Puerto Rico?

N. **¡Qué vanidad!** José Antonio es muy presumido. ¿Qué dice de su trabajo? Siga el modelo para saberlo.

> MODELO conocer a todo el mundo
> → Conozco a todo el mundo.

1. pertenecer a los círculos literarios de la ciudad

2. producir obras importantes

3. traducir poesía del inglés al español

4. dar muchas conferencias

5. siempre ofrecer ideas nuevas

6. merecer los aplausos de los oyentes

O. **¡Todos ayudamos!** En mi casa todo el mundo ayuda. Use **ir a** + el infinitivo dado para expresar lo que cada uno de nosotros va a hacer.

> MODELO tú / poner en orden la sala
> → Tú vas a poner en orden la sala.

Arreglando la casa	
barrer el suelo *to sweep the floor*	**lavar los platos** *to wash the dishes*
cortar el césped *to mow the lawn*	**limpiar la alfombra** *to clean the carpet*
hacer la cama *to make the bed*	**pasar la aspiradora** *to vacuum*
hacer la compra *to do the shopping*	**poner en orden** *to straighten up*
lavar la ropa *to do the laundry*	**sacar la basura** *to take out the garbage*

1. mi hermano y yo / cortar el césped

2. mi abuela / lavar la ropa

3. yo / barrer el suelo

4. mamá / hacer la compra

5. mis hermanas / lavar los platos

6. mi abuelo / sacar la basura

7. Uds. / hacer las camas

8. papá / pasar la aspiradora

9. tú / limpiar la alfombra

Nota cultural

En los países hispánicos, tradicionalmente, los abuelos vivían con sus hijos y nietos. Muy a menudo un tío o una tía vivía también con la familia. Los abuelos y los tíos tenían casi la misma autoridad en la disciplina de los hijos como los padres mismos. Cuando los hijos se casaban solían vivir muy cerca de sus padres. Hoy en día se nota más el fenómeno de la familia nuclear como en los Estados Unidos y una tendencia de parte de los ancianos de ir a vivir a un asilo de ancianos (*old age home*) en vez de ir a vivir con sus hijos.

P. La vida diaria. Exprese en español algunas de las cosas que Paco, sus amigos y sus familiares hacen todos los días.

1. I drive the car.
2. Mom and Dad sign papers.
3. My brother jogs.
4. You (*Ud.*) turn on the computer.
5. Federico and I attend lectures.
6. You (*tú*) read the newspaper.
7. David and Mateo swim in the pool.
8. My aunt and uncle receive their bills.
9. All the students discuss the topics.
10. You (*Uds.*) cook rice.
11. Jaime and I cross the street.
12. María Elena and Martín read until 1:00 A.M.

Q. Ejercicio oral. Haga una encuesta. Pregúntele a su amigo/amiga lo que le gusta hacer los fines de semana y en las vacaciones. Por ejemplo:

- ir al cine / a los conciertos / al teatro
- salir al campo / a las montañas
- acampar
- hacer turismo
- visitar los museos
- bailar
- pintar
- jugar al tenis / al béisbol / al fútbol
- tocar un instrumento musical
- ir de compras

R. Estructuras en acción. Lea este anuncio de un servicio de plancha a domicilio. Después, resuma su contenido combinando elementos de la columna A con los de la columna B. Escriba oraciones completas como en el modelo.

DON PLANCHÓN

Cuando Juan Marín descubrió que la tarea más ingrata para la mayoría de las mujeres es la plancha, decidió crear un servicio de plancha a domicilio. Recogen la ropa y la devuelven planchada el mismo día. Una camisa, dependiendo del tejido, cuesta entre 200 y 300 pesetas. Y el único requisito es que el pedido supere las mil pesetas. Funcionan en Madrid con un horario de 9.00 a 14.00 y de 15.00 a 19.30. El negocio se abrió en febrero de 1994 y próximamente se ampliará a Barcelona, Mallorca, Pontevedra y Valencia.   **Madrid: (91) 445 73 28**

MODELO   la gente   odiar la plancha de ropa
→ La gente odia la plancha de ropa.

A	B
1. Juan Marín	a. ... costar entre 200 y 300 pesetas
2. los empleados de Don Planchón	b. ... funcionar desde febrero de 1994
3. una camisa	c. ... ofrecer un servicio de plancha a domicilio
4. el pedido	d. ... tener que superar las mil pesetas
5. el negocio	e. ... recoger la ropa y devolverla planchada el mismo día

CHAPTER 2
SER & ESTAR

 A *The uses of* **ser**

- Spanish has two verbs that are equivalent to the English *to be:* **ser** and **estar.** Both verbs are irregular in the present tense. Both have **-oy** in the *yo* form, like **ir (voy)** and **dar (doy).**

ser		estar	
soy	somos	estoy	estamos
eres	sois	estás	estáis
es	son	está	están

- **Ser** is used before most phrases beginning with **de**; for example, in expressing origin:

Soy de los Estados Unidos.   *I'm from the United States.*

and possession:

La cartera **es de Felipe.**   *The wallet is Phillip's.*

and what material something is made of:

La blusa **es de seda.**   *The blouse is (made of) silk.*

- **Ser** is used before adjectives to indicate that the condition expressed by the adjectives does not result from a change. Thus, these adjectives express inherent qualities and characteristics such as nationality, age, physical and moral attributes, personality, religion, and color:

Mis amigas **son** españolas.	*My friends are Spanish.*
El presidente **es** joven.	*The president is young.*
Carlos **es** alto y rubio.	*Carlos is tall and blond.*
Nora **es** inteligente.	*Nora is intelligent.*
Mis primos **son** graciosos.	*My cousins are witty.*
Esos señores **son** protestantes/ judíos/católicos.	*Those men and women are Protestant/ Jewish/Catholic.*
Nuestro coche **es** azul.	*Our car is blue.*

- **Ser** is used to link two nouns or pronouns or a noun and a pronoun. Both nouns and pronouns may appear in the sentence or merely be understood. Unlike English, Spanish omits the indefinite article **un/una** with a profession:

El señor Lara **es arquitecto.**	*Mr. Lara is an architect.*
Pilar Suárez **es médica.**	*Pilar Suárez is a doctor.*
Somos ingenieros.	*We're engineers.*

- **Ser** is used to express time, dates, days of the week, and where an event takes place:

—¿Qué hora **es**?	*What time is it?*
—**Son** las ocho.	*It's eight o'clock.*
—¿Cuál **es** la fecha de hoy?	*What's today's date?*
—**Es** el seis de octubre.	*It's October 6th.*
—¿Qué día **es** hoy?	*What day is today?*
—**Es** miércoles.	*It's Wednesday.*
—¿El baile **es** en la universidad?	*Is the dance at the university?*
—No, **es** en el Hotel Palacio.	*No, it's at the Palacio Hotel.*

B   *The uses of* estar

- **Estar** is used to express location or position, whether it is permanent or temporary:

Santiago **está** en Chile.	*Santiago is in Chile.*
El perro **está** al lado del gato.	*The dog is next to the cat.*
La papelería **está** enfrente de la pastelería.	*The stationery store is opposite the pastry shop.*

- **Estar** is used before adjectives to indicate that the condition expressed by the adjective results from a change. The condition may be a phase of health, happiness, etc.; a temporary state of being tired, seated, etc.; or the result of an action such as a window being closed. **Estar** also may indicate that the adjective is the subjective impression of the speaker. **Estar** is therefore more common with adjectives that describe mental or physical states:

—¿Cómo **está** Inés?	*How's Inés?*
—La pobre **está** enferma.	*The poor girl is (has gotten) sick.*
—¿**Están** levantados los niños?	*Are the children up?*
—No, **están** acostados todavía.	*No, they're still in bed.*
—¿**Están** abiertas las ventanas?	*Are the windows open?*
—No, **están** cerradas.	*No, they are closed.*
—¿No reconoces a Luis?	*Don't you recognize Luis?*
—Apenas. **Está** muy gordo.	*Hardly. He's so fat. (He's gotten very fat./ He looks so fat to me.)*

- **Estar** is used in the formation of the progressive tenses: **estar** + the gerund. The gerund or **-ndo** form is equivalent to the *-ing* form in English:

Están esperando.	*They're waiting.*
Estaba viviendo en París.	*He was living in Paris.*

- **Ser** and **estar** are used with the past participle of the verb. **Ser** + the past participle is passive; it can have an agent phrase introduced by **por**. **Estar** + the past participle expresses the result of an action:

La puerta **fue abierta por** la chica.	*The door was opened by the girl.*
La puerta **está abierta.**	*The door is open.*
El trabajo **fue hecho por** él.	*The work was done by him.*
El trabajo **estaba hecho.**	*The work was done.*

- The choice of **ser** or **estar** in a sentence is crucial to the meaning. A change in the verb will change the meaning:

Lola **es** delgada.	*Lola is thin. (Lola is a thin person.)*
Lola **está** delgada.	*Lola is thin. (Lola has gotten thin./ Lola looks thin to me.)*
Mario **es** nervioso.	*Mario is nervous. (He is a nervous person.)*
Mario **está** nervioso.	*Mario is feeling nervous. (Mario has gotten nervous/seems nervous to me.)*
Esos profesores **son** aburridos.	*Those professors are boring.*
Esos profesores **están** aburridos.	*Those professors are bored.*
Fernando **es** listo.	*Fernando is clever.*
Fernando **está** listo.	*Fernando is ready.*
La actriz **es** vieja.	*The actress is old.*
La actriz **está** vieja.	*The actress looks old.*
Los hombres **son** vivos.	*The men are sharp/quick.*
Los hombres **están** vivos.	*The men are alive.*
Beatriz **es** pálida.	*Beatriz is pale-complexioned.*
Beatriz **está** pálida.	*Beatriz is pale.*
Es seguro.	*It's safe.*
Está seguro.	*He's sure.*
Paquito **es** bueno.	*Paquito is good (a good boy).*
La torta **está** buena.	*The cake is (tastes) good.*

- Note the difference in meaning between **ser** and **estar** when referring to food:

La carne **es** rica (mala).	*Meat is delicious (awful).* (in general)
La carne **está** rica (mala).	*The meat is/tastes delicious (awful).* (specific dish)

Note: Adjectives used with **ser** and **estar** must agree with the subject in number and gender:

- Commonly used expressions with **ser**:

¿Cómo es Ud.?   *What are you like?, What do you look like?*
¿Cuál es la fecha de hoy?   *What's today's date?*
¿Cuál es su nacionalidad?   *What is your nationality?*
¿De dónde es Ud.?   *Where are you from?*
¿De qué color es ...?   *What color is ...?*

¿De qué origen es Ud.?   *What is your background?*
es importante/necesario/posible   *it's important/necessary/possible*
es que   *the fact is that*
¿Qué hora es?   *What time is it?*

- Commonly used expressions with **estar**:

¿Cómo está Ud.?   *How are you?*
estar a punto de + *infinitive*   *to be about to*
estar conforme   *to be in agreement*
estar de acuerdo (con)   *to agree (with)*
estar de vacaciones   *to be on vacation*
estar de vuelta   *to be back*
estar para + *infinitive*   *to be about to*
estar por   *to be in favor of*
estar por + *infinitive*   *to be inclined to*

A. Soy yo. Escriba en español quién llama a la puerta. Siga el modelo empleando la forma correcta del verbo **ser**.

MODELO   —¿Quién es? (yo)
—Soy yo.

1. ¿Quién es? (ella)
2. ¿Quién es? (Uds.)
3. ¿Quién es? (nosotros)
4. ¿Quién es? (yo)
5. ¿Quién es? (tú)
6. ¿Quién es? (él)
7. ¿Quién es? (ellas)

B. ¿De dónde son? ¿De qué origen son? Escriba de dónde son y de qué origen son los amigos del Club Internacional. Siga el modelo.

MODELO   Tomás / Inglaterra / alemán
→ Tomás es de Inglaterra pero es de origen alemán.

1. Pablo / la Argentina / inglés
2. los gemelos / Francia / ruso
3. la licenciada / el Canadá / japonés
4. Ud. / los Estados Unidos / irlandés
5. Ramón y Virginia / Puerto Rico / polaco
6. tú / España / portugués
7. Ud. y Raquel / México / griego
8. yo / Venezuela / italiano

C. Una encuesta. Ud. prepara una encuesta y necesita hacerles unas preguntas a sus amigos hispanos. Exprese en español las preguntas que va a hacerles. Se usa el verbo **ser** en todas las oraciones.

1. Who are you?
2. Where are you from?

3. What is your nationality?

4. What is your background?

5. What are you like? / What do you look like?

6. What color are your eyes?

D. Están de vacaciones. Escriba dónde y cómo están las siguientes personas, empleando el verbo **estar** como en el modelo.

> MODELO   Alicia / Los Ángeles / ocupada
> → Alicia está en Los Ángeles y está ocupada.

1. Patricio / Madrid / contento

2. nosotros / Chile / cansados

3. los tíos / Tejas / nerviosos

4. Consuelo y su hermana / Suecia / aburridas

5. tú / Londres / enfermo

6. yo / París / feliz

E. ¿Cuál fue la pregunta? A continuación lea Ud. lo que escribió una persona al contestar las preguntas de un formulario. Luego escriba Ud. las preguntas. Para cada pregunta use el verbo **ser.**

1. Roberto Iglesias.

2. Canadiense.

3. Programador de computadoras.

4. Soltero. (*estado civil*)

5. El quince de febrero de 1970. (*fecha de nacimiento*)

6. Alto, moreno, de ojos castaños.

F. Biografías. Escriba la forma correcta del verbo **ser** o **estar** para terminar los textos biográficos de las siguientes personas.

A. Baltasar Estévez (1) _____ director de cine. Él (2) _____ célebre por sus comedias.

Sus películas (3) _____ realmente muy cómicas. Estévez (4) _____ muy gracioso.

(5) _____ mexicano pero (6) _____ en Barcelona este año porque filma una comedia

allí. Todos sus aficionados (7) _____ entusiasmados con esa nueva película.

B. Camila de la Renta (1) _____ diseñadora de ropa para mujeres. Su ropa (2) _____

de alta costura y (3) _____ muy cara. Este año los vestidos y los trajes que diseña

(4) _____ de seda y lana. (5) _____ blancos, negros y de otros colores claros.

La empresa de de la Renta (6) _____ en París, que (7) _____ la capital de la moda.

G. El museo de arte. Ud. es guía en un museo de arte y lleva a unos turistas a conocer el museo. Complete la descripción de la visita escribiendo las formas correctas de **ser** o **estar.**

Buenas tardes, señoras y señores. Aquí (nosotros) (1) _____ en la entrada

principal. A la derecha (2) _____ la librería. (3) _____ nueva y moderna. Y enfrente

de la librería (4) _____ la sala de conferencias y conciertos. Esta noche precisamente

hay una conferencia. Va a hablar Francisco Velázquez que (5) _____ profesor de

arte en la universidad. (6) _____ especialista en la pintura renacentista y (7) _____

muy inteligente. La conferencia (8) _____ a las ocho. Va a (9) _____ muy interesante.

Ahora, vamos a subir la escalera. Aquí a la derecha (10) _____ la sala de pintura

impresionista. Esta exposición (11) _____ muy importante. Muchos de los cuadros

que (12) _____ colgados aquí (13) _____ de otros museos europeos. Uds. (14) _____

viendo unas obras maestras que nunca habían salido de su país sino hasta ahora.

Bueno, ya (15) _____ las tres y me parece que (16) _____ hora de terminar nuestra

visita. Yo (17) _____ muy contenta de haber podido enseñarles el museo. Uds. que

(18) _____ aficionados al arte deben volver a menudo. El museo (19) _____ abierto

de martes a domingo. (20) _____ cerrado los lunes.

Nota cultural

El Museo del Prado, que se encuentra en Madrid, es una de las pinacotecas (*art museums*) más importantes del mundo. El Prado tiene la colección más completa de pintura española. Llaman la atención los cuadros de Velázquez, Goya, El Greco, Ribera, Zurbarán y Murillo. El museo tiene naturalmente obras de otros pintores célebres como Rembrandt, Bosco (*Bosch*), Brueghel, Rubens, Tiziano (*Titian*), Caravaggio, Gainsborough, etcétera. El edificio de estilo neoclásico fue construido por Juan de Villanueva por orden del rey español Carlos III (1716–88) que reinó a partir del año 1759.

H. Un semestre en el extranjero. Ud. está pasando un semestre en Madrid para perfeccionar su español. Toma clases en la universidad y vive en casa de una familia española. Ud. les escribe una carta a sus padres en la cual describe cómo es su vida en Madrid. Complete cada oración con la forma correcta de **ser** o **estar.**

Queridos padres:

Ya hace dos meses que (1) _____ en Madrid y (2) _____ muy contento. (3) _____ una

ciudad vieja y también moderna. Voy al Museo del Prado, al Parque del Retiro, a la Plaza

Mayor y a muchos lugares turísticos. Hay cafés, restaurantes, teatros, cines, y la vida

nocturna (4) _____ impresionante. ¡Claro que asisto a mis clases también! La clase de

literatura española (5) _____ un poco difícil a veces porque el profesor habla muy rápido.
Mi clase de historia (6) _____ muy buena. Los dos profesores (7) _____ inteligentes y
simpáticos. Por desgracia, la profesorá de lengua (8) _____ aburrida. La casa donde
vivo (9) _____ en la calle Serrano. Enfrente de la casa (10) _____ el Museo Arqueológico.
Algunas tiendas (11) _____ al lado de la casa también. Y la parada de autobuses (12) _____
delante de la casa. Así (13) _____ muy fácil viajar por la ciudad. La casa de la familia Ruiz
(14) _____ grande y bonita y mi cuarto (15) _____ muy cómodo. Los señores Ruiz tienen
cuatro hijos. (16) _____ siete personas en total porque la abuela vive con ellos también.
Esteban, el hijo mayor, (17) _____ un buen amigo mío. (18) _____ pequeño y moreno.
(19) _____ listo y simpático. Estela, la hija mayor, (20) _____ encantadora y muy guapa.
Tiene novio. ¡(21) _____ una pena porque creo que (22) _____ enamorado de ella!
(23) (¡_____ una broma!)

¿Cómo (24) _____ Uds.? Papá, (25) ¿_____ muy ocupado en la empresa? Mamá,
¿cómo (26) _____ la nueva computadora? ¿Y mis hermanos? Todos (27) _____ muy bien,
espero. Claudia debe (28) _____ contenta en el nuevo colegio, ¿verdad? ¿Cómo (29) _____
los abuelos y los tíos? ¿La tía (30) _____ enferma todavía? ¿Los tíos (31) _____ de vuelta
de Lisboa? ¿Y cómo (32) _____ el nuevo coche que compraron? Espero recibir muchas
noticias de Uds. Bueno, ya (33) _____ las cinco y media. Dos amigos que toman clases
conmigo van a pasar por mí a las seis. Jaime (34) _____ de Nueva York y Carlos (35) _____
de Nuevo México. Vamos a ir al cine. Faltan dos meses y voy a (36) _____ de vuelta en casa
con Uds. Hasta pronto.
Un abrazo muy fuerte de
Miguel

Nota cultural

Madrid, capital de España, se encuentra en una extensa llanura (*plain*) aproximadamente
en el centro de la Península. La ciudad, a orillas del río Manzanares, fue llamada Magerit
por los árabes. Éstos se apoderaron de la Península en 711 y se quedaron hasta 1492
cuando fueron derrotados definitivamente en Granada por los Reyes Católicos. El rey
Alfonso VI tomó Madrid definitivamente en 1084 y en 1561 Felipe II trasladó la Corte
a Madrid. En 1600, Felipe III llevó la Corte a Valladolid (ciudad al noroeste de Madrid)
pero volvió a llevarla a Madrid en 1605. Los reyes borbones (*Bourbons*), especialmente
Carlos III, hicieron construir muchos monumentos y edificios y convirtieron la ciudad en el
centro intelectual y artístico de España. Madrid no es solamente la capital de España,
sino también uno de los centros culturales de la Unión Europea.

I. **¿Qué preguntó?** A continuación hay unas respuestas que dio su amigo. Pero Ud. no oyó las preguntas que le hizo otro amigo. ¿Puede imaginarse cuáles son las preguntas? Escoja entre **ser** y **estar** al formular cada pregunta.

1. ¿La papelería? Enfrente del correo.

2. ¿Gloria? Rubia, alta y delgada.

3. ¿Los hermanos García? Brasileños.

4. ¿Juanito y Raúl? Preocupados y nerviosos.

5. ¿La familia Méndez? De origen español.

6. ¿Las primas de Paco? Encantadoras.

7. ¿El profesor Mora? En Costa Rica.

8. ¿El vestido? De algodón.

9. ¿La camisa y la corbata? Azules.

10. ¿Yo? Muy ocupado y cansado.

11. ¿Aquella casa? De los abuelos de Sara.

12. ¿Micaela? De Inglaterra.

J. **Unos nuevos estudiantes extranjeros.** Exprese en español una conversación entre dos amigas sobre los nuevos estudiantes extranjeros en su colegio.

1. Who are the new foreign students? Do you know where they're from?

2. I know María del Mar. She's in my math class. She's from Argentina.

3. Yes, and her background is Italian. She's very nice and smart.

4. But she's sad because she wants to go back to Buenos Aires.

5. Lorenzo Tomé is French, but his grandparents are of Spanish origin.

6. The family has been living in France for many years.

7. Lorenzo is studying biology and chemistry this year.

8. Yes. He says he wants to be a doctor.

K. **Ejercicio oral. La familia.** Pregúntele a su amigo/amiga cómo están y cómo son los miembros de su familia. Pregúntele también dónde están sus familiares ahora.

L. **Estructuras en acción.** Lea este anuncio que explica las ventajas de la tarjeta de abono a los transportes públicos de Madrid. Luego, copie las frases u oraciones donde aparecen formas de los verbos **ser** y **estar** y tradúzcalas al inglés.

Vocabulario

el abono *(here)*   subway and bus pass
la Comunidad de Madrid   city of Madrid and environs
el consorcio   consortium, association
constar de   to consist of
la tercera edad   old age

ESTOS SON TUS ABONOS

El Abono Transportes es la forma más práctica, cómoda y económica de disfrutar de las ventajas del transporte público.

Consta de **una tarjeta de Abono** personal y de carácter permanente, con tu foto, datos de identificación y número de abonado **más un cupón** que puede ser mensual o anual.

Con él podrás viajar por toda la Comunidad de Madrid o por la zona elegida, sin límite de viajes o combinaciones. Metro, tren, autobús y todos los transportes públicos están a tu disposición para moverte mejor.

CHAPTER 3

STEM-CHANGING VERBS & VERBS WITH SPELLING CHANGES

 A *Stem-changing verbs ending in -ar and -er*

- Stem-changing verbs that end in **-ar** or **-er** change the stem vowel in the present tense in two possible ways: **e > ie** and **o > ue** in all forms except *nosotros* and *vosotros*:

querer *to want, love*	
quiero	queremos
quieres	queréis
quiere	quieren

volver *to return*	
vuelvo	volvemos
vuelves	volvéis
vuelve	vuelven

pensar *to think*	
pienso	pensamos
piensas	pensáis
piensa	piensan

poder *can, to be able to*	
puedo	podemos
puedes	podéis
puede	pueden

*Remember that **pensar** + *infinitive* means *to intend to.*

Some common verbs that pattern like **querer** and **pensar** (e > ie):		
acertar *to be on target, guess right*	**confesar** *to confess*	**gobernar** *to govern*
apretar *to be tight, squeeze*	**defender** *to defend*	**helar*** *to freeze*
ascender *to go up, promote*	**descender** *to go down*	**nevar*** *to snow*
	despertar(se) *to wake up*	**perder** *to lose*
atravesar *to cross*	**empezar** *to begin*	**quebrar** *to break*
cerrar *to close*	**encender** *to light*	**recomendar** *to recommend*
comenzar *to begin*	**encerrar** *to lock in, contain*	**sentar(se)** *to seat, sit down*
	entender *to understand*	

*Impersonal verbs; conjugated only in the third-person singular.

Some common verbs that pattern like **volver** and **poder** (o > ue):		
acordarse *to remember*	**devolver** *to return, give*	**probar(se)** *to try, taste,*
acostar(se) *to put to bed, go*	*back*	*try on*
to bed	**doler** *to hurt, ache*	**recordar** *to remember*
almorzar *to eat lunch*	**encontrar** *to find*	**resolver** *to solve*
conmover *to move*	**envolver** *to wrap up*	**soler** *to be accustomed to*
(emotionally)	**jugar (u > ue)** *to play*	**tronar*** *to thunder*
contar *to count, tell*	**llover*** *to rain*	**volar** *to fly*
costar *to cost*	**mostrar** *to show*	
demostrar *to show*	**oler (o > hue)** *to smell*	

Note that **jugar** has the stem change **u > ue** and that **oler** has the change **o > hue**: **Huele bien.** *It smells good.*

A. ¿A qué juegan Uds.? Escriba el deporte al que juega cada persona.

> Modelo   Roberto / el fútbol
> → Roberto **juega** al fútbol.

1. yo / el tenis

2. Daniel y Felipe / el béisbol

3. Carlota / el vólibol

4. tú / el baloncesto

5. Jorge y yo / el fútbol americano

6. Uds. / el jai alai

Nota cultural

- **El fútbol** es el deporte más popular en los países hispánicos. Los resultados de los partidos de fútbol ocupan varias páginas, muchas veces con fotos grandes en colores, en los principales periódicos de estos países.

- **El béisbol** es ahora muy popular en México, Venezuela, Centroamérica y el Caribe gracias a la influencia estadounidense. Los periódicos de estos países hispánicos dan noticias de los equipos nacionales tanto como de los norteamericanos. Varios jugadores de béisbol venezolanos y de otros países hispánicos juegan en equipos estadounidenses. Muchas palabras que tienen que ver con este deporte norteamericano han pasado al español de los países donde se juega: **el jonrón, el fildeo.**

- **El jai alai** es un juego de pelota de origen vasco (*Basque*). El País Vasco o las provincias de Vascongadas quedan al norte de España; allí se habla el vascuence además del español. Los jugadores lanzan la pelota con una pala (*bat or paddle*), cesta (*basket*) o las manos contra un frontón (*wall*).

---

*Impersonal verbs; conjugated only in the third-person singular.

B. **¿A qué hora almuerzan?** Escriba a qué hora almuerzan estas personas.

> MODELO yo / a las dos
> → Yo **almuerzo** a las dos.

1. Uds. / a la una

2. Eva / a las doce y media

3. nosotros / a las tres

4. Mauricio y Beatriz / a la una y cuarto

5. tú / a las once y media

6. yo / a las dos y media

Nota cultural

El **almuerzo** se toma generalmente en los países hispanoamericanos a eso de la una o las dos de la tarde. En España, donde se llama **la comida,** se tomaba tradicionalmente entre las dos y las tres. Los españoles tenían la costumbre de volver a casa para comer, pero con los cambios en la sociedad en cuanto al horario, el tránsito, etcétera, ya no se hace mucho. En general, ya no se come tan fuerte a esa hora ni se duerme la siesta después. **La cena** en los países hispanoamericanos se toma a eso de las ocho, a veces algo más temprano o algo más tarde, pero casi nunca llega a la hora española—entre las diez y las once de la noche. Claro que los niños pequeños generalmente siguen un horario más conveniente. **El desayuno,** generalmente ligero, se toma en los países hispanos a más o menos la misma hora que en los Estados Unidos.

C. **¡No puedo!** Escriba que nadie puede hacer nada hoy.

> MODELO ¿Vas de compras hoy?
> → No, **no puedo.**

1. ¿Vienen Uds. conmigo hoy?

2. ¿Escribe Elena cartas hoy?

3. ¿Trabajan Josefa y Leonardo hoy?

4. ¿Toma Ud. el examen hoy?

5. ¿Voy a tu casa hoy?

6. ¿Visitamos el museo hoy?

D. **En un almacén.** Margarita va a un almacén para comprar ropa. Termine la conversación que tiene con la dependienta escribiendo la forma correcta de los verbos que aparecen entre paréntesis.

> MODELO Yo _____ (pensar) ir al almacén Princesa.
> → Yo **pienso** ir al almacén Princesa.

Dependienta —Señorita, ¿en qué _____ (1. poder) servirle?

Margarita —Es que yo no _____ (2. encontrar) los trajes.

Dependienta —Aquí están a la derecha. ¿Qué color _____ (3. querer) Ud.?

Margarita —_____ (4. Pensar) que el café o el azul marino.

Dependienta —Le _____ (5. mostrar) dos. Este azul es muy bonito, ¿verdad?

Margarita —Ah sí. ¿_____ (6. Poder) mostrarme el otro?

Dependienta —Cómo no. Aquí tiene el café. Yo _____ (7. encontrar) el estilo muy elegante.

Margarita —Los dos son hermosos. ¿Cuánto _____ (8. costar)?

Dependienta —El azul _____ (9. costar) ciento noventa dólares y el café _____ (10. costar) doscientos cinco dólares.

Margarita —De veras no sé. Creo que me _____ (11. probar) los dos. *(Margarita termina de probarse los trajes.)*

Margarita —Me llevo los dos trajes. ¿Ud. me los _____ (12. envolver), por favor?

Dependienta —Con gusto. ¿Ud. sabe que _____ (13. poder) pagar con tarjeta de crédito?

Margarita —Ah sí. Yo _____ (14. soler) pagar con mi tarjeta.

Dependienta —Bien. Yo _____ (15. volver) en unos minutos.

Nota cultural

Todos los países hispánicos tienen **almacenes.** También hay sucursales (*branches*) de algunos almacenes estadounidenses, como Sears, en muchos países. Tradicionalmente se cerraban las tiendas en España unas horas por la tarde. Coincidía con las horas de la comida y del calor máximo. Actualmente, se sigue el horario corrido, es decir, el almacén se mantiene abierto todo el día. Tradicionalmente, a muchas personas de las sociedades hispánicas les gusta la atención personal que encuentran en las tiendas pequeñas. Tienen la costumbre de este contacto personal, pero también les llama la atención lo grande y variado del almacén. Les son muy atractivos también los nuevos centros comerciales que se construyen por todas partes.

E. Sinónimos. Consulte la lista de verbos que tienen cambios radicales en las páginas 25–26 y escoja sinónimos para los verbos que aparecen en las siguientes oraciones. Escriba cada oración empleando la forma correcta del nuevo verbo.

> MODELO   El diccionario *vale* treinta dólares.
> → El diccionario **cuesta** treinta dólares.

1. Uds. *solucionan* los problemas de álgebra.

2. Los niños *cruzan* la calle con cuidado.

3. El concierto *empieza* a las ocho.

4. *Bajamos* al primer piso en ascensor.

5. Yo no *comprendo* su idea.

6. ¿*Regresas* el sábado o el domingo?

7. Pedro nos *enseña* el apartamento.

8. Los Salcedo *desean* salir esta noche.

9. Yo *prendo* la luz.

F. Un día típico. Escriba lo que hacen estas personas en un día típico.

> MODELO   Juana / cerrar las ventanas
> ➜ Juana **cierra** las ventanas.

1. mi papá / despertar a todos nosotros

2. mi mamá / contar lo que pasa

3. Uds. / almorzar en el centro

4. tú / devolver los libros a la biblioteca

5. los chicos / volver del colegio a las tres

6. Ana y yo / comenzar a estudiar a las cuatro

7. yo / jugar ajedrez

8. Federico / acostar a sus hermanitos

G. Hoy sí, mañana no. Escriba oraciones conjugando el segundo verbo de la construcción *verbo conjugado + infinitivo* para indicar que la acción ocurre hoy.

> MODELO   Mis tíos van a volver mañana.
> ➜ Mis tíos **vuelven** hoy.

1. Vas a recordar la fecha mañana.

2. Pablo y Lorenzo van a jugar fútbol mañana.

3. Vamos a probar el nuevo plato mañana.

4. Alicia va a encontrar su secador mañana.

5. Yo voy a devolver el paraguas mañana.

6. Ud. va a almorzar con Raquel mañana.

H. ¿Qué tiempo hace? Exprese en español el tiempo que hace hoy en varias ciudades.

¿Qué tiempo hace?

Hace sol/viento.   *It's sunny/windy.*
Hace calor/frío.   *It's warm/cold.*
Hace buen/mal tiempo.   *The weather's good/bad.*
Está nublado/despejado.   *It's cloudy/clear.*
llover (o > ue)   *to rain*
nevar (e > ie)   *to snow*

tronar (o > ue)   *to thunder*
el relámpago   *lightning*
escampar, despejar   *to clear up*
helar (e > ie)   *to freeze*
granizar   *to hail*

---

1. It's raining in Seville.

2. It's snowing in Montreal.

3. It's thundering in Santa Fe.

4. The rain is beginning to freeze in Nome.

5. It's beginning to snow in Moscow.

6. It's beginning to rain in Barcelona.

7. It's clear in Patagonia.

8. It's hailing in New York.

Nota cultural

- **Sevilla,** a orillas del río Guadalquivir, es la capital de la Comunidad Autónoma de Andalucía. Es una típica ciudad andaluza con su barrio antiguo (Santa Cruz) de hermosos patios y calles estrechas. Sus muchos monumentos llaman la atención: la Catedral, de arquitectura gótica, la Giralda, el Alcázar, el Archivo de Indias, la Biblioteca Colombina (de Cristóbal Colón), el museo de pintura, etcétera. Hay muchísimo turismo durante Semana Santa y las ferias de abril.

- **Santa Fe,** capital del estado de Nuevo México, fue nombrada por la ciudad española que se encuentra en la provincia de Granada. Fue en esa ciudad española donde Colón y los Reyes Católicos firmaron los convenios (*agreements*) en 1492.

- **Barcelona,** segunda ciudad de España, es la capital de la Comunidad Autónoma de Cataluña. Va desde las orillas del Mediterráneo hasta el monte Tibidabo. Es un puerto muy importante y tiene la industria más importante del país. La ciudad está dividida en dos partes por las Ramblas, una hermosa avenida que baja hasta el puerto. Allí hay un monumento de Colón que conmemora su regreso triunfal de América en 1493; fue recibido en Barcelona por los Reyes Católicos. Barcelona atrae a muchos turistas por su Catedral, iglesias, paseos, parques, plazas de toros, teatros, etcétera. Se habla catalán en Cataluña.

- **Patagonia** es una región de América del Sur, en la parte sur de la Argentina y Chile. Se extiende hasta el estrecho de Magallanes.

B Stem-changing verbs ending in *-ir*

- Stem-changing verbs that end in **-ir** have three types of possible changes in the vowel of the stem: **e > ie, o > ue, e > i**. These **-ir** verbs have the changes in the vowel of the stem in all persons of the present tense except *nosotros* and *vosotros*. Note that **morir(se)** is conjugated like **dormir**.

sentir *to regret*		**dormir** *to sleep*	
siento	sentimos	duermo	dormimos
sientes	sentís	duermes	dormís
siente	sienten	duerme	duermen

pedir *to ask for, request*	
pido	pedimos
pides	pedís
pide	piden

Verbs like **sentir** (e > ie):	
advertir *to notify, warn*	**hervir** *to boil*
convertir *to convert*	**mentir** *to lie*
divertirse *to have a good time*	**preferir** *to prefer*
	referirse (a) *to refer (to)*

Verbs like **pedir** (e > i):		
despedir *to fire*	**medir** *to measure*	**seguir** *to follow, continue*
despedirse (de) *to say good-bye*	**reír(se)** *to laugh*	**servir** *to serve*
gemir *to groan, moan*	**reñir** *to quarrel, scold*	**sonreír(se)** *to smile*
impedir *to prevent*	**repetir** *to repeat; have a second helping*	**vestir(se)** *to dress*

Note that **reír** and **sonreír** have **í** as the stem vowel in the singular and third-person plural: **(son)río, (son)ríes, (son)ríe, (son)reímos, (son)reís, (son)ríen.**

I. En el restaurante. Escriba lo que piden estas personas que salen a comer.

> **MODELO**   Francisco / carne ➜ Francisco pide carne.

1. Ud. y José María / piña
2. la familia Herrera / paella
3. Pili y yo / ensalada
4. tú / flan
5. los chicos / pollo
6. yo / arroz

J. ¿Quién sirve? Escriba quién sirve cada bebida.

> **MODELO**   Uds. / vino ➜ Uds. sirven vino.

1. yo / limonada
2. Susana / refrescos
3. nosotros / cerveza
4. Eduardo y Dolores / jugo
5. tú / agua mineral
6. Ud. y Pepe / té

Nota cultural

- **La paella** es un plato de arroz con carne, pollo, mariscos (*shellfish*) y pescado, guisantes, etcétera que se come en España. Es de origen valenciano, región conocida por su producción de arroz. Se usa el azafrán (*saffron*) para condimentar la paella y para darle al arroz su color amarillo.

- **El flan** es un plato dulce hecho con las yemas de huevo, leche y azúcar. Este postre español es parecido al dulce de leche hispanoamericano.

- España es un país vinícola (*wine-producing*). Hay **vinos** que se producen para exportación que son excelentes. Hasta los sencillos vinos de mesa que se sirven con la comida pueden ser buenísimos. El vino español más conocido en todo el mundo es el jerez (*sherry*) que se produce en la región de Jerez de la Frontera. Esta ciudad queda en la provincia de Cádiz, al sudoeste de Sevilla.

- **El agua mineral** se bebe corrientemente con la comida o en casa o en los restaurantes. Se puede pedir con gas (*carbonated*) o sin gas. Hay algunas regiones del país que tienen manantiales (*springs, sources*) conocidos por la calidad de su agua.

K. **¿Qué prefiere Ud. hacer?** Escriba lo que prefiere hacer cada persona.

> MODELO   Isabel / estudiar → Isabel prefiere estudiar.

1. los primos / salir al campo

2. Julia / leer novelas

3. mis hermanos y yo / ir a un concierto

4. Uds. / ver televisión

5. yo / jugar a las damas

6. tú / viajar

L. **Todos duermen la siesta.** Escriba cuándo duermen la siesta estas personas.

> MODELO   tú / los viernes. → Duermes la siesta los viernes.

1. el abuelo / todos los días

2. yo / los fines de semana

3. Uds. / una vez a la semana

4. nosotros / los lunes

5. los sobrinos / todas las tardes

6. Ud. / los días feriados

M. **En otras palabras.** Escriba lo que ocurre en las siguientes situaciones. Use la forma correcta de uno de los verbos que aparecen a continuación.

divertir	sentir	despedir	hervir
repetir	advertir	mentir	reír
sonreír	vestir	dormir	

> MODELO   Todos tienen hambre. Tú **sirves** la comida.

1. La abuela baña y _____ a sus nietos antes de llevarlos al parque.

2. Va a llegar una tempestad del norte. El locutor de radio _____ al público.

3. Las chicas dejan caer los vasos. Dicen que lo _____.

4. Ya _____ el agua. Ahora podemos meter las legumbres.

5. Ud. juega al tenis toda la mañana y siente un cansancio tremendo. Ud. _____ toda la tarde.

6. Ramona exagera mucho. En realidad, ella _____.

7. Diana _____ a sus amigos con sus cuentos graciosos. Sin embargo, hay algunos de ellos que no _____, ¡ni siquiera _____!

8. Hace dos años que la fábrica pierde dinero. Los dueños _____ a muchos obreros.

9. ¿Te gustó la torta? ¿Por qué no _____?

C *Verbs ending in -uir*

- Verbs ending in **-uir** (not including those ending in **-guir**) add **y** after the **u** in all forms except *nosotros* and *vosotros:*

construir *to build*	
construyo	construimos
construyes	construís
construye	construyen

Verbs that pattern like **construir**:

atribuir *to attribute*	**destruir** *to destroy*	**incluir** *to include*
concluir *to conclude*	**distribuir** *to distribute*	**influir** *to influence*
contribuir *to contribute*	**huir** *to flee*	**sustituir** *to substitute*

N. Vamos a contribuir. Hubo un terremoto que destruyó muchas casas en la Ciudad de México. Ud. y sus amigos deciden recaudar dinero para mandar medicinas a los mexicanos afectados. Escriba con cuánto dinero contribuyen estas personas.

> MODELO   Vera / diez dólares
> → Vera contribuye con diez dólares.

1. los padres de Vera / treinta dólares

2. mis hermanos y yo / quince dólares

3. el director del colegio / veinte dólares

4. Ud. / doce dólares

5. la tía Adriana / veinticinco dólares

6. los ciudadanos del pueblo / mil quinientos dólares

O. ¡Qué desastre! Hay un huracán en la Florida. Hay mucha gente sin casa. Escriba adónde huye la gente para escapar del peligro.

> MODELO   la familia Rivas / al norte
> → La familia Rivas huye al norte.

1. tú / a la estación de tren

2. Uds. / al oeste

3. Fernando / a casa de sus abuelos

4. nosotros / a la capital

5. la familia Ortega / a un hotel

6. yo / al interior del estado

P. Un proyecto. Unos amigos colaboran en realizar un proyecto para la clase de biología. Escriba lo que propone incluir cada persona del grupo.

> MODELO   yo / una bibliografía
> → Yo incluyo una bibliografía.

1. Roberto / investigaciones científicas

2. Uds. / fotos

3. Laura y yo / estadísticas

4. Ud. / buenas explicaciones

5. tú / un resumen

6. David y Ricardo / una introducción

D   Verbs ending in -iar and -uar

- Some verbs that end in **-iar** or **-uar** stress the **i** or the **u** (**í, ú**) in all forms except *nosotros* and *vosotros* in the present tense.

guiar *to guide*	
guío	guiamos
guías	guiáis
guía	guían

continuar *to continue*	
continúo	continuamos
continúas	continuáis
continúa	continúan

Verbs that pattern like **guiar**:		
confiar (en) *to rely (on), confide (in)*	**espiar** *to spy*	**variar** *to vary*
	fiarse (de) *to trust*	
enviar *to send*	**resfriarse** *to catch cold*	

Verbs that pattern like **continuar**:	
actuar *to act*	**graduarse** *to graduate*

Q. ¿Cuándo se resfrían Uds.? Las personas tienen ideas diferentes sobre cómo y cuándo se resfrían. Escriba lo que creen las siguientes personas.

> MODELO   Ud. / en diciembre → Ud. se resfría en diciembre.

1. Tomás / todos los inviernos

2. Uds. / cuando duermen poco

3. Lidia y Miguel / tres veces al año

4. Ud. / cuando come mal

5. yo / cuando me mojo

R. ¿Cuándo es su graduación? Escriba cuándo se gradúan sus amigos del colegio y de la universidad.

> **MODELO**   Daniela / en junio ➔ Daniela se gradúa en junio.

1. Micaela y Jorge / el año próximo
2. Ud. / dentro de dos años
3. Timoteo / en enero
4. Uds. / para el año dos mil
5. Anita / este mes

S. Los espías. Complete esta narración breve sobre el espionaje. Escriba la forma correcta de cada verbo que aparece entre paréntesis.

> **MODELO**   El espía **guía** (guiar) a sus colegas por el laberinto.

1. Los espías no _____ (fiarse) de nadie.
2. Todos los espías _____ (enviar) mensajes secretos.
3. El espía X _____ (confiar) solamente en el espía Y.
4. El espía Z _____ (continuar) su trabajo con los códigos.
5. El espía 003 _____ (resfriarse) trabajando bajo la lluvia.

T. ¿Qué dice Ud.? Conteste las siguientes preguntas personales.

1. ¿A Ud. le gustan las películas de espionaje y misterio? Describa lo que hacen los espías.
2. ¿A quiénes les envía cartas?
3. ¿Se fía Ud. en los anuncios de televisión? Explique.
4. ¿Qué hace y toma cuando se resfría?
5. ¿En quiénes confía Ud.?
6. ¿Cuándo se gradúa Ud.?

E *Verbs with spelling changes in the present tense*

- For verbs that end in **-ger** and **-gir, g** changes to **j** before **o** and **a**. In the present tense, the change occurs only in the first-person singular (*yo* form).

escoger *to choose*	
escojo	escogemos
escoges	escogéis
escoge	escogen

Verbs that pattern like escoger:

afligir *to afflict*	**elegir (e > i)** *to choose, elect*	**fingir** *to pretend*
coger *to grab, catch*		**proteger** *to protect*
corregir (e > i) *to correct*	**encoger** *to shrink*	**recoger** *to gather, pick up*
dirigir *to direct, conduct*	**exigir** *to demand*	

- For verbs that end in **-guir, gu** changes to **g** before **o** and **a**. In the present tense, the change occurs only in the first-person singular (*yo* form).

distinguir *to distinguish*	
distingo	distinguimos
distingues	distinguís
distingue	distinguen

Extinguir (*to extinguish*) is conjugated like **distinguir.**

- **Seguir** (*to follow, continue*) patterns like **distinguir** and also has the stem change **e > i.** This applies to related verbs ending in **-seguir: conseguir** (*to get, acquire*), **perseguir** (*to pursue, persecute*), **proseguir** (*to proceed*):

seguir *to follow*	
sigo	seguimos
sigues	seguís
sigue	siguen

- For most verbs that end in **-cer** or **-cir, c** changes to **z** before **o** and **a**. In the present tense, the change occurs only in the first-person singular (*yo* form):

convencer *to convince*	
convenzo	convencemos
convences	convencéis
convence	convencen

- **Mecer** (*to rock*), **ejercer** (*to exercise*) and **vencer** (*to conquer, overcome*) pattern like **convencer. Cocer** (*to cook*) and **torcer** (*to twist*) also follow this pattern and in addition have the stem change **o > ue**:

torcer *to twist*		cocer *to cook*	
tuerzo	torcemos	cuezo	cocemos
tuerces	torcéis	cueces	cocéis
tuerce	tuercen	cuece	cuecen

Most verbs are marked with their spelling changes in bilingual dictionaries. See for example: **coger** (**g > j/o, a**). When the verb has a stem change and a spelling change, it is usually marked: **torcer** (**o > ue, c > z/o, a**).

U. **¿Qué escoge Ud.?** Nuestros tíos van a celebrar su 25.º aniversario el sábado. Por eso vamos al almacén para comprarles unos regalos. Escriba qué regalos escogemos.

> **Modelo** Ud. / un florero
> → Ud. **escoge** un florero.

1. yo / una caja de bombones

2. mis padres / una bandeja de plata

3. nosotros / un perrito

4. tú / dos relojes

5. Uds. / un televisor

6. la abuela / un juego (*set*) de toallas

V. ¿Qué elige Ud.? Ahora escriba las oraciones del ejercicio U sustituyendo **elegir** por **escoger.**

W. ¿Cuál es su trabajo? Las siguientes personas hacen cierto trabajo. Escriba lo que hace cada persona escogiendo el verbo correcto de la lista abajo.

dirigir   extinguir   recoger   corregir   perseguir   cocer

1. Soy campesino. Yo _____ manzanas y tomates.

2. Soy policía. Yo _____ a los ladrones.

3. Soy bombero. Yo _____ incendios.

4. Soy cocinero. Yo _____ platos muy sabrosos.

5. Soy director de orquesta. Yo _____ una orquesta sinfónica.

6. Soy profesor. Yo _____ exámenes y composiciones.

X. Un misterio. Describa el terror que experimenta el narrador escribiendo la forma correcta de los verbos que aparecen entre paréntesis.

Es la una de la mañana. Yo _____ (1. seguir) por las calles vacías y desoladas de la ciudad. Yo me _____ (2. dirigir) al hotel. De repente oigo pasos. Tengo miedo. Me _____ (3. encoger) de hombros (*shrug*). Vuelvo la cabeza para ver quién camina detrás de mí, quizás en pos de mí (*after me*). Yo _____ (4. distinguir) una sombra de persona. No la _____ (5. reconocer). La persona deja de caminar y _____ (6. fingir) no verme. Yo _____ (7. conseguir) ver que la persona _____ (8. lucir) un vestido blanco que brilla a la luz de la luna. Yo _____ (9. proseguir) mi camino al hotel pero ahora camino más rápido. La situación me _____ (10. producir) mucha angustia pero yo _____ (11. fingir) no estar nervioso. Yo _____ (12. distinguir) un paquete que está a mis pies. Lo _____ (13. recoger). ¡Me da un escalofrío ver que yo soy el destinatario (*addressee*)! Trato de persuadirme que esto es una pesadilla. Por desgracia, no me _____ (14. convencer). ¡Aunque yo _____ (15. desconocer) el camino voy corriendo por las calles como un loco!

Y. Consiguen hacer algunas cosas. Escriba lo que consiguen hacer Ud. y sus amigos el sábado.

MODELO   Rosa y Margarita / terminar su tarea
→ Rosa y Margarita **consiguen** terminar su tarea.

1. Víctor / salir al centro comercial

2. Pablo y yo / reparar el coche

3. Ud. / ver la nueva exposición

4. yo / pasar la aspiradora

5. Uds. / arreglar los armarios

6. Teodoro y tú / colgar los cuadros

Z. **Sinónimos.** Escoja el sinónimo del verbo en cada oración de la lista abajo. Escriba la forma correcta del verbo en la nueva oración.

cocer	exigir	desconocer	elegir	conseguir
coger	producir	seguir	fingir	distinguir

1. *Continúa* con sus clases de pintura.

2. *Agarro* las monedas una por una.

3. *Ignoro* el motivo de los directores.

4. *Disimulo* tener interés en el proyecto.

5. *Cocinan* arroz para servir con el pollo.

6. No *diferencio* entre el mar y el cielo en el cuadro.

7. *Pido* más esfuerzos de parte de los estudiantes.

8. ¿*Seleccionas* tus clases para el próximo semestre?

9. No *logro* hablar con mis cuñados hoy.

10. *Cultivo* maíz y trigo en la finca.

AA. **Las noticias.** Exprese en español los titulares del periódico que Ud. lee. Trate de usar los verbos comprendidos en esta sección.

1. Leopoldo Soto is conducting the New York Philharmonic this week.

2. The firemen put out thirty fires each day.

3. The citizens are demanding better schools.

4. Senator Alonso is following the advice of his colleagues in the Senate.

5. The Americans elect a new president this year.

6. Young couple succeeds in winning the lottery!

7. A new recipe: chef cooks soup with ice cream!

8. News from abroad: the army of A vanquishes the army of B.

9. The campaign against illiteracy proceeds.

10. The governors are ignorant of many problems in their cities.

BB. **Ejercicio oral. ¿Qué piensan hacer Uds.?** Pregúnteles a sus amigos lo que piensan hacer y adónde quieren ir este fin de semana. Que digan también cómo se modificarán sus planes si llueve o nieva. Use verbos con cambios radicales donde sea posible, tales como **pensar, querer, preferir, volver, poder,** etc.

CC. **Estructuras en acción.** Lea estos dos anuncios para programas de televisión del canal *Antena 3* de España e indique en una hoja de papel a cuál de los dos programas se refieren las características dadas: **Manuel Campo Vidal** o **Farmacia de Guardia.**

Noticias
Comedia
Cambio de ideas
Hace pensar
Ya tiene muchos televidentes
Anuncio usa el estilo de la receta
   médica
Programa digno de confianza

CHAPTER 4
THE PRETERIT TENSE

 A *Regular verbs*

- The preterit tense is used to express events that were completed in the past. Preterit-tense endings are added to the stem of regular **-ar, -er,** and **-ir** verbs.

tomar *to take; drink*		**comer** *to eat*	
tom**é**	tom**amos**	com**í**	com**imos**
tom**aste**	tom**asteis**	com**iste**	com**isteis**
tom**ó**	tom**aron**	com**ió**	com**ieron**

vivir *to live*	
viv**í**	viv**imos**
viv**iste**	viv**isteis**
viv**ió**	viv**ieron**

Notes:

1. All preterit forms are stressed on the endings rather than on the stem.

2. For **-ar** verbs:
   - the first-person singular *(yo* form) in the present tense and the third-person singular *(él, ella, Ud.* form) are distinguished only by the stress: tom**o** / tom**ó.**
   - the first-person plural *(nosotros* form) is the same in the present tense and the preterit tense: **tomamos.** The meaning is clarified by context.

3. The preterit endings are the same for both **-er** and **-ir** verbs.

4. For **-ir** verbs:
   - the first-person plural *(nosotros* form) is the same in the present tense and the preterit tense: **vivimos.** The meaning is clarified by context.

5. For **-er** verbs:
   - the present and preterit of the *nosotros* forms are different: com**emos** / com**imos.**

6. **-Ar** and **-er** verbs that have changes in the vowel of the stem (**e** > **ie** or **o** > **ue**) in the present tense, do not have these changes in any of the preterit forms. For example: p**ie**nso / p**e**nsé, v**ue**lven / v**o**lvieron.

7. **-Ir** verbs that have a change in the vowel of the stem in the present tense also have a stem change in the preterit tense. In the preterit the vowel changes from **e** > **i** or from **o** > **u** in the third-person singular and plural.

pedir *to ask for*	
pedí	pedimos
pediste	pedisteis
pidió	pidieron

dormir *to sleep*	
dormí	dormimos
dormiste	dormisteis
durmió	durmieron

8. Some verbs that pattern like **pedir**: **servir** (*to serve*), **divertirse** (*to have a good time*), **repetir** (*to repeat*), **medir** (*to measure*), **advertir** (*to point out, warn*), **mentir** (*to lie*), **convertir** (*to convert*). Like **dormir**: **morir** (*to die*).

9. The verbs **reír** and **sonreír** have a written accent mark on the **i** of the endings of the *yo, tú, nosotros,* and *vosotros* forms in the preterit: (son)reí, (son)reíste, (son)rió, (son)reímos, (son)reísteis, (son)rieron.

10. **-Ir** verbs that have **ñ** directly before the ending drop the **i** of the ending in the third-person singular and plural: **gruñir** (*to grunt*): **gruñó/gruñeron**; **reñir** (*to scold*): **riñó/riñeron**.

 B *Verbs with spelling changes in the preterit*

- **-Ar** verbs whose stems end in the letters **c, g,** and **z** have spelling changes in the *yo* form of the preterit. While these verbs are regular in speech, the rules of Spanish spelling require that the sounds /k/, /g/, and /s/ (written **z**) be written differently before **e** and **i**:

/k/	ca, **que, qui,** co, cu
/g/	ga, **gue, gui,** go, gu
/s/ (written **z**)	za, **ce, ci,** zo, zu

- Compare the spelling of the *yo* form of the present and preterit of the verbs **buscar, llegar,** and **comenzar**: busco / **busqué,** llego / **llegué,** comienzo / **comencé.**

Some verbs like **buscar**:

acercarse *to approach*	**equivocarse** *to be mistaken*	**masticar** *to chew*
arrancar *to pull/root out; start up (vehicle)*	**explicar** *to explain*	**pescar** *to fish*
colocar *to put, place*	**fabricar** *to make, manufacture*	**publicar** *to publish*
dedicarse *to devote oneself*	**indicar** *to indicate*	**sacar** *to take out*
embarcarse *to embark, go on board*	**marcar** *to dial; mark*	**tocar** *to touch; play a musical instrument*
	mascar *to chew*	

Some verbs like **llegar**:

agregar *to add*	**colgar (o > ue)** *to hang*	**negar (e > ie)** *to deny*
ahogarse *to drown*	**encargar** *to put in charge, entrust, to order*	**pagar** *to pay*
apagar *to put out, extinguish*	**entregar** *to hand in/over*	**pegar** *to stick/beat*
cargar *to load*	**jugar (u > ue)** *to play*	**rogar (o > ue)** *to beg, ask*
castigar *to punish*	**madrugar** *to get up early*	**tragar** *to swallow*

Verbs like **comenzar**:

abrazar *to hug, embrace*	**deslizarse** *to slip*	**tranquilizarse** *to calm*
alcanzar *to reach, overtake*	**empezar (e > ie)** *to begin*	*down*
almorzar (o > ue) *to have lunch*	**gozar** *to enjoy*	**tropezar (e > ie)** *to trip, stumble*
	lanzar *to throw*	
amenazar *to threaten*	**realizar** *to fulfill*	
cruzar *to cross*	**rezar** *to pray*	

C *-Er and -ir verbs with stems ending in a vowel*

- **-Er** and **-ir verbs** that have a vowel immediately preceding the preterit ending, change **-ió** to **-yó** in the third-person singular and **-ieron** to **-yeron** in the third-person plural in the preterit. These verbs also add a written accent to the **i** of the *tú*, *nosotros*, and *vosotros* endings:

leer *to read*	
leí	leímos
leíste	leísteis
leyó	leyeron

oír *to hear*	
oí	oímos
oíste	oísteis
oyó	oyeron

- Verbs that end in **-uir** also pattern this way; however, there is no written accent on the *tú*, *nosotros*, and *vosotros* forms of the verbs:

construir *to build*	
construí	construimos
construiste	construisteis
construyó	construyeron

- **Traer**, which has an irregular preterit, verbs with prefixes added to **traer**, and verbs that end in **-guir** are exceptions to the above pattern.

Some verbs like **leer** and **oír**:

caer *to fall*	**creer** *to think, believe*	**poseer** *to have, possess*

Some verbs like **construir**:

concluir *to conclude*	**huir** *to flee*	**intuir** *to have a sense of, feel*
contribuir *to contribute*	**incluir** *to include*	
distribuir *to distribute*		

A. **¡Tanta tarea!** Escriba las cosas que Ud. y sus compañeros de clase hicieron ayer.

> MODELO   Bárbara / practicar el ruso en el laboratorio
> → Bárbara practicó el ruso en el laboratorio.

1. Esteban / estudiar la historia de la Edad Media

2. Rosa y Elena / solucionar problemas de cálculo

3. tú / escribir poemas

4. nosotros / trabajar en la librería

5. yo / visitar el museo de historia natural

6. Uds. / contestar preguntas de filosofía

7. Miguel / usar la computadora

8. Ud. / aprender fechas de historia de memoria

B. **¡Vaya un día de examen!** Escriba las formas correctas del pretérito de los verbos que aparecen entre paréntesis. Así describe lo que le pasó el día del examen.

> MODELO   Mamá me **despertó** (despertar) a las siete.

En seguida yo me _____ (1. levantar) y me _____ (2. arreglar). _____ (3. Bajar)

a la cocina donde _____ (4. saludar) a mis padres y a mi hermano. Mamá me

_____ (5. preparar) cereal y pan tostado. Yo _____ (6. tomar) jugo y

_____ (7. empezar) a repasar mi libro de química. Mi amigo Carlos _____ (8. pasar)

por mí y _____ (9. desayunar) con nosotros. Él y yo _____ (10. terminar) el desayuno

y yo _____ (11. coger) mi mochila de la sala. Carlos y yo _____ (12. salir) corriendo

para la parada de autobuses. El número once _____ (13. llegar) casi inmediatamente.

Los dos _____ (14. subir) y _____ (15. viajar) quince minutos hasta llegar al colegio.

Nosotros _____ (16. bajar) casi en la puerta principal. Tan pronto como el autobús

_____ (17. arrancar) yo _____ (18. buscar) mi mochila. No la _____ (19. encontrar).

¡Y con mis apuntes adentro! ¡Qué susto! "Yo _____ (20. colocar) la mochila en el

asiento y no _____ (21. recordar) cogerla al bajar!", yo _____ (22. pensar). Carlos

me _____ (23. mirar) con mi cara de angustia y _____ (24. hablar). "Chico,

no te preocupes. Aquí la tienes", me _____ (25. explicar). Mi mejor amigo me

_____ (26. entregar) la mochila y así me _____ (27. salvar) la vida.

C. **Salimos a cenar.** Escriba qué tal lo pasó Ud. cuando salió a cenar con sus amigos.

> MODELO   mis amigos y yo / salir a cenar / anoche
> → Mis amigos y yo salimos a cenar anoche.

1. Felipe / escoger / el Café Valencia

2. nosotros / llegar / al restaurante a las siete

3. nosotros / mirar / la carta

4. el mozo/ recomendar / la paella

5. Lorenzo / pedir / ternera y sopa

6. Eva y Diana / pedir / pescado y ensalada

7. yo / preferir / el arroz con pollo

8. tú / comer / torta de postre

9. todos / tomar/ vino

10. nadie / beber / café

11. Felipe / pagar / la cuenta

12. Jaime / dejar / la propina

13. todos nosotros / cenar / muy bien

14. yo / gozar / mucho

15. todos los amigos / divertirse

Nota cultural

El arroz con pollo es un plato que se sirve en casi todos los países del mundo hispánico. Varía de un país a otro o de una región a otra en cuanto a los otros ingredientes y los condimentos.

D. **¡Todo hecho ya!** Su amigo le pregunta si va a hacer ciertas cosas hoy. Para responderle, escriba que ya las hizo.

> **MODELO**   ¿Vas a apagar las luces?
> → Ya apagué las luces.

1. ¿Vas a sacar libros de la biblioteca?

2. ¿Vas a jugar al ajedrez?

3. ¿Vas a tocar la flauta?

4. ¿Vas a colocar los documentos en el archivo?

5. ¿Vas a arrancar la mala hierba del jardín?

6. ¿Vas a explicar lo que sucedió?

7. ¿Vas a colgar los cuadros?

8. ¿Vas a almorzar con Victoria?

9. ¿Vas a entregar el informe?

10. ¿Vas a empezar la novela inglesa?

E. **Pasaron los años.** Hace ocho años que Ud. no ve a unas personas. Ahora tiene noticias de ellas. Escriba lo que les pasó a lo largo de los años.

> MODELO   Jacinta / caer / enferma ➜ Jacinta cayó enferma.

1. los hermanos Serrat / construir / muchas casas

2. el profesor Burgos / influir / mucho en la política

3. Francisca / leer / libros para una casa editora

4. Marco e Isabel / huir / a otro pueblo por una tempestad

5. doña Elvira / contribuir / mucho dinero a las caridades

6. Leonardo / concluir / los trámites de la empresa

F. **¡Qué mala suerte!** Ayer todo le salió mal. Escriba lo que le pasó.

> MODELO   Yo me **caí** (caer) en la escalera.

1. Yo me _____ (equivocar) de número de teléfono

2. y _____ (marcar) mal cuatro veces.

3. Luego _____ (tropezar) con la pared

4. y me _____ (pegar) en el hueso de la alegría (*funny bone*).

5. Luego me _____ (deslizar) en una cáscara de plátano.

6. En la cena _____ (mascar) la carne demasiado rápido

7. y _____ (tragar) mal.

8. Para tranquilizarme, me _____ (bañar).

9. Casi me _____ (ahogar) en la bañera.

10. ¡Claro que no me _____ (tranquilizar)!

G. **Yo no hice eso.** Escriba las formas correctas de los verbos que aparecen entre paréntesis para describir lo que hicieron otras personas y lo que hizo o no hizo Ud.

> MODELO   Alicia **encargó** unos vestidos. (encargar)
> Yo no **encargué** nada.

1. Jorge _____ la pelota en el partido. (lanzar)

   Yo no _____ la pelota.

2. Álvaro _____ unos cuentos. (publicar)

   Yo no _____ cuentos sino una novela.

3. Tú te _____ a la pintura. (dedicar)

   Yo me _____ a la música.

4. Uds. _____ todos los cajones. (cargar)

   Yo no _____ ninguno.

5. Los Sierra _____ un viaje a Bruselas. (realizar)

   Yo _____ un viaje a Estocolmo, capital de Suecia.

6. Ud. se ＿＿＿ para Córcega (*Corsica*). (embarcar)

   Yo me ＿＿＿ para las islas de Grecia.

H. Una entrevista. Ud. acaba de volver de Puerto Rico donde pasó tres semanas con sus amigos. Ahora un periodista del periódico del colegio le hace unas preguntas sobre el viaje. Contéstelas.

> MODELO ¿Qué día llegó a Puerto Rico? (el 20 de diciembre)
> → Llegué el 20 de diciembre.

Turismo

el aeropuerto *airport*	**el mar** *sea, ocean*
almorzar *to have lunch*	**el museo** *museum*
aterrizar *to land*	**pescar** *to fish*
la estancia *stay*	**la playa** *beach*
la fortaleza *fortress*	**rezar** *to pray*
gozar (de) *to enjoy*	**la sinagoga** *synagogue*
la iglesia *church*	**visitar** *to visit*
el lugar turístico *tourist attraction*	

---

1. ¿Dónde aterrizaron Uds.? (el aeropuerto de San Juan)

2. ¿Qué lugares turísticos visitó? (fortalezas, museos e iglesias)

3. ¿Rezó Ud. en una iglesia? (yo en la iglesia de San Juan y Sara en una sinagoga)

4. ¿Almorzó Ud. en la playa? (en varias playas de la isla)

5. ¿Jugaron Uds. al tenis? (y al fútbol también)

6. ¿Pescó Ud. en el mar? (y en los ríos también)

7. ¿Avanzaron Uds. en su dominio del español? (mucho)

8. ¿Qué tal el viaje que realizaron? (maravilloso)

9. ¿Gozó de su estancia en Puerto Rico? (muchísimo)

Nota cultural

El **Estado Libre Asociado de Puerto Rico** es un país que tiene el océano Atlántico al norte y el mar Caribe al sur. Es la isla más oriental de las Antillas Mayores cuyas otras islas más grandes son La Española (la República Dominicana y Haití), Jamaica y Cuba. La isla fue llamada Borinquen por los indígenas (arawacos y caribes). Cristóbal Colón desembarcó en la isla en su segundo viaje en 1493. A los turistas les llaman la atención el Viejo San Juan, la fortaleza de El Morro, el museo de arte de Ponce, el Yunque (bosque), la Casa Blanca de Ponce de León, explorador de Puerto Rico y fundador de San Juan (1508), etcétera. Hay también muchos festivales por toda la isla como el Festival Casals de música clásica que tiene lugar a mediados de junio. El festival lleva el nombre del célebre violonchelista Pablo Casals, nacido en España de madre puertorriqueña y padre catalán, y nacionalizado puertorriqueño. Casals murió en Puerto Rico después de vivir allí casi veinte años. Los puertorriqueños llaman a Puerto Rico «la Isla».

I. ¿Cómo reaccionó la gente? Exprese en español cómo reaccionaron estas personas a una situación o a una noticia.

MODELO   Laura denied it. ➜ Laura lo negó.

1. You (*tú*) smiled.

2. The boys had a second helping. (*repetir*)

3. Patricio grunted.

4. We laughed.

5. You (*Uds.*) fell asleep. (*dormirse*)

6. Mrs. Gil served the soup.

7. Chelo scolded the children.

8. The thieves lied.

9. Our friends warned us.

10. Paquita had a good time.

11. They were sorry.

D *Irregular verbs in the preterit*

Many Spanish verbs have an irregular stem plus a special set of endings in the preterit. The endings for these verbs are: **-e, -iste, -o, -imos, -isteis, -ieron.** Note that the *yo* and *él* forms are stressed on the stem, not on the ending:

decir *to say, tell*		estar *to be*	
dije	dijimos	estuve	estuvimos
dijiste	dijisteis	estuviste	estuvisteis
dijo	dijeron	estuvo	estuvieron

hacer *to do, make*		poder *to be able, can*	
hice	hicimos	pude	pudimos
hiciste	hicisteis	pudiste	pudisteis
hizo	hicieron	pudo	pudieron

poner *to put*		querer *to want, love*	
puse	pusimos	quise	quisimos
pusiste	pusisteis	quisiste	quisisteis
puso	pusieron	quiso	quisieron

saber *to know*		tener *to have*	
supe	supimos	tuve	tuvimos
supiste	supisteis	tuviste	tuvisteis
supo	supieron	tuvo	tuvieron

traer *to bring*	
traje	trajimos
trajiste	trajisteis
trajo	trajeron

venir *to come*	
vine	vinimos
viniste	vinisteis
vino	vinieron

andar *to walk*	
anduve	anduvimos
anduviste	anduvisteis
anduvo	anduvieron

caber *to fit*	
cupe	cupimos
cupiste	cupisteis
cupo	cupieron

producir *to produce*	
produje	produjimos
produjiste	produjisteis
produjo	produjeron

Notes:

1. For the third-person singular of **hacer** in the preterit, the stem is spelled **hiz-** (**hizo**). The spelling change **c** > **z** before **o** retains the /s/.

2. Irregular preterits whose stem ends in **-j**, such as **dij-** (**decir**) and **traj-** (**traer**), have **-eron** and not **-ieron** in the third-person plural form: **dijeron, trajeron, produjeron.** Other verbs, ending in **-ducir,** are conjugated like **producir** in the preterit: **tradujeron** (**traducir** *to translate*), **condujeron** (**conducir** *to drive*), etc.

3. Compound forms of the verbs **hacer** (*rehacer, satisfacer,* etc.), **poner** (*proponer, reponerse,* etc.), **tener** (*mantener, sostener,* etc.), **traer** (*atraer, distraer,* etc.), **venir** (*convenir, prevenir*) are conjugated the same way as the main verb.

4. The preterit form of **hay** (*there is, there are*) is **hubo.**

5. **Dar** takes the endings of regular **-er** and **-ir** verbs in the preterit. Note that the first- and third-person singular forms are written without an accent mark. **Ver**, regular in the preterit, has no written accent marks, like **dar.**

dar *to give*	
di	dimos
diste	disteis
dio	dieron

ver *to see*	
vi	vimos
viste	visteis
vio	vieron

- **Ser** (*to be*) and **ir** (*to go*) have the same conjugation in the preterit tense. Although isolated sentences may be ambiguous (for example, **fue** means both *he was* and *he went*), context usually clarifies which verb is meant.

ser/ir	
fui	fuimos
fuiste	fuisteis
fue	fueron

- Some verbs take on a different meaning when they are used in the preterit. The distinction in meaning will be especially important when you study the difference between the preterit tense and the imperfect tense, which are two aspects or ways of looking at past time. In the case of these verbs used in the preterit, they focus on the beginning or completion of an action. For example, **conocí** means *I began to know*, that is, *I met*.

Verb	Spanish	English
saber *to know*	Supe la fecha hoy.	*I found out the date today.*
conocer *to know*	Conocimos a Carmen ayer.	*We met Carmen yesterday.*
tener *to have*	Tuvo una idea.	*He got an idea.*
poder *to be able to*	No pudieron salir.	*They didn't manage to go out.*
querer *to want*	No quisiste trotar.	*You refused to jog.*

J. El pronóstico meteorológico. Su amiga está leyendo el periódico y comenta sobre el tiempo que hace en varios lugares. Escriba que no ha cambiado desde ayer.

> **Modelo**   —Hace buen tiempo en Quito.
> —Hizo buen tiempo ayer también.

1. Está nublado en Bilbao.

2. Hace frío en Estocolmo.

3. Llueve en Montevideo.

4. Hace sol en Guadalajara.

5. Está despejado en Jerusalén.

6. Nieva en los Andes.

7. Hace ochenta grados en Miami.

8. Hace fresco en Roma.

9. Truena en Marruecos.

10. Hay mucho viento en Chicago.

Nota cultural

- **Quito,** capital de Ecuador, queda a algunos 25 kilómetros de la línea ecuatorial, pero tiene los días calurosos y las noches frescas porque tiene una altitud de 2.850 metros.

- **Bilbao** es una ciudad que queda al norte de España. En Bilbao suele haber cielos nublados y mucha lluvia.

- **Montevideo** es la capital de Uruguay, el país más pequeño de América del Sur. Es una estación veraniega (*summer resort*) y el punto de partida para llegar a los balnearios (*beach resorts*) de la costa uruguaya.

- **Guadalajara** es la segunda ciudad de México en población y la capital del estado de Jalisco. El clima es templado (*mild*), seco y despejado todo el año aunque las noches pueden ser tormentosas.

- **Los Andes,** cordillera (*mountain range*) de América del Sur que se extiende desde el mar de las Antillas o el Caribe hasta la Antártida. Va por la costa del Pacífico, y con sus 7.500 kilómetros de largo, es la mayor cadena (*chain*) del mundo, formando parte del paisaje de Argentina, Chile, Perú, Bolivia, Ecuador, Colombia y Venezuela. El clima varía de una parte de la cordillera a otra: lluvia en el sur, clima tropical y zonas de desierto en el centro, clima cálido y húmedo y nieves perpetuas a partir de los 4.000 metros en el norte. Hay mucha actividad volcánica también.

- **Marruecos** es un reino de África del Norte, que tiene el Mediterráneo al norte, el Atlántico al oeste y el Sáhara al sur y al sureste. Su capital es Rabat.

K. Escenas breves. Escriba las formas correctas en el pretérito de los verbos que aparecen entre paréntesis para saber lo que se dice en los diálogos breves.

1. —¿Qué _____ Ud. entonces? (decir)

   —Pues, no _____ nada.

2. —¿A qué hora _____ Uds. al cine? (ir)

   —_____ a las nueve.

3. —¿Dónde (tú) _____ el sábado? (estar)

   —_____ en el centro comercial.

4. —¿Las mozas les _____ los platos principales? (traer)

   —No, una moza _____ el pan y nada más.

5. —¿Uds. _____ en coche? (venir)

   —Yo _____ en coche pero Teri _____ en tren.

6. —Yo _____ con Catalina anteayer. (dar)

   —¿Ah sí? ¿Dónde la (Ud.) _____? (ver)

7. —¿Clara _____ lo que pasó? (oír)

   —Sí, lo _____ la semana pasada. (saber)

8. —Tú _____ la comida, ¿verdad? (hacer)

—Claro. Y _____ la mesa también. (poner)

9. —¿José _____ el informe? (leer)

—No, no _____. (querer)

10. —¿Quién _____ el postre? (hacer)

—¡_____ yo! (ser)

L. ¿Y qué pasó después? Para cada situación descrita abajo hay una reacción. Para saber cuál es, escoja la expresión de la lista y conjugue el verbo en el pretérito.

hacerse daño   decir que sí   poner la mesa   poder distinguir
tener frío   ir tras ella   estar feliz   hacerse médico

MODELO   Yo invité a Marta a mi casa. (venir a verme)
→ Marta **vino a verme.**

1. Matilde ganó la lotería. Ella _____.

2. Juan Carlos se graduó en la facultad de medicina. Él _____.

3. Bajó mucho la temperatura entre las cinco y las seis de la tarde. Los niños _____.

4. Preparamos una cena para veinte invitados. Nosotros _____.

5. El pintor se cayó de la escalera. Él _____.

6. Fue un día de mucha niebla. Yo ni _____ la carretera.

7. Uds. le pidieron prestado el coche a Rodrigo. Rodrigo _____.

8. Tu novia salió de la conferencia. Y tú _____.

M. Ayer, al contrario ... Generalmente Ud. hace cosas de cierta manera. Ayer, sin embargo, no fue así. Escriba cómo salieron sus actividades empleando la información que se encuentra entre paréntesis.

MODELO   Generalmente me acuesto a las diez. (las once)
→ Pero ayer me acosté a las once.

1. Generalmente me despierto a las ocho. (las siete)

2. Generalmente almuerzo en el Café Bélgica. (el Café Atenas)

3. Generalmente voy de compras por la tarde. (por la mañana)

4. Generalmente hago un plato de pollo. (un plato de pescado)

5. Generalmente juego al tenis con Roberto. (con Ricardo)

6. Generalmente sigo por la calle Toledo. (la calle Atocha)

7. Generalmente empiezo a trabajar después del desayuno. (antes del desayuno)

8. Generalmente vengo en tren. (en taxi)

N. Una merienda en el campo. Unos amigos recuerdan lo bien que lo pasaron ese domingo en julio cuando fueron a merendar en el campo. Escriba lo que dicen escogiendo los verbos correctos. Escriba los verbos en pretérito.

tener	oír	ver	comenzar	estar
hacer	conducir	poder	divertirse	
recoger	traer	ir	dar	

1. ¡Todos _____ tanto ese día!

2. Todos nosotros _____ en carro.

3. Antonio y Francisco _____ los carros.

4. Por desgracia Pedro no _____ acompañarnos.

5. _____ muy buen tiempo.

6. Diego _____ un paseo con los niños.

7. Lila y Berta _____ margaritas.

8. Yo _____ sándwiches y fruta.

9. Leticia y Manuel _____ ensaladas y jugo.

10. Los chicos _____ vacas y caballos

11. y _____ cantar los pájaros.

12. A las cinco de la tarde _____ a llover y

13. nosotros _____ que volver a la ciudad.

14. ¡Nosotros _____ muy contentos ese día!

O. ¡Qué suspenso! Ud. es escritor(a) de cuentos de misterio. Escriba un cuento de misterio expresando en español las siguientes frases.

1. The monster came to the city.

2. It smashed (*hacer pedazos*) cars and destroyed buildings.

3. When the people saw the monster they shouted (*dar gritos*).

4. I got (*ponerse*) pale.

5. My friend Lorenzo got a headache.

6. My friend Marisol got a stomachache.

7. We all started (*echarse a*) to run.

8. Some people didn't manage (*poder*) to escape.

9. The suspense became (*hacerse*) unbearable!

P. ¿Qué dice Ud.? Conteste las siguientes preguntas personales.

1. ¿Adónde fuiste el fin de semana?

2. ¿Qué hiciste el sábado (el domingo)?

3. ¿Adónde fuiste cuando saliste a comer?

4. ¿Con quiénes fuiste?

5. ¿Qué pidieron Uds.?

6. ¿Qué tal estuvo la comida?

7. ¿Qué tal sirvieron los mozos?

8. ¿Quién pagó la cuenta?

9. ¿Quién dejó la propina?

10. ¿Dónde pasó Ud. las vacaciones de verano (invierno)?

11. ¿Con quiénes fue?

12. ¿Qué hicieron Uds. allí?

Q. Ejercicio oral. Diálogos: El horario. Compare su horario diario con un amigo/ una amiga. Hable de las cosas que hizo ayer y diga a qué hora las hizo. Mencione cuándo se despertó, se acostó, almorzó, fue a la oficina, alquiló una película, etcétera. Luego describa lo que hizo el fin de semana.

R. Estructuras en acción. Lea el siguiente artículo sobre una exposición de violines robados. Fíjese en las formas del pretérito y conteste las preguntas que siguen.

1. Jean-Baptiste Vuillaume y Jacobus Steiner son _____.
   a. visitantes de la exposición
   b. policías parisienses
   c. marcas de violín

2. Vinieron a la exposición _____.
   a. personas a quienes les robaron el violín o el violoncelo
   b. varios parientes del rey de Francia
   c. ladrones de instrumentos musicales

3. _____ personas recuperaron su instrumento musical.
   a. Dos mil
   b. Unas cien
   c. Todas las

4. La primera mujer que entró en la exposición _____.
   a. vio que el violín número uno era el suyo
   b. no pudo evitar las risas
   c. fue Adelaida, hija del rey de Francia

5. La policía francesa organizó la exposición _____.
   a. para atrapar a los ladrones de violines
   b. para fomentar entusiasmo para la música
   c. para que los dueños de los instrumentos robados los recuperaran

¿Dónde está mi violín?

Más de 2.000 personas han visitado la exposición en cuatro días.

La policía de París organizó una exposición de mil violines y violoncelos robados para que sus dueños los identificaran. En los cuatro días que duró la exposición, cien personas recuperaron el suyo.

Algunos visitantes de la exposición estaban convencidos de que no encontrarían su violín, pero no renunciaron a intentarlo. Es el caso de André Miesch, de 73 años, que buscaba su violín Jean-Baptiste Vuillaume. Miesch aseguró que su violín, que fue robado hace 15 años, perteneció a la princesa Adelaida, hija del rey de Francia Luis XV. Otros tuvieron más suerte, como un músico de 70 años que encontró su Jacobus Steiner 1659 o como la primera mujer que entró en la exposición, quien inmediatamente señaló con el dedo el violín marcado con el número uno. Los expertos y policías presentes no pudieron evitar las risas, pensando que era un error fruto del entusiasmo, pero no. Era su violín.

No ha sido el caso de la mayoría. De las más de 2.000 personas que visitaron la exposición, sólo un centenar encontró su violín.

CHAPTER 5

THE IMPERFECT TENSE

A Formation of the imperfect

- The endings of the imperfect tense for **-ar** verbs have **-aba-** in all forms. The endings for **-er** and **-ir** verbs are formed by placing **-ía** in all forms:

viajar *to travel*	
viaj**aba**	viaj**ábamos**
viaj**abas**	viaj**abais**
viaj**aba**	viaj**aban**

correr *to run*		salir *to go out*	
corr**ía**	corr**íamos**	sal**ía**	sal**íamos**
corr**ías**	corr**íais**	sal**ías**	sal**íais**
corr**ía**	corr**ían**	sal**ía**	sal**ían**

Notes:

1. The first- and third-person singular forms are identical for all verbs in the imperfect: (*yo / él, ella, Ud.*) **viajaba, corría, salía.**

2. For **-ar** verbs, the *nosotros* form is the only one with a written accent.

3. For **-er** and **-ir** verbs, all forms have a written accent over the **í.**

4. The imperfect of **hay** is **había** (*there was, there were*).

- All verbs are regular in the imperfect tense with the exception of **ir, ser,** and **ver.**

ir *to go*		ser *to be*	
iba	íbamos	era	éramos
ibas	ibais	eras	erais
iba	iban	era	eran

ver *to see*	
veía	veíamos
veías	veíais
veía	veían

B   *Basic uses of the imperfect*

- The imperfect tense is used to express an event or action going on in the past without any reference to its beginning or end. Because the imperfect is not concerned with the beginning or completion of an action, it is the tense used for expressing repeated actions in past time. Adverbs and adverbial phrases such as **todos los días, siempre,** and **muchas veces** are often clues for the selection of the imperfect rather than the preterit. The imperfect is therefore also the tense used for description and expressing background in the past. Common English equivalents for the Spanish imperfect are *used to do, was doing:*

—¿**Eras** estudiante entonces?	***Were you** a student then?*
—No, yo **era** ingeniero ya.	*No, **I was** already an engineer.*
—**Querían** tocar en la orquesta.	***They wanted** to play in the orchestra.*
—¿No **querían** cantar en el coro?	***Didn't they want** to sing in the choir?*
—¿Dónde **estaban** anoche?	*Where **were you** last night?*
—**Estábamos** en el teatro.	*We **were** at the theater.*
—**Leía** el periódico todos los días, ¿no?	***You used to read** the newspaper every day, didn't you?*
—Sólo cuando **tenía** tiempo.	*Only when **I had** time.*
—¿Qué tiempo **hacía**?	*What **was** the weather like?*
—**Hacía** frío y **llovía**.	*It **was** cold and **it rained**.*

- The imperfect tense is used to tell what time it was in the past. The preterit is *never* used:

—¿Qué hora **era**?	*What time **was** it?*
—**Era** la una en punto.	*It **was** exactly one o'clock.*

- The imperfect tense is used in *indirect discourse* (in other words, to report what someone said) after the preterit form of verbs such as **decir, escribir, avisar, anunciar,** etc.:

¿Qué te dijo Loli?	*What did Loli tell you?*
Me **dijo** que **venía**.	*She **told** me she **was coming**.*
¿Les escribiste?	*Did you write to them?*
Sí, les **escribí** que **viajaba**.	*Yes, I **wrote** them that I **was traveling**.*
Paco nos **anunció** que **se casaba**.	*Paco **announced** to us he **was getting married**.*
¡Y a mí me **informó** que **pensaba** romper con su novia!	*And **he informed** me that **he intended** to break off with his fiancée!*

A. Cuando yo era niño(a) ... Ud. tiene nostalgia por esos años tan inolvidables de su niñez. Escriba sus recuerdos en su diario usando el imperfecto de los verbos que aparecen entre paréntesis.

> MODELO   Yo _____ (visitar) a mis amigos.
> → Yo visitaba a mis amigos.

El campo

al atardecer *at the end of the day*	**fresco** *fresh*
el bosque *woods*	**el lago** *lake*
el campo *field*	**merendar (e > ie)** *to picnic*
la casa de campo *country house*	**el monte** *mountain*
cultivar *to grow, raise*	**nadar** *to swim*
la flor *flower*	**la sierra** *mountains, mountain range*

Yo _____ (1. vivir) en Madrid con mis padres y mis hermanos Jaime y Marisol. Jaime _____ (2. ser) el mayor de los tres. Yo _____ (3. ir) al colegio y _____ (4. hacer) todas las cosas que _____ (5. soler) hacer los niños. Mis hermanos, mis amigos y yo _____ (6. ir) al cine, a los partidos de fútbol y a las fiestas. Lo que más me _____ (7. gustar) de aquellos años _____ (8. ser) la estancia en la casa de campo. Allí en la sierra de Guadarrama mis padres, mis hermanos y yo _____ (9. pasar) el mes de agosto. El aire _____ (10. ser) tan fresco y puro y no _____ (11. hacer) tanto calor como en Madrid. _____ (12. Haber) un campo detrás de la casa donde mis hermanos y yo _____ (13. jugar) al fútbol. Mi mamá _____ (14. cultivar) rosas y buganvillas en el jardín. ¡Qué hermosas _____ (15. ser)! Toda la casa _____ (16. oler) divinamente a flores. Nosotros _____ (17. salir) a merendar en el bosque todas las tardes. (Nosotros) _____ (18. Subir) en el monte hasta llegar a un lugar desde donde se _____ (19. ver) todo el valle. Mamá nos _____ (20. servir) los bocadillos más sabrosos del mundo. A veces papá nos _____ (21. leer) un cuento. Nosotros siempre _____ (22. ir) a nadar en uno de los lagos cristalinos de la sierra. Al atardecer (nosotros) _____ (23. estar) muy cansados. Mis hermanos _____ (24. volver) caminando a la casa pero papá me _____ (25. llevar) a mí en brazos porque yo _____ (26. ser) el bebé de la familia. ¡Qué felices recuerdos!

Nota cultural

- **La sierra de Guadarrama** es una cadena de montañas que queda en el centro de España, entre Madrid y Segovia. El pico más alto de la sierra es el de Peñalara, a 2.405 metros de alto. Muchos madrileños pasan sus vacaciones de verano o de invierno en la sierra. Casi todos los españoles, como casi todos los europeos, salen de vacaciones durante el mes de agosto.

- **El metro** equivale a 3.281 pies.

B. Reunión de la clase del año X. Ud. y sus compañeros de secundaria se reúnen después de no verse por muchos años. Se hacen preguntas para ponerse al tanto (*catch up on the news*). Escriba lo que contestan empleando el imperfecto, como en el modelo.

> MODELO   Oye, Clara, ¿todavía estudias arte?
> → Antes estudiaba arte, pero ya no.

1. Oye, Manolo, ¿todavía escribes para *El Tiempo?*

2. Oye, Dora, ¿todavía vas de vacaciones a Málaga?

3. Oye, Pepe, ¿todavía sales con Lola?

4. Oye, Jorge, ¿todavía te gusta la cocina tailandesa?

5. Oye, Ana María, ¿todavía cuidas a tu prima?

6. Oye, Paco, ¿todavía juegas en un equipo de fútbol?

7. Oye, Carmen, ¿todavía vienen al pueblo en invierno tú y tu marido?

8. Oye, Paula, ¿todavía almuerzas con tus padres los sábados?

9. Oye, Mario, ¿todavía eres socio del Club Atlántico?

10. Oye, Sofía, ¿todavía tocan la trompeta tus hijos?

11. Oye, Juan, ¿todavía le mandas bombones a Elena?

12. Oye, Laura, ¿todavía prefieres vivir en el centro?

13. Oye, Ramón, ¿todavía ves a los profesores?

14. Oye, Maribel, ¿todavía te despiertas a las cinco de la mañana?

C. Un vuelo. Ud. acaba de aterrizar en el aeropuerto donde lo (la) espera su familia. Mientras van a buscar su equipaje, Ud. les habla de los viajeros que conoció en el vuelo. Escriba qué eran y adónde iban. Use las formas del imperfecto de los verbos irregulares **ser** e **ir.**

> MODELO   Conocí al señor Torres. (abogado / Chicago)
> → El señor Torres era abogado. Iba a Chicago.

1. Conocí a la señorita Fajardo. (gerente de fábrica / Miami)

2. Conocí a unos señores italianos. (dueños de una pastelería / Uruguay)

3. Conocí a un señor. (profesor de economía / Irlanda)

4. Conocí a la señora Montoya. (banquera / Suiza)

5. Conocí a don Pedro Domínguez. (candidato a senador / Monterrey)

6. Conocí a Lorena Iglesias. (ama de casa / Costa Rica)

7. Conocí a los hermanos Machado. (músicos / Nueva York)

8. Conocí al señor Rubio. (cirujano / la India)

Nota cultural

- **Monterrey** queda al este de México, cerca de la frontera con Tejas. Es la capital del estado de Nuevo León y la tercera ciudad de México. Es un gran centro industrial y comercial.

- **Costa Rica,** país centroamericano, queda entre Nicaragua y Panamá con una costa en el Pacífico y otra en el Caribe. El país se destaca por su tradición democrática; en noviembre de 1989 celebró su centenario de la democracia. Costa Rica ha tenido más adelantos económicos y sociales que ningún otro país centroamericano y goza del nivel de vida más alto de toda esa región.

D. **¿Qué tal se veía?** La gente no podía ver ciertas cosas muy bien desde el lugar donde estaba. Escriba las formas correctas del imperfecto del verbo irregular **ver** al describir la situación de esas personas.

> MODELO   Pepe / el edificio suyo / la calle Mercado
> ➜ Pepe no veía el edificio suyo desde la calle Mercado.

1. Carolina y Ramón / el mar Caribe / el avión

2. nosotros / la cara de los actores / el paraíso (*highest balcony*) del teatro

3. doña Federica / el embotellamiento / la ventana del dormitorio

4. Uds. / toda la cancha de fútbol / la tribuna (*stand*) del estadio

5. yo / la cumbre de la montaña / el valle

6. Daniel / la discoteca / la esquina

7. tú / al público / la parte derecha de la escena

C *The imperfect and the preterit: two aspects of past time*

- The imperfect and preterit tenses express different ways of looking at past actions and events. The imperfect tense designates an action as going on in the past without any reference to its beginning or end. The preterit tense designates an action as completed in the past. Spanish speakers must select one of these two aspects—imperfect or preterit—for every past action they refer to. The differences between the tenses can be expressed in English, but it is not obligatory:

Cuando estaba en la universidad, **estudiaba** chino.	*When I was at the university, **I studied** Chinese. (or **I used to study** Chinese.)*
Ayer **estudié** chino.	*Yesterday **I studied** Chinese.*

- Sometimes English uses entirely different verbs to express the difference between the imperfect and the preterit of some Spanish verbs. For example, **tenía** means *I was in the process of having* or *I had;* **tuve** means *I began to have* or *I got, received:*

Sabía el precio.	*I knew the price.*
Supe el precio.	*I found out the price.*

Conocían a Sergio.	*They knew Sergio.*
Conocieron a Sergio.	*They met Sergio.*
No podíamos llegar para las cuatro.	*We couldn't arrive by four o'clock. (Doesn't say whether we arrived by four or not.)*
No **pudimos** llegar para las cuatro.	*We couldn't arrive by four o'clock. (We didn't arrive by four.)*
Laura **no quería** ir en metro.	*Laura didn't want to take the subway.*
Laura **no quiso** ir en metro.	*Laura refused to (didn't want to and didn't) take the subway.*

- The imperfect and the preterit can be used in two different clauses in the same sentence. The imperfect expresses the background, a continuing action, or an ongoing state, against which a completed action or event takes place:

Mientras **trabajábamos,** Julia **durmió** la siesta.	*While we were working, Julia took a nap.*

- It is possible to have sentences with all verbs in the imperfect if the speaker sees the past actions or events as ongoing processes:

Pilar **leía** mientras Marta **jugaba** al tenis.	*Pilar was reading while Marta was playing tennis.*

- It is possible to have sentences with all verbs in the preterit if the speaker views the actions mentioned as a series of completed events:

Cené, me arreglé y **fui** al teatro.	*I ate dinner, got ready, and went to the theater.*

E. ¿Qué tiempo hacía …? Sus amigos quieren saber qué tiempo hacía cuando sucedieron ciertas cosas. Use el imperfecto para hablar del tiempo y el pretérito para hablar de los sucesos al escribir los siguientes diálogos.

> MODELO   Ud. / salir / hacer buen tiempo
> → Hacía buen tiempo cuando Ud. salió.

1. Beatriz y tú / volver / llover

2. los Sorolla / levantarse / hacer frío

3. tú / ir a la biblioteca / estar despejado

4. José Antonio / venir a la casa / hacer viento

5. nosotros / terminar el trabajo / nevar

6. Ud. / entrar en el cine / tronar

7. yo / llegar a la universidad / hacer sol

F. ¿Qué hora era cuando …? Su amigo quiere saber a qué hora pasaron ciertas actividades. Use el imperfecto para hablar de la hora y el pretérito para hablar de las actividades.

> MODELO   Carmen y Víctor / llamar / las ocho
> → Eran las ocho cuando Carmen y Víctor llamaron.

1. Consuelo y Berta / despedirse / las nueve y media

2. el programa / comenzar / la una

3. Rosa / servir el almuerzo / mediodía

4. el empleado / abrir la taquilla / las diez en punto

5. nosotros / regresar de la estación / medianoche

6. Uds. / dormirse / muy tarde

7. el cartero / traer la correspondencia / temprano

8. los pintores / dejar de pintar la sala / las cinco y cuarto

G. Mientras estábamos de vacaciones ... Durante las vacaciones de invierno pasaron muchas cosas. Use el imperfecto para hablar del fondo (*background*) de las vacaciones y el pretérito para hablar de las cosas que sucedieron durante las vacaciones.

> MODELO   nosotros / estar de vacaciones / yo / leer cinco libros
>
> ➔ Mientras estábamos de vacaciones, yo leí cinco libros.

1. tú / viajar / acabar / la telenovela

2. Marta y Miguel / quedarse en un hotel / un ladrón / forzar la entrada (*break in*)

3. Eunice / vivir / en el extranjero / sus padres / vender su casa de campo

4. Uds. / hacer un viaje / sus vecinos / montar una nueva empresa

5. yo / ver / las siete maravillas del mundo / otras siete / añadirse a la lista

6. Benito / pasear por San Antonio / su novia / romper con él

7. el avión de Diego / aterrizar en Los Ángeles / el de su hermana / despegar en Atlanta

8. los turistas / conocer los Estados Unidos / la guerra / estallar en su país

9. nosotros / estar en el puerto / haber / un incendio en el barco

Nota cultural

Los españoles pusieron nombres españoles, y especialmente nombres de los santos, a muchos lugares de América, por ejemplo:

San Antonio, ciudad de Tejas, es donde ocurrió la batalla del Álamo en 1836. Cuando Tejas proclamó su derecho de separarse de México en 1835, Sam Houston asumió el mando del ejército tejano. En 1836 el general Santa Anna atacó el Álamo y mató a todos los soldados (23 febrero–6 marzo). Tejas declaró su independencia. Houston y los tejanos vencieron a los mexicanos en **San Jacinto.**

Donde hubo colonización española hay nombres españoles: *California, Tejas, la Florida.* Y en todo el sudoeste de los Estados Unidos: *Los Ángeles, Las Vegas, Santa Fe, San Francisco, San Diego, Santa Ana, San Antonio, El Paso, Alamogordo, Las Cruces,* etcétera.

H. Me sorprende. Su amiga le dice que varias personas ya no hacen ciertas cosas. A Ud. le sorprende porque antes las hacían. Para expresar esta idea Ud. dirá *Me sorprende* y cambiará las formas verbales del presente al imperfecto.

> MODELO —Juan Carlos ya no escucha discos.
> —Me sorprende. Antes escuchaba discos todos los días.

1. Felipe ya no corre quince millas al día.

2. Los tíos ya no duermen la siesta.

3. Anita ya no va al centro.

4. Martín ya no visita los museos.

5. El director ya no ensaya con la orquesta.

6. Las señoritas ya no ven la telenovela.

7. Carmen y Pablo ya no van al cine.

8. Felipe ya no conduce su coche.

I. Y al mismo tiempo ... Escriba las cosas que hacían las personas al mismo tiempo. Use el imperfecto para hablar de estas actividades. Escoja las actividades de la siguiente lista o invente otras.

trabajar en	ir de compras	jugar	divertirse
comer	bañarse	cocina	tocar
estudiar	esperar el tren	salir para	practicar
leer	ver una película	ensayar	arreglarse
escribir	caminar	dibujar	tomar algo

> MODELO   Sara escribía cartas mientras Teresa dibujaba.

J. Perspectivas. Las siguientes personas hablan de sus experiencias. Escriba el verbo en imperfecto o el verbo en pretérito para saber cómo ven el pasado estas personas.

El teatro

el/la acomodador(a) *usher*	**hacer el papel de** *to play the role of*
el/la aficionado(a) a la ópera *opera fan*	**la obra** *work, piece*
apagar las luces *to put out the lights*	**la ópera** *opera*
el/la cantante *singer*	**el programa** *playbill, program*
el decorado *scenery*	**sube el telón** *the curtain goes up*

A. Cuando yo (1. tenía / tuve) once años, mis padres me (2. llevaban / llevaron) por primera vez a ver una ópera. La acomodadora nos (3. sentaba / sentó) y nos (4. dio / daba) el programa. Mientras (5. leíamos / leímos) las notas sobre la obra,

las luces (6. se apagaban / se apagaron). Luego (7. subía / subió) el telón y
(8. veíamos / vimos) la escena. (9. Había / Hubo) un decorado de palacio.
Una cantante que (10. hizo / hacía) el papel de la reina (11. estaba / estuvo)
sentada en el trono. Ella (12. llevó / llevaba) una corona (*crown*) de oro y
(13. vestía / vistió) una capa de terciopelo (*velvet*) verde con armiño (*ermine*).
El cantante que (14. hacía / hizo) el papel del rey (15. salió / salía) a la escena y
(16. se ponía / se puso) a cantar. Yo (17. quedaba / quedé) tan impresionada con lo
que vi y oí que (18. me hice / me hacía) aficionada a la ópera para siempre.

Nota cultural

El Teatro Colón, lugar conocido de Buenos Aires, es uno de los teatros de ópera más
grandes del mundo. En este sitio todo dorado y de terciopelo (*velvet*) rojo, ponen ópera,
conciertos de la Orquesta Filarmónica de Buenos Aires, recitales y obras de ballet.
La temporada es de abril a primeros días de diciembre; está cerrado en enero y febrero.
Recuerde que las estaciones están al revés en el hemisferio austral (sur).

B. Hace ocho años (1. me gradué / me graduaba) de la universidad.
(2. Saqué / Sacaba) mi título en periodismo. (3. Esperaba / Esperé) encontrar
trabajo en uno de los periódicos grandes de la ciudad donde (4. nacía / nací).
(5. Quería / Quise) quedarme en Tejas porque mis padres y mis hermanos vivían
allí. Por desgracia, no (6. hubo / había) empleo en ningún periódico del estado.
Por lo tanto, yo (7. mandé / mandaba) mi currículum vitae a varios periódicos por
todo el país. (8. Tenía / Tuve) suerte. (9. Encontré / Encontraba) trabajo de
reportero en un periódico que (10. se publicaba / se publicó) en Maine. Al principio
la vida en Maine me (11. fue / era) muy difícil. Yo no (12. conocí / conocía) a
nadie donde (13. viví / vivía) y no (14. estaba / estuve) acostumbrado al
clima. ¡(15. Hacía / Hizo) un frío horrible en invierno! Pero un día yo
(16. conocía / conocí) a Marta quien (17. trabajó / trabajaba) en el periódico
también. Ella (18. fue / era) editora. ¡Y (19. era / fue) un flechazo para nosotros
(*love at first sight*)! En fin, Marta y yo (20. nos casamos / nos casábamos).
Yo (21. llegaba / llegué) a ser jefe de redacción (*editor-in-chief*) del periódico. Marta
y yo (22. tuvimos / teníamos) dos hijos. ¡Y todos (23. vivimos / vivíamos) muy
felices (*we all lived happily ever after*)!

K. Contrastes. Exprese las siguientes ideas en español. Los contrastes surgen de la diferencia entre el imperfecto y el pretérito.

1. Bárbara thought Tomás knew her sister Luz.
   Actually, he met Luz last night at dinner.

2. The businessmen wanted to discuss the issues, but their lawyers refused to.

3. The bride (*la novia*) didn't have any gifts.
   Then she got twenty gifts this morning.

4. We didn't know who had the documents.
   We found out yesterday.

5. I wasn't able to assemble (*armar*) the toy.
   Javier (tried but) couldn't assemble it either.

L. ¡Castillos de España! Para describir una visita a un castillo español escoja el imperfecto o el pretérito de los verbos que aparecen entre paréntesis.

El turismo	
el alcázar *citadel, fortress*	**hacer un viaje** *to take a trip*
el billete de avión *plane ticket*	**el lugar histórico** *historic site*
el castillo *castle*	**el palacio** *palace*
la gira *tour, excursion*	**el parador** *government-owned hotel (Spain)*
hacer la reservación *to book*	**patrocinado por** *sponsored by*

Yo siempre _____ (1. querer) visitar un castillo en España. Por eso cuando mi

esposo y yo _____ (2. ir) a hacer un viaje en mayo, yo le _____ (3. decir) a Rolando

que me _____ (4. interesar) visitar un castillo español. A Rolando le _____ (5. gustar)

la idea porque no _____ (6. conocer) España. Rolando _____ (7. comprar) los

billetes de avión y también _____ (8. hacer) la reservación para el hotel. Nosotros

_____ (9. pensar) hacer una gira de tres semanas con visitas a Madrid, Toledo,

Sevilla, Segovia y Santiago de Compostela. Nosotros _____ (10. tomar) el avión y

_____ (11. llegar) a Madrid el tres de mayo. Durante las tres semanas nosotros

_____ (12. visitar) varios lugares históricos y naturalmente _____ (13. conocer)

el Palacio Real en Madrid, el Alcázar de Sevilla, Segovia y Toledo y otros castillos y

palacios. Al llegar a Santiago de Compostela yo _____ (14. tener) una gran sorpresa.

En vez de simplemente visitar un castillo, nosotros _____ (15. poder) quedarnos en

uno por tres días. Es que el famoso castillo _____ (16. ser) un parador. Los paradores, es decir, hoteles patrocinados por el gobierno español, _____ (17. estar) por todas partes del país. ¡Por fin yo _____ (18. realizar) mi sueño de visitar un castillo en España!

Nota cultural

- **El Alcázar,** palabra de origen árabe, significa fortaleza, castillo o palacio real.

- **Sevilla,** a orillas del río Guadalquivir, es la capital de la Comunidad Autónoma de Andalucía. La construcción del **Alcázar de Sevilla** comenzó bajo los almohades, una dinastía árabe, en el siglo XII. Se siguió construyendo en época cristiana durante los reinos de Pedro I el Cruel, rey de Castilla y León (1334–69), Juan II, rey de Castilla (1405–54), los Reyes Católicos (Fernando II de Aragón [1452–1516] e Isabel I de Castilla [1451–1504]), Carlos V, rey de España y emperador de Alemania (1500–58) y Felipe II, rey de España (1527–98). Se puede visitar los apartamentos reales, el palacio de Pedro el Cruel, los jardines, etcétera.

- **El Alcázar de Segovia** fue construido en el siglo XIV por Alfonso XI, rey de Castilla y León (1312–50). Fue transformado en el siglo XV. En las salas hay exposición de armas, cuadros y muebles de época medieval. Se dice que el Alcázar de Segovia sirvió de modelo para el castillo de Disneylandia.

- **El Alcázar de Toledo** fue construido por Alfonso VI, rey de Castilla y León (1030–1109) cuando reconquistó la ciudad de los moros en 1085. El Cid fue su primer gobernador. En el siglo XIII fue reformado y embellecido. Carlos I (1500–58) confió la restauración del Alcázar al arquitecto español Covarrubias (1488–1570). Este arquitecto fue uno de los introductores del Renacimiento en España.

- **Juan de Herrera** (1530–97), otro gran arquitecto español, continuó con la restauración. Hubo otras restauraciones durante los siglos XVIII, XIX y XX por los destrozos de las guerras. La última restauración fue necesaria por la destrucción del Alcázar a principios de la Guerra Civil española (1936) cuando el coronel Moscardó se negó a rendirles el Alcázar a los republicanos. Ante la negativa de Moscardó, el Alcázar fue destruido y su propio hijo fue ejecutado.

- **Santiago de Compostela,** capital de la Comunidad Autónoma de Galicia, queda al noroeste de España. En la Edad Media fue un importante lugar de peregrinación (*pilgrimage*), especialmente a partir del siglo XI. El sepulcro del Apóstol Santiago se encuentra aquí. La magnífica catedral fue construida entre los siglos XI y XIII.

M. Del diario de un detective. Aquí tiene Ud. una página de la libreta de apuntes del famoso detective privado Samuel Espada. Para poder leer los apuntes e intentar desenredar el misterio, escriba el imperfecto o el pretérito de los verbos que aparecen entre paréntesis.

El crimen

la cita *appointment*	**la pandilla** *gang*
el/la chantajista *blackmailer*	**la policía** *police*
el detective privado *private detective*	**seguir la pista** *to follow the lead*
el ladrón *thief*	**sobresaltado** *startled*
maltés *Maltese*	

_____ (1. Ser) las diez de la mañana cuando _____ (2. sonar) el teléfono en mi oficina. Yo _____ (3. estar) despierto desde la noche anterior. (Yo) _____ (4. descolgar) y _____ (5. oír) la voz sobresaltada de una mujer. La mujer me _____ (6. decir) que una pandilla de ladrones le _____ (7. robar) su estatuilla (*figurine*) del halcón (*falcon*) maltés y que ahora le _____ (8. pedir) un rescate por el halcón. Además, la señorita me _____ (9. explicar) que _____ (10. tener) miedo de ir a la policía por razones especiales. Ella y yo _____ (11. quedar) en vernos en el vestíbulo del Hotel Casablanca. Ya _____ (12. ser) las siete de la tarde cuando yo _____ (13. llegar) al hotel. Toda la tarde yo _____ (14. seguir) la pista de los chantajistas hasta que _____ (15. llegar) la hora de la cita. En el vestíbulo yo _____ (16. ver) a una señorita guapísima que _____ (17. estar) sentada en un sofá. Ella _____ (18. tener) el pelo castaño y largo, los ojos verdes como dos esmeraldas y _____ (19. llevar) una gardenia en la chaqueta. Ella _____ (20. fumar) un cigarrillo igual que yo (¡porque todos los personajes de los años cuarenta fuman cigarrillos!). Yo me _____ (21. acercar) y me _____ (22. sentar) a su lado. Ella _____ (23. oler) a un perfume exótico. Yo le _____ (24. hablar) primero. "¿Es Ud. la señorita María Aster?", le _____ (25. preguntar). Ella se _____ (26. poner) a llorar y me _____ (27. decir) sollozando (*sobbing*): "Samuel, es que tú no comprendes …". Pero sí, yo _____ (28. comprender) muy bien. ¡Esto _____ (29. ir) a ser otro dramón (*sob story*)!

- Remember that the Spanish construction **hace** + *expression of time* + **que** + *verb in the present tense* is used to label an action that began in the past and is continuing in the present. Similarly, the construction **hacía** + *expression of time* + **que** + *verb in the imperfect tense* is used to label an action that was continuing in the past when something else happened. The corresponding question is **¿Cuánto tiempo hacía ...?** The word *tiempo* may be omitted:

—**¿Cuánto (tiempo) hacía que esperabas** cuando llegó el tren?	*How long had you been waiting when the train arrived?*
—**Hacía más de una hora** que esperaba.	*I had been waiting more than an hour.*

- A *verb in the imperfect tense* + **desde hacía** + *expression of time* is also used to label an action that was continuing in the past when something else happened:

—**¿Desde cuándo rodaban** la película cuando **hubo** un terremoto?	*How long had they been shooting the film when there was an earthquake?*
—**Rodaban** la película **desde hacía siete semanas** cuando **hubo** un terremoto.	*They had been shooting the film for seven weeks when there was an earthquake.*

N. **¿Cuánto tiempo hacía ...?** Haga preguntas y explique lo siguiente usando la construcción **hacía** + *expresión de tiempo* + **que** + *verbo en imperfecto* y **¿Cuánto (tiempo) hacía que ...?**

> MODELO   Leonor / estudiar inglés / salir para Inglaterra
> (dos años)
> —¿Cuánto tiempo hacía que Leonor estudiaba inglés
> cuando salió para Inglaterra?
> —Hacía dos años que estudiaba inglés.

1. Montserrat Pujol / cantar ópera / firmar un contrato con la Metropolitana (ocho años)

2. los señores Salazar / estar casados / su hija / nacer (cuatro años)

3. tú / vivir en París / tus padres / mudarse a Londres (once meses)

4. Susana y Lía / ser amigas / Susana / quitarle el novio a Lía (doce años)

5. Ud. / comprar billetes de lotería / ganar el premio (quince años)

6. Patricio y Ud. / tocar el violonchelo / el conservatorio / darles una beca (nueve años)

O. Cambios políticos y económicos. Pasaban unas cosas desde hacía tiempo cuando ocurrieron otras cosas en la vida política y económica del país. Use la construcción *verbo en imperfecto* + **desde hacía** + *expresión de tiempo* para describir los cambios. Junte las dos frases con *hasta que.*

MODELO   el gobierno / prometer muchas cosas / dos años / los ciudadanos / empezar a reclamar
→ El gobierno prometía muchas cosas desde hacía dos años hasta que los ciudadanos empezaron a reclamar.

Política y economía	
controlar la inflación *to control inflation*	
establecer la democracia *to establish democracy*	
explotar el petróleo *to exploit, develop oil*	
intentar *to try, attempt*	
privatizar la industria *to privatize industry*	
reclamar *to demand*	
los bienes *goods*	**el libre mercado** *free market*
la década *decade*	**el obrero** *worker*
el dictador *dictator*	**la prensa** *press*
el gobierno *government*	**el presidente** *president*
el golpe de estado *coup d'état*	**el pueblo** *the people*
el/la economista *economist*	**el sindicato** *union*
la libertad *liberty*	**el sueldo** *salary*

1. el gobierno / explotar el petróleo / treinta años / el presidente / privatizar la industria

2. la gente / sufrir por la inflación / cinco años / los economistas / intentar controlarla

3. la prensa / no ser libre / cincuenta años / haber / un golpe de estado

4. los obreros / no recibir un sueldo decente / cinco décadas / formarse los sindicatos

5. el país / no producir los bienes necesarios / varios años / el país establecer el mercado libre

6. el pueblo / no tener ninguna libertad / cuarenta y cinco años / morir el dictador y establecerse la democracia

P. ¿Qué dice Ud.? Conteste las siguientes preguntas personales.

1. ¿Cuántos años tenía cuando se vestía solo(a)?

2. ¿Cuántos años tenía cuando empezó a estudiar en el colegio?

3. Cuando era niño(a), ¿adónde iba de vacaciones?

4. ¿Qué le gustaba hacer cuando era niño(a)?

5. ¿Cómo era de niño(a)?

6. Hable de las cosas que solía hacer todos los días cuando asistía al colegio.

7. ¿Qué sueños quería realizar en la vida?

8. ¿Pudo realizar algunos ya?

Q. Un viaje a México. Exprese esta historia en español. Escoja entre el pretérito y el imperfecto para hablar del pasado.

1. The first day Beatriz and I spent in Mexico City we went to Chapultepec Park.

2. The weather was beautiful. It was sunny and warm.

3. There were many people in the park.

4. Little children were playing on the slides (*los resbalines*) and riding their bicycles.

5. As we walked through the park we saw Moctezuma's Tree and the Chapultepec Castle.

6. We arrived at the National Museum of Anthropology and went in.

7. We walked from room to room and saw the exhibit of pre-Columbian (*precolombino*) art.

8. We spent two hours in the museum.

9. Then we went to the bookstore where I bought a book about the Aztecs and the Mayans.

10. We had lunch in the museum cafeteria.

Nota cultural

- **El Bosque de Chapultepec** queda al final del Paseo de la Reforma en plena capital mexicana. El hermoso parque tiene miles de ahuehuetes (árboles coníferos), laberintos de caminos, lagos, un jardín botánico, un zoológico y varios museos.

- **El Castillo de Chapultepec,** situado en una colina, da hermosas vistas del valle de México desde sus balcones. La gran atracción del parque es el **Museo Nacional de Antropología** que presenta una espléndida exposición de las culturas mexicanas precolombinas, es decir, de los aztecas, los mayas y otros grupos que vivían allí antes de la llegada de Cristóbal Colón al Nuevo Mundo.

- Moctezuma II era el emperador azteca (1466–1520) cuando llegó Cortés a México en 1519. Fue hecho prisionero por los conquistadores españoles poco después de su llegada. **El Árbol de Moctezuma,** un poco más abajo del Castillo, era inmenso— de algunos 60 metros de alto. "El Sargento", como se le llama, se ha cortado hasta medir diez metros.

R. Ejercicio oral. Una encuesta. Prepare una lista de algunas actividades que Ud. hacía cuando era niño(a). Luego pregúnteles a unos amigos si también hacían esas actividades. Algunas posibilidades:

1. Jugaba al fútbol.

2. Pintaba cuadros al aire libre.

3. Pasaba los veranos en un campamento.

4. Cocinaba con mi mamá o papá.

5. Tocaba un instrumento musical.

6. Montaba en bicicleta.

7. Buceaba (*dive under water*) en el mar.

8. Iba de compras en el centro comercial.

S. **Estructuras en acción.** Lea el artículo sobre las catedrales españolas fijándose especialmente en los verbos en tiempo imperfecto. Luego haga el ejercicio.

Vocabulario	
el abad *abbot*	**girar en torno a** *to revolve around*
el animal de tiro *draft animal*	**impregnar** *to fill, pervade*
atar *to tie*	**el maestro de obras** *foreman*
la cal *limestone*	(construction)
el cantero *stonemason*	**mediados: a mediados de** *around*
el carro *cart*	*the middle of*
el cura *priest*	**el orfebre** *goldsmith*
diferencia: a diferencia de *in contrast to*	**el sacerdote** *priest*
la fachada *facade*	**semejante** *similar*
fiel *faithful*	**el tallista de madera** *wood carver*

1. El factor dominante en los siglos cuando se construyeron las catedrales era _____.
   a. la riqueza
   b. la religión
   c. el trabajo

2. La tarea central de una ciudad era _____.
   a. el transporte de vino
   b. la busca de curas competentes
   c. la construcción de su catedral

3. En la construcción de una catedral participaban _____.
   a. gente de todas las clases sociales
   b. varios dioses y sacerdotes paganos
   c. los obreros solamente

4. El interior de las catedrales era inmenso para _____.
   a. rivalizar con los templos paganos
   b. guardar la cal, la piedra y la madera
   c. recibir a todos los fieles que querían entrar

5. Hasta los nobles, hombres y mujeres, tiraban carros para _____.
   a. quitarles trabajo a los obreros
   b. transportar materiales de construcción
   c. llevar a los curas a la iglesia

PIEDRA SANTA

LAS CATEDRALES ESPAÑOLAS— CONSTRUCCIONES RELIGIOSAS Y COMUNITARIAS

En aquellos tiempos —el siglo XII, el XIII, inclusive el XIV— cuando se construyeron las grandes catedrales españolas, la religiosidad lo llenaba todo, y la vida entera de una ciudad giraba en torno a esa manifestación suprema de la religión que era el interminable y exaltante trabajo de la construcción de la catedral. A diferencia de los templos paganos, reservados a los dioses y a sus sacerdotes, las iglesias cristianas estaban construidas para recibir la comunión de los fieles: por eso no eran meras fachadas, sino grandes cavernas en donde cabían todos. Y se construían entre todos, ricos y pobres, curas y reyes, canteros y orfebres, y durante generaciones trabajaban en ellas de padres a hijos los escultores y los maestros de obra, los arquitectos y los tallistas de madera. Decía a mediados del siglo XII el abad de Saint Pierre sur Dive: «¿Quién vio u oyó alguna vez algo semejante, que grandes señores y príncipes de este mundo que tenían riquezas y de honores, que aun damas nobles inclinaron su orgullosa cabeza y se ataran a los carros como animales de tiro para transportar vino, aceite, cal, piedras y madera a los obreros que construían una iglesia?»

LA CATEDRAL DE LEÓN—SIGLOS XII–XV

CHAPTER 6
THE FUTURE &
CONDITIONAL TENSES

 A *Formation of the future tense*

- The future tense is formed in Spanish by adding a special set of endings to the infinitive. The endings are the same for **-ar, -er,** and **-ir** verbs.

firmar el documento *to sign the paper*	
Firmar**é** el documento.	Firmar**emos** el documento.
Firmar**ás** el documento.	Firmar**éis** el documento.
Firmar**á** el documento.	Firmar**án** el documento.

correr en el maratón *to run in the marathon*	
Correr**é** en el maratón.	Correr**emos** en el maratón.
Correr**ás** en el maratón.	Correr**éis** en el maratón.
Correr**á** en el maratón.	Correr**án** en el maratón.

asistir al concierto *to attend the concert*	
Asistir**é** al concierto.	Asistir**emos** al concierto.
Asistir**ás** al concierto.	Asistir**éis** al concierto.
Asistir**á** al concierto.	Asistir**án** al concierto.

- For some Spanish verbs the future tense endings are added on to modified versions of the infinitive. Some verbs have **-d-** in place of the infinitive vowel *-e-* or *-i-:*

  poner > **pondré** tener > **tendré** venir > **vendré**
  salir > **saldré** valer > **valdré**

- Some verbs lose the infinitive vowel *-e-:*

  caber > **cabré** querer > **querré**
  poder > **podré** saber > **sabré**

- Some verbs shorten the infinitive:

  decir > **diré** hacer > **haré**

- **-Ir** verbs that have an accent mark in the infinitive—**oír, reír, sonreír**—lose the accent mark in the future: **oiré, reiré, sonreiré.**

- The future of **hay** is **habrá** (*there will be*).

- Compounds of the irregular verbs have the same irregularities: componer (**compondré**), retener (**retendré**), prevenir (**prevendré**), contradecir (**contradiré**), satisfacer (**satisfaré**), etc.

B   *Uses of the future tense*

- The future tense is used in Spanish and English to express future time:

¿A qué hora **llegarán** Uds.?   *At what time **will you arrive**?*
Estaremos para las tres.   *We'll be there by three o'clock.*

- The future tense in Spanish is often replaced by the **ir a** + *infinitive* construction. This commonly used construction refers to the immediate future whereas the future tense refers to both the immediate and the remote future:

Esquiaré en los Pirineos.   *I'll ski in the Pyrenees.*
Voy a esquiar en los Pirineos.   *I'm going to ski in the Pyrenees.*

- The future tense is often replaced by the simple present tense when there is another element of the sentence that indicates future time:

Llamo **el jueves.**   *I'll call **on Thursday.***

- The future tense can be replaced by the present tense when asking for instructions; English *shall, should:*

¿**Doblo** aquí?   ***Shall (Should) I turn** here?*

- The future tense is commonly used in the main clause of a conditional sentence when the **si**-clause (*if-clause*) has the verb in the present tense:

Si Juana **va,** yo **iré** también.   *If Juana **goes**, **I'll go** too.*

- The order of the clauses can be reversed with the **si**-clause following the main clause: Yo **iré si va** Juana.

A. **Mis planes para el futuro.** Cambie los verbos del tiempo presente al futuro en la siguiente narración para saber lo que piensa hacer su amigo Daniel después de graduarse.

    MODELO   Trabajo en una oficina.
               → Trabajaré en una oficina.

1. Me gradúo en junio.

2. Mis amigos y yo celebramos con una fiesta.

3. Nuestros padres están muy contentos.

4. Yo hago un viaje a Europa en el verano.

5. Miguel me acompaña.

6. Nos encanta viajar.

7. Vamos a los países de la Europa oriental.

8. Andrés y Manuel quieren ir también.

9. Salimos para Polonia a mediados de junio.

10. Pasamos dos meses viajando.

11. Andrés vuelve antes porque

12. tiene que buscar empleo.

13. Al regresar yo empiezo a trabajar en una compañía internacional.

14. Miguel puede trabajar en la empresa de sus padres.

15. Manuel sigue con sus clases en la facultad de ingeniería.

16. ¡Tenemos tiempo de vernos, espero!

B. **¡Qué reacciones!** Ud. sabe cómo reaccionarán ciertas personas al oír unas noticias. Describa sus reacciones escribiendo los verbos en futuro.

> MODELO Luisa / sonreír
> ➜ Luisa sonreirá.

1. Mari Carmen / llorar

2. las tías / decir "¡ay de mí!" gimiendo (*groaning*)

3. Ramón / tener vergüenza

4. tú / volverse loco

5. Juan y Alicia / poner el grito en el cielo (*scream bloody murder*)

6. Uds. / enfadarse

7. Margarita / reírse a carcajadas

8. Ud. / ponerse de buen humor

9. nosotros / estar contento

C. **¡Qué día!** Mañana será un día sumamante ajetreado (*hectic*), con muchas ocupaciones para Ud. Diga lo que pasará, escribiendo los verbos en futuro.

> MODELO Estudiamos todo el día.
> ➜ Estudiaremos todo el día.

1. ¡Mañana es un ajetreo continuo (*hustle and bustle*)!

2. ¡Tenemos un día lleno de frenética actividad!

3. Hay clases todo el día

4. y tomamos exámenes también.

5. Además, yo voy al almacén.

6. Le compro un regalo a mi hermana.

7. Sarita cumple diecisiete años pasado mañana.

8. Mamá hace una comida y una torta.

9. Papá y yo salimos para comprar vino.

10. También quiero ir a la biblioteca.

11. Mis amigos y yo trabajamos hasta muy tarde.

12. ¡Trasnochamos (*We'll go to bed very late*) porque tenemos exámenes pasado mañana también!

D. Actividad y descanso. Ud. y sus amigos se dedicarán a ciertas cosas durante las vacaciones de invierno. Diga lo que piensan hacer, escribiendo los verbos en futuro.

> MODELO   Felipe / escuchar discos todo el día
> ➔ Felipe escuchará discos todo el día.

1. Yolanda y Ana / patinar

2. tú / cocinar yacu-chupe y un sancochado

3. Julio / bailar en la discoteca toda la noche

4. Consuelo / acostarse tarde

5. yo / pasear al perro

6. Uds. / jugar baloncesto

7. Magdalena / escribir cartas

8. nosotros / hacer una fiesta de disfraces (*costume party*)

9. Guillermo y Rodolfo / poder viajar al Canadá

10. Ud. / dormir la siesta todas las tardes

Nota cultural

La cocina peruana tiene muchos platos indígenas que les son exóticos a los extranjeros. **Yacu-chupe** es una sopa verde hecha a base de papas con queso, ajo, hojas de cilantro (*coriander*), perejil (*parsley*), pimentones, huevos, cebollas y menta. **El sancochado** es un guiso de carne y toda clase de legumbres y condimentado con ajo molido (*ground*).

E. Todo depende. ¡Ciertas cosas pasarán a condición de que pasen otras cosas! Para expresar esta idea escriba oraciones que tienen una cláusula con **si** con el verbo en presente y otra cláusula principal con el verbo en futuro.

> MODELO   tú / estudiar en la biblioteca: yo / trabajar allí también
> ➔ **Si** tú **estudias** en la biblioteca, yo **trabajaré** allí también.

1. María / querer salir : nosotros / salir con ella

2. ellos / ir : Ud. / poder verlos

3. yo / hacer la comida : tú / venir a almorzar

4. Uds. / trabajar mucho : Uds. / tener éxito

5. tú / no saber qué pasó : yo / decirte

6. nosotros / no comprar harina : no haber tortillas esta noche

7. hacer calor : Carlos y Pedro / ir a la playa

8. hacer fresco : Celeste / querer ir al cine

C *The future tense used to express probability or conjecture*

- The future tense in Spanish is also used to express probability or conjecture
  in present time. The English equivalents of the future of probability (*I wonder,
  it's probably, it might*, etc.) are usually very unlike the Spanish structures.

—¿Qué hora es?	*What time is it?*
—**Serán** las ocho.	*It's probably eight o'clock.*
—¿**Quién tendrá** las llaves?	*I wonder who has the keys.*
—Las **tendrá** Mario.	*Mario probably has them.*

- Context will determine whether a verb in the future tense refers to the future or
  to probability in present time. For example: ¿**Quién llamará?** means *Who will call?*
  as well as *I wonder who's calling*.

- **Deber de** + *infinitive* is also used to express probability in the present: **Deben de
  ser las diez.** = **Serán las diez.**

F. ¿**Qué será?** Su amiga no está segura de varias cosas. Ud. tampoco está seguro(a)
y por cada cosa expresa probabilidad o conjetura. Escriba los verbos en tiempo
futuro. Quite la palabra o las palabras que indican probabilidad.

> **MODELO**   *Probablemente* los Hidalgo están en casa.
> → Los Hidalgo estarán en casa.

1. *Probablemente* son las seis.

2. *Me imagino que* Teodoro tiene catorce años.

3. *Supongo que* el reloj vale mucho.

4. *Probablemente* hay problemas entre los socios.

5. *Supongo que* Teresa sabe la hora de la conferencia.

6. *Me imagino que* Esteban quiere ir a la reunión.

7. *Supongo que* las muchachas vuelven pronto.

G. ¿**Qué habrá en esa caja?** Ud. y sus amigos han visto a Juan Pedro que llevaba
una caja enorme. Todos se mueren por saber lo que hay adentro. Uds. hacen
conjeturas sobre el contenido usando el futuro de probabilidad.

> **MODELO**   *It's probably big.*   *I wonder if it's beautiful.*
> Será grande.   ¿Será hermoso?

1. I wonder if it's green (blue, red, yellow).

2. It probably has batteries.

3. I wonder if there are many parts.

4. Do you think it's made of wood (metal, plastic)?

5. Could it cost a lot?

6. It probably makes a noise.

7. It must be bigger than a breadbox (*una caja para el pan*).

8. Could everybody have one?

9. I wonder if it's alive.

10. It probably fits in your hand.

D *Formation of the conditional tense*

• The conditional tense (English *would*) is formed in Spanish by adding the endings of the imperfect tense of **-er** and **-ir** verbs to the infinitive. These endings are the same for the conditional of **-ar**, **-er**, and **-ir** verbs:

cobrar el cheque *to cash the check*	
Cobraría el cheque.	*I'd cash the check.*
Cobrarías el cheque.	*You'd cash the check.*
Cobraría el cheque.	*He'd/She'd/You'd cash the check.*
Cobraríamos el cheque.	*We'd cash the check.*
Cobraríais el cheque.	*You'd cash the check.*
Cobrarían el cheque.	*They'd/You'd cash the check.*

entender *to understand*	
Entendería.	*I'd understand.*
Entenderías.	*You'd understand.*
Entendería.	*He'd/She'd/You'd understand.*
Entenderíamos.	*We'd understand.*
Entenderíais.	*You'd understand.*
Entenderían.	*They'd/You'd understand.*

recibir cartas *to receive, get letters*	
Recibiría cartas.	*I'd receive letters.*
Recibirías cartas.	*You'd receive letters.*
Recibiría cartas.	*He'd/She'd/You'd receive letters.*
Recibiríamos cartas.	*We'd receive letters.*
Recibiríais cartas.	*You'd receive letters.*
Recibirían cartas.	*They'd/You'd receive letters.*

• Note that when *would* means *used to*, the imperfect tense rather than the conditional is used:

Cuando yo era niño, mi familia y yo **íbamos** al campo todos los veranos.

When I was a child, my family and I **would go** *to the country every summer.*

- The verbs that have modified infinitives in the future tense have the same changes in the conditional tense:

caber → **cabría**	poner → **pondría**	tener → **tendría**
decir → **diría**	querer → **querría**	valer → **valdría**
hacer → **haría**	saber → **sabría**	venir → **vendría**
poder → **podría**	salir → **saldría**	

- The conditional of **hay** is **habría** (*there would be*).

- Compounds of the irregular verbs have the same irregularities: componer (**compondría**), retener (**retendría**), prevenir (**prevendría**), contradecir **contradiría**), satisfacer (**satisfaría**), etc.

E *Uses of the conditional tense*

- The conditional is used commonly in subordinate (dependent) clauses after main verbs of communication (e.g., *decir*) and knowledge or belief (*saber, creer*) when the main verb is in one of the past tenses. Observe a similar correspondence of tenses in Spanish and English: *present / future* and *past / conditional*:

Juan **dice** que **irá**.	*Juan **says** he'll go.*
Juan **dijo** que **iría**.	*Juan **said** he'd go.*
Sé que **llamarán**.	*I **know** they'll call.*
Sabía que **llamarían**.	*I **knew** they'd call.*

- The conditional is commonly used in the main clause of a sentence that has the imperfect subjunctive in the **si**-clause (*if*-clause), that is, the subordinate or dependent clause. The condition expressed here is called *contrary-to-fact*. This pattern is practiced in greater depth in Chapter 12.

  Si Elena **saliera**, yo **saldría** también.   *If Elena **were to leave**, I'd **leave** too.*

- The conditional tense in Spanish is also used to express probability or conjecture in past time. The verbs most commonly used to express probability with the conditional are **estar, haber, ser,** and **tener**:

Sería la una.	*It **was probably** one o'clock.*
Habría algunas dificultades.	*There **were probably** some difficulties.*
El niño **tendría** nueve años.	*The boy **was probably** nine years old.*
El coche **costaría** un dineral.	*The car **probably cost** a fortune.*

- Context will determine whether a verb in the conditional tense refers to the conditional or to probability in past time. For example: **Serían las tres** = *It would be three o'clock (by the time we got there)* and *It was probably three o'clock.*

- **Deber de** in the imperfect + *infinitive* may be used to express probability in past time. **Debían de ser las diez** = **Serían las diez.**

H. Y Ud., ¿qué haría? ¿Qué harían ciertas personas en cada una de las siguientes situaciones? Escriba los verbos en tiempo condicional.

> MODELO   Estás en la clase de historia. El profesor hace preguntas. ¿Qué harías?
> a. contestar → **Yo contestaría.**
> b. cambiar el tema → **Yo cambiaría el tema.**

1. Ud. está en un almacén. Busca los abrigos y no puede encontrarlos. ¿Qué haría?
   a. buscar a la dependienta
   b. salir del almacén

2. Carolina cena en casa de los Cela. Le encanta el arroz con pollo. ¿Qué haría?
   a. repetir
   b. pedir la receta

3. Estamos en el metro. Un pasajero grita "¡fuego!". ¿Qué haríamos?
   a. salir muy rápido
   b. llamar a los bomberos

4. Osvaldo está en el teatro. Mientras busca su asiento le pisa el pie a una señora. ¿Qué haría?
   a. disculparse con la señora
   b. sentarse en su regazo (*lap*)

5. La madre quiere bañar a sus hijos pero no hay agua caliente. ¿Qué haría?
   a. acostarlos sin bañarlos
   b. llamar al fontanero

6. Pepe y Paco ven que hay diez pulgadas (*inches*) de nieve en la calle y hace buen tiempo. ¿Qué harían?
   a. hacer una figura de nieve
   b. lanzar (*throw*) bolas de nieve

7. Hay un choque de coches no muy serio. Ud. es testigo del accidente. ¿Qué haría?
   a. decirle al policía lo que pasó
   b. ponerles vendas a los heridos

I. ¡Qué bonanza! Ud. y sus amigos acaban de comprar un billete para la lotería que esta semana llegó a tres millones de dólares. ¿Qué harían Uds. con tres millones de dólares? Escriba algunas ideas empleando el tiempo condicional.

> MODELO   yo / comprar un chalet (*villa*) en el campo
> → **Yo compraría un chalet en el campo.**

1. Elena / pagar la matrícula en la universidad

2. mi primo Federico / venir a visitarnos

3. Uds. / hacer un viaje a China

4. Juan Pablo y Ana María / poner la plata en el banco

5. tú / no tener deudas (*debts*)

6. mi hermano y yo / querer darles dinero a los huérfanos (*orphans*)

7. nosotros / jugar a la Bolsa (*stock market*)

Nota cultural

La lotería es un juego público en el que se premian billetes que llevan ciertos números. A diferencia de los Estados Unidos donde las loterías son estatales, es decir, las dirigen los estados, España y los países latinoamericanos tienen loterías nacionales.

J. ¿Qué dijeron? Escriba lo que la gente dijo y preguntó sobre los planes para una fiesta. Use el condicional en las cláusulas subordinadas.

> MODELO   Pedro me dijo que **llamaría** (llamar).

1. Victoria nos dijo que le _____ (gustar) tener una fiesta en su casa.

2. Pablo le preguntó a Victoria si ella _____ (querer) planearla para el sábado.

3. Victoria nos aseguró que no _____ (haber) problema con esa fecha.

4. Isabel quería saber lo que nosotros _____ (poder) traer.

5. Victoria nos dejó saber que su mamá se _____ (ocupar) de la comida.

6. José y yo le dijimos que _____ (hacer) galletas y pasteles para la fiesta.

7. Marta y Carlos dijeron que _____ (poner) la mesa antes de la fiesta.

8. Todos le prometimos a Victoria que _____ (venir) muy temprano para ayudarla con los preparativos.

K. Probabilidad en el pasado. Exprese probabilidad o conjetura en el pasado al contestar las preguntas de su amiga. Use el condicional al contestar.

> MODELO   ¿Cuántos años tenía el primo de Fernando? (15 años)
> → Tendría quince años.

1. ¿Qué hora era cuando Uds. volvieron a casa? (las once)

2. ¿Cuántos invitados había en la fiesta? (60)

3. ¿Cómo estaban tus padres después del viaje? (cansados)

4. ¿Cuánto costó el carro de Felipe? (quince mil dólares)

L. Al contrario. Si ciertas personas fueran (*were going*) a la fiesta, algunas cosas pasarían. Para saber qué pasaría, escriba los verbos de la cláusula principal que aparecen entre paréntesis en el tiempo condicional.

> MODELO   **Si fuera Matilde a la fiesta,** Guillermo … también. (ir)
> **Si fuera Matilde a la fiesta,** Guillermo **iría** también.
> *If Matilde were going to the party, Guillermo would go too.*

1. Si fueran los Bello, nosotros _____ (estar) contentos.

2. Si fueran Uds., yo _____ (poder) llevarlos.

3. Si fuera Catalina, Tomás _____ (querer) bailar con ella.

4. Si fuéramos todos nosotros, los Herrera no _____ (caber) en el coche.

5. Si fuera Ud., _____ (venir) conmigo.

6. Si fueras, te _____ (poner) un esmoquin (*tuxedo*).

7. Si fueran todos los invitados, no _____ (haber) lugar en la pista de baile (*dance floor*).

M. Gustos e intereses. Use el tiempo condicional para expresar lo que le gustaría hacer y lo que a otros les gustaría hacer. Use estos verbos: **gustar, encantar, interesar, preferir, querer.**

1. I'd like to ...

2. My parents would prefer to ...

3. My sister would want to ...

4. My friend _____ would love to ...

5. My friend _____ would be interested in ...

6. My brother would like to ...

7. I'd love to ...

8. Our teachers would prefer to ...

9. My classmates would be interested in ...

10. My family would want to ...

N. Ejercicio oral. En la oficina. Haga un diálogo con un amigo/una amiga que tiene lugar en la oficina de la compañía donde trabajan. Uno de Uds. es el jefe y el otro es director de la empresa. El director le hace preguntas al jefe sobre el viaje de negocios que va a hacer. El jefe contesta sus preguntas. Use el tiempo futuro y el condicional lo más posible. Por ejemplo:

Director: ¿Adónde *iré* primero? *Me gustaría* hacer los preparativos para el viaje lo antes posible.

Jefe: Bueno, primero *visitarás* la oficina en Madrid. Luego *harás* el viaje a Barcelona.

Director: *Tendré* que comprar cheques de viajero. ¿Cuánto *valdrá* el viaje?

Jefe: ¿Sabes, Manuel? Te lo *podrían* calcular en contabilidad. Ahora, en cuanto al itinerario ...

O. Estructuras en acción. Lea el siguiente artículo sobre la boda de la infanta Elena de España fijándose especialmente en los verbos en futuro. Luego haga el ejercicio que le sigue.

Matrimonio—Sí, Quiero Pero Menos

El día 18 de marzo, a las 12.30, Sevilla y millones de españoles serán testigos de un "Sí, quiero" real. En ese momento, Elena de Borbón y Jaime de Marichalar entrarán a formar parte de las estadísticas. Serán una más de las 220.000 parejas que se calcula que este año contraerán matrimonio y como el 80 por ciento de ellas lo harán por la Iglesia, que en su caso es una Catedral.

El Rey paga

La tradición deja bien claro quién paga qué en una boda y don Juan Carlos I ha decidido ser fiel a ella en el enlace de su hija la Infanta Elena. Los padres de la novia deben costear las invitaciones, las fotografías y la ceremonia. Además del ajuar y el ágape para 1.500 invitados que se celebrará en los Reales Alcázares. Se calcula que el banquete nupcial costará 22 millones de pesetas.

La casa real también se hará cargo de cien entradas para que sus allegados disfruten del espectáculo ecuestre que tendrá lugar en la Maestranza el día anterior; y de los costos de la cena con que, esa noche, agasajará a las familias de los novios y la realeza en el Palacio de Villamanrique. Cerca de 500 comensales a 9.000 pesetas el cubierto.

El Rey correrá con los gastos de los adornos florales de la Catedral y el ramo de la novia, además de la factura del hotel Alfonso XIII de sus familiares cercanos. En total, Juan Carlos I tendrá que pagar 50 millones. El dinero saldrá de los 916 millones de pesetas de su asignación anual. La familia Marichalar, como también manda la tradición, costeará el traje de la Infanta Elena valorado en un millón de pesetas.

Vocabulario

el ágape   *banquet*
agasajar   *to receive warmly*
el ajuar   *trousseau*
los allegados   *entourage*
la asignación   *allowance*
los comensales   *guests at a meal*
contraer matrimonio   *to get married*
correr con los gastos   *to foot the bill*
costear   *to pay for*
el cubierto   *place setting*
ecuestre   *equestrian*
el enlace   *marriage*
las estadísticas   *statistics*

la factura   *bill*
hacerse cargo de   *to be responsible for*
la infanta   *princess*
los invitados   *guests*
los novios   *bride and groom (before the ceremony); newlyweds*
la pareja   *couple*
el ramo   *bouquet*
la realeza   *royalty*
sí quiero   *(marriage vow) I do*
tener lugar   *to take place*
el testigo   *witness*

Escoja la oración de la columna B que complete correctamente la frase de la columna A.

A	B
1. El Rey Juan Carlos I …	a. serán testigos de la boda real.
2. 220.000 parejas …	b. será costeado por la familia Marichalar.
3. El banquete …	c. contraerán matrimonio en la catedral de Sevilla.
4. El traje de la Infanta …	d. tendrá lugar el día anterior a la boda.
5. Millones de españoles …	e. tendrá que pagar 50 millones de pesetas por la boda.
6. El espectáculo ecuestre …	f. se quedarán en el hotel Alfonso XIII.
7. La Infanta Elena y Jaime de Marichalar …	g. costará 22 millones de pesetas.
8. Los parientes del Rey …	h. se casarán en España este año.

CHAPTER 7
REFLEXIVE VERBS

 A *Reflexive verbs—introduction and conjugation*

- Spanish has a large class of verbs called *reflexive verbs.* These verbs always have a reflexive pronoun that refers to the same person or thing as the subject. Most Spanish reflexive verbs correspond to English verbs that don't have a direct object (intransitive verbs) or English verb phrases consisting of *to be* or *to get* + an adjective or past participle. Reflexive verbs appear in vocabulary lists with the reflexive pronoun **se** attached to the infinitive: **acostarse** (*to go to bed*), **lavarse** (*to wash up*), **sentarse** (*to sit down*), **vestirse** (*to get dressed*).

- Observe that the reflexive pronoun precedes the conjugated verb:

acostarse (o > ue) *to go to bed* (present tense)	
me acuesto	nos acostamos
te acuestas	os acostáis
se acuesta	se acuestan

vestirse (e > i) *to dress, get dressed* (preterit)	
me vestí	nos vestimos
te vestiste	os vestisteis
se vistió	se vistieron

bañarse *to bathe, take a bath* (imperfect)	
me bañaba	nos bañábamos
te bañabas	os bañabais
se bañaba	se bañaban

- For most reflexive verbs there is a corresponding transitive verb in which the subject and direct object refer to different things or people:

Lavo el carro. *I wash the car. (I = subject; car = direct object)*
Me lavo. *I wash (up). (subject and direct object refer to **yo**)*

Acuestas a los niños. *You put the children to bed.*
  (you = subject; children = direct object)
Te acuestas. *You go to bed. (subject and direct object refer to **tú**)*

- The **se** of the infinitive must change to agree with the subject of the verb + infinitive construction. The reflexive pronoun may be placed either before the conjugated verb or after the infinitive. When placed after the infinitive, it is attached to it in writing:

quedarse *to stay, remain*	
Me quiero **quedar.**	Quiero **quedarme.**
Te quieres **quedar.**	Quieres **quedarte.**
Se quiere **quedar.**	Quiere **quedarse.**
Nos queremos **quedar.**	Queremos **quedarnos.**
Os queréis **quedar.**	Queréis **quedaros.**
Se quieren **quedar.**	Quieren **quedarse.**

B   *The reflexive pronoun as indirect object*

- With some verbs the reflexive pronoun is an indirect object rather than a direct object. These verbs, such as **ponerse** + article of clothing (*to put on an article of clothing*), have a direct object (the article of clothing) in addition to the reflexive pronoun:

Los niños se ponen **el abrigo.**	*The children put on **their coats.***
Y se ponen **las botas** también.	*And they put on **their boots** also.*
Marta se lavó **las manos.**	*Marta washed **her hands.***
Nos lavamos **la cara.**	*We washed **our faces.***

- Spanish uses a singular noun for articles of clothing and parts of the body, even with plural subjects. It is assumed that each person has one item. Only if each person has more than one item does Spanish use a plural noun.

Here are some common reflexive verbs and expressions that are used in this pattern:

ponerse + *article of clothing*	*to put on*
quitarse + *article of clothing*	*to take off*
romperse + *article of clothing*	*to tear*
lavarse + *part of the body*	*to wash*
quebrarse (e > ie) + *part of the body*	*to break*
quemarse + *part of the body*	*to burn*
romperse + *part of the body*	*to break*

abrocharse los cordones   *to tie one's shoelaces*
amarrarse los cordones   *to tie one's shoelaces*
atarse los cordones   *to tie one's shoelaces*
cepillarse los dientes   *to brush one's teeth*
cortarse el pelo   *to get a haircut*
desabrocharse los cordones   *to untie one's shoelaces*
desamarrarse los cordones   *to untie one's shoelaces*
desatarse los cordones   *to untie one's shoelaces*
lastimarse el dedo   *to hurt one's finger*
lavarse la cabeza   *to wash one's hair*
limarse las uñas   *to file one's nails*
limpiarse los dientes   *to brush one's teeth*
maquillarse la cara   *to put makeup on*
pintarse los labios   *to put lipstick on*
torcerse el tobillo (o > ue)   *to twist one's ankle*

A. ¿Reflexivo o no? Complete las siguientes oraciones escogiendo la forma transitiva o reflexiva del verbo que aparece entre paréntesis. Use el tiempo verbal indicado.

> **MODELO**   Rosita **bañó** a los niños y después ella **se bañó.**
> (bañar—*preterit*)

1. Mañana yo _____ a las siete y _____ a mi hermana a las siete y cuarto.
   (despertar—*present*)

2. Aunque el profesor Vélez _____ a sus estudiantes, Miguel y Carlota no _____.
   (aburrir—*imperfect*)

3. Los novios _____ en la catedral de Burgos. El cura de la novia los _____.
   (casar—*preterit*)

4. Al jugar al escondite (*hide-and-seek*) nosotros _____ a los niñitos y luego nosotros
   _____. (esconder—*future*)

5. ¿Tú _____ ahora mismo o _____ primero a Luisita? (vestir—*present*)

6. Nosotros ya _____ y _____ al perro también. (pasear—*preterit*)

7. La carta que Carmen recibió ayer no la _____. Sin embargo al leerla Martín
   _____. (tranquilizar—*preterit*)

8. Yo _____ durante el primer acto de la obra pero los otros dos actos no me _____.
   (divertir—*preterit*)

9. Pepe me hacía tantas preguntas que francamente yo _____. ¡Ese chico _____ a
   todo el mundo! (marear—*imperfect*)

10. Daniel no tiene ganas de hacer nada. A ver si nosotros lo _____. Vamos a
    invitarlo a jugar al tenis. A ver si él _____. (animar—*present*)

11. Cuando Pablo y Laura eran niños _____ al ver las películas de terror. Las
    películas con fantasmas (*ghosts*) los _____ más que nada. (asustar—*imperfect*)

12. Uds. _____ por cualquier cosa. Menos mal que no _____ a otras personas.
    (ofender—*present*)

B. Todavía no, abuelita. La abuela llama desde Buenos Aires para hablar con sus
nietos gemelos en Filadelfia. Ella les pregunta si pueden hacer ciertas cosas
solos (*by themselves*). Los niños le dicen a su abuela que no pueden hacerlas
solos todavía, que se las hace su mamá. Practique los verbos como verbos
transitivos y reflexivos.

> MODELO   **(bañarse)**
> abuelita: ¿Ustedes ya **se bañan** solos?
> nietos: No, abuelita. **Nos baña** mamá.

1. **(despertarse)**
   abuelita:
   nietos:

2. **(lavarse la cabeza)**
   abuelita:
   nietos:

3. **(peinarse)**
   abuelita:
   nietos:

4. **(quitarse los zapatos)**
   abuelita:
   nietos:

5. **(prepararse el desayuno)**
   abuelita:
   nietos:

6. **(acostarse)**
   abuelita:
   nietos:

Nota cultural

Buenos Aires figura en un huso horario (*time zone*) internacional una hora más tarde que
el huso horario de Filadelfia. La ciudad de México está en otro huso horario, una hora más
temprano que Filadelfia. Madrid está en otro, seis horas más tarde que Filadelfia.

C. Una excursión al campo. Ud. y sus amigos pasaron un día en el campo. Escriba
lo que cada persona llevó ese día. Practique el uso del verbo reflexivo **ponerse**
en pretérito.

> MODELO   tú / los zapatos de tenis
> ➜ Te pusiste los zapatos de tenis.

La ropa

el abrigo *overcoat*	**las medias** *socks (Latin America);*
la blusa *blouse*	*stockings (Spain)*
las botas *boots*	**los pantalones** *pants*
la bufanda *scarf*	**el saco** *jacket*
los calcetines *socks (Spain)*	**las sandalias** *sandals*
la camisa *shirt*	**el smoking** *tuxedo (also,* **el esmoquin***)*
la camiseta *T-shirt*	**el sombrero** *hat*
el cinturón *belt*	**el suéter** *sweater*
la corbata *tie*	**el traje** *suit*
la chaqueta *jacket*	**el traje de baño** *bathing suit*
el gorro *cap*	**el vestido** *dress*
los guantes *gloves*	**los zapatos** *shoes*
el impermeable *raincoat*	**de tacón alto** *high-heeled shoes*
los jeans, el pantalón vaquero *jeans*	**de tenis** *tennis shoes*

¿De qué es?: Las telas

el algodón *cotton*	**el nailon** *nylon*
el cuero *leather*	**el poliéster** *polyester*
el charol *patent leather*	**la seda** *silk*
la lana *wool*	**el terciopelo** *velvet*

1. Marina y yo / los jeans

2. Arturo / un traje de baño

3. Uds. / un impermeable

4. yo / un suéter de lana

5. Víctor y Paco / un gorro

6. todos nosotros / una camiseta

D. ¿Qué se llevará para ir al trabajo? Escriba lo que llevarán ciertas personas para ir al trabajo. Practique el uso del verbo reflexivo **ponerse** en futuro.

> MODELO   Alberto / un saco
> ➔ Alberto se pondrá un saco.

1. yo / un vestido

2. Alicia / una blusa

3. nosotros / zapatos de cuero

4. Uds. / una camisa de algodón

5. los jefes / un traje de lana

6. tú / una corbata

E. ¡Ya llega el baile de gala (*prom*)! Ud. y sus amigos están emocionados porque el baile de gala es el sábado. Todos Uds. necesitan probarse la ropa que van a llevar. Practique el uso del verbo reflexivo **probarse** en presente.

> MODELO   nosotros / los zapatos de charol
> ➔ Nos probamos los zapatos de charol.

1. Pilar y Luz / el traje largo

2. yo / el abrigo de terciopelo

3. Lorenzo / el smoking

4. Uds. / los zapatos de tacón alto

5. tú / la blusa de seda

6. Antonio y Esteban / la corbata

F. **¡Qué malas noticias!** Un amigo que acaba de volver de México pregunta por sus amigos. ¡Le toca a Ud. darle las malas noticias! Escriba los verbos reflexivos en pretérito.

> MODELO   Alfonso / caerse / cruzando la calle
> → Alfonso se cayó cruzando la calle.

1. Miguel / romperse la pierna / montando a caballo

2. Ana / quemarse la mano / cocinando

3. el perro de Bernardo / perderse / en las afueras

4. Eunice / torcerse el tobillo / patinando sobre el hielo

5. todos nosotros / enfermarse / comiendo hamburguesas poco cocidas

6. yo / hacerse daño / cortando el césped

7. los hermanos de Pedro / quebrarse el dedo / jugando al básquetbol

G. **Estimados televidentes …** Ud. es locutor(a) en la tele. Por desgracia las noticias de hoy son todas malas. Exprésela en oraciones completas usando los verbos reflexivos en pretérito y los otros elementos propuestos.

> MODELO   dos panaderos / quemarse las manos /
>   cuando hubo una explosión en el horno
> → Dos panaderos se quemaron las manos
>   cuando hubo una explosión en el horno.

1. la actriz Ramona Taylor / lastimarse / en el rodaje (*filming*) de su nueva película

2. el futbolista Diego Suárez / romperse el pie / en el partido de hoy

3. unos turistas norteamericanos / caerse / en la escalera mecánica del metro

4. un carpintero / cortarse la mano / aserruchando (*sawing*) madera

5. diez arqueólogos / hacerse daño / en una excavación en las pirámides

6. un bombero / quemarse / apagando un incendio

7. los bailarines / divorciarse / después de cuarenta años de bailar juntos

H. **El aseo personal** (*personal hygiene*). Escriba oraciones explicando cuándo y cómo algunas personas hacen su aseo personal. Practique el uso de los verbos reflexivos en presente.

> MODELO   Guillermo / limpiarse los dientes / dos veces al día
> → Guillermo se limpia los dientes dos veces al día.

El aseo personal	
afeitarse *to shave*	**lavarse** *to wash up*
arreglarse *to get ready to go out*	**limarse las uñas** *to file one's nails*
bañarse *to take a bath*	**lavarse los dientes** *to brush one's teeth*
cepillarse el pelo/los dientes *to brush one's hair/teeth*	**maquillarse** *to put makeup on*
	peinarse *to comb one's hair*
cortarse el pelo/las uñas *to cut one's hair/nails*	**pintarse** *to put makeup on*
	vestirse *to get dressed*
ducharse *to take a shower*	

1. Felisa / lavarse la cabeza / todos los días

2. yo / vestirse / rápidamente por la mañana

3. nuestros padres / ducharse / por la noche

4. Carlos / afeitarse / con una maquinilla de afeitar

5. Laura y Teresa / limarse las uñas / antes de ponerse el esmalte de uñas (*nail polish*)

6. tú / peinarse / con cuidado

7. Benjamín y yo / arreglarse / en el dormitorio

8. Ud. / cepillarse el pelo / después de maquillarse

I. Hay que hacerlo. Escriba oraciones en las cuales se expresa que las personas **quieren, van a, acaban de** (u otra expresión) hacer ciertas cosas. Practique la construcción del verbo conjugado con el verbo reflexivo en infinitivo. Escriba las oraciones de dos maneras.

> MODELO   Guillermo se afeita todos los días. (necesitar)
> ➔ Guillermo **necesita afeitarse** todos los días.
> ➔ Guillermo **se necesita afeitar** todos los días.

1. Samuel se coloca en una sucursal de la empresa. (querer)

2. Nosotros nos desayunamos antes de las ocho. (deber)

3. Los amigos se reúnen en casa de Felipe esta noche. (pensar)

4. Teresa se pesa todas las semanas. (necesitar)

5. Yo me voy de vacaciones en julio. (ir a)

6. Las señoras se aprovechan de las liquidaciones. (acabar de)

7. ¿Te sientas en esta fila? (querer)

8. Uds. se secan el pelo. (tener que)

 C *The imperative of reflexive verbs*

- Reflexive pronouns precede negative command forms but follow affirmative commands and are attached to them in writing. Observe that a written accent mark is added to affirmative command forms of more than one syllable when the reflexive pronoun is added:

Acuéstense ahora, chicos.   *Go to bed now, kids.*
No se levanten hasta las ocho.   *Don't get up until eight.*

- Here are some common reflexive verbs that refer to the daily routine. Their nonreflexive forms, usually transitive verbs, and meanings are also given:

acostar (o > ue) *to put (someone) to bed*
acostarse (o > ue) *to go to bed*

afeitar *to shave (someone)*
afeitarse *to shave*

arreglar *to arrange, fix*
arreglarse *to get ready (fix hair, clothing, etc.)*

bañar *to bathe (someone)*
bañarse *to bathe, take a bath*

cansar *to tire (someone)*
cansarse *to get tired*

colocar *to place, put*
colocarse *to get a job*

cortar *to cut*
cortarse *to cut oneself*

despedir (e > i) *to fire, dismiss*
despedirse de (e > i) *to say goodbye to*

despertar (e > ie) *to wake someone up*
despertarse (e > ie) *to wake up*

dormir (o > ue) *to sleep*
dormirse (o > ue) *to fall asleep*

enfermar *to make ill*
enfermarse *to get sick*

lastimar *to hurt*
lastimarse *to hurt oneself*

lavar *to wash someone, something*
lavarse *to wash up*

levantar *to raise, pick up*
levantarse *to get up*

maquillar *to put makeup on someone*
maquillarse *to put on makeup*

peinar *to comb someone's hair*
peinarse *to comb one's hair*

reunir *to join, gather*
reunirse (con) *to get together (with)*

vestir (e > i) *to dress (someone)*
vestirse (e > i) *to dress, get dressed*

- Here are some common reflexive verbs expressing feelings and emotions. Corresponding nonreflexive verbs are usually transitive:

aburrir *to bore someone*
aburrirse *to get, be bored*

alegrar *to make someone happy*
alegrarse *to be glad, happy*

animar *to cheer someone up, encourage someone*
animarse *to cheer up, take heart, feel like doing something*

asustar *to frighten someone*
asustarse *to get scared*

calmar *to calm someone down*
calmarse *to calm down*

decidir *to decide*
decidirse a *to make up one's mind*

divertir (e > ie) *to amuse*
divertirse (e > ie) *to have a good time*

enfadar *to make (someone) angry*
enfadarse *to get angry*

enojar *to make (someone) angry*
enojarse *to get angry*

entusiasmar *to excite, thrill, stir*
entusiasmarse *to get excited, feel thrilled*

exasperar *to exasperate, make (someone) lose his/her patience*
exasperarse *to get exasperated, lose one's patience*

interesar *to interest*
interesarse en *to be interested in*

marear *to make (someone) dizzy*
marearse *to get, feel dizzy*

molestar *to annoy, bother*
molestarse *to get annoyed*

ofender *to offend, insult, hurt someone*
ofenderse *to get offended, insulted; feel hurt*

preocupar *to worry someone*
preocuparse *to worry*

probar (o > ue) *to try, taste*
probarse (o > ue) *to try on*

sorprender *to surprise someone*
sorprenderse *to be surprised*

tranquilizar *to calm someone down, reassure*
tranquilizarse *to calm down, stop worrying*

J. Dando consejos. Lea las siguientes situaciones y luego dé algunos consejos empleando los verbos entre paréntesis con la forma formal e informal singular del mandato.

> Modelo   Tengo calor. (quitarse el suéter)
> ➔ Quítese el suéter. / Quítate el suéter.

1. Me gustan los dos trajes. (probarse los dos)

2. Tengo muchísimo sueño. (acostarse temprano)

3. ¡Tengo cita a las tres y ya son las tres menos cuarto! (darse prisa)

4. Empieza a llover. (ponerse el impermeable)

5. Voy a ver la nueva película española esta noche. (divertirse mucho)

6. ¡Me encanta París! (quedarse otra semana entonces)

7. Tengo que recoger a mis padres en el aeropuerto. (irse ahora mismo)

K. ¡No lo haga! Déle a la persona un mandato negativo empleando el verbo entre paréntesis con la forma formal e informal singular.

> Modelo   Me gusta el pelo largo. (no cortarse el pelo entonces)
> ➔ No se corte el pelo entonces.
> ➔ No te cortes el pelo entonces.

1. Tengo fiebre. (no levantarse todavía)

2. Tengo los pies mojados por la lluvia. (no enfermarse)

3. A Roberta se le rompió mi reloj. (no enfadarse con ella)

4. Voy a coger el tren de las ocho. (no despertarse tarde)

5. Necesito estudiar para un examen de biología. (no dormirse)

6. Yo no tengo la menor idea de lo que pasó. (no hacerse el desentendido)

7. Me como varios dulces todos los días. (no ponerse gorda)

L. ¡Niños, hagan esto! Empleando la forma del mandato de los verbos entre paréntesis, déles mandatos a los niños. Dígales las cosas que deben hacer.

> Modelo   bañarse ahora ➔ Niños, báñense ahora.

1. vestirse para salir

2. cepillarse los dientes

3. atarse los cordones

4. ponerse serios

5. lavarse las manos

M. ¡Niños, pórtense bien! Empleando la forma del mandato de los verbos entre paréntesis, déles mandatos a los niños. ¡Esta vez, dígales las cosas que *no* deben hacer!

> MODELO   no quitarse los guantes
> → Niños, no se quiten los guantes.

1. no ensuciarse la cara

2. no hacerse los sordos

3. no caerse patinando

4. no olvidarse de guardar sus juguetes

5. no irse del jardín

6. no pintarse los labios

7. no quejarse tanto

 D *The position of reflexive pronouns with the present participle*

- In the progressive tenses, the reflexive pronouns may either precede the forms of **estar** or follow the present participle (gerund). When they follow, they are attached in writing and a written accent is added to the vowel before the **-ndo** of the gerund.

Me estoy vistiendo.	*I'm getting dressed.*
Ana **está arreglándose.**	*Ana is getting ready.*

- Here are some commonly used reflexive verbs that refer to motion or to a change in position. In most cases, the corresponding nonreflexive verb is transitive:

acercar *to bring something closer, over*	**acercarse (a)** *to come closer, approach*
alejar *to move something away*	**alejarse (de)** *to move away from*
caer *to fall (usually figurative)*	**caerse** *to fall down*
correr *to move (an object)*	**correrse** *to move over, make room for*
detener *to stop, bring to a halt*	**detenerse** *to stop, come to a halt*
instalar *to install*	**instalarse** *to move in*
ir *to go*	**irse** *to go away*
levantar *to lift*	**levantarse** *to get up, rise*
mover (o > ue) *to move (put in motion)*	**moverse (o > ue)** *to move, stir, budge*
parar *to stop*	**pararse** *to stand up (especially Span. America)*
pasear *to take for a walk, to walk*	**pasearse** *to stroll*
perder (e > ie) *to lose*	**perderse (e > ie)** *to get lost*
quedar *to remain, be left*	**quedarse** *to stay, remain*
tirar *to throw*	**tirarse** *to jump, throw oneself; to lie down*
volcar (o > ue) *to knock over*	**volcarse (o > ue)** *to get knocked over*

- The following verbs of motion or change of position are used primarily as reflexives:

apresurarse de *to hurry*	**mudarse** *to move (change residence)*
echarse *to lie down*	**ponerse de pie** *to stand up (esp. Spain)*
escaparse *to escape*	**recostarse (o > ue)** *to lie down*
inclinarse *to bend over*	

- Here are some verbs that are used primarily or exclusively as reflexives in Spanish, at least in the meanings given. Verbs marked with an asterisk exist only as reflexives:

acordarse (o > ue) (de) *to remember*
apoderarse (de) *to take possession (of)*
aprovecharse (de) *to take advantage (of)*
apuntarse a/para *to register, sign up for*
arrepentirse de (e > ie) *to regret, repent*
***atreverse a** *to dare to do something*
ausentarse *to be out, away*
burlarse de *to laugh at, make fun of*
casarse (con) *to get married (to)*
comprometerse *to get engaged*
***desmayarse** *to faint*
***divorciarse** *to get divorced*
empeñarse (en) *to insist (on), persist (in)*
enamorarse (de) *to fall in love (with)*
enterarse (de) *to find out (about)*

fiarse de *to trust*
figurarse *to imagine*
fijarse (en) *to notice*
***jactarse de** *to boast about*
negarse a (e > ie) *to refuse to*
ocuparse de *to take care of*
olvidarse (de) *to forget*
oponerse a *to oppose, be against*
parecerse a *to resemble*
portarse bien/mal *to behave well/badly*
***quejarse de** *to complain about*
reírse de *to laugh at*
sentirse (e > ie) *to feel*
***suicidarse** *to commit suicide*

Note: **Olvidar** is followed by a direct object; **olvidarse** by the preposition **de**. **Olvidaron el número.** = **Se olvidaron del número.** *They forgot the number.* **Olvidarse** is also used with the indirect object pronoun: **Se les olvidó el número.** = *They forgot the number.* (See Chapter 19 on unplanned occurrences.)

N. **¡Haciendo diabluras (*Making mischief*)!** En una reunión dominical (*Sunday*), los niños están haciendo sus diabluras como siempre. ¡Y los adultos están reaccionando como siempre! Escriba oraciones con los verbos en presente progresivo para describir la escena. Escriba cada oración de dos maneras.

MODELO Sarita / mojarse con la sopa
➜ **Sarita está mojándose con la sopa.**
➜ **Sarita se está mojando con la sopa.**

la hermana de Sarita / quejarse
➜ **La hermana de Sarita está quejándose.**
➜ **La hermana de Sarita se está quejando.**

1. Luisito / portarse mal

2. los abuelos de Luisito / ponerse rojos

3. Adrianita / reírse como una loca

4. la tía de Adrianita / desmayarse

5. Fernandito / esconderse en un armario

6. el tío de Fernandito / asustarse

7. los gemelos (*twins*) / escaparse de su padre

8. el padre de los gemelos / enojarse

9. Pedrito / burlarse de sus primos

10. los primos de Pedrito / exasperarse

11. Mari Carmen / ensuciarse con el guacamole

12. la madre de Mari Carmen / avergonzarse

Nota cultural

El **guacamole** es una ensalada hecha con aguacate (*avocado*), tomate, cebolla y condimentos. Se come en México, América Central y Cuba.

O. Están en movimiento. Hay mucha actividad en el barrio hoy. Use el presente progresivo para decir lo que está haciendo cada persona.

> MODELO ¿Dónde está Juan Pedro? (levantarse de la mesa)
> → Se está levantando de la mesa. /
> Está levantándose de la mesa.

1. ¿Qué hace tu mamá? (apresurarse para salir)

2. ¿Qué hacen los Pereira? (mudarse a otro barrio)

3. ¿Dónde están los niños? (acercarse a la escuela)

4. ¿Qué hacen tus abuelos? (pasearse por el centro)

5. ¿Qué haces tú? (instalarse en un nuevo apartamento)

6. ¿Qué hacen Uds.? (irse al campo)

7. ¿Dónde está Elena? (quedarse en casa)

8. ¿Qué hace el señor Peña? (tirarse a la piscina)

E *Reflexive verbs with reciprocal meaning*

- The plural forms of reflexive verbs are used to express *reciprocal action* which corresponds to the English phrase "each other." Because **se ven** means either *they see each other* or *they see themselves* (e.g., in the mirror), the meaning must be clarified by the context:

—Jacinto y Laura **se quieren** mucho.	*Jacinto and Laura love each other very much.*
—**Se ven** todos los días.	*They see each other every day.*
—¿Dónde **se conocieron** Uds.?	*Where did you meet each other?*
—**Nos conocimos** en una conferencia.	*We met at a lecture.*

- Spanish uses the phrase **el uno al otro** (or **uno a otro**) to focus on or to clarify the meaning "each other." This phrase agrees with the gender and number of the people referred to: **el uno al otro / la una a la otra / los unos a los otros / las unas a las otras**:

Mis hermanos se ayudan **el uno al otro.**	*My brothers help each other.*
Las chicas se miran **la una a la otra.**	*The girls look at each other.*

- The reflexive pronoun is not used to express "each other" with prepositions other than **a**:

Diana y Felisa no pueden ir de compras **la una sin la otra.**	*Diana and Felisa can't shop without* ***each other.***

P. Mi mejor amigo(a) y yo. Escriba oraciones en las cuales describe cómo es la relación entre Ud. y su mejor amigo(a). Practique el uso del reflexivo con el significado *each other.* Use el tiempo presente del verbo.

> Modelo   Pablo y yo / conocer muy bien
> ➔ Pablo y yo nos conocemos muy bien.

1. Marisol y yo / hablar por teléfono cuatro veces al día

2. Jorge y yo / entender perfectamente

3. José María y yo / ver todos los días

4. Consuelo y yo / escribir mucho durante las vacaciones

5. Felipe y yo / ayudar con la tarea

6. Victoria y yo / prestar ropa

Q. Un gran amor. ¿Cómo llegaron Alejandra y Claudio a comprometerse? Escriba oraciones en pretérito con la forma recíproca del reflexivo para explicarlo.

> Modelo   ver por primera vez hace un año
> ➔ Se vieron por primera vez hace un año.

1. conocer en una fiesta
2. llamar a menudo
3. ver todos los días
4. hablar constantemente

5. comprar regalos
6. decir muchas cosas importantes
7. hacer promesas
8. llegar a querer

Nota cultural

En las sociedades tradicionales de los países hispánicos, las familias arreglaban el **matrimonio** para sus hijos. Los padres y abuelos sólo dejaban que la hija saliera con un joven bien educado y de ciertos medios económicos. Y cuando salía con el joven iban acompañados de una chaperona o dueña. Después de varios años de noviazgo (*courtship and engagement*), entre cinco y diez quizás, los novios se casaban. En las últimas décadas las cosas fueron cambiando, aunque todavía era necesario que la pareja esperara hasta que el esposo se ganara la vida para poder comprar un apartamento. Hoy en día los jóvenes se conocen, se enamoran y escogen un cónyuge (*mate*) sin tanta intervención de la familia. Y claro que ahora las mujeres trabajan también. Pero con todos estos cambios, la opinión de los familiares y su influencia en el matrimonio de los jóvenes sigue siendo más fuerte en el mundo hispánico que en los Estados Unidos.

R. **Travesuras (*Mischief*) en el parque.** Dos niños estaban en el parque ayer. Complete el siguiente relato con el pretérito de los verbos entre paréntesis para saber lo que les pasó. Ud. practicará el uso del reflexivo con el significado de *each other*.

Luisito y Juanito _____ (1. conocerse) en el parque ayer. _____ (2. Ponerse) a jugar. Pronto, Luisito le quitó el camión a Juanito. _____ (3. Enojarse) tanto que _____ (4. pegarse). Las dos mamás _____ (5. acercarse) y trataron de calmar a sus hijos. Los niños _____ (6. tranquilizarse) y _____ (7. abrazarse) y _____ (8. darse) un beso.

 How to say "become" in Spanish

- The English verb *to become* has several different translations in Spanish. When *to become* is followed by an adjective, the most common Spanish expression is **ponerse** + *adjective*. It is used for physical or emotional changes, where no effort is implied:

Esteban **se puso bravo** al leer la carta.	Esteban **got angry** *when he read the letter.*
Lidia y María **se pusieron pálidas** del susto.	*Lidia and María* **turned pale** *from fright.*
Juanita **se pone roja** porque es tímida.	*Juanita* **blushes (gets red)** *because she's shy.*

- **Volverse** + *adjective* is used to express a sudden, involuntary change, most commonly in the expression **volverse loco** *to go crazy, mad.* Changes indicated by **ponerse** may be superficial, while those indicated by **volverse** are more profound:

El psicólogo **se volvió loco.**	*The psychologist* **went mad.**
Los políticos **se volvieron muy arrogantes.**	*The politicians* **got very arrogant.**
¡Ese niño **se ha vuelto imposible!**	*That kid* **has become impossible!**

- **Hacerse** and **llegar a ser** also mean *to become* and are used with nouns expressing profession or adjectives expressing social status. They imply effort on the part of the subject. **Pasar a ser,** stressing the process of change, is also used:

Sarita **se hizo abogada.**	*Sarita* **became a lawyer.**
Lola **llegó a ser abogada** también.	*Lola* **became a lawyer** *also.*
Pedro y yo **nos hicimos amigos.**	*Pedro and I* **became friends.**
Pedro y Tomás nunca **llegaron a ser amigos.**	*Pedro and Tomás never* **got to be friends.**
Laura **pasó a ser directora ejecutiva** de la compañía.	*Laura* **got to be executive director** *of the company.*
Y **se hizo rica** también.	*And* **she got rich** *too.*

- The idioms **convertirse en (e > ie)** and **transformarse en** also express ideas related to the verb *to become:*

  Atlanta **se convirtió en** una ciudad importante.   *Atlanta **became** an important city.*

  El vino **se transformó en** vinagre.   *The wine **turned to** vinegar.*

- Very often the idea of *become* or *get* is expressed by a reflexive verb in Spanish. For example: **cansarse** (*to get tired*), **enojarse** (*to get angry*), **emocionarse** (*to get excited*). Some ideas can be expressed both with a verb meaning *to become* followed by an adjective and with a reflexive verb; the latter is more literary. Some examples: **hacerse rico / enriquecerse** (*to become rich*), **ponerse furioso / enfurecerse** (*to become furious*), **volverse orgulloso / enorgullecerse** (*to become haughty*).

- There are some verbs in Spanish that express a change of state similar to **cansarse** and **enojarse** that are *not reflexive*. These verbs have alternate constructions consisting of one of the verbs for *to become* followed by an adjective: **adelgazar / quedarse delgado** (*to get thin*), **enflaquecer / ponerse flaco** (*to get thin*), **engordar / ponerse gordo** (*to get fat*), **enloquecer / volverse loco** (*to go mad*), **enmudecer / volverse mudo** (*to become mute*), **ensordecer / volverse sordo** (*to go deaf*), **envejecer / ponerse viejo** (*to grow old*), **palidecer / ponerse pálido** (*to turn pale*).

S. **Cómo se dice *to become* en español.** Indique cuál de las expresiones que significan *to become* corresponde en cada oración.

1. Los chicos _____ contentísimos al ver su nueva bicicleta.
   a. se pusieron   b. se hicieron

2. Después de unas campañas políticas muy duras, Jorge Cuevas _____ senador.
   a. se volvió   b. llegó a ser

3. ¡_____ locos por la cantidad de trabajo!
   a. Nos volvemos   b. Nos hacemos

4. Rita _____ brava cuando el taxi chocó con su coche.
   a. se hizo   b. se puso

5. Este pueblo está _____ en un centro turístico.
   a. poniéndose   b. convirtiéndose

T. ***To become* y *to get*.** Exprese las siguientes oraciones en español escogiendo la expresión correcta para *become* or *get* en cada caso.

1. Ricardo became a millionaire.

2. The archaeologists got excited when they saw the ruins.

3. Magdalena often blushes (gets red) because she's very shy.

4. Daniel is marrying Tere because he wants to become an American citizen.

5. Carlitos has become impossible!

6. Felisa is getting very fat because of the cake and ice cream she eats every day!

7. The valley became an important technological center.

Nota cultural

Los **inmigrantes indocumentados** (*illegal aliens*) vienen a los Estados Unidos generalmente por razones económicas y políticas. Por no tener los documentos necesarios, tienen que aceptar trabajos que pagan mal y que no les dan ni beneficios ni seguridad. Les conviene solicitar la tarjeta verde (*Alien Registration Card*) porque con ella tienen todos los derechos de un ciudadano estadounidense salvo el de votar. Una manera de legalizar su estado de inmigrante indocumentado es casarse con un ciudadano de los Estados Unidos.

Other reflexive verbs

- There are cases of reflexive verbs that do not fit exactly into the categories given above and that require special attention:

- **Equivocarse** has a basic meaning of *to be mistaken, be wrong:*

Si crees que Paula te va a devolver el dinero, **te equivocas.**	*If you think Paula is going to return the money to you, **you're mistaken.***

- Note that **equivocarse** means to be wrong only when the subject is a person. **Estar equivocado** means *to be wrong* both for persons and things:

El físico **se equivocó.**	*The physicist **was wrong.***
El físico **estuvo equivocado.**	*The physicist **was wrong.***
La respuesta **está equivocada.**	*The answer **is wrong.***

  The expression **equivocarse de** can translate other uses of English *wrong:*

Ud. **se ha equivocado** de casa.	*You've come to the **wrong** house.*
Nos equivocamos de carretera.	*We took the **wrong** highway.*

- **Quedarse** has a basic meaning of *to remain, stay:*

Quédate en casa si no te sientes bien.	***Stay at home** if you don't feel well.*
Pensamos quedarnos en un parador en Segovia.	*We **intend to stay** at an inn in Segovia.*

- **Quedarse** can express *to become* to indicate a new state, either physical or emotional:

Todos **se quedaron atónitos.**	*Everyone **was astonished.***
Dos víctimas del terremoto **se quedaron ciegas y sordas.**	*Two victims of the earthquake **went blind and deaf.***

- Nonreflexive **quedar** is used to mean different things:

El cuarto **queda bien / mal** con las nuevas cortinas.	*The room **looks good / bad** with the new curtains.*
Tu corbata roja **queda bien** con tu camisa azul.	*Your red tie **goes well** with your blue shirt.*
Paco **quedó bien** regalándole flores a su suegra.	*Paco **made a good impression** giving flowers to his mother-in-law.*

El director de la orquesta **quedó mal** con los músicos.	*The conductor **made a bad impression** on the musicians.*

- **Hacerse,** when followed by the definite article and an adjective, means *to pretend to be, to act like:*

El ladrón **se hizo el desentendido** al ser encontrado por la policía.	*The thief **played dumb (pretended not to understand)** when he was found by the police.*
Lola **se hizo la sorda** cuando su hermana le pidió prestado el coche.	*Lola **pretended to be deaf (turned a deaf ear)** when her sister asked to borrow the car.*
Berta **se hizo la dormida** para no tener que hacer las labores domésticas.	*Berta **pretended to be asleep** so that she wouldn't have to do the household chores.*
Nicolás **se hacía el tonto** en la fiesta.	*Nicolás **was acting silly (playing the fool)** at the party.*

- Both **acordarse de** and **recordar** mean *to remember:*

Si no **me acuerdo** mal.	*If **I remember** correctly.*
Si no **recuerdo** mal.	*If **I remember** correctly.*

- **Recordar** also means *to remind:*

Les recuerdo que mañana tenemos ensayo.	***I'm reminding them*** *that we have a rehearsal tomorrow.*
Me recuerdas a tu mamá.	***You remind me*** *of your mother.*

Some expressions with reflexive verbs:

darse cuenta (de) *to realize*	**ponerse a** + *infinitive to begin to*
darse prisa *to hurry*	**ponerse de acuerdo** *to come to an agreement*
echarse a + *infinitive to begin to*	**quedarse con** *to keep, hold onto*
hacerse daño *to hurt oneself*	**tratarse de** *to be about, be a question of*
hacerse tarde *to get late*	

- Certain verbs are made reflexive to stress participation by the subject or to convey an intensification of the action:

Compré un coche.	*I bought a car.*
Me compré un coche.	*I bought (myself) a car.*
Leo **comió** los pasteles.	*Leo ate the pastries.*
Leo **se comió** los pasteles.	*Leo gobbled up the pastries.*

U. **Preposiciones con verbos reflexivos.** Complete las siguientes oraciones escribiendo las preposiciones correctas que faltan.

1. Este niño malcriado (*spoiled*) no se lleva bien _____ nadie.

2. Los turistas se fijaron _____ la arquitectura de los castillos.

3. No debemos aprovecharnos _____ las demás personas.

4. Jorge se arrepiente _____ haberles mentido a sus padres.

5. Yo me intereso mucho _____ la historia europea.

6. Los Cela se negaron _____ hacer cola en la taquilla.

7. ¿No te fías _____ tu abogado?

8. El vecino se ofreció _____ cortarnos el césped.

9. Los abuelos siempre se jactan (*brag*) _____ sus nietos.

10. Ud. se olvidó _____ desenchufar los aparatos eléctricos.

11. Daniel se casará _____ Luz en mayo.

12. No nos atrevemos _____ viajar de noche sin linterna.

V. En otras palabras. Vuelva a escribir las siguientes oraciones usando un sinónimo de los verbos o expresiones que aparecen en letra cursiva.

1. *Si me acuerdo bien,* los Aranda se mudaron a Los Ángeles.

2. Ud. *no tiene razón.* Lima es la capital del Perú, no de Ecuador.

3. Dos personas *perdieron la vista* a causa del accidente.

4. *Parece que* la niña *está dormida, pero no lo está.*

5. Juan Carlos *ha bajado mucho de peso.*

6. Creíamos que íbamos a *volvernos locos* por el desorden de la casa.

7. Todos los habitantes *están enfureciéndose* por el número de robos en el barrio.

8. Diego *se ponía pálido* corriendo la última milla de la carrera.

W. Ejercicio oral. Descríbale a un amigo/una amiga cómo es un día típico para Ud. Hable de sus actividades diarias y a qué hora las hace. Use verbos reflexivos. Por ejemplo: *despertarse, levantarse, vestirse, peinarse, bañarse, desayunarse, acostarse.*

X. Estructuras en acción. Lea el siguiente artículo sobre la contaminación del ambiente en la Ciudad de México, fijándose especialmente en los verbos reflexivos. Luego haga el ejercicio que lo sigue.

MÉXICO SE ASFIXIA

En la Ciudad de México ya no saben qué hacer para combatir la contaminación. Un estudio de la Organización Mundial de la Salud—OMS—afirma que respirar un día el aire de la Ciudad de México equivale a fumarse 40 cigarrillos. Otros especialistas aseguran que el ozono que deja la contaminación provoca el envejecimiento de los pulmones, lo que se traduce en aumento de infartos cardíacos.

En estos días, la temperatura aumentó a 30 grados, lo que junto a los escasos vientos, el intenso sol y la emisión diaria de 12.000 toneladas de gases, está convirtiéndose en un peligroso coctel para los 20 millones de habitantes.

En los últimos cuatro años el gobierno mejoró la calidad de los combustibles, obligó a las fábricas a filtrar sus gases y aplicó programas para restringir el tránsito de vehículos. Pero estas medidas no han logrado mejorar la situación.

La razón es que las políticas adoptadas por las autoridades poco se cumplen por la corrupción de las áreas de vigilancia y control, según ha denunciado el Centro de Ecología y Desarrollo de México.

Vocabulario

aplicar *to put into effect*	**el infarto cardíaco** *heart attack*
asegurar *to assure*	**la medida** *measure, step*
asfixiarse *to suffocate*	**obligar** *to force*
el aumento *increase*	**peligroso** *dangerous*
el combustible *fuel*	**la política** *policy*
cumplir *to do, accomplish*	**provocar** *to cause*
denunciar *to report*	**el pulmón** *lung*
el desarrollo *development*	**respirar** *to breathe*
el envejecimiento *aging*	**la vigilancia** *vigilance, watchfulness*
equivaler a *to be the equivalent of,*	**restringir** *to restrict, limit*
amount to	**la tonelada** *ton*
fumarse *to smoke*	**traducirse** *to result in, bring about*

Escoja la respuesta correcta para completar cada oración.

1. La población de la Ciudad de México es de _____ millones de habitantes.
   a. treinta
   b. veinte

2. Los pulmones envejecidos por la contaminación causan más _____.
   a. ataques al corazón
   b. enfermedades digestivas

3. Se afirma que respirar un día el aire de la Ciudad de México es equivalente a _____.
   a. tomarse un peligroso coctel
   b. fumarse cuarenta cigarrillos

4. _____ hace peligrar la salud de los habitantes de la capital.
   a. La emisión de doce mil toneladas de gases cada día
   b. La filtración de los gases emitidos por las fábricas

5. El gobierno mexicano _____ en los últimos cuatro años.
   a. ha eliminado la corrupción en los sectores de vigilancia y control
   b. ha mejorado la calidad de los combustibles

6. Aún la aplicación de programas para _____ no ha logrado reducir la contaminación del ambiente.
   a. limitar el tránsito de vehículos
   b. estudiar el ozono

7. Los gases emitidos en el aire son más dañinos cuando _____.
   a. las fábricas están obligadas a filtrar sus gases
   b. hace mucho calor y sol y poco viento

CHAPTER 8
PASSIVE CONSTRUCTIONS

 A *The passive voice—use and formation*

- The passive voice in Spanish consists of a form of **ser** + the past participle. This is often followed by the agent phrase introduced by the preposition **por.** The past participle agrees in number and gender with the subject of the sentence:

La cena fue servida *por Margarita.*	*Dinner was served by Margarita.*
Los paquetes serán entregados *por el cartero.*	*The packages will be delivered by the mailman.*
El coche ha sido reparado *por los mecánicos.*	*The car has been repaired by the mechanics.*

- The passive voice is used in Spanish when the speaker wishes to deemphasize the performer of the action. In the passive construction, the speaker can focus on the direct object by making it the subject of the passive sentence:

(active voice)	Los obreros construirán el rascacielos.
(passive voice)	El rascacielos será construido por los obreros.

Note that the direct object of the active sentence, **el rascacielos,** becomes the subject of the passive sentence. The subject of the active sentence, the performer of the action, **los obreros,** appears in the "agent phrase" introduced by **por.** In the rephrasing of the active sentence into a passive sentence, the speaker focuses on **el rascacielos** and on its building rather than on the performer of the action, **los obreros.**

A. En la oficina. Vuelva a escribir las siguientes oraciones, cambiándolas de construcción activa a construcción pasiva para describir las actividades que ocurren en la oficina. Mantenga el tiempo verbal de la oración en voz activa.

> MODELO   El secretario arregló los papeles.
> → Los papeles fueron arreglados por el secretario.

1. La recepcionista encontró el número de teléfono.
2. Los empleados llenarán los formularios.
3. El bibliotecario ha preparado el folleto.
4. La cajera cobra los cheques.
5. Las secretarias escribirán las cartas y las tarjetas postales.
6. Los agentes de viajes tradujeron los documentos.

7. El programador reparó la pantalla de la computadora.

8. Los mensajeros han puesto los recados en los escritorios.

B. Día de mudanza. Escriba oraciones con verbos en voz pasiva y en pretérito para describir lo que pasó en casa de los Pidal el día de su mudanza de San Salvador a Nueva York.

> MODELO   los muebles / llevar / cargadores (*movers*)
> → Los muebles fueron llevados por los cargadores.

1. las camas / subir a los dormitorios / tres hombres

2. la alfombra de la sala / correr / la señora Pidal

3. los cuadros / colgar en las paredes / Benito y Ramona

4. la secadora / bajar al sótano / un cargador

5. el sillón azul / colocar al lado de la ventana / el señor Pidal

6. las lámparas / poner en las mesas / la abuela

Nota cultural

- Hay mucha **emigración** de ciertos países hispánicos a los Estados Unidos por razones económicas, políticas y personales. Los inmigrantes hispanos más numerosos son de México, la República Dominicana, El Salvador, Colombia, Perú, Ecuador y Cuba.

- Muchos inmigrantes necesitan los servicios de las empresas de mudanza internacional. Por eso se ven tantos anuncios para las mudanzas en los periódicos hispánicos que se publican en los Estados Unidos; por ejemplo, en *El Diario/La Prensa* de Nueva York o *El Tiempo Latino* de Washington, D.C.

- El Salvador es el país centroamericano más pequeño y más densamente poblado. Muchos salvadoreños han emigrado a los Estados Unidos como resultado de los doce años de guerra civil que ha desgarrado (*torn apart*) El Salvador.

B *Se constructions with passive meaning*

- Spanish uses the construction **se** + verb in third-person singular or plural to deemphasize the subject. The agent phrase is not used in this construction. Notice that in English this **se**-construction (**se** + verb) can be translated in many different ways. The verb in this construction is either third-person singular or third-person plural depending on whether the grammatical subject is singular or plural:

El locutor **dio** los premios.	*The announcer **gave out (awarded)** the prizes.*
Los premios **fueron dados** por el locutor.	*The prizes **were given out (awarded)** by the announcer.*
Se dieron los premios.	*The prizes **were given out (awarded)**.*
Se sabe el motivo.	*The reason **is known**. / **You (They, People) know** the reason. / **One knows** the reason.*

Se entregó el informe.　　　　　　*The report **was handed in.***
Se entregaron los informes.　　　　*The reports **were handed in.***

- For intransitive verbs, that is, those that do not take a direct object, the verb is always in third-person singular:

Se sale por aquí.　　　　　　　　　*You **go out** this way. / This **is the way out.***

Se vive bien en este país.　　　　　*People **live** well in this country.*

Se trabaja con entusiasmo.　　　　*We (You, They) **work** enthusiastically.*

- Note that reflexive verbs such as **divertirse** and **despertarse** can only show an unidentified or deemphasized subject with the addition of **uno** (or **una** if the reference is feminine) to a third-person singular verb:

Uno se divierte mucho en el tiovivo.　*You have a lot of fun on the merry-go-round.*

Uno se despierta más tarde los domingos.　*People wake up later on Sundays.*

- Spanish also uses **la gente** with a third-person singular verb to label an indefinite subject. Compare this usage to English *people*. This Spanish construction is less common than its English equivalent:

Para divertirse, **la gente** va a un concierto.　*To have a good time, **people** go to a concert.*

- Spanish also uses the third-person plural of the verb to label an indefinite subject. In this case, the subject pronouns **ellos/ellas** cannot be used.

Dicen que va a llover.　　　　　　*They **say** it's going to rain.*

Me **van** a invitar a la boda.　　　　*They're going to invite me to the wedding. (I'm going to be invited to the wedding.)*

Lo **entrevistaron** la semana pasada.　*They **interviewed** him last week. (He was interviewed last week.)*

C. **¡Se están instalando todavía!** A los Pidal les quedan muchas cosas que hacer en instalarse. Diga qué son estas cosas formando oraciones con la construcción con **se** y el verbo en futuro. Fíjese que esta vez no hay agente en las oraciones.

MODELO　　correr / las cortinas
　　　　　　→ Se correrán las cortinas.

1. enchufar / la nevera

2. encender / las lámparas

3. guardar / las cajas

4. poner / el sofá / en la sala

5. colocar / el lavaplatos / en la cocina

6. meter / las sábanas / en el armario

7. poner / las sillas / con la mesa del comedor

D. Titulares y anuncios del periódico. Escriba oraciones usando la construcción con el sujeto indefinido **se** + la tercera persona singular o plural del verbo. Use el mismo tiempo verbal que en la oración original.

> MODELO   Los políticos estudian los problemas económicos.
> → Se estudian los problemas económicos.

1. La empresa busca programadores de computadoras.

2. La ley prohíbe el fumar en los restaurantes.

3. Los contadores (*accountants*) calculaban los impuestos.

4. Los inquilinos (*tenants*) alquilaron el apartamento en la playa.

5. El Café Alicante entrega comida a la casa hasta la una de la mañana.

6. Los clientes pagan con cheque o tarjeta de crédito.

7. Esta sucursal del Banco de Barcelona solicitará gerentes.

8. La compañía necesita secretarios bilingües.

Nota cultural

Otro servicio de conveniencia que recién empieza a tener un gran impacto en la sociedad de ciertos países hispánicos es **el servicio a domicilio.** Cada día hay más repartidores (*delivery people*) que, llamados por sus clientes, llegan a la casa de éstos en su furgoneta de reparto (*delivery van*). Actualmente en Madrid no sólo se entrega comida—paella, mariscos, pizza, bocadillos, comida china, comida congelada y vinos—sino también hay servicio de recoger y planchar ropa el mismo día, y de llevar a casa todo tipo de productos que venden las farmacias de guardia (*24-hour drugstores*). Se le envía al cliente cualquier cosa que necesite, que sea un fontanero (*plumber*), un chófer, reservas de billetes para espectáculos, etcétera. Hay empresas de servicio a domicilio en Barcelona, Valencia, (la isla de) Mallorca y otras ciudades españolas, tanto como en las ciudades grandes de los países hispanoamericanos.

E. Una excursión al zoológico. Escriba oraciones con el sujeto definido para describir una excursión al zoológico. Use los sujetos que aparecen entre paréntesis.

> MODELO   Se visita el zoológico. (nosotros)
> → Visitamos el zoológico.

1. Se va de excursión al zoológico. (mis amigos y yo)

2. Para llegar al zoológico, se toma el autobús en la calle Azorín. (nosotros)

3. Se ven leones, tigres, leopardos y panteras. (yo)

4. Se da de comer a los animales. (los guardianes)

5. Se entra en las jaulas para limpiarlas. (unos trabajadores)

6. Se comen las hojas de los árboles. (las jirafas)

7. Se tiran cacahuates a los elefantes. (tú)

8. Se juega tirando plátanos. (un mono)

9. Se grita en voz alta. (los loros)

10. Uno se baña en la piscina de la jaula. (los hipopótamos)

11. Se cura la pata de un jaguar. (una guardiana)

12. Se compran palomitas y refrescos. (Pilar y Arturo)

Nota cultural

Los grandes **zoológicos** que se encuentran en los Estados Unidos, como los de San Diego, Nueva York, Chicago o Washington, D.C., tienen sus equivalentes en algunos países hispánicos. Se destacan los zoológicos de la ciudad de México y de Madrid.

El jaguar es un félido (*gato*) grande, una especie de pantera de América.

C *Ser and estar with the past participle*

- Both **ser** and **estar** are used with the past participle of the verb. Passive sentences have **ser** + the past participle and usually have the agent phrase introduced by **por.** Sentences that have **estar** + the past participle express the result of an action. They do not have an agent phrase introduced by **por.**

La torta **fue hecha** por el cocinero.   *The cake **was made** by the chef.*
La torta **estaba hecha.**   *The cake **was made** (done, completed, finished).*

F. Todo estaba hecho. Cuando Ud. llegó todo estaba hecho ya. Dígaselo a su amigo siguiendo el modelo.

MODELO   ¿Quién abrió las ventanas?
→ No sé. Cuando yo llegué, las ventanas ya estaban abiertas.

1. ¿Quién arregló el cuarto?   5. ¿Quién puso la mesa?

2. ¿Quién preparó el almuerzo?   6. ¿Quién lavó los vasos?

3. ¿Quién cerró la puerta?   7. ¿Quién planchó el mantel?

4. ¿Quién apagó el microondas?   8. ¿Quién prendió las luces?

G. ¿Qué significa? Su amigo español está pasando las vacaciones de verano en su casa. Mientras Uds. se pasean por la ciudad, su amigo le pregunta qué quieren decir los letreros que ve. Explíquele lo que dicen en español usando la construcción con **se.**

1. Newspapers and magazines are sold here.

2. You park here.

3. You eat well.

4. One turns right.

5. You enter this way.

6. French is spoken here.

7. Travelers checks cashed.

8. The department store opens at ten.

H. ¿Qué dice Ud.? Un nuevo estudiante en su colegio le hace unas preguntas sobre la vida escolar y la de la calle. Conteste sus preguntas usando la construcción con **se.**

1. ¿Qué materias toman en el colegio?

2. ¿A qué hora almuerzan en el colegio?

3. ¿Cómo llegan al colegio?

4. ¿Dónde compran sus libros de texto?

5. ¿Cómo pueden sacar buenas notas?

6. ¿Qué hacen para divertirse los fines de semana?

7. ¿En qué restaurantes comen?

8. ¿Qué deportes juegan?

I. Ejercicio oral. Adivinanza (*guessing game*). En este juego de adivinanza sus amigos y Ud. intentan adivinar quién escribió una famosa obra literaria. Una persona dice el título de la obra, por ejemplo, *Don Quijote*, y los otros tienen que decir lo más rápido posible quién la escribió. Se contesta así: *Fue escrito por Cervantes.* Hay que contestar empleando la voz pasiva.

J. Estructuras en acción. Lea los siguientes anuncios de un periódico argentino sobre los cursos y conferencias que se dan. Luego haga el ejercicio.

Cursos y conferencias

Historia del arte. La Alianza Francesa de Mendoza organizó un curso de historia del arte "Desde Constantino el Grande hasta el fin de la Guerra de los Cien Años. El arte del occidente medieval". Estará a cargo del profesor Horacio Rosa y se desarrollará el 5, 12, 19 y 26, de 18.30 a 20.30. Mayores informes se ofrecen en la sede de la Alianza, Chile 1754.

Oratoria. Un curso sobre "Oratoria y comunicación oral" será ofrecido por el profesor Luis Osvaldo Perrotin y la licenciada Ana Gloria Ortega de Sevilla, en el Centro Cultural Matesis, Belgrano 29000, de Godoy Cruz, teléfonos 221864 y 240033.

Alemán. El Instituto Goethe anunció que hoy iniciará un ciclo de cursos de alemán. El primer año intensivo se desarrollará los lunes y miércoles de 16.30 a 19.45, mientras que de 15.15 a 17 tendrá lugar el de introducción a las técnicas de traducción simultánea. Para mayor información llamar al teléfono 340323.

Universidades

Facultad de Artes. La Escuela de Teatro informó sobre los seminarios internacionales que se ofrecerán este mes: del 12 al 14, Guillermo Heras (España), dictará uno sobre "Experiencia de montaje"; el 22 y 23, Alberto Isola (Perú) se referirá a "El training del actor" y Ramón Griffero (Chile) hablará sobre "Dramaturgia desde el espacio".

Se indicó que estos cursos se efectuarán en cooperación con el Teatro General San Martín, de Buenos Aires, y son coordinados por el Centro de Estudios e Investigación Teatral de la Escuela de Teatro. Las inscripciones se reciben de 15 a 20.

Vocabulario

la alianza *alliance*	**la inscripción** *registration*
a cargo de uno *to be in one's charge*	**la licenciada** *lawyer*
el ciclo *cycle*	**mayores informes** *more information*
desarrollar *to develop*	**el montaje** *staging*
dictar un seminario *to give a seminar*	**la oratoria** *oratory, oratorical art*
la dramaturgia *dramatic art*	**referirse** *to refer to, speak about*
efectuarse *to take place*	**la sede** *headquarters*
el espacio *space*	**la traducción** *translation*
la investigación *research*	

En una hoja de papel, escriba los ejemplos de construcción pasiva que se encuentran en los anuncios y tradúzcalos al inglés.

Historia del arte   **Oratoria**

1. _____   2. _____

Facultad de artes

3. _____   4. _____   5. _____   6. _____

CHAPTER 9

THE PERFECT TENSES

A The formation of the present perfect

- The perfect tenses in Spanish are similar to their English equivalents. They consist of a conjugated form of the auxiliary verb **haber** (*to have*) + the past participle, which is the form of the verb ending in **-do.** The past participle of regular verbs is formed by dropping the infinitive ending and adding **-ado** to **-ar** verbs and **-ido** to **-er** and **-ir** verbs:

mandar	**mandado**	*sent*
comprender	**comprendido**	*understood*
servir	**servido**	*served*

- The following verbs have irregular past participles:

abrir	**abierto**	hacer	**hecho**	ver	**visto**
cubrir	**cubierto**	morir	**muerto**	volver	**vuelto**
decir	**dicho**	poner	**puesto**		
escribir	**escrito**	romper	**roto**		

- When a prefix is added to any of the above verbs, the past participle shows the same irregularities:

describir	**descrito**	devolver	**devuelto**	predecir	**predicho**
descubrir	**descubierto**	imponer	**impuesto**	prever	**previsto**
deshacer	**deshecho**	posponer	**pospuesto**	revolver	**revuelto**

- **-Er** and **-ir** verbs that have stems ending in a vowel have an accent mark over the **-í-** in the past participle:

caer	**caído**	leer	**leído**	traer	**traído**
creer	**creído**	oír	**oído**		

- The past participle forms of **ser** and **ir** are **sido** and **ido** respectively.

- In the perfect tenses, object pronouns precede the forms of **haber** and are not attached to the *past participle.* In questions, subject pronouns follow the *past participle.* They are not placed between the auxiliary verb and the past participle as they are in English:

¿**Lo** has leído?	*Have you read **it**? (object pronoun)*
¿Qué han visto **Uds.**?	*What have **you** seen?*
¿Todavía no se ha levantado **Ud.**?	*Haven't **you** gotten up yet?*

- The present perfect consists of a conjugated form of the auxiliary verb **haber** + the past participle. The past participle does not change to show gender or number in compound tenses where the auxiliary verb is **haber**. The present perfect is used in Spanish, as in English, to mark or describe past events that have an influence on the present or that continue into the present.

ganar, comprender, salir	
(yo) **he** ganado, comprendido, salido	(nosotros) **hemos** ganado, comprendido, salido
(tú) **has** ganado, comprendido, salido	(vosotros) **habéis** ganado, comprendido, salido
(él/ella/Ud.) **ha** ganado, comprendido, salido	(ellos/ellas/Uds.) **han** ganado, comprendido, salido

A. **¿Listos para viajar?** Ud. y su familia se van de vacaciones. Antes de salir de la casa tienen que hacer ciertas cosas. Use el pretérito perfecto (*present perfect*) para escribir oraciones que explican quién hizo cada cosa.

MODELO   papá / comprar / el mapa
→ Papá ha comprado el mapa.

Preparándose para un viaje

el baúl *trunk (car)*	**la linterna** *flashlight*
el cheque de viajero *traveler's check*	**llenar el tanque del coche** *to fill the tank*
desenchufar los aparatos eléctricos *to unplug the appliances*	**el mapa** *map*
	la pila *battery (flashlight)*
el equipaje *luggage*	**prepararse** *to get ready*
hacer las maletas *to pack*	**la ventanilla** *car window*

1. Pedro / apagar / las luces

2. Cecilia y Pilar / hacer / las maletas

3. papá / llenar / el tanque del coche

4. Berta / desenchufar / los aparatos eléctricos

5. David y Juan Carlos / meter / el equipaje en el baúl

6. yo / decirles / a los vecinos / que nos vamos

7. mamá / poner / las pilas en la linterna

8. Paco y yo / comprar / los cheques de viajero

9. tú / limpiar / las ventanillas del coche

B. **Una receta de cocina** (*recipe*). Ud. y unos amigos están preparando un plato especial para servir en la cena. Use el pretérito perfecto para describir paso a paso lo que han hecho.

> MODELO   Vera / comprar / mariscos
> ➜ Vera ha comprado mariscos.

Una receta de cocina

el aguacate *avocado*	**freír** *to fry*
añadir *to add*	**la mayonesa** *mayonnaise*
la cacerola *saucepan*	**picar** *to chop*
el camarón *shrimp*	**la pimienta picante** *hot pepper*
la cebolla *onion*	**el pollo** *chicken*
cortar *to cut*	**poner al horno** *to put in the oven*
cubrir *to cover*	**quemar** *to burn*
encender el fuego *to turn on the flame*	**la sal** *salt*
la ensalada *salad*	**la salchicha** *sausage*
los espárragos *asparagus*	**la sartén** *frying pan*
freído *past participle* **freír**	
(**frito**—*more commonly used*)	

---

1. nosotros / leer / la receta

2. Jorge / encender / el fuego

3. yo / hacer / la mayonesa

4. Alicia y Juan Diego / picar / las pimientas picantes

5. Ud. / freír / las cebollas

6. Estrella y yo / cortar / la salchicha

7. tú / lavar / los espárragos y los aguacates

8. Marianela / añadir / sal

9. Uds. / poner / el pollo al horno

10. yo / mezclar / la ensalada de camarones

11. Martín / cubrir / la cacerola

12. Lupe y Julio / quemar / las sartenes

C. Vuelva a escribir las oraciones del *ejercicio B* cambiando los sustantivos que son complementos directos de los verbos a pronombres.

> MODELO   Vera ha comprado **mariscos.**
> ➜ Vera **los** ha comprado.

D. **¡Nos aburrimos como una ostra (*oyster*)! (*We're dying of boredom!*)** Ud. y sus amigos quieren escaparse de una fiesta muy aburrida. Describa lo que han hecho todos Uds. cambiando los verbos del tiempo presente al pretérito perfecto.

> MODELO   Pablo trata de huir.
> → Pablo ha tratado de huir.

1. María Dolores se duerme.

2. Ud. bosteza.

3. Yo me pongo el abrigo.

4. Carlos y Beatriz se despiden de la anfitriona (*hostess*).

5. ¡Nos matan de aburrimiento!

6. Tú te quejas que la comida te cayó mal.

7. Ud. y Clara dan excusas.

8. Ramón dice que se enferma.

E. **Preguntas personales.** Conteste las siguientes preguntas usando el pretérito perfecto.

1. ¿Qué materias ha tomado Ud. este año?

2. ¿Qué notas ha sacado en estas materias?

3. ¿Se ha hecho Ud. socio (*Have you joined*) de un club? ¿Del cuál?

4. ¿A qué países han viajado Ud. y sus padres?

5. ¿Qué planes han hecho Ud. y sus amigos para el verano?

6. ¿Ha decidido Ud. lo que va a estudiar en la universidad?

7. ¿Qué películas ha visto Ud. este año? ¿Cuál le ha gustado más?

8. ¿Cómo ha celebrado Ud. su último cumpleaños?

9. ¿Qué regalos ha recibido? ¿Quién le ha dado cada regalo?

10. ¿Qué cosas han hecho sus amigos y Ud. hoy?

F. **¡Hecho consumado! (*¡Cosa hecha!*)** Conteste las siguientes preguntas empleando el pretérito perfecto del verbo reflexivo en la oración original para explicar que las cosas ya están hechas.

> MODELO   ¿Cuándo van Uds. a mudarse?
> → Nos hemos mudado ya.

1. ¿Cuándo va Cristóbal a matricularse?

2. ¿Cuándo van Uds. a apoderarse de la finca?

3. ¿Cuándo vas a instalarte en la nueva casa?

4. ¿Cuándo van Irene y Jaime a comprometerse?

5. ¿Cuándo va Nora a enterarse de los líos de la familia?

6. ¿Cuándo vas a apuntarte en la lista de voluntarios?

7. ¿Cuándo van los Roldán a ausentarse de la ciudad?

B *The past perfect*

- The past perfect consists of the imperfect of the auxiliary verb **haber** + past participle. The English equivalent of the past perfect is *had done something*.

llegar, comer, subir	
(yo) **había** llegado, comido, subido	(nosotros) **habíamos** llegado, comido, subido
(tú) **habías** llegado, comido, subido	(vosotros) **habíais** llegado, comido, subido
(él/ella/Ud.) **había** llegado, comido, subido	(ellos/ellas/Uds.) **habían** llegado, comido, subido

- The past perfect or pluperfect tense designates an event that happened prior to another past event that is further removed in the past:

Yo ya me había despertado cuando sonó el despertador.

*I **had already awakened** when the alarm clock went off.*

María ya había ido al teatro cuando Pedro la llamó.

*María **had already gone to the theater** when Pedro called her.*

Nosotros habíamos vuelto a casa cuando empezó a nevar.

*We **had gotten back home** when it began to snow.*

G. No, fue antes. Escriba oraciones en las cuales explica que las cosas mencionadas no pasaron ayer sino antes. Ud. practicará el uso del pretérito pluscuamperfecto (*past perfect*).

> MODELO   ¿Llegó Lorenzo ayer? (la semana pasada)
> → No, **había llegado** la semana pasada.

1. ¿Fueron Uds. a ver la exposición en el museo ayer? (hace unos meses)

2. ¿Se cortó Amelia el pelo anteayer? (el sábado)

3. ¿Se casaron Ricardo y Leonor en abril? (dos meses antes)

4. ¿Hiciste el asado el cuatro de julio? (el primero de julio)

5. ¿Celebró Pepita su santo hace quince días? (hace un mes)

6. ¿Cambió Ud. de idea hace unos días? (hace mucho tiempo)

7. ¿Pusieron Uds. los papeles en orden este año? (el año pasado)

8. ¿Te devolvió Javier los libros esta semana? (la semana pasada)

9. ¿Escribimos los informes en febrero? (noviembre)

10. ¿Se rompió Ud. el codo hace seis meses? (hace casi un año)

Nota cultural

En los países hispánicos las personas celebran su **santo**, es decir, el día de su santo. El santo que se celebra depende del nombre de pila (*given name*) de la persona. El calendario hispánico incluye el santoral en el cual nombran a los santos de cada día del año. En ciertos países hispánicos no sólo se celebra el santo sino el cumpleaños también. El cumpleaños ha cobrado más importancia en algunos países por la influencia de los Estados Unidos.

H. Tomás, el holgazán (*loafer*). Es que los amigos de Tomás no pueden contar con él porque no le gusta trabajar y siempre llega tarde. Ya cuando Tomás llega, todo está hecho. ¡Los amigos lo habían hecho todo! Escriba oraciones en las cuales explica lo que ya habían hecho los amigos cuando llegó Tomás por fin.

> MODELO   Cuando Tomás llegó por fin … (los amigos / lavar el carro)
> → Cuando Tomás llegó por fin, los amigos ya habían lavado el carro.

1. Cuando Tomás llegó por fin … (Raúl / barrer el piso)

2. Cuando Tomás llegó por fin … (Uds. / poner la mesa)

3. Cuando Tomás llegó por fin … (Diana y Judit / recoger las manzanas)

4. Cuando Tomás llegó por fin … (Ud. / sacar la basura)

5. Cuando Tomás llegó por fin … (yo / subir las cajas a la buhardilla [*attic*])

6. Cuando Tomás llegó por fin … (tú / ir de compras)

7. Cuando Tomás llegó por fin … (Plácido y yo / pasar la aspiradora)

I. Ya habíamos hecho muchas cosas. Escriba oraciones que explican lo que Ud. y otras personas habían hecho ya cuando pasaron ciertas cosas. Use el pretérito para una frase y el pretérito pluscuamperfecto para la otra.

> MODELO   (sonar el teléfono) … (ellos / cenar)
> → Cuando sonó el teléfono, ellos ya habían cenado.

1. (Julia / venir a buscarnos) … (nosotros / hacer ejercicio)

2. (yo / ir a su casa) … (Virginia / dar una vuelta)

3. (Ud. / levantarse) … (sus padres / desayunarse)

4. (nosotros / volver a casa) … (Juanita / escribir su composición)

5. (los bomberos / llegar) … (Uds. / apagar el incendio en la cocina)

6. (los bisnietos / lograr ver a su bisabuelo) … (el bisabuelo / enfermarse)

J. Nunca habíamos visto … Ud., sus padres y hermanos vuelven mañana a los Estados Unidos después de pasar seis semanas en España. Ahora que se van se ponen a pensar en las cosas que no habían visto ni hecho en los viajes anteriores. Escriba oraciones usando el pretérito pluscuamperfecto en las cuales Uds. describen las cosas que no habían visto ni hecho antes.

MODELO   mamá / visitar la catedral de Burgos
→ Mamá no había visitado la catedral de Burgos hasta este viaje.

1. Laura / ver una corrida de toros en Madrid

2. Rodolfo y Eva / dar una vuelta en las carreteras gallegas

3. yo / hacer una excursión a El Escorial

4. tú y Susana / pasearse por el barrio de Santa Cruz

5. mamá, papá y yo / subir al monte Tibidabo

6. Jaime / conocer la Alhambra

7. tú / pasar Semana Santa en Sevilla

Nota cultural

- **La catedral de Burgos**—la ciudad de Burgos, capital de la provincia de Burgos, queda en Castilla la Vieja, al norte céntrico del país. Queda a las orillas del río Arlanzón. Su catedral, por sus dimensiones la tercera catedral española después de las de Sevilla y Toledo, se destaca por su estilo gótico. La construcción de la catedral empezó en el siglo XIII.

- **La corrida de toros** es el espectáculo nacional español. Las plazas de toros más importantes de España son las de Madrid, Sevilla y Barcelona.

- **Las carreteras gallegas**, es decir, de la región de Galicia al noroeste de España. Comprende las provincias de La Coruña, Lugo, Orense y Pontevedra.

- **El Escorial** es el monasterio y palacio construido por el rey español Felipe II en 1563. El plan del edificio fue supervisado por Felipe II al igual que la creación de un gran monumento para honrar la memoria de su padre, Carlos V. Se encuentra aquí el panteón de los reyes españoles donde están enterrados todos los reyes españoles salvo tres. El majestuoso edificio queda en la sierra de Guadarrama en la villa de San Lorenzo de El Escorial, a poca distancia al norte de Madrid.

- **El barrio de Santa Cruz,** que era el barrio judío en la Edad Media, es hoy el barrio más típico y pintoresco de Sevilla.

- **El monte Tibidabo** queda al noroeste de Barcelona. Desde la cima hay un hermoso panorama de Barcelona y el Mediterráneo. Hay un funicular (*cable car*) que lleva a la gente a lo alto del monte.

- **La Alhambra** es el hermoso palacio y fortaleza de los reyes moros en Granada. Se construyó en su mayor parte durante el siglo XIV.

- **La Semana Santa** es el período que precede al domingo de Resurrección. Las procesiones religiosas sevillanas son célebres. Muchos españoles van de vacaciones durante esta semana.

C *The future perfect*

- The future perfect consists of the future tense of the auxiliary verb **haber** + the past participle.

llegar, comer, subir	
(yo) **habré** llegado, comido, subido	(nosotros) **habremos** llegado, comido, subido
(tú) **habrás** llegado, comido, subido	(vosotros) **habréis** llegado, comido, subido
(él/ella/Ud.) **habrá** llegado, comido, subido	(ellos/ellas/Uds.) **habrán** llegado, comido, subido

- In Spanish, as in English, the future perfect tense designates an event that will be completed in the future before another event occurs or before some point in time in the future:

Habrán vuelto para finales del mes.   *They'll have returned by the end of the month.*

Lo habré terminado todo antes de irme.   *I'll have finished everything before I leave.*

- The future perfect is also used to express probability in past time. The future perfect of probability corresponds to the preterit or the present perfect:

Habrá pasado algo.
Probablemente pasó algo.   ⎫
Probablemente ha pasado algo. ⎬   *Something probably happened.*
                              ⎭

- **Deber de** + perfect infinitive, which is the infinitive **haber** + the past participle, can be used instead of the future perfect to express probability in past time:

Marta debe de haber llamado.   *Marta must have (probably) called.*

K. **¿Qué habrá ocurrido?** Escriba oraciones con el verbo en futuro perfecto para explicar para cuándo habrán ocurrido ciertas cosas.

MODELO   nosotros / almorzar / para las dos
→ Habremos almorzado para las dos.

1. Elena / graduarse / para el año próximo

2. Alfredo y Armando / mejorarse / antes de regresar al colegio

3. nosotros / ahorrar dinero / antes de las vacaciones de invierno

4. yo / darte tu regalo / antes de tu fiesta de cumpleaños

5. Ud. y Laura / mudarse / para mediados del mes

6. tú / sacar un pasaporte / para julio

L. Conjeturas (*Conjectures***).** Exprese sus conjeturas sobre lo que pasó usando el futuro perfecto para expresar probabilidad en el pasado.

> MODELO   *Probablemente* llegó el cartero.
> → **Habrá llegado** el cartero.

1. Su coche probablemente le costó un ojo de la cara.

2. Clara escribió la carta, probablemente.

3. Felipe y Eduardo probablemente ganaron la regata.

4. Uds. probablemente tomaron la merienda.

5. Martín y yo probablemente no entendimos el motivo.

6. Ud. probablemente no hizo cola por mucho tiempo.

D *The conditional perfect*

- The conditional perfect consists of the conditional tense of the auxiliary verb **haber** + the past participle. It corresponds to English *would have done something*.

llegar, comer, subir	
(yo) **habría** llegado, comido, subido	(nosotros) **habríamos** llegado, comido, subido
(tú) **habrías** llegado, comido, subido	(vosotros) **habríais** llegado, comido, subido
(él/ella/Ud.) **habría** llegado, comido, subido	(ellos/ellas/Uds.) **habrían** llegado, comido, subido

- The conditional perfect is used to designate an action or event that would have been completed in the past or when there is a real or implied condition:

Yo no lo **habría dicho.**	*I **wouldn't have said** it.*
Nosotros **nos habríamos quedado** más tiempo.	*We **probably would have stayed** longer.*

- The conditional perfect is also used to express probability in past time. It corresponds to the past perfect + *probably:*

Ya **se habría ido,** me imagino.	*He **had probably left,** I imagine.*

- The perfect infinitive consists of the infinitive **haber** + the past participle. It is used after prepositions and as the complement of some verbs:

Lorenzo ha sacado excelentes notas **por haber estudiado** tanto.	*Lorenzo has gotten excellent grades **for having studied** so much (because he studied so much).*
No recuerdo **haberlo visto.**	*I don't remember **having seen** him.*

M. No lo habríamos hecho. Escriba oraciones que expresan que Ud. y otras personas no habrían hecho las cosas que hicieron algunas personas.

> MODELO   Gregorio pidió el plato de langosta con salsa de chocolate. (yo)
> → Yo no lo habría pedido.

1. Diego y Jaime salieron a la calle durante la tormenta. (Patricia y yo)

2. Tere rompió su compromiso con su novio. (Sofía)

3. Uds. hicieron el viaje a California en autobús. (los turistas venezolanos)

4. Ariana se cortó el pelo en la peluquería Melenas. (tú)

5. Nosotros creímos lo que nos dijo Baltasar. (Ud.)

6. Te reíste cuando se te cayeron los vasos. (yo)

N. ¡Felicidades! Ud. es el maestro de ceremonias del programa de los Óscar. Les presenta la estatuilla del Óscar a los ganadores de las diferentes categorías artísticas de las películas del año. Practique el uso del infinitivo compuesto (*perfect infinitive*) tras (*after*) **por.**

> MODELO   Maribel Sánchez / trabajar en "Alma y corazón"
> → A Maribel Sánchez **por haber trabajado** en "Alma y corazón".

1. Lope Cernuda / dirigir "Plátanos y cerezas"

2. Ernesto del Olmo / componer la música de "Mosquitos mágicos"

3. Ela Pantoja y Roberto Campillo / escribir el guión de "Agua hervida"

4. Agustín Domingo / cantar en "Después de haber bailado"

5. Beatriz Perales / ser primera actriz en "Salchichas al sol"

6. Mateo de León y Diana Duque / producir "Grapadora en la mesa"

7. Silvia Siles / hacer la escenografía de "Narices al aire"

8. Memo Morado / actuar en "Langostas en el cielo"

9. Edit Revueltas / diseñar el vestuario de "Tijeras de poliéster"

10. Pepe del Oeste / maquillar a los actores de "Tamales quemados"

O. Allá en el rancho grande. Exprese en español sus conjeturas sobre el rancho o la estancia que tenía su familia hace muchos años. Escriba oraciones de probabilidad con el potencial compuesto (*conditional perfect*).

1. The ranch had probably been very big.

2. The farmers probably had had hens in a henhouse.

3. The farm workers probably had picked cherries and strawberries.

4. The landscape of the countryside probably had been beautiful.

5. My great-grandfather probably had gone fishing in the lake that was nearby.

6. My great-grandmother probably had cooked fresh fruits and vegetables from the harvest.

7. There probably had been horses and cows on the ranch.

8. The farmers had probably sowed seeds in the vegetable garden.

9. We probably would have loved life on the ranch.

P. Ejercicio oral. Diálogos. Hable con un amigo/una amiga de las cosas que Ud. *ha hecho* este año. Su amigo/amiga le dice lo que él/ella *habría hecho* este año. Por ejemplo, Ud. dice: *Yo he estudiado marketing este año.* Su amigo/amiga responde: *Yo habría estudiado informática.* Se puede hablar del trabajo, los pasatiempos, los deportes, las vacaciones, etcétera.

Q. Estructuras en acción. Lea este artículo sobre el turismo español en Portugal fijándose especialmente en los verbos en tiempos compuestos. Luego haga el ejercicio que sigue. (Se recomienda que el/la estudiante consulte un mapa de la península Ibérica para aprovechar al máximo el contenido cultural del artículo.)

La crisis no perdona:
Portugal espera menos turistas españoles

Lisboa. José María Moreiro

Las vacaciones de Semana Santa han sido siempre una de las épocas en que Portugal ha registrado una mayor afluencia de turistas españoles. Somos el primer cliente de este país, lo que en cifras viene a equivaler al 50 por ciento del turismo procedente de los restantes países. Sin embargo, durante la semana de Pascua de este año las perspectivas son menos halagüeñas y se teme aquí un notable descenso con respecto al largo medio millón de años anteriores, hecho que puede repetirse también durante el verano.

Las causas esenciales son dos: por un lado, la crisis económica, que lleva consigo un menor poder adquisitivo de los españoles; por otro, la última depreciación de nuestra moneda que, acompañada de la del escudo varios puntos por debajo, está aproximando la paridad, con el consiguiente encarecimiento.

A esto ha de sumarse el notabilísimo aumento del precio de los servicios en algunos casos, como es el de la vivienda, muy superior en Lisboa con respecto a ciudades como Madrid. Portugal, aunque dotado de los mismos encantos y de la ventaja de la proximidad para disfrutar de unas cortas vacaciones como las que se avecinan, ha dejado de ser el país de turismo barato que fue, esencialmente hasta 1986, año de su adhesión a la Unión Europea.

De todas formas, las previsiones señalan un mantenimiento del turismo que llega de Galicia a la región norte, con Viana do Castelo, Braga y Oporto como principales centros receptivos.

El área de la Gran Lisboa—Estoril, Cascais, Sintra y playa de Caparica, y el litoral de la zona centro—Peniche, Nazaré, Figueira da Foz son los destinos turísticos preferidos donde gozar del incipiente verano con que esta primavera nos regala.

Por lo que se refiere al Algarve, el mayor contingente de turistas hispanos siguen siendo los vecinos andaluces.

La entrada en vigor de un rigurosísimo código de circulación hacen indispensables dos esenciales consejos si los automovilistas no se quieren ver desagradablemente sorprendidos: el pago de las multas *ipso facto* y un moderadísimo consumo de alcohol, ya que la detección de 1,2 miligramos de alcoholemia está penado con prisión inmediata.

Vocabulario

la adhesión *membership*	el litoral *coast*
la afluencia *crowd, flow*	el mantenimiento *maintenance*
la alcoholemia *presence of alcohol in the blood*	la moneda *currency*
aproximar *to near*	la multa *fine, ticket*
el aumento *increase*	notabilísimo *very considerable*
avecinarse *to approach*	la paridad *parity (of currency)*
la cifra *figure*	la Pascua *Easter*
el código de circulación *highway code*	penar *to punish*
consigo *with it*	las perspectivas halagüeñas *promising prospects*
consiguiente *resulting*	el poder adquisitivo *purchasing power*
el consumo *consumption*	Por lo que se refiere al Algarve, ... *As for Algarve ..., As regards Algarve ...*
el descenso *decline*	la previsión *forecast*
el destino *destination*	la prisión *imprisonment*
dotado de *endowed with*	la proximidad *proximity, closeness*
el encanto *charm*	regalar *to treat well, royally*
el encarecimiento *rise, increase in price*	registrar *to note, notice*
la entrada en vigor *taking effect*	restante *remaining, rest*
equivaler *to be equivalent, mean*	el escudo *Portuguese unit of currency*
señalar *to point to*	
ha de sumarse *it has to be added*	sumarse *to add*
halagüeño *promising, flattering*	la ventaja *advantage*
el hecho *fact*	la vivienda *housing*
el largo medio millón *good half a million*	

1. Muchos turistas españoles pasan sus vacaciones de _____ en Portugal.
   a. Navidad
   b. Semana Santa
   c. Año Nuevo

2. Hay menos turismo español en Portugal por _____.
   a. los precios tan bajos
   b. el código de circulación
   c. la depreciación de la peseta

3. La mayor parte de los turistas españoles que van al Algarve son de _____.
   a. Galicia
   b. Andalucía
   c. la Gran Lisboa

4. Los turistas gallegos suelen hacer turismo en _____.
   a. Braga y Oporto
   b. Peniche y Nazaré
   c. Estoril y Sintra

5. La moneda portuguesa es _____.
   a. el escudo
   b. la peseta
   c. el franco

6. Según el artículo, Lisboa _____.
   a. no se encuentra en el área de la Gran Lisboa
   b. recibe más turismo que el litoral de la zona centro
   c. tiene mejor vivienda que Madrid

7. Se ofrecen consejos a los automovilistas en cuanto al pago de las multas y _____.
   a. a la adhesión a la Unión Europea
   b. al consumo de alcohol
   c. al poder adquisitivo de los españoles

8. Un 50 por ciento del turismo del Portugal _____.
   a. tiene 1,2 miligramos de alcoholemia
   b. goza de una disminución del precio de los servicios
   c. es procedente de España

CHAPTER 10
THE GERUND &
THE PROGRESSIVE TENSES

A *The formation of the gerund (present participle)*

- The gerund or **-ndo** form in Spanish corresponds to the *-ing* form in English. For **-ar** verbs, the ending of the gerund is **-ando**; for **-er** and **-ir** verbs, the ending is **-iendo**:

tomar	tom**ando**	aprender	aprend**iendo**	escribir	escrib**iendo**
ensayar	ensay**ando**	comer	com**iendo**	abrir	abr**iendo**

- **-Er** and **-ir** verbs whose stem ends in a vowel use **-yendo** and not **-iendo** to form the gerund:

caer	ca**yendo**	leer	le**yendo**	traer	tra**yendo**
creer	cre**yendo**	oír	o**yendo**		

- **-Ir** verbs that have a change in the vowel of the stem in the third-person singular of the preterit, have the same change in the gerund:

infinitive	*preterit*	*gerund*
decir	dijo	**diciendo**
dormir	durmió	**durmiendo**
morir	murió	**muriendo**
pedir	pidió	**pidiendo**
repetir	repitió	**repitiendo**
sentir	sintió	**sintiendo**
servir	sirvió	**sirviendo**
venir	vino	**viniendo**

- **Poder** and **ir** have irregular gerunds:

poder	**pudiendo**
ir	**yendo**

- Object and reflexive pronouns are attached to the present participle in writing and an accent mark is written over the **a** or **e** of the gerund ending:

esperándolo   **dándomelos**   **viéndolas**   **levantándose**

- The gerund in Spanish is usually equivalent to an English clause or gerund phrase beginning with *by, while, if, when,* or *because:*

Se aprende mucho **estudiando** con el profesor Padilla.	*You learn a lot **studying (when you study)** with Professor Padilla.*
Viajando en marzo, Nicolás ahorró mucho dinero.	***By traveling** in March, Nicolás saved a lot of money.*

- With verbs of perception, such as **ver, mirar, oír,** and **escuchar,** either the infinitive or the gerund can be used, as in English:

Los oímos cantar. ⎫ Los oímos cantando. ⎬	*We heard them sing/singing.*

A. **¡La vecina entremetida (*busybody*)!** ¡Su vecina se mete en todo! Ahora quiere saber lo que Ud. y otras personas hicieron hoy porque no los vio en todo el día. Contéstele usando **pasar** + el gerundio.

> **Modelo**   —¿Trabajó Ud. en la oficina hoy?
> —Sí, **pasé** el día **trabajando** en la oficina.

1. ¿Llamó Ud. por teléfono hoy?

2. ¿Estudiaron Carlos y Celeste en la biblioteca hoy?

3. ¿Durmió hoy el señor Marqués?

4. ¿Leyeron hoy Ud. y su hermano?

5. ¿Oíste las noticias hoy?

6. ¿Se bañó hoy la señora Pelayo?

B. **¡Cómo va volando el tiempo! (*How time flies!*)** Ud. piensa en las cosas que hizo ayer y en cuánto tiempo le llevó cada cosa. ¡Qué rápido se te fue el día! Escriba oraciones usando **pasar** + el gerundio para describir su horario de ayer.

> **Modelo**   yo / desayunar (media hora)
> → **Pasé** media hora **desayunando.**

1. yo / arreglarse (cuarenta y cinco minutos)

2. Estrella y yo / montar en bicicleta (hora y media)

3. yo / escribir un informe (dos horas)

4. Fernando, Chelo y yo / comprar cosas en el centro comercial (un par de horas)

5. mis amigos y yo / vestirse (una hora y cuarto)

6. yo / ver un documental (una hora)

B *The progressive tenses*

- The progressive tenses consist of the present, past, future, or conditional forms of the verb **estar** followed by the gerund:

Estoy oyendo música. *present progressive*	*I'm listening to music.*
Estaba oyendo música. *imperfect progressive*	*I was listening to music.*
Estuve oyendo música hasta que salimos. *preterit progressive*	*I was listening to music until we went out.*
Estaré oyendo música toda la tarde. *future progressive*	*I'll be listening to music all afternoon.*
Estaría oyendo música. *conditional progressive*	*I'd be listening to music.*

- The gerunds of **estar, ir,** and **venir** are not commonly used.

- The present, imperfect, and future progressive are different from the corresponding simple tenses in that they emphasize that the action is or was in progress. They may also suggest that the action is temporary, not habitual, or represents a change from the usual pattern:

Miguel juega al fútbol.	*Miguel plays soccer.* (habitual action)
Miguel está jugando al fútbol.	*Miguel's playing soccer.* (He's playing soccer right now *or* He's begun to play soccer.)

- The preterit progressive is used to show an action that was in progress in the past but is now completed:

  Estuvimos estudiando latín hasta que Óscar vino a buscarnos.
  We were studying Latin until Oscar came to pick us up.

- The present progressive in Spanish can never refer to the future as the present progressive in English does. To express future time, Spanish uses the simple present, the **ir a** + infinitive construction, or the future tense:

  Sacamos los boletos mañana. ⎫
  Vamos a sacar los boletos mañana. ⎬ *We're buying the tickets tomorrow.*
  Sacaremos los boletos mañana. ⎭

- In the progressive tenses, object and reflexive pronouns may either precede the form of **estar** or be attached to the gerund in writing, in which case a written accent is added:

  Isabel y Juan están paseándo**se**. ⎫
  Isabel y Juan **se** están paseando. ⎬ *Isabel and Juan are strolling.*

- The verb **seguir** is used with the gerund to mean *to be still doing something, to keep on doing something:*

Marta **sigue despertándose** antes de las seis.

*Marta **is still waking up** before six o'clock.*

Sigan buscando la llave.

Keep on looking for the key.

- **Ir** is commonly used with the gerund as well. It is used to convey the idea of *gradually* or *little by little:*

La empresa **va prosperando.**

*The company **is gradually prospering.***

Las flores **se fueron secando** poco a poco.

*The flowers **withered away** little by little.*

C. **En el campamento (***camp, campground***) de verano.** Escriba lo que están haciendo los niños en un día típico en el campamento. Use el verbo en presente progresivo.

> MODELO   Eva y Ángela trabajan en un campamento.
> → Eva y Ángela están trabajando en un campamento.

En el campamento

acampar *to camp*	**la mariposa** *butterfly*
apagar el fuego *to put out the fire*	**la mochila** *backpack, knapsack*
la araña *spider*	**el mosquito** *mosquito*
asar *to roast*	**nadar** *to swim*
atrapar *to catch*	**el perro caliente** *hot dog*
desenvolver *to unroll*	**la picadura** *bite*
encender el fuego *to light the fire*	**la pila** *battery*
la hormiga *ant*	**el saco (la bolsa) de dormir** *sleeping bag*
el hormiguero *anthill*	**la serpiente** *snake*
ir de camping *to go camping*	**la sierra** *mountains*
el lago *lake*	**la tienda de campaña** *tent*
la linterna *flashlight*	

---

1. Los niños acampan en la sierra.

2. Ricardo nada en el lago.

3. Lupe y yo llenamos la mochila.

4. Ester desenvuelve el saco de dormir.

5. Ud. y Andrés atrapan mariposas para su colección.

6. Pablo se acuesta en el saco de dormir.

7. Yo observo las hormigas en el hormiguero.

8. Tú enciendes el fuego para asar los perros calientes.

9. Pepe y Lucía meten las pilas en la linterna.

10. Todos nosotros nos quejamos de las picaduras de los mosquitos.

11. Ud. se asusta al ver las arañas en la tienda de campaña.

12. Consuelo grita al ver una serpiente.

D. Escriba oraciones con los verbos en presente, imperfecto o futuro progresivo. Cambie los sustantivos que son complementos directos a pronombres. Haga todos los cambios necesarios.

> MODELO   Carlos practica el ruso.
> → Carlos **está practicándolo.**
> → Carlos **lo está practicando.**

1. Leíamos los periódicos.

2. Uds. harán las maletas.

3. Me pongo el traje.

4. Ud. se lavaba la cabeza.

5. Nos dirás los planes.

6. Rita se viste en el dormitorio.

E. **¡Cuando estalló (*broke out*) el fuego, …!** Cuando estalló el fuego en la cocina del Hotel Dos Reyes en Cartagena, los huéspedes y los empleados del hotel estaban haciendo ciertas cosas. Escriba oraciones con el verbo en imperfecto progresivo que describen lo que estaban haciendo estas personas. Escriba cada oración de dos maneras cuando sea posible.

> MODELO   el señor Escudero / bañarse
> → El señor Escudero estaba bañándose.
> → El señor Escudero se estaba bañando.

En el hotel

el aire acondicionado *air conditioning*	**el lavado** *wash*
el ascensor *elevator*	**la lavandera** *laundress*
el botones *bellhop*	**el mozo** *waiter*
la camarera *chambermaid*	**el noveno piso** *ninth floor*
el equipaje *luggage*	**la recepción** *check-in desk*
el gerente *manager*	**registrarse** *to check in*
el huésped *guest (in hotel)*	**tocar el timbre** *to ring the bell*
el juego de toallas *set of towels*	

---

1. los señores Sotomayor / registrarse

2. la señorita Serrano / pedir un juego de toallas

3. el botones / subirles el equipaje a unos huéspedes

4. las camareras / arreglar los cuartos

5. los mozos / servirles la cena a los clientes

6. el gerente / prender el aire acondicionado

7. el doctor López / afeitarse

8. la lavandera / devolverle el lavado a la señora Casona

9. los huéspedes del noveno piso / bajar en el ascensor

10. los turistas ingleses / tocar el timbre en la recepción

11. los cocineros / ¡jactarse de los plátanos flameados que habían preparado!

F. ¡Qué va! Siguen haciéndolo. Su amiga acaba de volver de Bogotá donde pasó un semestre estudiando español. Ella supone que ha habido muchos cambios mientras estaba en el extranjero. Ud. le dice que *¡qué va!*, que todo sigue siendo igual. Escriba oraciones usando formas de **seguir** + el gerundio. Cambie los sustantivos que son complementos directos a pronombres.

MODELO   Ya no estudias química, ¿verdad?
→ ¡Qué va! **Sigo estudiándola.**

1. Elena ya no dice chismes (*gossip*), ¿verdad?

2. Ya no construyen la autopista, ¿verdad?

3. Ya no lees ciencia-ficción, ¿verdad?

4. Tus padres ya no duermen la siesta, ¿verdad?

5. Ud. ya no asiste a los conciertos de jazz, ¿verdad?

6. Nosotros, los Gatos Azules, ya no jugamos al fútbol en el estadio, ¿verdad?

G. ¡Nosotros, los trasnochadores (*night owls*)! A Ud. y a sus amigos les gusta trasnochar (*stay up late*). Escriba oraciones en futuro progresivo describiendo lo que Uds. estarán haciendo a esas horas.

MODELO   yo / hablar por teléfono / a la una de la mañana
→ Yo **estaré hablando** por teléfono a la una de la mañana.

1. Luisa / ver televisión / a las dos y media

2. Ud. / ducharse / a medianoche

3. mis amigos y yo / morirnos de sueño / a las cuatro

4. Pablo y Ramón / jugar al ajedrez / a las doce y media

5. yo / oír música / a la una y media

6. tú / comerse unos bocadillos / a las tres

C *The progressive tenses with **llevar** to express "have been doing"*

- In addition to **hace** + expression of time + **que** + verb in the present tense, Spanish expresses actions that begin in the past and that continue into the present with the present tense of **llevar** + the gerund:

  Llevo tres años **estudiando** español. ⎫
  Hace tres años que estudio español. ⎬ *I've been studying Spanish for three years.*
  Estudio español desde hace tres años. ⎭

- The gerund of **estar** is not used in the **llevar** + gerund construction. **Llevar** is used by itself:

  Llevo dos horas aquí.   *I've been here for two hours.*

H. Una entrevista. Un periodista le entrevista al famoso pintor-escultor peruano Pablo de Lima. Las preguntas se hacen con la construcción **hace** + expresión de tiempo y se contestan usando **llevar** + el gerundio.

MODELO   ¿Cuánto tiempo hace que Ud. hace esculturas?
            (quince años)
            → **Llevo** quince años **haciendo** esculturas.

La pintura

abstracto *abstract*	**el/la modelo** *model*
la cerámica *ceramics*	**el mural** *mural*
el cuadro *painting*	**el paisaje** *landscape*
dibujar *to draw*	**el pincel** *paintbrush*
el dibujo *drawing*	**pintar** *to paint*
el escultor/la escultora *sculptor*	**el pintor/la pintora** *painter*
la escultura *sculpture*	**la pintura** *painting; paint*
el fondo *background*	**el retrato** *portrait*
la galería *gallery*	

---

1. ¿Cuánto tiempo hace que Ud. pinta retratos? (doce años)

2. ¿Cuánto tiempo hace que Ud. usa estos pinceles? (unos meses)

3. ¿Cuánto tiempo hace que Ud. dibuja con modelos? (varios años)

4. ¿Cuánto tiempo hace que Ud. se dedica a la pintura? (toda la vida)

5. ¿Cuánto tiempo hace que Ud. cuelga sus cuadros de paisajes en la galería Olmo? (un año)

6. ¿Cuánto tiempo hace que Ud. se interesa en los murales? (poco tiempo)

7. ¿Cuánto tiempo hace que Ud. trabaja en cerámica? (nueve años)

8. ¿Cuánto tiempo hace que Ud. vive en París? (cinco años)

Nota cultural

Lima, capital del Perú, queda a orillas del río Rimac, no muy lejos del océano Pacífico. La ciudad fue fundada como "La ciudad de los Reyes" por Francisco Pizarro, conquistador español, en 1535. Lima tuvo una enorme importancia durante la época de la colonia hasta que se independizó Perú de España en 1821. Hay mucho que ver en Lima incluso la Universidad Nacional Mayor de San Marcos (fundada en 1551); la Catedral e iglesias; edificios públicos y casas históricas; varios museos de las culturas precolombinas e historia desde la conquista—el Museo Nacional de Antropología y Arqueología, el Museo de la Nación, el Museo de Oro, el Museo Nacional de Historia, el Museo del Tribunal de la Santa Inquisición, etcétera, y de arte—el Museo de Arte, el Museo de Arte Italiano, la Colección Pedro de Osma y la Pinacoteca (galería, museo de arte) Municipal donde hay una exposición grande de artistas peruanos, como Ignacio Merino (1817–76).

I. Un partido de fútbol. Un locutor de televisión describe un partido de fútbol empleando el presente progresivo de los verbos entre paréntesis.

1. Los aficionados _____ _____ sus equipos. (animar [*to cheer*])

2. Redondo _____ _____ el balón (*ball*). (robar)

3. Nosotros _____ _____ un partido emocionante. (ver)

4. Manrique _____ _____ un gol. (marcar [*to score*])

5. Los entrenadores (*trainers*) _____ _____ al campo de fútbol. (salir)

6. Cuéllar _____ _____ el balón. (regatear [*to dribble*])

7. Los técnicos (*managers*) _____ _____ un gran esfuerzo a los jugadores. (pedirles)

8. Los aficionados _____ _____. (entusiasmarse)

9. Uds., los televidentes, _____ _____ los gritos de los aficionados. (oír)

10. Este partido de campeonato _____ _____ mucha atención. (atraer)

J. Exprese en español las siguientes oraciones empleando el progresivo.

1. We're having a wonderful time!

2. You (*Ud.*) were jogging until it began to rain. (*use preterit progressive*)

3. They're still serving dinner at the Palacio Hotel.

4. I'm getting to know Madrid little by little.

5. Mateo and Victoria will be playing tennis all afternoon.

6. Pedro and I kept on reading.

K. **Ejercicio oral. ¿Qué están haciendo?** Use el presente progresivo para describir lo que Ud. y sus familiares y amigos están haciendo en este momento.

L. **Estructuras en acción.** Lea el siguiente anuncio sobre el aprendizaje de idiomas y haga los ejercicios.

Vocabulario

el dominio *command, mastery*   **lectivo** (adj.) *school*
gratuito *free*   **la plaza** *place, seat*
la jornada *working day*

¡BASTA YA DE PERDER AÑOS ESTUDIANDO IDIOMAS...!

En SEA hablará INGLÉS - Francés o Alemán en 4 semanas

Aprendiendo 2.000 palabras y toda la gramática básica.

USTED TIENE LA LIBERTAD DE ELEGIR

**Pero... ¿Para qué estudiar durante años? Si puedes comunicarte en un idioma
en 4 semanas o conseguir un cómodo dominio de él en 50 días lectivos**

¡RESERVE SU PLAZA ANTES DEL 30/04/95!
✓ PARKING GRATUITO   ✓ RESULTADOS GARANTIZADOS
¡¡LLÁMENOS!!... O VENGA A NUESTRAS JORNADAS INFORMATIVAS

al ☎ 308 36 69
en C/FERNANDO EL SANTO, 11

---

1. La idea principal del anuncio es _____.
   a. Hace falta aprender no más de 2.000 palabras de una lengua extranjera.
   b. El aprendizaje de una lengua extranjera debe ser rápido.
   c. Los idiomas extranjeros más importantes son el inglés, el francés y el alemán.

2. Según el anuncio, una persona puede entender y hacerse entendido en un idioma extranjero en _____.
   a. un año lectivo
   b. varios años
   c. cuatro semanas

3. Se pide información sobre los cursos _____.
   a. asistiendo a una sesión informativa
   b. reservando una plaza
   c. llamando a SEA solamente

4. *La libertad de elegir* se refiere a _____.
   a. optar entre francés e inglés
   b. llevar mucho o poco tiempo estudiando un idioma
   c. aprender gramática o vocabulario

5. En 50 días lectivos se puede _____.
   a. lograr un dominio de la lengua extranjera
   b. conseguir una plaza de parking
   c. escoger alemán u otro idioma

6. Fernando el Santo es _____.
   a. un profesor de inglés
   b. el telefonista
   c. la calle donde queda SEA

7. Escriba los dos gerundios que se encuentran en el anuncio.

   a. _____

   b. _____

8. Escriba la forma del gerundio de los verbos que se encuentran en el anuncio.
   El infinitivo de los verbos: **perder, hablar, elegir, poder, comunicarse, conseguir, reservar, llamarnos, venir.**

   a. _____

   b. _____

   c. _____

   d. _____

   e. _____

   f. _____

   g. _____

   h. _____

   i. _____

9. Escriba su propio anuncio cambiando el texto del anuncio que acaba de leer.
   Por ejemplo, los idiomas pueden cambiarse al chino, al hebreo, al italiano,
   al japonés, etcétera.

CHAPTER 11

THE SUBJUNCTIVE IN NOUN CLAUSES: PRESENT & PRESENT PERFECT SUBJUNCTIVE

 A *Forms of the present subjunctive: regular verbs*

- The present subjunctive is formed by changing the vowel **-a-** of the present indicative to **-e-** in **-ar** verbs and the vowels **-e-** and **-i-** of the present indicative to **-a-** in **-er** and **-ir** verbs. Regular **-er** and **-ir** verbs have identical endings in all persons of the subjunctive.

estudiar	
Quiere que estudi**e** idiomas.	*He wants me to study languages.*
estudi**es**	*He wants you to study languages.*
estudi**e**	*He wants her to study languages.*
estudi**emos**	*He wants us to study languages.*
estudi**éis**	*He wants you to study languages.*
estudi**en**	*He wants them to study languages.*

comprender	
Espera que comprend**a**.	*She hopes I'll understand.*
comprend**as**.	*She hopes you'll understand.*
comprend**a**.	*She hopes he'll understand.*
comprend**amos**.	*She hopes we'll understand.*
comprend**áis**.	*She hopes you'll understand.*
comprend**an**.	*She hopes they'll understand.*

vivir	
Prefieren que viv**a** aquí.	*They prefer me to live here.*
viv**as**	*They prefer you to live here.*
viv**a**	*They prefer her to live here.*
viv**amos**	*They prefer us to live here.*
viv**áis**	*They prefer you to live here.*
viv**an**	*They prefer them to live here.*

- In the present subjunctive the *yo* form and the *él* form are identical.

- **-Ar** and **-er** verbs that have changes in the vowel of the stem in the present indicative have these same changes in the present subjunctive:

Le aconsejan que p**ie**nse más.	*They advise her to think more.*
Nos aconsejan que pensemos más.	*They advise us to think more.*
Espera que yo enc**ue**ntre las llaves.	*He hopes that I find the keys.*
Espera que encontremos las llaves.	*He hopes that we find the keys.*

- **-Ir** verbs that have the change **e > ie** or **e > i** in the present indicative also have these changes in the present subjunctive. These verbs also have **i** in the stem of the *nosotros* and *vosotros* forms in the present subjunctive. **Dormir** and **morir** have the **o > ue** change in the present subjunctive and **u** in the stem of the *nosotros* and *vosotros* forms.

sentir	
sienta	sintamos
sientas	sintáis
sienta	sientan

seguir	
siga	sigamos
sigas	sigáis
siga	sigan

dormir	
d**ue**rma	durmamos
d**ue**rmas	durmáis
d**ue**rma	d**ue**rman

- Some verbs that end in **-iar** or **-uar** have an accent mark on the **í** or the **ú** in all forms except *nosotros* and *vosotros*. For example: **enviar**: envíe, envíes, envíe, enviemos, enviéis, envíen; **continuar**: continúe, continúes, continúe, continuemos, continuéis, continúen.

A. ¡Pero yo sí quiero! Un amigo suyo le menciona varias cosas que no están sucediendo. Ud. le dice que sí quiere que pasen. Use el presente del modo (*mood*) subjuntivo.

> MODELO   Alicia no estudia química.
> → Pero yo quiero que estudie química.

1. Marcos no trabaja.
2. Yo no consigo empleo.
3. Federico y Paula no nos escriben.
4. Juanita no sigue nuestros consejos.
5. Nosotros no comemos fuera hoy.
6. Yo no vuelvo temprano.
7. Los niños no duermen por la tarde.
8. Tú y yo no pedimos taxi.
9. Mis tíos no abren la tienda hoy.
10. Juan no entiende.
11. Amalia no piensa en nosotros.
12. La oficina no envía el paquete.
13. Yo no cierro las ventanas.
14. Tú y yo no nos divertimos.
15. Tú y yo no repetimos el vocabulario.

B Forms of the present subjunctive: irregular verbs

- Verbs that have an irregularity such as **-g-** or **-zc-** in the *yo* form of the present indicative have that irregularity in all persons of the present subjunctive. These irregularities occur only in **-er** and **-ir** verbs, and therefore all the present subjunctive endings have the vowel **-a-**.

- Here is a table of **-g-** verbs:

infinitive	present indicative (**yo** form)	present subjunctive
caer	**caig**o	caiga, caigas, caiga, caigamos, caigáis, caigan
decir	**dig**o	diga, digas, diga, digamos, digáis, digan
hacer	**hag**o	haga, hagas, haga, hagamos, hagáis, hagan
oír	**oig**o	oiga, oigas, oiga, oigamos, oigáis, oigan
poner	**pong**o	ponga, pongas, ponga, pongamos, pongáis, pongan
salir	**salg**o	salga, salgas, salga, salgamos, salgáis, salgan
tener	**teng**o	tenga, tengas, tenga, tengamos, tengáis, tengan
traer	**traig**o	traiga, traigas, traiga, traigamos, traigáis, traigan
venir	**veng**o	venga, vengas, venga, vengamos, vengáis, vengan

- Here is a table of the present subjunctive of other verbs that are irregular in the *yo* form:

infinitive	present indicative (**yo** form)	present subjunctive
caber	**quep**o	quepa, quepas, quepa, quepamos, quepáis, quepan
conocer	**conozc**o	conozca, conozcas, conozca, conozcamos, conozcáis, conozcan
nacer	**nazc**o	nazca, nazcas, nazca, nazcamos, nazcáis, nazcan
parecer	**parezc**o	parezca, parezcas, parezca, parezcamos, parezcáis, parezcan
construir	**construy**o	construya, construyas, construya, construyamos, construyáis, construyan
destruir	**destruy**o	destruya, destruyas, destruya, destruyamos, destruyáis, destruyan
ver	**ve**o	vea, veas, vea, veamos, veáis, vean

- **Dar** and **estar** are regular in the present subjunctive except for the accent marks. The first- and third-person singular forms of **dar** have the written accent (**dé**) and all of the present subjunctive forms of **estar** have the written accent, except the first-person plural form **estemos**:

dar		estar	
dé	demos	**esté**	estemos
des	deis	**estés**	**estéis**
dé	den	**esté**	**estén**

- **Haber, ir, saber,** and **ser** have irregular stems in the present subjunctive. However, their endings are regular:

infinitive	subjunctive stem	present subjunctive
haber	**hay-**	haya, hayas, haya, hayamos, hayáis, hayan
ir	**vay-**	vaya, vayas, vaya, vayamos, vayáis, vayan
saber	**sep-**	sepa, sepas, sepa, sepamos, sepáis, sepan
ser	**se-**	sea, seas, sea, seamos, seáis, sean

B. Le parece muy bien. Su amiga María se alegra de muchas cosas. Dígalo usando el presente del subjuntivo.

> MODELO   ¿Sabe María que viene Juan Carlos?
> → Sí. Se alegra de que venga.

1. ¿Sabe María que conoces a Pedro?

2. ¿Sabe María que tenemos un día libre?

3. ¿Sabe María que Alfredo le trae flores?

4. ¿Sabe María que yo no veo más películas de terror?

5. ¿Sabe María que los Ibáñez construyen una casa?

6. ¿Sabe María que Marcos y Julia salen juntos?

7. ¿Sabe María que tú y yo oímos mucha música clásica?

8. ¿Sabe María que su hermanito obedece a su profesor?

9. ¿Sabe María que Raquel compone música?

10. ¿Sabe María que la fiesta es mañana?

11. ¿Sabe María que hay reunión la semana que viene?

12. ¿Sabe María que sus primos van a España?

C *Spelling changes in the present subjunctive*

1. **-Ar** verbs whose stem ends in **c, g,** or **z** change those letters as follows in the present subjunctive:

   c → qu
   g → gu
   z → c

Lle**g**an el lunes.	→ Espero que lle**gu**en el lunes.
Bus**c**amos casa.	→ Es necesario que bus**qu**emos casa.
Almor**z**amos aquí.	→ Prefiero que almor**c**emos aquí.

2. **-Er** and **-ir** verbs whose stems end in **g, gu,** or **c** change those letters as follows in the present subjunctive:

   g → j
   gu → g
   c → z

Esco**g**es otro plato.	→ Queremos que esco**j**as otro plato.
Si**gu**en andando.	→ Es posible que si**g**an andando.
Te conven**c**e.	→ Espero que te conven**z**a.

3. **-Ar** verbs whose stem ends in **j** do not change **j** to **g** before **e**:

   Trabajo los domingos. → Quieren que trabaje los domingos.

4. Irregular verbs such as **hacer** and **conocer** don't follow the spelling change in the second rule above, but show the irregularities of the *yo* form of the present indicative:

Haces la cena.	→ Quiero que ha**g**as la cena.
Conocen a Marta.	→ No creo que cono**zc**an a Marta.

C. **Ortografía (*Spelling*).** Escriba en presente de subjuntivo los verbos que aparecen entre paréntesis recordando el cambio ortográfico.

1. Espero que tú _____ (realizar) tus planes.

2. Es necesario que Uds. _____ (acercarse) más.

3. ¡Qué lástima que _____ (comenzar) a llover!

4. Se alegran que yo _____ (dirigir) la orquesta.

5. Es probable que los chicos _____ (sacar) muy buenas notas.

6. Nos piden que _____ (recoger) las manzanas.

7. Es importante que Ud. _____ (dedicarse) a los negocios.

8. Me extraña que Vera no _____ (explicar) lo que pasó.

9. Te aconsejamos que _____ (entregar) el informe mañana.

10. Ojalá que Daniel _____ (conseguir) el puesto.

11. Tal vez Uds. _____ (organizar) la reunión.

12. No creo que Bárbara _____ (almorzar) antes de las dos.

13. Es difícil que yo los _____ (convencer).

14. Insisten en que nosotros _____ (apagar) las luces.

15. Tenemos miedo de que los soldados no _____ (vencer) a sus enemigos.

D   *Use of the present subjunctive in noun clauses*

- A noun clause is a clause that functions as a noun, that is, it can serve as either the subject or the object of a verb. Noun clauses that are incorporated into a longer sentence are called dependent or subordinate clauses and are introduced in Spanish by the conjunction **que.**

- All the Spanish tenses studied so far belong to the *indicative mood*. Verbs in the *indicative mood* express events or states that are considered factual, definite, or part of the speaker's experienced reality. The following examples have dependent noun clauses in the indicative. They show events perceived as part of reality because they are the objects of verbs such as **saber, parecer, oír, ver**:

Sabes **que lo hizo Sandra.**	*You know **that Sandra did it.***
Nos parece **que está lloviendo.**	*We think **it's raining.***
He oído **que hay una buena noticia.**	*I've heard **there's good news.***
Verán **que Juan no entiende.**	*You'll see **that Juan doesn't understand.***

- The *present subjunctive* in Spanish is used in dependent noun clauses that mark events or states that the speaker considers not part of reality or of his/her experience. These dependent noun clauses follow main clauses that express, as in the examples below, (1) expectation, skepticism, doubt, uncertainty; (2) demands, wants, needs, insistence, advice, impositions of will; (3) negated facts. The verbs in the main clauses are in the present, present perfect, future, or imperative:

(1) **Dudo** que Uds. **lleguen** para las tres.	*I **doubt** you'll **arrive** by three o'clock.*
(2) Paula **quiere** que la **visites.**	*Paula **wants** you **to visit** her.*
(3) **No es cierto** que **nos quedemos.**	*It's **not certain** that **we'll stay.***

- Verbs such as **desear** (*to want*), **esperar** (*to hope*), **insistir en** (*to insist*), **necesitar** (*to need*), **preferir** (*to prefer*), **querer** (*to want*) are followed by a dependent noun clause in the subjunctive and not by an infinitive *unless the subjects of both clauses are the same:*

Verb in main clause + dependent noun clause in subjunctive (two clauses: two different subjects)

Espero que Roberto **vaya.**	*I hope Roberto goes.*
Quieren que **salgamos.**	*They want us to go out.*
Insistimos en que Uds. **se queden.**	*We insist that you stay.*

Verb in main clause + infinitive (the same subject in both parts of the sentence)

Espero ir.	*I hope to go.*
Quieren salir.	*They want to go out.*
Insistimos en quedarnos.	*We insist on staying.*

- The verbs **decir** (*to tell someone to do something*) and **pedir** (*to ask someone to do something*) are followed by a subjunctive clause. They may occur with an indirect object:

Le dicen a Felipe que **tenga** cuidado.	*They tell Felipe to be careful.*
Susana **nos pide** que **traigamos** el periódico.	*Susana asks us to bring the newspaper.*

- **Decir** is followed by a dependent clause in the *indicative* when the dependent clause reports what someone said. For example, **José les dice: "Leo mucho"** or **"Leí mucho."** Contrast the use of the indicative and subjunctive after **decir**:

José les dice que **lee** mucho.	*José tells them he reads a lot.*
José les dijo que **leyó** mucho.	*José told them he read a lot.*
José les dice que **lean** mucho.	*José tells them to read a lot.*
José les dijo que **leyeran** mucho.	*José told them to read a lot.*

- Some verbs can be followed either by a noun clause in the subjunctive or by an infinitive without a change in meaning. An indirect object pronoun is optional if these verbs are followed by a subjunctive clause, but is obligatory when these verbs are followed by the infinitive. These verbs include: **aconsejar** (*to advise*), **exigir** (*to demand*), **impedir** (*to prevent*), **mandar** (*to order*), **permitir** (*to permit*), **prohibir** (*to forbid*), **recomendar** (*to recommend*), **rogar** (*to request, beg*), **sugerir** (*to suggest*):

(Les) aconsejo que **tomen** el tren. **Les aconsejo tomar** el tren.	} *I advise you to take the train.*
(Le) exigimos a Beatriz que **regrese.** **Le exigimos** a Beatriz **regresar.**	} *We demand that Beatriz return.*

- The verb **dejar** (*to let, allow*) can also be followed by a noun clause in the subjunctive or by an infinitive without a change in meaning. **Dejar** takes a direct object pronoun before a subjunctive clause:

(Los) **dejan** que **entren.** Los **dejan entrar.**	} *They let them come in.*

- Some verbs that express an emotional state, an attitude, or a bias are followed by dependent noun clauses in the subjunctive. These verbs include: **alegrarse (de)** (*to be glad, happy*), **extrañar** (*to surprise*), **gustar** (*to like*), **sentir** (*to regret*), **sorprender** (*to surprise*), **temer** (*to fear*), **tener miedo (de)** (*to be afraid [of]*).

Me alegro (de) que Uds. **visiten** Lima.	*I'm glad that you're visiting Lima.*
¿No **te extraña** que Claudia no **llame**?	*Aren't you surprised that Claudia doesn't call?*
Los Ayala **temen** que sus hijos no **saquen** buenas notas.	*Mr. and Mrs. Ayala are afraid their children aren't getting good grades.*

- **Gustar, extrañar,** and **sorprender** are usually used with an indirect object pronoun. (See Chapter 19 on the indirect object.)

D. ¿Indicativo o subjuntivo? Escoja entre el presente del indicativo y el presente del subjuntivo de los verbos que aparecen entre paréntesis para completar las siguientes oraciones.

MODELO   Creo que Fernando _____ el miércoles. (llegar)
→ Creo que Fernando **llega** el miércoles.

Prefiero que Fernando _____ el miércoles. (llegar)
→ Prefiero que Fernando **llegue** el miércoles.

1. Daniel quiere que nosotros le _____ lo que pasó. (decir)

2. Vemos que estos chicos _____ muchas fechas de memoria. (aprender)

3. Siento que Javier no _____ este año. (graduarse)

4. Nos extraña que Uds. no _____ el trabajo. (comenzar)

5. Piensan que tú _____ de todo. (quejarse)

6. Mis padres insisten en que yo _____ lo antes posible. (matricularse)

7. Me alegro de que Juan y Diana _____ a casarse. (ir)

8. Parece que Ud. no _____ hasta más tarde. (salir)

9. ¿Sabes que Raquel _____ razón? (tener)

10. Isabel comprende que nosotros no _____ ayudarla. (poder)

11. Le aconsejamos a Diego que _____ más responsable. (ser)

12. Les gusta que ya no _____ problemas con la casa. (haber)

13. Todo el mundo entiende que Uds. _____ ocupadísimos. (estar)

14. Yo exijo que tú me _____ caso. (hacer)

15. Pedro cree que yo lo _____ todo. (saber)

16. Debes darte cuenta que ya no se _____ ese libro. (conseguir)

E. ¡Viva México! Ud. y sus amigos están emocionados pensando en el viaje que van a hacer a México durante el verano. Escriba oraciones que expresen lo que quieren hacer en México. El sujeto de la cláusula principal y el de la subordinada (dependiente) deben ser el mismo; incluya el verbo conjugado + infinitivo.

MODELO   yo / querer / ver las pirámides de San Juan de Teotihuacán
→ Yo quiero ver las pirámides de San Juan de Teotihuacán.

1. Laura / esperar / perfeccionar su español

2. Ricardo y Beti / preferir / visitar la catedral del Zócalo

3. Ud. / deber / conocer Taxco

4. Pablo y yo / desear / ir a Puebla

5. tú / preferir / hacer una excursión a la Ciudad Universitaria

6. yo / sentir / no poder quedarme más tiempo en el Bosque de Chapultepec
7. Uds. / insistir en / escaparse un par de días a Mérida
8. todos nosotros / alegrarse de / estar en Oaxaca

Nota cultural

- **El Bosque de Chapultepec.** Este gran parque, hermoso con sus muchos ahuehuetes (árboles coníferos), queda al final del Paseo de la Reforma en la ciudad de México. Hay bellas vistas del Valle de México desde los balcones del Castillo de Chapultepec y también hay algunos museos interesantes. El más importante de éstos es el Museo Nacional de Antropología con su magnífica exposición de culturas precolombinas.

- **La catedral en el Zócalo.** El Zócalo, la Plaza Mayor de la parte más antigua de la ciudad de México, fue el sitio del gran templo azteca Teocalli. En ese mismo lugar los españoles construyeron la catedral más vieja y más grande de Latinoamérica. Fue concebida por Herrera, el arquitecto de El Escorial en España y de la catedral de Puebla. La construcción de la catedral empezó en 1525.

- **La Ciudad Universitaria.** De fama mundial, la Ciudad Universitaria queda a 18 kilómetros del centro de la capital. Se destaca la biblioteca de diez pisos con sus paredes de mosaicos en las cuales se narra la historia del saber científico. La Universidad de México fue fundada en 1551.

- **Mérida.** Capital del estado mexicano de Yucatán en la península de Yucatán, Mérida fue fundada en 1542 en el sitio de la ciudad maya de Tihoo. Esta península de la América Central, que queda entre el golfo de México y el mar Caribe, es un centro de turismo por su arqueología maya y sus playas.

- **Oaxaca.** Esta pintoresca ciudad de arquitectura del siglo XVII y mercados indígenas queda a 531 kilómetros al sureste de la ciudad de México.

- **Puebla (de los Ángeles).** "La ciudad de los Ángeles", una de las ciudades más antiguas y más famosas de México, queda al sur de la ciudad de México. Es una ciudad colonial muy atractiva por su catedral, las vistas de los volcanes y sus 60 iglesias, muchas de las cuales tienen tejas que brillan a la luz del sol. Por desgracia, la contaminación del ambiente, los embotellamientos y otros problemas causados por el desarrollo industrial, van destruyendo el hermoso aspecto colonial de la ciudad.

- **San Juan de Teotihuacán.** Las pirámides de San Juan de Teotihuacán quedan a unos 45 kilómetros al noreste de la ciudad de México. Estas enormes pirámides fueron construidas por los toltecas, quienes formaron una de las civilizaciones precolombinas del Valle de México. La Pirámide del Sol se construyó a fines del siglo primero y la Pirámide de la Luna se terminó alrededor del siglo dos. Teotihuacán fue un importante centro religioso y cultural. La civilización tolteca estaba ya en decadencia a principios del siglo XIII cuando llegaron los aztecas al Valle de México. Los aztecas fundaron su imperio en 1325 con su capital en Tenochtitlán, actualmente la ciudad de México.

- **Taxco.** Esta ciudad colonial muy pintoresca queda al sur de la ciudad de México. El primer envío (cargamento) de plata enviado a España desde el Nuevo Mundo fue de las minas de Taxco. Muchos turistas van a Taxco por los monumentos, las vistas y las platerías (*silversmiths*).

F. **¡Con la palomilla (*group of friends* [*Mexico*]) en México!** Ahora exprese lo que Ud. quiere que hagan los otros amigos en México. El sujeto de la cláusula principal es diferente del de la subordinada; por eso se usa el subjuntivo.

> MODELO   yo : querer / Paco y Mari : ver las pirámides de San Juan de Teotihuacán
> → Yo quiero que Paco y Mari vean las pirámides de San Juan de Teotihuacán.

1. Laura : esperar / nosotros : perfeccionar nuestro español

2. Ricardo y Beti : preferir / Ud. : visitar la Catedral del Zócalo

3. Ud. : necesitar / Leo : conocer Taxco

4. Pablo y yo : desear / Uds. : ir a Puebla

5. a ti : gustar / yo : hacer una excursión a la Ciudad Universitaria

6. yo : sentir / nosotros : no poder quedarse más tiempo en el Bosque de Chapultepec

7. Uds. : insistir en / los cuates (*pals* [*Mexico*]) : escaparse un par de días a Mérida

8. todos nosotros : alegrarse de / tú : estar en Oaxaca

G. **Una familia unida (*close*).** Los miembros de la familia Ayala son muy unidos. Todos se quieren mucho y comparten sus pensamientos y sentimientos. Escriba oraciones que expresen lo que quieren para los demás miembros de la familia. Use el subjuntivo.

Lazos familiares (*family ties*)	
la ahijada *goddaughter*	**el nieto** *grandson*
el ahijado *godson*	**los nietos** *grandchildren*
los ahijados *godchildren*	**la novia** *bride, fiancée*
la bisabuela *great-grandmother*	**el novio** *groom, fiancé*
el bisabuelo *great-grandfather*	**los novios** *bride and groom*
los bisabuelos *great-grandparents*	**la madrina** *godmother*
la cuñada *sister-in-law*	**el padrino** *godfather*
el cuñado *brother-in-law*	**los padrinos** *godparents*
los familiares *relatives*	**la suegra** *mother-in-law*
la nieta *granddaughter*	**el suegro** *father-in-law*

> MODELO   el abuelo : desear / su familia : vivir bien
> → El abuelo desea que su familia viva bien.

1. Elena : esperar / sus cuñados : tener éxito

2. el señor Ayala : pedirles / sus suegros : venir a verlos los domingos

3. la madrina : alegrarse / su ahijado : sacar buenas notas en el colegio

4. los padres : querer / sus hijos : ganarse la vida (*to earn a living*)

5. a la señora Ayala : gustarle / los bisabuelos : ser felices en la tercera edad (*old age*)

6. yo : aconsejarle / la nieta : hacerse arquitecta

7. Terencio : prohibirles / las ahijadas : ir solas al extranjero

8. tú : sentir / el cuñado : no estar contento con el nuevo empleo

9. la suegra : preferir / los novios : mudarse con ella

10. Uds. : rogarles / los padrinos : aceptar su regalo

11. Ricardo y yo : necesitar / los nietos : darnos muchos besos y abrazos

12. los hijos : no dejar / sus padres : trabajar demasiado manteniéndolos

H. Una carta. Ana María Vázquez vive en Bogotá, Colombia. Le escribe una carta a su amiga Isabel García que vive en Los Ángeles. Para enterarse de lo que Ana María dice, escriba el presente del subjuntivo o el presente del indicativo del verbo entre paréntesis.

Querida Isabel:

Espero que tú _____ (1. encontrarse) bien. Mis papás, hermanos y yo _____ (2. estar) perfectamente. Recibí tu carta ayer. Me alegro que tú _____ (3. poder) venir a verme durante las vacaciones. Creo que yo _____ (4. ir) a ir a la playa con mi familia todo el mes de julio. Por eso es mejor que tú _____ (5. llegar) a principios de agosto. Mis padres quieren que tus papás y hermanos _____ (6. pasar) el mes con nosotros también. Les recomiendo que _____ (7. comprar) los boletos de avión lo antes posible. Les aconsejo también que _____ (8. traer) ropa un poco gruesa (heavy), un impermeable y un paraguas porque _____ (9. hacer) fresco, _____ (10. estar) nublado y _____ (11. llover). Tú _____ (12. deber) recordar que Bogotá queda en las montañas. Yo _____ (13. saber) que tú no _____ (14. ir) a aburrirte en Bogotá. Tú _____ (15. ir) a ver que _____ (16. haber) tantas cosas que ver y hacer aquí. Voy a insistir en que Uds. _____ (17. despertarse) muy temprano todos los días aunque vamos a trasnochar (stay up late) oyendo música. Así yo _____ (18. poder) enseñarles las muchas cosas que hay en la ciudad y las afueras. Bueno, querida amiga, yo _____ (19. tener) muchas ganas de volver a verte. ¡Ojalá que tú me _____ (20. escribir) con la buena noticia de que _____ (21. venir) tu familia también!

Cariños de Ana María

Nota cultural

- Además de sus excelentes museos, edificios históricos y paisajes, **Bogotá** tiene también mucha vida nocturna. Hay clubes, discotecas y bares en la Zona Rosa, la región Carrera 15 con la calle 82. Este sistema de la carrera que cruza la calle a un ángulo cuadrado se usa por toda Colombia. Las avenidas, bulevares anchos e importantes, pueden ser calles o carreras.

- Colombia se conoce por su variedad de música **folklórica** debido a sus cuatro regiones musicales que van de los Andes al Caribe: montañas, costa del Pacífico, costa del Caribe y los llanos (*plains*) orientales. El instrumento nacional es **el tiple,** una pequeña guitarra de 12 cuerdas. El baile nacional es **el bambuco.** La música del Caribe, recién integrada en el repertorio de **la salsa,** es buena para bailar **la cumbia,** baile típico de esta región.

E   *The present subjunctive in noun clauses after impersonal expressions*

- Impersonal expressions (expressions with no specific subject) require the subjunctive in dependent noun clauses if they suggest that the event or state mentioned in the dependent clause is not part of perceived reality. For example: **es necesario que** (*it's necessary that*), **es importante que** (*it's important that*), **es imposible que** (*it's impossible that*), **es improbable que** (*it's improbable that*), **es posible que** (*it's possible that*), **es preciso que** (*it's necessary that*), **es probable que** (*it's probable that*), **Ojalá (que)** (*I hope [that]*).

—**Es necesario que discutamos** el asunto.	*It's necessary that we discuss the matter.*
—**Es posible que** yo **no tenga** tiempo hoy.	*It's possible I won't have time today.*
—Pero **es importante que resolvamos** algo.	*But it's important that we resolve something.*
—De acuerdo. **Es probable que podamos** discutirlo mañana.	*Agreed. It's probable we can discuss it tomorrow.*
—**Ojalá que tengas** razón.	*I hope you're right.*

- Impersonal expressions that show the speaker's emotional attitude or bias toward the event or state of the dependent clause also require the subjunctive: **es bueno que** (*it's good that*), **es inútil que** (*it's useless that*), **es malo que** (*it's bad that*), **es mejor que** (*it's better that*), **es peor que** (*it's worse that*), **es triste que** (*it's sad that*), **es útil que** (*it's useful that*), **más vale que** (*it's better that*). **Es una lástima que** (*It's a pity that*) and **¡qué lástima que!** (*what a pity that!*) are impersonal expressions that may be followed by the subjunctive or the indicative in the dependent clause:

—**Es triste** que José Luis **tenga** tantos problemas.	*It's sad that José Luis **has** so many problems.*
—**Es inútil** que **tratemos** de ayudarlo, ¿verdad?	*It's useless for us to try to help him, isn't it?*
—**Es una lástima** que no **haya** solución.	*It's a pity there's no solution.*

- When the speaker does not identify a specific subject in the dependent clause, the impersonal expression is followed by an infinitive. Study the following pairs of sentences:

Es preciso saber la fecha.	*It's necessary to know the date.*
Es preciso que sepamos la fecha.	*It's necessary that we know the date.*
Es útil hacer investigaciones.	*It's useful to do research.*
Es útil que hagas investigaciones.	*It's useful for you to do research.*

- There are certain verbs and expressions in Spanish that require the subjunctive in the dependent clause *only when they are negative,* that is, when they suggest that the event or state in the dependent clause is a negated fact. For example: **no es cierto que, no es evidente que, no es obvio que, no es que, no es/está seguro, no es verdad que, no creer que, no pensar que.** When they are not negative they are followed by the indicative.

  Note: The negative constructions of **creer** and **pensar** (**no creer que** and **no pensar que**), as well as **tal vez** (*perhaps*), may be followed by the indicative as well as the subjunctive. The choice of the indicative by the speaker suggests he/she thinks the event in the dependent clause is closer to reality while the use of the subjunctive suggests that the speaker is less certain about the event:

Creo que Lola y Paco **van** al cine.	*I think Lola and Paco are going to the movies.*
No creo que Lola y Paco **vayan** al cine.	*I don't think Lola and Paco are going to the movies. (Speaker isn't sure whether Lola and Paco are going to the movies—it's quite possible they're going.)*
No creo que Lola y Paco **van** al cine.	*I don't think Lola and Paco are going to the movies. (Speaker thinks Lola and Paco are probably not going to the movies.)*
Es verdad que Jaime **está** preocupado.	*It's true Jaime is worried.*
No es verdad que Jaime **esté** preocupado.	*It's not true Jaime is worried.*
Tal vez se enfadan.	*Perhaps they'll get angry.*
Tal vez se enfaden.	*Perhaps they might get angry. (Speaker is less certain.)*

- When they are used in the affirmative, **dudar** (*to doubt*) and **es dudoso** (*it's doubtful*), require the use of the subjunctive in the dependent clause. Conversely, when **dudar** and **es dudoso** appear in the negative, the verb in the dependent clause is in the indicative:

Dudamos que Andrés **vuelva** hoy.	*We doubt Andrés is coming back today.*
Es dudoso que Andrés **vuelva** hoy.	*It's doubtful Andrés is coming back today.*
No dudamos que Andrés **vuelve** hoy.	*We don't doubt Andrés is coming back today.*
No es dudoso que Andrés **vuelve** hoy.	*It's not doubtful Andrés is coming back today.*

I. ¡Qué desorden! ¡Y viene mamá! Ud. vive en un apartamento con tres compañeros(as) de cuarto. Este fin de semana vienen los padres a visitar a sus hijos en la universidad. Uds. están contentos(as) de ver a sus padres. ¡Están también un poco preocupados(as) porque mamá va a ver que el apartamento es una pocilga (*pigsty*)! Use las expresiones impersonales con el subjuntivo para describir la situación.

Haciendo la limpieza

barrer el piso   *to sweep the floor*
el cristal de ventana   *windowpane*
el desorden   *mess*
encerar el piso   *to wax the floor*
la estantería   *bookcase*
fregar las cacerolas   *to scour the pans*
guardar   *to put away*

meterse en   *to get involved in*
ordenar   *to clean up*
el producto para la limpieza   *cleaning product*
sacudir el polvo   *to dust*
la telaraña   *cobweb, spiderweb*
el trapo   *cleaning rag*

> **Modelo**   Vienen mis papás. (es bueno)
> → Es bueno que vengan mis papás.

1. Las mamás ven el desorden. (es malo)
2. Hacemos la limpieza del apartamento. (es necesario)
3. Lupe friega las cacerolas. (es importante)
4. Juan y Antonio barren los pisos. (es útil)
5. Uds. enceran los pisos. (es probable)
6. Las mamás traen trapos y productos para la limpieza. (más vale que)
7. Los papás no se meten en todo esto. (es dudoso)
8. Yo sacudo el polvo. (es preciso)
9. Leonor guarda los libros en las estanterías. (ojalá)
10. Mario y Griselda lavan los cristales de las ventanas. (es posible)
11. Tú quitas las telarañas del techo. (es mejor)
12. No nos relajamos en todo el día. (¡qué lástima que!)

J. Reacciones. Ud. reacciona a unas afirmaciones. Al reaccionar, tiene que escoger entre el presente del subjuntivo y el presente del indicativo.

> **Modelo**   Manuela trabaja de moza. (es verdad) / (no es verdad)
> → **Es verdad** que Manuela **trabaja** de moza.
> → **No es verdad** que Manuela **trabaje** de moza.

1. Lorenzo sigue enfermo. (no estoy seguro)
2. Teresa y Jesús se quieren mucho. (es obvio)
3. Uds. tienen problemas con el coche. (no es cierto)
4. Julia llega el sábado. (es que)

5. Alejandro es de origen ruso. (no es seguro)

6. Los niños están aburridos. (no es evidente)

7. Carmen lo sabe todo. (no es que)

8. Martín renuncia a su puesto. (es cierto)

K. Pereza del fin de año. Ahora que termina el año escolar y hace tan buen tiempo, sus amigos prefieren jugar al béisbol en vez de estudiar. ¡Le toca a Ud. convencerlos que deben trabajar más! Use el presente del subjuntivo.

> **MODELO**   Pedro: No quiero asistir a la clase de química hoy.
> (es necesario)
> Ud.:   Oye, Pedro, es necesario que asistas a la
> clase de química.

1. Anita: No voy a estudiar para los exámenes finales. (insisto en que)

2. Miguel: No deseo trabajar en la librería. (me sorprende)

3. Rebeca: No pienso escribir el informe para sociología. (más vale que)

4. Tomás: No me gusta practicar ruso en el laboratorio de lenguas. (es útil)

5. Graciela: No me interesa tomar apuntes en historia. (es importante)

6. Alfredo: Prefiero no hacer la tarea. (te ruego)

7. Carolina: No me importa sacar buenas notas. (espero)

8. Joaquín: Voy a jugar al béisbol todo el día. (te prohíbo)

L. En un coloquio (*discussion*). Use el presente del subjuntivo cuando sea necesario para expresar las ideas de los participantes de un coloquio sobre el mundo a fines del siglo veinte.

1. It's good there are so many technological advances (*adelantos*).

2. We prefer to use nuclear energy even more.

3. Everyone's happy to have the computer.

4. It's a pity that wars continue to break out (*estallar*).

5. We regret that the cities have so much crime.

6. I'm afraid new illnesses are killing many people.

7. It's probable that environmental pollution isn't doing so much harm.

8. It's obvious that the free market economy is best.

9. It's necessary to control inflation and unemployment.

10. We advise the political leaders to spend money more accountably (*con más responsabilidad*).

11. I hope (*Ojalá*) there will be free elections in every country.

12. Nobody doubts that the 21st century is going to bring many changes.

F *The present perfect subjunctive*

- The present perfect subjunctive is used in the same kinds of dependent clauses as the present subjunctive. It is used to indicate that the action of the dependent clause happens before the action of the main clause.

Me alegro de que Uds. **vayan.**	*I'm glad you are going.* *(two actions in the present)*
Me alegro de que **hayan venido.**	*I'm glad you came.* *(dependent clause action happens prior to action of main clause)*

- The present perfect subjunctive consists of the present subjunctive of **haber** + the past participle.

Esperan que lo

haya visto.	*They hope I saw him.*
hayas visto.	*They hope you saw him.*
haya visto.	*They hope he saw him.*
hayamos visto.	*They hope we saw him.*
hayáis visto.	*They hope you saw him.*
hayan visto.	*They hope they saw him.*

M. Escriba oraciones empleando la frase que aparece entre paréntesis en la cláusula principal y cambiando el verbo del pretérito al perfecto del subjuntivo.

> MODELO   Los Fernández llegaron. (es bueno)
> → Es bueno que los Fernández hayan llegado.

1. Uds. no vieron la exposición de arte. (Clara siente)

2. Patricia escribió las cartas. (dudamos)

3. Carlos se hizo ciudadano. (me alegro)

4. Viste la nueva película policíaca. (esperan)

5. Murió el bisabuelo de Paco. (es una lástima)

6. Las chicas no dijeron nada. (es mejor)

7. Hubo un incendio en el metro. (nos sorprende)

8. Luz se puso brava. (no piensan)

9. Me encantó el concierto. (se alegran)

N. Exprese las siguientes oraciones en español.

1. I'm glad Julia and Paco got married.

2. It's good that a bookstore opened in this neighborhood.

3. They doubt that the Tigers won the soccer championship.

4. We hope Fernando got rich.

5. Are you (*Ud.*) surprised that the Núñez family moved?

6. Ana doesn't think the boys broke the window.

O. Ejercicio oral. ¡Feliz año nuevo! Escríbales tarjetas a sus amigos expresando sus deseos para el año nuevo. Use el indicativo de los verbos *querer, esperar, desear,* etcétera en la cláusula principal y el presente del subjuntivo en la subordinada.

CHAPTER 12

THE IMPERFECT SUBJUNCTIVE & PAST PERFECT SUBJUNCTIVE; CONDITIONAL SENTENCES

A *Forms of the imperfect subjunctive*

- The forms of the imperfect subjunctive are derived from the third-person plural form of the preterit. Any irregularity or vowel change in the stem of the third-person plural of the preterit occurs in all persons of the imperfect subjunctive: **hablaron** → que yo **hablara, comieron** → que yo **comiera, escribieron** → que yo **escribiera, pidieron** → que yo **pidiera, hicieron** → que yo **hiciera, fueron** → que yo **fuera, durmieron** → que yo **durmiera, trajeron** → que yo **trajera.** The preterit ending **-ron** is replaced by the following endings in all verbs:

-ra		hablara	comiera	escribiera
-ras		hablaras	comieras	escribieras
-ra		hablara	comiera	escribiera
	Querían que			
-ramos		habláramos	comiéramos	escribiéramos
-rais		hablarais	comierais	escribierais
-ran		hablaran	comieran	escribieran

Meaning: *They wanted me/you/him/her/us/them to speak/eat/write.*

- The *yo* and *él* forms are identical in the imperfect subjunctive, and the *nosotros* form has a written accent mark on the vowel before the **-r**: **habláramos, comiéramos, escribiéramos.**

- There is an alternate form of the imperfect subjunctive that has endings in **-se**. The **-ra** and **-se** forms are largely interchangeable, but the **-se** forms are less common in colloquial speech:

-se		hablase	comiese	escribiese
-ses		hablases	comieses	escribieses
-se		hablase	comiese	escribiese
	Querían que			
-semos		hablásemos	comiésemos	escribiésemos
-seis		hablaseis	comieseis	escribieseis
-sen		hablasen	comiesen	escribiesen

A. Escriba los verbos que aparecen entre paréntesis en imperfecto del subjuntivo. Escriba cada verbo con las dos desinencias (*endings*) **-ra** y **-se.**

1. Yo esperaba que Manolo _____ / _____ cuenta. (darse)

2. Nos alegramos que Lorna _____ / _____ su collar de perlas. (encontrar)

3. Rita insistió en que los niños _____ / _____ las botas. (ponerse)

4. No era cierto que nosotros lo _____ / _____. (saber)

5. Ojalá que _____ / _____ pescado en la carta. (haber)

6. Te aconsejaron que _____ / _____ derecho. (seguir)

7. Dudaban que Ud. _____ / _____ la siesta. (dormir)

8. No fue posible que yo los _____ / _____ sino hasta el jueves. (ver)

9. Habíamos querido que Uds. _____ / _____ con nosotros. (reunirse)

10. Le gustaría que nosotros _____ / _____ esta sinfonía. (oír)

11. Preferiríamos que Elena nos lo _____ / _____. (decir)

12. No creían que los turistas _____ / _____ de Inglaterra. (ser)

13. Era preciso que se _____ / _____ nuevas casas en las afueras. (construir)

14. Yo querría que tú _____ / _____ los documentos. (traer)

15. Le dijeron a Mateo que no _____ / _____. (irse)

B *The imperfect subjunctive in noun clauses; the sequence of tenses*

- The imperfect subjunctive is used in dependent noun clauses instead of the present subjunctive when the verb in the main clause is in the imperfect, preterit, past perfect, or conditional:

Queríamos que lo **hicieras.** (*imperfect*)	We *wanted you to do it.*
Quisimos que lo **hicieras.** (*preterit*)	We *wanted you to do it.*
Habíamos querido que lo **hicieras.** (*past perfect*)	We *had wanted you to do it.*
Querríamos que lo **hicieras.** (*conditional*)	We *would want you to do it.*

- The present subjunctive is used when the verb in the main clause is in the present, present perfect, future, or imperative:

Queremos que lo **hagas.**	We *want you to do it.*
Hemos querido que lo **hagas.**	We've *wanted you to do it.*
Querremos que lo **hagas.**	We'll *want you to do it.*

- The English equivalents of many noun clauses in Spanish are in the infinitive so they do not show the tense distinctions seen in Spanish:

Queremos que lo **hagas**.	*We want you **to do** it.*
Queríamos que lo **hicieras**.	*We wanted you **to do** it.*

- Remember that in Spanish, if the subjects of the main clause and the dependent clause are the same, the infinitive is used, not the present or imperfect subjunctive:

Queremos **hacerlo**.	*We want **to do it**.*
Queríamos **hacerlo**.	*We wanted **to do it**.*

- **Ojalá** used with the present subjunctive means *I hope*. **Ojalá** used with the imperfect subjunctive means *I wish:*

Ojalá que **saquen** boletos.	*I hope they'll get tickets.*
Ojalá que **sacaran** boletos.	*I wish they'd get tickets.*

- Spanish uses the imperfect subjunctive, as well as the conditional, to soften a request or suggestion. The imperfect, used only with **querer, poder,** and **deber,** is more courteous than the conditional, which is used with any verb. In English, *would* is also used to soften a request: ¿Me lo **explicarías?** *Would you explain it to me?:*

Quisiera hablar con Ud.	*I'd like to speak with you.*
¿**Pudiera** prestármelo?	*Could you lend it to me?*
Uds. **debieran** volver a casa.	*You ought to return home.*

B. Un caso de celos. Narre la historia de dos chicos que quieren a Angélica. Cambie los verbos de la cláusula independiente según los verbos que aparecen entre paréntesis, y los verbos de las cláusulas dependientes de presente del subjuntivo a imperfecto del subjuntivo.

> MODELO   Felipe les **dice** a sus amigos que **salgan**. (dijo)
> → Felipe les **dijo** a sus amigos que **salieran**.

1. Felipe les sugiere que vayan a una discoteca. (sugirió)

2. Felipe espera que Angélica baile con él toda la tarde. (esperaba)

3. Teodoro también desea que Angélica pase la tarde con él. (deseaba)

4. Angélica teme que los chicos tengan celos. (temía)

5. Es posible que Felipe y Teodoro se peleen por Angélica. (Era)

6. Felipe no cree que sea una buena idea ir a la discoteca. (no creía)

7. Felipe le propone a Angélica que vean una película. (propuso)

8. A Angélica le agrada que Felipe y Teodoro la quieran (agradaba), ¡pero ella estaba enamorada de Julio!

C. Expectativas. Cuando Timoteo fue a pasar un semestre en la Ciudad de Guatemala para estudiar español, tenía ciertas expectativas y preocupaciones sobre cómo iba a ser su experiencia. Lea lo que pensaba y escriba los verbos que aparecen entre paréntesis en imperfecto del subjuntivo.

> MODELO   Timoteo deseaba que la casa donde iba a vivir
> **quedara** (quedar) cerca de la universidad.

1. Timoteo esperaba que _____ (haber) un chico de su edad en la familia.

2. Sentía que su mejor amigo no _____ (ir) a la Ciudad de Guatemala también.

3. Temía que nadie _____ (poder) comprender su español.

4. Era posible que Timoteo no _____ (llevarse) bien con sus compañeros de clase.

5. Tenía miedo que la comida le _____ (caer) mal.

6. Dudaba que sus profesores le _____ (aprobar) en todas las materias.

7. Era probable que Timoteo _____ (querer) mudarse a un hotel.

Nota cultural

Ciudad de Guatemala, capital de Guatemala, queda a 1.500 metros sobre el nivel del mar en una meseta de la Sierra Madre. La capital fue fundada por decreto (*decree*) de Carlos III de España en 1776 después que un terremoto acabó con la capital anterior, Antigua Guatemala, en 1773. **Antigua,** fundada en 1543, fue una de las ciudades más atractivas de Centroamérica con una población de 60.000, varias iglesias grandes, una universidad (1680), una imprenta (1660) y famosos pintores, escultores, escritores y artesanos. Ciudad de Guatemala es actualmente uno de los lugares más populares de Hispanoamérica para aprender español y muchos estudiantes norteamericanos y canadienses pasan el verano o el año académico allí estudiando el idioma.

D. ¿Qué tal le fue a Timoteo? Para saberlo, escriba los verbos que aparecen entre paréntesis en imperfecto del subjuntivo.

> MODELO   Los señores de la casa insistían en que Timoteo **se**
> **quedara** (quedarse) con ellos un mes más.

1. Era bueno que sus clases _____ (ser) tan interesantes.

2. Timoteo se alegró que sus profesores no lo _____ (colgar [*to fail*]).

3. Los señores permitían que Timoteo _____ (salir) con su hija Aurora.

4. La madre le pidió a Timoteo que los _____ (acompañar) a la sierra.

5. Los hijos de la familia le rogaron a Timoteo que _____ (jugar) al fútbol con ellos.

6. A Timoteo le sorprendió que todos lo _____ (tratar) tan bien.

7. El señor dejó que Timoteo _____ (conducir) el coche.

E. Vida de familia. Describa lo que los padres esperaban que sus hijos hicieran escribiendo los verbos de las oraciones en imperfecto del subjuntivo.

> MODELO   Mis papás querían que nosotros **estudiáramos** mucho. (estudiar)

1. Papá esperaba que yo _____ ingeniero. (hacerse)

2. Mamá insistía en que nosotros _____ sus tradiciones. (seguir)

3. Nuestros papás nos aconsejaban que _____ valores tradicionales. (tener)

4. Papá prefería que Pepe _____ con él en la empresa. (trabajar)

5. Nuestros padres deseaban que mis hermanos y yo _____. (casarse)

6. A nuestros papás les era importante que nosotros _____ responsables, honrados y trabajadores. (ser)

7. Mamá nos pedía que _____ a nuestra familia. (dedicarse)

8. Papá nos decía que _____ los unos a los otros. (ayudarse)

9. A nuestros padres les era necesario que mis hermanas _____ cerca. (vivir)

F. ¡Me sobra tiempo! (*I have plenty of time!*) Sus padres le pidieron que hiciera unas cosas para ayudarlos. Ud. creía que le sobraba tiempo para hacerlas y fue a jugar al béisbol con sus amigos. Al llegar a casa, sus padres ven que todo ha quedado sin hacer. Complete las oraciones empleando el imperfecto del subjuntivo del verbo que aparece entre paréntesis.

> MODELO   Hijo/Hija, yo quería que **buscaras** el correo. (buscar)

1. Hijo/Hija, te pedí que _____ el césped. (cortar)

2. Hijo/Hija, ¿no te dijimos que _____ la carne? (descongelar)

3. Hijo/Hija, te exigí que _____ los arbustos (*bushes*). (regar [*to water*])

4. Hijo/Hija, esperábamos que _____ la compra. (hacer)

5. Hijo/Hija, yo quería que _____ al perro. (bañar)

6. Hijo/Hija, te rogamos que _____ el garaje en orden. (poner)

7. Hijo/Hija, yo deseaba que _____ las herramientas (*tools*). (guardar)

8. Hijo/Hija, insistíamos en que _____ la basura. (sacar)

9. Hijo/Hija, tu hermanito necesitaba que le _____ su bicicleta. (reparar)

G. ¡Josefina, la muy pesada! A Josefina no le queda ni un solo amigo porque se porta mal con todo el mundo. Para saber lo que pasó con sus amigos, escriba el imperfecto del subjuntivo de cada verbo que aparece entre paréntesis.

> MODELO   Josefina le pidió al novio de Lola que la **llevara** al baile. (llevar)

1. Javier le dijo a Josefina que _____ con Arturo. (salir)

2. A los amigos no les gustaba que Josefina les _____. (mentir)

3. Josefina le aconsejó a Paquita que _____ con su novio. (romper)

4. Sus amigos sentían que Josefina _____ mala lengua (*vicious tongue*). (tener)

5. Josefina exigió que Pedro _____ la tarea de cálculo por ella. (hacer)

6. Josefina insistió en que los chicos la _____ a todas sus reuniones. (invitar)

7. Los amigos no querían que Josefina les _____ el pelo. (tomar)

8. Josefina les impidió a los amigos que _____ al cine sin ella. (ir)

9. A nadie le gustaba que Josefina _____ a los amigos en un lío. (meter)

H. ¡Ojalá! Ud. quiere que sucedan ciertas cosas pero duda que sea posible. Exprese lo que son esas cosas empleando el imperfecto del subjuntivo.

> **MODELO**   los primos / venir a visitarme
> → Ojalá que los primos vinieran a visitarme.

1. yo / encontrar / las llaves del coche

2. Uds. / recibir / el cheque

3. Diana / no quejarse / de todo

4. servirse / la cena / antes de las diez de la noche

5. Bernardo y Marta / no discutir / tanto

6. Lorenzo / vestirse / más rápido

7. tú y yo / ocuparse / del congreso (*conference*)

8. Timoteo / mantener / a sus padres

C *The past perfect (or pluperfect) subjunctive*

- The past perfect subjunctive consists of the imperfect subjunctive of **haber** + the past participle. The most important use of the past perfect subjunctive is in conditional sentences. The past perfect subjunctive is also used to express a contrary-to-fact wish in the past after **ojalá (que).**

Ojalá (que)	hubiera sabido.	*I wish I had known.*
	hubieras sabido.	*I wish you had known.*
	hubiera sabido.	*I wish she had known.*
	hubiéramos sabido.	*I wish we had known.*
	hubierais sabido.	*I wish you had known.*
	hubieran sabido.	*I wish they had known.*

- The past perfect subjunctive is used instead of the present perfect subjunctive to indicate that the action of the dependent clause happens before the action of the main clause when the main clause is in the preterit, imperfect, or conditional.

I. Escriba oraciones empleando la frase que aparece entre paréntesis en la cláusula principal y el verbo de la cláusula dependiente en pluscuamperfecto del subjuntivo.

MODELO   Néstor había ganado la lotería. (esperábamos)
→ **Esperábamos** que Néstor **hubiera ganado** la lotería.

1. Jorge había llegado a ser arquitecto. (era bueno)

2. Las hermanas Cela habían hecho un viaje a Santo Domingo. (nos gustó)

3. Uds. se habían quedado tanto tiempo. (me extrañó)

4. Tú habías comprado una pulsera de oro. (esperaban)

5. Yo había asistido a la conferencia en Roma. (era importante)

6. Juan y yo nos habíamos comprometido. (todos se alegraron)

Nota cultural

Santo Domingo, capital de la República Dominicana, es la más antigua de las ciudades americanas fundadas por los conquistadores. Fue fundada en 1496 por Bartolomé Colón, un hermano de Cristóbal Colón. La ciudad fue modernizada después que un huracán la dejó casi totalmente destruida, pero conserva cierto carácter colonial con sus muchos edificios y monumentos de interés histórico.

J. Exprese las siguientes oraciones en español.

1. You (*tú*) were hoping that they had been successful.

2. They were afraid that someone had told me.

3. We were sorry that you (*Ud.*) hadn't heard what happened.

4. Sarita doubted that we had come back from the country.

5. I was glad that it had been warm and sunny.

6. I wish you (*Uds.*) had told us as soon as possible.

D *Conditional sentences*

- In Spanish and English, conditional sentences include two clauses: a **si**-clause (*if*-clause) and a main clause. Both languages use similar tenses for the two clauses. The **si**-clause may come before or after the main clause.

- Possible conditions are expressed in both languages by using the present in the **si**-clause and the future in the main clause:

si-clause	*main clause*	
Si vas, *(present)*	**yo iré** también. *(future)*	*If you go, I'll go too.*

- To express a condition that is contrary to a fact or situation in present time, Spanish uses the imperfect subjunctive in the **si**-clause and the conditional in the main clause:

si-clause	*main clause*	
Si fueras, *(imperfect subjunctive)*	**yo iría** también. *(conditional)*	*If you were going, I'd go too.*

The sentence **Si fueras, yo iría también** expresses a condition that is *contrary-to-fact*. The fact is that *tú no vas* and the result is that *yo no voy*. The meaning is **(Pero) si fueras** (*But if you were going, which you're not*), **yo iría** también (*I'd go too*).

- Spanish expresses a condition that is contrary to a fact or situation in past time by using the past perfect subjunctive in the **si**-clause and the conditional perfect *or* the past perfect subjunctive in the main clause:

si-clause	*main clause*	
Si hubieras ido,	**yo habría ido** también.	*If you had gone, I would have*
Si hubieras ido,	**yo hubiera ido** también.	*gone too.*

K. **Todo está pendiente (*up in the air*).** Complete las siguientes oraciones con la forma correcta del verbo que aparece entre paréntesis. El verbo de la cláusula que empieza con **si** está en presente del indicativo.

   MODELO   Si Uds. **van** (ir), yo los **veré** (ver).

1. Si yo _____ (poder), los _____ (visitar).

2. Si ellos le _____ (ofrecer) el puesto a Daniel, lo _____ (aceptar).

3. Pepita y yo _____ (salir) si _____ tiempo. (tener)

4. Si Mario me _____ (llamar), yo se lo _____ (decir).

5. Si tú _____ (poner) la mesa , Isabel y Leo _____ (hacer) la cena.

6. _____ (Haber) mucha gente en la playa si _____ (hacer) un gran calor.

7. Tú _____ (tener) hambre si no _____ (comer) algo ahora.

8. Si Uds. no le _____ (preguntar) a Carlos, no lo _____ (saber).

9. Todos nosotros _____ (venir) en taxi si no _____ (haber) lugar en el coche de Manuel.

L. **Si fuera posible ...** Complete las siguientes oraciones con la forma correcta del verbo que aparece entre paréntesis. El verbo de la cláusula que empieza con **si** está en imperfecto del subjuntivo.

   MODELO   Si **fuera** (ser) posible, nosotros **iríamos** (ir).

1. Si yo _____ (tener) tiempo, _____ (hacer) un viaje a todos los países del mundo.

2. Los Madariaga _____ (venir) a visitarnos si nosotros los _____ (invitar).

3. Laura _____ (ver) esa obra de teatro si _____ (haber) entradas.

4. Si Diego _____ (ganar) la lotería, _____ (comprarse) un coche deportivo.

5. Si _____ (hacer) mucho viento, nosotros _____ (salir) con la cometa (*kite*).

6. Daniel _____ (dormir) la siesta si _____ (sentirse) cansado.

7. Si tú _____ (poder), _____ (resolver) el problema.

8. Uds. _____ (salir) más temprano si _____ (ser) posible, ¿no?

9. Si Ana María y Esteban _____ (saber) los motivos, se los _____ (decir) a Uds.

M. Cuentos de hadas. Recuerde lo que pasa en estos cuentos de hadas (*fairy tales*) y escriba la forma correcta del verbo que aparece entre paréntesis. El verbo de la cláusula que empieza con **si** emplea el imperfecto del subjuntivo.

> MODELO   Si Ricitos de Oro no **se durmiera** (dormirse) en la cama del osito, los tres osos no la **verían** (ver).

1. «Si yo _____ (encontrar) a la señorita que perdió la zapatilla de cristal,

   _____ (casarse) con ella», pensó el príncipe.

2. «Si una princesa me _____ (besar), yo _____ (dejar) de ser sapo (*toad*) y

   _____ (convertirse) en príncipe».

3. «Si _____ (haber) un guisante debajo de mi colchón, yo lo _____ (notar)», se dijo la princesa.

4. «Si Hansel y Gretel _____ (venir) a mi casa, yo me los _____ (comer)», pensó la bruja.

5. «Si yo no _____ (mentir), no se me _____ (crecer) la nariz», se dijo Pinocho.

6. «Si yo le _____ (dar) un beso a la bella durmiente, ella _____ (despertarse)», se dijo el príncipe.

7. «Si la reina no _____ (tener) celos de mí, no _____ (tener) que vivir con los siete enanos», pensó Blancanieves.

8. «Si yo _____ (soplar) fuerte, _____ (derrumbar) la casa de los tres cerditos», pensó el lobo.

N. ¡Viajes soñados! El verbo de la cláusula que empieza con **si** está en imperfecto del subjuntivo y la cláusula principal en condicional.

1. Si yo _____ (ir) a Costa Rica, me _____ (gustar) entrar en los bosques nacionales.

2. Si Graciela y Miguel _____ (hacer) un viaje al Brasil, _____ (ir) para el Carnaval.

3. Si Uds. _____ (poder) visitar Uruguay, _____ (quedarse) en Montevideo.

4. Si nosotros _____ (pasar) las vacaciones en Puerto Rico, _____ (tomar) el sol en la playa de Dorado.

5. Si tú _____ (visitar) Venezuela, _____ (probar) sancocho, arepas y cachapas.

6. Si Felipe _____ (querer) viajar al Ecuador, _____ (conocer) Quito.

Nota cultural

- Hay mucho ecoturismo en **Costa Rica** gracias a su red de bosques nacionales. En el de Monteverde, por ejemplo, hay más de 400 especies de aves (incluso el quetzal), monos, jaguares, pumas, reptiles y otros animales, 2.500 especies de plantas y más de 6.000 especies de insectos.

- **El Carnaval** es el período de diversiones que empieza el día de los Reyes y termina el martes anterior al miércoles de Ceniza (*Ash Wednesday*). Se celebra por toda Latinoamérica. El de Río de Janeiro es el más célebre.

- **Montevideo**, capital del Uruguay, es la única ciudad grande del país. Fue fundada por los españoles en 1726 como fortaleza contra los portugueses. Queda a orillas del río de la Plata, frente a Buenos Aires.

- **Dorado** es una hermosa playa de Puerto Rico. Queda en el océano Atlántico cerca de San Juan.

- El sancocho, las arepas y las cachapas son platos típicos de Venezuela. El **sancocho** es un guisado de yuca y legumbres con carne, pollo o pescado. Las **arepas** son un pan de maíz blanco y las **cachapas** son tortillas blandas de maíz. Las dos se llenan de un queso blanco u otras cosas.

- **Quito,** capital de Ecuador, queda a 25 kilómetros de la línea ecuatorial. Sin embargo, esta cuidad colonial, la segunda capital más alta de Latinoamérica, goza de días calurosos y noches frescas por su altitud. Quito era una ciudad del Imperio Inca cuando fue tomado en 1534 por los tenientes de Pizarro.

O. Si hubiera sido posible ... Complete las siguientes oraciones con la forma correcta del verbo que aparece entre paréntesis. El verbo de la cláusula que empieza con **si** está en pluscuamperfecto del subjuntivo. El verbo de la cláusula principal aparece en potencial compuesto (*conditional perfect*) o en pluscuamperfecto del subjuntivo.

> MODELO   Si **hubiera sido** (ser) posible, nosotros **habríamos ido** (ir).
> Si **hubiera sido** (ser) posible, nosotros **hubiéramos ido** (ir).

1. Si Uds. nos _____ (preguntar), les _____ / _____ (decir).

2. Yo te _____ / _____ (devolver) la cartera si te _____ (ver).

3. Si Jaime _____ (hacerse) médico, _____ / _____ (estar) más contento.

4. Eva y yo _____ / _____ (llamar) en seguida si lo _____ (saber).

5. Si yo _____ (jugar) béisbol en el parque, no _____ / _____ (romper) la ventana de la casa.

P. **¿Campo o ciudad?** Pablo se crió en el campo, su primo Gregorio, en la ciudad. Hablan de las maneras en las cuales hubiera sido diferente su vida si Pablo se hubiera criado en la ciudad y Gregorio en el campo. El verbo de la cláusula que empieza con **si** está en pluscuamperfecto del subjuntivo. El verbo de la cláusula principal aparece en potencial compuesto (*conditional perfect*) o en pluscuamperfecto del subjuntivo.

> MODELO   Pablo: estudiar en un colegio grande / criarse en la ciudad
> → Pablo **había/hubiera estudiado** en un colegio grande si **se hubiera criado** en la ciudad.

1. Pablo: asistir al teatro / vivir en la ciudad

2. Gregorio: ordeñar (*to milk*) las vacas / nacer en una finca

3. Pablo: ponerse más nervioso / oír tanto ruido todos los días

4. Gregorio: respirar aire no contaminado / vivir en el campo

5. Pablo: tomar el metro y los taxis / trabajar en la ciudad

6. Gregorio: aprender a montar a caballo / viajar por el campo

7. Pablo: comprar comida en el supermercado / ir de compras en la ciudad

8. Gregorio: comer frutas y legumbres muy frescas / criarse en el campo

9. Pablo: llevar un traje, camisa y corbata / ganarse la vida en una empresa

10. Gregorio: usar un sombrero de paja (*straw*) / cultivar la tierra

Q. **¡Julio el tardón (*slow poke*)!** A Julio le lleva tanto tiempo hacer cosas que siempre llega tarde a sus citas. Acaba de llegar a la fiesta de sus amigos. En vez de ver una fiesta, despierta a su amigo Memo que le explica que la fiesta terminó a las dos de la mañana. Julio piensa en cómo le habría salido si hubiera llegado antes. El verbo de la cláusula que empieza con **si** está en pluscuamperfecto del subjuntivo y el de la cláusula principal está en potencial compuesto (*conditional perfect*) o en pluscuamperfecto del subjuntivo.

> MODELO   Si yo **hubiera llegado** (llegar) antes, **habría/hubiera visto** (ver) a mis amigos.

1. Si yo _____ (terminar) mi trabajo para las diez, _____ (poder) llegar a tiempo.

2. Si yo _____ (planear) mejor mi horario, no me _____ (perder) la fiesta.

3. Si yo _____ (hacer) mi trabajo más eficazmente, _____ (bailar) con Julieta, la mujer de mis sueños.

4. Si yo no _____ (gastar) tanto tiempo echándome agua de colonia,

   _____ (disfrutar) de una comida rica.

5. Si yo _____ (manejar) más rápido, no _____ (atrasarse).

6. Si mis amigos _____ (divertirse) más, ellos _____ (quedarse) hasta las tres de la mañana.

7. Si Memo no _____ (acostarse) de inmediato, yo no _____ (tener) que tocar el timbre cien veces.

R. Exprese las siguientes oraciones en español.

1. If Victoria had had the key she would have opened the suitcase.

2. If you (*Ud.*) were to take a trip this summer, where would you go?

3. If they had been more careful, they wouldn't have lost their traveler's checks.

4. If you (*Uds.*) turn right at the corner, you'll see the museum.

5. I would pay attention to Roberto if he gave good advice.

S. **Ejercicio oral.** Converse con sus amigos de lo que harían en cada caso. Pregúnteles, por ejemplo: ¿Qué harías si tuvieras un millón de dólares? o ¿adónde irías si tuvieras un año de vacaciones?

T. **Estructuras en acción.** Lea los comentarios sobre los exámenes finales en España y luego haga el ejercicio.

Vocabulario

agobiarse *to get tired*	**insoportable** *unbearable*
el agobio *exhaustion, worry*	**la materia** *subject*
el aliado *ally*	**la pesadilla** *nightmare*
el aprobado *passing grade*	**procurar** *to try*
aprobar (o > ue) *to pass an exam*	**reñir (e > i)** *to scold*
la autoconfianza *self-confidence*	**la selectividad** *selective course taken*
la chuleta *(slang) cheating on exam*	*before technical studies in university*
dar de sí *to do one's best*	**sobresaliente** *excellent grade*
dar palo al agua *(here) to study, work*	**suspender** *to fail*
el dominio *mastery, good knowledge*	**el tema** *question (on an exam)*
el enemigo *enemy*	**el temario** *exam questions*
el esquema *outline*	**tumbado** *lying down*
lo hecho, hecho está *what's done is done*	**vago** *lazy*

Exámenes: La prueba final

El curso se acaba y estudiantes y padres sufren los agobios de los exámenes finales. El mejor aliado para aprobar es la autoconfianza, además del dominio de la materia. El peor enemigo son los nervios.

Hablan los estudiantes:

"No me gusta memorizar" (*Silvia Rivero, 17 años*)

> "Intento comprender los temas, no me gusta memorizar. Me hago esquemas, leo, procuro entender y escribo los temas porque así se te quedan mejor. Pongo en común los temas con la gente de clase y, si no entendemos algo, nos llamamos por teléfono. Mi madre me dice que me tranquilice y que 'lo hecho, hecho está'. Me pongo insoportable, no hay quien me hable".

"La selectividad es lo más difícil del mundo" (*Carlos Gustavo García, 18 años*)

> "Soy tranquilo para los exámenes, pero con la selectividad me pongo muy nervioso: es lo más difícil que hay. Tengo miedo de que me pregunten cosas que no han entrado en el temario. Las *chuletas* no ayudan".

"Tengo pesadillas" (*Silvia Heredia, 15 años*)

"Ante los exámenes me pongo muy nerviosa, muy nerviosa. Tomo mucho café y tengo pesadillas: sueño con los exámenes. Para estudiar copio los temas en un papel y luego me lo voy preguntando o le pido a mi madre que me lo pregunte ella. Estudio de todas las formas posibles: tumbada, de pie, andando … Pero siempre estudio sola, porque hablo mucho y si no, me distraigo".

Hablan los padres:

"No hay quien le hable" (*Josefa Sánchez*)

"Tengo dos hijos estudiando. Beatriz está muy nerviosa y se agobia mucho. Hasta que no acabe los exámenes no hay quien le hable. Mi marido es psicólogo y les dice a nuestros hijos que se tranquilicen y que no se agobien".

"No me gusta que estudie tanto" (*Germana Baile*)

"Mi hijo José Jorge está en segundo curso de Telecomunicaciones. Estudia demasiadas horas y hay que reñirle para que salga. La verdad, no me gusta que estudie tanto".

"Sólo les exijo lo que puedan dar de sí" (*Benito de Lucas*)

"Sólo les exijo lo que puedan dar de sí. Me da igual que saquen sobresalientes o aprobados. Si suspenden tampoco pasa nada. Lo que quiero es que trabajen, porque los buenos resultados vienen solos".

"Son un poco vagos" (*Carmen Martín*)

"Está claro que los que se ponen nerviosos es porque no han estudiado. Los que no han dado palo al agua en todo el curso es imposible que puedan aprobar, aunque se tomen cosas de la farmacia como hacen algunos. Yo les digo a mis hijos que no se preocupen porque otros saquen un 10 y ellos no. Pero la verdad es que son un poco vagos y podrían sacar más".

Empareje las cláusulas subordinadas (dependientes) con sus cláusulas independientes como ocurren en los comentarios. Use el subjuntivo, el indicativo o el infinitivo según sean necesarios.

A	B
1. Yo les digo a mis hijos _____	a. que no se agobien
2. Le pido a mi madre _____	b. lo que puedan dar de sí
3. Me da igual _____	c. comprender los temas
4. Tengo miedo de _____	d. memorizar
5. Procuro _____	e. que no se preocupen porque otros saquen un 10
6. Lo que quiero _____	f. para que salga
7. No me gusta _____	g. que puedan aprobar
8. Es imposible _____	h. que saquen sobresalientes o aprobados
9. Mi madre me dice _____	i. entender
10. Intento _____	j. que me lo pregunte ella
11. Les dice a nuestros hijos _____	k. es que trabajen
12. Les exijo _____	l. que me tranquilice
13. Hay que reñirle _____	m. que son un poco vagos
14. La verdad es _____	n. que me pregunten cosas que no han entrado en el temario

CHAPTER 13

THE SUBJUNCTIVE: ADVERB & ADJECTIVE CLAUSES

A *Adverb clauses that require the subjunctive*

- A clause that modifies a verb the way an adverb does is called an adverb clause. Compare the use of adverbs and adverb clauses in the following pairs of sentences:

Salimos **temprano**.	*We went out **early**.*
Salimos **cuando terminamos**.	*We went out **when we finished**.*
Cantaron **bien**.	*They sang **well**.*
Cantaron **como les habían enseñado**.	*They sang **as they had been taught**.*

- Adverb clauses are introduced by conjunctions, such as **cuando** and **como** in the above examples. The following conjunctions introduce adverb clauses in which the verb must be in the subjunctive: **a fin de que** (*in order that, so that*), **a menos que** (*unless*), **antes (de) que** (*before*), **con tal (de) que** (*provided that*), **en caso de que** (*in case*), **para que** (*so that*), **sin que** (*without*). The same sequence-of-tense rules apply in adverb clauses as in noun clauses:

Saldré **antes de que** vuelvan.	*I'll leave before they get back.*
Salí **antes de que** volvieran.	*I left before they got back.*
Tito va a comprar huevos **para que** hagamos la torta.	*Tito's going to buy eggs so we can make the cake.*
Tito compró los huevos **para que** hiciéramos la torta.	*Tito bought eggs so that we might make the cake.*
Escondemos el regalo **sin que** Olga sepa dónde.	*We're hiding the gift without Olga knowing where.*
Escondimos el regalo **sin que** Olga supiera dónde.	*We hid the gift without Olga knowing where.*

- **A menos que** and **con tal (de) que** are followed by the present subjunctive if the action of the dependent (subordinate) clause occurs *at the same time* as the action of the main clause. They are followed by the present perfect subjunctive if the action of the dependent clause occurs *before* the action of the main clause:

Estudiará matemáticas con tal que le **devuelvas** su libro.	*He'll study math provided that you return his book to him.*
Estudiará matemáticas con tal que le **hayas devuelto** su libro.	*He'll study math provided that you've returned his book to him.*

B *Adverb clauses with indicative or subjunctive*

- Certain conjunctions are followed by the indicative when the action of the dependent or subordinate clause is considered a known or established fact. They are followed by the subjunctive when the action of the dependent clause is considered uncertain or indefinite. In these dependent clauses with subjunctive, the conjunction often has the English equivalent of *ever* attached to it, as in *whenever, however, wherever*. These conjunctions include: **como** (*how*), **aunque** (*although, even though*), **según** (*according to*), **donde** (*where*), **mientras** (*while*), **de manera que** (*so that*), **de modo que** (*so that*):

Iremos **donde** tú **quieres**.	We'll go **where** you want. (*We know where you want to go.*)
Iremos **donde** tú **quieras**.	We'll go **wherever** you want to go. (*We don't know yet where you want to go.*)
Hágalo **como** ellos **dicen**.	Do it **how (the way)** they say. (*I know the way they say.*)
Hágalo **como** ellos **digan**.	Do it **however** they say. (*I don't know the way they say.*)
Aunque va Elena, yo no voy.	***Even though Elena is going,*** *I'm not going.* (*I know Elena is going.*)
Aunque vaya Elena, yo no voy.	***Even though Elena may go,*** *I'm not going.*

- Adverb clauses introduced by conjunctions of time such as **después (de) que** (*after*), **cuando** (*when*), **hasta que** (*until*), **tan pronto (como)** (*as soon as*), **en cuanto** (*as soon as*), **luego que** (*as soon as*), and **así que** (*as soon as*), are followed by the subjunctive when the main clause refers to the future or is a command:

Me quedaré **hasta que terminemos**.	*I'll stay until we finish.*
Díselo **cuando lleguen**.	*Tell it to them when they arrive.*

- If the action of the dependent clause is considered to be a habitual occurrence, the indicative, not the subjunctive, is used:

Se lo das **cuando llegan**.	*You (usually) give it to them when they arrive.*
Me quedo **hasta que terminamos**.	*I (usually) stay until we finish.*

- When the sentence relates a past action, the indicative is used after the conjunction of time as the event in the adverbial clause is considered to be part of reality:

Se lo dijiste **cuando llegaron**.	*You told it to them when they arrived.*
Me quedé **hasta que terminamos**.	*I stayed until we finished.*

- The conjunction of time **antes (de) que** is an exception because it is *always* followed by the subjunctive even when the verb of the main clause is in a past tense:

Nora **mandó** la carta **antes que** Pablo la **llamara.**   *Nora sent the letter before Pablo called her.*

- If the subject of the main clause and the dependent clause is the same, the clause is replaced by an infinitive:

Estudien *hasta que Beti lo entienda.*   *Study until Beti understands it.*
Estudien *hasta entenderlo.*   *Study until you understand it.*

Voy a leer *antes que juguemos* **tenis.**   *I'm going to read before we play tennis.*
Voy a leer *antes de jugar* **tenis.**   *I'm going to read before (playing) I play tennis.*

Salimos *sin que Uds. almorzaran.*   *We went out without your having lunch.*
Salimos *sin almorzar.*   *We went out without having lunch.*

A. No se sabe todavía. Diga que Ud. no sabe cómo son las cosas mencionadas completando las oraciones con las palabras que faltan en las cláusulas adverbiales. Se debe usar el presente del subjuntivo de los verbos.

1. Lo haré según Uds. _____. (mandar)

2. Viviremos donde Pepita _____. (aconsejar)

3. Aunque _____ habrá un partido de fútbol. (llover)

4. Guillermo quiere pintar los cuadros donde _____ mucha luz. (haber)

5. Realizarán el proyecto como tú _____. (querer)

6. Voy a leer el informe aunque no _____ muy interesante. (ser)

7. Vicente comerá donde Ud. _____. (preferir)

8. Prepara el plato según nosotros _____. (decir)

9. Van al cine aunque yo no _____. (ir)

B. Haciendo las diligencias (*Running errands*). Explique que algunas personas hicieron ciertas cosas **antes de que** otras personas hicieran otras. Use el pretérito para el verbo de la cláusula principal y el imperfecto del subjuntivo para la cláusula adverbial.

Las tiendas

la **carnicería** *butcher shop*	la **librería** *bookstore*
la **cita** *appointment, date*	el **mecánico** *mechanic*
el **correo** *post office*	la **pastelería** *pastry shop*
la **droguería** *drugstore*	la **peluquería** *beauty salon, barber shop*
los **frenos** *brakes*	**reparar** *to repair*
la **gasolinera** *gas station*	el **sello** *stamp*
la **joyería** *jewelry store*	la **tintorería** *dry cleaner's*
el **lavado** *wash*	la **zapatería** *shoe store*
la **lavandería** *laundry*	

> MODELO   Marta / ir a la pastelería : yo / ir a la carnicería
> → Marta fue a la pastelería **antes de que yo fuera** a la carnicería.

1. Elena y Mario / salir de la gasolinera : nosotros / entrar en la zapatería

2. Ud. / llevar el lavado a la lavandería : yo / volver a la droguería

3. Uds. / comprar los sellos : Consuelo / poder ir al correo

4. Fernando y yo / no hablar con el mecánico : él / repararnos los frenos

5. yo / sacar la ropa de la tintorería : Juana / tener su cita en la peluquería

6. tú / ir a la joyería : Arturo y Paco / buscar una librería

---

Nota cultural

- En el centro de las ciudades de habla hispana, se hace **la compra** tradicionalmente en las tiendas especializadas. La panadería, la carnicería, la pastelería, la tienda de comestibles, la lechería, la frutería son lugares frecuentados en los barrios antiguos. Todo el mundo conoce a los dueños de estas tiendas y a sus empleados. Sin embargo, el nuevo sistema de supermercados e hipermercados hace competencia con las tiendas tradicionales y poco a poco las va reemplazando. Ya en pleno centro se encuentran supermercados donde se vende todo.

- Hoy día hay mucha construcción de nuevas urbanizaciones y **centros comerciales** fuera de las ciudades. Estos centros de múltiples comercios, restaurantes y cines son muy atractivos y ya que todos tienen coche, es probable que mucha gente abandone las tiendas céntricas por el centro comercial.

- En las zonas rurales de Hispanoamérica, **el mercado campesino** que se realiza en los pueblos los domingos por la tarde es el centro para la compra de comida y también una institución social de mucha importancia.

C. Complete las siguientes oraciones con la forma correcta del verbo que aparece entre paréntesis. Escoja entre el indicativo y el subjuntivo (en presente o imperfecto).

> **MODELO**   No queremos ir al museo sin que tú **vayas.** (ir)

1. Llamaré a Julio para que él _____ lo que está pasando. (saber)

2. Se quedaron hasta que Federico _____. (venir)

3. Iremos al centro comercial a menos que Uds. nos _____. (necesitar)

4. Le presté el dinero a Marisol para que _____ comprarse el vestido. (poder)

5. Tú puedes venir a la casa sin que nosotros te _____. (invitar)

6. Los vimos tan pronto como nosotros _____ en la librería. (entrar)

7. No pensaban salir sin que mamá les _____ de comer. (dar)

8. Carmen se puso de pie en cuanto _____ la conferencia. (terminar)

9. Hazme saber cuando _____ los paquetes. (llegar)

10. Los muchachos iban al cine a menos que Clarita no _____ ganas de ver la película. (tener)

11. Hice el desayuno después de (yo) _____. (ducharse)

12. Uds. jugarán al béisbol así que _____ la tarea. (hacer)

D. Exprese las siguientes oraciones en español.

1. I'll call them when I get to the airport.

2. We'll watch the soccer match until it begins to rain.

3. Consuelo set the table an hour before her friends arrived.

4. They stood in line at the box office after they had lunch.

5. You (*Ud.*) didn't want to go shopping without our going too.

6. Do it (*Uds.*) whichever way they want.

7. Even though it's cold out, we should take a walk.

8. I'll lend you (*tú*) the book so that you won't have to take it out of the library.

9. Carlos is going to study for his exam before playing tennis.

C *Adjective clauses that require the subjunctive*

• An adjective clause modifies a noun the way an adjective does. All relative clauses are adjective clauses. In the example, **una obra que se titula** *Don Quijote,* "**que se titula** *Don Quijote*" modifies **obra** the way that **maravillosa** does in **una obra maravillosa.** The noun modified by an adjective clause is called the antecedent. Thus, **obra** is the antecedent of the **que**-clause.

- In Spanish, there are two types of antecedents—those considered part of reality, definite or existent, and those that are not part of reality, indefinite or nonexistent. In the sentence **Tenemos un profesor que habla chino,** the antecedent, **un profesor,** is a definite person who can be identified by name. Therefore, the indicative **habla** is used.

- For adjective clauses that modify antecedents that are not part of reality or the speaker's experience, the subjunctive is used. These include indefinite, undetermined, and negative antecedents:

Buscamos un profesor que **hable** chino.	*We're looking for a professor who speaks Chinese.*
Queremos un profesor que **hable** chino.	*We want a professor who speaks Chinese.*
Necesitamos un profesor que **hable** chino.	*We need a professor who speaks Chinese.*
No conozco a nadie que **hable** vasco.	*I don't know anyone who speaks Basque.*
No hay revista que le **guste.**	*There's no magazine he likes.*

- Note that **buscar, querer, necesitar,** and other such verbs may also have direct objects that are definite and identifiable. In this case, adjective clauses that modify these objects are in the *indicative.* In the example below, the professor being sought is known to the speakers:

Buscamos al profesor que **habla** chino.	*We're looking for the professor who speaks Chinese.*
Necesitamos al profesor que **habla** chino.	*We need the professor who speaks Chinese.*

- The sequence-of-tense rules apply in adjective clauses also:

Quiero una novela que **tenga** un buen argumento.	*I want a novel that **has** a good plot.*
Quería una novela que **tuviera** un buen argumento.	*I wanted a novel that **had** a good plot.*
No hay casa que les **guste.**	***There's no** house they **like.***
No había casa que les **gustara.**	***There was no** house they **liked.***

- In addition to **que,** other relative words such as **donde** and **quien** can introduce adjective clauses:

Buscan una florería **donde vendan** tulipanes.	*They're looking for a florist **where they sell** tulips.*
Tere quería un amigo **con quien pudiera** jugar tenis.	*Tere wanted a friend **with whom she could** play tennis.*

E. Se busca apartamento. Escriba oraciones que describan el apartamento que Ud. y sus amigos esperan encontrar. Use el presente de subjuntivo en la cláusula adjetival y el presente de indicativo en la cláusula principal.

> MODELO   nosotros / buscar un apartamento / tener cuatro dormitorios
> → Nosotros buscamos un apartamento que tenga cuatro dormitorios.

1. tú / querer un apartamento / tener dos baños

2. Mateo / necesitar un apartamento / donde / haber aire acondicionado

3. Javier y yo / buscar un apartamento / estar cerca de la universidad

4. Uds. / necesitar un apartamento / no costar un ojo de la cara (*not cost an arm and a leg*)

5. yo / querer un apartamento / no necesitar renovación

6. Pepe y Leo / desear un apartamento / ser moderno y fácil de limpiar

7. Octavio / buscar un apartamento / dar a una calle poco transitada (*a street with little traffic*)

8. Ud. / necesitar un apartamento / donde / caber todos los fiesteros (*party-lovers*)

F. ¡Mi novia ideal! Para saber lo que Esteban le cuenta a su amigo Felipe sobre la mujer ideal que busca, complete las cláusulas adjetivales de las oraciones con el presente del subjuntivo del verbo que aparece entre paréntesis.

1. Busco una novia que _____ ser una buena amiga. (saber)

2. Quiero una chica con quien _____ hablar fácilmente. (poder)

3. Me hace falta una mujer que me _____. (comprender)

4. Quiero tener una novia con quien yo _____. (divertirse)

5. Necesito una chica que _____ inteligente. (ser)

6. Estoy buscando una novia que _____ un buen sentido del humor. (tener)

G. ¡No hay candidatas al puesto! (*There are no candidates for the job!*)
Por desgracia, Felipe no puede ayudar a Esteban porque no tiene amigas que tengan todas estas cualidades. Complete las cláusulas adjetivales de las oraciones con el presente de subjuntivo del verbo que aparece entre paréntesis.

1. No conozco a ninguna chica que _____ todas estas características. (reunir)

2. No hay nadie que _____ tan perfecta. (ser)

3. No conozco a ninguna mujer con quien tú _____ salir. (querer)

4. No hay ninguna que te _____ a interesar mucho. (ir)

5. No conozco a ninguna muchacha que _____ un cociente intelectual (*I.Q.*) tan alto. (tener)

6. ¡No hay ninguna chica que _____ de ti en cuanto te vea! (enamorarse)

H. ¡En la cumbre! (*At the top of the ladder!*) Hacía varios años que Manuel trepaba en los peldaños del éxito hasta llegar a la cumbre. Ahora es presidente de su propia empresa internacional y conoce el éxito y la prosperidad. A veces Manuel se pone a pensar en el pasado. Complete las cláusulas adjetivales con el imperfecto del subjuntivo del verbo que aparece entre paréntesis para saber cómo eran las cosas.

Los negocios

compartir *to share*	**la fama** *name, reputation*
confiar en *to trust*	**el horario de trabajo** *work schedule*
la cumbre *the top*	**invertir (e > ie)** *to invest*
el dineral *fortune, a lot of money*	**los peldaños del éxito** *ladder of success*
la empresa *firm, company*	**la prosperidad** *prosperity*
esforzarse (o > ue) por *to strive to,*	**realizar** *to achieve*
try hard to	**trepar** *to climb*
el éxito *success*	

1. Yo buscaba una profesión que me _____ un dineral, fama y felicidad. (dar)

2. No había nadie que _____ más que yo por conseguir el éxito. (esforzarse)

3. Yo quería tener un horario de trabajo que me _____ pasar mucho tiempo con mi familia. (permitir)

4. Yo necesitaba una esposa que _____ mis ideas y opiniones sobre la vida. (compartir)

5. No conocía a nadie que _____ más plata en su compañía que yo. (invertir)

6. No había ninguna persona que _____ de vacaciones menos que yo. (ir)

7. Me hacían falta unos empleados en quienes _____ confiar. (poder)

8. ¡Mi esposa y yo buscábamos una casa donde _____ mucho lugar para mi oficina y para los niños! (haber)

9. Yo quería tener una empresa donde se _____ mis ambiciones. (realizar)

Nota cultural

En muchos países hispánicos las letras **S.A.** aparecen tras el nombre de una empresa. S.A. es la abreviatura de **Sociedad Anónima,** el equivalente en español de *Inc.*

 Adjective clauses with indicative or subjunctive

- In Spanish, a noun may be followed by a relative clause beginning with **que** that has a verb either in the indicative or the subjunctive. If the indicative is used, it suggests that the antecedent has already been identified. If the relative clause is in the subjunctive, it suggests that the antecedent has not been identified:

Traigo la torta que **quieres.**	*I'll bring the cake you want.*
(*Yo sé cuál de las tortas te gustó.*)	(*I know which of the cakes you liked.*)

Escoge la torta que **quieras.**   *Choose the cake you want.*
(Yo no conozco tus gustos.)   *(I don't know your tastes.)*

• The meaning of the subjunctive in these adjective clauses can be conveyed in English by words ending in *-ever:*

Iremos a la hora que tú **digas.**   *We'll go at **whatever** time you say.*

Ceno en el restaurante que ellos   *I'll have dinner in **whichever** restaurant*
  quieran.   *they want.*

I. Exprese las siguientes oraciones en español.

1. Mario and Carmen are looking for a house that has nine rooms.

2. There's no food that he likes!

3. I wanted a friend who would go to museums with me.

4. Don't you (*Ud.*) know anyone who's arriving before three o'clock?

5. Rosa will prepare whatever dish we choose.

6. They needed a secretary who worked on Saturdays.

7. We'll take the class with whichever professor teaches best.

J. Ejercicio oral. Hable con sus amigos de las cualidades que buscan en las personas. Complete las oraciones con cláusulas adjetivales como: Quiero un novio/una novia que …, Busco unos amigos que …, Necesito una jefe que …, etcétera.

K. Estructuras en acción. Lea los anuncios y haga el ejercicio que les sigue.

Costa Cruceros
Navegamos para divertirte.

Éstas pueden ser las vacaciones más divertidas de tu vida, o las más aburridas. Depende de si vienes o no.
Depende de las ganas que tengas de divertirte en Grecia. Porque hay muchas formas de conocerla. Pero ninguna tan mágica y diferente como a bordo del Costa Classica o del Costa Riviera. Dos hoteles flotantes de lujo con los que podrás descubrir lo mejor de las costas griegas. Y todo de una forma que jamás imaginaste. Este verano lo más fácil es pasárselo bien. Ven a Grecia con nosotros.

Tele ABC
Siempre junto a su televisor Tele ABC

Toda la información de todas las televisiones para que usted elija cómodamente su programación. Novedades, entrevistas y reportajes en TELEABC, cada fin de semana, sin aumento de precio, con *ABC* y *Blanco y Negro.*

SEAT

En la vida hay oportunidades que no puedes dejar escapar.
Este mes, el Seat Ibiza que tú quieras por sólo 9.900 Ptas. al mes, durante el primer año.

Olivetti

Le damos 50.000 ptas. por su viejo ordenador para que se compre un nuevo Olivetti.

Paradores
Haga realidad sus sueños por menos
de lo que imagina

Porque Paradores le ofrece, a usted y a su acompañante, un 35% de descuento en sus estancias en régimen de habitación y desayuno. Para que disfruten, desde 3.250 pesetas, de lugares de ensueño.

En una hoja de papel, escriba las oraciones de los anuncios que tengan cláusulas adverbiales o adjetivales y tradúzcalas al inglés.

CHAPTER 14
COMMANDS

A Command forms for **Ud.** and **Uds.**

- The command forms of a verb are used to tell someone to do or not to do something. The formal command forms for **Ud.** and **Uds.** are the same as the corresponding present subjunctive forms:

Escuche el ruido.	*Listen to the noise.*
Lea el libro.	*Read the book.*
Escriban el informe.	*Write the report.*
Traigan el periódico.	*Bring the newspaper.*

- Negative commands are formed by the addition of **no** before the affirmative command:

No escuche el ruido.	*Don't listen to the noise.*
No escriban el informe.	*Don't write the report.*

- A polite tone can be given to the command to soften it by the addition of **Ud.** or **Uds.** much as the addition of *please* does in English commands:

Espere.	*Wait.*
Espere Ud.	*Please wait.*
No griten.	*Don't shout.*
No griten Uds.	*Please don't shout.*

A. Una receta: La tortilla española. Póngase el gorro de cocinero y aprenda a preparar este plato español típico cambiando el infinitivo de los verbos al imperativo formal. ¡Trabajando paso a paso, Ud. llegará a ser un cocinero/ una cocinera de primera (*first rate*)!

> MODELO   Calentar el aceite de oliva en una sartén.
> → Caliente el aceite de oliva en una sartén.

La cocina	
el aceite de oliva *olive oil*	**el gorro de cocinero** *chef's hat*
a fuego lento *low heat, slowly*	**la patata (Spain)** *potato*
añadir *to add*	**pegar** *to stick*
batir *to beat*	**pelar** *to peel*
calentar (e > ie) *to heat*	**picar** *to chop*
la cebolla *onion*	**la pimienta** *pepper*
cocinar *to cook*	**rehogar (Spain)** *to brown*
dorar *to brown*	**remover (o > ue)** *to stir*
espolvorear *to sprinkle*	**la sal** *salt*
freír (e > i) *to fry*	**salpimentar** *to season*
la fuente *serving dish*	**la (or el) sartén** *frying pan*

1. Añadir las patatas y cebollas peladas y picadas.

2. Cocinar a fuego lento.

3. No rehogar las patatas y las cebollas.

4. Espolvorear con sal.

5. Batir los huevos.

6. Poner los huevos en la sartén.

7. Hacer dorar los huevos.

8. No dejar que se pegue la tortilla.

9. Servir en una fuente.

B. Una formación profesional (*Professional training*). Unos jóvenes ingenieros comienzan un programa de formación profesional con la empresa que acaba de contratarlos. Como jefe del programa, Ud. les dice lo que tienen que hacer usando el imperativo.

> **Modelo** Llegar a las nueve menos cuarto todos los días
> → **Lleguen** a las nueve menos cuarto todos los días.

1. Encontrarse en la oficina del señor Aguilar.

2. Traer la calculadora.

3. Hacer preguntas.

4. Usar la computadora.

5. Seguir los consejos del gerente.

6. Estudiar informática (*data processing*).

7. Leer el manual de telecomunicaciones.

8. Tener cuidado con la entrada y salida de datos (*data input and output*).

C. **Trámites de banco (*Bank procedures*).** Ud. está de vacaciones en Santiago de Chile. Mientras cambia unos cheques de viajero en el banco, oye algunas conversaciones. Escriba los verbos que aparecen en las preguntas en imperativo. Cambie los sustantivos complementos directos a pronombres. (See page 189 to review the position of object pronouns with command forms.)

En el banco	
calcular *to compute*	**el peso** *monetary unit of Chile and other*
la cuenta *(bank) account*	*Latin American countries*
cuenta corriente *checking account*	**la planilla de retiro** *withdrawal form, slip*
el cheque de viajero *traveler's check*	**la plata** *money*
firmar *to sign*	**el préstamo** *loan*
el formulario *form (paper)*	**retirar** *to withdraw*
el interés *interest*	**la ventanilla** *teller's window (station)*
llenar *to fill out*	

MODELO   —¿Debo abrir la cuenta?
—Sí, **ábrala.**
—No, **no la abra.**

1. ¿Debo retirar dinero?

2. ¿Puedo acercarme a la ventanilla?

3. ¿Tengo que firmar la planilla de retiro?

4. ¿Debo llenar el formulario?

5. ¿Le doy la plata en pesos?

6. ¿Puedo pedirles a Uds. un préstamo?

7. ¿Le calculo los intereses?

8. ¿Cierro la cuenta corriente?

9. ¿Le cobro los cheques de viajero?

Nota cultural

- **Santiago,** capital de Chile, queda a las orillas del río Mapocho. Tiene hermosos jardines públicos y se puede ver los picos de los Andes desde la ciudad. Fundada por Pedro de Valdivia en 1541, Santiago tiene una universidad del Estado, una universidad Católica y numerosas instituciones culturales, científicas y artísticas además de una pintoresca zona antigua.

- **El peso** es la moneda de Chile. El peso chileno está a 436 al dólar americano. Los otros países latinoamericanos que tienen el peso como moneda son Argentina, México, Colombia, Uruguay, Bolivia, la República Dominicana y Cuba.

B Command forms for **nosotros** (let's, let's not)

• The present subjunctive forms for **nosotros** are used as commands:

Tomemos el tren.	*Let's take the train.*
No hagamos nada.	*Let's not do anything.*

• The affirmative **nosotros** command is often replaced by **vamos a** + infinitive.
  Vamos a estudiar may mean either *We're going to study* or *Let's study.*
  No vamos a estudiar can only mean *We're not going to study.*

Vamos a salir esta noche. ⎫	
Salgamos esta noche. ⎭	*Let's go out tonight.*

• **Vamos** is used instead of **vayamos** for *let's go.* The regular present subjunctive
  form is used for the negative: **no vayamos.**

Vamos al centro.	*Let's go downtown.*
No vayamos al cine.	*Let's not go to the movies.*

• In affirmative **nosotros** commands the final **-s** of the verb ending is dropped
  when the reflexive pronoun **nos** or the indirect object pronoun **se** is added.
  An accent mark is written over the stressed syllable. For example: **Lavémonos**
  (Lavemos + **nos)** *Let's wash up* or **Prestémoselo (Prestemos** + **se** + **lo)** *Let's lend*
  it to her.

(quedarse)	**Quedémonos.**	*Let's stay.*
(sentarse)	**Sentémonos.**	*Let's sit down.*
(irse)	**Vámonos.**	*Let's go.*
(enseñarse)	**Enseñémosela.**	*Let's show it to them.*
(hacerse)	**Hagámoselos.**	*Let's make them for him.*

D. **¡Veámoslo todo en Perú!** Ud. y sus amigos están pasando las vacaciones
   en el Perú. Recién llegados a Lima, Uds. hablan de sus planes. Escriba oraciones
   empleando la primera persona del plural del imperativo.

> Modelo   viajar a Nasca
> **Viajemos** a Nasca.
> **Vamos a viajar** a Nasca.

1. dar un paseo por la zona de la Plaza de Armas

2. ir de compras en el Jirón de la Unión

3. conocer la Universidad de San Marcos

4. hacer una excursión a Machu Picchu

5. visitar la catedral y unas iglesias de Cuzco

6. quedarse en Miraflores

7. tomar un colectivo (*small van*) a una playa limeña

8. sentarse en el Malecón

Nota cultural

- **Lima,** capital del Perú, fue fundada por los españoles en 1535. Fue una ciudad rica e importante hasta que fue destruida por un terremoto en 1746. El casco antiguo (*old part*) de la ciudad conserva la arquitectura de la época colonial. Aquí se puede ver la Plaza de Armas alrededor de la cual se encuentran el Palacio de Gobierno, la Catedral y otros lugares históricos. Esta zona ha sido declarada patrimonio internacional por la UNESCO. Las nuevas zonas de Lima se encuentran en la Plaza San Martín, al sur del Jirón (calle larga) de la Unión, la principal calle comercial. Lima es también una ciudad moderna con rascacielos, contaminación del ambiente y "pueblos jóvenes" (*shanty settlements*).

- **La Universidad de San Marcos** fue fundada en 1551.

- **Machu Picchu,** una ciudad inca, queda en el departamento de Cuzco al sudeste de Lima. Las ruinas de la ciudad sagrada, que consiste en una fortaleza, terrazas, escaleras, templos, palacios, torres, fuentes y un reloj de sol, fueron descubiertas en 1911.

- La ciudad de **Cuzco** fue fundada en el siglo XI por Manco Cápac y era capital del Imperio Incaico hasta que los conquistadores españoles se apoderaron de la ciudad en 1533, nombrándola ciudad española en 1534. Hay varias iglesias incluso las de La Merced, San Francisco y Belén de los Reyes y una catedral de estilo barroco que data del siglo XVII.

- **Miraflores** es el suburbio más grande y más importante de la capital peruana. Con sus muchos comercios, excelentes restaurantes y hoteles, Miraflores, con San Isidro, constituyen ahora el centro social de Lima. Desde la Avenida Diagonal hay una magnífica vista del litoral (*coastline*) de Lima. El malecón (*jetty*) pasa por todas estas estaciones balnearias (*seaside resorts*).

- **Nasca** es una ciudad que queda al sudeste de Lima. A unos 22 kilómetros al norte de Nasca se pueden ver las famosas líneas nascas que son líneas paralelas, formas geométricas y las figuras de un perro, un mono, aves, una araña, un árbol y otras cosas. Se cree que fueron grabadas en las arenas de la Pampa Colorada por tres pueblos indígenas diferentes a partir de 900 antes de Jesucristo.

E. ¡Cómo no! Sus amigos le dicen que quieren hacer ciertas cosas hoy. Ud. les dice que está conforme expresando el imperativo para *nosotros* de dos maneras.

> MODELO   Quiero comprarle un regalo a Elisa.
> Cómo no. **Comprémoselo.**
> Cómo no. **Vamos a comprárselo.**

1. Quiero darle a Maximiliano la mochila.

2. Quiero sacar entradas para el concierto de la Sinfónica.

3. Me gustaría ir al museo por la tarde.

4. Sería agradable caminar por el parque.

5. Quiero inscribirme en la clase de computación.

6. Me gustaría jugar al tenis.

7. Quiero decirles a los chicos el motivo del disgusto (*argument*).

8. Sería lindo tumbarse (*to lie down*) en la playa.

C *Command forms for* **tú** *and* **vosotros**

- Negative informal commands for **tú** and **vosotros** are derived from the present subjunctive:

tú	**No compres** más.	*Don't buy more.*
	No comas tanto.	*Don't eat so much.*
	No pidas cerveza.	*Don't order beer.*
	No digas eso.	*Don't say that.*
vosotros	**No compréis** más.	*Don't buy more.*
	No comáis tanto.	*Don't eat so much.*
	No pidáis cerveza.	*Don't order beer.*
	No digáis eso.	*Don't say that.*

- Affirmative informal commands for **tú** and **vosotros** have their own endings. The affirmative informal commands are derived from the present indicative **tú** form minus the person ending **-s**:

present indicative	*command*	
Contestas el teléfono.	→ **Contesta** el teléfono.	*Answer the telephone.*
Vendes el coche.	→ **Vende** el coche.	*Sell the car.*
Abres la ventana.	→ **Abre** la ventana.	*Open the window.*
Sirves la cena.	→ **Sirve** la cena.	*Serve dinner.*

- Affirmative **vosotros** commands are formed by replacing the **-r** of the infinitive by **-d**. They lose their final **-d** when the reflexive pronoun **os** is attached: **Acordaos** (*Remember*). The one exception to this rule is **idos** (*go away*).

(contestar)	→ Contesta**d** el teléfono.	*Answer the telephone.*
(vender)	→ Vende**d** el coche.	*Sell the car.*
(abrir)	→ Abri**d** la ventana.	*Open the window.*
(servir)	→ Servi**d** la cena.	*Serve dinner.*
(arreglarse)	→ Arregla**os**.	*Get ready.*

F. ¡Venid a la fiesta! Vosotros estáis en España donde estáis organizando una fiesta para esta noche. Decid lo que los demás tienen que hacer usando la segunda persona del plural (*vosotros*) del imperativo.

> MODELO   preparar las ensaladas / no cocinar la carne todavía
> → **Preparad** las ensaladas, pero **no cocinéis** la carne todavía.

1. hacer la torta / no ponerle el glaseado (*icing*) todavía

2. abrir las botellas de sangría / no cortar las rebanadas (*slices*) de naranja todavía

3. sacar los platitos para las tapas / no preparar el chorizo y el pulpo todavía

4. poner la mesa / no colocar los claveles todavía

5. salir a comprar aceitunas / no ir todavía

6. destapar (*uncork*) el vino / no servirlo en un jarro todavía

7. colgar los globos / no dejarlos en la entrada

8. escoger los discos compactos / no poner música con palabrotas (*bad words*)

Nota cultural

- **La sangría** es una bebida española hecha con vino tinto, agua y azúcar a la cual se puede añadir rebanadas de naranja, durazno y otras frutas.

- **Las tapas** son bocados (*snacks*) que acompañan las bebidas en España. Algunas tapas que se sirven comúnmente son las aceitunas (*olives*), la tortilla española, el salchichón (*seasoned pork sausage*), el chorizo (*sausage seasoned with red peppers*), el pulpo en su tinta (*octopus in its ink*).

- **El clavel** (*carnation*) es una flor muy apreciada por los españoles. Hay una canción española tradicional titulada *Clavelitos*.

G. Exprese en español los siguientes mandatos usando la segunda persona del plural del imperativo (*vosotros*).

1. Be patient.
2. Go away.
3. Tell the truth.
4. Be charming.
5. Take a bath.
6. Write a short story.
7. Attend the lecture.
8. Play the piano.
9. Go to bed early.

- The following verbs have irregular affirmative **tú** commands. Note that the negative **tú** commands of these verbs are regular: they are derived from the present subjunctive forms: **no digas, no hagas, no vayas,** etc.

decir → di salir → sal
hacer → haz ser → sé
ir → ve tener → ten
poner → pon venir → ven

Note: The affirmative **tú** commands for **ir** and **ver** are the same: **ve.**

H. ¡Tengo los nervios de punta! (*I'm all on edge!*) Manuela está nerviosísima estos días por los exámenes y el trabajo, y se peleó con su novio. Dígale lo que debe hacer para calmarse usando el imperativo.

MODELO salir a divertirse
→ **Sal** a divertirte.

1. dar un paseo todos los días
2. hacer ejercicio
3. tomar una infusión de manzanilla (*chamomile tea*)
4. tranquilizarse escuchando música
5. no beber mucha cafeína
6. dormir la siesta todas las tardes
7. reunirse con los amigos
8. no preocuparse por tonterías
9. buscarse otro novio

Nota cultural

La infusión de manzanilla se toma mucho en España para curar toda clase de problemas digestivos. Se conoce como calmante natural.

I.   ¡Paquito, deja de poner el grito en el cielo! (*Paquito, stop kicking up a fuss!***)**
Ud. está cuidando a un niño malcriado (*spoiled*) que hace diabluras (*is up to mischief*). Emplee el imperativo para decirle que haga o no haga ciertas cosas.

MODELO   limpiar la mancha del jugo
→ **Limpia** la mancha del jugo.

1. portarse bien
2. no hacer payasadas (*to clown around*)
3. no ser terco
4. dejar al perro en paz (*to leave alone*)
5. recoger las migas de las galletas
6. no derramar el perfume de tu mamá
7. hacerme caso
8. no encerrarse en el baño
9. venir acá inmediatamente

J.   ¡Tito el desgraciado (*unlucky guy***)!** Todo le pasa a Tito porque tiene mala suerte.
Ayúdele a hacer o no hacer ciertas cosas con consejos escritos en imperativo.

MODELO   Tito, **mira.** (mirar)
Tito, **no corras.** (no correr)

1. Tito, _____. (darse prisa)
2. Tito, _____. (no lastimarse)
3. Tito, _____. (no cortarse el dedo)
4. Tito, _____. (tener cuidado)
5. Tito, _____. (no romperse el pie)
6. Tito, _____. (no encender los fósforos)
7. Tito, _____. (conducir más lentamente)
8. Tito, _____. (ponerse una armadura [*suit of armor*])

K.   El médico aconseja ... Carlitos se quebró el tobillo jugando al fútbol. Su mamá
lo lleva al consultorio donde el médico les da consejos a Carlitos y a su mamá.
Escriba el verbo en imperativo para expresar lo que dice el médico a la señora y
a Carlitos.

MODELO   Señora, **póngale** esta crema. (ponerle)
Carlitos, **anda** con cuidado. (andar)

Las fracturas

la quebradura *fracture, break*	**quebrarse (***e* > **ie)** *to break*
escayolado *in a plaster cast*	**el tobillo** *ankle*
la muleta *crutch*	**el vendaje** *dressing*

---

1. Señora, _____ ir al colegio. (dejarlo)

2. Carlitos, no _____ la pierna escayolada. (mojarse)

3. Señora, _____ estas pastillas si le duele el tobillo. (darle)

4. Carlitos, no _____ deportes por ahora. (jugar)

5. Señora, _____ la receta. (hacerle)

6. Carlitos, no _____ el vendaje. (quitarse)

7. Señora, _____ al consultorio la semana próxima. (traerlo)

8. Carlitos, _____ a verme el miércoles o el jueves. (venir)

9. Carlitos, _____ a la calle con muletas. (salir)

 The position of object pronouns with command forms

- Object pronouns (direct, indirect, reflexive) are placed in their usual position *before* the verb in *negative* commands.

No **lo** hagas.	*Don't do it.*
No **se lo** digas.	*Don't tell it to him.*
No **me la** traiga.	*Don't bring it to me.*
No **se** preocupen Uds.	*Please don't worry.*
No **nos** sentemos.	*Let's not sit down.*
No **te los** pongas. (los = guantes)	*Don't put them on.*

- Object pronouns *follow* affirmative commands and are attached to them. When attached, an accent mark is placed over the stressed syllable, except when a single object pronoun is added to a one-syllable command form: **dime** (*tell me*); **dímelo** (*tell me it*). However, **dé, esté,** and **está** may keep their accent marks when a single object pronoun is added: **deme** or **déme.**

Hazlo.	*Do it.*
Díselo.	*Tell it to him.*
Tráigamela.	*Bring it to me.*
Quédense Uds.	*Please stay.*
Sentémonos.	*Let's sit down.*
Póntelos. (los = guantes)	*Put them on.*

L. Sí, hágalo. Conteste las preguntas con la forma adecuada del imperativo—*Ud.,* *tú, Uds.* Cambie los sustantivos que son complementos directos a pronombres y haga todos los cambios necesarios.

> **MODELO**   ¿Quieres que yo te traiga las revistas?
> → Sí, **tráemelas.**

1. ¿Quieres que yo les dé los informes a los jefes?

2. ¿Uds. quieren que yo les mande las cartas (a Uds.)?

3. ¿Ud. necesita que le entreguemos la tarea (a Ud.)?

4. ¿Quieres que te ponga el abrigo?

5. ¿Uds. necesitan que yo les prepare los bocadillos?

6. ¿Uds. quieren que les sirvamos el postre?

7. ¿Prefieres que te explique la idea?

8. ¿A Ud. le interesa que le diga los motivos?

9. ¿Debemos enseñarle los cuadros a Pedro?

M. **No, no lo haga.** Ahora, conteste las preguntas del *ejercicio L* con imperativos negativos.

> MODELO   ¿Quieres que yo te traiga las revistas?
> → No, **no me las traigas.**

1. ¿Quieres que yo les dé los informes a los jefes?

2. ¿Uds. quieren que yo les mande las cartas (a Uds.)?

3. ¿Ud. necesita que le entreguemos la tarea (a Ud.)?

4. ¿Quieres que te ponga el abrigo?

5. ¿Uds. necesitan que yo les prepare los bocadillos?

6. ¿Uds. quieren que les sirvamos el postre?

7. ¿Prefieres que te explique la idea?

8. ¿A Ud. le interesa que le diga los motivos?

9. ¿Debemos enseñarle los cuadros a Pedro?

E *Indirect commands*

- Indirect commands in Spanish consist of **que** + present subjunctive. Object and reflexive pronouns are placed before the verb. English equivalents are *Let* or *Have him/her/it/them do something*. Sometimes *I hope* is suggested in these sentences:

Que pase.	*Have him come in.*
Que espere.	*Let her wait.*
Que me llamen.	*Have them call me.*
Que se matriculen.	*Let them register.*
Que no se lo dé.	*Don't let him give it to them.*

- Subject pronouns are added to indirect commands for emphasis: Que lo haga **él.** (*Let **him** do it.*)

- Indirect commands of **se** constructions with indirect object pronouns (see Chapter 19—Unplanned occurrences) are usually the equivalents of regular commands in English. For example: **Que no se te olvide** el carnet (*Don't forget your driver's license*) or **Que no se les acaben** los cheques de viajero (*I hope you don't run out of traveler's checks*).

N. **¡Que lo hagan los otros!** Rosario se niega a colaborar con sus compañeros de clase en el proyecto de ciencias. Incluso manda que los amigos se ocupen de todo. Escriba lo que Rosario propone que los otros hagan, usando el imperativo indirecto.

> MODELO   No quiero participar en el proyecto. (los demás)
> → **Que participen** los demás.

1. No voy a leer los libros de consulta (*reference books*). (Manolo)

2. No me interesa dibujar tablas (*charts*). (Terencio y Elena)

3. No quiero observar los experimentos en el laboratorio. (Paulina)

4. Me niego a hacer los gráficos (*plot graphs*). (los otros)

5. No tengo ganas de investigar estas teorías. (Samuel)

6. No quiero dedicarme a las ciencias. (mis amigos)

7. No pienso escribir un informe. (Federico)

O. Exprese los siguientes mandatos indirectos en español.

1. Have her give it to you. (it = *el cheque*, to you = *a Ud.*)

2. Let them go away.

3. Have him send them to her. (them = *las tarjetas*)

4. I hope you don't lose your wallet. (use **se** construction with indirect object pronoun, you = *tú*)

5. Let them come back in the afternoon.

6. I hope you don't run out of soft drinks. (use **se** construction with indirect object pronoun; you = *Uds.*)

F Other ways of giving commands

- Often in newspaper ads for employment, recipes, notices, instructions, etc., the infinitive of the verb is used as an imperative rather than the command form:

Interesados **mandar** currículum vitae.	*Interested persons, **send** your curriculum vitae.*
Enviar historial con fotografía a …	*Send résumé with photograph to …*
Interesados **llamar** al teléfono …	*Interested persons, **call** …*
Secar las berenjenas, **pasarlas** por harina y **freírlas** en aceite hirviendo.	*Dry the eggplants, **dip them** into flour and **fry them** in boiling oil.*

- The infinitive rather than the command form is used with the following expressions that convey formality and politeness. They are the English equivalent of asking something with *please:*

Favor de llamarme mañana.	*Please call me tomorrow.*
Favor de esperar.	*Please wait.*
Tenga la bondad de sentarse.	*Please sit down.*
Haga el favor de firmar el documento.	*Please sign the paper.*
Hágame el favor de enviar el cheque.	*Please send the check.*

P. Libro de cocina. Escriba los siguientes verbos en imperativo como infinitivos.

      MODELO   Limpie el pollo.
                   → **Limpiar** el pollo.

1. Córtelos a tiritas (*in strips*).
2. Añada el vino.
3. Déjelo evaporar.
4. Pártalos en trozos.
5. Tape las patatas.
6. Seque los tomates.
7. Añádalas a la salsa.
8. Remuévalo (*stir*).
9. Póngala en una fuente (*serving dish*).

Q. El primer día de clase. El profesor de español les dice a sus estudiantes que hagan unas cosas. Escriba los verbos en imperativo como infinitivos usando las expresiones que aparecen entre paréntesis.

      MODELO   Estudien el primer capítulo. (favor de)
                   → **Favor de estudiar** el primer capítulo.

1. Vayan al laboratorio de lenguas. (hagan el favor de)
2. Aprendan los diálogos de memoria. (tengan la bondad de)
3. Traigan el diccionario. (favor de)
4. Matricúlense si no lo han hecho. (tengan la bondad de)
5. Compren el libro de texto y el cuaderno de trabajo. (háganme el favor de)

6. Apúntense en esta lista. (favor de)

7. Hagan hincapié (*emphasize*) en los ejercicios de fonética todos los días. (hagan el favor de)

8. No actúen mucho en grupo. (tengan la bondad de)

9. Vean películas y lean periódicos en español. (favor de)

R. Busque empleo. Complete los siguientes anuncios de periódico para empleos con los mandatos que faltan. Use el infinitivo en cada caso. Elija entre: **enviar, dirigirse, llamar, mandar, concertar, remitir, escribir, ponerse en contacto, adjuntar, presentarse.**

MODELO   Interesados **enviar** curriculum vitae. (*send*)

1. Interesados _____ lunes día 3 al teléfono 91-742-42-63. (*call*)

2. _____ historial y fotografía al Apto. (apartado = *box*) 36492, 28080 Madrid. (*Send*)

3. Interesados _____ a: ARA Publicidad, 08008 Barcelona. (*write*)

4. Interesados _____, lunes 3 de 9,30 a 14 horas y de 15,30 a 17,30 horas, en C/Alcalá, 54, Srta. Núñez. (*apply*)

5. Interesados _____ a: PAR-7. Avda. del Mediterráneo, 22, 28007 Madrid. (*go to*)

6. Interesados _____ fotografía reciente al apartado de Correos número 2.059 de Madrid. (*attach*)

7. Los interesados deben _____ con Ignacio Doncel llamando de 9 a 14 horas y de 16 a 18 horas al teléfono (91) 585-83-64. (*get in touch*)

8. Las personas interesadas, _____ entrevista en el teléfono (91) 653-95-00. (*arrange*)

S. Ejercicio oral. Escenas de teatro. Sus amigos y Ud. crean escenas en las cuales los personajes emplean el imperativo. Por ejemplo: en el consultorio, el médico aconseja a sus pacientes sobre sus problemas de salud; en la oficina, un programador le enseña a un compañero cómo hacer funcionar la computadora; en casa, los padres les dicen a sus hijos que arreglen su cuarto.

T. Estructuras en acción. Lea los siguientes anuncios de periódicos y haga el ejercicio.

A.

> **No permitas que dejen sin bosques a tu hijo.** Por sólo 3.000 Ptas., hazle socio del Club del Árbol. Plantaremos un árbol en su nombre, en la Comunidad de Madrid. Planta un árbol para tu hijo. Llámanos al (91) 308 23 09 para más información. Regálale un árbol.

B.

> BELLSOUTH CELULAR (CHILE)
>
> **Aproveche los precios de otoño.** No se pierda esta oportunidad. Compre ahora su celular y pague el equipo en julio a precio contado. Exija su casilla (*box*) de mensajes gratis. Llame hoy mismo al 339-5050.

C.

> **Acer ¡No se la pierda!**
>
> ¡Nuestra experiencia de 15 años es su garantía! Surtimos (*we supply*) a toda la República.
>
> Llame primero a: Asesoría en Cómputo, S.A.
>
> Visítenos en el stand 104 de la Feria de la ciudad de México 12:00 a 9:00 P.M., 16 de abril.

D.

> **AMERICAN LANGUAGE COMMUNICATION CENTER**
>
> **APRENDA INGLÉS de una manera rápida, fácil y divertida.** ¡Mejore sus oportunidades y obtenga una vida mejor en Nueva York! Certificado por el departamento de educación del estado de Nueva York.
>
> ¡Matricúlese ahora y reciba una semana gratis!
>
> ¡Llame hoy! Pregunte por María. (212) 736-2373

En una hoja de papel, escriba las formas del imperativo que aparecen en los anuncios y tradúzcalas al inglés.

CHAPTER 15
THE INFINITIVE

 A *The conjugated verb + infinitive*

- In Spanish, an important function of the infinitive of the verb is to serve as a complement or completion form in verb + infinitive constructions. The conjugated verb can be followed directly by an infinitive:

Debe cursar durante el verano.	*He should take courses during the summer.*
Necesitamos tomar una decisión.	*We had to make a decision.*
Querían salir a cenar.	*They wanted to go out to have dinner.*
¿Has podido encontrarlos?	*Have you been able to find them?*
Prefiero ir al concierto.	*I prefer to go to the concert.*
Procure llegar para las siete.	*Try to arrive by seven o'clock.*
Creo poder tenerlo listo para mañana.	*I think I can have it ready for tomorrow.*

These verbs may be followed directly by an infinitive:

conseguir (e > i) *to succeed in, manage to*
creer *to think, believe*
deber *should, ought to*
decidir *to decide*
dejar *to let, allow*
desear *to want*
esperar *to hope, expect, wait*
hacer *to make*
impedir (e > i) *to prevent from*
intentar *to try to*
lograr *to succeed in*
mandar *to order to*

merecer *to deserve to*
necesitar *to need, have to*
ofrecer *to offer*
oír *to hear*
olvidar *to forget*
ordenar *to order*
parecer *to seem to*
pensar (e > ie) *to intend*
permitir *to allow*
poder (o > ue) *can, to be able to*
preferir (e > ie) *to prefer*
pretender *to try to*
procurar *to try to*
prohibir *to prohibit*

prometer *to promise to*
querer (e > ie) *to want*
recordar (o > ue) *to remember to*
resolver (o > ue) *to resolve to*
saber *to know how to*
sentir (e > ie) *to regret, be sorry*
soler (o > ue) *to be used to, accustomed to*
temer *to be afraid to*
ver *to see*

A. Fiestas y celebraciones. Practique la construcción del verbo conjugado + infinitivo. Desarrolle unas nuevas oraciones añadiendo a las oraciones originales los verbos que aparecen entre paréntesis. Guarde el tiempo verbal de la oración original.

> MODELO   Los Arriaga pasan la Nochebuena en casa. (preferir)
> → Los Arriaga **prefieren pasar** la Nochebuena en casa.

1. Los españoles celebraron el santo del Rey Juan Carlos el 24 de junio. (querer)

2. Uds. siempre iban de vacaciones en Semana Santa. (procurar)

3. Paco no salió con su novia el Día de los Enamorados. (poder)

4. Comes una uva por cada campanada (*bell ringing*) el 31 de diciembre. (soler)

5. Raúl y Pepita no asistieron a la Misa del Gallo este año. (conseguir)

6. Los niñitos recibían muchos regalos lindos el Día de Reyes. (esperar)

7. No gastas bromas el Día de los Inocentes. (resolver)

8. Hay unas fiestas grandes el Día de la Raza. (deber)

9. Les traje flores y bombones a los tíos por el Año Nuevo. (decidir)

Nota cultural

- **La Nochebuena,** es decir, el 24 de diciembre, se celebra en todos los países hispánicos. Las familias suelen festejarla con una cena tradicional. Muchas personas van a la **Misa del Gallo** a las doce de la noche.

- Para el 31 de diciembre, **el Fin de Año,** cuando se oyen las campanadas a las doce de la noche, la gente come una uva por cada campanada. ¡Así asegura la buena suerte para el año nuevo!

- El 6 de enero es la Epifanía o **el Día de Reyes.** Este día, cuando los Reyes Magos (*Magi*) les traen regalos a los niños, señala el fin de las fiestas de Navidad.

- **Semana Santa** es el período de la Pascua Florida (*Easter*) cuando mucha gente toma sus vacaciones.

- **El Día de la Raza (o el Día de la Hispanidad)** se celebra el 12 de octubre en el mundo hispánico y coincide con el Día de Cristóbal Colón en los Estados Unidos.

- Para muchas personas hispánicas **el santo** es más importante que el cumpleaños. Hay gente que celebra las dos cosas. En España, el 24 de junio es el día de San Juan y también se celebra el santo del Rey Juan Carlos.

- **El Día de los Enamorados** se celebra en el mundo hispánico el 14 de febrero tanto como el Día de San Valentín en los Estados Unidos.

- **El Día de los Inocentes** se celebra en los Estados Unidos como *April Fool's Day*.

B. Expansión de oraciones. Practique la construcción del verbo conjugado
+ infinitivo. Desarrolle unas nuevas oraciones añadiendo a las oraciones
originales los verbos que aparecen entre paréntesis. Guarde el tiempo verbal
de la oración original.

> MODELO   Sirvió la comida. (mandar)
> → **Mandó servir** la comida.

1. Nadaban muy bien. (saber)

2. Ud. ganó más plata. (merecer)

3. Terminé el proyecto. (lograr)

4. Felipe está solo en la casa. (temer)

5. Se sale por esa puerta. (prohibir)

6. Han tocado un vals. (ofrecer)

7. Limpiábamos la casa. (hacer)

8. No escuchaste los discos compactos. (dejar)

B *The conjugated verb + preposition + infinitive*

- Some verbs require a preposition before an infinitive. The most common
  prepositions are **a** and **de,** but some verbs require **en** or **por:**

Van a pedir paella.	*They're going to order paella.*
Comenzó a llover hace media hora.	*It began to rain half an hour ago.*
Yo me encargué de hacer las investigaciones.	*I took charge of doing the research.*
No insistas en sentarte en la primera fila.	*Don't insist on sitting in the first row.*
¿Uds. no se interesaban por coleccionar sellos?	*Weren't you interested in collecting stamps?*

The following verbs take **a** before an infinitive:

acercarse a *to approach*	**dedicarse a** *to devote oneself to*	**llevar a** *to lead to*
acostumbrarse a *to be accustomed to*	**disponerse a** *to get ready to*	**meterse a** *to start to*
animar a *to encourage to*		**negarse a (e > ie)** *to refuse to*
aprender a *to learn to*	**echar(se) a** *to begin to*	**obligar a** *to force, compel to*
atreverse a *to dare to*	**empezar a (e > ie)** *to begin to*	
ayudar a *to help*		**persuadir a** *to persuade*
bajar a *to go down to*	**enseñar a** *to show how, teach to*	**ponerse a** *to begin to*
comenzar a (e > ie) *to begin to*	**invitar a** *to invite to*	**prepararse a** *to get ready to*
cuidar a/de *to take care of*	**ir a** *to be going to*	**renunciar a** *to renounce*
decidirse a *to decide to*	**llegar a** *to get to, succeed in*	**volver a (o > ue)** *to do (something) again*

Some examples:

—¿Te decidiste **a** seguir trabajando
en esta oficina?

*Did you make up your mind to continue
working in this office?*

—Sí. Ya me he acostumbrado **a**
trabajar aquí.

*Yes. I've already gotten used to working
here.*

—Mañana empiezo **a** estudiar en
serio.

Tomorrow I'll start studying seriously.

—Yo también debo ponerme **a**
trabajar.

I also ought to begin working.

—¿Volvieron **a** pedirte dinero?

Did they ask you for money again?

—No. No se atrevieron **a** pedirme
nada.

No. They didn't dare ask me for anything.

- After verbs of motion **a** indicates the purpose of the action:

Bajo/Subo **a** ayudarte.

*I'm coming downstairs/upstairs (in order)
to help you.*

The following verbs take **de** before an infinitive:

acabar de *to have just (done something)*	**encargarse de** *to take charge of*
acordarse de (o > ue) *to remember*	**jactarse de** *to boast of*
arrepentirse de (e > ie) *to regret*	**olvidarse de** *to forget*
avergonzarse de (o > üe) *to be ashamed of*	**presumir de** *to boast about*
cuidar de/a *to take care of*	**terminar de** *to stop*
dejar de *to stop*	**tratar de** *to try to*

—No te olvides **de** venir a cenar el
jueves.

*Don't forget to come have dinner on
Thursday.*

—No te preocupes. Acabo **de** anotar
el día y la hora.

*Don't worry. I've just written down the day
and the hour.*

The following verbs take **en** before an infinitive:

consentir en (e > ie) *to consent, agree to*	**interesarse en/por** *to be interested in*
consistir en *to consist of*	**quedar en** *to agree to*
dudar en *to hesitate over*	**tardar en** *to delay in, be long in*
empeñarse en *to insist on, be determined to*	**vacilar en** *to hesitate over*
insistir en *to insist on*	

—Carlos se interesa mucho **en**
hablarme.

Carlos is very interested in talking to me.

—¿Consentiste **en** verlo?

Did you consent to see him?

—Sí. Quedamos **en** vernos mañana.

Yes. We agreed to see each other tomorrow.

The following verbs take **con** before an infinitive:

amenazar con *to threaten to*	**soñar con (o > ue)** *to dream of, about*
contar con (o > ue) *to count on, rely on*	

—En vez de trabajar, Juanita sueña todo el día **con** hacerse actriz.

Instead of working, Juanita dreams all day of becoming an actress.

—Por eso el jefe amenazó **con** despedirla.

That's why the boss threatened to fire her.

- The verb **tener** is followed by **que** before an infinitive. **Tener que** means *to have to do something*:

Teníamos que estacionar el coche.

We had to *park the car.*

- Many of the above verbs take the same preposition before a noun object as well:

—¿Se dedica la señora Gómez **a su familia**?

Does Mrs. Gómez devote herself to her family?

—Sí, se encarga **de la casa** y **de sus hijos**.

Yes, she's in charge of the house and her children.

C. ¿Qué hacen los estudiantes? Practique el uso de las preposiciones. Complete cada oración con la preposición correcta.

MODELO   Empiezan **a** estudiar francés.

1. Ricardo se prepara _____ tomar los exámenes.

2. Carolina y Miguel quedaron _____ verse en la clase de física.

3. Jorge se empeña _____ sacar buenas notas este semestre.

4. Isabel se ha dedicado _____ hacer investigaciones.

5. Marco presume _____ saberlo todo.

6. Fernanda volverá _____ cursar biología.

7. Uds. se interesan _____ leer literatura inglesa.

8. Tú y yo nos encargaremos _____ organizar los archivos.

9. Pablo sueña _____ graduarse el año que viene.

10. Teresa se decidió _____ matricularse en la escuela de verano.

11. Yo trato _____ ir a la biblioteca todas las tardes.

12. Pancho cuenta _____ terminar la carrera (*course of study*) este año.

13. Julia y Lorenzo acaban _____ completar sus requisitos (*requirements*).

14. Nosotros tendríamos _____ buscar otras optativas (*electives*).

D. Exprese las siguientes oraciones en español.

1. We were accustomed to having dinner at 9:00 P.M.

2. Why did they take so long in calling us?

3. Esteban refused to lend Diego money.

4. Try to pay with a credit card. (you = Ud.)

5. Sing that song again. (you = Uds.)

6. I'm going to attend the lecture.

7. Silvia threatened to leave immediately.

8. They dream about becoming millionaires!

E. Sinónimos. Escoja un sinónimo de las listas de verbos con y sin preposiciones para cada expresión escrita en bastardilla (*italics*).

> MODELO   Los miembros del comité *acuerdan* reunirse el martes.
> → Los miembros del comité **convienen en** reunirse el martes.

1. Pedro *logró* hacerse presidente de la empresa.

2. Consuelo *se jacta de* ser la mejor futbolista del equipo.

3. Los Arcos *se prepararán a* recibir a sus tíos.

4. El profesor *mandó* cerrar los libros.

5. Uds. *sintieron* perderse la boda.

6. Yo no *recordé* recoger los pasteles.

7. ¿Cómo es que *te pusiste a* hacer la tarea a las dos de la mañana?

8. No se *dejaba* entrar en las salas de escultura.

9. Están *dudando en* invertir dinero en la compañía.

C The infinitive after prepositions

- The infinitive can be used after many prepositions, such as: **a, al, antes de, a pesar de, con el objeto de, con tal de, después de, en caso de, en lugar de, en vez de, hasta, para, por, sin.**

Almorcemos **después de montar** en bicicleta.	*Let's have lunch after we go for a bicycle ride.*
Estudie más **para aprender** más.	*Study more (in order) to learn more.*
Me alegré **al oír** la buena noticia.	*I became happy when I heard the good news.*
Mario irá **con tal de ver** a Susana.	*Mario will go provided that he sees Susana.*
Llenen el formulario **antes de firmarlo.**	*Fill out the form before you sign it.*
¿Entraste **sin vernos**?	*Did you come in without seeing us?*

F. Exprese las siguientes oraciones en español. Use el infinitivo después de ciertas preposiciones.

1. We'll call you before we go out. (*tú*)

2. They traveled to Ponce by car without stopping.

3. Children, go to bed after you brush your teeth. (*Uds.*)

4. Bernardo should read a book instead of watching television.

5. I'll be in the library until I come home.

6. Elena will skate provided that Daniel skates too.

7. Invite them in case you see them. (*Ud.*)

8. When we got to the party we started to dance.

Nota cultural

Ponce, ciudad de Puerto Rico, es un puerto en el Caribe. Es un centro de las industrias petrolera, agrícola, textil y del cemento. Ponce tiene una universidad y un museo de arte.

D *The infinitive after verbs of perception*

- The infinitive is used after verbs of perception such as **ver** and **oír** to signal a completed action. The gerund rather than the infinitive is used to show an incomplete or in-progress action:

Los **oí cantar.**	*I heard them sing.*
¿Uds. no nos **vieron entrar?**	*Didn't you see us come in?*

G. ¿Qué oyó? Lorenzo tiene problema del oído y va con un audioprotesista (*hearing aid specialist*) porque necesita un aparato. El especialista le pregunta lo que oyó.

> **MODELO** ¿Oyó Ud. el ruido de los coches? (frenar [*to brake*])
> ➔ Sí, los oí frenar.

1. ¿Oyó Ud. el trueno? (retumbar [*to thunder*])

2. ¿Oyó Ud. el maullido del gato? (maullar [*to meow*])

3. ¿Oyó Ud. el despegue y el aterrizaje de los aviones? (despegar [*to take off*] y aterrizar [*to land*])

4. ¿Oyó Ud. el susurro de las hojas? (susurrar [*to whisper*])

5. ¿Oyó Ud. los gritos de sus hijos? (gritar)

6. ¿Oyó Ud. los ronquidos de su mujer? (roncar [*to snore*])

H. ¿Qué vieron Uds.? Forme oraciones usando **ver,** un verbo de percepción.

> **MODELO** María / bailar
> ➔ La vimos bailar.

1. José y Pablo / trotar

2. Anita y Rosita / hacer los bocadillos

3. Roberto / entrar en la discoteca

4. la señorita Barba / dictar una conferencia

E The infinitive preceded by *que*

- The infinitive is often preceded by **que**. However, the **que** + infinitive construction cannot be used with verbs of searching, needing, and requesting:

Me queda mucho **que hacer.**	*I have a lot left to do.*
Nos han dado tantas cosas **que/para hacer.**	*They've given us so many things to do.*
Compra algo **que/para leer.**	*Buy something to read.*
Pidió algo **para aplacar** su sed.	*He ordered something to slake his thirst.*
Queríamos algo **para comer.**	*We wanted something to eat.*

I. Complete las siguientes oraciones escogiendo **que** o **para** antes del infinitivo como sea necesario.

1. Teníamos mucho _____ hacer.

2. Están buscando algo _____ comer.

3. Compraré algo _____ leer.

4. Hay muchas cosas _____ ver.

F Adjective + *de* + infinitive

- The construction adjective + **de** + infinitive is used when the infinitive of a transitive verb is not followed by an object or a clause. The **de** is omitted when an object or a clause appears:

El vasco es muy difícil **de** aprender.	*Basque is very difficult to learn.*
Es muy difícil aprender vasco.	*It's very difficult to learn Basque.*
Su teoría es imposible **de** comprobar.	*His theory is impossible to prove.*
Es imposible comprobar su teoría.	*It's impossible to prove his theory.*

J. Complete las siguientes oraciones escribiendo **de** antes del infinitivo cuando sea necesario. Si no es necesario, escriba una X.

1. No es posible _____ comprenderlo.

2. Eso es fácil _____ ver.

3. Es triste _____ pensar que ya no vuelven.

4. El japonés no es difícil _____ aprender.

K. **Ejercicio oral. Juego de expansión de oraciones.** Se juega entre dos equipos. Uno de los equipos da una oración y un verbo para expandirla al otro equipo como en el *ejercicio B* de este capítulo. Se juega hasta que uno de los equipos tenga 20 puntos.

PART TWO

Nouns and Their Modifiers; Pronouns

CHAPTER 16
NOUNS & ARTICLES

 A *Gender of nouns*

- In Spanish, all nouns are either masculine or feminine. There are some clues to the gender of nouns.

- Most nouns that end in **-o** or that refer to males are masculine:

el libro	el hijo	el hombre
el banco	el señor	el duque
el laboratorio	el profesor	el toro
el padre	el doctor	el piano

- Most nouns that end in **-a** or that refer to females are feminine:

la revista	la hija	la duquesa
la librería	la señora	la vaca
la oficina	la profesora	la cartera
la madre	la mujer	la flauta

- There are many nouns that end in **-a** and **-ma** that are masculine and some nouns that end in **-o** that are feminine. The gender of these words must be memorized:

masculine

el día	el mediodía	el problema
el mapa	el idioma	el programa
el tranvía	el planeta	el sistema
el panda	el clima	el poema

feminine
la mano
la radio
la foto (*abbreviation of* la fotografía)
la moto (*abbreviation of* la motocicleta)

- The gender of most nouns that end in **-e** or a consonant cannot be predicted and must therefore be memorized:

masculine

el lápiz	el examen	el jarabe (*syrup*)
el papel	el buzón (*mailbox*)	el desván (*attic*)
el arroz (*rice*)	el cobre (*copper*)	el alfiler (*pin*)
el aceite (*oil*)	el disfraz (*disguise*)	el cine

feminine

la clase	la llave	la piel (*skin*)
la gente	la torre (*tower*)	la luz

- Nouns that have endings in **-dad, -tad, -tud, -umbre, -ión, -ie, -cia, -ez, -eza, -nza, -sis,** and **-itis** are usually feminine:

la ciudad	la serie (*series*)
la verdad	la superficie (*surface*)
la felicidad (*happiness*)	la presencia (*presence*)
la libertad	la diferencia
la fraternidad	la sencillez (*simplicity*)
la juventud (*youth*)	la pereza (*laziness*)
la multitud	la esperanza (*hope*)
la cumbre ([*mountain*] *top*)	la tesis (*thesis*)
la certidumbre (*certainty*)	la crisis
la nación	la faringitis (*pharyngitis*)
la reunión (*meeting*)	

- Nouns that refer to people (and some animals) that end in **-or, -és, -ón,** and **-ín** are usually masculine and add **-a** to make the feminine form. The accent mark of the masculine form is dropped in the feminine:

masculine	*feminine*
el doctor	la doctora
el profesor	la profesora
el francés	la francesa
el anfitrión (*host*)	la anfitriona (*hostess*)
el campeón (*champion*)	la campeona
el león (*lion*)	la leona (*lioness*)
el bailarín (*dancer*)	la bailarina (*dancer*)

- Nouns that end in **-aje, -ambre, -or, -án,** or a stressed vowel are usually masculine:

el equipaje (*luggage*)	el amor
el paisaje (*landscape*)	el refrán (*proverb*)
el calambre (*cramp*)	el champú (*shampoo*)
el enjambre (*swarm* [*of bees, etc.*])	el rubí (*ruby*)
el valor (*value*)	

- In forming the feminine, some nouns that refer to people (or some animals) change only their article but not their form. Many of these nouns end in **-e, -a, -ista, -nte,** or a consonant:

el/la joven (*young man/woman*)	el/la artista
el/la líder (*leader*)	el/la turista
el/la intérprete (*interpreter*)	el/la agente
el/la atleta (*athlete*)	el/la cantante
el/la mártir (*martyr*)	el/la dependiente
el/la tigre (*tiger* [*also, tigresa*])	el/la estudiante
el/la dentista	

A feminine form ending in **-nta** is common: **la dependienta, la estudianta.**

- The days of the week are masculine:

Iremos a la sierra **el jueves** y volveremos **el lunes.**	*We'll go to the mountains on Thursday and we'll come back on Monday.*

- The months of the year are masculine:

el enero más frío	*the coldest January*
el agosto más caluroso	*the hottest August*

- The names of languages are masculine:

El español se habla en veinte países.	*Spanish is spoken in twenty countries.*
El inglés es la lengua de muchos países también.	*English is the language of many countries also.*

- Compound nouns that consist of a verb and a noun are masculine:

el paraguas	*umbrella*	el limpiacristales	*window cleaner*
el lavaplatos	*dishwasher*	el tocadiscos	*record player*
el salvavidas	*lifeguard, life preserver*	el sacacorchos	*corkscrew*
el parachoques	*bumper*		

- Numbers (*el número*) are masculine:

El veintisiete de enero es el cumpleaños de Mozart.	*January 27 is Mozart's birthday.*
Mi número de suerte es **el 15.**	*My lucky number is 15.*

- Colors are masculine when used as nouns:

Me gusta **el azul** más que **el marrón.**	*I like blue more than brown.*

- Many names of trees are masculine while their fruit is feminine:

el árbol		*la fruta*
el almendro	*almond tree*	la almendra
el castaño	*chestnut tree*	la castaña
el cerezo	*cherry tree*	la cereza
el manzano	*apple tree*	la manzana
el naranjo	*orange tree*	la naranja
el peral	*pear tree*	la pera

- All infinitives used as nouns are masculine:

El fumar hace daño.	***Smoking** is harmful.*

- Nouns that begin with stressed **a** or **ha** are feminine but take the masculine article in the singular, but **las** in the plural:

el agua	*water*	el hambre	*hunger*
el águila	*eagle*	el hacha	*hatchet*
el ave	*bird*		

el agua fría del lago	*the cold water of the lake*
las aguas tibias del Caribe	*the warm waters of the Caribbean*

- The names of rivers, seas, and oceans are masculine:

Los Estados Unidos tiene costa en **el (océano) Atlántico** y **el Pacífico.**	*The United States has coasts on the Atlantic Ocean and on the Pacific.*
El (río) Amazonas atraviesa el Brasil.	*The Amazon River passes through Brazil.*

- Some Spanish nouns have both a masculine and feminine gender, but with a difference in meaning:

masculine		*feminine*	
el capital	*money*	la capital	*capital city*
el mañana	*tomorrow*	la mañana	*morning*
el frente	*front (weather, military)*	la frente	*forehead*
el orden	*order (tidiness)*	la orden	*order (command)*
el policía	*policeman*	la policía	*policewoman, police force*

- The word **arte** is masculine in the singular but feminine in the plural:

el arte español	*Spanish art*
las bellas artes	*fine arts*

- Foreign words that enter Spanish, usually from English, are almost always masculine. Some words remain feminine when borrowed into Spanish:

el jazz
el marketing
el (e)spray   *aerosol*
el campus
el/la cassette   *cassette player/cassette tape*

- Some nouns do not vary in gender and are applied to males and females, in some cases with a change in article:

el ángel
el bebé
la persona
el personaje   *character (in a book, play)*
la víctima
el/la testigo   *witness*
el/la modelo

Thus you say **Juan fue *la* víctima más joven del accidente** but **Marta es *la* testigo más importante.**

- Sometimes an inanimate feminine noun can be applied to a male person with a change in meaning. In this case, the new noun is masculine:

la cámara	*camera*	**el** cámara	*cameraman*
la trompeta	*trumpet*	**el** trompeta	*trumpet player*
las medias	*socks*	**los** Medias Rojas	*the Red Sox*

A. ¿Masculino o femenino? Escriba la forma masculina o femenina del artículo definido para cada sustantivo de la lista.

1. _____ concierto
2. _____ sistema
3. _____ escritor
4. _____ tierra
5. _____ drama
6. _____ mano
7. _____ natación
8. _____ día
9. _____ natalidad (*birthrate*)
10. _____ parque
11. _____ legumbre
12. _____ guión (*script*)
13. _____ capital (*capital city*)

14. _____ pararrayos (*lightning rod*)
15. _____ computadora
16. _____ seguridad (*security*)
17. _____ rompecabezas (*riddle*)
18. _____ idioma
19. _____ dirección (*address*)
20. _____ escocés
21. _____ banano
22. _____ verde
23. _____ frente (*forehead*)
24. _____ ascensor
25. _____ parabrisas (*windshield*)

B. Por parejas. Escriba quién es la pareja femenina (*counterpart*) de cada hombre. Practique usando la forma femenina de los sustantivos. Escriba el artículo también.

1. el profesor / _____
2. el rey / _____
3. el artista / _____
4. el abogado / _____
5. el príncipe / _____
6. el gobernador / _____
7. el representante / _____
8. el policía / _____

9. el emperador / _____
10. el actor / _____
11. el estadista (*statesman*) / _____
12. el holandés (*Dutchman*) / _____
13. el cliente / _____
14. el atleta / _____
15. el programador / _____

C. Exprese las siguientes oraciones en español.

1. Mr. Galíndez is leaving on a business trip on Tuesday and will return on Thursday.

2. Don't put the frying pan in the dishwasher. (*Ud.*)

3. English and French are the official languages of Canada.

4. Beethoven was born on December 16, 1770.

5. My favorite colors are green and blue.

6. Let's pick apples from that (apple) tree.

7. The official bird of the United States is the eagle.

8. Did they like the cruise (*crucero*) in the Mediterranean or the Caribbean better?

9. Reading is so pleasant.

10. A tropical front will arrive tomorrow.

11. We'll invest our capital in an international company.

12. What are the names of the characters in the novel?

13. The cameraman lost his camera.

14. In the film we saw, the angels saved the baby.

15. The witnesses talked to the victim of the accident.

B   *Number of nouns*

- In Spanish, nouns that end in a vowel form the plural by adding **-s**:

singular	*plural*
el hermano	los hermanos
el espejo *mirror*	los espejos
la carretera *highway*	las carreteras
la placa *license plate*	las placas
el clarinete	los clarinetes
el café	los cafés

- Nouns that end in a consonant, including **y**, form the plural by adding **-es**:

el titular *headline*	los titulares
la ley *law*	las leyes
el huracán *hurricane*	los huracanes
el peatón *pedestrian*	los peatones
el limón	los limones
la opinión	las opiniones
el inglés	los ingleses
el mes	los meses
el país	los países
el pez *fish*	los peces
la voz *voice*	las voces
el lápiz	los lápices
el examen	los exámenes
el origen	los orígenes

Notes on the formation of the plural:

Nouns stressed on the last syllable in the singular lose their accent mark in the plural: **limón ➜ limones, inglés ➜ ingleses, autobús ➜ autobuses.** Exception: **país ➜ países.**

Lápices and all nouns that have a written accent on the next to the last syllable in the singular retain that accent in the plural: **azúcar ➜ azúcares.**

Examen and **origen** add an accent mark in the plural: **exámenes, orígenes.**

A few common nouns shift their stress in the plural: **el carácter → los caracteres, el régimen → los regímenes, el espécimen → los especímenes.**

When **-es** is added to final **z**, the **z** is changed to **c: pez → peces, voz → voces, lápiz → lápices.**

Nouns that end in a stressed **-í** or **-ú** add **-es** to form the plural: **el rubí → los rubíes, el tabú → los tabúes.**

Nouns of more than one syllable ending in an unstressed vowel plus **s** do not add a plural ending:

el viernes	→	los viernes
el miércoles	→	los miércoles
la crisis	→	las crisis
el atlas	→	los atlas
el paraguas	→	los paraguas
el abrelatas *can opener*	→	los abrelatas

- The masculine plural of nouns referring to people includes both males and females:

  los hijos   *children, sons and daughters*
  los hermanos   *brothers and sisters*
  los Reyes de España   *The King and Queen of Spain*

- If a proper name refers to a family, it has no plural form. If a group of individuals happen to have the same name, a plural form is used. Names that end in **-z** are usually invariable:

Los Prado viven en esta calle.	*The Prado family lives on this street.*
La guía telefónica tiene tantos **Morelos** y **Blancos.**	*The telephone book has so many Morelos and Blancos (people named Morelo and Blanco).*
¿No conoces a **los Fernández**?	*Don't you know the Fernándezes?*

- Some nouns are always plural in Spanish as they are in English:

  los anteojos   *eyeglasses*
  las gafas   *eyeglasses*
  los gemelos   *twins, binoculars, cuff links*
  las tijeras   *scissors*
  los auriculares   *earphones*

- Some nouns are usually plural in Spanish. Many of them appear in set expressions, for example: **hacerle cosquillas a alguien** *to tickle someone.*

  las vacaciones   *vacation*
  los bienes   *goods*
  las afueras   *outskirts*
  los alrededores   *surroundings*
  las cosquillas   *tickling*
  las ganas   *urge, desire*

  Note that **las ganas** appears in singular in **No me da la gana** *I don't feel like it.*

- The Spanish equivalent of *They washed their hair* is **Se lavaron la cabeza.** Notice that Spanish uses the singular noun **la cabeza** implying there is one for each person.

Se cortaron **la rodilla.**	*They cut their knees.*
Se pusieron **la chaqueta.**	*They put on their jackets.*
¿Tienen Uds. **novia**?	*Do you have girlfriends?*

D. En plural. Escriba la forma en plural de estos sustantivos y de su artículo.

1. el guante
2. el lavaplatos
3. la religión
4. el origen
5. el pizarrón
6. el color
7. la amistad
8. el rey
9. la tos
10. el martes
11. el irlandés
12. el paréntesis
13. el señor Sánchez
14. la luz
15. el té

E. El arca de Noé. ¡No se olvide que hay dos animales de cada especie que suben al arca de Noé! Practique usando el plural de los sustantivos.

Modelo   caballo **caballos**

1. vaca
2. orangután
3. elefante
4. avestruz (*ostrich*)
5. león
6. castor (*beaver*)
7. loro (*parrot*)
8. cóndor
9. delfín (*dolphin*)
10. gorrión (*sparrow*)
11. faisán (*pheasant*)
12. pantera (*panther*)
13. tigre
14. oveja
15. mono (*monkey*)

F. Sobre gustos no hay nada escrito. (*Everyone to his/her own taste.*) Escriba oraciones en las cuales Ud. explica lo que le gusta comer a cada persona. Cambie el sustantivo (la comida) al plural.

Modelo   Carlos / comer / haba (*beans*)
→ Carlos come **habas.**

1. Lucía / pedir / guisante (*peas*)
2. yo / preferir / el espárrago (*asparagus*)
3. tú / ordenar / papa frita
4. Claudia y Jesús / querer / macarrón (*macaroni*)
5. nosotros / tener ganas de comer / espinaca

6. Ud. y Lourdes / pedir / frijol

7. Ud. / querer / palomita de maíz

Nota cultural

Los frijoles (*kidney beans*), alimento básico de la dieta mexicana, es la misma planta que cultivaron los indios precolombinos de México. Los frijoles se comen en muchos platos en todos los países hispanoamericanos. En España se llaman judías o alubias. La papa (la patata en España), indígena de América, fue llevada a España y Europa por los conquistadores en el siglo XVI. La palabra es de origen quechua, el idioma hablado por los incas del Perú.

G. **¡Que toque la orquesta!** Vuelva a escribir estos instrumentos en el plural con el artículo definido.

1. piano

2. flauta

3. viola

4. clarinete

5. violonchelo

6. violín

7. trompeta

8. trombón

9. arpa

10. oboe

11. tambor

12. tuba

C *The definite article: forms, uses*

- In Spanish, the definite article, English *the,* changes its form to agree with the noun in gender (masculine/feminine) and number (singular/plural):

	masculine	*feminine*
singular	**el**	**la**
plural	**los**	**las**

    el cuerpo   **la** cabeza
    los cuerpos   **las** cabezas

- In Spanish, unlike English, the definite article is used before a noun to refer to something in a general way (mass or uncountable nouns) or to refer to all the members of its class. Colors, like abstract nouns, also require the article:

La democracia es el mejor sistema de gobierno.	*Democracy is the best system of government.*
El agua mineral es buena para la digestión.	*Mineral water is good for digestion.*
El verde es el color que más me gusta.	*Green is the color I like best.*
No le gustan **las espinacas**.	*She doesn't like spinach.*

Note that the sentence **No le gustan las espinacas** is ambiguous out of context because it can mean she doesn't like all spinach, that is, spinach in general, or she doesn't like a particular spinach already mentioned in the conversation.

- The definite article **el** is used before the names of languages except directly after **hablar** and after the prepositions **de** and **en.** It is also commonly omitted directly after the verbs **aprender, enseñar, estudiar, leer, practicar,** and **saber.**

Hablamos español.	*We speak Spanish.*
Hablamos bien **el** español.	*We speak Spanish well.*
Escribió la carta **en** francés.	*He wrote the letter in French.*
Te presto el diccionario **de** chino.	*I'll lend you the Chinese dictionary.*
Saben hebreo y estudian japonés.	*They know Hebrew and they're studying Japanese.*

- The definite article is used before titles except when the person is being addressed directly. It is not used before **don / doña** and **Santo / San / Santa:**

El señor Lerma está bien.	*Mr. Lerma is well.*
Señor Lerma, ¿cómo está Ud.?	*Mr. Lerma, how are you?*
Don Juan nació el día de **San** Juan.	*Juan was born on St. John's day.*

- The definite article is used to express the time of day:

Son **las cuatro** y media.	*It's four thirty.*
Se acostaron a **la una** de la mañana.	*They went to bed at one A.M.*

- The definite article is used with the days of the week except after the verb **ser** when expressing dates:

El concierto fue **el sábado.**	*The concert was on Saturday.*
Los lunes el museo está cerrado.	*On Mondays the museum is closed.*
Hoy **es miércoles.**	*Today is Wednesday.*

- The definite article is used with the names of the seasons. It can be omitted after the preposition **en** when it is suggested that the event mentioned occurs in that season every year:

Me encanta **el verano.**	*I love summer.*
Alano va a Madrid **en el otoño.**	*Alano is going to Madrid in the fall.*
Gonzalo viaja a Barcelona **en invierno.**	*Gonzalo travels to Barcelona in winter.*

- Spanish uses the definite article rather than the possessive adjective that English prefers with parts of the body and articles of clothing, especially with reflexive verbs:

Sofi se puso **los jeans.**	*Sofi put on her jeans.*
Mauricio está cepillándose **los dientes.**	*Mauricio is brushing his teeth.*

- The definite article is used before infinitives that function as nouns. The article is often omitted when the infinitive is the subject of the sentence:

(El) robar es malo.	*Stealing is bad.*
El estafar es también un vicio.	*Cheating is also a vice.*

- The definite article is used with the names of rivers, oceans, and mountains:

El Sena pasa por París y **el Támesis** por Londres.	*The Seine flows through Paris and the Thames through London.*
Los Pirineos quedan entre España y Francia.	*The Pyrenees are between Spain and France.*

- The definite article is traditionally used before the names of some countries, although it tends to be omitted more and more in the modern language. The definite article *must* be used before the name of a country, city, or continent that is modified:

en **(los)** Estados Unidos	*in the United States*
a través de **(del)** Canadá	*through Canada*
por **(la)** Argentina	*through Argentina*
hacia **(el)** Perú	*toward Peru*
sobre **(el)** Japón	*about Japan*
la Europa central	*Central Europe*
la España medieval	*Medieval Spain*

- The definite article is used before nouns of measurement:

un dólar **la libra**	*a dollar a/the pound*
cincuenta centavos **el kilo**	*fifty centavos a/the kilo*

- In Spanish, many set phrases that require the definite article do not have it in their English equivalents:

a/en/de **la** iglesia	*to/in/from church*
en **la** televisión	*on television*
en **el** mar	*at sea, on/in the sea*

H. El artículo definido. Para cada sustantivo, escriba lo siguiente: (a) el artículo definido singular, (b) el artículo definido plural, (c) el plural del sustantivo.

1. aceituna	11. salvavidas	21. tenedor
2. ensayo	12. origen	22. pirámide
3. agua	13. foto	23. raíz
4. árbol	14. mes	24. sacapuntas
5. dulce	15. serpiente	25. pensión
6. demora	16. sillón	26. pintor
7. sal	17. miel	27. jardín
8. pasaporte	18. lápiz	28. jugador
9. volcán	19. francés	29. esquí
10. actividad	20. vez	30. pan

I. **¡Retrato de la heroína romántica!** Armando, un pintor romántico, pinta el retrato de la mujer ideal. ¿Cómo es? Para saberlo, escriba la forma correcta del artículo definido y el sustantivo.

> MODELO   La mujer ideal tiene: **los pies** pequeños (*feet*)

1. _____ azules (*eyes*)
2. _____ rosadas (*cheeks* [mejillas])
3. _____ suaves (*hands*)
4. _____ largos (*fingers*)
5. _____ como cerezas (*lips*)
6. _____ como perlas (*teeth*)
7. _____ como el oro (*hair*)
8. _____ como cisne (*swan*) (*neck*)
9. _____ bien formadas (*ears*)

J. **¿Artículo definido o no?** Complete las oraciones con la forma correcta del artículo definido donde sea necesario.

1. Bogotá, _____ capital de Colombia, se encuentra en las montañas.
2. Nos interesa _____ cine.
3. Laura y Encarnación saben perfectamente _____ ruso.
4. Hay multa por _____ ensuciar las calles.
5. ¿Adónde va Ud., _____ señorita Maldonado?
6. Volvimos a casa a _____ diez y cuarto.
7. Estas revistas están escritas en _____ catalán.
8. La comida fue _____ miércoles.
9. _____ legumbres son buenas para _____ salud.
10. _____ verano es la estación más agradable del año.
11. Hoy es _____ domingo.
12. Hicimos investigaciones sobre _____ España contemporánea.
13. _____ duraznos se venden a 79 centavos _____ libra en verano.
14. ¿Habrá algo interesante en _____ televisión?
15. _____ señorita Suárez llega de _____ iglesia.

Nota cultural

El catalán se habla en Cataluña, la región al noreste de España. El español y el catalán son oficiales en Cataluña. El catalán también se habla en Valencia (el dialecto se llama valenciano) y en las islas Baleares (el dialecto es el mallorquín).

K. Exprese las siguientes oraciones en español.

1. The Sánchez family is going to Florida in the spring.
2. Florencia put on her socks.
3. Give (*Ud.*) us the Latin books.

4. Juli and Nicolás love swimming.

5. What did the tourists do at sea?

6. The twins washed their faces.

7. Elías knows Portuguese, speaks Italian, reads Russian, and is learning German.

8. The masked ball was on Saturday. It began at 9:30 P.M.

9. The novel was written in Polish and translated into Greek.

D The definite article: omissions

- The definite article is omitted before mass or count nouns which do not refer to the whole of their class, but only to some of it or a part of it (an unspecified quantity):

Guadalupe tiene paciencia.	*Guadalupe is patient.*
Toman aspirinas.	*They're taking aspirin.*
Amparo compró carne.	*Amparo bought meat.*

- Spanish usually omits the definite article after **haber**:

Hay gente en el comedor.	*There are people in the dining room.*

- When two nouns are joined by **de** to form a compound noun, the definite article is omitted before the *second* noun:

la carne de res	*beef*
el dolor de cabeza	*headache*
libros de historia	*history books*

- The definite article is usually omitted in apposition:

Caracas, capital de Venezuela	*Caracas, the capital of Venezuela*
Santa Fe, capital de Nuevo México	*Santa Fe, the capital of New Mexico*
Simón Bolívar, libertador de Sudamérica	*Simón Bolívar, the liberator of South America*
Mario Vargas Llosa, novelista	*Mario Vargas Llosa, the novelist*

- The definite article is omitted before ordinal numbers with kings and other rulers:

Alfonso X (décimo)	*Alfonso the Tenth*
Carlos V (quinto)	*Charles the Fifth*

- In Spanish, there are many set adverbial phrases that do not take the definite article whereas their English equivalents usually do:

en nombre de	*in the name of*
a corto/largo plazo	*in the short/long run*
en camino	*on the way*

L. ¿Falta el artículo definido? Escriba el artículo definido donde sea necesario.

1. Plácido Domingo, _____ tenor, y Montserrat Caballé, _____ soprano, son españoles.

2. Juan Carlos _____ I (primero) subió al trono español en 1975.

3. ¡Alfonsito tiene dolor de _____ estómago y Luisito tiene dolor de _____ muelas por los bombones que se comieron!

4. Los chicos compraron _____ refrescos más naturales para la fiesta.

5. Aurelia no está en casa porque ya está en _____ camino.

6. No hay _____ sillones en la sala todavía.

7. Tomamos _____ vitaminas para tener _____ energía.

Nota cultural

Hay varios artistas hispanos que tienen una fama internacional en la música clásica. Plácido Domingo y José Carreras, dos de "los tres tenores" (con Pavarotti), son españoles. Montserrat Caballé y Victoria de los Ángeles, sopranos, son españolas. Alicia de Larrocha, pianista española. Pablo Casals, violonchelista español. Rafael Frühbeck de Burgos, director español. Claudio Arrau, pianista chileno. Jaime Laredo, violinista, nació en Bolivia. José Gutiérrez, pianista, nació en Cuba. El director de orquesta Eduardo Mata nació en México.

E The neuter article lo

• Spanish has a neuter article **lo** which is placed before an adjective used as a noun to express an abstract idea or a certain quality. The form **lo** is invariable and is used with masculine and feminine and singular and plural adjectives + **que** to express *how*. **Lo** is also used with adverbs and adverbial phrases:

lo bueno	*the good part, what's good*
lo fácil	*the easy part, what's easy*
Lo importante es que nosotros pensamos **lo mismo.**	*The important thing is that we think the same.*
Vi **lo listo/lista** que es.	*I saw how clever he/she is.*
Oí **lo graciosos/graciosas** que son.	*I heard how witty they are.*
Pensaban en **lo bien** que lo iban a pasar.	*They were thinking about the good time they were going to have.*

• **Lo** is used before a **de** phrase which means *the matter concerning:*

lo del ingeniero	*the matter concerning the engineer*
lo de tus documentos	*the business about, situation of your papers*

Lo is used in the phrases **lo más/menos posible** *as much as possible/as little as possible* and **lo antes posible** *as soon as possible.*

M. **¡Artículos en el museo!** Cuando Ud. fue al museo con su amiga vieron muchas cosas interesantes. Escriba la forma correcta del artículo que falte. Escoja entre el artículo neutro **lo,** el definido y el indefinido. No se olvide de escribir las contracciones **al** y **del** cuando sean necesarias. ¡Tenga en cuenta que es posible que no sea necesario el artículo!

_____ (1) viernes yo fui con Edita a _____ (2) museo de _____ (3) arte. Todo

_____ (4) de _____ (5) arte nos interesa mucho. _____ (6) bello de _____ (7) museo

son _____ (8) salas de _____ (9) escultura. Hay tantos *artículos* y piezas de

_____ (10) gran valor. No pudimos ver _____ (11) esculturas porque _____ (12) mes

pasado hubo _____ (13) robo en _____ (14) museo. Parece que _____ (15) ladrones

entraron a _____ (16) museo a _____ (17) tres de _____ (18) mañana. Se llevaron

_____ (19) estatuas preciosas. _____ (20) guardia muy simpático nos dijo que

_____ (21) de _____ (22) seguridad en _____ (23) museo es _____ (24) problema.

F *The indefinite article: forms, uses, and omissions*

* The Spanish indefinite article (English *a, an*) appears as **un** before a masculine noun and as **una** before a feminine noun.

	masculine	*feminine*
singular	**un**	**una**
plural	**unos**	**unas**

* The plural indefinite articles **unos/unas** are the equivalent of English *some, a few, a couple of.*

* **El** and **un** are always used before feminine nouns that begin with a stressed **a-** or **ha-**. The plural of these nouns always uses **las** and **unas**. This rule does not apply where the first vowel is not stressed: **la alfombra, la ambición.** Also, the name of letter **a** is **la a** and the letter **h** is **la hache**:

el/un agua	**las/unas** aguas
el/un águila *eagle*	**las/unas** águilas
el/un alma *soul*	**las/unas** almas
el/un arca *ark*	**las/unas** arcas
el/un área	**las/unas** áreas
el/un arma *arm, weapon*	**las/unas** armas
el/un arpa *harp*	**las/unas** arpas
el/un haba *bean*	**las/unas** habas
el/un habla *language*	**las/unas** hablas
el/un hambre *hunger*	**las/unas** hambres

- The indefinite article is omitted before predicate nouns that denote profession, occupation, nationality, religion, social status, gender, etc. If, however, the noun is modified by a phrase or an adjective, the indefinite article is expressed:

Amparo es violinista.	*Amparo is a violinist.*
Es una violinista brillante.	*She's a brilliant violinist.*
Francisco es carpintero.	*Francisco is a carpenter.*
Esos chicos son argentinos.	*Those kids are Argentine.*
Ester es judía/católica/protestante.	*Ester is Jewish/Catholic/Protestant.*

- The indefinite article is usually omitted after the verbs **tener, llevar** (*to wear*), **usar, comprar, buscar, sacar**:

Asunción tiene jardín.	*Asunción has a garden.*
Nieves y Julián usan anteojos.	*Nieves and Julián wear glasses.*
Compra pasteles.	*Buy pastries.*

- The indefinite article is omitted in phrases with **¡qué …!** (*what a …!*) and before **otro** (*another*), **cierto** (*a certain*), **tal** (*such a*), **medio** (*half a*), **ciento** (*a hundred*), and **mil** (*a thousand*). The English equivalents of these words have the indefinite article:

¡Qué día!	*What a day!*
otro color y otro estilo	*another color and another style*
cierta persona	*a certain person*
tal problema	*such a problem*
medio kilo	*half a kilo*
cien/mil dólares	*a hundred/a thousand dollars*

N.   El artículo indefinido. Para cada sustantivo, escriba lo siguiente: (a) el artículo indefinido singular, (b) el artículo indefinido plural, (c) el plural del sustantivo.

1. mar	11. papel	21. voz
2. optimista	12. volibol	22. desfile
3. orden	13. menú	23. nación
4. parador	14. cereal	24. lavaplatos
5. olor	15. buzón	25. lema
6. oboe	16. irlandés	26. sucursal
7. área	17. alma	27. ascensor
8. mochila	18. paraguas	28. habla
9. joven	19. camarón	29. postal
10. nadador	20. garaje	30. agua

O. En el taller. El pintor Dionisio está pintando en su taller donde se encuentran las siguientes cosas. Escriba la forma correcta del artículo indefinido al lado del sustantivo.

1. _____ cuadro

2. _____ artista (*masc.*)

3. _____ pinceles

4. _____ mural

5. _____ modelos (*fem.*)

6. _____ colección

7. _____ paisajes

8. _____ escultura

9. _____ retratos

P. ¿Artículo indefinido o no? Escriba la forma correcta del artículo indefinido donde sea necesario.

1. Sergio es _____ ingeniero.

2. Es _____ día muy caluroso.

3. Gabriel es _____ judío y Carmen es _____ católica.

4. Verónica tiene entre _____ cien y _____ mil sellos en su colección.

5. ¿Puede Ud. enseñarme _____ otro estilo de abrigo, por favor?

6. Simón Colón es _____ pianista muy talentoso.

7. La nueva vecina es _____ mexicana.

8. Todos los niños de esa familia usan _____ gafas.

9. No se puede encontrar _____ paraguas grande.

G Contractions **del** and **al**

- There are two contractions in Spanish. The masculine article **el** combines with the preposition **de** to form **del** *of the* and with **a** to form **al** *to the.* These prepositions do not contract with the other forms of the definite article **la, los, las.** The contractions are not used if the definite article is part of a proper name:

Mateo es el gerente **del** hotel.	*Mateo is the manager of the hotel.*
Álvaro fue **al museo.**	*Álvaro went to the museum.*
Sol fue **a El Prado.**	*Sol went to El Prado.*

Q. ¿Dónde están todos? Diga que las personas no están porque fueron a distintos lugares. Use la contracción **al** cuando sea necesario.

MODELO   Nieves / teatro ➔ Nieves fue al teatro.

1. Concepción y Simón / puesto de periódicos

2. yo / ayuntamiento (*town hall*)

3. Domingo y Brígida / supermercado

4. Ud. / parque de atracciones

5. Lourdes / iglesia

6. mi hermano / la bolsa (*stock exchange*)

7. nosotros / estación de tren

8. tú / centro comercial

H Possession

- In Spanish, possession is expressed by the use of a prepositional phrase with **de.** Spanish titles such as **señor** and **profesora** must be preceded by the definite article when referring to the specific person. (When directly addressing a person with a title, the definite article is not used.)

Leí el informe **de Jacobo.**	*I read Jacobo's report.*
Leí todos los capítulos **del libro.**	*I read all the chapters of the book.*
Hoy es el día **del** examen final.	*Today is the day of the final exam.*
Cenaron en el restaurante **del** hotel.	*They had dinner in the hotel restaurant.*
¿Conoces el comercio **del** señor Bermúdez?	*Are you familiar with Mr. Bermúdez' store?*

- In Spanish, **¿De quién?** followed by **ser** is equivalent to English *Whose?*

¿De quién es el cinturón?	*Whose belt is it?*
¿De quién son estos pendientes?	*Whose earrings are these?*
¿De quién(es) es el barco?	*Whose boat is it?*
¿De quién son estas postales?	*Whose postcards are these?*

A form **¿De quiénes?** also exists to refer to a plural possessor but is not common in the spoken language.

R. **¿De quién es?** Escriba preguntas y respuestas que demuestran posesión.

> Modelo   los libros de texto / el profesor
> → ¿De quién son los libros de texto?
> → Son del profesor.

1. el almacén / el señor Acosta
2. los peines / Adela y Matilde
3. el equipaje / las turistas
4. los discos compactos / el pianista
5. este llavero / la empleada
6. las sartenes / el cocinero
7. las raquetas / estas tenistas
8. el reloj / el doctor Villanueva

S. Exprese las siguientes frases en español.

1. Mr. Valle's florist shop
2. the (*masc.*) president's office
3. the programmer's disks
4. the shop's windows
5. the nuclear plant's energy
6. the students' notebooks
7. Professor (*fem.*) Salas' lectures

T. **Ejercicio oral. Un programa de concursos (*Quiz show*).** Como presentador/a del programa, Ud. lee sustantivos a los dos equipos que luego tienen que ponerles el artículo definido o indefinido correcto. Se puede variar con frases de posesión, las contracciones **al** y **del,** etc. ¡Al final se calculan los puntos ganados por cada equipo para saber quiénes sacaron el premio gordo (*grand prize*)!

U. Estructuras en acción. Lea el siguiente anuncio sobre una velada literaria con Carlos Fuentes, el célebre escritor mexicano. El anuncio aparece sin algunos artículos. Escriba los artículos donde sean necesarios. (El ejercicio sigue en la página 224.)

Veladas Literarias

Carlos Fuentes en Círculo de Lectores

Jueves, 6 de julio de 1995, a las 8 de la tarde.

Círculo de Lectores organiza un encuentro con **Carlos Fuentes,** con motivo de la presentación de la **Biblioteca Carlos Fuentes** y de la biografía ilustrada *Retrato de Carlos Fuentes,* escrita por Julio Ortega.

La presentación correrá a cargo de **Julio Ortega,** profesor de literatura latinoamericana en la Universidad de Brown, Estados Unidos.

Carlos Fuentes intervendrá con una charla titulada *Vida de la obra, obra de la vida.*

La velada tendrá lugar en el Centro Cultural de Círculo de Lectores en Madrid, calle de O'Donnell, 10.

Las invitaciones pueden recogerse en el mismo Centro Cultural a partir de las 10 de la mañana del lunes 3 de julio. Teléfono: (91) 435 37 40
Información a los medios, teléfono: (91) 435 83 44

CÍRCULO DE LECTORES

Vocabulario

a partir de   *from*
el círculo   *circle*
con motivo de   *because of, on the occasion of*
correr a cargo de   *to be the responsibility of, in the hands of*
la charla   *informal talk*
el encuentro   *meeting*
intervenir   *to participate, take part*
el lector   *reader*
los medios   *media*
recoger   *to pick up*
la velada literaria   *literary evening*

Círculo de Lectores organiza _____ (1) encuentro con Carlos Fuentes, con _____ (2) motivo de _____ (3) presentación de _____ (4) Biblioteca Carlos Fuentes y de _____ (5) biografía ilustrada *Retrato de Carlos Fuentes,* escrita por Julio Ortega.

_____ (6) presentación correrá a _____ (7) cargo de Julio Ortega, _____ (8) profesor de _____ (9) literatura latinoamericana en _____ (10) Universidad de Brown, _____ (11) Estados Unidos.

Carlos Fuentes intervendrá con _____ (12) charla titulada *Vida de* _____ (13) *obra,* *obra de* _____ (14) *vida.*

La velada tendrá _____ (15) lugar en _____ (16) Centro Cultural de Círculo de Lectores en Madrid, calle de O'Donnell, 10.

_____ (17) invitaciones pueden recogerse en _____ (18) mismo Centro Cultural a partir de _____ (19) 10 de _____ (20) mañana del lunes 3 de _____ (21) julio. Teléfono: (91) 435 37 40. Información a los medios, teléfono: (91) 435 83 44.

CHAPTER 17
ADJECTIVES

A Agreement of adjectives

- Spanish adjectives agree in gender and number with the nouns they modify. Adjectives that have a masculine singular form ending in **-o** have four forms:

bonito	masculine	feminine
sing.	bonito	bonita
pl.	bonitos	bonitas

maravilloso	masculine	feminine
sing.	maravilloso	maravillosa
pl.	maravillosos	maravillosas

- Adjectives that have a masculine singular ending in a consonant or in **-e** have only two forms, a singular and a plural. They do not change for gender:

difícil	masculine & feminine
sing.	difícil
pl.	difíciles

triste	masculine & feminine
sing.	triste
pl.	tristes

- A small number of adjectives of nationality end in **-a** or in stressed **-í** or **-ú**. These also have only two forms:

belga *Belgian*	masculine & feminine
sing.	belga
pl.	belgas

israelí *Israeli*	masculine & feminine
sing.	israelí
pl.	israelíes

hindú *Hindu*	masculine & feminine
sing.	hindú
pl.	hindúes

Other similar adjectives: **azteca** (*Aztec*), **marroquí** (*Moroccan*), **iraní** (*Iranian*), **pakistaní** (*Pakistani*), **bantú** (*Bantu*). There are also adjectives ending in **-ista, -sta,** and **-ita** that follow the above pattern: **realista, entusiasta, nacionalista, cosmopolita.**

- Adjectives ending in the suffixes **-dor, -ón,** and **-án** add **-a** to form the feminine, and therefore have four forms like adjectives ending in **-o.** These adjectives form their masculine plural by adding **-es** and their feminine plural by adding **-as.** The accented suffixes lose their accent when an ending is added.

hablador *talkative*	masculine	feminine
sing.	hablador	habladora
pl.	hablador**es**	hablador**as**

preguntón *inquisitive*	masculine	feminine
sing.	preguntón	preguntona
pl.	preguntones	preguntonas

- Spanish adjectives usually follow the nouns they modify:

—En esa tienda de ropa venden cosas **maravillosas.**	*In that clothing store they sell wonderful things.*
—Sí. Veo que te has comprado unos vestidos muy **bonitos.**	*Yes. I see that you've bought yourself some very pretty dresses.*

A. ¿Cómo están? Su amigo le pregunta cómo están ciertas personas. Contéstele usando los adjetivos que aparecen entre paréntesis haciendo la concordancia necesaria.

> **MODELO** ¿Cómo está tu hermana? (ocupado)
> → Está ocupada.

1. ¿Cómo están tus padres? (feliz)

2. ¿Cómo estás? (contento)

3. ¿Cómo se encuentra Raquel? (nervioso)

4. ¿Cómo se siente Claudio? (deprimido)

5. ¿Cómo se encuentran las hermanas de Augusto? (triste)

6. ¿Cómo están Uds.? (cansado)

7. ¿Cómo se sienten los primos de Paco? (enfermo)

8. ¿Cómo está Matilde? (preocupado)

9. ¿Cómo está tu tía? (aburrido)

B. ¡Don de gentes! Jacobo y su hermana Luisa son estudiantes de intercambio que llegaron de Tegucigalpa, capital de Honduras, el año pasado. Viven con una familia norteamericana y se llevan muy bien con todo el mundo. ¿Qué piensa la gente de los hermanos hondureños? Para saberlo, escriba oraciones usando los adjetivos que aparecen entre paréntesis. Haga las concordancias necesarias.

> **MODELO** Elena cree / Luisa / honesto
> → Elena cree que Luisa es honesta.

Carácter y personalidad

buena gente   nice (person/people)
cortés   courteous
el don de gentes   charm, getting on well with people
encantador   charming
generoso   generous
gracioso   witty
honesto   honest
independiente   independent

inteligente   intelligent
listo   clever
responsable   reliable
serio   serious
simpático   nice, pleasant
sincero   sincere
tener personalidad   to have personality or character
trabajador   hard-working

1. Paco cree / Jacobo / listo

2. la señora Alvarado piensa / Luisa / encantador

3. el profesor de cálculo encuentra / a los hermanos / inteligente y trabajador

4. Nieves cree / Jacobo / sincero

5. el señor Alvarado dice / Luisa / gracioso y generoso

6. las profesoras de literatura europea encuentran a Jacobo / serio y responsable

7. los hijos de los Alvarado creen / Luisa / independiente y simpático

8. todo el mundo dice / Jacobo y Luisa / buena gente y cortés

Nota cultural

Tegucigalpa, capital de Honduras, fue fundada como campamento de minas en 1578. Los españoles empezaron a poblar la ciudad en este año aunque los indígenas ya llamaban la ciudad Tisingal. Tegucigalpa quiere decir "montaña de plata" en el idioma indígena original. La ciudad se convirtió en capital en 1880. A diferencia de la ciudad de Guatemala que fue casi totalmente destruida por terremotos, Tegucigalpa conserva mucha de su arquitectura original porque no queda en una falla (fault) geológica. La ciudad tiene plazas grandes, hermosos jardines, una universidad nacional, un paraninfo (salón) universitario donde tienen lugar muchos eventos culturales, una catedral del siglo XVIII tardío, el Teatro Nacional Manuel Bonilla, etcétera.

C. **¿Qué se piensa de ellos?** Juan y Teresa no le caen bien a nadie. ¿Qué piensa la gente de ellos? Escriba oraciones usando los adjetivos que aparecen entre paréntesis. Haga las concordancias necesarias.

MODELO   Laura dice: No soporto a Juan porque es **antipático.**

Más carácter y personalidad

aguantar   to stand
antipático   unpleasant
desleal   disloyal
engañoso   deceitful
Me cae mal.   I don't like her.
mentiroso   lying

molesto   annoying
No los puedo ver.   I can't stand them.
odiar   to hate
soportar   to stand
tonto   silly, stupid

1. Ramón dice: Creo que Teresa es muy _____. (arrogante)

2. Patricio dice: No aguanto a Juan porque es _____. (molesto)

3. Matilde dice: Los encuentro _____. (tacaño)

4. Ana dice: No los puedo ver porque son _____. (tonto)

5. Luisa dice: Teresa me cae mal porque es _____. (mentiroso)

6. Joaquín dice: Yo odio a los dos porque son _____. (desleal)

7. Adela dice: Yo encuentro a los dos _____. (engañoso)

D. Pintura mexicana. Los estudiantes de «Pintura mexicana del siglo XX» están viendo unas diapositivas (*slides*). Comentan sobre los colores del cuadro titulado *Campamento Zapatista*. Escriba adjetivos de color haciendo las concordancias necesarias.

1. Es impresionante la capa _____ (*blue*) de la Virgen de Guadalupe.

2. Salta a la vista (*stands out*) el sombrero _____ (*yellow*).

3. Es bonita la piel _____ (*brown*) de los campesinos.

4. Me encanta la camisa _____ (*pink*).

5. Los pantalones _____ (*white*) tienen pliegues (*folds*) _____ (*blue*).

6. Los ojos _____ (*black*) de los campesinos son muy sensibles.

7. El campesino tiene en la mano un fusil (*rifle*) _____ (*brown*).

8. Llama la atención la jarra (*jug*) _____ (*red*).

9. Se nota la piña _____ (*green*) y _____ (*brown*).

Nota cultural

- **Campamento Zapatista** fue pintado por el pintor mexicano Fernando Leal en 1922. Leal, que nació en 1900 y murió en 1964, fue uno de los primeros pintores en usar temas indigenistas para los murales grandes. Otros grandes muralistas mexicanos fueron Orozco, Rivera y Siqueiros. El campamento zapatista se refiere a Emiliano Zapata, político y revolucionario mexicano (1883–1919), que reclamó tierras para los campesinos.

- **La Virgen de Guadalupe** fue símbolo de los zapatistas. La Virgen apareció al indio Juan Diego y su imagen quedó grabada (*imprinted*) en su manta (*poncho*). Desde 1910, año que empezó la Revolución Mexicana, la Virgen de Guadalupe es patrona (*patron saint*) de Hispanoamérica.

E. ¡El Príncipe Azul (*Prince Charming*)! El Príncipe Azul estudia su ropa. Escriba lo que tiene en su armario empleando los adjetivos de color. ¡Fíjese bien si tiene ropa apropiada para pescar una princesa (*to catch a princess*)!

Para montar a caballo:

1. una chaqueta _____ (rojo)

2. unos pantalones _____ (amarillo)

3. unas botas _____ (marrón)

4. unos guantes _____ (negro) o _____ (rojo)

5. un sombrero con plumas _____ (amarillo) _____ (anaranjado) y _____ (verde)

Para ir a un baile de etiqueta (*dress ball*):

6. un esmoquin (*tuxedo*) _____ (negro)

7. un sombrero de copa (*top hat*) _____ (negro)

8. una faja (*cummerbund*) _____ (morado)

9. unos calcetines _____ (morado) y _____ (gris)

 B *Position of adjectives; shortened forms of adjectives*

- Although descriptive adjectives in Spanish usually follow the noun they modify, descriptive and other adjectives can also appear before nouns in certain cases:

   1. When they express an inherent characteristic of the noun that is known to all and does not add any new information about the noun:

la **blanca** nieve	*white snow*
el **tímido** cordero	*the timid lamb*
una **olorosa** rosa	*a fragrant rose*

   2. When they express a subjective judgment of the speaker. **Bueno, malo,** and their comparatives **mejor** and **peor** fall into this category:

Vivimos en una **pequeña** ciudad.	*We live in a small city.*
Tenemos que leer una **larga** novela.	*We have to read a long novel.*
Sobrevolaron la **enorme** selva.	*They flew over the huge jungle.*
Es el **peor** libro que leímos.	*It's the worst book that we read.*
Prepararon una **buena** comida.	*They prepared a good meal.*

   3. Adjectives that express quantity precede the noun: **mucho, poco, bastante, suficiente, cuánto, alguno, ninguno, ambos** (*both*), **varios** (*several*):

Alberto siempre tiene **muchas** ideas.	*Alberto always has a lot of ideas.*
¿Hay **alguna** farmacia por aquí?	*Is there a (any) drugstore around here?*
No ganan **suficiente** dinero.	*They don't earn enough money.*

   4. After exclamations with **¡Qué!**:

¡Qué **mala** suerte!	*What bad luck!*
¡Qué **hermosa** plaza!	*What a beautiful square!*

When an adverb such as **más, tan, muy,** etc. modifies the adjective, the adjective usually follows the noun:

¡Qué plaza **más hermosa**!	*What a beautiful square!*
Prepararon una comida **muy buena.**	*They prepared a very good meal.*
Fue una clase **especialmente interesante.**	*It was an especially interesting class.*

- The adjectives **bueno, malo, primero, tercero, uno, alguno,** and **ninguno** lose their final **-o** before a masculine singular noun. **Alguno** and **ninguno** add an accent mark when shortened: **algún, ningún**:

—¿No conoces a **ningún** estudiante?	*Don't you know any students?*
—No conozco a nadie todavía. Es mi **primer** día aquí.	*I don't know anyone yet. It's my first day here.*
—¿Hay **algún** consejo que te puedo dar?	*Is there any advice that I can give you?*
—No, he tenido **un mal** día, nada más.	*No, I've had a bad day, that's all.*

- The adjectives **grande** and **cualquiera** (*any*) shorten to **gran** and **cualquier,** respectively, before any singular noun:

Cualquier restaurante por aquí es un **gran** restaurante.	*Any restaurant around here is a great restaurant.*

- The adjective **Santo** shortens to **San** before all masculine saints' names except those that begin with **To-** and **Do-** as in **Santo Tomás** and **Santo Domingo.**

Some adjectives have different English equivalents depending on whether they precede or follow the nouns they modify:

nuestro **antiguo** jefe *our former boss*	una ciudad **antigua** *an old, ancient city*
cierto país *a certain country, some countries*	una cosa **cierta** *a sure thing, a true thing*
una **nueva** casa *another house*	una casa **nueva** *a new house*
el **mismo** profesor *the same teacher*	el profesor **mismo** *the teacher himself*
un **pobre** hombre *a poor man (unfortunate)*	un hombre **pobre** *a poor man (penniless)*
un **gran** presidente *a great president*	un hombre **grande** *a big man*
diferentes libros *various books*	libros **diferentes** *different books*
Paco es **medio** español. *Paco is half Spanish.*	el español **medio** *the average Spaniard*
Este café es **pura** agua. *This coffee is nothing but water.*	Prefiero beber agua **pura.** *I prefer to drink pure water.*
Juan es un **simple** camarero. *Juan is just a waiter.*	Juan es un muchacho **simple.** *Juan is a simple boy.*

Me interesa **cualquier** película
española.
I'm interested in any Spanish film.

Vamos a alquilar una película
cualquiera.
Let's rent any old film.

María es la **única** mexicana aquí.
María is the only Mexican here.

María es una chica **única.**
María is a unique girl.

F. Adjetivos pre- y pospuestos. Ponga el adjetivo o antes o después del sustantivo.
Haga los cambios necesarios.

1. ¡Éste es el _____ día _____ de mi vida! (mejor)

2. Hay _____ discos compactos _____ en el escritorio. (alguno)

3. Ha habido _____ días _____ de lluvia este año. (mucho)

4. Los estudiantes leyeron unos _____ poemas _____. (renacentista)

5. Los franceses usan mucho la _____ energía _____. (nuclear)

6. El profesor dará el examen a _____ clases _____ el miércoles. (ambos)

7. Pili tiene los _____ ojos _____. (castaño)

8. No retiraron _____ plata _____ de su cuenta de ahorros. (suficiente)

9. Nos encanta el _____ vino _____. (tinto)

10. No se sabe _____ horas _____ de trabajo quedan. (cuánto)

11. Pedro tomó la _____ decisión _____ posible. (peor)

12. Miguel y Víctor se dedican al análisis de _____ teorías _____. (político)

G. ¡Qué exclamación! Amplíe cada exclamación con la forma correcta del adjetivo
que aparece entre paréntesis. Haga los cambios necesarios.

   MODELO   ¡Qué casa! (lindo) → ¡Qué linda casa!

1. ¡Qué situación! (absurdo)

2. ¡Qué clima! (tan perfecto)

3. ¡Qué partido! (más emocionante)

4. ¡Qué paella! (tan rico)

5. ¡Qué zapatos! (hermoso)

6. ¡Qué ideas! (más estupendo)

7. ¡Qué problemas! (más complicado)

8. ¡Qué legumbres! (fresco)

9. ¡Qué niños! (cariñoso)

10. ¡Qué reunión! (tan animado)

H. Adjetivos: ¿forma apócope (*shortened*) o no? Complete las siguientes oraciones
con la forma correcta del adjetivo que aparece entre paréntesis.

1. El cinco de septiembre es el _____ día del semestre. (primero)

2. No es _____ idea llevar el paraguas hoy. (malo)

3. Estos estadistas son _____ hombres. (grande)

4. Unas canicas (*marbles*) son un _____ juguete para Paquito. (bueno)

5. Ya es la _____ vez que me han invitado a salir. (tercero)

6. Esperamos que vengan a vernos _____ día. (alguno)

7. No hemos hecho _____ plan hasta ahora. (ninguno)

8. Yo nací el día de _____ Juan. (santo)

9. Sánchez dictó una serie de _____ conferencias. (bueno)

10. Albéniz fue un _____ compositor español. (grande)

11. No les gustó _____ bicicleta. (ninguno)

12. Pruebe _____ recetas de este libro de cocina italiana. (alguno)

13. _____ librería tendrá el libro que buscas. (Cualquiera)

14. ¿No celebras tu santo el día de _____ Rosa? (santo)

15. Jesús y Pepe fueron los _____ jugadores en llegar al estadio. (primero)

16. Carlos es el _____ rey de la dinastía. (tercero)

17. ¡No des _____ ejemplo para los niños! (malo)

I. Adjetivos: antes o después del sustantivo. Exprese en español el adjetivo que aparece entre paréntesis poniéndolo antes o después del sustantivo.

1. Beti y yo vamos al _____ dentista _____. (*same*)

2. Atenas es una _____ ciudad _____. (*ancient*)

3. La fecha de su boda es una _____ cosa _____. (*sure*)

4. Tino es _____ portugués _____ y _____ mexicano _____. (*half/half*)

5. Bolívar fue un _____ soldado _____. (*great*)

6. Habla con un _____ funcionario _____. (*any old*)

7. ¡El _____ dramaturgo _____ no aguanta su obra! (*himself*)

8. La sopa que pedí es _____ agua _____. (*nothing but*)

9. Ricardo es una _____ persona _____. (*unique*)

10. _____ empresa _____ sigue perdiendo dinero. (*A certain*)

11. Los hermanos Ayala son _____ hombres _____ desde que su compañía quebró (*went bankrupt*). (*poor*)

12. La _____ casa _____ de Daniela y Pablo quedaba en las afueras de la ciudad. (*former*)

13. Mi biblioteca tiene _____ libros _____ sobre el _____ tema _____. (*several/same*)

14. A Leonor le va a encantar _____ regalo _____ que le demos. (*any*)

15. Agustín y Patricia son los _____ pianistas _____ que tocan con la orquesta. (*only*)

16. Le dimos el pésame (*we offered our sympathy*) a la _____ señora _____. (*poor* [*sad, in mourning*])

C *Adjectives of nationality*

- Adjectives of nationality that end in **-o** in the masculine singular have the regular four forms:

chileno *Chilean*	masculine	feminine
sing.	chileno	chilena
pl.	chilenos	chilenas

mexicano *Mexican*	masculine	feminine
sing.	mexicano	mexicana
pl.	mexicanos	mexicanas

- Adjectives of nationality or of origin that end in a consonant also have four forms. An **-a** is added to form the feminine. The masculine plural ends in **-es**, not **-os**. Adjectives of nationality that have an accent mark on the last syllable of the masculine singular lose that accent mark when an ending is added:

español *Spanish*	masculine	feminine
sing.	español	española
pl.	españoles	españolas

inglés *English*	masculine	feminine
sing.	inglés	inglesa
pl.	ingleses	inglesas

alemán *German*	masculine	feminine
sing.	alemán	alemana
pl.	alemanes	alemanas

andaluz *Andalusian*	masculine	feminine
sing.	andaluz	andaluza
pl.	andaluces	andaluzas

- Adjectives of nationality or of origin that end in a vowel other than **-o** have only two forms. Many of these have the suffix **-ense** such as **canadiense** (*Canadian*), **bonaerense** (from Buenos Aires). *See also section **A** of this chapter.*

Adjetivos de nacionalidad (gentilicios)

continente		*islas*	
África	africano	las Antillas	antillano
la Antártida	antártico	las Bahamas	bahamiano
el Ártico	ártico	las Baleares	balear
Asia	asiático	Mallorca	mallorquín
Australia	australiano	las Canarias	canario
Europa	europeo	las Filipinas	filipino
Norteamérica	norteamericano (= estadounidense)		
Sudamérica	sudamericano		

país	*gentilicio*	*país*	*gentilicio*
Alemania	alemán	Israel	israelí
Arabia Saudita	saudí/saudita	Jamaica	jamaicano
Argelia	argelino	Jordania	jordano
(la) Argentina	argentino	(el) Japón	japonés
Australia	australiano	Kuwait/Kuweit	kuwaití
Austria	austríaco	Líbano	libanés
Bélgica	belga	Luxemburgo	luxemburgués
Bolivia	boliviano	Madagascar	malgache
(el) Brasil	brasileño	(República Malgache)	
Camboya	camboyano	Marruecos	marroquí
(el) Canadá	canadiense	México	mexicano
Chile	chileno	Nicaragua	nicaragüense
China	chino	Noruega	noruego
Colombia	colombiano	Nueva Zelanda	neocelandés
Corea	coreano	los Países Bajos	holandés
Costa Rica	costarricense	(el) Panamá	panameño
Cuba	cubano	(el) Paraguay	paraguayo
Dinamarca	danés	(el) Perú	peruano
(el) Ecuador	ecuatoriano	Polonia	polaco
Egipto	egipcio	Portugal	portugués
Escocia	escocés	Puerto Rico	puertorriqueño
España	español	(la) República Dominicana	dominicano
(los) Estados Unidos	norteamericano, estadounidense	Rusia	ruso
		El Salvador	salvadoreño
Finlandia	finlandés	Siria	sirio
Francia	francés	Sudán	sudanés
Grecia	griego	Suecia	sueco
Guatemala	guatemalteco	(la) Suiza	suizo
Haití	haitiano	Tailandia	tailandés
Holanda	holandés	Taiwán	taiwanés
Honduras	hondureño	Túnez	tunecino
Hungría	húngaro	Turquía	turco
(la) India	indio, hindú	(el) Uruguay	uruguayo
Inglaterra	inglés	Venezuela	venezolano
Irak/Iraq	iraquí	Vietnám	vietnamita
Irán	iraní	Yemen	yemení
Irlanda	irlandés		

ciudad	*gentilicio*	*ciudad*	*gentilicio*
Bogotá	bogotano	Málaga	malagueño
Buenos Aires	bonaerense/porteño	Nueva York	neoyorquino
Caracas	caraqueño	París	parisiense/parisino
Florencia	florentino	Quito	quiteño
Lima	limeño	Roma	romano
Londres	londinense	Sevilla	sevillano
Madrid	madrileño	Toledo	toledano

J. ¿De dónde son? Ud. y su amigo están preparando una lista de los estudiantes extranjeros de la facultad de ingeniería (*school of engineering*). Su amigo le pregunta si son de cierto país y Ud. lo confirma con el adjetivo de nacionalidad.

> **MODELO** Catalina es de Italia, ¿verdad?
> → Sí, es italiana.

1. Abrahán es de Rusia, ¿verdad?
2. Rosalinda y Arturo son del Canadá, ¿verdad?
3. David es de Israel, ¿verdad?
4. Mercedes es de Costa Rica, ¿verdad?
5. Hugo es de Guatemala, ¿verdad?
6. Xavier y Paula son de Bélgica, ¿verdad?
7. Alano es del Japón, ¿verdad?
8. Bárbara es de la India, ¿verdad?
9. Isabel y Lucía son de Egipto, ¿verdad?
10. Margarita es de Inglaterra, ¿verdad?
11. Gerardo es de Corea, ¿verdad?
12. Cristina y Oliverio son de Francia, ¿verdad?

K. ¡De muchos uno solo! Estados Unidos es un país de habitantes de miles de orígenes distintos. ¡Sin embargo, son todos *americanos*! Escriba oraciones que dicen de qué origen son estos habitantes usando el adjetivo del nombre del país.

> **MODELO** Josefa e Ignacio / Panamá
> Josefa e Ignacio son de origen panameño.

1. yo / Nueva Zelanda
2. Teodoro e Irene / El Salvador
3. Uds. / Líbano
4. Gabriel / Vietnám
5. Adela y Rosa / Irán
6. Estanislao y Sofía / Grecia
7. tú / Marruecos
8. Ud. y yo / Taiwán
9. Gualterio / Hungría

Nota cultural

Panamá tiene al norte el océano Atlántico o mar Caribe, al este Colombia, al sur el océano Pacífico y al oeste Costa Rica. El Canal de Panamá es una gran encrucijada (*crossroad*) estratégica del mundo que hace comunicar los dos mares. El Canal, construido por los Estados Unidos, fue abierto en 1914. Estados Unidos controlaba la Zona del Canal hasta 1978 cuando Estados Unidos y Panamá ratificaron un nuevo tratado (*treaty*) cambiando el nombre de la Zona al Área del Canal y dando soberanía (*sovereignty*) sobre el Canal a Panamá. Estados Unidos mantiene bases militares en el área. A partir del año 2000 el Canal será propiedad de Panamá.

D *More on the agreement of adjectives*

- Adjectives modifying two plural nouns of the same gender are in the plural of that gender:

  libros y periódicos argentin**os**   *Argentine books and newspapers*
  ciudades y provincias argentin**as**   *Argentine cities and provinces*

- If two nouns of different genders, whether singular or plural, are modified by a single adjective, the adjective is masculine plural:

  pantalones y chaquetas barat**os**   *inexpensive pants and jackets*
  un colegio y una universidad antigu**os**   *an ancient school and university*

- When a noun is used as an adjective, it usually does not agree in gender and number with the noun it modifies:

  una visita **relámpago**   *a quick visit*
    (relámpago *lightning*)
  la luz **piloto** (piloto *pilot*)   *pilot light (stove)*
  apartamentos **piloto**   *model apartments*

- Some of these nouns eventually become adjectives and show agreements. This is especially true of some nouns used as adjectives of color:

  zapatos **marrón/marrones**   *brown shoes*
  medias **café/cafés**   *light brown stockings*

L. Sustantivos en plural. Escriba la forma correcta del adjetivo en plural.

1. Hay _____ almacenes y restaurantes en el centro comercial. (bueno)

2. Conocimos varios pueblos y aldeas _____. (español)

3. Queremos manzanas y cerezas recién _____. (recogido)

4. Tengo mapas y guías _____. (inglés)

5. En la sala hay un sofá y dos sillones _____. (blanco)

6. Compre pan y torta _____. (fresco)

7. Laura necesita una blusa y unas medias _____. (rojo)

8. Busquen un lavaplatos y una máquina de lavar _____. (rebajado)

9. No se vende ni agua ni sales _____. (mineral)

10. El resultado del choque fueron un parachoques y una puerta _____. (nuevo)

11. Hay ofertas y liquidaciones _____ toda esta semana. (magnífico)

12. Clara tiene el pelo y las pestañas _____. (negro)

E *Two or more adjectives modifying a noun*

- Typically, if two adjectives modify a noun, they both follow it and are joined by **y**:

  | una chica inteligente **y** simpática | *a nice, intelligent girl* |
  | un día caluroso **y** agradable | *a warm, pleasant day* |

- If **y** is left out, the adjective that the speaker wishes to emphasize comes last:

  | artistas europeos **modernos** | *modern European artists (out of all European artists, the modern ones)* |
  | artistas modernos **europeos** | *modern European artists (out of all modern artists, the European ones)* |

- However, if one of the two adjectives usually precedes the noun, it is placed there:

cierto país europeo	*a certain European country*
el **único** estudiante español	*the only Spanish student*
diferentes libros científicos	*various scientific books*
otra ciudad moderna	*another modern city*
ese **pobre** hombre enfermo	*that poor sick man*

M. **El rodaje de una película.** (*The shooting of a film.*) Para comentar sobre el rodaje de una película por el director de cine Federico Felino, ponga los elementos de cada grupo en su orden correcto. Cada grupo consiste en un sustantivo, un adjetivo descriptivo y un adjetivo que aparece antes del sustantivo. Escriba la oración completa.

1. Federico Felino es director de cine / mejor / joven

2. Es su film / primero / doblado (*dubbed*)

3. Será una película / grande / extranjero

4. Tiene escenas / alguno / romántico

5. Se oye diálogo / uno / bueno

6. Hay efectos / alguno / especial

7. Escribieron guión (*script*) / uno / inteligente

8. Trabajaron en el film intérpretes (*masc. and fem.*) / principal (*star, lead*) / alguno

9. Hay subtítulos / alguno / bien traducido

10. La película tiene argumento (*plot*) / interesante / uno

11. La película ganará un premio / importante / cinematográfico

F   The past participle as an adjective

- The past participle of most verbs can function as an adjective:

El ladrón entró por la ventana **abierta.**   *The thief got in through the open window.*

Quiero dominar la lengua **escrita** y la lengua **hablada.**   *I want to master the written language and the spoken language.*

Encontré los documentos **perdidos.**   *I found the lost documents.*

- The Spanish past participle is used to describe positions of people and objects where the present participle is used in English:

Todos están **sentados** en el comedor.   *Everyone is **sitting** in the dining room.*

A estas horas hay mucha gente **parada** en el metro.   *At this hour there are a lot of people **standing** in the subway.*

N. Diálogos. Termine los siguientes diálogos con la forma correcta del adjetivo del modismo. Todos los adjetivos son participios pasados. El adjetivo se encuentra en el modismo o se deriva del verbo del modismo.

> MODELO   **estar loco de contento**   *to be wild with joy*
>
> Felipe —¿Sabes? Gané la lotería. ¡Estoy *loco* de contento!
> Isabel —¡Enhorabuena, chico! Si yo la ganara estaría *loca* de contento también.

1. **estar frito**   *to be all washed up*

   Diana: ¡Qué mala nota saqué en el examen! ¡Estoy _____!

   Mateo: Yo también. ¡Los dos estamos _____!

2. **estar hecho una sopa**   *to be soaking wet*

   Raúl: Está lloviendo a cántaros. (*It's raining cats and dogs.*) Estoy _____ una sopa.

   Sara: ¡Yo estoy _____ una sopa también!

3. **morirse de risa**   *to die laughing*

   Roberto: Mira a Clara e Inés. Están _____ de risa.

   Dorotea: Fíjate que Pepe y Esteban también están _____ de risa.

4. **comerse de envidia**   *to be eaten up with envy*

   Julia: ¿Sabes que Aurelia está _____ de envidia porque yo salgo con Matías?

   Anita: ¡No sólo Aurelia sino todas las chicas están _____ de envidia!

5. **meterse en lo que no le importa**   *to butt in*

   Lola: Como siempre, Raúl está _____ en lo que no le importa.

   Paco: Así son sus hermanos también, siempre _____ en lo que no les importa.

6. **estar muy pagado de sí mismo**   *to have a high opinion of oneself*

   Alfredo: Chico, ya no salgo con Brígida porque está muy _____ de sí misma.

   Nicolás: Haces muy bien. ¡Yo rompí con Tere, Eva y Paloma porque están

   muy _____ de sí mismas!

7. **dormirse en los laureles**   *to rest on one's laurels*

   Tito: Veo que no te esfuerzas porque estás _____ en los laureles.

   José: Cuando logres algo como yo, ¡tú también estarás _____ en los laureles!

8. **estar hecho una lástima**   *to be a sorry sight, in a sad state*

   Leonor: ¿Qué les pasa a Paula y Dora? Están _____ una lástima.

   Alicia: A lo mejor tienen lo que tiene Mari que también está _____ una lástima.

O. ¿Qué están haciendo? Use adjetivos que terminan en **-do** para explicar la posición de ciertas personas. Termine las oraciones con la forma correcta del adjetivo y del verbo **estar.**

> Modelo   Mario **está levantado** (levantar) ya.

1. Rosario _____ (acostar) durmiendo la siesta.

2. Clemente _____ (parar [*to stand*]) en la puerta de la casa esperando a su novia.

3. Los García _____ (sentar) a la mesa todavía por la sobremesa.

4. Pili _____ (asomar [*to lean out*]) en la ventana.

5. Los niños _____ (arrodillar) en el suelo jugando con sus cochecitos.

6. Adolfo y Javier _____ (tirar) en el suelo por los puñetazos que se dieron.

7. Paloma _____ (inclinar [*to bow*]) mientras el público aplaude.

Nota cultural

La sobremesa se refiere a la conversación alrededor de la mesa después de comer. Es una costumbre española tradicional.

P. ¡Preparados! ¡Listos! ¡Ya! (*Ready! Set! Go!*) Su amiga le pregunta cuándo Ud. y otras personas van a hacer ciertas cosas porque tiene prisa por salir. Escriba oraciones que dicen que Uds. están listos porque esas cosas ya están hechas. Practique usando adjetivos que terminan en **-do.**

> Modelo   ¿Cuándo van Uds. a arreglarse?
> → Ya estamos arreglados(as).

1. ¿Cuándo va Gerardo a bañarse?

2. ¿Cuándo van Elías e Isaac a afeitarse?

3. ¿Cuándo va Juliana a maquillarse?

4. ¿Cuándo van Uds. a vestirse?

5. ¿Cuándo va Ud. a peinarse?

6. ¿Cuándo van Simón y Martín a ducharse?

7. ¿Cuándo vas a pintarte?

Q. ¡A comer pues! Ya es hora de comer. Su mamá les dice a Ud. y a los otros miembros de su familia que hagan ciertas cosas. Pero parece que todo está ya. Explique eso derivando el adjetivo del verbo en el mandato.

> MODELO   Polo, prende el horno, por favor.
> → Ya está prendido.

1. Margara, pon los cubiertos (*place settings*), por favor.

2. Benjamín, sirve el agua, por favor.

3. Abuela, prepara el dulce de leche, por favor.

4. Pancho, rompe los huevos, por favor.

5. Pepe y Nano, corten el pan, por favor.

6. Trini, haz la ensalada, por favor.

7. Tía, bate las natillas, por favor.

8. Toni, pela unos dientes de ajo, por favor.

Nota cultural

Natillas, un postre español, es un dulce que contiene huevo, leche y azúcar.

G   *Adjectives used as nouns (nominalization of adjectives)*

- Spanish adjectives can be used as nouns when the noun they modify is deleted:

—Las camisas verdes son más caras que **las rojas.**	*The green shirts are more expensive than the red ones.*
—De acuerdo. Pero prefiero **las verdes.**	*OK. But I prefer the green ones.*
—La casa vieja es más grande que **la moderna.**	*The old house is bigger than the modern one.*
—Por eso vamos a comprar **la vieja.**	*That's why we're going to buy the old one.*

R. Opciones y preferencias. Sus amigos le preguntan qué cosas prefiere. Conteste sus preguntas escribiendo una de las dos posibilidades primero y luego la otra. ¡Es que, en realidad, le gustan ambas cosas! Use los adjetivos como sustantivos.

> MODELO   ¿Cuál prefieres, la novela histórica o la novela fantástica?
> → Prefiero la histórica. *and* Prefiero la fantástica.

1. ¿Cúal te gusta más, la música instrumental o la música vocal?

2. ¿Cuáles prefieres, los programas serios o los programas cómicos?

3. ¿Dónde prefieres comer, en un restaurante chino o en un restaurante francés?

4. ¿Cuáles te gustan más, los trajes azules o los trajes marrones?

5. ¿Prefieres un apartamento moderno o un apartamento viejo?

6. ¿Cuál te gusta más, una universidad particular (*private*) o una universidad estatal (*state*)?

7. ¿Cuál prefieres, las películas norteamericanas o las películas extranjeras?

8. ¿Dónde quieres vivir, en una ciudad grande o en una ciudad pequeña?

9. ¿Cuál te interesa más, las ciencias políticas o las ciencias naturales?

H *Comparative of adjectives*

- One object or person may be seen as having more, less, or the same amount of a characteristic as another. To express this, Spanish and English use the comparative construction:

  Comparison of superiority (**más** + adjetivo + **que**):

La avenida es **más ancha que** nuestra calle.	*The avenue is **wider than** our street.*

  Comparison of inferiority (**menos** + adjetivo + **que**):

Pero la avenida es **menos ancha que** la autopista.	*But the avenue is **less wide than** the superhighway.*

  Note that in English the comparison of inferiority is usually expressed as *not as*: The avenue is *not as wide as* the superhighway.

  Comparison of equality (**tan** + adjetivo + **como**):

La avenida es **tan ancha como** el Paseo de Miraflores.	*The avenue is as wide as Miraflores Boulevard.*

- The adjectives **bueno** and **malo** have irregular comparative forms:

  bueno → **mejor**   malo → **peor**

Este restaurante es **mejor** que el otro.	*This restaurant is better than the other one.*
El ruido aquí es **peor** que en el barrio mío.	*The noise is worse here than in my neighborhood.*

  Más bueno and **más malo** are used to refer to moral qualities.

- **Grande** and **pequeño** have irregular comparative forms when they refer to age:

  grande → **mayor** *older*   pequeño → **menor** *younger*

Mi hermano **menor** es más alto que mi hermana **mayor**.	*My younger brother is taller than my older sister.*

- Adverbs are compared in the same way as adjectives:

Ella contesta **más cortésmente que** él.	*She answers **more politely than** he does.*
Ella contesta **menos cortésmente que** él.	*She answers **less politely than** he does.*
Ella contesta **tan cortésmente como** él.	*She answers **as politely as** he does.*

- In comparing verbs and nouns, **tan** changes to **tanto**. **Tanto** is invariable with verbs, but agrees with nouns that follow it:

Comparing verbs:

Yo trabajo **más que** tú.	*I work **more than** you do.*
Yo trabajo **menos que** tú.	*I work **less than** you do.*
Yo trabajo **tanto como** tú.	*I work **as much as** you do.*

Comparing nouns:

—Creo que tú tienes **menos exámenes que** Amalia.	*I think you have **fewer exams than** Amalia.*
—Te equivocas. Tengo **tantos exámenes como** ella, y **más trabajos** escritos.	*You're mistaken. I have **as many exams as** she has, and **more papers**.*

- **Que** (*than*) is followed by *subject pronouns* unless the pronoun is the direct or indirect object of the verb. In that case, **que** is followed by **a** + stressed pronoun:

Yo estudio más **que tú.**	*I study more **than you do.***
A mí me gusta más **que a ti.**	*I like it more **than you do.***

- **Que** is followed by **nada** and **nadie** where English uses *anything, anyone*:

El curso es difícil, más **que nada.**	*The course is hard, more **than anything.***
Luis Alberto baila mejor **que nadie.**	*Luis Alberto dances better **than anyone.***

- **Que** is replaced by **de** before a numeral:

Ganan más **de** ochocientos dólares por semana.	*They earn more than eight hundred dollars a week.*

- **Que** is replaced by **de lo que** before a clause implying a standard for comparison:

—Este libro es más difícil **de lo que** cree el profesor.	*This book is more difficult than the teacher thinks.*
—Y menos interesante **de lo que** yo me imaginaba.	*And less interesting than I imagined.*

How difficult the teacher thought the book was or *how interesting I imagined the book was* is the basis for comparison.

- **Que** is replaced by **de** before **el que, la que, los que, las que.** The article represents a deleted noun:

Necesito más plata **de la que** me prestaste. (*la que = la plata que*)	*I need more money than (the money) you lent me.*
Encontramos menos problemas **de los que** esperábamos. (*los que = los problemas que*)	*We found fewer problems than (the problems) we expected.*

S. En comparación. Combine las dos oraciones de cada grupo en una sola que expresa una comparación. Escriba dos oraciones de comparación para cada grupo.

> MODELO   Loren es listo./Julio es más listo.
> → Julio es **más** listo que Loren.
> → Loren es **menos** listo que Julio.

1. Ana es astuta./Luisa es más astuta.

2. El museo de arte es bueno./El museo de historia natural es mejor.

3. Mi novio (Mi novia) es inteligente./Yo soy más inteligente.

4. El cuarto de Elena es hermoso./Tu cuarto es más hermoso.

5. La película inglesa es aburrida./La película francesa es más aburrida.

6. Los bailarines son talentosos./Los cantantes son más talentosos.

7. Las blusas de algodón son elegantes./Las blusas de seda son más elegantes.

8. Tu hermano es grande./Tu hermana es mayor.

T. Comparación de adverbios. Escriba una comparación de adverbios de tres maneras: **más, menos** e **igual.**

> MODELO   Él corrió **más** rápidamente **que** ella.
> Ella corrió **menos** rápidamente **que** él.
> Él corrió **tan** rápidamente **como** ella.

1. José habló _____ francamente _____ Consuelo.

   Consuelo habló _____ francamente _____ José.

   José habló _____ francamente _____ Consuelo.

2. Los enfermeros trabajaron _____ cuidadosamente _____ los médicos.

   Los médicos trabajaron _____ cuidadosamente _____ los enfermeros.

   Los enfermeros trabajaron _____ cuidadosamente _____ los médicos.

3. Virginia resolvió los problemas _____ fácilmente _____ Cristina.

   Cristina resolvió los problemas _____ fácilmente _____ Virginia.

   Virginia resolvió los problemas _____ fácilmente _____ Cristina.

U. Adjetivos: igualdad. Escriba oraciones que demuestran la comparación de igualdad de los dos sustantivos.

> MODELO   Eduardo/diligente/Memo
> → Eduardo es tan diligente como Memo.

1. la obra de teatro/divertida/la película

2. las clases de física/fáciles/las clases de cálculo

3. los documentales/artísticos/los reportajes

4. los platos griegos/sabrosos/los platos húngaros

5. esta actriz/célebre/ese actor

6. el arroz/bueno/el maíz

7. el príncipe/valiente/el rey

8. Francisca/aburrida/su hermana María

9. la inflación/baja/la inflación de hace tres años

I   Superlative of adjectives; absolute superlative

- Spanish has no special superlative form. Usually, the definite article (or possessive adjective) is used with the noun that the adjective modifies to imply a superlative. Compare the following comparative and superlative sentences:

  —Quiero ver una película **más emocionante.** (*comparative*)

  *I want to see a **more exciting** film.*

  —Ésta es **la película más emocionante** que alquilé. (*superlative*)

  *This is **the most exciting film** that I rented.*

- After a superlative, *in* is translated by **de**:

  —Estamos en la ciudad más importante **del** país.

  *We're in the most important city **in the** country.*

  —Y ésta es la calle más elegante **de** la ciudad.

  *And this is the most elegant street **in the** city.*

- Spanish has a suffix **-ísimo,** called the absolute superlative, that is added to adjectives. This suffix adds the idea of *very* to the adjective. Note that **c** and **g** change to **qu** and **gu,** and **z** changes to **c** when **-ísimo** is added. Adjectives in **-ísimo** are four-form adjectives:

  lindo ➔ lindísimo   feo ➔ feísimo   largo ➔ larguísimo
  fácil ➔ facilísimo   rico ➔ riquísimo   feliz ➔ felicísimo

V. Nuestra clase. Use los signos aritméticos para formar superlativos que describan a los estudiantes de la clase.

> **MODELO**   Carlos / − atento
> ➔ Carlos es el estudiante menos atento.

1. Juan Pablo / + aplicado

2. Fermín y Cosme / − obediente

3. Silvia / + simpático

4. Irene y María / − trabajador

5. Verónica / + inteligente

6. Íñigo y Esteban / + hablador

7. Sergio / + encantador

8. Rosa y Jacinto / − preparado

W. **¡Qué parque más precioso!** Confirme las observaciones de su amigo respecto al parque que están visitando con el superlativo absoluto del adjetivo.

> MODELO   El parque es lindo.
> → Sí. Es **lindísimo.**

1. La vegetación es interesante.
2. Ese árbol es viejo.
3. Esas flores son hermosas.
4. El zoológico del parque es grande.
5. Ese león parece feroz.
6. Los monos son simpáticos.
7. Las veredas (*paths*) son largas.
8. El lago es bello.

X. **Visitando la ciudad.** Raquel les enseña su ciudad a sus amigos. Les explica todo lo que ven con superlativos. Escriba lo que les dice a los amigos.

> MODELO   aquí está/biblioteca/importante/ciudad
> → Aquí está la biblioteca más importante de la ciudad.

1. allí se encuentra/plaza/imponente/ciudad
2. aquí ven/catedral/antiguo/estado
3. en frente hay/universidad/conocido/país
4. ésta es/calle/largo/ciudad
5. en esta calle hay/tiendas/hermoso/zona
6. allí está/tienda de comestibles/estimado/barrio
7. delante de nosotros hay/hotel/internacional/país
8. en este barrio se encuentran/restaurantes/concurrido (*busy, much frequented*)/ciudad
9. aquí ven/casa/viejo/ciudad
10. pronto veremos/estadio/grande/región

Y. **La clase de literatura.** El profesor y los estudiantes describen las obras que estudian con superlativos. Escriba lo que dicen.

> MODELO   novela/interesante/siglo
> → Es la novela más interesante del siglo.

1. poema/conocido/literatura europea
2. obra de teatro/presentado/año
3. comedia/aplaudido/teatro nacional
4. novela/vendido/literatura moderna
5. tragedia/estimado/nuestro teatro
6. poeta/respetado/su siglo
7. novelista/leído/mundo
8. dramaturgo/apreciado/nuestra época

Z. Exprese las siguientes ideas en español.

1. I read more than you (*Ud.*) do.

2. They know less than we do.

3. Ignacio complains as much as his wife does.

4. I have more compact discs than Federico.

5. Eva sees fewer films than Margarita.

6. We take as many trips as they do.

7. We have more than ten thousand books in our library.

8. The soccer game was more exciting than they expected.

9. I want more jewels than you gave me!

10. This is the most expensive coat that I've bought.

11. Ruiz is the best programmer in the company.

12. This is the most beautiful beach in the country.

AA. **Ejercicio oral.** Converse con un amigo/una amiga en describir a sus parientes y a sus amigos. Describa cómo son (carácter, personalidad, lo físico), cómo están, de dónde son, de qué origen son, etcétera.

BB. **Estructuras en acción.** Lea el pronóstico meteorológico de un periódico español fijándose mucho en los adjetivos. Luego haga los ejercicios. Pero antes de hacerlos, unos consejos:

- repase el vocabulario sobre el tiempo y los puntos cardinales (*directions*)
- relacione adjetivos con sus sustantivos correspondientes (piense en la familia lingüística)
- consulte un mapa en el cual figuran España, las islas españolas y el norte de África (Marruecos)

El tiempo

a lo largo del día *throughout the day*	**la nube** *cloud*
a última hora *at the end of the day*	**nuboso** *cloudy*
el carácter *kind, nature*	**occidental** *western*
costero *coastal*	**parcialmente** *partially*
cubierto *overcast*	**el predominio** *prevalence, predominance*
el chubasco *downpour, shower*	**el pronóstico (meteorológico)** *(weather) forecast*
el descenso *decline*	
despejado *clear*	**el riesgo** *risk*
disperso *scattered*	**salvo** *except*
flojo *light*	**soleado** *sunny*
la granizada *hailstorm*	**el tercio norte** *the northern third*
ligero *light*	**el litoral** *coast*	**el tiempo** *weather*
matinal *morning*	**la tormenta** *storm*
la mitad sur *the southern half*	**tormentoso** *stormy*
la niebla *mist, fog*	

Términos geográficos

Andalucía *región del sur de España*
Asturias *región del norte de España*
Baleares *islas españolas del Mediterráneo (Mallorca, Menorca, Ibiza, etcétera)*
las Canarias *islas españolas del Atlántico (cerca de Marruecos [Morocco])*
Castilla y León *Castilla la Vieja, región del centro de España*
Cataluña *región del nordeste de España*
Ceuta *plaza de soberanía (city enclave) española en Marruecos*
la Comunidad Valenciana *Comunidad Autónoma y provincia de España en el Mediterráneo*
Extremadura *Comunidad Autónoma y región que queda al oeste de España*
Galicia *Comunidad Autónoma y región que queda al noroeste de España*
Murcia *Comunidad Autónoma y región que queda al sudeste de España*
Navarra *Comunidad Autónoma y región que queda al norte de España*
Madrid *capital de España y de la provincia de Madrid; Comunidad Autónoma*
Melilla *plaza de soberanía (city enclave) española en Marruecos*
los Pirineos *cadena de montañas entre España y Francia*

EL TIEMPO
Tormentas, más irregulares en el tercio norte

El cielo estará casi despejado en Canarias y parcialmente nuboso en Ceuta, Melilla y litoral andaluz. Predominio del cielo nuboso en el resto de la mitad sur de la Península con intervalos muy nubosos. Podrán producirse granizadas muy locales. Nieblas matinales y temperaturas en ligero descenso.

Área de Madrid: Núcleos nubosos que irán aumentando a lo largo del día, con algunos chubascos tormentosos a última hora. Vientos flojos.

Andalucía: Nubes dispersas, con cielos más despejados por la mitad occidental.

Asturias: Cielos muy nubosos o cubiertos, con algunos chubascos de carácter débil a moderado.

Baleares: Nuboso, especialmente en la isla de Menorca, donde habrá alguna precipitación.

Canarias: Ambiente soleado, aunque con núcleos nubosos por la zona norte.

Castilla y León: Cielos muy nubosos, con algunas precipitaciones, que pueden ser de origen tormentoso.

Cataluña: Cielos muy nubosos, sobre todo en el Pirineo, donde hay riesgo de tormentas.

Comunidad Valenciana: Soleado en la mayor parte de la Comunidad.

Extremadura: Soleado, excepto en la parte norte, donde se formarán núcleos nubosos.

Galicia: Cielos nubosos, con precipitaciones de carácter débil.

Murcia: Predominio de los cielos poco nubosos o despejados, salvo nubes dispersas por la zona costera.

Navarra: Muy nuboso, con tormentas, más abundantes por la tarde.

1. Escriba adjetivos que aparecen en el pronóstico que están relacionados con las siguientes palabras.

1. sol	8. abundancia
2. tormenta	9. despejar
3. costa	10. mañana
4. occidente	11. debilidad
5. cubrir	12. ligereza
6. nube	13. dispersar
7. Andalucía	14. flojera

2. Escriba frases que describan el tiempo que hace en ciertas regiones de España. Haga una paráfrasis de lo que está escrito en el pronóstico. Por ejemplo, en Cataluña, **está muy nublado, es posible que haya tempestades.**

1. En Castilla y León

2. En la Comunidad Valenciana

3. En el área de Madrid

4. En Asturias

5. En las Baleares

6. En Ceuta y Melilla

7. En Galicia

8. En Murcia

CHAPTER 18
DEMONSTRATIVES & POSSESSIVES

A Demonstrative adjectives

- Spanish has three demonstrative adjectives: **este** *this* (*near the speaker*), **ese** *that* (*near the person spoken to*), and **aquel** *that* (*removed from both the speaker and the person spoken to*). The demonstrative adjectives agree in gender and number with the noun they modify:

	masculine	*feminine*
singular	**este**	**esta**
plural	**estos**	**estas**

	masculine	*feminine*
singular	**ese**	**esa**
plural	**esos**	**esas**

	masculine	*feminine*
singular	**aquel**	**aquella**
plural	**aquellos**	**aquellas**

Este apartamento tiene más habitaciones que **aquellas** casas.

This apartment has more rooms than those houses (over there).

Préstame **ese** bolígrafo que tienes. **Este** bolígrafo que tengo ya no escribe.

Lend me that ballpoint pen that you have. This ballpoint that I have doesn't write any more.

Note that the three demonstratives correspond to the three place words for *here* and *there*:

este ~ aquí
ese ~ ahí
aquel ~ allí

- The demonstrative **ese** can be placed after the noun to convey a note of contemptuousness:

No sé por qué una muchacha tan inteligente como Margarita saldría con el chico **ese.**

I don't know why a girl as intelligent as Margarita would go out with a guy like that.

A. Útiles de escuela. Cambie el artículo definido o indefinido a la forma correcta del adjetivo demostrativo para hablar de sus útiles de escuela. Escriba cada oración de tres maneras.

Útiles de escuela	
el atlas *atlas*	**la goma de borrar** *eraser*
el bolígrafo *ballpoint pen*	**el libro de texto** *textbook*
el compás *compass*	**el papel cuadriculado** *graph paper*
el diccionario *dictionary*	**la regla** *ruler*
la enciclopedia *encyclopedia*	**el sacapuntas** *pencil sharpener*

> MODELO   Necesito un cuaderno.
> → Necesito **este** cuaderno.
> → Necesito **ese** cuaderno.
> → Necesito **aquel** cuaderno.

1. Los libros de texto están bien escritos.

2. Compré el compás anteayer.

3. Consultaré el atlas.

4. Prefiero el papel cuadriculado.

5. La marca de sacapuntas es conocida.

6. Me gusta el diccionario de español.

7. Los bolígrafos no sirven.

8. Encontré las reglas en la papelería.

9. Las enciclopedias no tienen información sobre el tema.

B. De compras en El Corte Inglés. Complete los siguientes diálogos entre unos amigos que van de compras. Llene los espacios en blanco con la forma correcta del adjetivo demostrativo.

En la sección de ropa para mujeres

1. Irene —Oye, Trini, ¿qué te parece _____ (*this*) traje?

2. Trini —¿Cuál? ¿_____ (*That*) traje azul?

3. Irene —Sí. ¿Verdad que _____ (*this*) color es muy bonito?

4. Trini —Francamente me gusta más _____ (*that, over there*) traje verde.

5. Pero me gustan _____ (*these*) blusas y no hacen juego con el traje verde.

6. Trini —Bueno chica, llévate _____ (*that*) traje azul y _____ (*those*) blusas entonces.

   Y si te queda dinero todavía, cómprate el traje verde con _____ (*that, over there*)

   blusa negra. ¡El conjunto (*outfit*) te quedará fenómeno!

En la sección de ropa para hombres

7. Lupe —Bueno, Tito, ayúdame. ¿Qué le regalo a Mateo por su cumpleaños?

   ¿_____ (*This*) corbata roja o _____ (*that*) cinturón negro?

8. Tito —Querida hermana, no me gustan ni _____ (*these*) corbatas ni _____ (*those*) cinturones. Mateo es un gran chico. _____ (*This*) novio tuyo se merece algo más interesante e importante. Mira _____ (*this*) sección de deportes … _____ (*that*) bate, o _____ (*that, over there*) guante para jugar béisbol … o quizás _____ (*that*) raqueta de tenis, o …

9. Lupe —Tito, yo comprendo lo que estás haciendo. ¡Quieres que Mateo te preste su nuevo bate o guante o raqueta! _____ (*This*) no puede ser. ¡Es mejor que escoja el regalo yo!

Nota cultural

El Corte Inglés es uno de los grandes almacenes españoles con sucursales por todo el país. Se vende de todo en el almacén—ropa, muebles, aparatos electrodomésticos (*appliances*), etcétera. Tiene hasta un supermercado completo también.

B Demonstrative pronouns

- Demonstrative pronouns in Spanish have the same form as demonstrative adjectives. The noun is deleted and an accent mark is added over the stressed vowel of the demonstrative:

—Estas tortas son más ricas que **aquéllas.**	*These cakes are more delicious than **those** (over there).*
—Pero aquellas galletas no son tan buenas como **éstas.**	*But those cookies (over there) aren't as good as **these**.*
—¿Qué camisa prefiere Ud.? ¿**Ésta** o **ésa**?	*Which shirt do you prefer? **This one** or **that one**?*
—Creo que me gusta más **aquélla** que está en el otro mostrador.	*I think that I like **that one** on the other counter best.*
—Aquellos anteojos son más bonitos que **ésos.**	*Those eyeglasses (over there) are prettier than **those**.*
—Puede ser, pero **éstos** tienen la montura que más me gusta.	*That may be, but **these** have the frame I like best.*
—¿Quiénes son los dos muchachos que figuran en la foto?	*Who are the two boys in the photograph?*
—**Éste** es mi primo Carlos y **ése** es su amigo.	***This one** is my cousin Carlos and **that one** is his friend.*

Note: In modern usage, the written accent is sometimes left off demonstrative pronouns.

- Spanish has three neuter demonstrative pronouns ending in **-o**: **esto, eso, aquello.** These never have a written accent. They refer to situations or ideas, not to specific nouns:

—Dicen que Pedro toma y que después maneja.	*They say that Pedro drinks and then drives.*
—No hay nada más peligroso que **eso.**	*There's nothing more dangerous than **that.** (**eso** = drinking and driving)*
—El tío Marcos tenía antes una tienda de ropa en el centro.	*Uncle Marcos used to have a clothing store downtown.*
—**Aquello** fue hace muchos años, ¿verdad?	***That** was many years ago, wasn't it? (**aquello** = that he had a clothing store downtown)*

- The neuter demonstratives can be followed by **de** to express *this/that situation regarding* or *this/that matter of/about:*

Esto de trabajar demasiado no te hace ningún bien.	***This situation of (your) working too much** is not doing you any good.*
Aquello de tu hermano Íñigo me puso triste.	***That business about your brother Íñigo** made me sad.*

C. **Un crítico de restaurantes.** Ud. es crítico de restaurantes. Alguien le hace una entrevista sobre ciertas comidas que probó. Contéstele usando los pronombres demostrativos en su respuesta.

> MODELO   ¿Qué queso le gustó más? ¿Este queso o ese queso?
> → Me gustó **éste** más que **ése.**
> *or* Me gustó **ése** más que **éste.**

1. ¿Qué salsa de champiñones (*mushrooms*) le gustó más? ¿Esa salsa o aquella salsa?

2. ¿Qué fideos le gustaron más? ¿Aquellos fideos o estos fideos?

3. ¿Qué bizcocho le gustó más? ¿Este bizcocho o ese bizcocho?

4. ¿Qué salchichas le gustaron más? ¿Esas salchichas o aquellas salchichas?

5. ¿Qué guisado (*stew*) le gustó más? ¿Este guisado o ese guisado?

6. ¿Qué panes le gustaron más? ¿Estos panes o aquellos panes?

7. ¿Qué sopa de legumbres le gustó más? ¿Esta sopa de legumbres o esa sopa de legumbres?

 Possessive adjectives

- Possessive adjectives in Spanish agree with the noun they modify. Possessive adjectives referring to the singular pronouns and to the third-person plural have only two forms: a singular and a plural. The possessives **nuestro** and **vuestro** are four-form adjectives. On the next page is a chart of the short-form or unstressed possessive adjectives in Spanish.

(yo) **mi/mis**	(nosotros) **nuestro/-a/-os/-as**
(tú) **tu/tus**	(vosotros) **vuestro/-a/-os/-as**
(él/ella/Ud.) **su/sus**	(ellos/ellas/Uds.) **su/sus**

- The possessive adjective **su/sus** means *his, her, its, your, their*. To clarify who is referred to, a phrase consisting of **de** + pronoun may be added:

  —¡Qué bueno! Allí están Sergio y
  Marisa. Necesito su libro.

  Great! There are Sergio and Marisa. I need (his/her/their) book.

  —¿El libro **de él** o el libro **de ella**?

  His book or her book?

  —¿Qué cinta te gustó más?

  Which tape did you like best?

  —La cinta **de Uds.** La cinta **de ellos** no me gustó tanto.

  Your tape. I didn't like their tape so much.

- Spanish has a set of long-form or stressed possessive adjectives that can be used to contrast one possessor with another (*It's **my** book, not **your** book.*). These are all four-form adjectives and follow the noun they modify:

el libro **mío**	la cinta **mía**	el libro **nuestro**	la cinta **nuestra**
los libros **míos**	las cintas **mías**	los libros **nuestros**	las cintas **nuestras**
el libro **tuyo**	la cinta **tuya**	el libro **vuestro**	la cinta **vuestra**
los libros **tuyos**	las cintas **tuyas**	los libros **vuestros**	las cintas **vuestras**
el libro **suyo**	la cinta **suya**	el libro **suyo**	la cinta **suya**
los libros **suyos**	las cintas **suyas**	los libros **suyos**	las cintas **suyas**

The phrases consisting of **de** + pronoun clarify the person **suyo** refers to:

  —Rogelio y Paula escribieron muchos artículos.

  Rogelio and Paula wrote a lot of articles.

  —**Los** artículos **de él** se publicaron en España y **los** artículos **de ella** en México.

  His articles were published in Spain and her articles in Mexico.

  —**La** pluma **mía** no tiene tinta. ¿Me prestas **la** pluma **tuya**?

  My pen doesn't have any ink. Can you lend me your pen?

  —Lo siento. **La** pluma **mía** no funciona tampoco.

  I'm sorry. My pen doesn't work either.

- The long-form possessive adjectives can also occur with the indefinite article:

  unos amigos **míos**   *some friends of mine*
  una idea **tuya**   *an idea of yours*

D. **¡En el depósito de artículos perdidos** (*lost and found*)! ¿Adónde van a parar las cosas perdidas? Ud. y su amigo buscan esos artículos en el depósito donde suelen acabar. Dígale a su amigo que las cosas pertenecen a otra persona de la que creía. Use un adjetivo posesivo en su respuesta.

> MODELO   Esta bufanda será de Paco, ¿no? (Jorge)
> ➜ No, no es suya. Será de Jorge.

1. Este guante será de Rebeca, ¿no? (Martina)

2. Estas llaves serán de Carlos y Pepe, ¿no? (nosotros)

3. Este cepillo para el pelo será de Amparo, ¿no? (Rosita)

4. Estos apuntes de historia serán del nuevo estudiante de intercambio, ¿no? (Uds.)

5. Estas calculadoras serán de Fernando y Graciela, ¿no? (tú)

6. Este pañuelo será de Anita, ¿no? (la profesora Márquez)

7. Esta agenda (*appointment book*) será de Uds., ¿no? (Eduardo)

E. Viajes. ¿Qué se lleva en un viaje? Escriba cada frase empleando un adjetivo posesivo de forma larga.

> MODELO   el paquete/(yo)
> → el paquete mío

Hacer un viaje

el billete de ida y vuelta *round-trip ticket*	**el maletín** *small suitcase*
la bolsa de viaje *travel bag*	**la mochila** *backpack*
el cheque de viajero *traveler's check*	**el paquete** *package*
el equipaje de mano *hand luggage*	**la visa** *visa*
la maleta *suitcase*	

1. las maletas/(tú)

2. el equipaje de mano/(nosotros)

3. los cheques de viajero/(ellos)

4. la bolsa de viaje/(Ud.)

5. los maletines/(tú y yo)

6. la mochila/(Uds.)

7. el pasaporte/(yo)

8. las visas/(ellas)

9. los billetes de ida y vuelta/(tú)

 Possessive pronouns

• Spanish possessive pronouns consist of the definite article plus the long-form possessive adjective. The noun is deleted:

—Javier se compró un coche espléndido.

Javier bought himself a terrific car.

—Sí, **el suyo** costó mucho más que **el nuestro.**

*Yes, **his** cost much more than **ours** did.*

—Los estudiantes míos son muy buenos este semestre. ¿Y **los suyos**?

*My students are very good this semester. What about **yours**?*

—**Los míos** también son excelentes.

***Mine** are excellent too.*

—Mira mi computadora nueva.

Look at my new computer.

—Es fabulosa. Creo que **la tuya** tiene más memoria que **la mía.**

*It's fabulous. I think **yours** has more memory than **mine**.*

- The masculine plural of the possessive pronoun can refer to family members or to teams:

  —¿Cómo están **los tuyos**?   *How's your family?*
  —¿**Los míos**? Perfectamente, gracias.   *My family? Just fine, thanks.*

  —Espero que ganen **los nuestros**.   *I hope our team wins.*
  —Vamos a ver. Los otros son muy   *Let's see. The others are very good too.*
  buenos también.

- The neuter article **lo** + the masculine singular of the long-form possessive forms a neuter possessive pronoun meaning *whose part, whose task, etc.*:

  —Denme **lo mío** y me voy.   *Give me **my share** and I'll leave.*
  —**Lo tuyo** son veinte dólares.   ***Your part** is twenty dollars.*

  —No encontramos **lo nuestro,** señor.   *We can't find **our things,** sir.*
  —**Lo suyo** está en la oficina.   ***Your things** are in the office.*

F. **¡Fernando el fanfarrón (braggart)!** ¡Cada vez que alguien dice que tiene algo bueno, Fernando se jacta (*brags*) de tener algo mejor! Escriba lo que dice Fernando usando los pronombres posesivos.

> **MODELO**   Martín —Mi coche es muy lujoso.
>   Fernando —¡Pero el mío es más lujoso que el tuyo!

1. Lorenzo: Mi raqueta de tenis es muy moderna.

   Fernando: _____

2. Patricia: Mis discos compactos son nuevos.

   Fernando: _____

3. Ricardo: Mi novia es muy simpática.

   Fernando: _____

4. Dalia: Mi computadora funciona muy bien.

   Fernando: _____

5. Carlos: Mis revistas de deportes son muy interesantes.

   Fernando: _____

6. Clara: Mis notas son muy buenas.

   Fernando: _____

7. Leo: Mi perro es sumamente inteligente.

   Fernando: _____

G. ¿Dónde está? Use pronombres posesivos para explicar dónde cree Ud. que
están ciertas cosas.

> MODELO   ¿Dónde está el anillo de Virginia? (en el dormitorio)
> → El suyo estará en el dormitorio.

1. ¿Dónde están los manuales de José? (en el estante [*shelf*])

2. ¿Dónde está tu permiso de manejar? (en mi cartera)

3. ¿Dónde están las pulseras de Lola y Nieves? (en la cómoda)

4. ¿Dónde están los sellos de Uds.? (en la gaveta [*drawer*])

5. ¿Dónde está nuestra agenda? (en el escritorio)

6. ¿Dónde están vuestros frascos de agua de colonia? (en el baño)

7. ¿Dónde está su (de Ud.) guitarra? (encima del piano)

H. ¡Qué niño más repipí (*precocious brat*)! Angelito siempre se sale con la suya
(*gets his own way*). ¿Y estas otras personas? ¿Siempre se salen con la suya? Use
el pronombre posesivo apropiado en contestar que sí o que no.

> MODELO   la hermanita de Angelito (sí)
> → Sí, se sale con la suya.

1. las hermanas mayores de Angelito (no)

2. Rafaelito (no)

3. Ud. (sí)

4. Bárbara (no)

5. Uds. (no)

6. tú (sí)

7. vosotros (sí)

I. Exprese las siguientes oraciones en español.

1. This business about the company is difficult to understand.

2. That situation regarding our trip has to be resolved.

3. We'll have to talk about that matter of buying a new car.

4. An old friend of mine is arriving on Saturday.

5. How's your (*tú*) family? (use a possessive pronoun)

6. We hope our team wins. (use a possessive pronoun)

7. Your part (task) is to bring the flowers. (*Ud.*)

8. My part is to make copies (*fotocopiar*).

J. Ejercicio oral. Practique el uso de los demostrativos y los posesivos. Pregúnteles
a sus amigos a quiénes pertenecen ciertas cosas. Por ejemplo, Ud. pregunta
«¿De quién es este disco compacto?» Un amigo contesta: «Es mío» o «Es suyo
(Es de él)», señalando a otro amigo.

CHAPTER 19

PERSONAL PRONOUNS: SUBJECT, OBJECT, PREPOSITIONAL

A *Subject pronouns*

- The subject pronouns in Spanish are:

singular	plural
yo *I*	**nosotros, nosotras** *we*
tú *you (informal singular)*	**vosotros, vosotras** *you (informal plural, Spain only)*
él *he, it*	**ellos** *they, masculine*
ella *she, it*	**ellas** *they, feminine*
Ud. (usted) *you* (*formal singular*)	**Uds. (ustedes)** *you* (*formal and informal plural in Latin America, formal plural in Spain*)

- There are several important differences between the personal pronouns in English and Spanish:

  1. Spanish has four forms for *you* that show politeness and number. However, **vosotros/vosotras** is used only in Spain, giving Latin American Spanish three forms for *you:* two singular forms **tú** (informal) and **usted** (formal), and one plural form **ustedes** that can be used for any group of two or more people.

  2. Since all Spanish nouns are either masculine or feminine, **él** and **ella** refer to things as well as to people.

  3. **Ud.** and **Uds.** are often abbreviated **Vd.** and **Vds.** in Spain.

  4. Subject pronouns are less common in Spanish than in English because the verb endings show who is performing the action. They are used, however, to contrast or emphasize the subject of the verb.

—¿Qué haces mañana?	*What are you doing tomorrow?*
—Trabajo.	*I'm working.*
—¿Qué hacen (Uds.) mañana?	*What are you doing tomorrow?*
—**Ella** tiene el día libre, pero **yo** trabajo.	*She has the day off, but **I**'m working.*

- Note the following use of the subject pronouns with **ser** (colloquial English translations appear in parentheses):

Soy yo. *It is I. (It's me.)*	**Somos nosotros, Somos nosotras.** *It is we. (It's us.)*
Eres tú. *It is you.*	**Sois vosotros, Sois vosotras.** *It is you.*
Es él. *It is he. (It's him.)*	**Son ellos.** *It is they. (masculine) (It's them.)*
Es ella. *It is she. (It's her.)*	**Son ellas.** *It is they. (feminine) (It's them.)*
Es Ud. *It is you.*	**Son Uds.** *It is you.*

A. Identifique el sujeto de cada oración. Escriba el pronombre sujeto al lado de la oración. Si hay más de una posibilidad, escriba todos los pronombres posibles.

> MODELO   ¡Lees una cantidad de libros! **tú**

1. Estacionemos en esta calle.
2. Es español.
3. Sois simpáticas.
4. Buscaban casa.
5. Tengo razón.
6. Está contentísima.
7. Cenasteis a las nueve.
8. Lo verás.
9. Eran bellas.
10. Es inglesa.

B. Yo ... pero tú ... Practique usando el pronombre sujeto en combinar las dos oraciones en una.

> MODELO   Estudias español. Estudia (ella) francés.
> → *Tú* estudias español, pero *ella* estudia francés.

1. Trabajo de lunes a viernes. Trabajas los fines de semana.
2. Estudiamos en una universidad particular. Estudian (Uds.) en una universidad estatal.
3. Viven (ellas) en pleno centro. Vive (Ud.) en las afueras.
4. Vas de compras el sábado. Vamos de compras el jueves.
5. Es (él) abogado. Soy profesor.
6. Desayuna (Ud.) fuerte. Desayuna (ella) poco.
7. Escuchan (ellos) música clásica. Escucháis rock.

B *Pronouns after prepositions (prepositional pronouns)*

- After a preposition, Spanish uses the subject pronouns, except for **yo** and **tú**:

para **mí**	para **nosotros/nosotras**
para **ti**	para **vosotros/vosotras**
para **él**	para **ellos**
para **ella**	para **ellas**
para **Ud.**	para **Uds.**

Note that **mí** has a written accent but **ti** does not.

- Two irregular forms exist with the preposition **con**: **conmigo** (*with me*) and **contigo** (*with you*) (*informal singular*). There is also a form **consigo** (*with himself, with herself, with themselves*).

—¿Puedes ir conmigo?	*Can you go with me?*
—Hoy no. Mañana voy contigo.	*Not today. Tomorrow I'll go with you.*
—Alicia está enojada con nosotros.	*Alicia is angry with us.*
—Debería estar enojada consigo misma. Ella tiene la culpa de todo.	*She should be angry with herself. She's to blame for everything.*

- After the prepositions **como** (*like*), **según** (*according to*), **salvo** (*except*), **excepto** (*except*), **menos** (*except*), **entre** (*between, among*), subject pronouns are used even in the first- and second-persons singular: **entre tú y yo** (*between you and me*), **todos menos tú** (*everyone except you*), **según yo** (*according to me*). **Yo** and **tú** replace **mí** and **ti** after **y** with other prepositions:

Lo dijo delante de Ud. y **yo.**	*He said it in front of you and me.*

C. Pronombres preposicionales. Escriba la forma correcta de la preposición.

> MODELO   de **mí** (yo)

1. para _____ (él)
2. con _____ (tú)
3. según _____ (tú)
4. por _____ (nosotros)
5. salvo _____ (yo)
6. sobre _____ (Ud.)
7. con _____ (yo)
8. de _____ (vosotros)
9. para _____ (ellas)
10. por _____ (tú)
11. menos _____ (tú)
12. como _____ (yo)
13. en _____ (ella)
14. entre _____ y yo (tú)

D. Pronombres preposicionales. Conteste las siguientes preguntas usando los pronombres preposicionales correctos.

> MODELO   ¿Trajiste algo para Elenita?
> → Sí, traje algo para **ella.**

1. ¿Vive Ud. cerca de las tiendas?
2. ¿Trabajaba Timoteo en esa oficina?
3. ¿Lograron Uds. hablar sobre esos asuntos?
4. ¿Pagaste un dineral (*fortune*) por el estéreo?
5. ¿Salió Ud. con Isabel y Alfonso?
6. ¿Hay mucho trabajo para la clase de filosofía?
7. ¿Se casó María Elena con el pintor?
8. ¿Felicitaste a los jugadores por la victoria?

E. ¡Te equivocas! Su amigo cree que Ud. hizo algunas cosas con ciertas personas o para ellas. Dígale que no hizo las cosas ni con las personas que él cree ni para ellas. Use pronombres preposicionales en sus respuestas.

> MODELO   Saliste con Gabriela, ¿verdad?
> → No, con ella, no.

1. Almorzaste con Paquita y Laura, ¿verdad?

2. Fuiste al cine con Víctor, ¿verdad?

3. Hiciste el informe para la profesora Godoy, ¿verdad?

4. Trabajaste en la librería por tu hermana, ¿verdad?

5. Compraste un regalo para tus padres, ¿verdad?

6. Escribiste el trabajo por Daniel, ¿verdad?

7. Jugaste tenis con los Vilas, ¿verdad?

8. Preparaste el almuerzo para mí, ¿verdad?

C *Personal **a** and direct objects*

- A direct object noun in Spanish is joined to its verb directly, without a preposition, if it refers to a thing. Direct object nouns that refer to specific people are preceded by **a.** This use of **a** is called *personal a:*

—No veo **a tu abuela.**	*I don't see your grandmother.*
—Está en la cocina **ayudando a mi madre.**	*She's in the kitchen helping my mother.*
—¿Alquilaste **la película**?	*Did you rent the film?*
—Sí, y compré **palomitas de maíz.**	*Yes, and I bought popcorn.*

  In the above examples, the nouns **abuela, madre, película, palomitas de maíz** are direct objects.

- Several verbs that take a direct object in Spanish have English equivalents that have prepositions:

aprovechar algo	*to take advantage of something*
buscar algo/a alguien	*to look for something/for someone*
escuchar algo/a alguien	*to listen to something/to someone*
esperar algo/a alguien	*to wait for something/for someone*
mirar algo/a alguien	*to look at something/at someone*
pagar algo	*to pay for something*
pedir algo	*to ask for something*

- Personal **a** is also used before **alguien** and **nadie,** and before **alguno, ninguno, cualquiera,** and any other pronoun or, optionally, a number that refers to people:

—¿**A quién** llamas?	*Whom are you calling?*
—No puedo llamar **a nadie.** El teléfono está descompuesto.	*I can't call anyone. The telephone is out of order.*

—¿Despidieron **a alguien?**	*Did they fire anyone?*
—No, no despidieron **a ningún empleado.**	*No, they didn't fire a single employee.*
—¿**A cuántos** invitaste a la fiesta?	*How many did you invite to the party?*
—Invité **(a) quince.**	*I invited fifteen.*
—Hoy llevo **a los míos** al centro.	*Today I'm taking my family downtown.*
—¿Puedo ir con Uds.? Me encantaría conocer **a los tuyos.**	*Can I go with you? I would love to meet your relatives.*

- Personal **a** is not used before nouns referring to people if they are not specific:

—Este restaurante busca **camareros.**	*This restaurant is looking for waiters.*
—También necesitan **un cajero.**	*They also need a cashier.*

- Personal **a** is usually not used with **tener**:

—¿Cuántos hijos tienen los Sánchez?	*How many children do the Sanchezes have?*
—Tres. Tienen dos muchachas y un muchacho.	*Three. They have two girls and a boy.*

F. La *a* personal. Escriba la **a** personal donde sea necesario para completar las siguientes oraciones. No se olvide de escribir la contracción **al (a + el)** cuando haga falta.

1. Yo buscaba _____ los sobres.

2. Encontré _____ los niños en el patio.

3. Busquen _____ los documentos en el escritorio.

4. Encontraron _____ el arquitecto en su oficina.

5. Paco conoció _____ su novia hace seis meses.

6. ¿_____ quién viste en el teatro?

7. Llevamos _____ nuestros amigos a la sierra.

8. ¿No comprendes _____ el problema todavía?

9. Me gustaría conocer _____ la ciudad.

10. Llévate _____ el paquete.

11. Vamos a buscar _____ Mari Carmen.

12. No he encontrado _____ el número de teléfono.

13. Jesús y Tito llevan _____ la camiseta de su equipo.

14. ¿Quién llamó _____ el médico?

15. Ayuda _____ tu hermano.

16. ¿Conoce Ud. _____ ese centro comercial?

17. Voy a ver _____ mis tíos mañana.

18. Nadie comprende _____ el profesor Delgado.

19. ¿Es verdad que no pudiste encontrar _____ el hotel?

20. ¿_____ quiénes llamaste?

G. **¡Un flechazo!** (*Love at first sight!*) Simón le explica a su amigo cómo se enamoró en Palma de Mallorca. Escriba la **a** personal cuando sea necesario.

1. Pedro: Entonces, ¿ya conocías _____ algunos estudiantes de la facultad de ciencias sociales?

2. Simón: Por desgracia, las primeras semanas no conocí _____ ninguno de los estudiantes.

3. Pedro: ¿Pero no viste _____ tantos chicos en la universidad?

4. Simón: Claro que los vi pero no me presenté _____ ellos porque no dominaba el español.

   Pedro: ¿Cómo es que cambió la situación entonces?

5. Simón: Bueno, después de un mes más o menos conocí _____ alguien de la facultad de ingeniería que me llevó a una fiesta.

6. Pedro: Allí conociste _____ mucha gente, ¿verdad?

7. Simón: _____ muchas personas, no, pero _____ una muy especial sí. Es que vi _____ tantas chicas muy lindas.

8. Pedro: Y querías sacar a bailar _____ todas, ¿no?

   Simón: Sí, al principio. ¡Hasta que me fijé en una que me dejó boquiabierto!

9. Pedro: ¡Un flechazo! Total, no invitaste _____ ninguna a salir ...

10. Simón: ¡Excepto _____ Josefa!

Nota cultural

Palma de Mallorca es la capital de la provincia de Baleares, las islas españolas en el Mediterráneo. Es también capital de la isla de Mallorca, la mayor de las Baleares. Por su hermoso paisaje y clima perfecto, Mallorca es un gran centro de turismo internacional. Un lugar de visita es la Cartuja de Valldemosa, un convento donde el compositor Federico Chopin (1810–49) y la escritora francesa la baronesa Dudevant, cuyo seudónimo era Jorge (George) Sand, pasaron el invierno de 1838.

H. **Verbos.** Exprese las siguientes oraciones en español. No se olvide que varios verbos en español que tienen complemento directo y no tienen preposición corresponden a verbos con preposición en inglés.

1. Ask for another bottle of wine. (*Ud.*)

2. Let's take advantage of this sale.

3. Look at the beautiful ocean. (*tú*)

4. I'll wait for them until three o'clock.

5. He's looking for his brother and sister.

6. Did their parents pay for the furniture?

7. Let's listen to the orchestra.

D *Direct object pronouns: forms and position*

- Direct object nouns can be replaced by direct object pronouns. The direct object pronouns in Spanish are:

me	nos
te	os
lo	los
la	las

Note the following:

1. **Lo, la, los, las** refer to both people and things.

2. **Lo, la, los, las** are also the direct object pronouns for **Ud.** and **Uds.,** so they mean *you* as well as *him, her, it, them.*

3. In Spain, **lo** is replaced by **le** when referring to people.

- Direct object pronouns precede the conjugated verb in Spanish (they follow in English):

—¿Dónde estarán los niños? Hace quince minutos que **los** busco y no **los** encuentro.	*Where can the children be? I've been looking for them for fifteen minutes and I can't find them.*
—**Los** vi en el parque.	*I saw them in the park.*
—¡Ay! No tengo el libro de química. **Lo** dejé en el colegio.	*Oh! I don't have the chemistry book. I left it at school.*
—Aquí tengo el mío. ¿**Lo** quieres?	*I have mine here. Do you want it?*
—**Me** avisará si hay un cambio en el horario de mañana.	*You'll inform me if there's a change in tomorrow's schedule.*
—Cómo no, señora. Cualquier cosa y **la** llamo en seguida.	*Of course, madam. If anything comes up I'll call you immediately.*
—¿Vas al centro ahora? ¿**Nos** llevas?	*Are you going downtown now? Will you take us?*
—Con mucho gusto. **Los** dejo delante del correo. ¿Está bien?	*Gladly. I'll leave you in front of the post office. Is that all right?*

- In compound tenses the direct object pronouns are placed before the auxiliary verb **haber:**

—Carlos, ¡qué milagro! No **te** hemos visto por tanto tiempo.	*Carlos, what a surprise! We haven't seen you for such a long time.*
—Es que **me** han contratado en una empresa de las afueras.	*That's because they've hired me at a firm in the suburbs.*

- In verb + infinitive constructions, the direct object pronoun may either precede the first verb or be attached to the infinitive:

—¿Has visto la nueva película española?	*Have you seen the new Spanish film?*
—No, pero **la** quiero ver. *or* No, pero quiero ver**la.**	*No, but I want to see it.*

- In the progressive tenses, the direct object pronoun can be placed either before the form of **estar** or be attached to the present participle. When the pronoun is attached to the present participle, an accent mark is added to the vowel before the **-ndo**:

—¿Has leído la nueva novela de Atienza?	*Have you read the new novel by Atienza?*
—**La** estoy leyendo ahora. *or* Estoy leyéndo**la** ahora.	*I'm reading it now.*

- The direct object pronoun is also attached to affirmative command forms. An accent mark is added to the stressed vowel of the command form, except in the case of one-syllable commands:

—Ah, tienes el periódico. **Ponlo** en la mesa.	*Ah, you have the newspaper. Put it on the table.*
—No, **cógelo** tú y **llévalo** arriba.	*No, you get it and take it upstairs.*
—Éstas son las palabras nuevas, chicos. **Apréndanlas** de memoria.	*These are the new words, kids. Learn them by heart.*
—Por favor, **repáselas** con nosotros, profesor.	*Please, review them with us, sir.*

- To emphasize or contrast direct object pronouns referring to people, a phrase consisting of **a** + the corresponding stressed pronoun is added to the sentence:

—¿Reconociste a Laura y a Marcos?	*Did you recognize Laura and Marcos?*
—**La** reconocí **a ella,** pero no **lo** vi **a él.**	*I recognized **her,** but I didn't see **him.***
—Parece que las secretarias son más simpáticas que el jefe.	*It seems that the secretaries are nicer than the boss.*
—Sí, **a ellas las** encuentro encantadoras, pero **a él** no **lo** aguanto.	*Yes, I find **them** delightful, but I can't stand **him.***

- When a direct object noun *precedes* the verb, the direct object pronoun must be present. Compare Veo **a Juan** *with* **A Juan lo** veo. This is true even if the direct object is a thing. Compare: Dejé **los libros** en la mesa *with* **Los libros los** dejé en la mesa.

I. **¡A jugar pues!** Sus amigos quieren pasar la tarde jugando juegos en casa porque está lloviendo. Diga si quiere jugar los juegos que proponen. Escriba la respuesta de dos maneras usando un complemento directo.

Juegos			
la batalla naval *battleship*		**la lotería** *lotto*	
la charada *charades*		**el monopolio** *monopoly*	
las damas *checkers*		**las palabras cruzadas** *crossword puzzle*	
los dardos *darts*		**el rompecabezas** *riddle*	
el dominó *dominoes*		**el tres en raya** *tic-tac-toe*	

> MODELO ¿Quieres jugar damas? (sí)
> → Sí, quiero jugar**las.** *or* Sí, **las** quiero jugar.

1. ¿Quieres jugar dominó? (sí)

2. ¿Prefieres jugar batalla naval? (sí)

3. ¿Quieres hacer un tres en raya? (no)

4. ¿Prefieres tirar dardos? (no)

5. ¿Quieres hacer la charada? (sí)

6. ¿Prefieres jugar lotería? (no)

7. ¿Quieres ver unas palabras cruzadas? (sí)

8. ¿Prefieres jugar monopolio? (no)

9. ¿Quieres hacer rompecabezas? (no)

Nota cultural

El **dominó** se juega mucho en los países hispánicos. Se usa la palabra **crucigrama** también para palabras cruzadas.

J. Mi coche. Conteste las siguientes preguntas sobre el cuidado de su coche cambiando el sustantivo a un pronombre complemento directo. Escriba dos oraciones para cada respuesta.

> **Modelo** ¿Compraste la bomba de aire (*air pump*)?
> → No, no **la** compré. Voy a comprar**la**.

El coche

la caja de herramientas *toolbox*		**las piezas de repuesto** *spare parts*	
el faro *headlight*		**la placa de matrícula** *license plate*	
el gato *jack*		**el silenciador** *muffler*	
el parachoques *bumper*		**el volante** *steering wheel*	

1. ¿Cambiaste el aceite?

2. ¿Reparaste el parachoques?

3. ¿Pediste las placas de matrícula?

4. ¿Llevaste una caja de herramientas y piezas de repuesto?

5. ¿Usaste el gato?

6. ¿Pusiste otros faros?

7. ¿Arreglaste el volante?

8. ¿Instalaste el silenciador?

K. Bernardo y los coches. Bernardo acaba de sacar su licencia de conducir y piensa mucho en su coche. Escriba oraciones sobre la afición de Bernardo cambiando el sustantivo a un pronombre complemento directo. Escriba cada oración de dos maneras.

> MODELO   Bernardo quiere limpiar el baúl.
> → Bernardo quiere limpiarlo. / Bernardo lo quiere limpiar.

El coche

la avería *breakdown*	**el coche todo terreno** *jeep*
el baúl *trunk*	**el pinchazo** *blowout*
cargar la batería *to charge the battery*	**la señal de tráfico** *road sign*
el coche descapotable *convertible*	

---

1. Piensa comprar el coche todo terreno.

2. Tiene que llenar el tanque de gasolina.

3. Trata de leer todas las señales de tráfico.

4. Prefiere conducir un coche descapotable.

5. Debe cargar la batería.

6. Teme tener un pinchazo.

7. Procura evitar las averías.

L. Lo significa *you.* El complemento directo **lo, la, los, las** también reemplaza *Ud.* y *Uds.* Conteste las preguntas empleando el complemento directo en su respuesta.

> MODELO   ¿Me conoce Ud.?
> → Sí, señor, **lo conozco.**

1. ¿Me conoce Ud.?

   Sí, señorita, _____.

2. ¿Nos comprende Ud.?

   Sí, señores, _____.

3. ¿Me llama Ud.?

   No, señora, no _____.

4. ¿Nos busca Ud.?

   No, señoras, no _____.

5. ¿Me lleva Ud.?

   Sí, señor, _____.

6. ¿Nos conoce Ud.?

   No, señoritas, no _____.

7. ¿Me ayuda Ud.?

   Sí, profesor, _____.

8. ¿Nos ve Ud.?

   No, señores, no _____.

M. ¡Míralo! Dé mandatos a varias personas diciéndoles lo que deben hacer en ciertos deportes. Escriba mandatos afirmativos y negativos colocando el pronombre complemento directo en su posición correcta.

> MODELO   ver / Ud. / los Juegos Olímpicos
> → Véalos. / No los vea.

1. marcar / Ud. / goles

2. llamar / tú / al árbitro (*umpire*)

3. jugar / Uds. / béisbol

4. saltar / Ud. / vallas (*hurdles*)

5. hacer / tú / gimnasia

6. mirar / Uds. / la cancha

7. lanzar / tú / la pelota

8. ser / Ud. / plusmarquista (*masc.*) (*record holder*)

9. levantar / Uds. / las pesas

N. ¿Lo ha visto Ud.? Unos amigos quieren saber si Ud. ha visto a ciertas personas y cosas hoy. Conteste usando el pronombre complemento directo.

> MODELO   ¿Ha visto a Paulina hoy? (sí / no)
> → Sí, la he visto.
> → No, no la he visto.

1. ¿Has visto al señor Domínguez hoy? (sí)

2. ¿Ha visto Ud. a los decanos de la universidad? (no)

3. ¿Han visto Uds. la cámara? (sí)

4. ¿Ha visto Ud. los alicates (*pliers*)? (no)

5. ¿Has visto a las hermanas Moya? (no)

6. ¿Han visto Uds. las tarjetas de crédito? (sí)

7. ¿Ha visto Ud. el recibo? (sí)

8. ¿Has visto a la ortodontista? (no)

O. La catedral de Sevilla. La catedral se remonta (*dates back*) al siglo XV cuando se empezó a construir. Ud. vive en la Edad Media y es testigo de la construcción. Describa las actividades que está viendo en oraciones que cambian el sustantivo al pronombre complemento directo. Escriba las oraciones de dos maneras.

La catedral de Sevilla: su construcción

el albañil *bricklayer*	**el fraile** *monk*
los andamios *scaffolding*	**el maestro de obras** *master builder*
la argamasa *mortar* (*mezcla de arena y agua*)	**la mezquita** *mosque*
el dibujante *draftsman*	**la monja** *nun*
echar los cimientos *to lay the foundation*	**rezar las oraciones** *to say prayers*

> MODELO   Yo estoy viendo la construcción.
> → Yo estoy viéndola.
> → Yo la estoy viendo.

1. Los arquitectos están empleando el estilo gótico.

2. Los constructores van destruyendo la mezquita.

3. Los dibujantes están dibujando las ventanas.

4. Los maestros de obras están echando los cimientos.

5. Los frailes y las monjas siguen rezando sus oraciones.

6. Los trabajadores siguen colocando los andamios.

7. Los albañiles van trayendo piedras.

8. Los obreros están poniendo argamasa.

Nota cultural

La catedral de Sevilla es por sus dimensiones la primera de España y la tercera del mundo cristiano después de San Pedro del Vaticano y San Pablo de Londres. Es una de las últimas catedrales góticas españolas y tiene algunas influencias renacentistas. La catedral fue comenzada en 1402 y terminada a principios del siglo XVI.

Hubo influencia árabe en España a partir de la batalla de Guadalete en 711 en la cual los árabes derrotaron a Don Rodrigo, el último rey visigodo, y se apoderaron de la península Ibérica. Duró la influencia árabe en España ocho siglos hasta que perdieron la campaña (*campaign*) de Granada en 1492. Sin embargo, la influencia árabe en España perdura en la onomástica (nombres de lugares), comida, lingüística y arquitectura. La catedral de Sevilla fue construida sobre las ruinas de una **mezquita.**

P. Una criada *muy* trabajadora. El señor Salas vuelve a su casa y quiere saber dónde están las cosas y la gente. Su criada Pepa le contesta con oraciones que tienen el complemento directo en primer lugar. ¿Qué le dice Pepa al señor Salas?

> **MODELO**   ¿Dónde está mi esposa? (ver salir hace una hora)
> → A su esposa la vi salir hace una hora.

1. ¿Dónde está la revista? (poner en su mesa de trabajo)

2. ¿Dónde están los chicos? (llevar al cine)

3. ¿Dónde está el balón de fútbol? (dejar en el jardín)

4. ¿Dónde está el bebé? (acostar)

5. ¿Dónde están mis libros? (arreglar en su cuarto)

6. ¿Dónde están las cartas que escribí? (echar al correo)

7. ¿Dónde está mi camisa amarilla? (colgar en su armario)

8. ¿Dónde están las galletas que compré? (comer)

E   *Indirect object pronouns: forms and position*

- Indirect objects are joined to the verb by the preposition **a**. Indirect objects most commonly refer to people.

- The indirect object pronouns in Spanish are:

me	nos
te	os
le	les

- Indirect object pronouns follow the same rules of position as direct object pronouns:

  Te dije la verdad.
  Le debo decir la verdad. *or* Debo decir**le** la verdad.
  Les estoy diciendo la verdad. *or* Estoy diciéndo**les** la verdad.
  Nos han dicho la verdad.
  Díg**ame** la verdad.

- An indirect object noun in Spanish is usually accompanied by the corresponding indirect object pronoun (**le** or **les,** depending on whether the noun is singular or plural):

—¿**Les** escribiste **a tus padres**?	*Did you write to your parents?*
—Sí, y también **le** mandé una carta **a mi hermana**.	*Yes, and I also sent my sister a letter.*

Some verbs that take an indirect object in Spanish take a direct object in English:

contestarle a alguien	*to answer someone*
pedirle algo a alguien	*to ask someone for something*
preguntarle a alguien	*to ask someone*
recordarle a alguien	*to remind someone*

Many verbs take an indirect object of the person (le ... a alguien) and a direct object that is a thing (algo):

contarle algo a alguien	*to relate, recount something to someone*
darle algo a alguien	*to give something to someone*
decirle algo a alguien	*to tell, say something to someone*
devolverle algo a alguien	*to return something to someone*
enseñarle algo a alguien	*to show something to someone*
escribirle algo a alguien	*to write something to someone*
entregarle algo a alguien	*to hand over something to someone*
enviarle algo a alguien	*to send something to someone*
explicarle algo a alguien	*to explain something to someone*
mandarle algo a alguien	*to send something to someone*
mostrarle algo a alguien	*to show something to someone*
ofrecerle algo a alguien	*to offer something to someone*
pedirle algo a alguien	*to ask someone for something*
recordarle algo a alguien	*to remind someone of something*
regalarle algo a alguien	*to give something to someone as a gift*
traerle algo a alguien	*to bring something to someone*

The indirect object is often the equivalent of English *from* with verbs meaning *take away*, *steal*, *remove*, etc.:

arrebatarle algo a alguien	*to snatch, grab something from someone*
comprarle algo a alguien	*to buy something from someone*
esconderle algo a alguien	*to hide something from someone*
exigirle algo a alguien	*to demand something of someone*
ganarle algo a alguien	*to win something from someone*
ocultarle algo a alguien	*to hide something from someone*
pedirle prestado algo a alguien	*to borrow something from someone*
quitarle algo a alguien	*to take something away from someone*
robarle algo a alguien	*to steal something from someone*
sacarle algo a alguien	*to get something out of someone*
solicitarle algo a alguien	*to ask, request something of someone*
suspenderle algo a alguien	*to revoke, cancel something of someone*

¿A quién le compraste el coche?	*Whom did you buy the car from?*
Me exigieron mis documentos de identidad.	*They demanded my identification papers (of/from me).*
Le solicité trabajo **al padre de Lucas.**	*I applied for work with/from Lucas's father.*
Al turista le quitaron el pasaporte.	*They took the tourist's passport from him.*

- To emphasize or contrast indirect object pronouns, a phrase consisting of **a** + the corresponding stressed pronoun is added to the sentence:

—¿Qué **les** pidieron los aduaneros **a ustedes**?	*What did the customs officers ask **you** for?*
—**A mí me** pidieron el pasaporte, pero **a él le** pidieron todos los documentos.	*They asked for **my** passport, but they asked for all of **his** documents.*
—¿**A ustedes les** regalaron algo?	*Did they give **you** anything as a gift?*
—**A nosotros nos** regalaron muchas cosas, pero **a ellos no les** dieron nada.	*They gave **us** many things, but they didn't give **them** anything.*

Q. **El complemento indirecto.** Cambie el pronombre del complemento indirecto en cada oración.

> MODELO   Yo le pedí unas revistas. (a ellos)
> → Yo les pedí unas revistas.

1. Les traje los refrescos. (a ti)

2. Me dieron flores. (a nosotros)

3. Le mandó una tarjeta postal. (a mí)

4. Nos dijeron los precios. (a Ud.)

5. Te ofrecimos el escritorio. (a él)

6. Les preguntó la hora. (a ella)

7. Le expliqué mis ideas. (a vosotros)

8. Me recordaron el cumpleaños de Leo. (a Uds.)

R. Salir ganando o salir perdiendo. Añada a cada oración una frase que consiste en **a** + el pronombre enfático para hacer énfasis en o contraste de los pronombres de complemento indirecto.

> MODELO **A mí** me enviaron mucha plata, pero **a ella** (Roberta) no le enviaron nada.

1. _____ nos mostraron el castillo, pero _____ (Ud. y Felipe) les mostraron solamente el establo de caballos.

2. Marta me contó _____ la pura verdad, pero _____ te contó puras mentiras.

3. Yo le escribí una carta de amor _____ (Daniel), pero le escribí una carta de odio _____ (su novia).

4. _____ te dimos la llave de la casa, pero _____ (Catarina y Jorge) les dimos una carta de despedida.

5. _____ os regalaron unos discos compactos fabulosos, pero _____ nos regalaron unos discos rayados (*scratched*).

6. _____ (Elena y Margarita) les trajo unos bombones, pero _____ (Ud.) le trajo una caja vacía.

S. Un mal día en el barrio. Muchas cosas malas sucedieron hoy en el barrio. Miguel pasó todo el día en el barrio y cuenta los lamentables sucesos a los amigos que regresan de sus clases en la universidad. Haga oraciones con los elementos dados para completar la narración de Miguel. Debe haber un pronombre complemento indirecto en cada oración que Ud. escribe.

1. ¿Conocen a la señora de Pacheco?
   un joven/arrebatar el bolso

2. ¿Conocen a los Caballero, los dueños de la bodega?
   dos hombres enmascarados/robar treinta mil pesos

3. ¿Se acuerdan de que Martín vendió su estéreo?
   los compradores/pagar con billetes falsos

4. Mi hermanito jugaba en el parque.
   alguien/quitar la bicicleta

5. La señora de Parrondo está molesta.
   su hijo de cuatro años/esconder las llaves del coche

6. Un policía pilló (*caught*) al hijo de Galván manejando borracho.
   el juez/suspender el permiso de manejar

7. El señor Ribera está furioso con su hijo.
   éste/ocultar sus salidas con Elvira Camacho

8. Matilde Peña está preocupada.
   su sobrino/pedir prestado mucho dinero

F   *Verbs usually appearing with an indirect object pronoun (e.g., **gustar**)*

- Certain verbs in Spanish are almost always used with an indirect object pronoun. This construction is different from the English equivalents of these verbs. The most common of these is **gustar**:

Me gusta la torta. *I like the cake.* **Me gustan** las galletas. *I like the cookies.*	**Nos gusta** la torta. *We like the cake.* **Nos gustan** las galletas. *We like the cookies.*
Te gusta la torta. *You like the cake.* **Te gustan** las galletas. *You like the cookies.*	**Os gusta** la torta. *You like the cake.* **Os gustan** las galletas. *You like the cookies.*
Le gusta la torta. *He, She likes/You like the cake.* **Le gustan** las galletas. *He, She likes/You like the cookies.*	**Les gusta** la torta. *They/You like the cake.* **Les gustan** las galletas. *They/You like the cookies.*

- Note that the verb agrees with the subject of the Spanish sentence, **torta** or **galletas**.

- When the grammatical subject of a verb like **gustar** is an infinitive, the verb is always third-person singular:

—**Me encanta patinar** sobre el hielo.   *I love to ice skate.*
—A mí **me gusta más esquiar.**   *I like skiing better.*

Here are some other verbs that function like **gustar**:

convenirle a alguien	*to suit someone, be good for someone*
encantarle a alguien	*to love something*
entusiasmarle a alguien	*to be excited about something*
faltarle a alguien	*to be missing something, not to have something*
fascinarle a alguien	*to be fascinated*
hacerle falta a alguien	*to need something*
importarle a alguien	*to care about something, to mind*
interesarle a alguien	*to be interested in something*
quedarle a alguien	*to have something left*
sobrarle a alguien	*to have more than enough of something*
tocarle a alguien	*to be someone's turn*

—¿**Te importa** acompañarme a la exposición de arte?   *Would you mind accompanying me to the art show?*
—**Me encantaría. Me interesa** mucho la pintura.   *I'd love to. I'm very interested in painting.*

—Creo que **te convendría** salir un poco.   *I think it would be good for you to go out a little.*
—Sé que **me hace falta,** pero **me sobra** trabajo.   *I know I need to, but I have too much work.*

—Parece que no **te entusiasman** mucho estos juegos.	*It seems that you're not very excited about these games.*
—Cada vez que **me toca a mí,** pierdo.	*Every time it's my turn, I lose.*

• To emphasize or contrast the indirect object pronouns, a phrase consisting of **a** + the corresponding stressed pronoun is added to the sentence. This prepositional phrase is also used for "short responses":

—¿Cuánto dinero nos queda?	*How much money do we have left?*
—A mí me quedan doscientos pesos. ¿**Y a ti?**	*I have two hundred pesos left. How about you?*
—Chicos, ¿a quién le gusta la torta de chocolate?	*Kids, who likes chocolate cake?*
—**¡A mí! ¡A mí! ¡A mí!**	*I do! I do! I do!*

The phrase **¿Y a ti?** is short for **Y a ti, ¿cuánto dinero te queda?** The phrase **¡A mí!** is short for **A mí me gusta la torta de chocolate.**

T. En plural. Cambie el sujeto de las siguientes oraciones al plural. Todos los verbos son del tipo **gustar.** No se olvide de hacer todos los cambios necesarios.

> MODELO   Me gusta ese suéter.
> ➔ Me gustan esos suéteres.

1. Le encanta su perfume.

2. Nos interesa esta novela.

3. Les queda un examen.

4. Te entusiasma la comedia.

5. Os importa la idea.

6. Me hace falta una guía.

7. Les fascina esta materia.

8. Le falta un cuaderno.

U. En el futuro. Añada la construcción **ir a** + infinitivo a las siguientes oraciones con verbos como **gustar.**

> MODELO   Me gusta esa película. ➔ Me va a gustar esa película.
> Me gustan esas películas. ➔ Me van a gustar esas películas.

1. Nos importan sus problemas.

2. No les queda mucho dinero.

3. Le encanta visitar a sus abuelos.

4. No les sobra comida.

5. Os conviene viajar en tren.

6. Te fascinan esos cuadros.

7. Me entusiasman sus obras.

8. No le interesan esos programas.

V. Conteste cada pregunta escogiendo entre el pronombre sujeto y la frase con **a.**

> MODELO   ¿Quién estudia chino? (Yo./A mí.)
> ➔ Yo.

1. ¿A quién le gusta jugar baloncesto? (Él./A él.) _____

2. ¿Quiénes vieron a los niños? (Ellos./A ellos.) _____

3. ¿A Juana le quedan cincuenta dólares? (Ella no./A ella no.) _____

4. ¿Conociste a Diana? (Yo no./A mí no.) _____

5. ¿Comprendieron al profesor? (A nosotros sí./Nosotros sí.) _____

6. ¿A quién le interesan estos poemas? (Ud./A Ud.) _____

7. ¿Te hace falta manejar? (A mí sí./Yo sí.) _____

8. ¿Devolvieron los libros a la biblioteca? (A mí sí./Yo sí.) _____

W. Los Castellón planean un viaje. Exprese en español la conversación que tienen los señores Castellón y sus tres hijos sobre el viaje que piensan hacer en el verano. Escriba oraciones usando en cada caso un verbo como **gustar.**

1. Alicia Castellón: I'd like to take a trip to Spain.

2. Rafael Castellón: I'd love to visit my relatives in Venezuela and Argentina.

3. Lorenzo: I'd be interested in going camping in New Mexico or Arizona.

4. Nora: And I'd be fascinated to see the new Italian fashions.

5. Carlos: I'd be very enthusiastic about following Miguel Induraín in *el Tour de Francia.*

6. Rafael Castellón: It's good for us (suits us) to make a decision as soon as possible.

7. Lorenzo: We have more than enough suggestions. Let's draw lots! (*echar suertes*)

8. Nora: It's my turn first!

G *Other uses of the indirect object*

- The indirect object in Spanish is often the equivalent of the English possessive with parts of the body and articles of clothing. This is also true of reflexive pronouns:

  —¿**Te quito** el abrigo?
  —No, gracias. Siempre **me haces daño** en el brazo cuando me lo quitas.

  Shall I help you off with your jacket?
  No, thank you. You always hurt my arm when you help me off with it.

  —Ven, Carlitos. **Te lavo** las manos.
  —No, no. Yo mismo **me las lavo.**

  Come, Carlitos. I'll wash your hands.
  No, no. I'll wash them myself.

- The indirect object tells for whose benefit or for whose disadvantage something is done:

  —¿**Me haces** el almuerzo, mamá?
  —Sí, si **me llevas** las bolsas de comida a la cocina.

  Can you make my lunch for me, Mom?
  Yes, if you carry the bags of food to the kitchen for me.

  —Espero que no **nos** caiga otra vez la vecina con sus dos hijos.
  —Sí, la última vez esos dos diablos casi **nos** destruyeron la casa.
  —¡Y **nos** comieron todas las galletas que teníamos!

  I hope the neighbor doesn't drop in on us again with her two children.
  Yes, the last time those two rascals almost destroyed our house.
  And they ate up all the cookies that we had.

- The indirect object pronouns can be added to certain impersonal expressions:

Es difícil caminar cuando nieva.	*It's hard to walk when it snows.*
Me es difícil caminar cuando nieva.	*It's hard for me to walk when it snows.*
Es necesario estudiar más.	*It's necessary to study more.*
Nos es necesario estudiar más.	*It's necessary for us to study more.*

- The indirect object pronoun can be added to a **se** construction with certain verbs to express *unplanned occurrences*. These constructions focus on the object affected rather than on the person involved:

---

acabársele a alguien	*to run out of*
caérsele a alguien	*to drop*
ocurrírsele a alguien	*to dawn on, get the idea of*
olvidársele a alguien	*to forget*
perdérsele a alguien	*to lose*
quedársele a alguien	*to leave something behind*
rompérsele a alguien	*to break*

—Veo que **se te rompieron** los anteojos.	*I see that you broke your glasses.*
—Sí, **se me cayeron** en la calle.	*Yes, I dropped them in the street.*
—¿Cómo **se les ocurrió** venir ayer?	*How did they get the idea to come yesterday?*
—**Se les había olvidado** que la reunión era mañana.	*They had forgotten that the meeting was tomorrow.*
—**Se nos está acabando** la gasolina. Tenemos que comprar.	*We're running out of gas. We have to buy some.*
—Pero **se me perdió** la tarjeta de crédito.	*But I lost my credit card.*

X. Sucesos inesperados. Escriba los elementos de la oración que faltan. Todas las oraciones expresan la idea de un suceso inesperado, es decir, complemento directo + construcción con **se**. Use el pretérito de los verbos entre paréntesis.

1. No pudimos hacer los sándwiches. (acabársele)

   _____ el pan.

2. Plácido no pudo entrar en su casa. (perdérsele)

   _____ las llaves.

3. No le mandé una tarjeta a Beatriz. (olvidársele)

   _____ la fecha de su cumpleaños.

4. ¡Pero estáis mojadísimos! (quedársele)

   ¿_____ el paraguas en casa?

5. ¡Cuidado de no cortarte la mano! (rompérsele)

   ¿Cómo _____ los vasos?

6. ¡Pasando por Madrid, Uds. no visitaron a los tíos! (ocurrírsele)

¿Ni ____ llamarlos?

7. Los niños están recogiendo todos los papeles en el suelo. (caérsele)

¿Cómo ____?

Y. Prevenir (*to warn*) **contra lo inesperado.** Escriba oraciones previniendo a unas personas contra ciertas cosas. Fíjese que el imperativo de los verbos como **acabársele** es un mandato indirecto.

> MODELO   tú/no caérsele/los platos
> → Que no se te caigan los platos.

1. Uds./no olvidársele/asistir a la conferencia

2. él/no perdérsele/los anteojos

3. Ud./no acabársele/la paciencia

4. vosotros/no quedársele/los cheques de viajero

5. ella/no rompérsele/las estatuillas de porcelana (*china figurines*)

6. tú/no ocurrírsele/tales cosas

7. ellos/no caérsele/la torta de chocolate

Z. Exprese los siguientes diálogos en español usando la construcción del suceso inesperado.

1. —Did you (*Ud.*) lose your wallet?
—No, I had left it at home.

2. —They're running out of pastries at the bake shop.
—Didn't it occur to you (*tú*) to buy them this morning?

3. —Be careful! You're (*Uds.*) going to drop the cups!
—We already broke two!

4. —I forgot to pick Tere and Leo up.
—Didn't it dawn on you (*tú*) that they were waiting all night?

H Double object pronouns

- In Spanish a direct object pronoun and an indirect object pronoun can appear together with a verb. The indirect object pronoun precedes the direct object pronoun:

—Necesito mil pesos. ¿**Me los** prestas?   *I need a thousand pesos. Will you lend them to me?*

—**Te los** presto con tal de que **me los** devuelvas la semana que viene.   *I'll lend them to you as long as you return them to me next week.*

—Nos interesa tu colección de sellos. ¿**Nos la** enseñas?   *We're interested in your stamp collection. Will you show it to us?*

—Claro. Ahora **se la** traigo.   *Of course. I'll bring it to you right now.*

- When a third-person indirect object pronoun (**le** or **les**) precedes a third-person direct object pronoun (**lo, la, los, las**), the indirect object pronoun changes to **se.**

le/les + lo → se lo
le/les + la → se la
le/les + los → se los
le/les + las → se las

- Double object pronouns cannot be separated from each other. Double object pronouns follow the same rules of position as single object pronouns. When double object pronouns are added to an infinitive, present participle, or affirmative command, an accent mark is always added, even to infinitives and command forms of one syllable: **Quiero dártelo, Dámelo**:

—¿Cuándo le va a entregar Ud. el informe al jefe? | *When are you going to submit the report to the boss?*
—Ya **se lo** he entregado. | *I've already submitted it to him.*

—Hay un problema que no comprendo. | *There's a problem that I don't understand.*
—**Mué**stra**melo.** A ver si **te lo** puedo explicar. *or* A ver si puedo **explicártelo.** | *Show it to me. Let's see if I can explain it to you.*

—¿Dónde están nuestras maletas? | *Where are our suitcases?*
—El botones **nos las** está subiendo ahora. *or* El botones está subi**é**ndo**noslas** ahora. | *The bellhop is bringing them up for us now.*

- Sentences with **se** out of context can be ambiguous. Context or a phrase consisting of **a** + prepositional pronoun clarifies who **se** refers to:

—¿La niñita se puso los zapatos? | *Did the little girl put on her shoes?*
—Sí, **se los** puso. (**se** = reflexive pronoun referring to **la niña**) | *Yes, she put them on.*

—¿La niñita se puso los zapatos? | *Did the little girl put on her shoes?*
—No, **yo se los puse.** (**se** = indirect object pronoun referring to **la niña**) | *No, I put them on (for her).*

—¿El gerente y la directora tienen copias del informe? | *Do the manager and the director have copies of the report?*
—Sí, a él **se lo** mandé por correo y a ella **se lo** di personalmente. | *Yes, I sent it to him by mail and I gave it to her personally.*

AA. Dos pronombres complementos directo e indirecto. Escriba oraciones cambiando el sustantivo complemento directo a un pronombre y haga todos los cambios necesarios.

MODELO   Les entregaré las cartas el martes.
→ Se las entregaré el martes.

1. Me dijeron los motivos.

2. Le hemos puesto los zapatos.

3. Está explicándoles la idea.

4. Os muestro el paquete.

5. ¿Te darían una beca?

6. Les cuentas los chismes.

7. Nos ha hecho las chuletas de cordero.

8. Devuélvame el cortacésped (*lawnmower*).

9. Me estaban enseñando las fotos.

10. ¿A quién le vendiste tu velero?

11. Os había escrito una tarjeta postal.

12. ¿Nos prestarás unos disquetes?

13. Apréndanse las fechas de memoria.

14. ¿Estáis preguntándole el por qué?

15. Le pusieron una multa.

16. Les preparó arroz y maíz.

17. Estará bajándome el equipaje.

18. Vendámosles la casa.

19. Estuvimos trayéndole los periódicos ingleses.

20. Te apagaré la televisión.

BB. **Algo pasará./Algo pasó.** Añada la construcción **ir a** + infinitivo o **acabar de** + infinitivo a las siguientes oraciones. Haga los cambios necesarios respecto a los verbos y a los pronombres complementos directo e indirecto. Escriba cada oración de dos maneras.

MODELO	Se los doy.	**(ir a)**	**(acabar de)**
		Voy a dárselos.	Acabo de dárselos.
		Se los voy a dar.	Se los acabo de dar.

1. Me la traen. (ir a)

2. Te lo dice. (acabar de)

3. Se los hacemos. (ir a)

4. Os las pongo. (acabar de)

5. Se lo muestra. (ir a)

6. Nos la compráis. (acabar de)

7. Me los cuentas. (ir a)

8. Se las arreglo. (acabar de)

9. Te la suben. (ir a)

10. Os lo damos. (acabar de)

11. Se lo describimos. (ir a)

12. Se la pruebas. (acabar de)

13. Te los limpia. (ir a)

14. Se las encuentro. (acabar de)

15. Me la piden. (ir a)

16. Nos lo buscas. (acabar de)

17. Os los llevamos. (ir a)

18. Se las sirve. (acabar de)

19. Se lo devolvéis. (ir a)

20. Te la canto. (acabar de)

CC. ¡Mami, papi, cómprenmelo! ¡Esta niña Rita vuelve loca a toda su familia! No deja de pedir cosas y por desgracia, sus familiares se lo conceden todo. Por eso es una niña mal criada (*spoiled brat*). Escriba diálogos entre Rita y sus familiares en los cuales Ud. emplea los pronombres complementos directo e indirecto con mandatos y verbos en tiempo presente.

> **MODELO** Mami / comprarme / una bicicleta
> → Rita: Mami, cómpramela.
>   Mamá: Sí, hijita, te la compro.

1. Papi / darme / bombones

   Rita: Papi, _____

   Papá: Sí, hijita, _____

2. Rita: Mami / comprarme / canicas (*marbles*)

   Rita: Mami, _____

   Mamá: Sí, hijita, _____

3. Rita: Juan / prestarme / tu patineta (*scooter*)

   Rita: Juan, _____

   Juan: Sí, hermanita, _____

4. Rita: Amparo / comprarme / soldaditos de plomo (*tin soldiers*)

   Rita: Amparo, _____

   Amparo: Sí, hermanita, _____

5. Rita: Abuelo / regalarme / un billete de cien dólares

   Rita: Abuelo, _____

   Abuelo: Sí, hijita, _____

6. Rita: Elvira / servirme / todo el helado de chocolate

   Rita: Elvira, _____

   Elvira: Sí, hermanita, _____

7. Rita: Tía / ponerme / tus joyas de oro

   Rita: Tía, _____

   Tía: Sí, hijita, _____

DD. **¿Las cosas claras?** Exprese las siguientes oraciones en inglés aclarando a quién(es) se refiere el ambiguo **se.** Unas oraciones pueden tener más de una sola traducción.

1. a. Se la dio Fernando.
   b. Se la dio a Fernando.

2. a. Se lo dijeron los profesores.
   b. Se lo dijeron a los profesores.

3. a. Se las prestó el vecino.
   b. Se las prestó al vecino.

4. a. Se los pidieron mis colegas.
   b. Se los pidieron a mis colegas.

5. a. Se la devolvió Laura.
   b. Se la devolvió a Laura.

I Special uses of the object pronouns

- The object pronoun **lo** is used to replace a clause or an adjective or a predicate noun of both genders and numbers. This **lo** has no equivalent in English:

  —Los Ochoa se mudaron a Ecuador.   *The Ochoas moved to Ecuador.*
  —Sí, **lo sé.** (**lo** = que se mudaron a   *Yes, I know.*
  Ecuador)

  —¿María Elena es simpática?   *Is María Elena nice?*
  —Sí, **lo es.** (**lo** = simpática)   *Yes, she is.*

  —¿Son profesoras Marta y Sara?   *Are Marta and Sara teachers?*
  —**Lo** fueron. Ahora son abogadas.   *They were. Now they're lawyers.*
  (**lo** = profesoras)

- The object pronouns **la** and **las** appear in many idioms without any antecedent. They must be memorized as part of the idiom:

apañárselas	*to manage, get by*
arreglárselas	*to manage, get by*
componérselas	*to manage, get by*
echárselas de + adjective, noun	*to boast of being*
habérselas con	*to be up against, face, have to deal with*
tenérsela jurada a alguien	*to have it in for someone*
vérselas con	*to explain oneself to*

—Creo que el profesor Méndez **me la tiene jurada.**	*I think Professor Méndez has it in for me.*
—No te preocupes. **Te las arreglarás** bien en su clase.	*Don't worry. You'll manage fine in his class.*
—Oscar siempre **se las echa de rico.**	*Oscar always boasts of being rich.*
—Y no tiene dónde caerse muerto. No sé cómo **se las apaña.**	*And he doesn't have a penny. I don't know how he manages.*
—Este profesor tiene que **habérselas con una clase mediocre.**	*This teacher has to face a class of mediocre students.*
—Y si no hacen progresos, tiene que **vérselas con el director.**	*And if they don't do well, he has to explain why to the principal.*

EE. **¡En español, por favor!** Exprese estas oraciones en español.

1. —Do you (*tú*) know if the stores are open?
   —I couldn't (*sabría*) tell you.

2. I don't know how Raúl manages. He thinks that everyone has it in for him.

3. Any student who behaves badly will have to explain himself to me.

4. —Are Ramón and Sergio students?
   —No, they're not. They're programmers.
   —I think they're very intelligent.
   —Yes, they are.

5. Pedrito couldn't put on his coat so I helped him on with it.

6. —Should I ask Alicia and Pablo for their history notes?
   —Ask him for them. Don't ask her for them. (*tú*)

FF. **Ejercicio oral.** Hable con un amigo/una amiga de los libros que leyeron y las películas que vieron este año. Usen pronombres de complemento directo e indirecto.

GG. **Estructuras en acción.** Lea el siguiente anuncio sobre una inmobiliaria (*real estate company*) y haga los ejercicios.

I. Conteste las siguientes preguntas.

1. ¿Qué es lo que se vende en este anuncio?

2. ¿Cuál es el regalo que se le da al comprador?

3. ¿Cuál es el regalo que se le da al cliente por conocer el chalet piloto?

4. ¿Qué es Satafi?

II. Exprese las siguientes frases del artículo en inglés.

1. Sólo tendrá que ocuparse de cómo decorarla.

2. Huarte le hace un regalo de lujo.

3. o si Vd. lo prefiere

4. Visítenos o llámenos.

5. Le obsequiaremos con dos fantásticas noches en el Hotel Alcora de Sevilla.

CON UNA CASA ASÍ SÓLO TENDRÁ QUE OCUPARSE DE CÓMO DECORARLA

Y DE DÓNDE INSTALAR LA SAUNA.

Porque ahora, al comprar su casa en SATAFI, HUARTE le hace un regalo de lujo*. Una maravillosa sauna, totalmente equipada e instalada, para relajarse 365 días al año, o si Vd. lo prefiere, un descuento por importe equivalente.

*Promoción válida hasta el 30 de septiembre 1995.

Residencial SATAFI GETAFE MADRID

Visítenos o llámenos, concertaremos hora de visita. **Y además le obsequiaremos con dos fantásticas noches en el Hotel Alcora de Sevilla,** sólo por conocer nuestro chalet piloto, decorado con estilo propio.

10 a 14'30 h. y de 17 a 20'30 h. Tel. 682 49 30

CHAPTER 20
RELATIVE PRONOUNS

 A *The relative pronoun* **que**

- Relative pronouns are used to join two sentences into a single sentence. The clause introduced by the relative pronoun is the relative clause.

- The relative pronoun **que** can refer to animate or inanimate antecedents (persons or things) and can be either the subject or direct object of the verb of the relative clause it introduces. **Que** can refer to both singular and plural nouns and is the most common relative pronoun in everyday conversation:

el hombre **que** trabaja aquí (*que refers to* **hombre** *and is the subject of its clause*)	*the man who works here*
los paquetes **que** están en la mesa (*que refers to* **paquetes** *and is the subject of its clause*)	*the packages that are on the table*
los abogados **que** conozco (*que refers to* **abogados** *and is the direct object of its clause*)	*the lawyers whom I know*
la casa **que** compré (*que refers to* **casa** *and is the direct object of its clause*)	*the house that I bought*

- In English the relative pronoun can be omitted when it is the object of the verb: *the lawyers I know, the house I bought.* In Spanish, **que** is never omitted.

- **Nadie** and **alguien,** when antecedents, have **que** as the subject or direct object of a relative clause. **Todo** takes **lo que**:

—Si hay **alguien que** comprende, es él.	*If there's someone who understands, it is he.*
—No, él no comprende tampoco. No hay **nadie que** comprenda.	*No, he doesn't understand either. There's no one who understands.*
Esto es **todo lo que** tengo.	*This is all (everything) I have.*

A. Seamos precisos. Conteste las preguntas de su amigo con una cláusula relativa para que él sepa de qué objeto o persona se trata.

> MODELO   ¿Qué libro quieres? (El libro está en la estantería.)
> → Quiero el libro que está en la estantería.
>
> ¿Qué suéter lleva Paula? (Su novio le compró el suéter en Ecuador.)
> → Lleva el suéter que su novio le compró en Ecuador.

1. ¿A qué médico ves? (Tiene su consulta en aquel edificio.)

2. ¿Qué película quieres ver? (La película se rodó en Perú.)

3. ¿Qué revistas te gustan más? (Las revistas se publican en Asunción.)

4. ¿Qué restaurante prefieres? (El restaurante sirve comida del Caribe.)

5. ¿A qué peluquería vas? (La peluquería está en la calle del Conde.)

6. ¿Qué libros quieres comprar? (El profesor nos recomendó los libros.)

7. ¿Qué abrigo llevas? (Mis padres me regalaron el abrigo para Navidad.)

8. ¿Con qué secretaria hablaban Uds.? (Contratamos a esa secretaria la semana pasada.)

9. ¿Qué mecánico repara tu coche? (El vecino conoce al mecánico.)

10. ¿Qué carta estás leyendo? (Silvia me mandó esta carta ayer.)

Nota cultural

- **Asunción,** capital del Paraguay, fue fundada en 1537 por Juan de Salazar y Gonzalo de Mendoza. Fue una importante base de penetración de la Conquista española por la cuenca (*basin*) del río de la Plata. Es una ciudad colonial que tiene monumentos interesantes y jardines lindos. Muchas avenidas están bordeadas (*lined*) de árboles del caucho (*rubber*), naranjos y lapachos (*árbol americano*).

- Casi todos los paraguayos hablan no sólo el español sino también **el guaraní,** la lengua de los indígenas. El guaraní es el segundo idioma oficial después del español. Se enseña en los colegios particulares, se publican periódicos y revistas en guaraní y hay un teatro guaraní.

B. Más precisiones. La persona que habla usa cláusulas relativas para indicar exactamente a qué objeto o persona se refiere. Escriba sus precisiones según el modelo.

> MODELO   ¿Qué computadora?
> (Olivia la usa.) → La computadora que usa Olivia.
> (Tiene mucha memoria.) → La computadora que tiene mucha memoria.

1. ¿Qué profesora?
   (Todos los estudiantes la admiran.)
   (Enseña francés y español.)
   (Acaba de casarse.)
   (Mis padres la conocen.)

2. ¿Qué casa?
   (Juana y Rafael la compraron.)
   (Tiene patio y piscina.)
   (La construyeron en 1975.)
   (Es de ladrillos.)

3. ¿Qué regalo?
   (Mis hermanos y yo lo recibimos hace dos días.)
   (Mis tíos nos lo mandaron.)
   (Te lo enseñé ayer.)
   (Nos gustó tanto.)

4. ¿Qué restaurante?
   (Nuestros amigos lo abrieron el año pasado.)
   (Sirve comida española.)
   (Tiene manteles rojos.)
   (Muchos artistas lo frecuentan.)

5. ¿Qué senador?
   (El pueblo lo eligió el año pasado.)
   (Prometió combatir la inflación.)
   (Está casado con una extranjera.)
   (Los obreros lo apoyan.)

B *The relative pronoun* **quien**

- When **que** is the direct object of the verb in its clause and it has an antecedent that is a person, it can be replaced by **a quien** or, if the antecedent is plural, **a quienes**:

El empleado **a quien** conocíamos ya no trabaja aquí.	*The employee (whom) we knew doesn't work here any longer.*
Busqué a los estudiantes **a quienes** vi ayer, pero no los encontré.	*I looked for the students (whom) I saw yesterday, but I couldn't find them.*

- **Quien** and **quienes** can also serve as the subject of a relative clause if that clause is set off by commas (nonrestrictive clause):

José Pedro fue a hablar con la profesora Umbral, **quien** siempre tiene tiempo para sus estudiantes.	*José Pedro went to speak with Professor Umbral, who always has time for her students.*

C. El profesor, quien ... Quien y **quienes** sirven también de sujeto de una cláusula relativa si esa cláusula está apartada con unas comas. Combine las siguientes oraciones con **quien / quienes** para describir a algunas personas que están en la universidad.

La universidad

aprobar (o > ue) *to pass*	**dictar una conferencia** *to deliver a lecture*
los archivos *files*	**jubilarse** *to retire*
el ayudante *assistant*	**el salón de actos** *assembly hall, auditorium*
el congreso *conference*	**el secretario general** *registrar*
el decano *dean*	**el tribunal de exámenes** *board of examiners*

> MODELO   Cajal, Toledano y Puche aprobaron sus exámenes./ Ellos son compañeros de cuarto en una residencia universitaria.
> → Cajal, Toledano y Puche, quienes son compañeros de cuarto en una residencia universitaria, aprobaron sus exámenes.

1. El señor Mora es secretario general de la universidad./Él se encarga de los archivos.

2. El profesor Uriarte enseña química./Él asistió a un congreso en la UNAM.

3. Los estudiantes tienen que entregar una tesis./Ellos se gradúan en junio.

4. La doctora Arrieta tiene dos ayudantes de laboratorio./Ella figura en el tribunal de exámenes.

5. Estos decanos trabajan en la facultad de ingeniería./Ellos planean el programa.

6. El rector de la universidad es abogado./Él dicta conferencias de ciencias políticas.

7. Algunos estudiantes de medicina fueron a hablar con el profesor Quijano./ Él estaba ya en el salón de actos.

8. La profesora Arenas se jubila el año que viene./Ella hace investigaciones de biología.

Nota cultural

• La **UNAM** es la Universidad Nacional Autónoma de México. La universidad mexicana fue fundada en 1551. La primera universidad fundada en América fue la de Santo Domingo (1538). Las universidades hispanoamericanas fundadas después fueron las de San Marcos de Lima (1551), Córdoba (1621), Javierana de Bogotá (1622), Caracas (1721), La Habana (1728), Buenos Aires (1821).

• La **Ciudad Universitaria mexicana,** que queda a 18 kilómetros al sur de la ciudad de México, tiene una fama mundial por su arquitectura, obra del arquitecto mexicano Juan O'Gorman (1905–82). Se destaca la torre de la biblioteca cubierta por fuera de mosaicos que narran la historia del conocimiento científico desde la astronomía azteca hasta la teoría molecular. La Rectoría (edificio administrativo del presidente de la universidad) es notable por su mural de David Siqueiros y el estadio Olímpico por su pintura-escultura de Diego Rivera.

D. **... a quien/... a quienes.** **A quien** y **a quienes** se usan como complemento directo de un verbo cuando el antecedente es una persona. Combine las siguientes oraciones en una con **a quien** o **a quienes** para describir a ciertas personas.

> MODELO   Las chicas vinieron a vernos./Las conocimos en el teatro.
> → Las chicas a quienes conocimos en el teatro vinieron a vernos.

1. Mis primos están de vacaciones en Estados Unidos./Los vi en Caracas hace dos años.

2. La pintora sólo pinta acuarelas./La vieron en la exposición.

3. La muchacha me dio las gracias hoy./Yo le di un regalo ayer.

4. Los amigos no quisieron salir./Los llamamos a la una de la mañana.

5. Los vecinos se habían mudado./Los buscábamos.

6. La dependiente ya no trabaja en esta tienda./Ud. la conoció el año pasado.

7. El señor es mi profesor de cálculo./Lo encontraste en la calle.

Nota cultural

- **Caracas,** capital de Venezuela, queda a 25 kilómetros de La Guaira, que le sirve de puerto en el Caribe. Esta ciudad modernísima fue fundada en 1567 por Diego de Losada. La ciudad ha crecido enormemente en los últimos 50 años extendiéndose de su centro en la Plaza de Bolívar a los alrededores por hermosas avenidas. Hubo un boom económico causado por la nacionalización de la industria petrolera en 1976. La nacionalización fue llevada a cabo con compensación para los Estados Unidos y los otros países. Las grandes reservas de petróleo se encuentran en la región del lago Maracaibo en la parte occidental de Venezuela cerca de su frontera con Colombia. Venezuela sufrió una crisis económica durante los años ochenta porque el precio del petróleo bajó en el mercado internacional y Venezuela no había desarrollado una industria y tecnología nacionales. Por eso el gobierno ha tratado de reducir la dependencia del país en el petróleo. Venezuela ayudó a formar la OPEP (Organización de Países Exportadores de Petróleo) y es el tercer país en producción de petróleo de la OPEP. Desde 1959, Venezuela ha tenido gobiernos elegidos democráticamente.

- **Simón Bolívar,** *el Libertador,* nació en Caracas (1783–1830). Formado en las ideas de los escritores de la Ilustración europea (el Siglo de las Luces [*The Enlightenment*]), Bolívar fue el gran líder del movimiento independentista de los países sudamericanos.

- Caracas, como casi todas las ciudades hispánicas, ha nombrado sus grandes avenidas y calles por sus héroes nacionales. Por ejemplo, uno se pasea en **la avenida Bolívar** o en **la avenida Andrés Bello.** Bello fue un gran escritor, filólogo, poeta y político que nació en Caracas en 1781. Bello fundó y fue rector de la Universidad de Chile y murió en Santiago en 1865. Naturalmente hay una avenida Andrés Bello en Santiago. En ciertas ciudades hispánicas también se conmemoran las fechas más importantes de la historia del país. La ciudad de México no sólo tiene muchas avenidas como la de Benito Juárez, nombrada por el gran político (1806–72), sino también muchas calles con fechas como la del 16 de septiembre, fecha en la que el cura Hidalgo pronunció el "Grito de Dolores" en 1810 comenzando así la guerra de la Independencia mexicana.

E. **¿Sujeto u objeto?** Complete las siguientes oraciones escogiendo **quien(es)** si se refiere al sujeto de una cláusula relativa o **a quien(es)** si se refiere al complemento directo del verbo.

1. Te presento al señor quien/a quien conocimos ayer.

2. Llamemos a aquella señorita, quien/a quien siempre está dispuesta a ayudarnos.

3. Voy a la casa de los señores, a quienes/quienes compraron la casa de enfrente.

4. ¿Conoces a los chicos a quienes/quienes invité a la fiesta?

5. Esos arquitectos, a quienes/quienes trabajan en el rascacielos nuevo, son mis cuñados.

6. ¿Comprende Ud. a la locutora quien/a quien yo no comprendo bien?

7. Jorge llama a su novia a quien/quien quiere muchísimo.

8. La novia de Jorge está enamorada de Alfredo, quien/a quien es el mejor amigo de Jorge.

C *The relative pronouns el que, el cual*

- The relative pronouns **el que** and **el cual** have four forms each: **el que, la que, los que, las que; el cual, la cual, los cuales, las cuales.** They can replace **que** or **a quien/a quienes** when the antecedent is animate and the relative pronoun is the object of the verb:

los españoles **a los que** he conocido	*the Spaniards (whom) I met*
el electricista **al que** he llamado	*the electrician (whom) I called*
la vecina **a la que** no soportamos	*the neighbor (whom) we can't stand*

- In nonrestrictive clauses (those set off by commas), **el que** and **el cual** can function as both subject and object and can refer to either people or things. Since **el que** and **el cual** show gender and number distinctions, they are used to avoid confusion when there is more than one possible antecedent for **que** or **quien**:

El amigo de mi prima, **el cual/el que** estudia física, llega mañana de Caracas.	*My (female) cousin's (male) friend, who (refers to the male friend) studies physics, is arriving from Caracas tomorrow.*
El amigo de mi prima, **la cual/la que** estudia física, llega mañana de Caracas.	*My (female) cousin's (male) friend, who (refers to the female cousin) studies physics, is arriving from Caracas tomorrow.*

- The neuter relative pronouns **lo que** and **lo cual** refer to a preceding clause or idea. They only occur in clauses set off by commas (nonrestrictive clauses):

Su hija le dijo que no quería seguir estudiando, **lo que/lo cual** no le gustó para nada al señor Lara.	*His daughter told him that she didn't want to continue with her studies, which Mr. Lara didn't like at all.*

F. **¿El que o lo que?** Escoja el pronombre **el que (la que, los que, las que)** o **lo que** para completar las siguientes oraciones.

1. Me cayeron muy bien los turistas a _____ conocimos en la excursión.

2. Los Merino nos invitaron a pasar el fin de semana en su barco, _____ nos agradó mucho.

3. La hermana de Federico, _____ vive en Bogotá, estudiará administración de empresas en Estados Unidos.

4. Nadie vio llegar a Isabel, _____ nos sorprendió.

5. ¡Por fin fuimos en la montaña rusa, _____ nos dejó medio muertos!

6. El amigo de mi primo, _____ trabaja en Barcelona, se casará en mayo.

7. Esas chicas tan antipáticas con _____ saliste son mis primas.

G. **¿El cual o lo cual?** Ahora reemplace los pronombres relativos del ejercicio anterior con **el cual (la cual, los cuales, las cuales)** o **lo cual.**

1. Me cayeron muy bien los turistas a _____ conocimos en la excursión.

2. Los Merino nos invitaron a pasar el fin de semana en su barco, _____ nos agradó mucho.

3. La hermana de Federico, _____ vive en Bogotá, estudiará administración de empresas en Estados Unidos.

4. Nadie vio llegar a Isabel, _____ nos sorprendió.

5. ¡Por fin fuimos en la montaña rusa, _____ nos dejó medio muertos!

6. El amigo de mi primo, _____ trabaja en Barcelona, se casará en mayo.

7. Esas chicas tan antipáticas con _____ saliste son mis primas.

D *Relative pronouns after prepositions*

- **Que** may be used after the prepositions **a, de,** and **con** when the antecedent is not a person:

Éste es el tema **a que** nos limitamos.	*This is the subject to which we will limit ourselves.*
¿Comprendes los problemas **de que** te hablé?	*Do you understand the problems that I spoke to you about?*
Mi abuelo me mostró el bastón **con que** camina.	*My grandfather showed me the cane he walks with.*

- **En que** is common after expressions of time and to express imprecise location:

el mes **en que** se fueron	*the month they went away*
un siglo **en que** la vida era muy difícil	*a century in which life was very difficult*
el edificio **en que** trabajamos	*the building we work in*
la materia **en que** se interesa	*the subject she's interested in*

- When **en** expresses physical location inside an object, **en el que/en la que/en los que/en las que** are used:

  Abrió la gaveta **en la que** había metido las llaves.

  He opened the drawer in which he had put the keys.

  Donde can replace these relatives with **en**: see *section E* of this chapter.

- **Quien/quienes** or **el que** are used after prepositions for human antecedents. Some speakers also use **el cual**:

  el tío **a quien/al que** Pablito se parece

  the uncle (whom) Pablito looks like

  la chica **con quien/con la que** se casó mi hermano

  the girl (whom) my brother married

  los amigos **de quienes/de los que** me fío

  the friends (whom) I trust

- After prepositions other than **a, de, con,** and **en,** the relative pronoun **que** is not used. **Quien/quienes** may be used for people, **el que** and **el cual** for both people and things. **El cual** is especially common after prepositions of more than one syllable (**para, según, hacia, desde, contra, mediante, durante, sobre**) and with compound prepositions (**a causa de, delante de, detrás de, encima de, debajo de, por medio de, enfrente de, al frente de, antes de, después de,** etc.):

  una guerra **durante la cual** cayeron muchos soldados

  a war during which many soldiers fell

  el edificio **delante del cual** la vi

  the building in front of which I saw her

  los problemas **a causa de los que** dejé de estudiar

  the problems because of which I stopped studying

  los señores **para quienes (para los que/para los cuales)** trabajo

  the men for whom I work

  las ancianas al lado **de quienes (al lado de las que/al lado de las cuales)** vivimos

  the old ladies next door to whom we live

H. Te enseño mi ciudad. Ud. le enseña su ciudad a un amigo extranjero. Exprese la información dada con una cláusula relativa como en el modelo.

> MODELO   Hay un festival de teatro durante el verano.
> El verano es la estación …
> → El verano es la estación durante la cual hay un festival de teatro.

1. Hay varias líneas de metro debajo de estas calles.

   Éstas son las calles _____

2. Vivimos cerca de la facultad.

   Allí ven la facultad _____

3. Hay un restaurante enfrente de ese cine.

   Allí está el cine _____

4. Solemos pasar los domingos aquí.

   Ven y te presento a los muchachos _____

5. Hay una exposición de arte en medio de la plaza.

Ésta es la plaza _____

6. Hay un mercado al aire libre detrás de aquellos edificios.

Aquéllos son los edificios _____

7. Ahora caminamos hacia un barrio muy antiguo.

El barrio _____

8. Unas tiendas elegantes se encuentran al otro lado de este río.

Éste es el río _____

I. *En* **de varios significados.** Escoja el pronombre relativo correcto en cada caso. Recuerde que hay una diferencia entre el **en** concreto que significa *dentro de* y el **en** que expresa una relación abstracta.

1. los libros _____ me intereso (en que/en los que)

2. el armario _____ cuelgo mi ropa (en que/en el que)

3. la exactitud _____ insiste el profesor (en que/en la que)

4. el arreglo _____ quedaron (en que/en el que)

5. el bolsillo _____ tengo mis llaves (en que/en el que)

6. los cuadernos _____ escribo (en que/en los que)

7. los métodos _____ creemos (en que/en los que)

8. las bolsas _____ llevaban la comida (en que/en las que)

J. Exprese las siguientes oraciones en inglés.

1. El concierto benéfico fue un evento mediante el cual la universidad recibió mucho dinero.

2. Se ha construido un nuevo rascacielos desde el cual hay fabulosas vistas de la ciudad.

3. Éstos son los libros según los cuales el profesor Sorolla sacó sus conclusiones.

4. Siempre me acuerdo de las ruinas griegas entre las cuales caminamos.

5. Se abrió una librería al lado de la cual se abrirá una heladería.

6. Vamos a reunirnos en la confitería enfrente de la cual nos conocimos.

7. ¡Allí está la fuente delante de la cual nos enamoramos!

8. ¿Cómo se llama la empresa para la cual Antonio trabaja?

9. ¿Sabe Ud. cuáles son las ideas sobre las cuales los investigadores formularon sus teorías?

E   *The relative pronoun* **cuyo;** **donde** *as a relative pronoun*

- **Cuyo** means *whose*. It agrees in gender and number with the following noun:

La doctora Paredes es la profesora **cuyas clases** cursé con mucho provecho.	*Dr. Paredes is the teacher whose classes I took and benefited greatly from.*
Ése es el autor **cuyos libros** leemos en la clase de literatura.	*That's the author whose books we read in literature class.*
Él es un hombre sobre **cuya vida** se comenta mucho.	*He's a man about whose life people comment a lot.*

- **Donde** is used after prepositions to refer to a place. It can also replace **en el que** when the relative pronoun refers to a concrete place. As a relative pronoun, **donde** does not take a written accent.

la avenida **donde** hay muchos cafés	*the avenue on which/where there are many cafés*
la puerta **por donde** salieron	*the door through which they went out*
la playa **hacia donde** caminábamos	*the beach toward which we were walking*

K. Cuyo. Complete las siguientes oraciones escribiendo la forma correcta del pronombre relativo **cuyo.**

1. Éste es el nuevo cantante _____ canciones han ganado muchos premios.

2. Éstos son los señores _____ hijos asisten a la universidad con los nuestros.

3. Tengo que buscar a la persona _____ coche está estacionado delante de mi garaje.

4. Quieren conocer al compositor _____ sinfonía será estrenada el sábado.

5. Habla con tu vecino _____ perro ladra (*barks*) toda la noche.

6. Se habla mucho de la profesora de arqueología _____ clases son tan interesantes.

7. Es un país _____ historia no se estudia lo suficiente.

8. Ésos son los técnicos _____ equipos han llegado al campeonato.

L. Exprese las siguientes oraciones en inglés.

1. Ahora sabes la razón por la cual me enfadé.

2. Vivíamos en un barrio donde había muchas tiendas.

3. Allí a la derecha está la puerta por donde entran y salen los actores.

4. Yo no entiendo los motivos por los cuales el sindicato declaró la huelga.

5. Los muchachos no me dijeron para donde iban.

6. Son las horas durante las cuales Menchu hace su tarea.

7. Aquí está el kiosko detrás del cual Sergio y Sol quedaron en verse.

PART THREE

Other Elements of the Sentence

CHAPTER 21
ADVERBS

A *The formation of adverbs*

- Spanish adverbs are formed by adding **-mente** to the feminine form of the adjective. Spanish **-mente** corresponds to the English adverbial suffix *-ly:*

histórico *historic*	→ históricamente *historically*
intenso *intense*	→ intensamente *intensely*
lento *slow*	→ lentamente *slowly*
loco *crazy*	→ locamente *crazily*
profundo *deep*	→ profundamente *deeply*
serio *serious*	→ seriamente *seriously*

- Adjectives that do not have a distinct feminine form add **-mente** to the masculine/feminine singular:

amable *kind*	→ amablemente *kindly*
fácil *easy*	→ fácilmente *easily*
feliz *happy*	→ felizmente *happily*
inteligente *intelligent*	→ inteligentemente *intelligently*
triste *sad*	→ tristemente *sadly*

- Several adverbs either have irregular forms or are identical to the corresponding adjectives:

bueno *good*	→ bien *well*
malo *bad*	→ mal *badly*
mejor *better*	→ mejor *better*
peor *worse*	→ peor *worse*

- Many adverbs of quantity have no suffix but are identical to the masculine singular of the adjective:

mucho	demasiado	más
poco	tanto	menos

- Adverbs referring to loudness and softness have no ending:

hablar alto/bajo	*to speak loudly, softly*
hablar fuerte	*to speak loudly*

A. Para describir acciones. Escriba el adverbio que corresponde a los adjetivos siguientes.

MODELO   maravilloso → maravillosamente

1. alegre
2. descuidado
3. cruel
4. artístico
5. normal
6. abierto
7. franco
8. nervioso
9. evidente
10. responsable
11. débil
12. verdadero
13. torpe

14. violento
15. perspicaz (*perceptive*)
16. burlón (*mocking*)
17. comercial
18. sagaz (*wise*)
19. honrado
20. humilde
21. difícil
22. admirable
23. estupendo
24. afectuoso
25. vulgar

B. ¿Cómo hablaron? Escriba oraciones que describan cómo algunas personas hablaron en ciertas situaciones. Se practica formando adverbios.

MODELO   Marisol hablaba. ¿Fue sincera?
→ Sí, habló sinceramente.

1. Hernán pidió un préstamo en el banco. ¿Estaba nervioso?
2. Matías pidió disculpas (*apologized*). ¿Fue honesto?
3. Anita y Bárbara contaron sus problemas. ¿Estaban tristes?
4. Ud. se enojó con un compañero de clase. ¿Estuvo furiosa?
5. La señorita Cortés se quejó. ¿Estaba malhumorada (*peevish*)?
6. A Uds. se les rompieron nueve vasos. ¿Estuvieron incómodos (*embarrassed*)?
7. Hablaste por teléfono. ¿Estabas distraído?
8. Gladis chocó con un árbol montando en bicicleta. ¿Estuvo incoherente?

B   *The use of adverbs of manner; adverbs as intensifiers*

- Adverbs of manner (adverbs that tell *how* something is done), such as the ones presented in the previous section, come right after the verbs they modify, or as close to the verb as possible:

—Hiciste **mal** el trabajo.	*You did the work poorly.*
—¿Qué dices? Lo hice **bien.** De todas formas, lo hice **mejor** que tú.	*What are you talking about? I did it well. Anyway, I did it better than you did.*
—Mentira. Yo trabajé **cuidadosamente.**	*Not true. I worked carefully.*
—A mí me parece que no hiciste nada **sistemáticamente.**	*I think you didn't do anything systematically.*

- Adverbs cannot come between an auxiliary verb and the main verb, as they often do in English:

El huracán ha destruido el pueblo **totalmente.**	*The hurricane has **totally** destroyed the town.*
El enfermo está mejorando **rápidamente.**	*The patient is **rapidly** improving.*

- Direct objects, including negative and indefinite words such as **algo, nada, nadie,** and neuter demonstratives, often come between the verb and the adverb:

Leyó **el artículo** atentamente.	*He read the article attentively.*
No explicó **nada** claramente.	*He didn't explain anything clearly.*
Dijo **eso** torpemente.	*He said that awkwardly.*

- When two or more adverbs ending in **-mente** modify the same verb, the suffix **-mente** is dropped from all but the last adverb:

Nos habló **franca** y **abiertamente.**	*He spoke to us frankly and openly.*
Hay que explicar las cosas **clara** e **inteligentemente.**	*One has to explain things clearly and intelligently.*

- Adverbs ending in **-mente** can be replaced by **con** + the corresponding noun:

alegremente ➜ con alegría	elegantemente ➜ con elegancia
claramente ➜ con claridad	inteligentemente ➜ con inteligencia
cuidadosamente ➜ con cuidado	torpemente ➜ con torpeza

- Intensifiers, or adverbs that modify adjectives and other adverbs, precede the adjective or adverb they modify:

muy bonito	*very pretty*
extremadamente inteligente	*extremely intelligent*
totalmente ridículo	*totally ridiculous*
completamente inútil	*completely useless*
elegantemente vestido	*elegantly dressed*
sumamente bien	*extremely well*
muy rápidamente	*very quickly*

C. Cada adverbio en su lugar. Ordene los elementos para formar oraciones colocando los adverbios en su lugar debido (*right*).

> MODELO problema/claramente/el/explicó
> → Explicó claramente el problema.

1. las/mal/frases/pronunciaron

2. responsablemente/trabajaron/muy

3. bien/cosas/las/andaban

4. hijos/que/felizmente/mis/quiero/vivan

5. su/interesante/última/fue/película/muy

6. padres/inocentemente/a/niño/miraba/el/sus

7. esos/sumamente/Patricia/difíciles/encontró/problemas

8. salgan/la/rápidamente/de/muy/casa

9. totalmente/proyecto/encontramos/ridículo/el

D. En otras palabras. Vuelva a escribir estas oraciones, utilizando el verbo que corresponda al sustantivo y el adverbio que se forma del adjetivo.

> MODELO Juan es un hablador apasionado.
> → Juan habla apasionadamente.

1. Martín y Fernando son unos trabajadores inteligentes.

2. Lola es una cantante maravillosa.

3. Carmen y Pilar son escritoras hábiles.

4. El señor Ibáñez es un conductor prudente.

5. Lucas es un estudiante diligente.

6. Marcos es un pintor divino.

7. Carla y Pedro son viajeros frecuentes.

8. Alfonso es un jugador enérgico.

E. *Con* + sustantivo = adverbio + *-mente*. Cambie el adverbio que termina en **-mente** a una frase que consiste en la preposición **con** + sustantivo.

1. inteligentemente

2. armónicamente

3. elegantemente

4. diligentemente

5. delicadamente

6. cariñosamente

7. alegremente

8. ligeramente

9. lealmente

10. suavemente

11. fuertemente

12. felizmente

13. tristemente

14. calurosamente

15. claramente

C   *Adverbs of time and place*

- **Ya** means *already, now, right now.* **Ya no** means *no longer.*

—Tocan a la puerta.	*Someone's at the door.*
—**Ya** voy.	*I'll be right there.*
—¿**Ya** has visto la nueva película?	*Have you already seen the new film?*
—No, **ya** no voy al cine.	*No, I don't go to the movies anymore.*

- The adverb **recién** appears before past participles with the meaning *newly, just, recently.*

un niño **recién** nacido	*a newborn child*
los **recién** casados	*the recently married couple*
una casa **recién** construida	*a newly built house*

- Other common adverbs of time are **ahora** (*now*), **ahora mismo** (*right now*), **antes** (*before*), **mucho antes** (*a long time before*), **anteriormente** (*formerly*), **apenas** (*hardly, scarcely*), **posteriormente** (*subsequently*), **luego** (*then, afterwards*), **en seguida** (*right away*), **todavía** (*still*), **todavía no** (*not yet*), **siempre** (*always*), **aún** (*still, yet*), etc.

- The basic adverbs of place in Spanish are **aquí** (*here*), **ahí** (*there* [*near the person spoken to*]), and **allí** (*there* [*not near the speaker or the person spoken to*]). The adverbs **acá** and **allá** are used in the phrases **para acá** (*this way, in this direction*) and **para allá** (*that way, in that direction*). **Allá** means *way over there, somewhere over there.* In South America, **acá** often replaces **aquí** in speech:

—**Aquí** hay excelentes escuelas.	*There are excellent schools here.*
—**Allá** en mi país también.	*Back in my country also.*
—¿Qué veo **ahí** en tu mecedora?	*What do I see there on your rocking-chair?*
—Es mi gato.	*It's my cat.*

Other common adverbs of place:

arriba	*up, upstairs*
abajo	*down, downstairs*
en lo alto	*up, up there, up high*
(a)delante	*in front*
atrás	*in back*
cerca	*nearby*
lejos	*far off*
al fondo	*in back, at the bottom*
a la derecha/izquierda	*on the right/left*
al lado	*next door, next to it*
por algún sitio/lado	*somewhere*
por ningún sitio/lado	*nowhere, not anywhere*

- Adverbs of place combine with various prepositions and with each other:

por aquí	*around here*	hasta allí	*up to there*
por ahí	*around there*	hacia allá	*toward that place far away*
por allí	*around there*	allí arriba	*up there*
por allá	*around there (far away)*	aquí abajo	*down here*
desde aquí	*from here*	aquí cerca	*near here*

- Adverbs of place can also express time in certain phrases:

de aquel momento para acá	*from that time until now*
por allá por el año 1920	*around the year 1920*
de ayer acá	*from yesterday until now*
allá en mi juventud	*back then in my youth*

F. Exprese los siguientes diálogos en español. Tenga presente especialmente el uso de los adverbios.

1. —Did you (*Uds.*) go to the supermarket already?
   —Not yet.

2. —I'll be back right away.
   —Come here right now! (*tú*)

3. —Mariana can't find her cat anywhere.
   —Look (*Ud.*) up there! The cat's in the tree.

4. —Are the boys around here?
   —They're probably inside the house.
   —Do you (*tú*) know if they're upstairs or downstairs?
   —They're probably hiding behind some piece of furniture.

Nota cultural

En muchos países hispánicos, la planta baja se refiere al *ground floor* de un edificio.
El primer piso de un edificio es generalmente lo que llamamos en inglés *the second floor*.

G. Un adverbio más otro. Escriba frases con dos adverbios para describir cómo se hicieron ciertas cosas. Cambie los adjetivos a la forma correcta del adverbio.

1. elegante y cuidadoso
2. lento y suave
3. cariñoso y caluroso
4. oportuno y apasionado

5. ligero y perezoso
6. fiel y leal
7. sabio y astuto
8. deprimido y triste

H. Ejercicio oral. Diálogos con adverbios. Pregúntele a un amigo/una amiga cómo se hicieron ciertas acciones. Ud. pregunta por ejemplo: ¿Cómo te habló tu hermana? Su amigo/amiga contesta usando un adverbio: *Me habló abiertamente.* Luego cambian de papel para que los dos tengan la oportunidad de preguntar y contestar.

CHAPTER 22

PREPOSITIONS

 Basic prepositions: **a, de, en, con**

1. The preposition **a**:

▶ indicates motion toward a place:

ir a la ciudad   *to go to the city*
llegar a la oficina   *to arrive at the office*
regresar a casa   *to return home*

▶ labels the animate, specific direct object (*personal* **a**):

ver a Consuelo   *to see Consuelo*
ayudar a los niños   *to help the children*

▶ labels the indirect object, usually accompanied by the indirect object pronoun, especially in American Spanish:

Le di el paquete a Carla.   *I gave Carla the package.*
Les compré helado a los chicos.   *I bought the children ice cream.*

▶ connects verbs of motion to a following infinitive (*conveys the idea of purpose*):

salir a comer   *to go out to eat*
venir a vernos   *to come to see us*

▶ labels the rate or price:

¿A cuánto está el dólar hoy?   *What's the exchange rate of the dollar today?*
a sesenta millas por hora   *at sixty miles an hour*
Estos camiones se venden a veinte mil dólares.   *These trucks sell at/for $20,000.00.*
dos veces al día, a la semana   *twice a day, a week*

▶ labels the manner:

a pie   *on foot*
a caballo   *on horseback*
andar a gatas   *to crawl on all fours*
a regañadientes   *reluctantly*
a doble espacio   *double-spaced*
escribir a lápiz   *to write in pencil*
hecho a mano   *made by hand*
a la española   *Spanish-style*
a la americana, a lo americano   *American-style*

▶ expresses location (instead of **en**) in certain fixed expressions of place and time:

estar sentados a la mesa *to be seated at the table*
tocar a la puerta *to knock at the door*
a la izquierda/derecha, a mano izquierda/derecha *on the left/right*
a la salida del pueblo *at the edge of town*
a la salida del trabajo *upon leaving work*
al final de la calle *at the end of the street*
Mi colegio está a dos kilómetros de aquí. *My school is two kilometers from here.*
a la vuelta de la esquina *around the corner*
a(l) mediodía/a medianoche *at noon/midnight*
a las dos de la tarde *at two in the afternoon*
a nuestra llegada *upon our arrival*
estar a dieta, a régimen *to be on a diet*

▶ is found in idiomatic expressions:

al mes de trabajar aquí *after working here for one month*
paso a paso *step by step*
uno a uno *one by one*
a veces *sometimes*
a escondidas *stealthily, behind someone's back*
a espaldas de uno *behind someone's back*
a mi juicio, a mi parecer *in my opinion*

A. **¿A o nada?** Complete cada oración añadiendo la preposición **a** donde sea necesaria.

1. Les envié unas tarjetas _____ mis amigos.

2. ¿Conociste _____ la Alhambra?

3. No pudimos ir _____ verlos.

4. Leonardo habló con nosotros _____ dos veces.

5. Llegué _____ pueblo _____ la una.

6. Ya han viajado _____ cien millas.

7. ¿_____ cuánto está el peso hoy?

8. Ya son _____ las ocho.

9. La parada queda _____ seis cuadras de mi casa.

B. Exprese las siguientes oraciones en español.

1. I wrote the paper double-spaced.

2. Upon his arrival at midnight, he went to bed.

3. The baby crawls on all fours.

4. I love the clothing that's made by hand.

5. The children ate all the cookies behind our backs.

2. The preposition **de**:

▶ indicates motion from place:

El avión llega de Colombia.   *The plane is arriving from Colombia.*
Vengo de la farmacia.   *I'm coming from the drugstore.*
Salgo de casa a las ocho menos diez.   *I leave home at ten to eight.*

▶ indicates origin and possession:

Son de Venezuela.   *They're from Venezuela.*
el tren de Buenos Aires   *the train from Buenos Aires*
la mochila de Pedrito   *Pedrito's backpack*
la casa de mis tíos   *my aunt and uncle's house*

▶ indicates the material of which something is made or the content of a container:

una casa de ladrillos   *a brick house*
un reloj de oro   *a gold watch*
una camisa de algodón   *a cotton shirt*
una taza de café   *a cup of coffee*
un vaso de agua   *a glass of water*
una caja de juguetes   *a box of toys*

▶ is often the equivalent of English *with* or *in* in descriptive expressions such as the following:

lleno de agua   *filled with water (also: full of water)*
cubierto de nieve   *covered with snow*
forrado de plumón   *down lined, lined with down*
vestido de negro   *dressed in black*
pintado de azul   *painted (in) blue*

▶ forms noun phrases that are the equivalent of noun + noun or present participle + noun constructions in English:

una lección de música   *a music lesson*
una exposición de arte   *an art show*
la máquina de lavar   *the washing machine*
la facultad de medicina   *the medical school*
el cuarto de baño   *the bathroom*
el libro de biología   *the biology book*

▶ indicates a characteristic:

una persona de dinero   *a wealthy person*
la mujer del sombrero rojo   *the woman in the red hat*
una chica de talento   *a talented girl*
un hombre de porte medio   *a man of medium build*

▶ indicates a limitation or restriction on a verb or adjective:

Trabajo de programador.   *I work as a programmer.*
ciego del ojo izquierdo   *blind in one's left eye*
alto de estatura   *tall*
ancho de espaldas   *broad-shouldered*
un metro de largo, de ancho, de alto   *a meter long, wide, high*

▶ indicates time in certain fixed expressions:

trabajar de día, de noche   *to work days, nights*
Es de día, de noche.   *It's daytime, nighttime.*
muy de mañana   *very early in the morning*

▶ indicates the manner in which something is done:

ponerse de pie, de rodillas   *to stand up, get on one's knees*
estar de luto   *to be in mourning*
Se viste, se disfraza de policía.   *He dresses as, disguises himself as a policeman.*
servir de intérprete   *to serve as interpreter*
hacer algo de buena fe, de mala gana   *to do something in good faith, unwillingly*
beber algo de un trago   *to drink something in one gulp*

▶ connects nouns in humorous or mocking descriptions of people:

el loco de Pedro   *crazy Pedro*
la muy tonta de Marta   *silly Marta*
el pobre de mi cuñado   *my poor brother-in-law*
aquel burro de recepcionista   *that jerk of a receptionist*

▶ indicates the cause or reason:

saltar de alegría   *to jump for joy*
gritar de dolor   *to scream in pain, because of the pain*
morir de hambre   *to starve to death*
estar loco de alegría   *to be mad with joy*
no poder moverse de miedo   *to be paralyzed with fear*

▶ indicates the topic (English *about*):

hablar de filosofía   *to talk about philosophy*
saber poco de aquella familia   *to know little about that family*

C. *¿De o nada?* Complete cada oración añadiendo la preposición **de** donde sea necesaria.

1. ¡Qué hermosa es tu blusa _____ seda!

2. Esos turistas son _____ chilenos.

3. Diana lleva un vestido _____ azul.

4. Éstos son los documentos _____ ingeniero.

5. La niñita saltó _____ alegremente.

6. Salieron _____ casa a las diez y cuarto.

7. Pedro tomará su lección _____ piano el jueves.

8. Sírvame una taza _____ té, por favor.

D. Exprese las siguientes oraciones en español.

1. They gave me (as a gift) a gold bracelet and silver earrings.

2. Bernardo is tall and broad-shouldered.

3. Do you (*tú*) want to work days or nights?

4. Her poor aunt is in mourning.

5. They got down on their knees.

3. The preposition **en**:

▶ indicates location (English *at, in, on*):

en el comedor   *in the dining room*
en la mesa   *on the table*
en el aeropuerto   *at the airport*

▶ indicates extent of time:

Vuelvo en unos minutos.   *I'll be back in a few minutes.*
Roma no se construyó en un día.   *Rome wasn't built in a day.*

▶ is used in some expressions of manner:

en serio   *seriously*
en broma   *not seriously, as a joke*
estar en contra   *to be against something, to be against it*

▶ labels the amount by which:

más alto que yo en una cabeza   *a head taller than I*
Los precios han aumentado en un 20 por ciento.   *Prices have gone up (by) 20%.*

▶ labels the price:

Te lo doy en diez dólares.   *I'll give it to you for ten dollars.*

▶ labels the means by which:

Te reconocí en la voz, en el andar.   *I recognized you by your voice, by your way of walking.*
ir en avión, en barco, en tren, en coche   *to go by plane, by boat, by train, by car*

E. Exprese las siguientes oraciones en inglés.

1. La reconocí en la voz.

2. Me lo vendieron en dos mil dólares.

3. El valor ha subido en un quince por ciento.

4. Los obreros están en contra de la huelga.

F. Exprese las siguientes oraciones en español.

1. We plan to go by plane.

2. I'll pick you (*Uds.*) up at the airport.

3. Miguel is taller than Juan by a head.

4. Are you saying this seriously or as a joke?

4. The preposition **con**:

▶ expresses accompaniment:

salir con los amigos   *to go out with friends*
llegar con un ramillete de flores   *to arrive with a bouquet of flowers*
té con limón   *tea with lemon*

▶ expresses attitude (sometimes **para con**):

Es muy amable conmigo.   *He's very nice to me.*
generoso con uno   *generous to someone*
insolente para con el maestro   *fresh to the teacher*

▶ labels the means:

abrir la puerta con una llave   *to open the door with a key*
atar el paquete con cuerda   *to tie the package with string*

When preceding an infinitive, **con** labels the action as a means:

Con pulsar esta tecla, se guarda el archivo.   *By pushing this key, you save the file.*

▶ labels the manner:

Nos recibió con una sonrisa.   *He received us with a smile.*
Lo hice con mucho esfuerzo.   *I did it with a great deal of effort.*

▶ expresses *in spite of* or *notwithstanding*:

Con todos sus problemas, se hizo abogado.   *In spite of all his problems, he
    became a lawyer.*
Con tener tanto dinero de su tío, acabó sin un centavo.   *In spite of all the money
    he had from his uncle, he wound up penniless.*

▶ can label the content of a container and is less ambiguous than **de**:

una cesta con ropa   *a basket of clothing*
una bolsa con cebollas   *a bag of onions*

G. ¿Con qué? Complete las siguientes oraciones con una de las expresiones con
con. Escoja entre *con caramelos / sonrisa / cuerda / llave / esfuerzo / leche*.

1. Tomó café _____.

2. Abrieron la puerta _____.

3. Se ató el paquete _____.

4. Nos saludó _____.

5. Búscame la bolsa _____.

6. Lo hacen todo _____.

H. ¿Qué falta? Complete estas oraciones con la preposición que falta. Escoja entre
a, de, en y **con**. No se olvide de escribir las contracciones **al** y **del** donde sean
necesarias.

1. ¿Viste a la señora _____ el vestido rojo?

2. _____ todos sus defectos, José me parece una buena persona.

3. Vivo _____ dos cuadras de la oficina.

4. ¿Hablas _____ serio?

5. Tengo que terminar mi tesis _____ una semana.

6. El señor Salas es muy generoso _____ sus hijos.

7. Es una mujer _____ estatura media.

8. El dólar está _____ veintiocho pesos.

9. Las calles están cubiertas _____ nieve.

10. Limpio el suelo _____ un trapo.

11. ¿Me puedes dar agua _____ hielo?

12. Hay un buen restaurante _____ la estación de trenes.

13. Ahora me voy. Hablaremos _____ mi regreso.

14. Vengan a sentarse _____ la mesa.

15. La reconocí _____ la voz.

16. El inocente _____ mi hermano se compró un coche usado que no funciona.

17. Este jarro fue hecho _____ máquina.

18. Hace frío. Ponte el gorro _____ lana.

19. No comprendo _____ ese profesor.

20. La sala es grande. Tiene cinco metros _____ largo.

21. _____ mes de trabajar en la empresa, Víctor renunció a su puesto.

22. _____ principio, no nos gustaba la casa.

B *Por and* *para*

1. The preposition **para**:

▶ labels the destination, the time by which, or the figurative goal:

Tomaron el tren para Córdoba.	*They took the train for Cordoba. (destination)*
Los chicos salieron para el colegio.	*The kids left for school. (destination)*
Terminaré para el martes.	*I'll finish by Tuesday. (time by which)*
El regalo es para ti.	*The gift is for you. (figurative goal)*
Estudio para médico.	*I'm studying to be a doctor. (figurative goal)*
Es un honor para nosotros.	*It's an honor for us. (figurative goal)*
Leo para mejorar mi español.	*I read to improve my Spanish. (infinitive as figurative goal)*
Busqué otro empleo para ganar más plata.	*I looked for another job in order to earn more money. (infinitive as figurative goal)*

▶ labels the standard for comparison:

Para profesor tiene poca paciencia.	*For a teacher, he doesn't have much patience.*
Para médico sabe poco.	*For a doctor, he doesn't know much.*

▶ labels the information in the sentence as someone's opinion:

Para mí, la obra fue excelente.	*In my opinion, the play was excellent.*
Para ella, el precio es bueno.	*In her opinion, the price is good.*

▶ appears in some common expressions and idioms:

para entonces   *by that time*
para otra vez   *for another (later) occasion*
¿Para qué echar la soga tras el caldero?   *Why throw good money after bad?*
para siempre   *forever*
para variar   *just for a change*
ser tal para cual   *to be two of a kind*

2. The preposition **por**:

▶ expresses motion through a place or location somewhere in a place (imprecise location):

Salga por esa puerta.	*Go out through that door. (motion through)*
Hay varios restaurantes por este barrio.	*There are several restaurants in (around) this neighborhood. (imprecise location)*
por todas partes, por todos lados	*everywhere (imprecise location)*
No lo he visto por aquí.	*I haven't seen him around here. (imprecise location)*

▶ expresses duration of time or imprecise point in time:

Trabajó por muchos años.	*He worked for many years. (duration)*
Tuve que hacer cola por tres horas.	*I had to stand in line for three hours. (duration)*
Ayer por la tarde.	*Yesterday in the afternoon. (imprecise point in time)*
Nos veremos por Navidad.	*We'll see each other around Christmas. (imprecise point in time)*

▶ designates the cause or reason:

Se ofenden por cualquier cosa.	*They get insulted at/over any little thing.*
Te felicito por tus buenas notas.	*I congratulate you on your good grades.*
Lo pasé mal en Panamá por el calor.	*I had a bad time of it in Panama because of the heat.*

▶ designates the means:

Mándeme un mensaje por correo electrónico.	*Send me a message by e-mail.*

▶ designates the motivation or inducement, or the person for whose sake something is done:

Brindaron por el equipo vencedor.	*They toasted the winning team.*
Todo lo hice por mi familia.	*Everything I did was for my family.*
Me callé por ti.	*I kept quiet for your sake.*

▶ expresses exchange or substitution:

Pagamos mucho dinero por el coche. *We paid a lot of money for the car.*

Enseñé la clase por el profesor. *I taught the class for the teacher.*
  (instead of him)

▶ adds the idea of motion to prepositions of location:

El caballo saltó **por encima de** la valla. *The horse jumped over the hurdle.*

El mozo pasó **por detrás de** las sillas. *The waiter passed behind the chairs.*

El perro corrió **por debajo de** la mesa. *The dog ran under the table.*

▶ labels the agent in passive constructions (see Chapter 8).

▶ appears in many common expressions:

por acá/ahí/allá/aquí *around here/there/there/here*
por ahora *for now*
por añadidura *in addition*
por aquel entonces *at that time*
por casualidad *by chance*
por cierto *certainly*
por completo *completely*
por lo común *usually*
por consecuencia *consequently*
por consiguiente *consequently*
por culpa de *the fault of*
por lo demás *furthermore*
por lo mismo *for that very reason*
por lo pronto *for the time being*
por lo que a mí me toca *as far as I'm concerned*
por lo tanto *therefore*
por lo visto *apparently*
por mi parte *as far as I'm concerned*

por dentro y por fuera *inside and outside*
por desgracia *unfortunately*
por ejemplo *for example*
por esa época *around that time*
por escrito *in writing*
por eso *therefore, that's why*
por excelencia *par excellence*
por favor *please*
por fin *finally*
por lo general *generally*
por lo menos *at least*
por primera vez *for the first time*
por poco *almost*
por si acaso *just in case*
por su cuenta *on one's own*
por su parte *as far as one is concerned*
por supuesto *of course*
por último *finally*
por un lado, por otro *on the one hand, on the other*

▶ appears in many useful idioms:

dar gato por liebre *to put something over on someone*
(de) una vez por todas *once and for all*
en un dos por tres *in a jiffy*
poner por las nubes *to praise to the skies*
por las buenas o por las malas *whether one likes it or not*
por los cuatro costados *on both sides*
escaparse por un pelo *to have a narrow escape, to escape by the skin of one's teeth*
Pasó el examen por los pelos. *He barely got through the exam.*
traído por los pelos *far-fetched*
por motivo de *on account of*

por si las moscas   *just in case*
siete por dos son catorce   *seven times two are fourteen*
trabajar por cuatro   *to work like a slave*

▶ **Por** and **para** contrast with each other in certain contexts:

por esa época	*around that time*
para esa época	*by that time*
Por algo lo hizo.	*He did it for some reason or other.*
Para algo lo hizo.	*He did it for some purpose.*
¿Para quién trabaja Ud.?	*For whom are you working?*
Trabajo para el señor Domínguez.	*I'm working for Mr. Domínguez.* *(he's my boss)*
¿Por quién trabaja Ud.?	*For whom are you working?*
Trabajo por el señor Domínguez.	*I'm working for Mr. Domínguez.* *(in his place)*

I. ¡Pepita la preguntona (*busybody*)! Pepita pregunta muchas cosas por ser curiosa. Conteste sus preguntas usando la preposición **por** en sus respuestas.

> **Modelo**   —¿Por qué se durmió Ud. tan temprano?
> (un tremendo sueño)
> —Me dormí tan temprano por un tremendo sueño.

1. ¿Por qué fue Ud. al almacén? (un par de zapatos)

2. ¿Por qué felicitaron Uds. a Verónica? (su cumpleaños)

3. ¿Por qué te duele la espalda? (jugar tenis / cuatro horas)

4. ¿Por qué no terminó Javier el informe? (pereza)

5. ¿Cuándo veremos a Carlos y Elena? (la tarde)

6. ¿Cómo salieron los Salcedo de la ciudad? (el puente más céntrico)

7. ¿Por qué cosas irán Uds. a la bodega? (salchicha y queso)

8. ¿Cómo tendrás que hacer la tarea? (escrito)

9. ¿Por dónde darán un paseo los muchachos? (el bulevar Alameda)

10. ¿Por quiénes vas a pasar por la casa de los Granados? (Micaela y Angustias)

Nota cultural

Hay varios nombres que se usan para el *grocery store* norteamericano. Además de **bodega** en América se dice: **tienda de abarrotes, pulpería, colmado, almacén**; y en España: **mantequería, tienda de comestibles, tienda de ultramarinos**.

J. ¿Una película encantadora? A su amiga le gustó tanto la película *Mangos del Caribe* que la vio cinco veces. Ud. quiere saber por qué le gustó tanto porque Ud. la encontró francamente aburrida. Se contesta usando la preposición **por**.

> **Modelo**   ¿Por qué te gustó la película tanto? (los actores principales)
> → Fue por los actores principales.

1. ¿Por qué la viste cinco veces? (la fotografía)

2. ¿Por qué te interesa tanto? (el argumento)

3. ¿Por qué quedaste tan impresionada? (la dirección)

4. ¿Por qué te llamó la atención? (el guión [*script*])

5. ¿Por qué estás loca por ella? (los decorados [*scenery*])

6. ¿Por qué la encontraste tan buena? (la banda sonora [*soundtrack*])

7. ¿Por qué le haces un relato entusiasta (*rave review*)? (los efectos especiales)

8. ¿Por qué estás tan entusiasmada por ella? (el diálogo)

Nota cultural

El centenario del **cine español** se celebró el 14 de mayo de 1996, fecha de la primera proyección en Madrid. Algunos directores españoles han logrado una fama internacional, entre ellos, Luis Buñuel, Luis García Berlanga, Víctor Erice, Carlos Saura y Pedro Almodóvar.

K. ¿Para qué? ¡Ud. es el hermano modelo para su hermanito! Por eso él tiene interés en saber todo lo que Ud. hace y por qué lo hace. Ud. le contesta dándole muy buenos consejos. Use la preposición **para** + infinitivo en su respuesta.

> MODELO   ¿Para qué estudias tanto? (sacar buenas notas)
> → Para sacar buenas notas.

1. ¿Para qué trabajas en la biblioteca? (ganar plata)

2. ¿Para qué lees tantos libros? (aprender mucho)

3. ¿Para qué te quedas en casa los sábados hasta las tres? (ayudar a mamá y a papá)

4. ¿Para qué le compras flores y bombones a tu novia? (demostrarle mi cariño)

5. ¿Para qué practicas español cuatro horas al día todos los días? (perfeccionarlo)

6. ¿Para qué votas en todas las elecciones? (ser buen ciudadano)

7. ¿Para qué hablas de los principios éticos? (llevar una vida moral y feliz)

L. ¡Una semana muy ocupada! Hay tantas cosas que hacer y tan poco tiempo para hacerlas. Escriba para cuándo todas las cosas se tienen que hacer. Use **para** en su respuesta.

> MODELO   ¿Para cuándo te cortas el pelo? (el jueves)
> → Para el jueves.

1. ¿Para cuándo tienes que entregar el informe? (pasado mañana)

2. ¿Para cuándo arreglaste cita con el dentista? (la semana entrante)

3. ¿Para cuándo vas a entrevistarte para el empleo? (el martes)

4. ¿Para cuándo necesitas devolver los libros a la biblioteca? (finales del mes)

5. ¿Para cuándo precisas el regalo para el aniversario de tus papás? (el mes próximo)

6. ¿Para cuándo debes recoger la ropa en la tintorería? (las cinco de la tarde)

7. ¿Para cuándo vas a alquilar un coche? (el fin de semana)

M. **¿Por o para?** Complete los siguientes diálogos con **por** o **para**.

1. —¿Cuándo sale el tren de Madrid _____ Barcelona?

   —Sale _____ la mañana pasando _____ Zaragoza _____ la tarde.

2. —¿Van tú y Mari Carmen al centro comercial _____ ver los escaparates?

   —Ah, sí, una vez _____ semana.

3. —_____ peluquera, Teresa no sabe cortar el pelo.

   —_____ eso ya no voy a esa peluquería.

4. —Hagamos una excursión _____ la sierra _____ mediados de julio.

   —_____ variar, viajemos _____ las islas _____ principios de agosto.

5. —¿_____ quién es este hermoso traje hecho a la medida?

   —Es _____ mi hermana Rosa. Fue hecho _____ Gabriela, la famosa modista.

6. —¿Le dijiste a Juan lo de Armando _____ teléfono?

   —¡Qué va! _____ darle esta noticia tengo que hacerlo _____ escrito.

   —¿_____ cuándo va a recibir la carta?

   —¡Será _____ el 30 de febrero del año 2000 _____ el hecho de que no la he escrito todavía!

7. —¿Cuánto pagaste _____ los boletos?

   —_____ mí, un precio especial—¡el doble del precio normal!

8. —Parece que el ladrón se escapó _____ los pelos.

   —¿_____ dónde entró en la tienda?

   —_____ lo que leí en el periódico, entró _____ una ventana del sótano.

9. —Rodrigo estuvo enfermo _____ la leche estropeada que tomó.

   —Yo sé. Él me llamó para pedirme que fuera al trabajo _____ él.

Nota cultural

- **Zaragoza** es la capital de la Comunidad Autónoma de Aragón, que queda a orillas del río Ebro en el noreste de España. Su monumento más importante es la basílica de Nuestra Señora del Pilar. Zaragoza fue una ciudad ibera (pueblo europeo antiguo), una colonia romana, fue conquistada por los árabes (714) y ganada por Alfonso I (1118). En 1808 y 1809 resistió con gran heroísmo el ataque de las tropas francesas.

- En España, una gran parte de **la ropa** fue tradicionalmente hecha a la medida (*made to order, tailor-made*) por modistos (*couturiers*). Luego llegó la industria ropera con ropa ya confeccionada en las fábricas. Los españoles empezaron a comprar sus prendas de vestir en los almacenes y tiendas pequeñas igual que en los países latinoamericanos. La ropa suele costar mucho dinero en España tanto como en Latinoamérica. Por eso, muchos hispanoamericanos viajan a menudo a Estados Unidos en busca de precios más módicos y gangas. Hoy en día España goza de mucha fama en la alta costura.

N. Exprese las siguientes oraciones en inglés. Fíjese especialmente en las preposiciones **por** y **para.**

1. Soy norteamericano por los cuatro costados.

2. Iremos con Uds. más temprano por si las moscas.

3. Ponen a la tía Natalia por las nubes.

4. Ricardo habrá llamado para algo.

5. Tres por ocho son veinticuatro.

6. Mortadelo y Filemón son tal para cual.

7. «Te querré para siempre» le dijo don Quijote a Dulcinea.

Nota cultural

- **Mortadelo y Filemón** son los espías tan populares de las historietas españolas. Su creador, Francisco Ibáñez, empezó a escribir y dibujar estas historias en forma de tiras cómicas (*comic strips*) en los tebeos, publicaciones infantiles ilustradas, hace casi 40 años.

- **Don Quijote** es el protagonista de la novela *El ingenioso hidalgo Don Quijote de la Mancha* que fue escrita por Miguel de Cervantes Saavedra. Cervantes escribió la novela para burlarse de las novelas de caballerías cuyos protagonistas eran los caballeros andantes (*knights errant*). Se publicó la primera parte del Quijote en Madrid en 1605 y la segunda en Madrid en 1615. Don Quijote trata de hacer justicia en el mundo en nombre de su dama Dulcinea.

O. **¡Vivan los fiesteros!** (*Hooray for the party lovers!*) Les toca a los estudiantes hacer una fiesta del fin de curso. Cada persona salió a comprar algo y ahora cuenta lo que compró y cuánto costó. Use la preposición **por** en las respuestas.

>   MODELO   yo/ir/los manteles : pagar/doce dólares
>   → Yo fui por los manteles. Pagué doce dólares por
>   ellos.

1. Beatriz/ir/panecillos : pagar/treinta dólares

2. Carlos y Leo/ir/refrescos : pagar/cincuenta y cinco dólares

3. Paula y yo/ir/servilletas : pagar/siete dólares

4. tú/ir/fiambres (*cold cuts*) : pagar/ciento setenta y nueve dólares

5. yo/ir/torta : pagar/dieciocho dólares

6. Uds./ir/vino : pagar/cuarenta y tres dólares

7. Ud./ir/fruta : pagar/veintidós dólares

C *Other simple prepositions*

desde	*from*	**menos**	*except*
durante	*during*	**salvo**	*except*
entre	*between, among*	**según**	*according to*
excepto	*except*	**sin**	*without*
hacia	*toward*	**sobre**	*above, about*
hasta	*until*		

- **Desde** is more specific than **de** in labeling the starting point:

Lo vi desde la ventana.	*I saw him from the window.*
Desde aquel día hemos sido buenos amigos.	*From that day on we have been good friends.*

- **Hacia** can refer to attitudes and feelings as well as direction:

Siente mucho cariño hacia sus sobrinos.	*He feels deep affection for his nieces and nephews.*

Note the following combinations of **hacia** + adverb:

hacia atrás   *backward; toward the rear*
hacia adelante   *toward the front*
hacia arriba   *upward*
hacia abajo   *downward*

- **Hasta** can mean *even* as well as *until:*

Hasta mis abuelos vinieron a la fiesta.	*Even my grandparents came to the party.*

- **Sin** + infinitive has a variety of English equivalents:

El trabajo quedó sin hacer.	*The work remained undone.*
Las calles están sin pavimentar.	*The streets are unpaved.*

Habla sin parar.	*He talks without a stop.*
Quedamos sin comer.	*We ended up not eating.*

- **Sobre** means *about* as well as *above, on top of.* It can also mean *about* in the sense of *approximately:*

un artículo sobre la industria mexicana	*an article on (about) Mexican industry*
Vamos a comer sobre las siete.	*We'll eat at about seven o'clock.*

P. En español, por favor. Exprese estas oraciones en español.

1. My homework is unfinished.
2. I put one book on top of the other.
3. I saw him go out toward the rear.
4. She lived for (= during) many years among the Indians.
5. It's hot even in the mountains.
6. The immigrants feel love for their new country.
7. They followed us from the door of the movie theater.
8. I'm reading a book about Puerto Rico.

D Sets of prepositions and compound prepositions

1. **Ante, antes de** (*before*), **delante de** (*in front of*)

   Antes de is used to mean *before* with time expressions; **ante** is figurative. **Delante de** expresses physical location:

antes de su llegada	*before your arrival*
antes de Navidad	*before Christmas*
antes de las ocho	*before eight o'clock*
comparecer ante el juez	*to appear before the judge*
ante todo	*first of all, above all*
No sé qué hacer ante tantas posibilidades.	*I don't know what to do faced with so many possibilities.*
Hay un jardín delante de la casa.	*There's a garden in front of the house.*

2. **Bajo** and **debajo de** (*under*)

   Bajo is mostly figurative; **debajo de** is usually literal:

bajo la administración de González	*under the Gonzalez government*
bajo Carlos V	*under Charles the Fifth*
bajo ningún concepto	*in no way*
diez grados bajo cero	*ten degrees below zero*
bajo llave	*under lock and key*
bajo juramento	*on oath, under oath*
debajo del puente	*under the bridge*

3. **Contra** and **en contra de** (*against*)

   En contra de usually expresses being against someone's ideas, policies, or political views. **Contra** means against in most other contexts:

apoyarse contra el árbol	*to lean against the tree*
pastillas contra la gripe	*pills for the flu*
luchar contra el enemigo	*to fight against the enemy*
escribir un artículo en contra de la guerra	*to write an article against (opposing) the war*
hablar en contra del proyecto	*to speak against the plan*
Los hechos van en contra de sus ideas.	*The facts run counter to your ideas.*

4. **Frente a** and **enfrente de** (*opposite, facing, across from*) are synonyms. Note that **delante de** should be used to mean *in front of*:

Hay una parada de autobuses enfrente de/frente a nuestra casa.	*There's a bus stop across from our house.*

5. **Tras** means *behind, after* in certain set expressions. Generally, **detrás de** means *behind* and **después de** means *after*:

año tras año	*year after year*
un artículo tras otro	*one article after another*
detrás de la casa	*behind the house*
después de la clase	*after class*

6. Other compound prepositions:

   a causa de   *because of*
   acerca de   *about (concerning)*
   al lado de   *next to*
   a lo largo de   *along*
   a pesar de   *in spite of*
   a través de   *through*
   cerca de   *near; about (approximately)*
   dentro de   *inside of*
   encima de   *on, upon, on top of (similar to* sobre, *but cannot mean "approximately")*
   (a)fuera de   *outside of*
   junto a   *close to, right next to*
   lejos de   *far from*
   por medio de   *by means of (a synonym of* mediante*)*
   respecto a   *about (concerning)*

Q. **Ejercicio de conjunto.** Escoja la preposición que complete correctamente las oraciones.

1. No pudieron lanzar el nuevo cohete _____ mal tiempo que hacía.
   a. por medio del
   b. junto al
   c. a causa del

2. Todo lo que sé lo supe _____ noticiero del Canal 7.
   a. encima del
   b. sobre el
   c. a través del

3. No puedo salir de la oficina a las cinco. Llegaré al restaurante _____ las seis.
   a. a pesar de
   b. respecto a
   c. después de

4. El señor Aranda tuvo un ataque de nervios _____ la perspectiva de perder su empleo.
   a. ante
   b. para
   c. al lado de

5. Ricardo mandó carta _____ carta y nunca recibió una respuesta.
   a. tras
   b. atrás
   c. detrás de

6. Si alquilas un apartamento tan _____ la oficina, tendrás que viajar por lo menos una hora para llegar al trabajo.
   a. junto a
   b. lejos de
   c. por medio de

7. En la radio están hablando constantemente _____ peligro de un ciclón.
   a. sobre el
   b. encima del
   c. cerca del

8. El coche resbaló, salió de la carretera, y fue _____ por la cuesta.
   a. afuera
   b. hacia abajo
   c. cerca

9. Miré por la ventana mientras mi avión volaba _____ Nueva York.
   a. entre
   b. por encima de
   c. antes de

10. Alfredo tiene gripe. _____ lo tanto, no viene hoy.
    a. Por
    b. En
    c. De

11. El tren de alta velocidad viaja _____ 270 kilómetros _____ hora.
    a. por/de
    b. en/para
    c. a/por

12. Bueno, eso es todo _____ ahora.
    a. para
    b. hacia
    c. por

13. _____ culpa de él, el proyecto quedó _____ terminar.
   a. Para/en
   b. Con/hasta
   c. Por/sin

14. A ese sobrino mío lo quiero _____ todo.
   a. a pesar de
   b. a lo largo de
   c. frente a

15. Los ciclistas tienen que pasar _____ los coches cuando hay mucho tráfico.
   a. por entre
   b. ante
   c. después de

16. Varios senadores se expresaron _____ Tratado de Libre Comercio con México.
   a. por medio del
   b. en contra del
   c. dentro del

17. Todos estos sarapes están hechos _____ mano.
   a. a
   b. con
   c. de

18. Pedro Camacho es el señor _____ traje gris.
   a. con el
   b. dentro del
   c. del

19. —¿No vino Zenaida?
   —No. Vinieron todos _____ ella.
   a. con
   b. después de
   c. menos

20. Este autor vivió _____ los Reyes Católicos.
   a. debajo de
   b. sin
   c. bajo

R. **Ejercicio oral. Preposiciones: por y para.** Hágale preguntas a su amigo/amiga que empiezan con ¿por qué? o ¿para qué? Su amigo/amiga contesta con por o para. Por ejemplo: —¿Por qué te interesó la novela tanto? —*Por el argumento.* o —¿Para qué compraste bombones? —*Para regalar.*

S. **Estructuras en acción.** Lea el siguiente anuncio fijándose especialmente en las preposiciones. Luego haga el ejercicio.

Vocabulario

ajustar   *to fit*
asesorar   *to advise*
el corredor   *agent*
dar gato por liebre a uno   *to take someone in, sell a pig in a poke*
los seguros   *insurance*

**Un agente de seguros
nunca le dará gato por liebre.**

etrás de un buen seguro siempre hay un buen agente o corredor de seguros. Porque sólo ellos son los profesionales que más saben de seguros. Porque sólo ellos son los que le asesorarán y aconsejarán sobre el seguro que mejor se ajuste a sus necesidades. Porque sólo ellos estarán allí donde usted lo necesite y en el momento que lo precise, para resolver sus problemas. Y porque sólo ellos saben, en todo momento, qué compañías son las que dan mejor servicio y cuáles son las más seguras.

Es un mensaje de Winterthur, Schweiz y Equitativa.

Grupo Winterthur está formado por Winterthur, Schweiz, Equitativa e Hispasalud.

Grupo Winterthur

Escriba la preposición que falta. Escoja entre las dos dadas, una de las cuales aparece en el texto del anuncio.

Un agente _____ (1. de/en) seguros nunca le dará gato _____ (2. para/por) liebre. Detrás _____ (3. a/de) un buen seguro siempre hay un buen agente o corredor _____ (4. de/para) seguros. Porque sólo ellos son los profesionales que más saben _____ (5. en/de) seguros. Porque sólo ellos son los que le asesorarán y aconsejarán _____ (6. sobre/hacia) el seguro que mejor se ajuste _____ (7. a/hasta) sus necesidades. Porque sólo ellos estarán allí donde usted lo necesite y _____ (8. con/en) el momento que lo precise, _____ (9. para/por) resolver sus problemas. Y porque sólo ellos saben, _____ (10. a/en) todo momento, qué compañías son las que dan mejor servicio y cuáles son las más seguras.

CHAPTER 23
INTERROGATIVE WORDS & QUESTION FORMATION

A Interrogative words in information questions

- Questions that begin with an interrogative word such as **¿Cuándo?** or **¿Quién?** ask for a piece of information (*When is the party?*, *Who is your teacher?*, *Which one do you want?*). They are called *information questions*.

- Interrogative words have a written accent. The most important interrogative words are:

¿cuál?, ¿cuáles?	*which one(s)?*	**¿de dónde?**	*from where?*
¿cuándo?	*when?*	**¿qué?**	*what?, which?*
¿cuánto?	*how much?*	**¿por qué?**	*why?*
¿cuántos?	*how many?*	**¿para qué?**	*for what purpose?*
¿cómo?	*how?*	**¿quién?, ¿quiénes?**	*who? (subject)*
¿dónde?	*where? (at what place?)*	**¿a quién?, ¿a quiénes?**	*whom? (object)*
¿adónde?	*where? (to what place?)*	**¿de quién?, ¿de quiénes?**	*whose?*

- Some of the interrogatives are not used exactly like their English equivalents:

  ▶ **¿Cómo?**

  1. **¿Cómo?** is used to ask for repetition of something you didn't understand or to express surprise at something you have just heard (English uses *what* for this purpose):

     —Hay examen de física hoy.   *There's a physics exam today.*
     —¿Cómo?   *What?*

  2. Unlike English *how* in questions such as *How heavy is the package?*, *How wide is the river?*, *How fast does he run?*, **¿cómo?** cannot precede adjectives or adverbs directly. Here are the ways Spanish asks for measurements:

     ¿Cuánto pesa el paquete?
     ¿Cómo es de pesado el paquete?   } *How heavy is the package?*
     ¿Cuánto es de pesado el paquete?

     ¿Cómo es el río de ancho?
     ¿Cuánto es el río de ancho?
     ¿Cuánto tiene el río de ancho?   } *How wide is the river?*
     ¿Qué anchura tiene el río?
     ¿Cuánto mide el río de ancho?

     ¿Con qué rapidez corre?   *How fast does he run?*

     In Spanish America, a colloquial form **¿Qué tan ancho es el río?** exists.

3. **¿Cómo?** has different meanings depending on whether it is used with **ser** or **estar**:

¿Cómo está tu hermano?	*How is your brother? (asks about health or mental state)*
¿Cómo es tu hermano?	*What does your brother look like? or What is your brother like? (character, personality)*

▶ **¿Cuál?**

1. **¿Cuál?** and **¿Cuáles?** are replaced by **¿Qué?** before a noun in standard Spanish:

¿Qué libros leíste?	*Which books did you read?*
¿Qué materias escogiste?	*Which subjects did you choose?*

In parts of Spanish America, such as Mexico and Cuba, sentences such as **¿Cuáles materias escogiste?** are acceptable.

2. **¿Cuál?** is used for English *what* when an identification is asked for:

¿Cuál es la diferencia?	*What's the difference?*
¿Cuál es la capital de Nicaragua?	*What's the capital of Nicaragua?*
¿Cuál es la fecha de hoy?	*What's today's date?*
¿Cuál fue el resultado?	*What was the result?*
¿Cuál fue el año de la crisis económica?	*What was the year of the crisis in the economy?*

Note that **¿qué?** before **ser** asks for a definition:

¿Qué es filosofía?	*What is philosophy?*
¿Qué es programación?	*What is programming?*

▶ **¿Dónde?** *vs.* **¿Adónde?**

1. **¿Dónde?** is used to ask about location. **¿Adónde?** asks direction and is used with verbs of motion:

¿Dónde trabaja Jimena?	*Where does Jimena work?*
¿Adónde va Jimena?	*Where is Jimena going?*

Many speakers use **¿dónde?** with both meanings.

2. Note also **¿para dónde?** and **¿hacia dónde?** *toward where?*

▶ **¿De quién(es)?**

Questions beginning with **¿De quién(es)?** have a different word order than their English equivalents:

¿De quién es el libro?	*Whose book is this?*

▶ Prepositions always precede the interrogative word in Spanish:

¿Con cuántas personas llegó?	*How many people did he arrive with?*
¿Para quiénes es el regalo?	*Whom is the gift for?*
¿Sobre qué habló el profesor?	*What did the teacher talk about?*
¿En qué casa vive Nélida?	*Which house does Nélida live in?*

A. Los detalles, por favor. Cuando su amiga le habla de lo que hacen unas personas, Ud. le pide más detalles usando las palabras interrogativas con las preposiciones apropiadas.

> MODELO   Francisca se lamenta de todo.
> → ¿De qué se lamenta?

1. Monserrat se quejaba de todo.
2. Jorge y Maribel se interesan en todo.
3. Eduardo se jacta de todo.
4. Carlota se casó en mayo.
5. Cristóbal y Tere se metieron en todo.
6. Luz se fija en todo.
7. Hernán se ríe de todo.
8. Elvira se enamoró.
9. Pablo soñó con muchas personas.

B. ¿Quiénes son? Lea la información dada sobre cada persona y derive preguntas con palabras interrogativas de ella. Escriba más preguntas cuando sea posible.

> MODELO   Es venezolano.
> → ¿De dónde es? *or* ¿De qué nacionalidad es?

A. Leonardo Gustavo Sáenz

1. Es argentino.
2. Es ingeniero.
3. Trabaja para una compañía argentina con sucursales en los Estados Unidos.
4. Vive en Nueva York.
5. Está casado con una norteamericana.
6. Tienen tres hijos.

B. Delmira Danielo

7. Nació en Francia.
8. Sus abuelos son de España.
9. Se mudó al Canadá cuando tenía cuatro años.
10. Hace estudios posgraduados en química en una universidad canadiense.
11. Estudia para química.
12. Vive con sus padres y hermanos en las afueras de Montreal.

C. Claudio del Mundo

13. Ganó la gran carrera de bicicletas.
14. Es un héroe nacional en España.
15. Fue condecorado por el rey español.
16. Tiene cuarenta y dos bicicletas.

17. Le gusta más su italiana amarilla.

18. Quiere descansar.

19. Irá de vacaciones al Caribe.

20. Llevará a su mujer y a sus dos hijas.

Nota cultural

Miguel Induraín fue otra vez un héroe nacional de España cuando ganó el 82 Tour de Francia en julio de 1995. Induraín triunfó sobre algunos 188 ciclistas en esta famosa carrera de bicicleta, la del jersey amarillo—¡por quinta vez!

C. **¿Cómo? ¡Habla más fuerte!** Su amiga llama para invitarlo/la a ir de compras con ella. Por desgracia, hay interferencias en la línea y Ud. le pregunta lo que dijo usando las palabras interrogativas apropiadas. Escriba más de una pregunta donde sea posible.

   MODELO   —Voy al centro comercial.
                —¿Adónde?

1. —Pienso ir al centro comercial que queda en la carretera de Salamanca.

    —_____

2. —Hay ochenta y siete tiendas en el centro comercial.

    —_____

3. —Hay unos veintiséis restaurantes y cafés en el centro comercial.

    —_____

4. —Voy a comprar dos pares de zapatos.

    —_____

5. —Necesito comprarle un regalo a mi cuñada.

    —_____

6. —Trataré de gastar menos de cincuenta dólares.

    —_____

7. —Quizás le compre una blusa de seda.

    —_____

8. —No sé si le guste más la azul o la verde.

    —_____

9. —Pagaré con tarjeta de crédito o con cheque.

    —_____

10. —Voy a llegar en coche.

    —_____

11. —Saldré para el centro comercial a eso de las dos.

    —_____

12. —Volveré a casa antes de la cena.

    —_____

D. Estudiantes. Complete los siguientes diálogos con las palabras interrogativas que faltan.

A.

1. Nati: ¿_____ materias estás tomando este semestre?

   Sergio: Estoy tomando cuatro.

2. Nati: ¿_____ son?

   Sergio: Historia de los Estados Unidos, literatura inglesa, física y español.

3. Nati: ¿_____ enseña la clase de historia?

   Sergio: El profesor Durán.

4. Nati: ¿_____ es la clase?

   Sergio: ¡Excelente, y fuerte! El profe es estupendo. No hay cosa que no sepa.

5. Nati: ¿_____ estudiantes hay en la clase?

6. Sergio: Creo que somos veintidós. ¿_____ te interesa tanto?

7. Nati: Es que soy aficionada a la historia norteamericana. Es posible que tome la clase de oyente (*auditor*). ¿_____ se reúnen Uds.?

   Sergio: En el edificio de ciencias políticas, aula número 387.

8. Nati: ¿_____ días?

   Sergio: Lunes, miércoles y jueves.

9. Nati: ¿_____ hora?

   Sergio: De las diez y media hasta las doce.

B.

10. Diego: Oye, Paco, ¿_____ es esta carpeta (*briefcase*)? ¿De Baltasar?

11. Paco: ¿_____ dice adentro? ¿No tiene nombre ni papeles?

12. Diego: ¿_____? (*Where?*) Yo no veo nada. Mira.

13. Paco: ¿_____ color es la de Jaime? ¿No tiene él una así?

14. Diego: No me acuerdo. Vamos a llamarlo. ¿_____ es su número de teléfono?

    Paco: No creo que lo encontremos en la casa porque lo vi hace poco por aquí.

15. Diego: ¿_____ iba?

    Paco: No tengo la menor idea.

16. Diego: ¿Con _____ estaba?

    Paco: Ni te puedo decir porque yo hablaba con Aurelia.

17. Diego: ¿_____? (*What?*) ¿_____ dices? ¿Tú y Aurelia otra vez?

18. Paco: Ay, chico, ¿_____ quieres que yo haga? La quiero mucho. ¿_____ me
    hablas de esto ahora?

19. Diego: Bueno, es tema de otro día. Por ahora, ¿_____ estará Jaime?

E. Un testigo. Ud. estaba paseándose por la calle cuando vio un choque de
coches. Un policía acaba de llegar a la escena del accidente y quiere hacerle unas
preguntas. Forme las preguntas escribiendo las palabras interrogativas que
faltan.

1. ¿_____ estaba Ud. cuando vio ocurrir el accidente?

2. ¿_____ pasó? Déme todos los detalles.

3. ¿_____ pasó? Dígame la hora exacta.

4. ¿_____ de los dos coches fue responsable del accidente?

5. ¿_____ pasó la luz roja sin parar?

6. ¿_____ iba el conductor del coche blanco?

7. ¿_____ venía el conductor del coche rojo?

8. ¿_____ peatones (*passersby*) se acercaron a la escena?

9. ¿_____ minutos transcurrieron (*elapsed*) entre el choque y la llegada de la policía?

F. Una conversación telefónica. Ud. está escuchando lo que dice su amigo
mientras habla por teléfono. Porque no oye lo que dice la otra persona, Ud. tiene
que imaginarse lo que ésta le pregunta a su amigo. Escriba las preguntas que
habrá hecho.

> MODELO —¿Qué tiempo hace?
> —Hace calor.

1. —_____

   —De parte de Jaime Vega.

2. —_____

   —La casa queda en la calle Olmo.

3. —_____

   —El coche es de Roberto.

4. —_____

   —Es verde oscuro.

5. —_____

   —Voy a llevar a Ofelia.

6. —_____

   —Llegaremos a las nueve.

7. —_____

   —Tengo cincuenta y uno.

8. —_____

   —Pienso ver a Leo y a Matilde.

9. —_____

   —Será el sábado.

10. —_____

    —Llegan mis primos.

11. —_____

   —Gasté mucha plata.

12. —_____

   —Está lloviendo.

13. —_____

   —Tito y César se encuentran muy bien.

14. —_____

   —Me quedo hasta el domingo.

15. —_____

   —No quiero ninguno de los dos.

16. —_____

   —Jugaron tenis.

G. Vamos a comprar boletos. Exprese las siguientes oraciones en español. Preste mucha atención a las palabras interrogativas.

1. When are we going to buy the tickets for the play?

2. How about going tomorrow? Where's the box office?

3. On Pamplona Avenue. How many tickets do we need?

4. Six. How much do they cost?

5. Eighteen dollars each. Who's paying for them?

6. Each one will pay for his/her ticket. What day are we going?

7. Thursday. What time does the show start?

8. At eight o'clock. Whom are you inviting?

9. Nobody! The ticket is too expensive! How are we getting there?

10. By car or by train.

H. ¡Maravillas naturales de las Américas!: para expresar la magnitud. Con los elementos dados, forme preguntas acerca de la magnitud de estos lugares tan conocidos.

1. el río Iguazú / tener 1.320 kilómetros / largo

   ¿_____?

2. el río Amazonas / tener 6.500 kilómetros / longitud

   ¿_____?

3. el río Mississippi / medir 3.780 kilómetros / largo

   ¿_____?

4. el lago Titicaca / ser 3.815 metros / altura

   ¿_____?

5. el desierto de Atacama / tener 600 millas / largo

   ¿_____?

6. el monte McKinley / tener 6.096 metros / altura

   ¿_____?

7. la cumbre Aconcagua / medir 6.959 metros / alto

   ¿_____?

Nota cultural

- **Un kilómetro** (1.000 metros) equivale aproximadamente a 5/8 de una milla. Un metro equivale a 39.37 pulgadas (*inches*).

- **El río Iguazú** se encuentra al sur del Brasil y desemboca en (*flows into*) el Paraná donde se unen Argentina, Brasil y Paraguay.

- **El río Amazonas** nace en los Andes de Perú y atraviesa (*crosses*) Brasil.

- **El río Mississippi** (en español **Misisipí**) desemboca en el golfo de México por un ancho delta.

- **El lago Titicaca** se encuentra en la altiplanicie (*high plateau*) andina de Perú y Bolivia.

- **El desierto de Atacama**, que queda al norte de Chile, es una región rica en cobre y nitrato (*saltpeter*).

- **El monte McKinley** es la cumbre (*peak*) más alta de las montañas Rocosas (*Rocky*). La sierra se extiende desde Alaska, donde se encuentra el monte McKinley, hasta México.

- **Aconcagua**, la cumbre más alta de América, se encuentra en los Andes argentinos.

I. Complete las siguientes oraciones con las palabras interrogativas correctas. Escoja **¿cuál?, ¿cómo?** o **¿qué?**

1. ¿_____ es la capital de Costa Rica?

2. ¿_____ es computación?

3. ¿_____ son tus hermanos?

4. ¿_____ fue el problema?

5. ¿_____ están por tu casa?

6. ¿_____ es la fecha de hoy?

7. ¿_____ es guacamole?

J. Escriba preguntas derivadas de las oraciones. Tenga presente que la preposición precede la palabra interrogativa.

> **Modelo** Van *para el mar.*
> → ¿Para dónde van?

1. Estas rosas son *para Susana.*

2. Los ingenieros hablaron *sobre el nuevo puente.*

3. Celeste trabaja *en aquella oficina.*

4. Alberto fue *con otras siete personas.*

5. Los disquetes son *de Uds.*

6. Caminabas *hacia el río.*

7. Jeremías entró *por aquí.*

8. Soñó *con su novia.*

9. Se metieron *en un lío.*

B *Yes/no questions*

- Questions that do not begin with a question word require either *yes* or *no* as an answer. In English, they are called *yes/no questions* (in Spanish, **preguntas generales**).

- To make a statement into a *yes/no question* in Spanish, the intonation changes from falling to rising at the end of the sentence without changing the word order:

¿Los chicos tienen juguetes?	*Do the children have toys?*
¿Alfonsina trabaja mañana?	*Is Alfonsina working tomorrow?*
¿Martín sacó las entradas?	*Did Martín buy the tickets?*

- *Yes/no questions* can also be formed from statements by inverting the subject and the verb:

¿Tienen los chicos juguetes?	*Do the children have toys?*
¿Trabaja Alfonsina mañana?	*Is Alfonsina working tomorrow?*
¿Sacó Martín las entradas?	*Did Martín buy the tickets?*

- The subject can also be placed at the end of the sentence to emphasize it:

¿Trabaja Alfonsina mañana?	*Is Alfonsina working* tomorrow? (*focus on* tomorrow)
¿Trabaja mañana Alfonsina?	*Is* Alfonsina *working tomorrow?* (*focus on* Alfonsina)

- In *yes/no questions* consisting of just a subject and verb, either the subject or the verb may come at the end, depending on which element is the focus of the question. Thus, the questions **¿Carlos se va?** and **¿Se va Carlos?** require different answers, since their focus is different:

—¿Carlos se va?	*Is Carlos leaving?* (*focus on the verb*)
—No, se queda.	*No, he's staying.*
—¿Se va Carlos?	*Is Carlos leaving?* (*focus on who's leaving*)
—No, Carlos no. Se va Raúl.	*No, not Carlos. Raúl is leaving.*

- Statements consisting of a subject, **ser** or **estar,** and an adjective are usually made into *yes/no questions* by placing the subject at the end of the sentence, not right after the verb as in English:

El coche es caro.	*The car is expensive.*
¿Es caro el coche?	*Is the car expensive?*
Las tiendas están cerradas.	*The stores are closed.*
¿Están cerradas las tiendas?	*Are the stores closed?*

- Spanish can add phrases such as **¿verdad?, ¿no es verdad?, ¿no es cierto?, ¿no?** to statements to turn them into questions. The added phrases are called *tags.* These *tag questions* signal that the speaker expects the answer *yes.* Note that if the statement is negative, only **¿verdad?** can be used as a tag.

Vienes con nosotros, ¿no es cierto?	*You're coming with us, aren't you?*
Te gustó la clase, ¿no?	*You liked the class, didn't you?*
No tienes hambre, ¿verdad?	*You're not hungry, are you?*

K. **¿Cuál es la pregunta?** Derive preguntas generales de las oraciones enunciativas colocando el sujeto inmediatamente después del verbo.

> MODELO   Raúl estudia arquitectura.
> → ¿Estudia Raúl arquitectura?

1. Gustavo y Melinda aprenden francés.

2. Pepe trabaja en una tienda de videos.

3. Ud. toca piano.

4. Los niños se han vestido.

5. Cristóbal jugará tenis.

6. Elena se matriculó anteayer.

7. Uds. deben quedarse unos días más.

8. Ramona está a dieta.

L. **¿*Ser/estar* + adjetivo + sujeto?** Derive preguntas generales de las siguientes oraciones. Ponga el verbo **ser** o **estar** primero seguido del adjetivo y al final el sujeto.

> MODELO   El edificio es alto.
> → ¿Es alto el edificio?

1. Estos niños son traviesos.

2. Las margaritas (*daisies*) son bonitas.

3. El televisor estaba descompuesto.

4. El museo está abierto.

5. La revista es italiana.

6. Las joyas fueron robadas.

7. Los pantalones están rotos (*torn*).

8. Esta marca es buena.

9. El espectáculo fue impresionante.

M. **Para hacer un picnic.** Unos amigos quieren hacer un picnic y necesitan hacer ciertas cosas para que resulte bien. ¿Quién se ocupa de cada cosa? Para saberlo, conteste las siguientes preguntas generales usando el nombre o los nombres que aparece(n) entre paréntesis en su respuesta.

> MODELO   ¿Trae la carne Marianela? (Clarita)
> → No, Marianela no. La trae Clarita.

1. ¿Compra los panes Pedro? (Memo)

2. ¿Domingo y Toni nos llevan en coche? (Salvador y Bartolo)

3. ¿Dora va a preparar las ensaladas? (Leonor)

4. ¿Traerá Jorge el bate y la pelota? (Miguel)

5. ¿Piensa Carmen llevar los manteles? (Marcos)

6. ¿Harán Uds. los bocadillos? (Olivia y Nacho)

7. ¿Jesús y Marta invitarán a los amigos? (tú)

8. ¿Te ocupas tú de la fruta? (Mari)

C Questions in indirect speech

- When a question is not asked directly, but incorporated into a larger sentence as a dependent clause, it is called an indirect question. Compare the following examples. The first one has a question quoted directly, the second one has the same question reported indirectly by being incorporated into a larger sentence:

  She asked me, "Where is the post office?"
  She asked me where the post office was.

- Information questions are turned into indirect questions as subordinate clauses. The question word retains its accent mark.

Me preguntaron: —¿De dónde vienes?	*They asked me, "Where are you coming from?"*
Me preguntaron de dónde venía.	*They asked me where I was coming from.*
Te pregunté: —¿Cuándo regresarás?	*I asked you, "When will you return?"*
Te pregunté cuándo regresarías.	*I asked you when you would return.*
Siempre nos preguntan: —¿Qué quieren?	*They always ask us, "What do you want?"*
Siempre nos preguntan qué queremos.	*They always ask us what we want.*

- *Yes/no questions* are turned into indirect questions by means of **si** (*whether, if*).

Direct question: ¿Sales, Juan?	*Are you going out, Juan?*
Indirect: Le pregunté a Juan si salía.	*I asked Juan if he was going out.*

- If **preguntar** is in the present or future, then the tense of the original question is kept in the indirect questions:

Me pregunta para qué lo hago.	*He asks me why I do it.*
Nos pregunta cuándo vendrá Marta.	*He asks us when Marta will come.*
Me preguntará cuándo regresaron.	*He'll ask me when they returned.*

- The following table sums up the changes in tense in indirect questions.

  If the verb of the main clause (**preguntar**) is in the preterit:

The tense of the original question	changes to:
present ¿Para qué lo haces?	→ *imperfect* Me preguntó para qué lo hacía.
future ¿Cuándo vendrá Marta?	→ *conditional* Me preguntó cuándo vendría Marta.
preterit ¿Por qué regresaron?	→ *pluperfect* Me preguntó por qué habían regresado. or → *preterit* Me preguntó por qué regresaron.

N. ¡Cuántas preguntas! ¡Unas personas le machacaron los oídos (*repeated over and over again*) con tantas preguntas hoy que Ud. se encuentra mareado(a) (*dizzy*)! Ahora Ud. le cuenta a otro amigo lo que le preguntaron usando la pregunta indirecta.

> MODELO   Anita me preguntó: —¿Adónde vas?
> → Anita me preguntó adónde iba.

1. Felipe me preguntó: —¿Qué harás en la tarde?

2. Isabel me preguntó: —¿Con quiénes saliste?

3. Carlos me preguntó: —¿Por qué no quieres jugar baloncesto?

4. Sol me preguntó: —¿A qué hora volviste a casa?

5. Claudio me preguntó: —¿Para cuándo necesitas escribir el informe?

6. Mi hermanita me preguntó: —¿Cuándo me llevas a una discoteca?

7. Mis primos me preguntaron: —¿Por qué no nos invitas al parque de atracciones?

8. Mi mamá me preguntó: —¿Por qué tienes dolor de cabeza?

9. Yo me pregunté a mí mismo: —¿Por qué te levantaste de la cama?

O. Ejercicio oral: Una adivinanza. (*Guessing game.*) Ud. piensa en una persona, una cosa o un acontecimiento histórico. Sus amigos tienen que hacerle preguntas hasta adivinar lo que es. Le toca a la persona que lo adivina pensar en otra persona, cosa o acontecimiento.

P. Estructuras en acción. Lea el siguiente anuncio sobre una corrida de toros. Luego, escriba las preguntas con palabras interrogativas que se pueden hacer a base de la información dada en el anuncio. En algunos casos se pueden formar dos o más preguntas.

Plaza de Toros, Madrid Las Ventas

Gran novillada (corrida con toros jóvenes)
con picadores (toreros que montados a caballo hieren [*wound*] al toro con una pica para debilitarlo)

1. Plaza de Toros—Las Ventas, Madrid

2. sábado, 29 de julio

3. a las 10,30 de la noche

4. seis novillos

5. novillo = toro joven

6. toreros E. Martínez "Chapurra", Juan Muriel, Carlos Pacheco

7. niños acompañados, gratis

Gran corrida de toros

8. domingo, 30 de julio

9. a las siete de la tarde

10. seis toros

Venta de localidades (se venden billetes en taquilla)

11. para los dos festejos (fiestas)

12. para el público en general

13. viernes, día 28

14. de 10 a 2 y de 5 a 8

CHAPTER 24
NEGATIVE & INDEFINITE WORDS

A Negative words and expressions

- Study the following list of Spanish negative words and expressions and their affirmative counterparts:

	alguna vez *sometime*
	algunas veces *sometimes*
nunca, jamás *never*	**a veces** *sometimes*
	muchas veces, a menudo *often*
	siempre *always*

nunca más *never again*	**otra vez** *again*
nada *nothing*	**algo** *something*
nadie *no one, nobody*	**alguien** *someone, somebody*
tampoco *neither, not either*	**también** *also*
ni, ni siquiera *not even*	**o** *or*
ni … ni *neither … nor*	**o … o** *either … or*
en/por ninguna parte *nowhere*	**en/por alguna parte** *somewhere*
en/por ningún lado / sitio / lugar *nowhere*	**en/por algún lado / sitio / lugar** *somewhere*
ya no *no longer*	**todavía** *still*
de ninguna manera, de ningún modo *in no way*	**de alguna manera, de algún modo** *somehow, in some way*

- Spanish also has negative and affirmative adjectives: **ninguno** (*no, not a*) and **alguno** (*some*). **Ninguno** and **alguno** are shortened to **ningún** and **algún** before a masculine singular noun:

Laura trabaja en **algún** edificio del centro.	*Laura works in some building downtown.*
Mercedes trabaja en **alguna** oficina.	*Mercedes works in some office.*
Hay **algunos** anuncios en el periódico.	*There are some ads in the newspaper.*
Conozco **algunas** tiendas elegantes por aquí.	*I know some elegant stores around here.*

- **Ninguno** is not used in the plural unless the noun it modifies is always used in the plural such as **anteojos, tijeras, vacaciones,** etc.:

No hay **ningún** hospital aquí.	*There is no hospital here. (There are no hospitals ...)*
No recibí **ninguna** respuesta.	*I didn't receive any answer.*
Este año no tenemos **ningunas** vacaciones.	*This year we don't have any vacation.*

- When negative words follow the verb, **no** precedes it:

No hice **nada** hoy.	*I didn't do anything today.*
Catalina **no** hizo **nada tampoco.**	*Catalina didn't do anything either.*
No vamos **nunca** a esquiar.	*We never go skiing.*

  However, if a negative word precedes the verb, then **no** is not used:

—**Nunca** voy al cine.	*I never go to the movies.*
—Yo **tampoco** voy mucho.	*I don't go much either.*

- Personal **a** is used before **alguien** and **nadie** when they are direct objects and also before forms of **alguno** and **ninguno** when they refer to people and are direct objects:

—¿Viste **a alguien** en la plaza?	*Did you see anyone in the square?*
—No, no vi **a nadie.**	*No, I didn't see anyone.*
—¿Invitaste **a alguno** de los vecinos?	*Did you invite any of the neighbors?*
—No, no llamé **a ninguno.**	*No, I didn't call any (of them).*

- When words joined by **ni ... ni** or **o ... o** are the subject of a sentence, the verb can be either singular or plural:

—Debe venir **o Pepe o Rosa.**	*Either Pepe or Rosa should be coming.*
—¿Y si no vienen **ni él ni ella**?	*And what if neither he nor she comes?*

- A single **ni** means *not even*. **Ni siquiera** is a more emphatic form:

—¿Cuántos asistieron a la reunión?	*How many attended the meeting?*
—**Ni** uno./**Ni siquiera** uno.	*Not even one.*
—¿Te ofrecieron algo?	*Did they offer you anything?*
—**Ni** un vaso de agua.	*Not even a glass of water.*

A. **¡No!** Conteste las preguntas negativamente usando **no** y las palabras negativas que corresponden a las afirmativas.

> MODELO —¿Quieres tomar *algo?*
> —No, no quiero tomar **nada.**

1. ¿Fuiste *alguna vez* a la Isla de Pascua?

2. ¿Aprendieron Uds. chino *también?*

3. ¿*Alguien* ha llamado esta tarde?

4. ¿Va Isabel a tomar álgebra *otra vez?*

5. ¿Leerás *o* la novela *o* el guión de la película?

6. ¿*Algunos* jefes renunciaron al puesto?

7. ¿Conoció Osvaldo *a alguien* por fin?

8. ¿Quedan *algunos* duraznos?

9. ¿*Siempre* limpias la casa los sábados?

10. ¿Has visto *a alguna* de las empleadas?

Nota cultural

Isla de Pascua, que queda en el Pacífico, pertenece a Chile. La isla, que es de 180 kilómetros cuadrados, tiene un observatorio meteorológico. Se conoce por sus enormes estatuas de piedra que fueron construidas probablemente por gente primitiva de origen polinesio.

B. **¡Angustias, la aguafiestas** (*the wet blanket*)! Angustias lo ve todo negro, es decir, es muy pesimista. Lea sus comentarios sobre una fiesta y cambie el orden de la palabra negativa.

> MODELO **Nadie** se divierte.
> → **No** se divierte **nadie.**

1. Nada queda de la comida.

2. Tampoco hay refrescos.

3. Ni los chicos ni las chicas bailan.

4. Ninguno de los chicos se acerca para hablarme.

5. Ningún cantante canta bien.

6. Nadie tiene ganas de quedarse.

7. Nunca dan fiestas divertidas.

C. **¡Qué iluso** (*dreamer*)! ¡Humberto pasa la vida soñando ... pero son mirlos blancos (*impossible dreams* [mirlo *blackbird*]). Dígale que no puede ser empleando las palabras negativas apropiadas.

> MODELO Siempre gano becas.
> → ¡Qué va! **Nunca/Jamás** ganas becas.

1. Alguien me regaló dos millones de dólares.

2. Algunas chicas dicen que soy un Adonis.

3. Muchas veces saco un diez en mis exámenes.

4. Yo nado y patino mejor que nadie.

5. Los reyes de España me mandaron algo.

6. Yo también voy a la luna.

7. Conchita va a salir conmigo otra vez.

8. Mis padres me van a regalar o un Jaguar o un Ferrari.

B *Further uses of negative words*

- Spanish, unlike English, allows two or more negative words in a sentence:

  Nadie trae **nada nunca.**   *Nobody ever brings anything.*

- **Alguno** can have an emphatic *negative* meaning when placed after the noun:

  No hay problema **alguno.**   *There is no problem at all.*

  No recibimos carta **alguna.**   *We received no letter at all.*

- In Spanish, negatives are used in certain constructions where English uses indefinite words rather than negatives:

  1. after **que** (*than*) in comparatives:

     —La lluvia fue peor **que nada.**   *The rain was worse than anything.*
     —Sí, y yo me mojé más **que nadie.**   *Yes, and I got wetter than anyone.*
     —Lo que es la guerra lo sabe este   *This country knows better than any other*
       país mejor **que ningún otro.**   *what war is.*
     —Se ha sufrido más aquí **que en**   *People have suffered more here than*
       ningún otro lugar.   *anywhere else.*
     —Hoy habló el profesor mejor **que**   *Today the teacher spoke better than ever.*
       nunca.
     —Y aprendimos más cosas **que en**   *And we learned more than at any other*
       ningún otro momento.   *time.*

  2. after **sin, antes de,** and **antes que:**

     Lo hizo **sin** pedir **nada a nadie**   *He did it without ever asking anything*
       nunca.   *of anyone.*
     Antes de hacer **nada,** lee las   *Before doing anything, read the*
       instrucciones.   *instructions.*
     Has llegado **antes que nadie.**   *You've arrived before anyone else.*

  3. after **imposible, poco probable, inútil,** expressions of doubt, and other similar words that imply negation:

     Es **imposible** hacer **nada** aquí.   *It's impossible to do anything here.*
     Es **inútil** pedirle **nada.**   *It's useless to ask him for anything.*
     Dudo que venga **nadie.**   *I doubt that anyone will come.*

- The conjunction **pero** is replaced by **sino** after a negative clause:

  No viene ella, **sino** él.   *Not she, but he, is coming.*

  Note also **no solamente (sólo) ... sino también** *not only ... but also.*

D. Hay que ser negativo. Complete las siguientes oraciones con las expresiones negativas o indefinidas apropiadas.

1. Es imposible decirle _____ a este chiquillo porque no le hace caso a _____.

2. ¡_____ he oído tantas barbaridades!

3. El programa no fue _____ bueno pero los locutores sí fueron _____ interesantes.

4. ¿No probaste la sopa? Y salió mejor que _____.

5. No sólo visitamos Córdoba _____ nos quedamos ocho días en Granada.

6. Aunque Diego y yo nos conocimos hace un año es como si él no me conociera _____.

7. ¡Qué señora más distinguida! Será _____.

8. ¡Ay, sus cuentos tan largos y siempre con los mismos temas! Son los cuentos de _____.

9. Maribel es tan torpe; no sabe nada _____.

10. Mauricio es siempre el primero en llegar. Llega antes que _____.

11. —¿Vino Alicia Delgado?

    —Sí, y _____ ella, _____ su hermano Francisco.

12. Muchos dicen que Toledo es más interesante por su arte e historia que _____ otra ciudad española.

Nota cultural

- **Córdoba** es una pintoresca ciudad andaluza que queda a orillas del río Guadalquivir. Sus monumentos más importantes incluyen la catedral (que era mezquita [*mosque*]), el Alcázar (fortaleza, palacio real) y un puente romano sobre el Guadalquivir. Córdoba y Granada impresionan por su arquitectura y arte árabes.

- **Granada** es otra hermosa ciudad andaluza. Queda al pie de la Sierra Nevada. Algunos monumentos que destacan son la Alhambra (el palacio de los reyes moros), el palacio de Carlos V, la Catedral y el Generalife (el palacio y jardines de los reyes moros). Granada, la última defensa de los moros en España, fue conquistada por los Reyes Católicos en 1492.

- **Toledo,** una gran ciudad rica en historia y arte, queda al sur de Madrid en Castilla. A orillas del río Tajo, Toledo fue la capital visigoda (*Visigoth*) y residencia de la Corte española hasta 1560. Toledo se destaca como lugar turístico por su catedral gótica, la sinagoga del Tránsito, la iglesia de Santo Tomé, el puente romano de Alcántara y la casa de El Greco. Este famoso pintor que nació en Creta en 1541 (o 1542), vivió muchos años en Toledo y allí murió en 1614. La ciudad influyó mucho en su obra (véase *La vista de Toledo*). Se puede ver su obra maestra *El entierro del Conde de Orgaz* en la iglesia de Santo Tomé.

C   Negative words in conversation

- Negative words frequently serve as one-word answers to questions:

—¿Vas a menudo al café estudiantil?	*Do you often go to the student café?*
—**Nunca.**	*Never.*
—¿Quién te ayudó con el trabajo?	*Who helped you with the work?*
—**Nadie.**	*Nobody.*

- Negative words, including **no,** often appear with subject pronouns or with phrases consisting of **a** + prepositional pronoun as short answers to questions:

—¿Cursan tú y Carla español?	*Are you and Carla taking Spanish?*
—Yo, sí. **Ella, no.**	*I am. She's not.*
—No voy a la fiesta hoy. ¿Y tú?	*I'm not going to the party today. What about you?*
—**Yo tampoco.**	*Neither am I.*
—A mí no me gusta este plato.	*I don't like this dish.*
—**A nosotros tampoco.**	*We don't either.*
—A mí siempre me escriben.	*People are always writing to me.*
—**A nosotros nunca.**	*Never to us.*

- Some non-negative expressions such as **en absoluto** and **en la vida** can function as negatives:

—**En la vida** he visto un espectáculo tan bueno.	*I have never in my life seen such a good show.*
—Yo tampoco.	*Neither have I.*
—¿Contrataría Ud. a ese señor?	*Would you hire that man?*
—**En absoluto.**	*Absolutely not.*

- **Algo** and **nada** can function as adverbs and modify adjectives and verbs:

—El discurso fue **algo** confuso.	*The speech was somewhat confusing.*
—Y no fue **nada** interesante.	*And it wasn't at all interesting.*
—Tomás trabaja **algo.**	*Tomás works a little.*
—Pero no se concentra **nada.**	*But he doesn't concentrate at all.*

Para nada is an emphatic replacement for **nada: No se concentra para nada.**

- **Algo de** and **nada de** are used before nouns:

—¿Quieres **algo de** chocolate?	*Do you want a little chocolate?*
—No, no debo comer **nada de** dulces.	*No, I'm not supposed to eat any sweets.*

Algo de is a synonym for **un poco de.**

Negative and indefinite words appear in many idiomatic expressions:

Expressions with negative words:

nunca *and* **jamás**

jamás de los jamases   *never ever*
el cuento de nunca acabar   *the never-ending story*
casi nunca   *hardly ever*
¡Hasta nunca!   *Good-bye forever!*
nunca jamás   *never ever*
nunca más   *never again, no more*

ni

ni hablar, ni modo   *nothing doing*
No lo puedo ver ni en pintura.   *I can't stand him at all.*
No tengo ni idea.   *I haven't the slightest idea.*

nada

No por nada vendimos la casa.   *We had good reason to sell the house.*
No por nada le llaman 'tonto'.   *They don't call him 'dumb' for nothing.*
¡De eso nada, monada! (*slang*)   *None of that!, No way!*
De nada. Por nada.   *You're welcome./Don't mention it.*
¡Nada de salir antes de terminar la tarea!   *Forget about going out before you finish your homework!*
No me conoce de nada.   *He doesn't know me from Adam.*
antes de nada   *first of all*
casi nada   *hardly*
como si nada   *as if it were nothing at all*
dentro de nada   *in a moment*
más que nada   *more than anything*
nada de eso   *nothing of the sort*
nada de extraordinario   *nothing unusual*
nada de nada   *nothing at all*
nada más   *that's all*
no servir para nada   *to be useless*
no tener nada de + noun   *to not have _____ at all*
no tener nada de particular   *to have nothing special about*
por nada del mundo   *for nothing in the world*
quedarse en nada   *to come to nothing*
tener en nada   *to think very little of; take no notice of*

nadie

Es un don nadie.   *He's a nobody.*

Expressions with indefinite words:

Algo es algo. Más vale algo que nada.   *Something is better than nothing.*
Ya es algo.   *That's something at least./It's a start.*
¡Por algo será!   *There must be a reason.*
De algo lo conozco.   *I know you from somewhere.*
algo así   *something like that*
tener algo que ver con   *to have something to do with*
ser alguien   *to be somebody*
Nos vemos a la hora de siempre.   *We'll see each other at the usual time.*
Es lo de siempre.   *It's the same old story.*
Para siempre.   *Forever.*

E. **¿Cómo se dice eso en inglés?** Exprese las siguientes oraciones en inglés. Tenga en cuenta especialmente las expresiones con palabras negativas e indefinidas.

1. ¡No la puedo ver ni en pintura!

2. ¡De eso nada, monada!

3. Van a verse a la hora de siempre.

4. No por nada la llaman encantadora.

5. Guillermo dice que no tiene ni idea.

6. Todo el tiempo y todos los planes se quedaron en nada.

7. Al fin y al cabo todo el discutir no sirvió para nada.

8. Lo que dices no tiene nada que ver con la situación actual.

F. **¿Algo? ¿Nada? ¿Nunca?** Exprese las siguientes ideas escogiendo una de las expresiones con **nunca/jamás, algo** o **nada.**

1. Eso es inútil.
   a. No sirve para nada.
   b. Por nada del mundo.

2. ¿Ir al cine? ¡Ni hablar!
   a. Algo es algo.
   b. ¡Nada de salir!

3. Es lo de siempre.
   a. Nunca jamás.
   b. Nada de extraordinario.

4. X está relacionado con Y.
   a. X tiene algo que ver con Y.
   b. X se queda en nada.

5. No volveremos a vernos.
   a. Nos veremos más que nunca.
   b. Nunca más nos veremos.

6. Se le acabó la paciencia.
   a. No tiene nada de paciencia.
   b. Más vale algo que nada.

7. Camilo tendrá algún motivo.
   a. Por algo será.
   b. Por nada.

8. Van poco a ese café.
   a. Como si nada.
   b. Casi nunca.

9. Olga vuelve muy pronto.
   a. Dentro de nada.
   b. Antes de nada.

D *Other indefinite words and constructions*

- The pronoun **cualquiera** means *anyone* or *any one* and can refer to people or things:

  —¿Cuál de los dos pasteles quieres?   *Which of the two pastries do you want?*
  —**Cualquiera** de los dos.   *Any one (either one) of the two.*

  —**No cualquiera** podría hacer esto.   *Not just anyone would be able to do this.*
  —Al contrario. **Cualquiera** lo habría   *On the contrary. Anyone would have done*
  hecho mucho mejor.   *it much better.*

  Note also the idiomatic use of **cualquiera** as a noun: **Él es un cualquiera.** *He's a nobody.*

- When used as an adjective, **cualquiera** becomes **cualquier**:

El tren puede llegar en **cualquier** momento.	*The train can arrive at any moment.*
La vida es más fácil en **cualquier** otro lugar.	*Life is easier anywhere else.*
Está contento con **cualquier** cosa.	*He's happy with anything.*

- Spanish also indicates "indefiniteness" by the subjunctive. English often uses *whatever, wherever,* etc. in these cases. Compare the following pairs of sentences:

Lee el libro que recomiendan.	*Read the book that they recommend. (indicative: speaker knows which book it is)*
Lee el libro que **recomienden.**	*Read whatever book they recommend. (subjunctive: speaker does not know which book it is)*
Haga lo que quiere.	*Do what you want. (indicative: we already know what you want to do)*
Haga lo que **quiera.**	*Do whatever you want. (subjunctive: we don't yet know what you want to do)*

- Note that **todo** is usually followed by the definite article and noun:

Por **todo el** país.	*Throughout the whole country.*
Toda la casa.	*The whole house.*
Todos los estudiantes.	*All the students.*
Todas las calles.	*Every street.*

- When **todo** is followed directly by a *singular* noun, it means *every* or *any*:

Todo jugo de fruta es bueno.	*Any fruit juice is good.*
Todo mexicano apoya el tratado.	*Every Mexican supports the treaty.*
Nos sirvieron **toda** clase de fruta.	*They served us every kind of fruit.*

- Note also the use of **todo** with place names:

Hay paradores por **toda España.**	*There are government inns all over Spain.*
En casi **todo Santiago** hay servicio de metro.	*The subway serves almost all of Santiago.*

- **Todo** can also be used as a pronoun or in pronominal phrases:

Todo es interesante en España.	*Everything is interesting in Spain. (**Todo** takes a singular verb.)*
Todos son amables.	*Everyone is nice. (**Todos** takes a plural verb.)*
Todo el mundo trata de ayudar.	*Everyone, everybody tries to help. (**Todo el mundo** takes a singular verb.)*

G. ¡En español, por favor! Exprese las siguientes oraciones en español. Tenga en cuenta especialmente las expresiones con palabras negativas o indefinidas.

1. He had good reason to quit his job.

2. They'll call at any moment.

3. We walked the whole day through the whole city.

4. Anyone could help us with the work.

5. Every avenue is blocked during rush hour.

6. There are Roman ruins all over Spain.

Nota cultural

Las ruinas romanas. Al comenzar los tiempos históricos, España estaba poblada por los iberos y los celtas que se fundieron entre sí creando los celtíberos. Luego los fenicios y los griegos fundaron colonias en España. Hacia el siglo VI antes de Jesucristo, llegaron los cartagineses. Los romanos vencieron a los cartagineses en España en 202 a. de J.C. A pesar de la heroica resistencia de las poblaciones indígenas, Roma logró someterlas a su poder unificador (*unifying*) a través de su lengua y su legislación. Los romanos construyeron acueductos, caminos, puentes, anfiteatros y arcos de triunfo, algunos de los cuales se han conservado espléndidamente en Segovia, Sagunto, Mérida, Toledo, etcétera.

H. ¡Finales dramáticos o "Lo que el viento se llevó"! Le toca a Ud. como guionista (*scriptwriter*) escribir las últimas palabras de unas películas. Escríbalas expresando las siguientes ideas en español. Tenga en cuenta las expresiones con palabras negativas e indefinidas.

1. Although I'll love you forever, I must say: "good-bye forever!"

2. Something is better than nothing.

3. Forget about going to Mars before you graduate! (use *tú*)

4. And here ends the never-ending story!

5. I know you from somewhere. You must be somebody. (use *Ud.*)

6. Do whatever you want! Go wherever you want! I shall never ever forget you! (use *tú*)

7. This ending? That ending? I'm happy with either one!

8. That's all. Tomorrow is another day!

I. Ejercicio oral. Ud. afirma algo. Su amigo/amiga contesta haciendo negativa la afirmación. Luego, se hace al inverso, es decir, uno dice algo usando palabras o expresiones negativas y el otro contesta con una respuesta afirmativa.

J. Estructuras en acción. Lea el siguiente anuncio que salió en un periódico mexicano y haga los ejercicios que se encuentran a continuación.

Exprese las siguientes frases en inglés.

1. ¿Ha soñado alguna vez con estar en …?

2. Tierra Santa

3. Viaje por los Caminos de la Fe.

4. Galilea, Tiberíades, Nazaret, Belén, Jerusalén

5. Audiencia Papal, Roma, Asís, Florencia

Conteste las siguientes preguntas.

6. ¿Cuándo hay salidas a Jerusalén?

7. ¿Cómo son los hoteles incluidos?

8. ¿Qué idioma habla el/la guía?

9. ¿Qué comidas se sirven en todo el viaje?

10. ¿Qué cosa no se incluye?

11. ¿Cómo se llaman las dos líneas aéreas mencionadas en el anuncio? ¿De qué país es cada una?

CHAPTER 25
NUMBERS; DATES; TIME

 A *Cardinal numbers*

- Cardinal numbers are used for counting. The Spanish cardinal numbers from 1 to 99 are:

0 cero	10 diez	20 veinte
1 uno (una)	11 once	21 veintiuno (-una)
2 dos	12 doce	22 veintidós
3 tres	13 trece	23 veintitrés
4 cuatro	14 catorce	24 veinticuatro
5 cinco	15 quince	25 veinticinco
6 seis	16 dieciséis	26 veintiséis
7 siete	17 diecisiete	27 veintisiete
8 ocho	18 dieciocho	28 veintiocho
9 nueve	19 diecinueve	29 veintinueve
30 treinta	40 cuarenta	70 setenta
31 treinta y uno (una)	50 cincuenta	80 ochenta
32 treinta y dos	60 sesenta	90 noventa

- Numbers ending in *one* agree in gender with the following noun. **Uno** shortens to **un** before a masculine noun. The number **veintiún** has a written accent in the masculine:

veintiún libros   *21 books*
veintiuna revistas   *21 magazines*
cincuenta y un estudiantes   *51 students*
cincuenta y una profesoras   *51 female teachers*

- **Una** also shortens to **un** before a noun beginning with a stressed **a** sound:

un águila   *one eagle*
veintiún aulas   *21 lecture halls*
cuarenta y un hachas   *41 axes*

- Numbers ending in **uno** are used in counting and when no masculine noun follows directly:

—¿Cuánto es? ¿Treinta y dos pesos?   *How much is it? 32 pesos?*
—No, treinta y uno.   *No, 31.*

- The numbers from 16 to 19 and from 21 to 29 can be written as three words: **diez y seis, diez y siete, diez y ocho, diez y nueve, veinte y uno (una), veinte y dos, veinte y tres,** etc. No accent marks are used when these numbers are spelled as three words. Compare **veintiséis** and **veinte y seis.**

- The Spanish numbers from 100 to 999 are:

100	cien	400	cuatrocientos/cuatrocientas
101	ciento uno (una)	500	quinientos/quinientas
110	ciento diez	600	seiscientos/seiscientas
167	ciento sesenta y siete	700	setecientos/setecientas
200	doscientos/doscientas	800	ochocientos/ochocientas
300	trescientos/trescientas	900	novecientos/novecientas

Notes:

1. **cien** becomes **ciento** before another number: **ciento sesenta** *160.*

2. Spanish does not use **y** to connect hundreds to the following number the way English may use *and: two hundred **and** forty* **doscientos cuarenta.**

3. The hundreds from 200 to 900 agree in gender with the noun they modify. This agreement takes place even when other numbers come between the hundreds and the noun.

doscient**os** edificios	*two hundred buildings*
doscient**as** casas	*two hundred houses*
doscient**as** treinta y cuatro casas	*two hundred thirty-four houses*

- Numbers above 1,000:

1.000	mil	100.000	cien mil
2.000	dos mil	250.000	doscientos cincuenta mil
6.572	seis mil quinientos setenta y dos	1.000.000	un millón
10.000	diez mil	2.000.000	dos millones

Notes:

1. Numerals ending in **-cientos** agree across the word **mil**: seiscient**as** cincuenta mil pesetas.

2. Spanish uses the period to separate thousands in writing numbers and the comma as a decimal point: $7.560 = **siete mil quinientos sesenta dólares;** $7,50 = **siete dólares cincuenta centavos.**

3. Spanish does not count by hundreds above 1,000. Thus, *seventeen hundred* must be rendered **mil setecientos;** *thirty-two hundred* as **tres mil doscientos.**

4. **Millón** is a noun and is followed by **de** before a noun unless another number comes between **millón** and the following noun: **un millón de pesos; dos millones de pesos; un millón doscientos mil pesos.**

5. *A billion* in Spanish is **mil millones. Un billón** means *a trillion.*

6. The word **o** *or* is written **ó** between figures to avoid confusion with zero: **5 ó 6.**

A. Para hacer un inventario. Ud. trabaja de empleado de tiempo parcial en una papelería. Hoy le toca hacer el inventario de las existencias (*stock*). Ponga en la lista la cantidad de cada cosa que encuentra, escribiendo el número en letras.

La papelería

la agenda de entrevistas *appointment book*	**hacer un inventario** *to take inventory*
el bloc de papel *writing pad*	**el papel de escribir** *stationery*
el bolígrafo *ballpoint pen*	**el pegamento** *glue*
la caja *box*	**el rotulador** *felt-tip pen*
el calendario *calendar*	**el sobre** *envelope*
la etiqueta *label*	**los sujetalibros** *bookends*
las existencias *stock*	**los sujetapapeles** *paper clips*
la goma *rubber band*	**el taco** *writing pad (Spain)*
la goma de borrar *eraser*	**tiempo parcial** *part-time*
la grapa *staple*	**tiempo completo** *full-time*
la grapadora *stapler*	**el tubo** *tube*

> MODELO   gomas de borrar/386
> → trescientas ochenta y seis gomas de borrar

1. grapadoras/100

2. tacos/1.821

3. rotuladores y bolígrafos/1.549

4. cajas de gomas, grapas y sujetapapeles/751

5. cajas de papel de escribir y sobres/467

6. agendas de entrevistas y calendarios/909

7. tubos de pegamento y etiquetas/1.000

8. sujetalibros de metal y de plástico/1.381

Nota cultural

Hay palabras españolas cuyo significado varía mucho de un país a otro. Por ejemplo, en España, **el taco** es un bloc de papel o un librito de billetes de metro. Siendo una palabra de múltiples significados, también significa un pedazo de madera o comida, un bocado ligero, un trago de vino, un calendario trepado (*tear-off*), un lío, una palabrota, etcétera. En ciertos países de Hispanoamérica, **el taco** es una tortilla rellena o un tacón de zapato. En Chile, es una persona rechoncha (gruesa y baja). En Centroamérica significa una preocupación o un temor. A pesar de las diferencias de vocabulario, todos los hispanos de todos los países de habla española se entienden debido a la unidad fundamental del idioma.

B. El censo: población de países. Ud. se encarga de escribir el número de habitantes de los siguientes países hispánicos, según su último censo de 1990 ó 1992.

1. Argentina: 32.901.000
2. Colombia: 34.296.000
3. Chile: 13.528.000
4. Ecuador: 10.933.000
5. España: 39.118.000
6. México: 92.380.000

B *Ordinal numbers*

- Ordinal numbers are used for ranking (*first, second, etc.*). In conversation, usually only the ordinal numbers through *tenth* are used in Spanish. Spanish ordinal numbers are adjectives that agree with the noun they modify in gender and number:

primero	*first*	sexto	*sixth*
segundo	*second*	séptimo	*seventh*
tercero	*third*	octavo	*eighth*
cuarto	*fourth*	noveno	*ninth*
quinto	*fifth*	décimo	*tenth*

- Ordinal numbers usually precede the noun. **Primero** and **tercero** become **primer** and **tercer** before a masculine singular noun:

el **primer** día   *the first day*   el **tercer** capítulo   *the third chapter*
la **segunda** hija   *the second daughter*   la **séptima** casa   *the seventh house*

- Ordinals often follow nouns such as **siglo** and the names of kings and queens:

el siglo segundo   *the second century*   Carlos Quinto   *Charles the Fifth*

- Above *tenth*, Spanish generally uses the cardinal numbers after the noun instead of the ordinals. Sometimes the cardinal numbers are used even below *tenth*:

Vive en el piso quince.   *He lives on the fifteenth floor.*
Vamos a leer el capítulo tres.   *We're going to read the third chapter.*

- Ordinals are abbreviated in various ways in Spanish: 1er, 1era, 1o, 2a, 3ro, 5to, 7ma, 8o.

C. ¡Todos juntos en los Estados Unidos! Alberto y un grupo de amigos chilenos están en los Estados Unidos para estudiar inglés durante el verano. Y todos viven en la misma residencia. Alberto les escribe a sus padres y les dice en qué piso está cada uno de los amigos.

      MODELO   Ramón/6
            → Ramón vive en el sexto piso.

1. Silvia y Adela/12
2. Carlos/5
3. yo/1
4. Margarita/9
5. Ana María/10
6. Patricio/4
7. Lucía/3
8. Daniela/14

C Days, dates, and years

- The days of the week and the months of the year are not capitalized in Spanish. Note that the Hispanic week begins with Monday:

Days of the Week

lunes *Monday*	jueves *Thursday*	sábado *Saturday*
martes *Tuesday*	viernes *Friday*	domingo *Sunday*
miércoles *Wednesday*		

Months of the Year

enero *January*	mayo *May*	septiembre *September*
febrero *February*	junio *June*	octubre *October*
marzo *March*	julio *July*	noviembre *November*
abril *April*	agosto *August*	diciembre *December*

Seasons

la primavera *spring*	el otoño *fall, autumn*
el verano *summer*	el invierno *winter*

- In Spanish there are several patterns for using the above words in expressions of time:

  1. The singular definite article **el** means *on* before the days of the week.

     Nos vamos **el** lunes.   *We're leaving on Monday.*

  2. The plural definite article **los** indicates repeated action or regular occurrence.

     Van a la iglesia **los** domingos.   *They go to church on Sundays.*

  3. The preposition **en** is used before months of the year and the names of the seasons: **en enero, en otoño.** The definite article is sometimes used after **en** with the names of the seasons: **en la primavera.**

- To express dates, Spanish uses cardinal numbers, except for **el primero** (some speakers say **el uno**). The definite article **el** precedes the date. The order is day-month-year and the preposition **de** is placed before the month and also the year, if it is given. Note that as with days of the week, no preposition is used for *on*.

  —Creía que tus primos llegaban el   *I thought your cousins were arriving on*
    treinta de noviembre.   *November thirtieth.*
  —No, vienen el primero de diciembre.   *No, they're coming December first.*

Notes:

1. The definite article **el** in dates is usually left out after the day of the week: **martes, 5 de mayo.**

2. When abbreviating dates, the Spanish order day-month-year is used. Roman numerals are often used for the month: **25-VIII-44,** el veinticinco de agosto de mil novecientos cuarenta y cuatro.

3. As in English, the last two numbers are often used in speech to express the years of the present century. In this case the definite article **el** precedes the year:

   Llegamos en el setenta y dos.   *We arrived in '72.*

Some useful expressions for talking about the days and dates or that use the days and months in idiomatic ways:	
¿Cuál es la fecha de hoy?	*What's today's date?*
¿A cuánto estamos hoy?	*What's today's date?*
Es el primero de junio.	*It's June first.*
Estamos a diez de octubre.	*It's October tenth.*
¿Qué día es hoy?	*What day is today?*
Hoy es jueves.	*Today is Thursday.*
pasando un día, un día de por medio	*every other day*
a principios de marzo	*toward the beginning of March*
a mediados de julio	*toward the middle of July*
a finales de septiembre	*toward the end of September*
No es cosa del otro jueves.	*It's nothing special.*
martes trece	*Tuesday the 13th (equivalent of Friday the 13th)*

D. El premio Nobel. Diez escritores hispánicos han recibido el premio Nobel en literatura desde que el premio se comenzó a otorgar (*award*) en 1901. Aquí tiene Ud. una lista de cinco de los galardonados (*prize winners*) con el año del premio y las fechas de nacimiento y muerte. Escriba estos números en letras.

1. Octavio Paz (México)

   premio Nobel: 1990 _____

   nacimiento: 1914 _____

2. Camilo José Cela (España)

   premio Nobel: 1989 _____

   nacimiento: 1916 _____

3. Gabriel García Márquez (Colombia)

   premio Nobel: 1982 _____

   nacimiento: 1928 _____

4. Vicente Aleixandre (España)

   premio Nobel: 1977 _____

   nacimiento: 1898 _____

   muerte: 1984 _____

5. Pablo Neruda (Chile)

   premio Nobel: 1971 _____

   nacimiento: 1904 _____

   muerte: 1973 _____

E. ¡Qué desastre! A lo largo de los años ha habido huracanes originados en el Caribe que han hecho mucho daño. Aquí tiene Ud. una lista de algunos huracanes con su año y el número de muertos que causaron. Escriba los números en letras.

1. *Nombre del huracán: Celia*
   País, región o estado: Cuba, la Florida, Tejas

   Fecha: 30/VII–5/VIII/1970 _____   *Causó (31)* _____ muertos.

2. *Nombre del huracán: Fifi*
   País, región o estado: Honduras

   Fecha: 19–20/IX/1974 _____   *Causó (2.000)* _____ muertos.

3. *Nombre del huracán: Gilbert*
   País, región o estado: Caribe, Golfo de México

   Fecha: 10–17/IX/1988 _____   *Causó (260)* _____ muertos.

4. *Nombre del huracán: Andrew*
   País, región o estado: la Florida, Luisiana

   Fecha: 24–26/VIII/1992 _____   *Causó (14)* _____ muertos.

D Telling time

- All times begin with **Son las,** except for **Es la una** (*It's one o'clock*). To ask the time say, **¿Qué hora es?** In Spanish America **¿Qué horas son?** is very common.

  Son las tres.   *It's three o'clock.*
  Son las tres y diez.   *It's ten after three.*
  Son las tres y cuarto/y quince.   *It's a quarter after three./It's three fifteen.*
  Son las tres y media/y treinta.   *It's three thirty.*
  Son las cuatro menos veinte.   *It's twenty to four.*
  Son las cuatro menos cuarto/menos quince.   *It's a quarter to four.*

- An alternative system for expressing the times between the half hour and the following hour is very common in Spanish America. The verbs used are **faltar** and **ser:**

  Faltan/Son quince (minutos) para las cuatro.   *It's a quarter to four.*
  Falta/Es un cuarto para las cuatro.   *It's a quarter to four.*

- The equivalents of English A.M. and P.M. in Spanish are the phrases **de la mañana, de la tarde, de la noche** added to the expression of time. Spanish-Americans often use A.M. and P.M. as in English. For noon and midnight, people say **Son las doce del día, Son las doce de la noche** or **Es mediodía, Es medianoche.**

  Son las diez de la mañana.   *It's 10 A.M.*
  Son las seis de la tarde.   *It's 6 P.M.*
  Son las once y media de la noche.   *It's 11:30 P.M.*

- To express time, Spanish uses the preposition **a:**

  A las ocho de la mañana.   *At 8 A.M.*
  A veinte para las siete.   *At twenty to seven.*

- In Spanish-speaking countries, a 24-hour clock is used for official purposes: train and plane schedules, show times. In the 24-hour clock, the minutes past the hour are counted from 1 to 59. **Cuarto** and **media** are replaced by **quince, treinta,** and **cuarenta y cinco**; and the phrases **de la mañana, de la tarde, de la noche** are not used.

  Mi avión sale a las **trece treinta.**   *My plane leaves at one thirty P.M.*
  La película es a las **veinte cuarenta.**   *The film is at 8:40 P.M.*

- The word **horas** often appears when using the 24-hour clock:

  El programa es a las dieciocho horas.   *The program is at 6 P.M.*

Some useful expressions for talking about the time of day:	
Son las seis en punto.	*It's six o'clock sharp.*
Es tarde./Es temprano.	*It's late./It's early.*
Se levanta tarde/temprano.	*He gets up late/early.*
Siento llegar tarde.	*I'm sorry to be late.*
Llego con anticipación.	*I'm early.*
Llego puntualmente.	*I'm on time.*
Mi reloj está adelantado/retrasado.	*My watch is fast/slow.*
Son las tres pasadas.	*It's after three, past three.*
ser madrugador(a)	*to be an early riser*
pegársele a uno las sábanas	*to sleep late, sleep in*

F. En el tren turístico. La Renfe, la sociedad nacional de trenes españoles, ofrece al público viajes turísticos en tren desde Madrid a los lugares históricos más importantes de España. Lea el programa de esta excursión de dos días a las tierras del Cid en Castilla la Vieja y conteste las preguntas con la hora oficial.

ren tierras del Cid.

Burgos. Tierra del Campeador. Punto de encuentro de Románico y Gótico. Punto de encuentro con el arte Medieval. Con el tren Tierras del Cid conócela a fondo. Recorre Covarrubias, Silos y La Yecla. Sal a su encuentro.

PROGRAMA

Sábado

07:30 h.- Recepción de viajeros en el punto de información de la estación de Madrid Chamartín.

08:00 h.- Salida hacia Burgos.

11:36 h.- Llegada a Burgos. Traslado en autocar a Covarrubias, visita a la Colegiata. Tiempo libre para almorzar.

16:00 h.- Salida en autocar para visitar Santo Domingo de Silos y la Yecla.

20:00 h.- Llegada a Burgos. Traslado al hotel. Tiempo libre.

21:30 h.- Saludo del Ayuntamiento en el antiguo Monasterio de San Juan. Vino, aperitivos y actuaciones folklóricas. Elección de la madrina del tren.

Domingo

09:30 h.- Desayuno en el hotel.

10:30 h.- Salida en autocar para visitar el Monasterio de las Huelgas. San Pedro de Cardeña (posibilidad de oír Misa) y Cartuja.

14:00 h.- Tiempo libre para el almuerzo.

16:30 h.- Concentración en la puerta de la Catedral para visitarla. Traslado en autocar a la estación de ferrocarril.

18:39 h.- Salida de la estación de Burgos hacia Madrid.

21:55 h.- Llegada a Madrid Chamartín. Fín de viaje.

MODELO   ¿Cuándo es la salida en autocar a Santo Domingo de
Silos?
→ El sábado a las dieciséis horas.

1. ¿Cuándo se reúnen los viajeros para empezar la excursión?

2. ¿Cuándo se llega a Burgos?

3. ¿Cuándo es el saludo del Ayuntamiento?

4. ¿Cuándo salen para visitar el Monasterio de las Huelgas?

5. ¿Cuándo es el almuerzo el domingo?

6. ¿Cuándo es la visita de la Catedral de Burgos?

7. ¿Cuándo sale el tren de Burgos a Madrid?

Nota cultural

- **Tierra del Cid Campeador.** Rodrigo Díaz nació en Vivar, a nueve kilómetros de Burgos, en 1026 y murió en 1099. Dado el título Cid (señor) por los musulmanes, fue el héroe de la Reconquista (los cristianos españoles lucharon por retomar la Península de los musulmanes). Fue un personaje semihistórico cuya fama aumentó a través de poemas como **El Cantar del Mío Cid,** escrito hacia 1180. Las hazañas (*deeds*) de este caballero castellano que luchó fielmente por su rey (Sancho II, luego su hermano Alfonso VI), marcan la historia de Castilla de finales del siglo XI.

- **Burgos,** capital de la provincia de Burgos, tiene la tercera catedral española por sus dimensiones. En este magnífico edificio gótico se encuentran los restos del Cid Campeador y de su esposa doña Jimena.

E *Arithmetic operations, fractions, percentages*

- The basic arithmetic operations are read as follows in Spanish:

$15 + 12 = 27$	quince **más** doce **son/es igual a** veintisiete
$40 - 24 = 16$	cuarenta **menos** veinticuatro **son/es igual a** dieciséis
$10 \times 15 = 150$	diez **por** quince **son/es igual a** ciento cincuenta
$120 \div 12 = 10$	ciento veinte **dividido por** doce **son/es igual a** diez

  For division, the preposition **entre** is also used: **ciento veinte entre doce son diez.**

- Except for **un medio** (*one half*) and **un tercio** (*one third*), fractions have the same form as masculine ordinal numbers:

  un cuarto   *one-fourth*
  tres quintos   *three-fifths*

- Above one-tenth, the suffix **-avo** is added to the cardinal number to form the corresponding fraction: **un onceavo** (*one-eleventh*), **tres veinteavos** (*three-twentieths*).

  Note also **un centavo** or **un centésimo** (*one-hundredth*) and **un milésimo** (*one-thousandth*).

- Percentages in Spanish usually have an article (either **un** or **el**) before the figure:

Dan un veinte por ciento de   *They give a twenty percent discount.*
  descuento.

El diez por ciento de la población   *Ten percent of the population speaks*
  habla español.   *Spanish.*

The words for mathematical operations are:

sumar *to add*	el quebrado *fraction*
restar *to subtract*	por ciento *percent*
multiplicar *to multiply*	el porcentaje *percentage*
dividir *to divide*	

G. Operaciones matemáticas. Ayude a un amigo hispano que no habla inglés a resolver estos problemas. Primero, escriba los problemas con números y luego resuélvalos.

1. ciento setenta y cuatro más ochenta y nueve son _____

2. seiscientos tres menos doscientos ochenta y uno son _____

3. cuarenta y nueve por cinco son _____

4. mil doscientos ochenta y cuatro dividido por cuatro son _____

5. tres cuartos de ochenta son _____

6. Juan ganó $15.000 en la lotería. Tiene que pagar un 30% de impuestos. ¿Cuánto tiene que pagar de impuestos? _____

Nota cultural

- **El álgebra** fue introducida en Europa hacia 950 por los árabes que la aprendieron de los griegos. El tratado de álgebra más antiguo fue escrito por el griego Diofante de Alejandría.

- **Álgebra** es una de las 4.000 palabras que entraron en el español del árabe a través de ocho siglos de dominación árabe en la Península. Por medio del español muchas de estas palabras han pasado a las otras lenguas europeas. Otras palabras traídas por los árabes en el campo de las matemáticas incluyen: **cero, cifra, cenit.**

H. Ejercicio oral. ¿Cuál es la fecha? Ud. menciona un acontecimiento histórico y sus amigos tienen que decir la fecha. Por ejemplo, Ud. dice Colón descubre América. Otra persona dice el doce de octubre de mil cuatrocientos noventa y dos. O un amigo/una amiga dice Pearl Harbor atacado por los japoneses. Ud. dice el siete de diciembre de mil novecientos cuarenta y uno.

PART FOUR

Idiomatic Usage

CHAPTER 26
IDIOMS, EXPRESSIONS, & PROVERBS

A *Idioms and expressions with* **tener**

tener ángel/mal ángel	*to be charming/lack charm*
tener buena/mala estrella	*to be lucky/unlucky*
tener calor/frío	*to be warm/cold*
tener corazón de piedra	*to be hard-hearted*
tener cuidado	*to be careful*
tener dolor de cabeza/estómago	*to have a headache, stomachache*
tener en la punta de la lengua	*to have on the tip of one's tongue*
tener éxito	*to be successful*
tener ganas de	*to feel like*
tener hambre/sed	*to be hungry/thirsty*
tener inconveniente	*to mind, object to*
tener la culpa de	*to be to blame for*
tener la palabra	*to have the floor*
tener la razón de su parte	*to be in the right*
tener líos	*to have difficulties*
tener los huesos molidos	*to be exhausted*
tener los nervios de punta	*to have one's nerves on edge*
tener lugar	*to take place*
tener madera para	*to be cut out for, made for*
tener mala cara	*to look bad*
tener malas pulgas	*to be short-tempered*
tener miedo de	*to be afraid of*
tener mundo	*to be sophisticated, know how to act in society*
tener ojo de buen cubero (*cooper*)	*to have a sure, accurate eye*
tener ojos de lince	*to have (sharp) eyes like a hawk* (literally, *lynx*)
tener pájaros en la cabeza	*to have bats in the belfry*
tener palabra	*to keep one's word*
tener por	*to consider someone to be*
tener prisa	*to be in a hurry*
tener que ver con	*to have to do with*
tener razón	*to be right*
tener sueño	*to be sleepy*
tener suerte	*to be lucky*
tener un disgusto	*to have a falling out*

tener vergüenza de	*to be ashamed of*
no tener arreglo	*not to be able to be helped*
no tener donde caerse muerto	*not to have a penny to one's name*
no tener nombre	*to be unspeakable*
no tener pelo de tonto	*to be nobody's fool*
no tener pelos en la lengua	*to be very outspoken*
no tener pies ni cabeza	*to not make any sense, have no rhyme or reason*

A. Tener. Complete cada oración con una expresión o un modismo con **tener** como reacción lógica a la escrita. Puede haber más de una expresión en algunos casos. Escriba las dos.

1. A Manolo le dieron un ascenso en la empresa y le dieron un aumento de sueldo también.

   Tuvo _____.

2. Yo no comprendo nada de este libro.

   Para mí, el libro no tiene _____.

3. El nombre del actor es ...

   ¡Caramba! Lo tengo _____.

4. Este niño es muy listo.

   ¿Verdad que no tiene _____?

5. Pablo corrió tanto que ni puede levantarse por cansado.

   El chico tiene _____.

6. Carmen ganó el premio gordo de la lotería.

   Esta señorita tiene _____.

7. Rebeca siempre está molesta y se queja de todo.

   Ella tiene _____.

8. El detective Sierra lo ve todo. No se le pierde nada.

   En efecto. Él tiene _____.

9. Álvaro se ve mal y está nerviosísimo.

   El pobre chico tiene _____ y tiene _____.

10. Los padres de Gonzalito se sienten avergonzados porque su hijo siempre causa problemas en el colegio.

    Los señores tienen _____ porque Gonzalito tiene muchos _____ en el colegio.

B *Idioms and expressions with* **tomar**

tomar algo a bien/a mal	*to take something well/badly*
tomar a broma/risa	*to take as a joke*
tomar a pecho	*to take to heart*
tomar aliento	*to catch one's breath*
tomar en serio	*to take seriously*
tomar la palabra	*to take the floor*
tomar partido por	*to side with*
tomar la delantera	*to get ahead of*
tomarle el pelo	*to pull someone's leg*
tomárselo con calma	*to take it easy*

B. Tomar. Escriba una paráfrasis de cada oración empleando una expresión con **tomar.**

1. Amparo lo aceptó tranquilamente.

2. Los García se pusieron tristes por la muerte del vecino.

3. Pedro se rió viendo las diabluras de su hijo.

4. La profesora se enojó por lo que le dijo Marianela.

5. Paco apoyó a Juan Carlos en la discusión.

C *Idioms and expressions with* **estar**

está despejado/claro	*it's clear*
está nublado	*it's cloudy*
estar a sus anchas	*to be comfortable*
estar calado/mojado hasta los huesos	*to be soaked to the skin*
estar como el pez en el agua	*to be right at home*
estar con el alma en un hilo/en vilo	*to be in suspense*
estar de más/de sobra	*to be in excess*
estar en condiciones	*to be in good shape, be able (to do something)*
estar en la luna	*to have one's head in the clouds*
estar en las nubes	*to be in the clouds, daydreaming*
estar fuera de sí	*to be beside oneself emotionally (positive and negative)*
estar hecho polvo	*to get worn out*
estar hecho una fiera	*to get furious*
estar hecho una sopa	*to get soaked*
estar loco de atar/de remate	*to be completely crazy*
estar sin blanca	*to be flat broke*

C. Estar. Escriba una expresión con **estar** que sea sinónimo de la escrita.

1. cansarse _____

2. mojarse _____

3. no tener dinero _____

4. ponerse furioso _____

5. sentirse cómodo _____

D Idioms and expressions with echar

echar a perder	to ruin, spoil
echar chispas	to be furious, get angry
echar de menos	to miss
echar flores	to flatter, sweet-talk
echar la bronca a uno	to give someone a dressing down
echar la culpa	to blame
echarse a	to start to
echárselas de	to fancy oneself as, boast of being

D. ¿Qué le pasó a don Juan? Complete cada oración usando una de las expresiones con **echar.**

1. Lorenzo le dijo a Beti que la echaba _____ cuando ella estaba de vacaciones.

2. Al mismo tiempo, Lorenzo echaba _____ a Marisol y a Gloria.

3. Lorenzo _____ de ser don Juan.

4. Al volver, Beti se enteró de la situación y echó _____.

5. Beti le echó _____ a Lorenzo y rompió con él.

E Idioms and expressions with dar

dar a	to face
dar a luz un niño	to give birth
dar asco	to disgust
dar calabazas	to jilt; to flunk
dar carta blanca a uno	to give someone a free hand, carte blanche
dar cuerda a	to wind
dar con	to find; run into
dar de comer/beber	to feed/give a drink to
dar el golpe de gracia	to finish someone off, give the coup de grâce
dar gritos	to shout
dar guerra	to cause, make trouble
dar la hora	to strike the hour

dar la lata	*to make a nuisance of oneself*
dar las gracias	*to thank*
dar por sentado	*to take for granted; regard as settled*
dar rienda suelta a	*to give free rein to*
dar un abrazo	*to hug, embrace*
dar un paseo	*to take a walk, ride*
dar una vuelta	*to take a walk, ride*
dar vueltas a algo	*to think something over, thoroughly examine*
darse cuenta de	*to realize*
darse la mano	*to shake hands*
darse por vencido	*to give up*
darse prisa	*to hurry*

E. ¿Qué se dio en cada caso? Complete cada oración usando una de las expresiones con **dar.**

1. Paquita era tan molesta y mal criada. Ella daba _____.

2. Los soldados dejaron de luchar. Se dieron _____.

3. Los soldados ultimaron a sus enemigos. Les dieron _____.

4. No deje que los chicos hagan esas cosas. No les dé _____.

5. Creo que ya tomamos la decisión. Di el asunto _____.

F *Idioms and expressions with* ***hacer***

hace + time expression + preterit	*ago*
hace buen/mal tiempo	*it's good/bad weather*
hace calor/frío	*it's warm/cold*
hace viento	*it's windy*
hacer caso	*to pay attention, heed*
hacer (buenas) migas	*to hit it off with someone*
hacer de las suyas	*to be up to one's old tricks*
hacer un papel	*to play a role*
hacer juego	*to match*
hacer la vista gorda	*to turn a blind eye, pretend not to notice*
hacer las paces	*to make peace*
hacer época	*to be sensational, attract public attention*
hacer pedazos (añicos)	*to break to pieces*
hacer su agosto	*to make a killing*
hacer un viaje	*to take a trip*
hacerse + profession, status, etc.	*to become*
hacerse daño	*to hurt oneself*
hacerse tarde	*to become late*
hacérsele agua la boca	*to make someone's mouth water*

F. ¿Qué quieren hacer? Complete cada oración usando una de las expresiones con **hacer.**

1. dos amigos que se han peleado

   Quieren _____.

2. una persona que estudia la Bolsa e invierte mucho dinero

   Quiere _____.

3. una actriz que no ha trabajado en una película exitosa

   Quiere _____.

4. unos padres que tienen vergüenza de las diabluras de sus hijos

   Quieren _____.

5. un niñito travieso que ha tratado de portarse bien

   Quiere _____.

G   Idioms and expressions with *ir, llevar,* and **quedar**

Ir

ir al grano	*to go straight to the point*
ir de juerga	*to be out on a spree*
ir sobre ruedas	*to run smoothly*
ir tirando	*to get by*

Llevar

llevar a cabo	*to carry out*
llevar la contraria	*to take an opposite point of view, contradict*
llevar leña al monte	*to carry coals to Newcastle*
llevarse como el perro y el gato	*to be always squabbling*
llevarse un chasco	*to be disappointed*

Quedar

quedar boquiabierto	*to be left agape in bewilderment*
quedarse con	*to keep*
quedarse con el día y la noche	*to be left penniless*
quedarse de una pieza	*to be dumbfounded*
quedar en	*to agree on*
quedarse sin blanca	*to be flat broke, to go broke*

G. Ir, llevar, quedar. Reescriba las oraciones con uno de los modismos de esta sección.

1. El proyecto está progresando sin problemas.

   El proyecto _____.

2. Nos pusimos de acuerdo para vernos delante del cine.

   _____ vernos delante del cine.

3. No me gusta ir a su casa. Siempre están discutiendo.

   No me gusta ir a su casa. _____.

4. Si viniste a ver a Micaela, vas a quedar sin satisfacción. Ella no está.

   Si viniste a ver a Micaela, vas a _____. Ella no está.

5. Es difícil hablar con Alfonso. Nunca está de acuerdo con nadie.

   Es difícil hablar con Alfonso. Siempre _____.

6. No sé si vamos a poder realizar este plan.

   No sé si vamos a poder _____ este plan.

7. Cuando me dijo eso, no pude hacer nada más que mirarlo en silencio.

   Cuando me dijo eso, _____.

8. El negocio del señor Ortega quebró y su familia quedó sin un centavo.

   El negocio del señor Ortega quebró y su familia _____.

H Idioms and expressions with *meter* and *poner*

Meter

meter la pata	*to put one's foot in one's mouth*
meter las narices	*to snoop around*
meterse en donde no le llaman	*to meddle, snoop around*
meterse en la boca del lobo	*to enter the lion's den*
meterse en un callejón sin salida	*to get into a jam*

Poner

poner en ridículo	*to make look ridiculous*
poner las cartas sobre la mesa	*to put one's cards on the table*
poner los puntos sobre las íes	*to dot the i's and cross the t's*
poner a alguien por las nubes	*to heap praise on someone*
poner pleito	*to sue*
ponérsele a uno la carne de gallina	*to get goose pimples*
ponérsele los cabellos/los pelos de punta	*to have one's hair stand on end, be terrified*

H. Definiciones. Escriba al lado de cada definición la letra del modismo que le corresponda.

Definiciones

_____ 1. entrar en un lugar peligroso

_____ 2. llevar ante el juez, al tribunal

_____ 3. sentir mucho miedo

_____ 4. decir o hacer algo inapropiado y ofensivo

_____ 5. sentir pánico

_____ 6. buscarse un problema que no tiene solución

_____ 7. explicar las cosas para que no haya dudas

_____ 8. alabar a alguien con entusiasmo

Modismos

a. meterse en un callejón sin salida
b. meter la pata
c. poner en ridículo
d. meterse en la boca del lobo
e. poner pleito
f. ponérsele a uno la carne de gallina
g. poner por las nubes
h. poner las cartas sobre la mesa
i. ponérsele los cabellos, los pelos de punta
j. poner los puntos sobre las íes
k. meterse en donde no le llaman

I   *Idioms and expressions with* **ser**

ser de buena pasta	*to be a good guy, have a nice disposition*
ser de película	*to be sensational*
ser de poca monta	*to be of little value*
ser el colmo	*to be the limit*
ser harina de otro costal	*to be a horse of a different color*
ser el ojo derecho	*to be someone's pet*
ser la flor y nata	*to be the cream/best*
ser otro cantar	*to be a horse of a different color*
ser pan comido	*to be as easy as pie*
ser para chuparse los dedos	*to taste delicious*
ser todo oídos	*to be all ears*
ser un cero a la izquierda	*to be of no value, count for nothing (a person)*
ser un mirlo (*blackbird*) blanco	*to be an impossible dream*
ser una lata	*to be annoying*
ser una perla	*to be a jewel, treasure*
ser uña y carne	*to be close as can be*
no ser cosa del otro jueves	*to be nothing out of the ordinary*

I. **¿Cuál es?** Indique cuál de los modismos con **ser** significa lo mismo que la oración prinicipal.

1. Ya has llegado al límite.
   a. Esto es pan comido.
   b. Esto es un mirlo blanco.
   c. Esto es el colmo.

2. Esta situación me fastidia mucho.
   a. Es una lata.
   b. Es de película.
   c. Es otro cantar.

3. Esas dos chicas son muy buenas amigas. Siempre están juntas.
   a. Son la flor y la nata.
   b. Son de buena pasta.
   c. Son uña y carne.

4. Lo que me dices ahora es algo totalmente distinto.
   a. Es una perla.
   b. Es harina de otro costal.
   c. Es de poca monta.

5. Este flan está riquísimo.
   a. Es todo oídos.
   b. Es para chuparse los dedos.
   c. Es un cero a la izquierda.

J *Otras expresiones verbales*

andar de boca en boca	*to be generally known*
andarse por las ramas	*to beat around the bush*
armarse un escándalo	*to cause a row*
buscar tres pies al gato	*to split hairs*
no caber en sí/su piel	*to be beside oneself with joy, anger, etc.; to be presumptuous*
caerse el alma a los pies	*to be down in the dumps*
consultar con la almohada	*to sleep on it*
decirle cuatro verdades	*to tell someone a thing or two*
no decir ni pío	*not to say a word*
dejar caer	*to drop*
dejar de + infinitive	*to stop (doing something)*
dejar plantado	*to stand up*
no dejar piedra por (sin) mover	*to leave no stone unturned*
dorar la píldora	*to sugarcoat something*
dormir a pierna suelta	*to sleep like a log*
dormir la mona	*to sleep off a hangover*
dormirse en/sobre los laureles	*to rest on one's laurels*
faltarle a uno un tornillo	*to have a screw loose*
hablar hasta por los codos	*to talk incessantly*
llamar al pan pan y al vino vino	*to call a spade a spade*

mandar a freír espárragos	*to tell someone to go jump in the lake/go fly a kite*
matar la gallina de los huevos de oro	*to kill the goose that lays the golden eggs*
matar dos pájaros de un tiro	*to kill two birds with one stone*
no importar un bledo/un comino/ un pepino	*to not give a damn about*
pasar las de Caín	*to go through hell*
pedir peras al olmo	*to expect the impossible*
no pegar ojo en toda la noche	*to not sleep a wink all night*
quemarse las cejas	*to burn the midnight oil*
querer decir	*to mean*
no saber a qué carta quedarse	*to be unable to make up one's mind*
sacar/salir a luz	*to publish*
sacar en limpio/en claro	*to make clear*
salirse con la suya	*to get one's own way*
saltar a la vista	*to be obvious*
tocar en lo vivo	*to hurt deeply*
tragarse la píldora	*to be taken in, swallow a lie*
valer la pena	*to be worthwhile*
valer un mundo/un ojo de la cara/ un Potosí	*to be worth a fortune*
venir de perlas	*to be just the thing, just right*
verlo todo color de rosa	*to see life through rose-tinted glasses*
verlo todo negro	*to be pessimistic*
no poder verlo ni en pintura	*to not be able to stand the sight of someone*
volver a las andadas	*to go back to one's old ways*
volver en sí	*to regain consciousness*

J. Sinónimos. Escoja en la columna B un sinónimo para cada modismo de la columna A.

A

_____ 1. llamar al pan pan y al vino vino

_____ 2. costar un ojo de la cara

_____ 3. dormir a pierna suelta

_____ 4. faltarle un tornillo

_____ 5. no decir ni pío

_____ 6. pedir peras al olmo

_____ 7. saltar a la vista

_____ 8. andarse por las ramas

B

a. ser evidente
b. buscar tres pies al gato
c. dormir profundamente
d. no abrir la boca
e. exigir lo imposible
f. llamar las cosas por su nombre
g. no ir al grano
h. valer un Potosí
i. no estar completamente bien de la cabeza
j. volver en sí

K. Antónimos. Escoja en la columna B un antónimo para cada modismo de la columna A.

A

_____ 1. andar de boca en boca

_____ 2. no importarle un bledo

_____ 3. no pegar ojo

_____ 4. volver a las andadas

_____ 5. dejar plantado

_____ 6. no saber a qué carta quedarse

_____ 7. no poder verlo ni en pintura

_____ 8. hablar hasta por los codos

B

a. comportarse mejor que antes
b. no decir ni pío
c. tomar una decisión
d. caerse el alma a los pies
e. preocuparse mucho
f. ser muy amigo de uno
g. ser una cosa ignorada de todos
h. sacar en limpio
i. dormir a pierna suelta
j. acudir a la cita

K *Otros modismos*

¡A otro perro con ese hueso!	*Nonsense!, Don't give me that!* (literally, *to another dog with that bone*)
a pedir de boca	*perfectly, smoothly*
como el que más	*as well or better than anyone else*
contra viento y marea	*against all odds* (literally, *against wind and tide*)
dar gato por liebre	*to sell a pig in a poke, take someone in*
de buenas a primeras	*right off the bat*
de carne y hueso	*flesh and blood*
de categoría	*of importance*
de mal en peor	*from bad to worse*
de segunda mano	*second hand*
desde que el mundo es el mundo	*since the world began*
Dios mediante	*God willing*
el qué dirán	*what people say*
entre la espada y la pared	*between the devil and the deep blue sea* (la espada *sword*)
en un abrir y cerrar de ojos	*in the twinkling of an eye*
está chupado/tirado	*it's a piece of cake*
Hay gato encerrado.	*There's something fishy.*
Hay moros en la costa.	*The coast isn't clear, careful.* (literally, *There are Moors on the coast.*)
Más vale cuatro ojos que dos.	*Two heads are better than one.*
¡Ojo!	*Be careful!*
peces gordos	*big shots, important people*
sin más ni más	*without further hesitation*
tocar madera	*to touch wood, to knock on wood*
todo el santo día	*the whole darn day*
Trato hecho.	*It's a deal.*

L. Sinónimos. Escoja en la columna B un sinónimo para cada modismo de la columna A.

A	B
_____ 1. está chupado	a. engañar
_____ 2. el qué dirán	b. existe una cosa que no vemos
	c. con mucha rapidez
_____ 3. dar gato por liebre	d. la opinión de los demás
_____ 4. hay gato encerrado	e. en seguida
	f. con gran esfuerzo
_____ 5. de segunda mano	g. es pan comido
_____ 6. en un abrir y cerrar de ojos	h. entre dos peligros
	i. usado, no nuevo
_____ 7. de categoría	j. de mucha importancia
_____ 8. de buenas a primeras	

L   Dichos y refranes (Sayings and proverbs)

A caballo regalado no se le mira el colmillo.	Don't look a gift horse in the mouth. (colmillo canine tooth)
A lo hecho, pecho.	It's no use crying over spilled milk. (literally, Chest out to what has been done.)
Al que madruga, Dios le ayuda.	The early bird catches the worm. (madrugar to get up early)
Antes que te cases, mira lo que haces.	Look before you leap.
Aunque la mona se vista de seda, mona se queda.	You can't make a silk purse out of a sow's ear. (literally, Although the she-monkey may dress in silk, she remains a monkey.)
Cuando a Roma fueres/Allá donde fueres, haz como vieres.	When in Rome, do as the Romans do. (Fueres and vieres are old future subjunctive forms.)
Del dicho al hecho hay gran trecho.	There's many a slip 'twixt the cup and the lip. (el trecho distance)
De tal palo, tal astilla.	A chip off the old block. (el palo stick; la astilla splinter)
Desgraciado en el juego, afortunado en amores.	Unlucky in cards, lucky in love.
Dios los cría y ellos se juntan.	Birds of a feather flock together.
El infierno está lleno de buenos propósitos, y el cielo de buenas obras.	The road to hell is paved with good intentions.
El sapo a la sapa tiénela por muy guapa.	Beauty is in the eye of the beholder. (el sapo toad; la sapa female toad; tiénela = la tiene)
En tierra de ciegos, el tuerto es rey.	In the land of the blind, the one-eyed is king. (tuerto one-eyed)
En una hora no se ganó Zamora.	Rome wasn't built in a day.

Eso es el cuento de la lechera/Hacer las cuentas de la lechera.	*Don't count your chickens before they've hatched.*
Las paredes oyen.	*Walls have ears.*
Los dineros del sacristán, cantando se vienen y cantando se van.	*Easy come, easy go.* (el sacristán *church sexton*)
Más vale pájaro en mano que ciento volando.	*A bird in the hand is worth two in the bush.*
No es oro todo lo que reluce (brilla).	*All that glitters isn't gold.*
Obras son amores, que no buenas razones.	*Actions speak louder than words.* (razones *speech, talk*)
Ojos que no ven, corazón que no siente.	*Out of sight, out of mind.*
Poderoso caballero es don Dinero.	*Money talks.*
Quien mala cama hace, en ella se yace.	*You made your bed, now lie in it!* (yacer [old] *to lie down*)
Sobre gustos no hay nada escrito.	*Everyone to his own taste.*
Ver y creer.	*Seeing is believing.*

Nota cultural

- **Zamora** es una ciudad de León, región de España situada al oeste de Castilla. En la Edad Media, Zamora fue el teatro de muchas batallas entre musulmanes y cristianos y entre facciones de cristianos hasta que se impuso el dominio de los castellanos en 1072.

- **El cuento de la lechera** está incluido en una antología de la Edad Media, *El conde Lucanor.* En este cuento, una lechera (*dairymaid*) va al mercado llevando en la cabeza una jarra de leche para vender. Mientras camina, piensa en el dinero que le va a traer la venta de la leche. De repente se cae, y con ella la jarra. Con la jarra rota y la leche desparramada terminan sus sueños y las cuentas que sacaba con dinero que todavía no había ganado.

M. ¿Qué se diría? Escoja el refrán apropiado para cada situación.

1. Uno nota que un muchacho se comporta exactamente como su padre.
   a. No es oro todo lo que reluce.
   b. De tal palo, tal astilla.
   c. Obras son amores, que no buenas razones.

2. Uno advierte a su compañero que deben ser discretos porque no se sabe quién escucha.
   a. Las paredes oyen.
   b. Ver y creer.
   c. Aunque la mona se vista de seda, mona se queda.

3. Uno quiere decirle a un amigo que hay que olvidar los errores del pasado.
   a. A lo hecho, pecho.
   b. Sobre gustos no hay nada escrito.
   c. Cuando a Roma fueres, haz como vieres.

4. Uno quiere advertirle a su amigo que debe actuar con prudencia en una situación complicada.
   a. Más vale pájaro en mano que ciento volando.
   b. El sapo a la sapa tiénela por muy guapa.
   c. Antes que te cases, mira lo que haces.

5. Un muchacho reprocha a su novia el no haberle escrito cuando estaba ella en el extranjero.
   a. Los dineros del sacristán cantando se vienen y cantando se van.
   b. Del dicho al hecho hay gran trecho.
   c. Ojos que no ven, corazón que no siente.

N. **¡El zoológico de expresiones!** Los siguientes proverbios y expresiones nombran a ciertos animales. Consulte las listas de proverbios y expresiones para completarlos con los nombres de los animales que faltan. Luego exprese la oración en inglés.

1. Aunque _____ se vista de seda, _____ se queda.

2. Más vale _____ en mano que ciento volando.

3. A otro _____ con ese hueso.

4. Que no le dé _____ por _____.

5. _____ por _____ tiénela por muy guapa.

6. Son los _____ gordos de la industria.

7. A _____ regalado no se le mira el colmillo.

8. Creo que hay _____ encerrado.

CHAPTER 27
WORD FORMATION & DIMINUTIVES

A Forming nouns from verbs

- Some nouns related to verbs consist of the verb stem + **-o** or **-a**:

aumentar *to increase*	→	el aumento *increase*
ayudar *to help*	→	la ayuda *help*
contar *to count*	→	la cuenta *bill*
charlar *to chat*	→	la charla *chat, talk*
dudar *to doubt*	→	la duda *doubt*
encontrar *to meet*	→	el encuentro *meeting, sports match*
espantar *to frighten*	→	el espanto *fright, scare*
esperar *to wait*	→	la espera *waiting*
fracasar *to fail*	→	el fracaso *failure*
gastar *to spend*	→	el gasto *expense*
practicar *to practice*	→	la práctica *practice*
regresar *to return*	→	el regreso *return*
volar *to fly*	→	el vuelo *flight*

- Many nouns are formed from the past participle of verbs. These can also be seen as the verb stem + the suffixes **-ada** (for **-ar** verbs), **-ida** (for **-er, -ir** verbs):

bajar *to go down(stairs)*	→	la bajada *way down; decline*
caer *to fall*	→	la caída *fall*
comer *to eat*	→	la comida *meal, food*
correr *to run*	→	la corrida (de toros) *running (of bulls = bullfight)*
entrar *to enter*	→	la entrada *entrance*
ir *to go*	→	la ida *trip to somewhere, first leg of journey*
llegar *to arrive*	→	la llegada *arrival*
mirar *to look (at)*	→	la mirada *look, glance*
salir *to go out*	→	la salida *exit*
subir *to go up*	→	la subida *way up, rise*
volver *to go/come back*	→	la vuelta *return, trip back*

- Many nouns are formed from **-ar** verbs with the suffix **-ción**. Most of these have English cognates ending in *-tion:*

  admirar ➜ la admiración   organizar ➜ la organización
  invitar ➜ la invitación   separar ➜ la separación

  Note that not all English words ending in *-tion, -sion* have Spanish equivalents ending in **-ción, -sión**:

  transportation ~ el transporte (**la transportación** is rare)

A. ¿Y el verbo original? Escriba al lado de cada sustantivo el verbo de que se deriva.

1. la formación _____   5. la conversión _____

2. la comprensión _____   6. la decisión _____

3. la dominación _____   7. la obligación _____

4. la preparación _____   8. la complicación _____

- The suffixes **-ancia** and **-encia** are used to form nouns from verbs. Most of the nouns have English cognates:

  coincidir ➜ la coincidencia   tolerar ➜ la tolerancia
  preferir ➜ la preferencia   vigilar ➜ la vigilancia

  Note also **la estancia** (*stay*) from **estar.**

- The suffix **-miento** is widely used to form nouns from verbs. **-Ar** verbs have the vowel **a** before this suffix; both **-er** and **-ir** verbs have the vowel **i**:

  agotar *to exhaust*   ➜ el agotamiento *exhaustion*
  entender *to understand* ➜ el entendimiento *understanding*

B. El sustantivo que falta. Complete la tabla siguiente con los sustantivos que faltan.

1. **comportarse** *to behave*	_____ behavior
2. **encarcelar** *to jail, imprison*	_____ jailing
3. **consentir** *to consent*	_____ consent
4. **mover** *to move*	_____ movement
5. **pensar** *to think*	_____ thought
6. **plantear** *to pose (a problem)*	_____ posing
7. **tratar** *to treat*	_____ treatment
8. **nombrar** *to nominate*	_____ nomination
9. **crecer** *to grow, increase*	_____ growth

B *Forming verbs from nouns*

- The suffix **-ear** is one of the most common ways to convert a noun into a verb. It can convey the impression of repeated movement or action of the noun:

  párpado *eyelid* ➔ parpadear *to blink*
  paso *step* ➔ pasear *to walk*

  Most of these verbs can then form a noun ending in **-eo**: **el parpadeo** *blinking,* **el paseo** *walk.*

C. Verbos nuevos. Adivine el significado de los verbos en negrita (*boldface*) partiendo de los sustantivos de los cuales se han formado.

1. el sabor *taste*

   Come lentamente y **saborea** estos platos. _____

2. la gota *drop (of liquid)*

   El agua **goteaba** del techo de la casa. _____

3. el golpe *blow, hit*

   El hombre **golpeaba** al perro cruelmente. _____

4. la tecla *key (on a keyboard)*

   La pianista **tecleaba** la sonata. _____

5. la hoja *leaf, sheet of paper*

   La bibliotecaria **hojeaba** las páginas del libro. _____

6. el zapato *shoe*

   Todos **zapateaban** al compás (*rhythm*) de la música. _____

7. la pata *paw; foot (slang)*

   Para jugar fútbol, hay que saber **patear.** _____

- Some nouns can be transformed into verbs by the prefix **en-** + infinitive ending **-ar**:

  la cadena *chain* ➔ encadenar *to chain*
  la máscara *mask* ➔ enmascarar *to mask*
  el veneno *poison* ➔ envenenar *to poison*

  Some of these verbs allow a new noun to be formed by adding **-miento**:

  el encadenamiento *chaining*
  el envenenamiento *poisoning*

D. Complete esta tabla de palabras relacionadas. Siga el modelo de **cadena—encadenar—encadenamiento; veneno—envenenar—envenenamiento.**

1. Sp. la casilla	**Sp.** _____	**Sp. encasillamiento**
Eng. mailbox, pigeonhole	*Eng. to pigeonhole*	*Eng. pigeonholing*
2. Sp. la grasa	**Sp. engrasar**	**Sp.** _____
Eng. _____	*Eng.* _____	*Eng. lubrication*
3. Sp. la saña	**Sp.** _____	**Sp. ensañamiento**
Eng. rage, fury	*Eng. to enrage, infuriate*	*Eng. raging, fury*
4. Sp. la botella	**Sp.** _____	**Sp.** _____
Eng. bottle	*Eng. to bottle (up)*	*Eng. traffic jam*
5. Sp. la pareja	**Sp. emparejar**	**Sp.** _____
Eng. couple	*Eng. to match, pair*	*Eng. pairing, mating*
6. Sp. la frente	**Sp. enfrentar**	**Sp.** _____
Eng. forehead, brow, face	*Eng. to face, confront*	*Eng. clash, confrontation*

 Forming verbs from adjectives

- Certain adjectives can be transformed into verbs by the prefix **a-** + infinitive ending **-ar**:

fino *fine* → afinar *to refine, tune*
llano *flat* → allanar *to flatten, level*
liso *smooth* → alisar *to smooth*
manso *tame* → amansar *to tame, domesticate*

E. **El detective del diccionario.** Empareje los verbos de la columna A con su equivalente inglés de la columna B. Cada verbo deriva de un adjetivo que Ud. ya sabe.

A	B
_____ 1. acertar	a. assure
_____ 2. aclarar	b. lengthen
	c. enlarge
_____ 3. achicar	d. drive mad (with joy or delight)
_____ 4. aflojar	e. guess right, hit the mark
	f. clarify
_____ 5. agrandar	g. loosen
_____ 6. alargar	h. reduce in size
_____ 7. alocar	
_____ 8. asegurar	

- The suffix **-ecer** is added to the stem of some adjectives and nouns to create a new verb:

  oscuro ➔ oscurecer *to get dark*
  pálido ➔ palidecer *to grow pale*

  Like all **-ecer** verbs, the first-person singular and the present subjunctive have **-zc-** before the endings: Temo que **oscurezca** antes de que lleguemos. *I'm afraid it will get dark before we arrive.*

F. **Acertijos** (*riddles*) **léxicos.** Adivine qué significan estas palabras.

1. florecer _____

2. fortalecer _____

3. humedecer _____

4. robustecer _____

5. What household appliance is **la humedecedora**? _____

- Many adjectives can be made into verbs with the prefix **en-** (**em-** before **b** and **p**) and the suffix **-ecer**. Adjectives whose stems end in **c** change the **c** to **qu** before **-ecer**:

  triste ➔ entristecer *to sadden*
  pobre   ➔ empobrecer *to impoverish*
  rico   ➔ enriquecer *to enrich*

G. **Formación de verbos.** ¿Cuáles son los verbos que derivan de estos adjetivos?

1. duro _____

2. bello _____

3. flaco _____

4. noble _____

5. loco _____

6. negro _____

7. rojo _____

8. ronco (*hoarse*) _____

9. sordo _____

D *Suffixes added to nouns to form new nouns*

- The suffix **-ada** can have three different meanings:

  1. the full measure of the noun, the amount that the noun holds (**-ado** is used with some nouns)

     la cuchara *spoon* → la cucharada *spoonful*
     la pala *shovel* → la palada *shovelful*
     el puño *fist* → el puñado *fistful*
     la boca *mouth* → el bocado *mouthful;* (also, la bocanada *mouthful, swallow*)

  2. a blow with the object designated by the noun

     el cuchillo *knife* → la cuchillada *a slash made with a knife*
     el puñal *dagger* → la puñalada *stab*
     la pata *foot, paw* → la patada *kick*

  3. an act typical of the object or person designated by the noun

     el animal *animal* → una animalada *a stupid or gross thing to do*
     el payaso *clown* → una payasada *clown-like action, action worthy of a clown*
     el muchacho *boy, kid* → una muchachada *kid's prank*

- The suffix **-astro** is the equivalent of English *step-* with relatives:

  el hermanastro *stepbrother*

- The suffix **-azo,** like **-ada,** can signify a blow with the object designated by the noun. In Latin America, **-azo** can also be an augmentative suffix:

  la bala *bullet* → el balazo *a shot, a bullet wound*
  el codo *elbow* → el codazo *nudge, push with the elbow*
  los ojos *eyes* → los ojazos *big eyes*

- The suffix **-era** designates the container for the object expressed by the noun. Some nouns use **-ero** as the suffix for this meaning:

  la sopa *soup* → la sopera *soup bowl*
  la pimienta *pepper* → el pimentero *pepper shaker*

- The suffix **-ero** has other important functions:

  1. the owner or person in charge

     la cárcel *jail* → el carcelero *jailer*
     el molino *mill* → el molinero *miller*

  2. the person who makes or sells the object denoted by the noun

     el libro *book* → el librero *bookseller*
     el reloj *watch* → el relojero *watchmaker*

  3. the person fond of whatever the noun designates

     el queso *cheese* → quesero *fond of cheese, cheese-loving*
     el café *coffee* → cafetero *fond of coffee, coffee-drinker, coffee-lover*

  The suffix **-ería,** derived from **-ero,** designates the corresponding store or place of business:

  la librería *bookstore*
  la relojería *watchmaker's store, watch store*

H. **¿Qué significa?** Escriba el significado de las siguientes palabras, analizando la raíz y el sufijo.

1. el pastelero _____

2. la cucharada _____

3. la sombrerería _____

4. la cafetera _____

5. la ensaladera _____

6. el lapicero _____

7. la bobada _____

8. la barcada _____

9. el portazo _____

10. la hijastra _____

11. el salero _____

12. fiestero _____

E Diminutives and augmentatives

- Diminutives are widely used in Spanish to add a note of smallness or endearment to the noun. The most common diminutive suffix is **-ito/-ita,** added to nouns and personal names. The following spelling changes occur when **-ito/-ita** is added: **c → qu, g → gu, z → c**:

  la silla *chair* → la sillita *small chair*
  el hermano *brother* → el hermanito *little brother, younger brother*
  la cuchara *spoon* → la cucharita *teaspoon*
  el gato *cat* → el gatito *kitten*
  abuela *grandmother* → abuelita *grandma*
  Paco → Paquito
  Diego → Dieguito
  Lorenza → Lorencita

- The diminutive suffix **-ito/-ita** changes to **-cito/-cita** if the noun ends in **-n** or **-r,** or if the noun ends in **-e** and has more than one syllable:

  el pintor *painter* → el pintorcito *painter, third-rate painter (often sarcastic)*
  la joven *young girl, teenage girl* → la jovencita *young girl (endearing)*
  la madre *mother* → la madrecita *dear mother*
  el puente *bridge* → el puentecito *little bridge*

- Nouns of two syllables whose first syllable has **ie** or **ue** and which end in **-o** or **-a** drop the **-o** or **-a** and add **-ecito/-ecita** to form the diminutive. The same is true of one-syllable nouns ending in a consonant:

  la piedra *stone* → la piedrecita *little stone*
  la fiesta *party* → la fiestecita *little party*
  el cuerpo *body* → el cuerpecito *little body (could be sarcastic)*
  la puerta *door* → la puertecita *little door*
  la flor *flower* → la florecita *little flower*

- Other diminutive endings are **-ico** (a regional variant of **-ito**), **-illo** (which can convey contempt as well as endearment), and **-uelo** (a diminutive ending that often conveys a note of contempt). These endings add **c** or **ec** (**z** or **ez** in the case of **-uelo**) the way **-ito** does:

  la cuesta *slope* → la cuestecilla *slight slope*
  un abogado *lawyer* → un abogadillo *third-rate lawyer*
  una república *republic* → una republiquilla *a miserable government*
  la cosa *thing* → la cosilla *insignificant thing*
  un rey *a king* → un reyezuelo *a poor excuse for a king*
  un escritor *a writer* → un escritorzuelo *a very bad writer*
  un muchacho *boy* → un muchachuelo *small boy*

- Words with a diminutive suffix may take on an independent meaning:

  el zapato *shoe* → la zapatilla *slipper*
  la mano *hand* → la manecilla *hand of a watch or clock*
  la bolsa *bag* → el bolsillo *pocket*

Nota cultural

- El diminutivo **-ico/-ica** se usa tanto en la república centroamericana de Costa Rica que se les ha apodado (*nicknamed*) a los costarricenses **«los ticos»**.

- **Costa Rica** es una nación democrática cuya estabilidad presenta un contraste con el trágico desorden político y social del resto de Centroamérica. El ex-presidente de Costa Rica, Oscar Arias, que se esforzó incansablemente por resolver de una manera pacífica los conflictos de Nicaragua y El Salvador, recibió el premio Nobel de la Paz en 1987.

- The suffix **-ucho/-ucha** conveys the idea of ugliness:

  la casa *house* → la casucha *hovel*
  el cuarto *room* → el cuartucho *small, miserable, uncomfortable room*

- The most common augmentative suffix in Spanish is **-ón/-ona**:

  la mancha *stain* → el manchón *big, dirty stain*
  la mujer *woman* → la mujerona *big, hefty woman*
  la novela *novel* → el novelón *long, boring novel*

  Note, however, that in **el ratón** (*mouse*) from **la rata** (*rat*) the suffix **-ón** functions as a diminutive.

- The suffix **-ón/-ona** can also be added to some verb stems to form adjectives meaning *given to doing the action of the verb*:

  contestar *to answer* → contestón *given to answering back*
  llorar *to cry* → llorón *crybaby, always crying*
  mirar *to look at* → mirón *given to staring*
  preguntar *to ask* → preguntón *inquisitive, given to asking too many questions*
  responder *to answer* → respondón *fresh, insolent, given to answering back*
  burlarse *to make fun of* → burlón *mocking, derisive*
  comer *to eat* → comilón *big eater, glutton*
  dormir *to sleep* → dormilón *sleepy-head*
  gritar *to shout, scream* → gritón *loud-mouthed, always yelling*

- The suffix **-azo/-aza** is also augmentative, especially in Spanish America:

  el perro *dog* ➔ el perrazo *big dog*
  el éxito *success* ➔ el exitazo *great success, hit*

- The augmentative suffix **-ote/-ota** often adds a note of contempt to the idea of bigness:

  la palabra *word* ➔ la palabrota *bad word, dirty word*
  el animal *animal* ➔ el animalote *big animal; gross, ignorant person*

- As with diminutives, the addition of an augmentative suffix sometimes creates an independent word:

  soltero *unmarried* ➔ el solterón *old bachelor,* la solterona *old maid*
  la silla *chair* ➔ el sillón *armchair*
  la caja *box* ➔ el cajón *drawer; crate*

- Diminutive and augmentative suffixes can be added to adjectives and some adverbs. The suffixes vary in form as with nouns:

  pobre *poor* ➔ pobrecito/a *an unfortunate person*
  feo *ugly* ➔ feíto *somewhat ugly, a little ugly*
  viejo *old* ➔ viejito *rather old, getting on in years*
  flaco *thin* ➔ flacucho *skinny*
  inocente *innocent* ➔ inocentón *naive, gullible*
  guapo *good-looking* ➔ guapote *really good-looking*
  poco *little, not much* ➔ poquito *very little, rather little*
  ahora *now* ➔ ahorita *right now*
  tarde *late* ➔ tardecito *rather late, a little late*
  cerca *nearby* ➔ cerquita *really close, not at all far away*
  en seguida *right away* ➔ en seguidita *in just a moment*

I. Diminutivos. Escriba el diminutivo en **-ito/-ita** que corresponda a estas palabras.

1. la voz	11. el lago
2. la carta	12. suave
3. el traje	13. el viento
4. el pez	14. el jugo
5. el cuento	15. el carro
6. la pierna	16. fuerte
7. el caballo	17. chico
8. el bosque	18. nuevo
9. el dolor	19. fresco
10. la cabeza	20. la luz

CHAPTER 28
¡OJO! COMMON ERRORS & PITFALLS

A Dejar vs. salir

- **Dejar** and **salir** both mean *to leave*, but they are not interchangeable. **Dejar** is a transitive verb that means *to leave something or someone behind:*

  —¿Dónde **dejaste las llaves** del coche? — *Where did you leave the car keys?*

  —Creo que **las dejé** en la mesa del comedor. — *I think I left them on the dining room table.*

  —¿Dónde **los puedo dejar**? — *Where can I leave you (off)?*

  —**Déjeme a mí** delante del cine y **deje a mi marido** en la estación. — *Leave me in front of the movie theater and drop (= leave) my husband at the station.*

- **Salir** is an intransitive verb that means *to go out* or *leave*. The preposition **de** follows **salir** before the place being left:

  —Nuestro tren **sale** a las tres y media. — *Our train leaves at three thirty.*

  —En ese caso debemos **salir de casa** a las tres para no llegar tarde. — *In that case we should leave the house at three in order not to be late.*

Compare the following examples where **salir** and **dejar** contrast:

Salió de la casa a las cinco. — *He left the house at five o'oclock.*
Dejó la casa hecha un desastre. — *He left the house in a mess.*

- Note that **irse** and **marcharse** also mean *to leave* in the sense of *to go away*. They also require **de** before the name of the place. **Marcharse** may imply leaving forever or for a long period of time:

  —**Me voy** de la oficina a las cinco. — *I'm leaving the office at five o'clock.*

  —Ayer **te fuiste** a las cuatro, ¿verdad? — *Yesterday you left at four, didn't you?*

  —**Se marchó** porque odiaba el trabajo aquí. — *He left because he hated the work here.*

  —A ver si yo también **me marcho** pronto. — *Let's see if I (can) leave soon too.*

- **Dejar** + infinitive means *to let*. **Dejar** + **de** + infinitive means *to stop doing something:*

  —¿Cuándo me **dejarás** salir, mamá? — *When will you let me go out, Mom?*

  —Cuando **deje de** llover. — *When it stops raining.*

- **Salir** + adjective or adverb means *to turn out*. An indirect object is often added:

Ese coche **te saldrá** muy caro.	*That car will turn out to be very expensive for you.*
Nos salió mal el proyecto.	*The project turned out badly for us.*
Los nuevos empleados **salieron** muy trabajadores.	*The new employees turned out to be very hard-working.*

A. **¿Cómo se dice?** Complete estas oraciones con la forma correcta de **salir, dejar, irse, marcharse,** según convenga.

1. No debemos _____ nada en el cuarto de hotel.

2. Si llueve, no quiero _____ a la calle. Prefiero esperar a que _____ de llover.

3. No _____ (*tú-imperative*), por favor. No me _____ solo aquí en el parque.

4. Ese sinvergüenza (*scoundrel*) _____ (*preterit*) del país y _____ a su mujer y a sus hijos sin un centavo.

5. Juan y yo _____ del correo y nos dirigimos al banco.

6. Oye, Carlitos, _____ de molestarme. Te dije que no podías _____ a jugar.

7. La fiesta de Francisca _____ estupenda. Yo lo pasé muy bien.

8. Casi todos los estudiantes _____ mal en el examen de física porque fue muy difícil.

9. Mis padres no me _____ manejar de noche.

B   *Saber vs. conocer*

- **Saber** and **conocer** both mean *to know*. **Saber** is used for facts, information, or knowledge that can be stated:

—¿**Sabes** la dirección de Marta?	*Do you know Marta's address?*
—No, pero **sé** su número de teléfono.	*No, but I know her phone number.*

- **Conocer** means *to know a person, to be familiar with a place*. With places, **conocer** is often translated as *to have been* in English:

—¿**Conoces** a Pedro Gómez?	*Do you know Pedro Gómez?*
—No, pero **conozco** a su hermana.	*No, but I know his sister.*
—¿**Conocen** Uds. la universidad?	*Are you familiar with the university?*
—No, no la **conocemos.**	*No, we've never been there.*

- **Saber** + infinitive means *to know how to do something*:

—¿**Sabes** cocinar?	*Do you know how to cook?*
—**Sé** preparar algunas cosas sencillas.	*I know how to prepare some simple things.*

B. *¿Saber o conocer?* Indique cuál de las formas verbales dadas completa correctamente las oraciones.

1. Alfredo no _____ a nadie en esta ciudad. (sabe / conoce)

2. ¿No _____ Galicia? Entonces, tienen que ir. (saben / conocen)

3. ¿_____ Ud. cuántos habitantes hay en Caracas? (Sabe / Conoce)

4. No _____ esta computadora. ¿Cómo funciona? (sé / conozco)

5. Mi abuela no _____ manejar. (sabe / conoce)

C   *Oreja vs. oído*

- **Oreja** and **oído** both mean *ear*. **Oreja** refers to the outer ear; **oído** refers to the inner ear, thus the sense of hearing or the ear canal.

El peluquero me cortó **la oreja.**	*The hairdresser cut my ear.*
El bebé tiene una infección de **los oídos.**	*The baby has an ear infection.*

C. *¿Oyes?* Complete las oraciones siguientes con **oreja** u **oído,** escogiendo entre las posibilidades dadas.

1. —¿Por qué llora tu hijo?

   —Creo que tiene dolor de _____. (orejas / oídos)

2. Después de la corrida de toros, le ofrecen _____ del toro al torero. (la oreja / el oído)

3. Tiene _____ para la música. (buena oreja / buen oído)

4. Le dio un golpe en _____. (la oreja / el oído)

5. Mi abuelo no oye bien. Es duro de _____. (oreja / oído)

Nota cultural

En **la corrida de toros,** si el torero torea bien según los jueces, le conceden una de las orejas del toro. Si torea sumamente bien, existe la posibilidad de que los jueces le premien con las dos orejas y el rabo (*tail*) del toro.

D   *Meanings of quedar*

- **Quedar** means to remain. One of its most frequent uses is to ask for the location of places:

—¿Dónde **queda** el estadio?	*Where's the stadium?*
—**Queda** lejos, cerca del aeropuerto.	*It's far away, near the airport.*

- When referring to people, **quedar** means *to remain, be in a certain emotional or physical state:*

quedar boquiabierto	*to be open-mouthed with astonishment*
quedar ciego, sordo, cojo	*to go blind, deaf, lame*
quedar en ridículo	*to look foolish*
quedar bien	*to come off well, make a good impression*
quedar mal	*to come off badly, make a bad impression*
hacer algo por quedar bien	*to do something to make a good impression*

- **Quedar** means *to have left*, often with an indirect object pronoun:

—¿Cuánto dinero **te queda**?	*How much money do you have left?*
—**Me quedan** mil pesos.	*I have a thousand pesos left.*
Quedan cinco kilómetros.	*There are five kilometers left (to go).*
Quedan seis estudiantes en la clase.	*There are six students left in the class.*
Quedan pocos días para las vacaciones.	*There aren't many days left until vacation.*
Me quedan tres páginas por escribir.	*I have three pages left to write.*

- **Quedarse** means *to stay, remain:*

quedarse en un hotel, en casa de sus amigos	*to stay at a hotel, at one's friends' house*

- **Quedarse con** means *to keep*; **quedarse sin** means *to run out of:*

Se quedó con mi libro de química.	*He kept my chemistry book.*
Me quedo con éste.	*I'll take this one. (in a store)*
Quédese Ud. con la vuelta.	*Keep the change.*
Me he quedado sin azúcar.	*I've run out of sugar.*
Lidia **se ha quedado sin** trabajo.	*Lidia has lost her job.*

Some expressions with **quedar(se)**:

No me queda más remedio.	*I have no choice, no alternative.*
Queda a tres kilómetros de aquí.	*It's three kilometers from here.*
Quedar con uno para ir al cine.	*To make a date with someone to go to the movies.*
Quedan en salir el domingo.	*They agree, arrange to go out on Sunday.*
¿En qué quedamos?	*What did we decide to do?*
No se queda con la cólera dentro.	*He can't hide his anger.*
No quise quedarme en menos.	*I refused to be outdone.*
Se quedó en nada.	*It came to nothing.*

D. Quedar. Exprese estas oraciones en español. En todas use el verbo **quedar(se)**.

1. We have two weeks left in Puerto Rico.

2. Keep the money. I don't need it. (*tú*)

3. I have run out of job opportunities. (*salidas*)

4. They stayed with a Mexican family.

5. You (*Uds.*) have three sentences left to translate.

6. He went deaf because of the explosion.

7. Where's the post office, please?

8. Paula and I agreed to go to the movies.

E   *"To break" and "to tear"*

- The Spanish verb **romper** covers the meanings of English *to break* and *to tear*:

La ventana está rota.	*The window is broken.*
Mi camisa está rota./Tengo la camisa rota.	*My shirt is torn.*

- **Romperse** + article of clothing is often used with the meaning *to tear something*:

Cuidado, o te vas a romper el pantalón.	*Careful or you'll tear your pants.*

- *To be broken* in the sense of *to be out of order* is usually **estar descompuesto.** The verb is **descomponerse** and it may also appear with an indirect object pronoun (the unplanned occurrences construction): **descomponérsele a uno**:

El ascensor está descompuesto.	*The elevator is broken (out of order).*
Se descompuso el aire acondicionado.	*The air conditioner went on the blink.*
Se me descompuso el coche.	*My car broke down.*

Some expressions with **romper**:

romper con alguien   *to break off with someone*
romper a llorar, romper en llanto   *to burst out crying*
romper el fuego   *to open fire*
romper las hostilidades   *to start hostilities*
Quien rompe paga.   *Actions have consequences.*
No te preocupes. No te vas a romper.   *Don't worry. You're not so fragile.*

E. ¿Cómo se dice eso en español? Exprese las siguientes ideas en español.

1. Who tore my newspaper?

2. My chair is broken.

3. The radio is broken.

4. My coat is torn.

5. I hope the car doesn't break down on us.

6. We don't understand why she burst out crying.

7. Don't tear your jacket. (*tú*)

8. Elena broke off with her boyfriend.

9. The enemy opened fire.

10. Actions have consequences.

Nota de vocabulario

Note that **el radio** often refers to the radio as an appliance while **la radio** means *radio* as a medium of communication. Some speakers use **la radio** for both meanings.

F *"Wrong"*

- There is no one Spanish word that covers all the meanings of English *wrong*. When *wrong* means *morally* or *ethically wrong*, Spanish often uses **malo**:

Hiciste algo muy **malo**.	*You did something very wrong.*
¿Qué tiene eso de **malo**?	*What's wrong with that?*

- When *wrong* means *incorrect*, Spanish has several possibilities, not all interchangeable:

  1. When said of people, Spanish uses **no tener razón, equivocarse,** or **estar equivocado**:

     —Mónica dijo que la lámpara costaba cincuenta dólares.   *Monica said that the lamp cost fifty dollars.*

     —**No tiene razón.** Cuesta cuarenta.   *She's wrong. It costs forty.*

     —Quisiera hablar con el señor Lares.   *I'd like to speak with Mr. Lares.*

     —Aquí no vive ningún señor Lares. Ud. ha marcado un número **equivocado.**   *There's no Mr. Lares (living) here. You've dialed the wrong number.*

     —¿Aquí no vive la familia Laínez?   *Doesn't the Laínez family live here?*

     —No. Ud. **se ha equivocado de casa.**   *No. You've come to the wrong house.*

     —Creo que la respuesta es cinco y tres octavos.   *I think the answer is five and three eighths.*

     —Ud. **está equivocado.** La respuesta es seis.   *You're wrong. The answer is six.*

  2. When said of information, answers, etc., Spanish uses **incorrecto, inexacto, equivocado,** and **mal.**

La respuesta es incorrecta, inexacta.	*The answer is wrong.*
La receta está mal.	*The recipe is wrong.*
Mi reloj anda mal.	*My watch is wrong.*
Estos datos están equivocados.	*These data are wrong.*

Escribió Ud. mal mi dirección.	*You wrote my address wrong.*
Me comprendió Ud. mal.	*You didn't understand me correctly.*
El estudiante contestó mal.	*The student answered incorrectly.*

3. When *wrong* means *inopportune, unwanted* it is often translated as **no ... adecuado** or **no ... apropiado, impropio**:

No es el momento **adecuado/ apropiado** para hablar de esas cosas.	*It's the wrong time to speak about those things.*
Decir algo **inoportuno** en español es *meter la pata*.	*To say the wrong thing in Spanish is* meter la pata.

4. When *wrong* expresses a result or outcome not desired or sought, it can have a variety of translations:

This is the wrong book.	*Éste no es el libro que hacía falta.*
This is the wrong train.	*Éste no es el tren que debíamos tomar./ Nos hemos equivocado de tren.*
Your socks are wrong side out.	*Tienes los calcetines al revés.*
I'm in the wrong profession.	*Mi profesión no me conviene.*
He played a wrong note.	*Tocó una nota falsa.*
The chair is in the wrong place.	*La silla está mal colocada.*
You're driving on the wrong side of the road.	*Ud. maneja por el lado prohibido.*

5. When *wrong* means *amiss, to have something wrong*, the verb **pasar** is used:

—¿Qué te pasa, Luis?	*What's wrong with you, Luis?*
—No me pasa nada.	*Nothing is wrong with me.*
—¿Pasa algo aquí?	*Is something wrong here?*
—No, profesora, no pasa nada.	*No, ma'am. Nothing is wrong.*
—Le pasa algo a la computadora.	*Something's wrong with the computer.*
—Hay que llamar al técnico.	*We have to call the repairman.*

6. Note also the following expressions:

Distinguir entre el bien y el mal.	*To tell right from wrong.*
Entiéndeme bien.	*Don't get me wrong.*
Todo salió mal.	*Everything went wrong.*
Hiciste mal en prestarle el dinero.	*You were wrong to lend him the money.*

F. Está mal. Exprese estas oraciones en español.

1. I dialed the wrong number.
2. We took the wrong plane.
3. What's wrong with the tape recorder?
4. This is not the right time.
5. I read the title wrong.
6. Your gloves are wrong side out.
7. He's got the wrong job.
8. The definition is wrong.
9. I was wrong not to believe him.
10. You added wrong.

G   *"To miss"*

- The verb *to miss* has several very different meanings in English, each of which is translated by a different Spanish verb. When *miss* means *to long for a person or thing*, Spanish uses **echar de menos** or, especially in Spanish America, **extrañar**:

  —Echo de menos a mi familia.   *I miss my family.*
  —Yo también extraño a mis padres.   *I also miss my parents.*

- Spanish uses the verb **perder** for *to miss a plane, train*, etc.:

  —Date prisa. Vamos a perder el   *Hurry up. We're going to miss the bus.*
    autobús.
  —Ya lo hemos perdido. Tomaremos   *We've already missed it. We'll take the*
    el siguiente.   *next one.*

- Spanish uses the verb **perderse** for *to miss a show*, etc.:

  —Me perdí la nueva película.   *I missed the new film.*
  —Te has perdido algo muy bueno.   *You've missed something very good.*

  Note that *to miss class* is usually **faltar a clase**.

- For *to miss the target, not to hit, to miss the mark,* etc. Spanish uses **errar el tiro** or **fallar (el blanco)**:

  El ladrón disparó, pero falló el blanco.   *The thief shot, but missed.*

  Es un método que nunca falla.   *It's a method that never misses, never fails.*

- *To be missing* can be expressed in two ways in Spanish, depending on the meaning:

  Encontraron a los estudiantes   *They found the missing students.*
    desaparecidos.

  Nos faltan tres cartas.   *We're missing three letters.*

  Complete las oraciones con las   *Complete the sentences with the missing*
    palabras que faltan.   *words.*

- Other uses of *to miss:*

  You can't miss it.   No puedes dejar de encontrarlo.
  I arrived late so I missed him.   Llegué tarde y no lo encontré.
  Don't miss the museums when you're No dejes de ir a los museos cuando
    in Mexico.   estés en México.
  I missed what you said.   No entendí lo que dijiste.

G. **¡A completar!** Complete estas oraciones con una expresión adecuada que exprese la idea de *to miss.*

1. Anoche mi hermana no pudo salir. Por eso _____ la obra de teatro.

2. Si Alfonso _____ tantas veces a clase, va a salir muy mal en el curso.

3. Vamos rápido. No quiero _____ el avión.

4. El pillo (*hoodlum*) trató de romper la ventana con una piedra, pero _____.

5. Otra vez, por favor. Hay tanto ruido aquí que _____ lo que dijiste.

6. Con estas cintas, tienes que aprender inglés. Dicen que es un sistema que nunca

   _____.

7. —¿Todos los socios del club ya han llegado?

   —No, todavía _____ dos o tres.

8. Ojalá pudiera ver a mi novia. No sabes cuánto la _____.

9. Hubo muchos soldados _____ al terminar la guerra.

Verb Charts

Regular Verbs

-ar verbs

cantar *to sing*	
indicative mood	
PRESENT	canto, cantas, canta, cantamos, cantáis, cantan
IMPERFECT	cantaba, cantabas, cantaba, cantábamos, cantabais, cantaban
PRETERIT	canté, cantaste, cantó, cantamos, cantasteis, cantaron
FUTURE	cantaré, cantarás, cantará, cantaremos, cantaréis, cantarán
CONDITIONAL	cantaría, cantarías, cantaría, cantaríamos, cantaríais, cantarían
PRESENT PERFECT	he cantado, has cantado, ha cantado, hemos cantado, habéis cantado, han cantado
PLUPERFECT	había cantado, habías cantado, había cantado, habíamos cantado, habíais cantado, habían cantado
PRETERIT PERFECT	hube cantado, hubiste cantado, hubo cantado, hubimos cantado, hubisteis cantado, hubieron cantado
FUTURE PERFECT	habré cantado, habrás cantado, habrá cantado, habremos cantado, habréis cantado, habrán cantado
CONDITIONAL PERFECT	habría cantado, habrías cantado, habría cantado, habríamos cantado, habríais cantado, habrían cantado
subjunctive mood	
PRESENT	cante, cantes, cante, cantemos, cantéis, canten
IMPERFECT	cantara, cantaras, cantara, cantáramos, cantarais, cantaran
	cantase, cantases, cantase, cantásemos, cantaseis, cantasen
PRESENT PERFECT	haya cantado, hayas cantado, haya cantado, hayamos cantado, hayáis cantado, hayan cantado
PLUPERFECT	hubiera/hubiese cantado, hubieras/hubieses cantado, hubiera/hubiese cantado, hubiéramos/hubiésemos cantado, hubierais/hubieseis cantado, hubieran/hubiesen cantado
imperative mood	
	canta/no cantes (tú), cante (Ud.), cantemos (nosotros), cantad/no cantéis (vosotros), canten (Uds.)

-er verbs

comer *to eat*	
indicative mood	
PRESENT	como, comes, come, comemos, coméis, comen
IMPERFECT	comía, comías, comía, comíamos, comíais, comían
PRETERIT	comí, comiste, comió, comimos, comisteis, comieron
FUTURE	comeré, comerás, comerá, comeremos, comeréis, comerán
CONDITIONAL	comería, comerías, comería, comeríamos, comeríais, comerían
PRESENT PERFECT	he comido, has comido, ha comido, hemos comido, habéis comido, han comido
PLUPERFECT	había comido, habías comido, había comido, habíamos comido, habíais comido, habían comido
PRETERIT PERFECT	hube comido, hubiste comido, hubo comido, hubimos comido, hubisteis comido, hubieron comido
FUTURE PERFECT	habré comido, habrás comido, habrá comido, habremos comido, habréis comido, habrán comido
CONDITIONAL PERFECT	habría comido, habrías comido, habría comido, habríamos comido, habríais comido, habrían comido
subjunctive mood	
PRESENT	coma, comas, coma, comamos, comáis, coman
IMPERFECT	comiera, comieras, comiera, comiéramos, comierais, comieran
	comiese, comieses, comiese, comiésemos, comieseis, comiesen
PRESENT PERFECT	haya comido, hayas comido, haya comido, hayamos comido, hayáis comido, hayan comido
PLUPERFECT	hubiera/hubiese comido, hubieras/hubieses comido, hubiera/hubiese comido, hubiéramos/hubiésemos comido, hubierais/hubieseis comido, hubieran/hubiesen comido
imperative mood	
	come/no comas (tú), coma (Ud.), comamos (nosotros), comed/no comáis (vosotros), coman (Uds.)

-ir verbs

vivir *to live*

indicative mood

PRESENT	vivo, vives, vive, vivimos, vivís, viven
IMPERFECT	vivía, vivías, vivía, vivíamos, vivíais, vivían
PRETERIT	viví, viviste, vivió, vivimos, vivisteis, vivieron
FUTURE	viviré, vivirás, vivirá, viviremos, viviréis, vivirán
CONDITIONAL	viviría, vivirías, viviría, viviríamos, viviríais, vivirían
PRESENT PERFECT	he vivido, has vivido, ha vivido, hemos vivido, habéis vivido, han vivido
PLUPERFECT	había vivido, habías vivido, había vivido, habíamos vivido, habíais vivido, habían vivido
PRETERIT PERFECT	hube vivido, hubiste vivido, hubo vivido, hubimos vivido, hubisteis vivido, hubieron vivido
FUTURE PERFECT	habré vivido, habrás vivido, habrá vivido, habremos vivido, habréis vivido, habrán vivido
CONDITIONAL PERFECT	habría vivido, habrías vivido, habría vivido, habríamos vivido, habríais vivido, habrían vivido

subjunctive mood

PRESENT	viva, vivas, viva, vivamos, viváis, vivan
IMPERFECT	viviera, vivieras, viviera, viviéramos, vivierais, vivieran
	viviese, vivieses, viviese, viviésemos, vivieseis, viviesen
PRESENT PERFECT	haya vivido, hayas vivido, haya vivido, hayamos vivido, hayáis vivido, hayan vivido
PLUPERFECT	hubiera/hubiese vivido, hubieras/hubieses vivido, hubiera/hubiese vivido, hubiéramos/hubiésemos vivido, hubierais/hubieseis vivido, hubieran/hubiesen vivido

imperative mood

	vive/no vivas (tú), viva (Ud.), vivamos (nosotros), vivid/no viváis (vosotros), vivan (Uds.)

Verbs with Changes in the Vowel of the Stem

pensar (e > ie) to think	
PRESENT INDICATIVE	pienso, piensas, piensa, pensamos, penséis, piensan
PRESENT SUBJUNCTIVE	piense, pienses, piense, pensemos, penséis, piensen
IMPERATIVE	————, piensa, piense, pensemos, pensad, piensen

Other tenses and forms present no changes in the vowel of the stem.

entender (e > ie) *to understand*	
PRESENT INDICATIVE	entiendo, entiendes, entiende, entendemos, entendéis, entienden
PRESENT SUBJUNCTIVE	entienda, entiendas, entienda, entendamos, entendáis, entiendan
IMPERATIVE	————, entiende, entienda, entendamos, entended, entiendan

Other tenses and forms present no changes in the vowel of the stem.

recordar (o > ue) *to remember*	
PRESENT INDICATIVE	recuerdo, recuerdas, recuerda, recordamos, recordáis, recuerdan
PRESENT SUBJUNCTIVE	recuerde, recuerdes, recuerde, recordemos, recordéis, recuerden
IMPERATIVE	————, recuerda, recuerde, recordemos, recordad, recuerden

Other tenses and forms present no changes in the vowel of the stem.

volver (o > ue) *to return*	
PRESENT INDICATIVE	vuelvo, vuelves, vuelve, volvemos, volvéis, vuelven
PRESENT SUBJUNCTIVE	vuelva, vuelvas, vuelva, volvamos, volváis, vuelvan
IMPERATIVE	————, vuelve, vuelva, volvamos, volved, vuelvan

Other tenses and forms present no changes in the vowel of the stem.

Stem-changing **-ir** verbs have three types of possible changes in the vowel of the stem **e > ie, e > i, o > ue.** In addition to the expected changes in the present subjunctive and imperative, verbs having the change **e > ie** and **e > i** have **i** as the stem vowel and verbs having the change **o > ue** have **u** as the stem vowel in the following forms:

a. the **nosotros** and **vosotros** forms of the present subjunctive

b. the **nosotros** command and the negative **vosotros** commands

c. the third-person singular and third-person plural forms of the preterit

d. all persons of the imperfect subjunctive (both **-ra** and **-se** forms)

e. the present participle

Sample Conjugations

sentir (e > ie) *to feel, regret*	
PRESENT INDICATIVE	siento, sientes, siente, sentimos, sentís, sienten
PRESENT SUBJUNCTIVE	sienta, sientas, sienta, sintamos, sintáis, sientan
IMPERATIVE	———, siente, sienta, sintamos, sentid, sientan
PRETERIT	sentí, sentiste, sintió, sentimos, sentisteis, sintieron
IMPERFECT SUBJUNCTIVE	sintiera, sintieras, sintiera, sintiéramos, sintierais, sintieran
	sintiese, sintieses, sintiese, sintiésemos, sintieseis, sintiesen
PRESENT PARTICIPLE	sintiendo

Other tenses and forms present no changes in the vowel of the stem.

pedir (e > i) *to ask for*	
PRESENT INDICATIVE	pido, pides, pide, pedimos, pedís, piden
PRESENT SUBJUNCTIVE	pida, pidas, pida, pidamos, pidáis, pidan
IMPERATIVE	———, pide, pida, pidamos, pedid, pidan
PRETERIT	pedí, pediste, pidió, pedimos, pedisteis, pidieron
IMPERFECT SUBJUNCTIVE	pidiera, pidieras, pidiera, pidiéramos, pidierais, pidieran
	pidiese, pidieses, pidiese, pidiésemos, pidieseis, pidiesen
PRESENT PARTICIPLE	pidiendo

Other tenses and forms present no changes in the vowel of the stem.

dormir (o > ue) *to sleep*	
PRESENT INDICATIVE	duermo, duermes, duerme, dormimos, dormís, duermen
PRESENT SUBJUNCTIVE	duerma, duermas, duerma, durmamos, durmáis, duerman
IMPERATIVE	———, duerme, duerma, durmamos, dormid, duerman
PRETERIT	dormí, dormiste, durmió, dormimos, dormisteis, durmieron
IMPERFECT SUBJUNCTIVE	durmiera, durmieras, durmiera, durmiéramos, durmierais, durmieran
	durmiese, durmieses, durmiese, durmiésemos, durmieseis, durmiesen
PRESENT PARTICIPLE	durmiendo

Other tenses and forms present no changes in the vowel of the stem.

Verbs with Spelling Changes

1. Verbs ending in **-car** (**c** > **qu** before **e**)
   The change occurs in the first-person singular of the preterit, in all persons of the present subjunctive, and in imperative forms derived from the present subjunctive.

tocar *to touch, play an instrument*	
PRETERIT	toqué, tocaste, tocó, tocamos, tocasteis, tocaron
PRESENT SUBJUNCTIVE	toque, toques, toque, toquemos, toquéis, toquen

2. Verbs ending in **-gar** (**c** > **gu** before **e**)
   The change occurs in the first-person singular of the preterit, in all persons of the present subjunctive, and in imperative forms derived from the present subjunctive.

llegar *to arrive*	
PRETERIT	llegué, llegaste, llegó, llegamos, llegasteis, llegaron
PRESENT SUBJUNCTIVE	llegue, llegues, llegue, lleguemos, lleguéis, lleguen

3. Verbs ending in **-zar** (**z** > **c** before **e**)
 The change occurs in the first-person singular of the preterit, in all persons of the present subjunctive, and in imperative forms derived from the present subjunctive.

cruzar *to cross*	
PRETERIT	crucé, cruzaste, cruzó, cruzamos, cruzasteis, cruzaron
PRESENT SUBJUNCTIVE	cruce, cruces, cruce, crucemos, crucéis, crucen

4. Verbs ending in **-ger** and **-gir** (**g** > **j** before **a** and **o**)
 The change occurs in the first-person singular of the present indicative, in all persons of the present subjunctive, and in imperative forms derived from the present subjunctive.

recoger *to pick up*	
PRESENT INDICATIVE	recojo, recoges, recoge, recogemos, recogéis, recogen
PRESENT SUBJUNCTIVE	recoja, recojas, recoja, recojamos, recojáis, recojan

exigir *to demand*	
PRESENT INDICATIVE	exijo, exiges, exige, exigimos, exigís, exigen
PRESENT SUBJUNCTIVE	exija, exijas, exija, exijamos, exijáis, exijan

5. Verbs ending in **-guir** (**gu** > **g** before **a** and **o**)
 The change occurs in the first-person singular of the present indicative, in all persons of the present subjunctive, and in imperative forms derived from the present subjunctive.

seguir *to follow*	
PRESENT INDICATIVE	sigo, sigues, sigue, seguimos, seguís, siguen
PRESENT SUBJUNCTIVE	siga, sigas, siga, sigamos, sigáis, sigan

6. Verbs ending in a consonant + **-cer, -cir** (**c** > **z** before **a** and **o**)
 The change occurs in the first-person singular of the present indicative, in all persons of the present subjunctive, and in imperative forms derived from the present subjunctive.

convencer *to convince*	
PRESENT INDICATIVE	convenzo, convences, convence, convencemos, convencéis, convencen
PRESENT SUBJUNCTIVE	convenza, convenzas, convenza, convenzamos, convenzáis, convenzan

7. **-Er** verbs having stems ending in a vowel

*These verbs change the **i** of the preterit endings **-ió** and **-ieron** and the **i** of the present participle ending **-iendo** to **y**. The **y** appears in all persons of the imperfect subjunctive. These verbs also add written accents to the endings of the second-person singular and the first- and second-persons plural of the preterit.*

creer *to believe*	
PRETERIT	creí, creíste, creyó, creímos, creísteis, creyeron
IMPERFECT SUBJUNCTIVE	creyera (creyese), creyeras, creyera, creyéramos, creyerais, creyeran
PRESENT PARTICIPLE	creyendo

Irregular Verbs

1. Verbs ending in a vowel + **-cer** or **-cir**

*These verbs change the final **c** of the stem to **-zc-** before **a** and **o**. The **-zc-** appears in the first-person singular of the present indicative, in all persons of the present subjunctive, and in imperative forms derived from the present subjunctive.*

conocer *to know*	
PRESENT INDICATIVE	conozco, conoces, conoce, conocemos, conocéis, conocen
PRESENT SUBJUNCTIVE	conozca, conozcas, conozca, conozcamos, conozcáis, conozcan

2. Verbs ending in **-uir** (not including those ending in **-guir**)

*These verbs add **y** before a vowel other than **i** and change the unaccented **i** between vowels to **y**. The **y** appears in all singular forms and the third-person plural of the present, in the third-persons singular and plural of the preterit, in all persons of the present and imperfect subjunctive, and in all imperative forms except the affirmative **vosotros** command.*

construir *to build*	
PRESENT INDICATIVE	construyo, construyes, construye, construimos, construís, construyen
PRETERIT	construí, construiste, construyó, construimos, construisteis, construyeron
IMPERATIVE	construye, construya, construyamos, construid, construyan
PRESENT SUBJUNCTIVE	construya, construyas, construya, construyamos, construyáis, construyan
IMPERFECT SUBJUNCTIVE	construyera (construyese), construyeras, construyera, construyéramos, construyerais, construyeran

Other Irregular Verbs

andar   *to walk*

PRETERIT	anduve, anduviste, anduvo, anduvimos, anduvisteis, anduvieron
IMPERFECT SUBJUNCTIVE	anduviera (anduviese), anduvieras, anduviera, anduviéramos, anduvierais, anduvieran

caer   *to fall*

PRESENT INDICATIVE	caigo, caes, cae, caemos, caéis, caen
PRETERIT	caí, caíste, cayó, caímos, caísteis, cayeron
IMPERATIVE	cae (no caigas), caiga, caigamos, caed (no caigáis), caigan
PRESENT SUBJUNCTIVE	caiga, caigas, caiga, caigamos, caigáis, caigan
IMPERFECT SUBJUNCTIVE	cayera (cayese), cayeras, cayera, cayéramos, cayerais, cayeran
PRESENT PARTICIPLE	cayendo
PAST PARTICIPLE	caído

dar   *to give*

PRESENT INDICATIVE	doy, das, da, damos, dais, dan
PRETERIT	di, diste, dio, dimos, disteis, dieron
IMPERATIVE	da (no des), dé, demos, dad (no deis), den
PRESENT SUBJUNCTIVE	dé, des, dé, demos, deis, den
IMPERFECT SUBJUNCTIVE	diera (diese), dieras, diera, diéramos, dierais, dieran
PAST PARTICIPLE	dado

decir   *to say, tell*

PRESENT INDICATIVE	digo, dices, dice, decimos, decís, dicen
PRETERIT	dije, dijiste, dijo, dijimos, dijisteis, dijeron
FUTURE	diré, dirás, dirá, diremos, diréis, dirán
CONDITIONAL	diría, dirías, diría, diríamos, diríais, dirían
IMPERATIVE	di (no digas), diga, digamos, decid (no digáis), digan
PRESENT SUBJUNCTIVE	diga, digas, diga, digamos, digáis, digan
IMPERFECT SUBJUNCTIVE	dijera (dijese), dijeras, dijera, dijéramos, dijerais, dijeran
PRESENT PARTICIPLE	diciendo
PAST PARTICIPLE	dicho

estar *to be*

PRESENT INDICATIVE	estoy, estás, está, estamos, estáis, están
PRETERIT	estuve, estuviste, estuvo, estuvimos, estuvisteis, estuvieron
IMPERATIVE	está (no estés), esté, estemos, estad (no estéis), estén
PRESENT SUBJUNCTIVE	esté, estés, esté, estemos, estéis, estén
IMPERFECT SUBJUNCTIVE	estuviera (estuviese), estuvieras, estuviera, estuviéramos, estuvierais, estuvieran

haber *to have (auxiliary verb)*

PRESENT INDICATIVE	he, has, ha, hemos, habéis, han
PRETERIT	hube, hubiste, hubo, hubimos, hubisteis, hubieron
FUTURE	habré, habrás, habrá, habremos, habréis, habrán
CONDITIONAL	habría, habrías, habría, habríamos, habríais, habrían
PRESENT SUBJUNCTIVE	haya, hayas, haya, hayamos, hayáis, hayan
IMPERFECT SUBJUNCTIVE	hubiera (hubiese), hubieras, hubiera, hubiéramos, hubierais, hubieran

hacer *to do, to make*

PRESENT INDICATIVE	hago, haces, hace, hacemos, hacéis, hacen
PRETERIT	hice, hiciste, hizo, hicimos, hiciste, hicieron
FUTURE	haré, harás, hará, haremos, haréis, harán
CONDITIONAL	haría, harías, haría, haríamos, haríais, harían
IMPERATIVE	haz (no hagas), haga, hagamos, haced (no hagáis), hagan
PRESENT SUBJUNCTIVE	haga, hagas, haga, hagamos, hagáis, hagan
IMPERFECT SUBJUNCTIVE	hiciera (hiciese), hicieras, hiciera, hiciéramos, hicierais, hicieran
PAST PARTICIPLE	hecho

ir *to go*

PRESENT INDICATIVE	voy, vas, va, vamos, vais, van
PRETERIT	fui, fuiste, fue, fuimos, fuisteis, fueron
IMPERATIVE	ve (no vayas), vaya, vamos/(no) vayamos, id (no vayáis), vayan
PRESENT SUBJUNCTIVE	vaya, vayas, vaya, vayamos, vayáis, vayan
IMPERFECT SUBJUNCTIVE	fuera (fuese), fueras, fuera, fuéramos, fuerais, fueran
PRESENT PARTICIPLE	yendo

oír *to hear*

PRESENT INDICATIVE	oigo, oyes, oye, oímos, oís, oyen
PRETERIT	oí, oíste, oyó, oímos, oísteis, oyeron
IMPERATIVE	oye (no oigas), oiga, oigamos, oíd (no oigáis), oigan
PRESENT SUBJUNCTIVE	oiga, oigas, oiga, oigamos, oigáis, oigan
IMPERFECT SUBJUNCTIVE	oyera (oyese), oyeras, oyera, oyéramos, oyerais, oyeran
PRESENT PARTICIPLE	oyendo
PAST PARTICIPLE	oído

poder *to be able, can*

PRESENT INDICATIVE	puedo, puedes, puede, podemos, podéis, pueden
PRETERIT	pude, pudiste, pudo, pudimos, pudisteis, pudieron
FUTURE	podré, podrás, podrá, podremos, podréis, podrán
CONDITIONAL	podría, podrías, podría, podríamos, podríais, podrían
IMPERATIVE	puede, pueda, podamos, poded, puedan
PRESENT SUBJUNCTIVE	pueda, puedas, pueda, podamos, podáis, puedan
IMPERFECT SUBJUNCTIVE	pudiera (pudiese), pudieras, pudiera, pudiéramos, pudierais, pudieran
PRESENT PARTICIPLE	pudiendo

poner *to put*

PRESENT INDICATIVE	pongo, pones, pone, ponemos, ponéis, ponen
PRETERIT	puse, pusiste, puso, pusimos, pusisteis, pusieron
FUTURE	pondré, pondrás, pondrá, pondremos, pondréis, pondrán
CONDITIONAL	pondría, pondrías, pondría, pondríamos, pondríais, pondrían
IMPERATIVE	pon (no pongas), ponga, pongamos, poned (no pongáis), pongan
PRESENT SUBJUNCTIVE	ponga, pongas, ponga, pongamos, pongáis, pongan
IMPERFECT SUBJUNCTIVE	pusiera (pusiese), pusieras, pusiera, pusiéramos, pusierais, pusieran
PAST PARTICIPLE	puesto

producir *to produce*	
PRESENT INDICATIVE	produzco, produces, produce, producimos, producís, producen
PRETERIT	produje, produjiste, produjo, produjimos, produjisteis, produjeron
IMPERATIVE	produce (no produzcas), produzca, produzcamos, producid (no produzcáis), produzcan
PRESENT SUBJUNCTIVE	produzca, produzcas, produzca, produzcamos, produzcáis, produzcan
IMPERFECT SUBJUNCTIVE	produjera (produjese), produjeras, produjera, produjéramos, produjerais, produjeran

querer *to want*	
PRESENT INDICATIVE	quiero, quieres, quiere, queremos, queréis, quieren
PRETERIT	quise, quisiste, quiso, quisimos, quisisteis, quisieron
FUTURE	querré, querrás, querrá, querremos, querréis, querrán
CONDITIONAL	querría, querrías, querría, querríamos, querríais, querrían
IMPERATIVE	quiere (no quieras), quiera, queramos, quered (no queráis), quieran
PRESENT SUBJUNCTIVE	quiera, quieras, quiera, queramos, queráis, quieran
IMPERFECT SUBJUNCTIVE	quisiera (quisiese), quisieras, quisiera, quisiéramos, quisierais, quisieran

saber *to know*	
PRESENT INDICATIVE	sé, sabes, sabe, sabemos, sabéis, saben
PRETERIT	supe, supiste, supo, supimos, supisteis, supieron
FUTURE	sabré, sabrás, sabrá, sabremos, sabréis, sabrán
CONDITIONAL	sabría, sabrías, sabría, sabríamos, sabríais, sabrían
IMPERATIVE	sabe (no sepas), sepa, sepamos, sabed (no sepáis), sepan
PRESENT SUBJUNCTIVE	sepa, sepas, sepa, sepamos, sepáis, sepan
IMPERFECT SUBJUNCTIVE	supiera (supiese), supieras, supiera, supiéramos, supierais, supieran

salir *to go out*

PRESENT INDICATIVE	salgo, sales, sale, salimos, salís, salen
FUTURE	saldré, saldrás, saldrá, saldremos, saldréis, saldrán
CONDITIONAL	saldría, saldrías, saldría, saldríamos, saldríais, saldrían
IMPERATIVE	sal (no salgas), salga, salgamos, salid (no salgáis), salgan
PRESENT SUBJUNCTIVE	salga, salgas, salga, salgamos, salgáis, salgan

ser *to be*

PRESENT INDICATIVE	soy, eres, es, somos, sois, son
PRETERIT	fui, fuiste, fue, fuimos, fuisteis, fueron
FUTURE	seré, serás, será, seremos, seréis, serán
CONDITIONAL	sería, serías, sería, seríamos, seríais, serían
IMPERATIVE	sé (no seas), sea, seamos, sed (no seáis), sean
PRESENT SUBJUNCTIVE	sea, seas, sea, seamos, seáis, sean
IMPERFECT SUBJUNCTIVE	fuera (fuese), fueras, fuera, fuéramos, fuerais, fueran

tener *to have*

PRESENT INDICATIVE	tengo, tienes, tiene, tenemos, tenéis, tienen
PRETERIT	tuve, tuviste, tuvo, tuvimos, tuvisteis, tuvieron
FUTURE	tendré, tendrás, tendrá, tendremos, tendréis, tendrán
CONDITIONAL	tendría, tendrías, tendría, tendríamos, tendríais, tendrían
IMPERATIVE	ten (no tengas), tenga, tengamos, tened (no tengáis), tengan
PRESENT SUBJUNCTIVE	tenga, tengas, tenga, tengamos, tengáis, tengan
IMPERFECT SUBJUNCTIVE	tuviera (tuviese), tuvieras, tuviera, tuviéramos, tuvierais, tuvieran

traer *to bring*

PRESENT INDICATIVE	traigo, traes, trae, traemos, traéis, traen
PRETERIT	traje, trajiste, trajo, trajimos, trajisteis, trajeron
IMPERATIVE	trae (no traigas), traiga, traigamos, traed (no traigáis), traigan
PRESENT SUBJUNCTIVE	traiga, traigas, traiga, traigamos, traigáis, traigan
IMPERFECT SUBJUNCTIVE	trajera (trajese), trajeras, trajera, trajéramos, trajerais, trajeran
PRESENT PARTICIPLE	trayendo
PAST PARTICIPLE	traído

valer *to be worth*	
PRESENT INDICATIVE	valgo, vales, vale, valemos, valéis, valen
FUTURE	valdré, valdrás, valdrá, valdremos, valdréis, valdrán
CONDITIONAL	valdría, valdrías, valdría, valdríamos, valdríais, valdrían
IMPERATIVE	vale (no valgas), valga, valgamos, valed (no valgáis), valgan
PRESENT SUBJUNCTIVE	valga, valgas, valga, valgamos, valgáis, valgan

venir *to come*	
PRESENT INDICATIVE	vengo, vienes, viene, venimos, venís, vienen
PRETERIT	vine, viniste, vino, vinimos, vinisteis, vinieron
FUTURE	vendré, vendrás, vendrá, vendremos, vendréis, vendrán
CONDITIONAL	vendría, vendrías, vendría, vendríamos, vendríais, vendrían
IMPERATIVE	ven (no vengas), venga, vengamos, venid (no vengáis), vengan
PRESENT SUBJUNCTIVE	venga, vengas, venga, vengamos, vengáis, vengan
IMPERFECT SUBJUNCTIVE	viniera (viniese), vinieras, viniera, viniéramos, vinierais, vinieran
PRESENT PARTICIPLE	viniendo

ver *to see*	
PRESENT INDICATIVE	veo, ves, ve, vemos, veis, ven
PRETERIT	vi, viste, vio, vimos, visteis, vieron
IMPERFECT INDICATIVE	veía, veías, veía, veíamos, veíais, veían
IMPERATIVE	ve (no veas), vea, veamos, ved (no veáis), vean
PRESENT SUBJUNCTIVE	vea, veas, vea, veamos, veáis, vean
IMPERFECT SUBJUNCTIVE	viera (viese), vieras, viera, viéramos, vierais, vieran
PAST PARTICIPLE	visto

Answers

CHAPTER 1
The Present Tense

A. En la clase de español.

1. Daniel pronuncia muy bien.
2. Nosotros abrimos el libro de texto.
3. Tú levantas la mano.
4. Los chicos comprenden la lección.
5. Ud. toma apuntes.
6. Yo leo el diálogo.
7. Isabel y tú aprenden los modismos.
8. Vosotros escribís un ejercicio.

B. ¿En esta clase? ¡Qué va!

1. Uds. nunca corren.
2. Nosotros nunca faltamos.
3. Juan Carlos nunca masca chicle.
4. Yo nunca salto.
5. Laura y Carmen nunca empujan.
6. Tú nunca interrumpes.
7. Las chicas nunca beben refrescos.
8. Ud. y yo nunca tardamos en llegar.

C. ¿Qué hacen sus profesores?

Answers will vary.

D. ¡Las quince primaveras!

1. planean	10. beben
2. cocina	11. bailan
3. compra	12. toca
4. colocan	13. cantan
5. invita	14. abre
6. Llega	15. recibe
7. vive	16. saca
8. llega	17. felicitan
9. comen	18. brindan

E. ¡Un lío telefónico!

1. desea	9. debe
2. tarda	10. espera
3. busca	11. funciona
4. Queda	12. mete
5. mete	13. comunican
6. marca	14. dejan
7. contestan	15. decide
8. cree	

F. Un viaje de negocios.

1. Sí, salgo la semana próxima.
2. Sí, vengo a la oficina el viernes.
3. Sí, voy a Francia y España.
4. Sí, conozco Italia.
5. Sí, hago las maletas mañana.
6. Sí, sé cuándo regreso.

G. ¡Cuánto trabajo tenemos!

1. Las chicas vienen si tienen tiempo.
2. Ud. viene si tiene tiempo.
3. Tú y yo venimos si tenemos tiempo.
4. Sara viene si tiene tiempo.
5. Uds. vienen si tienen tiempo.
6. Yo vengo si tengo tiempo.

H. ¿Oyes lo que dicen?

1. Yo oigo lo que Uds. dicen.
2. Tú oyes lo que nosotros decimos.
3. Guillermo oye lo que Teresa dice.
4. Rosa y yo oímos lo que Ud. dice.
5. Ud. y su primo oyen lo que yo digo.
6. Carmen y Paco oyen lo que tú dices.

I. ¡Lo hago yo!

1. Yo pongo la mesa.
2. Yo traigo las flores.
3. Yo doy un paseo.
4. Yo veo televisión.
5. Yo traduzco el libro.

J. ¿Hablan en serio?

1. Merezco recibir el premio Nobel.
2. Compongo una obra maestra mozartiana.
3. Obtenemos una beca de dos millones de dólares.
4. Traduzco novelas del vasco al sánscrito.
5. Conduzco la limosina presidencial.
6. Supongo que yo tengo razón siempre.

K. ¿Cuánto tiempo hace?

1. ¿Cuánto tiempo hace que Uds. cocinan a la francesa? ¿Desde cuándo cocinan Uds. a la francesa?

2. ¿Cuánto tiempo hace que Mario y Federico nadan? ¿Desde cuándo nadan Mario y Federico?
3. ¿Cuánto tiempo hace que Consuelo toca el violín? ¿Desde cuándo toca Consuelo el violín?
4. ¿Cuánto tiempo hace que haces carpintería? ¿Desde cuándo haces carpintería?
5. ¿Cuánto tiempo hace que Esteban baila flamenco? ¿Desde cuándo baila Esteban flamenco?
6. ¿Cuánto tiempo hace que sus hermanos coleccionan monedas? ¿Desde cuándo coleccionan sus hermanos monedas?

L. *Hace mucho tiempo que …*

1. Hace un año que Uds. cocinan a la francesa. Uds. cocinan a la francesa desde hace un año.
2. Hace tres años que Mario y Federico nadan. Mario y Federico nadan desde hace tres años.
3. Hace seis años que Consuelo toca el violín. Consuelo toca el violín desde hace seis años.
4. Hace siete semanas que haces carpintería. Haces carpintería desde hace siete semanas.
5. Hace ocho meses que Esteban baila flamenco. Esteban baila flamenco desde hace ocho meses.
6. Hace dos años y medio que sus hermanos coleccionan monedas. Sus hermanos coleccionan monedas desde hace dos años y medio.

M. *¿Cómo son?*

1. No, no conozco a esos muchachos.
2. No, ellos no conocen a los señores Gorostiza.
3. No, no conocemos a la profesora de economía.
4. No, no conocemos a aquel médico.
5. No, no conozco a Alfredo Parra.
6. No, ella no conoce a Agustín.

N. *¡Qué vanidad!*

1. Pertenezco a los círculos literarios de la ciudad.
2. Produzco obras importantes.
3. Traduzco poesía del inglés al español.
4. Doy muchas conferencias.
5. Siempre ofrezco ideas nuevas.
6. Merezco los aplausos de los oyentes.

O. *¡Todos ayudamos!*

1. Mi hermano y yo vamos a cortar el césped.
2. Mi abuela va a lavar la ropa.
3. Yo voy a barrer el suelo.
4. Mamá va a hacer la compra.
5. Mis hermanas van a lavar los platos.
6. Mi abuelo va a sacar la basura.
7. Uds. van a hacer las camas.
8. Papá va a pasar la aspiradora.
9. Tú vas a limpiar la alfombra.

P. *La vida diaria.*

1. Yo conduzco el coche.
2. Mamá y Papá firman papeles.
3. Mi hermano trota.
4. Ud. prende (pone) la computadora.
5. Federico y yo asistimos a conferencias.
6. Tú lees el periódico.
7. David y Mateo nadan en la piscina.
8. Mis tíos reciben sus cuentas.
9. Todos los estudiantes hablan de los temas.
10. Uds. cuecen (cocinan) arroz.
11. Jaime y yo cruzamos la calle.
12. María Elena y Martín leen hasta la una de la mañana.

Q. *Haga una encuesta.*

Answers will vary.

R. *Estructuras en acción*

1. c	4. d
2. e	5. b
3. a	

CHAPTER 2
Ser *and* Estar

A. *Soy yo.*

1. Es ella.	5. Eres tú.
2. Son Uds.	6. Es él.
3. Somos nosotros.	7. Son ellas.
4. Soy yo.	

B. *¿De dónde son? ¿De qué origen son?*

1. Pablo es de la Argentina pero es de origen inglés.
2. Los gemelos son de Francia pero son de origen ruso.

3. La licenciada es del Canadá pero es de origen japonés.
4. Ud. es de los Estados Unidos pero es de origen irlandés.
5. Ramón y Virginia son de Puerto Rico pero son de origen polaco.
6. Tú eres de España pero eres de origen portugués.
7. Ud. y Raquel son de México pero son de origen griego.
8. Yo soy de Venezuela pero soy de origen italiano.

C. *Una encuesta.*

1. ¿Quién eres?
2. ¿De dónde eres?
3. ¿De qué nacionalidad eres?
4. ¿De qué origen eres?
5. ¿Cómo eres?
6. ¿De qué color son tus ojos?

D. *Están de vacaciones.*

1. Patricio está en Madrid y está contento.
2. Nosotros estamos en Chile y estamos cansados.
3. Los tíos están en Tejas y están nerviosos.
4. Consuelo y su hermana están en Suecia y están aburridas.
5. Tú estás en Londres y estás enfermo.
6. Yo estoy en París y estoy feliz.

E. *¿Cuál fue la pregunta?*

1. ¿Cuál es su nombre?
2. ¿Cuál es su nacionalidad?
3. ¿Cuál es su profesión?
4. ¿Cuál es su estado civil?
5. ¿Cuál es su fecha de nacimiento?
6. ¿Cómo es Ud.?

F. *Biografías.*

A.	1. es	B.	1. es
	2. es		2. es
	3. son		3. es
	4. es		4. son
	5. Es		5. Son
	6. está		6. está
	7. están		7. es

G. *El museo de arte.*

1. estamos	11. es
2. está	12. están
3. Es	13. son
4. está	14. están
5. es	15. son
6. Es	16. es
7. es	17. estoy
8. es	18. son
9. ser	19. está
10. está	20. Está

H. *Un semestre en el extranjero.*

1. estoy	19. Es
2. estoy	20. es
3. Es	21. Es
4. es	22. estoy
5. es	23. Es
6. es	24. están
7. son	25. estás
8. es	26. es
9. está	27. están
10. está	28. estar
11. están	29. están
12. está	30. está
13. es	31. están
14. es	32. está
15. es	33. son
16. Son	34. es
17. es	35. es
18. Es	36. estar

I. *¿Qué preguntó?*

1. ¿Dónde está la papelería?
2. ¿Cómo es Gloria?
3. ¿De dónde son los hermanos García? / ¿De qué nacionalidad son los hermanos García?
4. ¿Cómo están Juanito y Raúl?
5. ¿De qué origen es la familia Méndez?
6. ¿Cómo son las primas de Paco?
7. ¿Dónde está el profesor Mora?
8. ¿De qué es el vestido?
9. ¿De qué color son la camisa y la corbata?
10. ¿Cómo está(s)?
11. ¿De quién(es) es aquella casa?
12. ¿De dónde es Micaela?

J. *Unos nuevos estudiantes extranjeros.*

1. ¿Quiénes son los nuevos estudiantes extranjeros? ¿Sabes de dónde son?
2. Yo conozco a María del Mar. Está en mi clase de matemáticas. Es de la Argentina.

3. Sí, y es de origen italiano. Es muy simpática e inteligente.
4. Pero está triste porque quiere volver a Buenos Aires.
5. Lorenzo Tomé es francés pero sus abuelos son de origen español.
6. Hace muchos años que la familia vive en Francia.
7. Lorenzo estudia biología y química este año.
8. Sí. Él dice que quiere ser médico.

K. La familia.

Answers will vary.

L. Estructuras en acción

1. Éstos son tus abonos. *These are your passes.*
2. El Abono Transportes es la forma más práctica, cómoda y económica de disfrutar de las ventajas del transporte público. *The Abono Transportes is the most practical, comfortable, and economical way of enjoying the advantages of public transportation.*
3. ... un cupón que puede ser mensual o anual. *... a coupon that can be monthly or yearly.*
4. Metro, tren, autobús y todos los transportes públicos están a tu disposición. *Subway, train, bus and all forms of public transportation are at your disposal.*

CHAPTER 3
Stem-Changing Verbs and Verbs with Spelling Changes

A. ¿A qué juegan Uds.?

1. Yo juego al tenis.
2. Daniel y Felipe juegan al béisbol.
3. Carlota juega al vólibol.
4. Tú juegas al baloncesto.
5. Jorge y yo jugamos al fútbol americano.
6. Uds. juegan al jai alai.

B. ¿A qué hora almuerzan?

1. Uds. almuerzan a la una.
2. Eva almuerza a las doce y media.
3. Nosotros almorzamos a las tres.
4. Mauricio y Beatriz almuerzan a la una y cuarto.
5. Tú almuerzas a las once y media.
6. Yo almuerzo a las dos y media.

C. ¡No puedo!

1. No, no podemos.
2. No, no puede.
3. No, no pueden.
4. No, no puedo.
5. No, no puedes.
6. No, no podemos. (No, no pueden.)

D. En un almacén.

1. puedo	9. cuesta
2. encuentro	10. cuesta
3. quiere	11. pruebo
4. Pienso	12. envuelve
5. muestro	13. puede
6. Puede	14. suelo
7. encuentro	15. vuelvo
8. cuestan	

E. Sinónimos.

1. resuelven	6. Vuelves
2. atraviesan	7. muestra
3. comienza	8. quieren
4. Descendemos	9. enciendo
5. entiendo	

F. Un día típico.

1. Mi papá despierta a todos nosotros.
2. Mi mamá cuenta lo que pasa.
3. Uds. almuerzan en el centro.
4. Tú devuelves los libros a la biblioteca.
5. Los chicos vuelven del colegio a las tres.
6. Ana y yo comenzamos a estudiar a las cuatro.
7. Yo juego ajedrez.
8. Federico acuesta a sus hermanitos.

G. Hoy sí, mañana no.

1. Recuerdas la fecha hoy.
2. Pablo y Lorenzo juegan fútbol hoy.
3. Probamos el nuevo plato hoy.
4. Alicia encuentra su secador hoy.
5. Yo devuelvo el paraguas hoy.
6. Ud. almuerza con Raquel hoy.

H. ¿Qué tiempo hace?

1. Llueve (Está lloviendo) en Londres.
2. Nieva (Está nevando) en Montreal.
3. Truena (Está tronando) en Santa Fe.
4. La lluvia empieza a helar en Nome.
5. Empieza a nevar en Moscú.
6. Comienza a llover en Barcelona.

7. Está despejado (claro) en Patagonia.
8. Graniza (Está granizando) en Nueva York.

I. *En el restaurante.*

1. Ud. y José María piden piña.
2. La familia Herrera pide paella.
3. Pili y yo pedimos ensalada.
4. Tú pides flan.
5. Los chicos piden pollo.
6. Yo pido arroz.

J. *¿Quién sirve?*

1. Yo sirvo limonada.
2. Susana sirve refrescos.
3. Nosotros servimos cerveza.
4. Eduardo y Dolores sirven jugo.
5. Tú sirves agua mineral.
6. Ud. y Pepe sirven soda.

K. *¿Qué prefiere Ud. hacer?*

1. Los primos prefieren salir al campo.
2. Julia prefiere leer novelas.
3. Mis hermanos y yo preferimos ir a un concierto.
4. Uds. prefieren ver televisión.
5. Yo prefiero jugar a las damas.
6. Tú prefieres viajar.

L. *Todos duermen la siesta.*

1. El abuelo duerme la siesta todos los días.
2. Yo duermo la siesta los fines de semana.
3. Uds. duermen la siesta una vez a la semana.
4. Nosotros dormimos la siesta los lunes.
5. Los sobrinos duermen la siesta todas las tardes.
6. Ud. duerme la siesta los días feriados.

M. *En otras palabras.*

1. viste
2. advierte
3. sienten
4. hierve
5. duerme
6. miente
7. divierte / ríen / sonríen
8. despiden
9. repites

N. *Vamos a contribuir.*

1. Los padres de Vera contribuyen treinta dólares.
2. Mis hermanos y yo contribuimos quince dólares.
3. El director del colegio contribuye veinte dólares.
4. Ud. contribuye doce dólares.

5. La tía Adriana contribuye veinticinco dólares.
6. Los ciudadanos del pueblo contribuyen mil quinientos dólares.

O. *¡Qué desastre!*

1. Tú huyes a la estación de tren.
2. Uds. huyen al oeste.
3. Fernando huye a casa de sus abuelos.
4. Nosotros huimos a la capital.
5. La familia Ortega huye a un hotel.
6. Yo huyo al interior del estado.

P. *Un proyecto.*

1. Roberto incluye investigaciones científicas.
2. Uds. incluyen fotos.
3. Laura y yo incluimos estadísticas.
4. Ud. incluye buenas explicaciones.
5. Tú incluyes un resumen.
6. David y Ricardo incluyen una introducción.

Q. *¿Cuándo se resfrían Uds.?*

1. Tomás se resfría todos los inviernos.
2. Uds. se resfrían cuando duermen poco.
3. Lidia y Miguel se resfrían tres veces al año.
4. Ud. se resfría cuando come mal.
5. Yo me resfrío cuando me mojo.

R. *¿Cuándo es su graduación?*

1. Micaela y Jorge se gradúan el año próximo.
2. Ud. se gradúa dentro de dos años.
3. Timoteo se gradúa en enero.
4. Uds. se gradúan para el año noventa y ocho.
5. Anita se gradúa este mes.

S. *Los espías.*

1. se fían
2. envían
3. confía
4. continúa
5. se resfría

T. *¿Qué dice Ud.?*

Answers will vary.

U. *¿Qué escoge Ud.?*

1. Yo escojo una caja de bombones.
2. Mis padres escogen una bandeja de plata.
3. Nosotros escogemos un perrito.
4. Tú escoges dos relojes.
5. Uds. escogen un televisor.
6. La abuela escoge un juego de toallas.

V. *¿Qué elige Ud.?*

1. elijo
2. eligen
3. elegimos
4. eliges
5. eligen
6. elige

W. *¿Cuál es su trabajo?*

1. recojo
2. persigo
3. extingo
4. cuezo
5. dirijo
6. corrijo

X. *Un misterio.*

1. sigo
2. dirijo
3. encojo
4. distingo
5. reconozco
6. finge
7. consigo
8. luce
9. prosigo
10. produce
11. finjo
12. distingo
13. recojo
14. convenzo
15. desconozco

Y. *Consiguen hacer algunas cosas.*

1. Víctor consigue salir al centro comercial.
2. Pablo y yo conseguimos reparar el coche.
3. Ud. consigue ver la nueva exposición.
4. Yo consigo pasar la aspiradora.
5. Uds. consiguen arreglar los armarios.
6. Teodoro y tú consiguen colgar los cuadros.

Z. *Sinónimos.*

1. Sigue
2. Cojo
3. Desconozco
4. Finjo
5. Cuecen
6. distingo
7. Exijo
8. Eliges
9. consigo
10. Produzco

AA. *Las noticias.*

1. Leopoldo Soto dirige la Filarmónica de Nueva York esta semana.
2. Los bomberos extinguen treinta fuegos cada día.
3. Los ciudadanos exigen mejores escuelas.
4. El senador Alonso sigue los consejos de sus colegas en el senado.
5. Los americanos eligen un nuevo presidente este año.
6. ¡Joven pareja consigue ganar la lotería!
7. Una nueva receta: ¡cocinero cuece sopa con helado!
8. Noticias del extranjero: ejército de A vence al ejército de B.
9. La campaña contra el analfabetismo prosigue.

10. Los gobernadores desconocen muchos problemas que tienen sus ciudades.

BB. *¿Que piensan hacer Uds.?*

Answers will vary.

CC. *Estructuras en acción*

Manuel Campo Vidal: Noticias, Cambio de ideas, Hace pensar, Programa digno de confianza.
Farmacia de Guardia: Comedia, Ya tiene muchos televidentes, Anuncio usa el estilo de la receta médica.

CHAPTER 4
The Preterit Tense

A. *¡Tanta tarea!*

1. Esteban estudió la historia de la Edad media.
2. Rosa y Elena solucionaron problemas de cálculo.
3. Tú escribiste poemas.
4. Nosotros trabajamos en la librería.
5. Yo visité el museo de historia natural.
6. Uds. contestaron preguntas de filosofía.
7. Miguel usó la computadora.
8. Ud. aprendió fechas de historia.

B. *¡Vaya un día de examen!*

1. levanté
2. arreglé
3. Bajé
4. saludé
5. preparó
6. tomé
7. empecé
8. pasó
9. desayunó
10. terminamos
11. cogí
12. salimos
13. llegó
14. subimos
15. viajamos
16. bajamos
17. arrancó
18. busqué
19. encontré
20. coloqué
21. recordé
22. pensé
23. miró
24. habló
25. explicó
26. entregó
27. salvó

C. *Salimos a cenar.*

1. Felipe escogió el Café Valencia.
2. Nosotros llegamos al restaurante a las siete.
3. Miramos la carta.
4. El mozo recomendó la paella.
5. Lorenzo pidió ternera y sopa.

6. Eva y Diana pidieron pescado y ensalada.
7. Yo preferí el arroz con pollo.
8. Tú comiste torta de postre.
9. Todos tomaron (tomamos) vino.
10. Nadie bebió café.
11. Felipe pagó la cuenta.
12. Jaime dejó la propina.
13. Todos nosotros cenamos muy bien.
14. Yo gocé mucho.
15. Todos los amigos se divirtieron.

D. *¡Todo hecho ya!*

1. Ya saqué los libros de la biblioteca. (Ya los saqué de la biblioteca.)
2. Ya jugué (al) ajedrez. (Ya lo jugué.)
3. Ya toqué la flauta. (Ya la toqué.)
4. Ya coloqué los documentos en el archivo. (Ya los coloqué en el archivo.)
5. Ya arranqué la mala hierba del jardín. (Ya la arranqué del jardín.)
6. Ya expliqué lo que sucedió. (Ya lo expliqué.)
7. Ya colgué los cuadros. (Ya los colgué.)
8. Ya almorcé con Victoria. (Ya almorcé con ella.)
9. Ya entregué el informe. (Ya lo entregué.)
10. Ya empecé la novela inglesa. (Ya la empecé.)

E. *Pasaron los años.*

1. Los hermanos Serrat construyeron muchas casas.
2. El profesor Burgos influyó mucho en la política.
3. Francisca leyó libros para una casa editora.
4. Marco e Isabel huyeron a otro pueblo por una tempestad.
5. Doña Elvira contribuyó mucho dinero a las caridades.
6. Leonardo concluyó los trámites de la empresa.

F. *¡Qué mala suerte!*

1. equivoqué
2. marqué
3. tropecé
4. pegué
5. deslicé
6. masqué
7. tragué
8. bañé
9. ahogué
10. tranquilicé

G. *Yo no hice eso.*

1. lanzó / lancé
2. publicó / publiqué

3. dedicaste / dediqué
4. cargaron / cargué
5. realizaron / realicé
6. embarcó / embarqué

H. *Una entrevista.*

1. Aterrizamos en el aeropuerto de San Juan.
2. Visité fortalezas, museos e iglesias.
3. Yo recé en la iglesia de San Juan y Sara rezó en una sinagoga.
4. Almorcé en varias playas de la Isla.
5. Jugamos al tenis y al fútbol también.
6. Pesqué en el mar y en los ríos también.
7. Avanzamos mucho en nuestro dominio del español.
8. Realizamos un viaje maravilloso.
9. Gocé muchísimo de mi estancia en Puerto Rico.

I. *¿Cómo reaccionó la gente?*

1. Tú sonreíste.
2. Los chicos repitieron.
3. Patricio gruñó.
4. Nosotros reímos.
5. Uds. se durmieron.
6. La señora Gil sirvió la sopa.
7. Chelo regañó a los niños.
8. Los ladrones mintieron.
9. Nuestros amigos nos advirtieron.
10. Paquita se divirtió.
11. Ellos lo sintieron.

J. *El pronóstico meteorológico.*

1. Estuvo nublado ayer también.
2. Hizo frío ayer también.
3. Llovió ayer también.
4. Hizo sol ayer también.
5. Estuvo despejado ayer también.
6. Nevó ayer también.
7. Hizo ochenta grados ayer también.
8. Hizo fresco ayer también.
9. Tronó ayer también.
10. Hubo mucho viento ayer también.

K. *Escenas breves.*

1. dijo / dije
2. fueron / Fuimos
3. estuviste / Estuve
4. trajeron / trajo
5. vinieron / vine / vino
6. di / vio
7. oyó / supo
8. hiciste / puse
9. leyó / quiso
10. hizo / Fui

L. *¿Y qué pasó después?*

1. estuvo feliz
2. se hizo médico
3. tuvieron frío
4. pusimos la mesa
5. se hizo daño
6. pude distinguir
7. dijo que sí
8. fuiste tras ella

M. *Ayer, al contrario …*

1. Pero ayer me desperté a las siete.
2. Pero ayer almorcé en el Café Atenas.
3. Pero ayer fui de compras por la mañana.
4. Pero ayer hice un plato de pescado.
5. Pero ayer jugué al tenis con Ricardo.
6. Pero ayer seguí por la calle Atocha.
7. Pero ayer empecé a trabajar antes del desayuno.
8. Pero ayer vine en taxi.

N. *Una merienda en el campo.*

1. se divirtieron
2. fuimos
3. condujeron
4. pudo
5. Hizo
6. dio
7. recogieron
8. hice
9. trajeron
10. vieron
11. oyeron
12. comenzó
13. tuvimos
14. estuvimos

O. *¡Qué suspenso!*

1. El monstruo llegó (vino) a la ciudad.
2. Hizo pedazos a los coches y destruyó edificios.
3. Al ver el monstruo la gente dio gritos. (Cuando la gente vio el monstruo dio gritos.)
4. Me puse pálido(a).
5. A mi amigo Lorenzo le dio dolor de cabeza.
6. A mi amiga Marisol le dio dolor de estómago.
7. Todos nos echamos a correr.
8. Algunas (Unas) personas no pudieron escaparse.
9. ¡El suspenso se hizo insoportable (inaguantable)!

P. *¿Qué dice Ud.?*

Answers will vary.

Q. *El horario.*

Answers will vary.

R. *Estructuras en acción*

1. c
2. a
3. b
4. a
5. c

CHAPTER 5
The Imperfect Tense

A. *Cuando yo era niño(a) …*

1. vivía
2. era
3. iba
4. hacía
5. solían
6. íbamos
7. gustaba
8. era
9. pasábamos
10. era
11. hacía
12. Había
13. jugábamos
14. cultivaba
15. eran
16. olía
17. salíamos
18. Subíamos
19. veía
20. servía
21. leía
22. íbamos
23. estábamos
24. volvían
25. llevaba
26. era

B. *Reunión de la clase del año X.*

1. Antes escribía para *El tiempo,* pero ya no.
2. Antes iba de vacaciones a Málaga, pero ya no.
3. Antes salía con Lola, pero ya no.
4. Antes me gustaba la cocina tailandesa, pero ya no.
5. Antes cuidaba a mi prima, pero ya no.
6. Antes jugaba en un equipo de fútbol, pero ya no.
7. Antes veníamos al pueblo en invierno, pero ya no.
8. Antes almorzaba con mis padres los sábados, pero ya no.
9. Antes era socio del Club Atlántico, pero ya no.
10. Antes mis hijos tocaban la trompeta, pero ya no.
11. Antes le mandaba bombones a Elena, pero ya no.
12. Antes prefería vivir en el centro, pero ya no.
13. Antes veía a los profesores, pero ya no.
14. Antes me despertaba a las cinco de la mañana, pero ya no.

C. *Un vuelo.*

1. La señorita Fajardo era gerente de fábrica. Iba a Miami.
2. Unos señores italianos eran dueños de una pastelería. Iban a Uruguay.
3. Un señor era profesor de economía. Iba a Irlanda.
4. La señora Montoya era banquera. Iba a Suiza.
5. Don Pedro Domínguez era candidato a senador. Iba a Monterrey.
6. Lorena Iglesias era ama de casa. Iba a Costa Rica.
7. Los hermanos Machado eran músicos. Iban a Nueva York.
8. El señor Rubio era cirujano. Iba a la India.

D. *¿Qué tal se veía?*

1. Carolina y Ramón no veían el mar Caribe desde el avión.
2. Nosotros no veíamos la cara de los actores desde el paraíso del teatro.
3. Doña Federica no veía el embotellamiento desde la ventana del dormitorio.
4. Uds. no veían toda la cancha de fútbol desde la tribuna del estadio.
5. Yo no veía la cumbre de la montaña desde el valle.
6. Daniel no veía la discoteca desde la esquina.
7. Tú no veías al público desde la parte derecha de la escena.

E. *¿Qué tiempo hacía … ?*

1. Llovía cuando Beatriz y tú volvieron.
2. Hacía frío cuando los Sorolla se levantaron.
3. Estaba despejado cuando fuiste a la biblioteca.
4. Hacía viento cuando José Antonio vino a la casa.
5. Nevaba cuando nosotros terminamos el trabajo.
6. Tronaba cuando Ud. entró en el cine.
7. Hacía sol cuando yo llegué a la universidad.

F. *¿Qué hora era cuando … ?*

1. Eran las nueve y media cuando Consuelo y Berta se despidieron.
2. Era la una cuando el programa comenzó.
3. Era mediodía cuando Rosa sirvió el almuerzo.
4. Eran las diez en punto cuando el empleado abrió la taquilla.
5. Era medianoche cuando regresamos de la estación.
6. Era muy tarde cuando Uds. se durmieron.
7. Era temprano cuando el cartero trajo la correspondencia.
8. Eran las cinco y cuarto cuando los pintores dejaron de pintar la sala.

G. *Mientras estábamos de vacaciones …*

1. Mientras tú viajabas, acabó la telenovela.
2. Mientras Marta y Miguel se quedaban en un hotel, un ladrón forzó la entrada.
3. Mientras Eunice vivía en el extranjero, sus padres vendieron su casa de campo.
4. Mientras Uds. hacían un viaje, sus vecinos montaron una nueva empresa.
5. Mientras yo veía las siete maravillas del mundo, se añadieron otras siete a la lista.
6. Mientras Benito se paseaba por San Antonio, su novia rompió con él.
7. Mientras el avión de Diego aterrizaba en Los Ángeles, el de su hermana despegó en Atlanta.
8. Mientras los turistas conocían los Estados Unidos, la guerra estalló en su país.
9. Mientras nosotros estábamos en el puerto, hubo un incendio en el barco.

H. *Me sorprende.*

1. Me sorprende. Antes corría quince millas al día.
2. Me sorprende. Antes dormían la siesta.
3. Me sorprende. Antes iba al centro.
4. Me sorprende. Antes visitaba los museos.
5. Me sorprende. Antes ensayaba con la orquesta.
6. Me sorprende. Antes veían la telenovela.
7. Me sorprende. Antes iban al cine.
8. Me sorprende. Antes conducía su coche.

I. *Y al mismo tiempo …*

Answers will vary.

J. Perspectivas.

A.
1. tenía
2. llevaron
3. sentó
4. dio
5. leíamos
6. se apagaron
7. subió
8. vimos
9. Había
10. hacía
11. estaba
12. llevaba
13. vestía
14. hacía
15. salió
16. se puso
17. quedé
18. me hice

B.
1. me gradué
2. Saqué
3. Esperaba
4. nací
5. Quería
6. había
7. mandé
8. Tuve
9. Encontré
10. se publicaba
11. fue
12. conocía
13. vivía
14. estaba
15. Hacía
16. conocí
17. trabajaba
18. era
19. fue
20. nos casamos
21. llegué
22. tuvimos
23. vivimos

K. Contrastes.

1. Bárbara creía que Tomás conocía a su hermana Luz. En realidad, él conoció a Luz anoche en la cena.
2. Los hombres de negocios querían hablar de los asuntos pero sus abogados no quisieron.
3. La novia no tenía regalos. Entonces tuvo veinte regalos esta mañana.
4. No sabíamos quién tenía los documentos. Lo supimos ayer.
5. Yo no podía armar el juguete. Javier no pudo armarlo tampoco.

L. ¡Castillos de España!

1. quería
2. íbamos
3. dije
4. interesaba
5. gustó
6. conocía
7. compró
8. hizo
9. pensábamos
10. tomamos
11. llegamos
12. visitamos
13. conocimos
14. tuve
15. podíamos
16. era
17. estaban
18. realicé

M. Del diario de un detective.

1. Eran
2. sonó
3. estaba
4. descolgué
5. oí
6. dijo
7. robó
8. pidieron
9. explicó
10. tenía
11. quedamos
12. eran
13. llegué
14. seguía
15. llegó
16. vi
17. estaba
18. tenía
19. llevaba
20. fumaba
21. acerqué
22. senté
23. olía
24. hablé
25. pregunté
26. puso
27. dijo
28. comprendí
29. iba

N. ¿Cuánto tiempo hacía … ?

1. ¿Cuánto tiempo hacía que Montserrat Pujol cantaba ópera cuando firmó un contrato con la Metropolitana? / Hacía ocho años que cantaba ópera.
2. ¿Cuánto tiempo hacía que los señores Salazar estaban casados cuando nació su hija? / Hacía cuatro años que estaban casados.
3. ¿Cuánto tiempo hacía que vivías en París cuando tus padres se mudaron a Londres? / Hacía once meses que yo vivía en París.
4. ¿Cuánto tiempo hacía que Susana y Lía eran amigas cuando Susana le quitó el novio a Lía? / Hacía doce años que eran amigas.
5. ¿Cuánto tiempo hacía que Ud. compraba billetes de lotería cuando ganó el premio? / Hacía quince años que yo compraba billetes de lotería.
6. ¿Cuánto tiempo hacía que Patricio y Ud. tocaban el violonchelo cuando el conservatorio les dio una beca? / Hacía nueve años que tocábamos el violonchelo.

O. Cambios políticos y económicos.

1. El gobierno explotaba el petróleo desde hacía treinta años hasta que el presidente privatizó la industria.
2. La gente sufría por la inflación desde hacía cinco años hasta que los economistas intentaron controlarla.
3. La prensa no era libre desde hacía cincuenta años hasta que hubo un golpe de estado.
4. Los obreros no recibían un sueldo decente desde hacía cinco décadas hasta que se formaron los sindicatos.

5. El país no producía los bienes necesarios desde hacía varios años hasta que el país estableció el mercado libre.

6. El pueblo no tenía ninguna libertad desde hacía cuarenta y cinco años hasta que murió el dictador y se estableció la democracia.

P. *¿Qué dice Ud.?*

Answers will vary.

Q. *Un viaje a México.*

1. El primer día que Beatriz y yo pasamos en la Ciudad de México fuimos al Bosque de Chapultepec.
2. Hacía muy buen tiempo. Hacía sol y calor.
3. Había mucha gente en el parque (el bosque).
4. Unos niñitos jugaban en los resbalines y montaban en bicicleta.
5. Mientras caminábamos por el parque (el bosque) vimos el Árbol de Moctezuma y el Castillo de Chapultepec.
6. Llegamos al Museo Nacional de Antropología y entramos.
7. Caminábamos de una sala a otra y vimos la exposición de arte precolombino.
8. Pasamos dos horas en el museo.
9. Entonces fuimos a la librería donde yo compré un libro sobre los aztecas y los mayas.
10. Almorzamos (Tomamos el almuerzo) en la cafetería del museo.

R. *Una encuesta.*

Answers will vary.

S. *Estructuras en acción*

1. b
2. c
3. a

4. c
5. b

CHAPTER 6
The Future and Conditional Tenses

A. *Mis planes para el futuro.*

1. Me graduaré en junio.
2. Mis amigos y yo celebraremos con una fiesta.
3. Nuestros padres estarán muy contentos.
4. Yo haré un viaje a Europa en el verano.
5. Miguel me acompañará.

6. Nos encantará viajar.
7. Iremos a los países de la Europa oriental.
8. Andrés y Manuel querrán ir también.
9. Saldremos para Polonia a mediados de junio.
10. Pasaremos dos meses viajando.
11. Andrés volverá antes porque
12. tendrá que buscar empleo.
13. Al regresar yo empezaré a trabajar en una compañía internacional.
14. Miguel podrá trabajar en la empresa de sus padres.
15. Manuel seguirá con sus clases en la facultad de ingeniería.
16. ¡Tendremos tiempo de vernos, espero!

B. *¡Qué reacciones!*

1. Mari Carmen llorará.
2. Las tías dirán "¡ay de mí!" gimiendo.
3. Ramón tendrá vergüenza.
4. Tú te volverás loco.
5. Juan y Alicia pondrán el grito en el cielo.
6. Uds. se enfadarán.
7. Margarita se reirá a carcajadas.
8. Ud. se pondrá de buen humor.
9. Nosotros estaremos contentos.

C. *¡Qué día!*

1. ¡Mañana será un ajetreo continuo!
2. ¡Tendremos un día lleno de frenética actividad!
3. Habrá clases todo el día
4. y tomaremos exámenes también.
5. Además, yo iré al almacén.
6. Le compraré un regalo a mi hermana.
7. Sarita cumplirá diecisiete años pasado mañana.
8. Mamá hará una comida y una torta.
9. Papá y yo saldremos para comprar vino.
10. También querré ir a la biblioteca.
11. Mis amigos y yo trabajaremos hasta muy tarde.
12. ¡Trasnocharemos porque tendremos exámenes pasado mañana también!

D. *Actividad y descanso.*

1. Yolanda y Ana patinarán.
2. Tú cocinarás yacu-chupe y un sancochado.
3. Julio bailará en la discoteca toda la noche.
4. Consuelo se acostará tarde.
5. Yo pasearé al perro.
6. Uds. jugarán baloncesto.
7. Magdalena escribirá cartas.

8. Nosotros haremos una fiesta de disfraces.
9. Guillermo y Rodolfo podrán viajar al Canadá.
10. Ud. dormirá la siesta todas las tardes.

E. Todo depende.

1. Si María quiere salir, nosotros saldremos con ella.
2. Si ellos van, Ud. podrá verlos.
3. Si yo hago la comida, tú vendrás a almorzar.
4. Si Uds. trabajan mucho, tendrán éxito.
5. Si tú no sabes qué pasó, yo te diré.
6. Si nosotros no compramos harina, no habrá tortillas esta noche.
7. Si hace calor, Carlos y Pedro irán a la playa.
8. Si hace fresco, Celeste querrá ir al cine.

F. ¿Qué será?

1. Serán las seis.
2. Teodoro tendrá catorce años.
3. El reloj valdrá mucho.
4. Habrá problemas entre los socios.
5. Teresa sabrá la hora de la conferencia.
6. Esteban querrá ir a la reunión.
7. Las muchachas volverán pronto.

G. ¿Qué habrá en esa caja?

1. ¿Será verde (azul, rojo, amarillo)?
2. ¿Tendrá pilas?
3. ¿Habrá muchas partes?
4. ¿Será de madera (metal, plástico)?
5. ¿Costará (Valdrá) mucho?
6. ¿Hará un ruido?
7. ¿Será más grande que una caja para el pan?
8. ¿Todo el mundo tendrá uno? (¿Todos tendrán uno?)
9. ¿Estará vivo?
10. ¿Cabrá en la mano?

H. Y Ud., ¿qué haría?

1. a. Buscaría a la dependienta. / b. Saldría del almacén.
2. a. Repetiría. / b. Pediría la receta.
3. a. Saldríamos muy rápido. / b. Llamaríamos a los bomberos.
4. a. Se disculparía con la señora. / b. Se sentaría en su regazo.
5. a. Los acostaría sin bañarlos. / b. Llamaría al fontanero.
6. a. Harían una figura de nieve. / b. Lanzarían bolas de nieve.
7. a. Yo le diría al policía lo que pasó. / b. Yo les pondría vendas a los heridos.

I. ¡Qué bonanza!

1. Elena pagaría la matrícula en la universidad.
2. Mi primo Federico vendría a visitarnos.
3. Uds. harían un viaje a China.
4. Juan Pablo y Ana María pondrían la plata en el banco.
5. Tú no tendrías deudas.
6. Mi hermano y yo querríamos darles dinero a los huérfanos.
7. Jugaríamos a la bolsa.

J. ¿Qué dijeron?

1. gustaría	5. ocuparía
2. querría	6. haríamos
3. habría	7. pondrían
4. podríamos	8. vendríamos

K. Probabilidad en el pasado.

1. Serían las once cuando volvimos a casa.
2. Habría sesenta invitados.
3. Estarían cansados.
4. Costaría quince mil dólares.

L. Al contrario.

1. estaríamos	5. vendría
2. podría	6. pondrías
3. querría	7. habría
4. cabrían	

M. Gustos e intereses.

Answers will vary.

N. En la oficina.

Answers will vary.

O. Estructuras en acción

1. e	5. a
2. h	6. d
3. g	7. c
4. b	8. f

CHAPTER 7
Reflexive Verbs

A. ¿Reflexivo o no?

1. me despierto / despierto
2. aburría / se aburrían
3. se casaron / casó
4. esconderemos / nos esconderemos
5. te vistes / vistes

6. nos paseamos / paseamos
7. tranquilizó / se tranquilizó
8. me divertí / divirtieron
9. me mareaba / mareaba
10. animamos / se anima
11. se asustaban / asustaban
12. se ofenden / ofenden

B. *Todavía no, abuelita.*

1. ¿Uds. ya se despiertan solos? / No, abuelita. Nos despierta mamá.
2. ¿Uds. ya se lavan la cabeza solos? / No, abuelita. Nos lava la cabeza mamá. (Nos la lava mamá.)
3. ¿Uds. ya se peinan solos? / No, abuelita. Nos peina mamá.
4. ¿Uds. ya se quitan los zapatos solos? / No, abuelita. Nos quita los zapatos mamá. (Nos los quita mamá.)
5. ¿Uds. ya se preparan el desayuno solos? / No, abuelita. Nos prepara el desayuno mamá. (Nos lo prepara mamá.)
6. ¿Uds. ya se acuestan solos? / No, abuelita. Nos acuesta mamá.

C. *Una excursión al campo.*

1. Marina y yo nos pusimos los jeans.
2. Arturo se puso un traje de baño.
3. Uds. se pusieron un impermeable.
4. Yo me puse un suéter de lana.
5. Víctor y Paco se pusieron un gorro.
6. Todos nosotros nos pusimos una camiseta.

D. *¿Qué se llevará para ir al trabajo?*

1. Yo me pondré un vestido.
2. Alicia se pondrá una blusa.
3. Nosotros nos pondremos zapatos de cuero.
4. Uds. se pondrán una camisa de algodón.
5. Los jefes se pondrán un traje de lana.
6. Te pondrás una corbata.

E. *¡Ya llega el baile de gala!*

1. Pilar y Luz se prueban el traje largo.
2. Yo me pruebo el abrigo de terciopelo.
3. Lorenzo se prueba el smoking.
4. Uds. se prueban los zapatos de tacón alto.
5. Te pruebas la blusa de seda.
6. Antonio y Esteban se prueban la corbata.

F. *¡Qué malas noticias!*

1. Miguel se rompió la pierna montando a caballo.
2. Ana se quemó la mano cocinando.
3. El perro de Bernardo se perdió en las afueras.
4. Eunice se torció el tobillo patinando sobre el hielo.
5. Todos nosotros nos enfermamos comiendo hamburguesas poco cocidas.
6. Yo me hice daño cortando el césped.
7. Los hermanos de Pedro se quebraron el dedo jugando al básquetbol.

G. *Estimados televidentes …*

1. La actriz Ramona Taylor se lastimó en el rodaje de su nueva película.
2. El futbolista Diego Suárez se rompió el pie en el partido de hoy.
3. Unos turistas norteamericanos se cayeron en la escalera mecánica del metro.
4. Un carpintero se cortó la mano aserruchando madera.
5. Diez arqueólogos se hicieron daño en una excavación en las pirámides.
6. Un bombero se quemó apagando un incendio.
7. Los bailarines se divorciaron después de cuarenta años de bailar juntos.

H. *El aseo personal.*

1. Felisa se lava la cabeza todos los días.
2. Yo me visto rápidamente por la mañana.
3. Nuestros padres se duchan por la noche.
4. Carlos se afeita con una maquinilla de afeitar.
5. Laura y Teresa se liman las uñas antes de ponerse el esmalte de uñas.
6. Te peinas con cuidado.
7. Benjamín y yo nos arreglamos en el dormitorio.
8. Ud. se cepilla el pelo después de maquillarse.

I. *Hay que hacerlo.*

1. Samuel quiere colocarse en una sucursal de la empresa. / Samuel se quiere colocar …
2. Nosotros debemos desayunarnos antes de las ocho. / Nosotros nos debemos desayunar …
3. Los amigos piensan reunirse en casa de Felipe esta noche. / Los amigos se piensan reunir …

4. Teresa necesita pesarse todas las semanas. / Teresa se necesita pesar …
5. Yo voy a irme de vacaciones en julio. / Yo me voy a ir …
6. Las señoras acaban de aprovecharse de las liquidaciones. / Las señoras se acaban de aprovechar …
7. ¿Quieres sentarte en esta fila? / ¿Te quieres sentar … ?
8. Uds. tienen que secarse el pelo. / Uds. se tienen que secar …

J. *Dando consejos.*

1. Pruébese los dos. / Pruébate los dos.
2. Acuéstese temprano. / Acuéstate temprano.
3. Dése prisa. / Date prisa.
4. Póngase el impermeable. / Ponte el impermeable.
5. Diviértase mucho. / Diviértete mucho.
6. Quédese otra semana entonces. / Quédate otra semana entonces.
7. Váyase ahora mismo. / Vete ahora mismo.

K. *¡No lo haga!*

1. No se levante todavía. / No te levantes todavía.
2. No se enferme. / No te enfermes.
3. No se enfade con ella. / No te enfades con ella.
4. No se despierte tarde. / No te despiertes tarde.
5. No se duerma. / No te duermas.
6. No se haga el desentendido. / No te hagas el desentendido.
7. No se ponga gorda. / No te pongas gorda.

L. *¡Niños, hagan esto!*

1. Niños, vístanse para salir.
2. Niños, cepíllense los dientes.
3. Niños, átense los cordones.
4. Niños, pónganse serios.
5. Niños, lávense las manos.

M. *¡Niños, pórtense bien!*

1. Niños, no se ensucien la cara.
2. Niños, no se hagan los sordos.
3. Niños, no se caigan patinando.
4. Niños, no se olviden de guardar sus juguetes.
5. Niños, no se vayan del jardín.
6. Niños, no se pinten los labios.
7. Niños, no se quejen tanto.

N. *¡Haciendo diabluras!*

1. Luisito está portándose mal. / Luisito se está portando mal.
2. Los abuelos de Luisito están poniéndose rojos. / Los abuelos de Luisito se están poniendo rojos.
3. Adrianita está riéndose como una loca. / Adrianita se está riendo como una loca.
4. La tía de Adrianita está desmayándose. / La tía de Adrianita se está desmayando.
5. Fernandito está escondiéndose en un armario. / Fernandito se está escondiendo en un armario.
6. El tío de Fernandito está asustándose. / El tío de Fernandito se está asustando.
7. Los gemelos están escapándose de su padre. / Los gemelos se están escapando de su padre.
8. El padre de los gemelos está enojándose. / El padre de los gemelos se está enojando.
9. Pedrito está burlándose de sus primos. / Pedrito se está burlando de sus primos.
10. Los primos de Pedrito están exasperándose. / Los primos de Pedrito se están exasperando.
11. Mari Carmen está ensuciándose con el guacamole. / Mari Carmen se está ensuciando con el guacamole.
12. La madre de Mari Carmen está avergonzándose. / La madre de Mari Carmen se está avergonzando.

O. *Están en movimiento.*

1. Se está apresurando para salir. Está apresurándose para salir.
2. Se están mudando a otro barrio. Están mudándose a otro barrio.
3. Se están acercando a la escuela. Están acercándose a la escuela.
4. Se están paseando por el centro. Están paseándose por el centro.
5. Me estoy instalando en un nuevo apartamento. Estoy instalándome en un nuevo apartamento.
6. Nos estamos yendo al campo. Estamos yéndonos al campo.
7. Se está quedando en casa. Está quedándose en casa.
8. Se está tirando a la piscina. Está tirándose a la piscina.

P. Mi mejor amigo(a) y yo.

1. Marisol y yo nos hablamos …
2. Jorge y yo nos entendemos …
3. José María y yo nos vemos …
4. Consuelo y yo nos escribimos …
5. Felipe y yo nos ayudamos …
6. Victoria y yo nos prestamos …

Q. Un gran amor.

1. Se conocieron en una fiesta.
2. Se llamaron a menudo.
3. Se vieron todos los días.
4. Se hablaron constantemente.
5. Se compraron regalos.
6. Se dijeron muchas cosas importantes.
7. Se hicieron promesas.
8. Se llegaron a querer. (Llegaron a quererse.)

R. Travesuras en el parque.

1. se conocieron
2. Se pusieron
3. Se enojaron
4. se pegaron
5. se acercaron
6. se tranquilizaron
7. se abrazaron
8. se dieron

S. Cómo se dice to become *en español.*

1. a
2. b
3. a
4. b
5. b

T. To become y to get.

1. Ricardo se hizo (llegó a ser) millonario.
2. Los arqueólogos se entusiasmaron al ver las ruinas.
3. Magdalena se pone roja a menudo porque es muy tímida.
4. Daniel se casa con Tere porque quiere llegar a ser (hacerse) ciudadano americano.
5. ¡Carlitos se ha vuelto imposible!
6. ¡Felisa está poniéndose muy gorda por la torta y helado que come todos los días!
7. El valle se convirtió en un importante centro de tecnología.

U. Preposiciones con verbos reflexivos.

1. con
2. en
3. de
4. de
5. en
6. a
7. de
8. a
9. de
10. de
11. con
12. a

V. En otras palabras.

1. Si no recuerdo mal, …
2. Ud. se equivoca.
3. Dos personas se quedaron ciegas …
4. La niña se hace la dormida.
5. Juan Carlos se ha enflaquecido.
6. Creíamos que íbamos a enloquecernos …
7. Todos los habitantes están poniéndose furiosos …
8. Diego se palidecía …

W. Ejercicio oral.

Answers will vary.

X. Estructuras en acción

1. b
2. a
3. b
4. a
5. b
6. a
7. b

CHAPTER 8
Passive Constructions

A. En la oficina.

1. El número de teléfono fue encontrado por la recepcionista.
2. Los formularios serán llenados por los empleados.
3. El folleto ha sido preparado por el bibliotecario.
4. Los cheques son cobrados por la cajera.
5. Las cartas y las tarjetas postales serán escritas por las secretarias.
6. Los documentos fueron traducidos por los agentes de viajes.
7. La pantalla de la computadora fue reparada por el programador.
8. Los recados han sido puestos en los escritorios por los mensajeros.

B. Día de mudanza.

1. Las camas fueron subidas a los dormitorios por tres hombres.
2. La alfombra de la sala fue corrida por la señora Pidal.
3. Los cuadros fueron colgados en las paredes por Benito y Ramona.
4. La secadora fue bajada al sótano por un cargador.

5. El sillón azul fue colocado al lado de la ventana por el señor Pidal.
6. Las lámparas fueron puestas en las mesas por la abuela.

C. *¡Se están instalando todavía!*

1. Se enchufará la nevera.
2. Se encenderán las lámparas.
3. Se guardarán las cajas.
4. Se pondrá el sofá en la sala.
5. Se colocará el lavaplatos en la cocina.
6. Se meterán las sábanas en el armario.
7. Se pondrán las sillas con la mesa del comedor.

D. *Titulares y anuncios del periódico.*

1. Se buscan programadores de computadoras.
2. Se prohíbe el fumar en los restaurantes.
3. Se calculaban los impuestos.
4. Se alquiló el apartamento en la playa.
5. Se entrega comida a la casa hasta la una de la mañana.
6. Se paga con cheque o tarjeta de crédito.
7. Se solicitarán gerentes.
8. Se necesitan secretarios bilingües.

E. *Una excursión al zoológico.*

1. Mis amigos y yo vamos de excursión al zoológico.
2. Para llegar al zoológico, tomamos el autobús en la calle Azorín.
3. Yo veo leones, tigres, leopardos y panteras.
4. Los guardianes dan de comer a los animales.
5. Unos trabajadores entran en las jaulas para limpiarlas.
6. Las jirafas comen las hojas de los árboles.
7. Tú tiras cacahuates a los elefantes.
8. Un mono juega tirando plátanos.
9. Los loros gritan en voz alta.
10. Los hipopótamos se bañan en la piscina de la jaula.
11. Una guardiana le cura la pata a un jaguar.
12. Pilar y Arturo compran palomitas y refrescos.

F. *Todo estaba hecho.*

1. No sé. Cuando yo llegué, el cuarto ya estaba arreglado.
2. No sé. Cuando yo llegué, el almuerzo ya estaba preparado.
3. No sé. Cuando yo llegué, la puerta ya estaba cerrada.

4. No sé. Cuando yo llegué, el microondas ya estaba apagado.
5. No sé. Cuando yo llegué, la mesa ya estaba puesta.
6. No sé. Cuando yo llegué, los vasos ya estaban lavados.
7. No sé. Cuando yo llegué, el mantel ya estaba planchado.
8. No sé. Cuando yo llegué, las luces ya estaban prendidas.

G. *¿Qué significa?*

1. Se venden periódicos y revistas aquí.
2. Se estaciona aquí.
3. Se come bien.
4. Se dobla a la derecha.
5. Se entra por aquí.
6. Aquí se habla francés.
7. Se cobran cheques de viajero.
8. Se abre el almacén a las diez.

H. *¿Qué dice Ud.?*

Answers will vary. Suggested responses:
1. Se toman física, historia y matemáticas.
2. Se almuerza a la una. (Se toma el almuerzo a la una.)
3. Se llega andando o en autobús.
4. Se compran los libros de texto en la librería Academia.
5. Se sacan buenas notas estudiando mucho.
6. Se va a un concierto o al cine.
7. Se come en el Café Miraflores o en el restaurante Cuatro Caminos.
8. Se juegan fútbol, tenis y béisbol.

I. *Adivinanza.*

Answers will vary.

J. *Estructuras en acción*

1. (mayores informes) se ofrecen—*more information is offered, is available*
2. (un curso) será ofrecido por el profesor—*a course will be given by the professor*
3. (seminarios) se ofrecerán—*seminars will be given*
4. Se indicó que ...—*It was said, indicated that ...*
5. (cursos) son coordinados por el Centro—*courses are coordinated by the Center*
6. (inscripciones) se reciben—*registrations are received, taken*

CHAPTER 9
The Perfect Tenses

A. *¿Listos para viajar?*

1. Pedro ha apagado las luces.
2. Cecilia y Pilar han hecho las maletas.
3. Papá ha llenado el tanque del coche.
4. Berta ha desenchufado los aparatos eléctricos.
5. David y Juan Carlos han metido el equipaje en el baúl.
6. Yo les he dicho a los vecinos que nos vamos.
7. Mamá ha puesto las pilas en la linterna.
8. Paco y yo hemos comprado los cheques de viajero.
9. Tú has limpiado las ventanillas del coche.

B. *Una receta de cocina.*

1. Hemos leído la receta.
2. Jorge ha encendido el fuego.
3. Yo he hecho la mayonesa.
4. Alicia y Juan Diego han picado las pimientas picantes.
5. Ud. ha frito (freído) las cebollas.
6. Estrella y yo hemos cortado la salchicha.
7. Tú has lavado los espárragos y los aguacates.
8. Marianela ha añadido la sal.
9. Uds. han puesto el pollo al horno.
10. Yo he mezclado la ensalada de camarones.
11. Martín ha cubierto la cacerola.
12. Lupe y Julio han quemado las sartenes.

C.

1. La hemos leído.
2. Jorge lo ha encendido.
3. Yo la he hecho.
4. Alicia y Juan Diego las han picado.
5. Ud. las ha frito (freído).
6. Estrella y yo la hemos cortado.
7. Tú los has lavado.
8. Marianela la ha añadido.
9. Uds. lo han puesto al horno.
10. Yo la he mezclado.
11. Martín la ha cubierto.
12. Lupe y Julio las han quemado.

D. *¡Nos aburrimos como una ostra!*

1. María Dolores se ha dormido.
2. Ud. ha bostezado.
3. Yo me he puesto el abrigo.
4. Carlos y Beatriz se han despedido de la anfitriona.

5. ¡Nos han matado de aburrimiento!
6. Tú te has quejado que la comida te cayó mal.
7. Ud. y Clara han dado excusas.
8. Ramón ha dicho que se enferma.

E. *Preguntas personales.*

Answers will vary. Suggested responses:
1. He tomado historia europea, literatura inglesa, cálculo, español y química.
2. He sacado una A en historia europea y cálculo, A menos en español y química y B más en literatura inglesa.
3. Me he hecho socio del club de ajedrez.
4. Hemos viajado a España, Francia, Chile, la Argentina, Israel y Taiwán.
5. Hemos hecho planes para ir a la playa.
6. He decidido que voy a estudiar biología.
7. He visto _____. Me ha gustado más _____.
8. He celebrado mi último cumpleaños con una fiesta.
9. He recibido _____. Mis padres me han dado _____.
10. Hemos tomado dos exámenes y hemos jugado fútbol.

F. *¡Hecho consumado!*

1. Cristóbal se ha matriculado ya.
2. Nos hemos apoderado de la finca ya.
3. Yo me he instalado en la nueva casa ya.
4. Irene y Jaime se han comprometido ya.
5. Nora se ha enterado de los líos de la familia ya.
6. Yo me he apuntado en la lista de voluntarios ya.
7. Los Roldán se han ausentado de la ciudad ya.

G. *No, fue antes.*

1. No, habíamos ido a ver la exposición hace unos meses. (habíamos ido a verla)
2. No, Amelia se había cortado el pelo el sábado. (se lo había cortado)
3. No, Ricardo y Leonor se habían casado dos meses antes.
4. No, yo había hecho el asado el primero de julio. (lo había hecho)
5. No, Pepita había celebrado su santo hace un mes. (lo había celebrado)
6. No, yo había cambiado de idea hace mucho tiempo.
7. No, habíamos puesto los papeles en orden el año pasado. (los habíamos puesto)

8. No, Javier me había devuelto los libros la semana pasada. (me los había devuelto)
9. No, habíamos (habían) escrito los informes en noviembre. (los habíamos escrito / los habían escrito)
10. No, me había roto el codo hace casi un año. (me lo había roto)

H. *Tomás, el holgazán.*

1. Cuando Tomás llegó por fin, Raúl ya había barrido el piso.
2. … , Uds. ya habían puesto la mesa.
3. … , Diana y Judit ya habían recogido las manzanas.
4. … , Ud. ya había sacado la basura.
5. … , yo ya había subido las cajas a la buhardilla.
6. … , tú ya habías ido de compras.
7. … , Plácido y yo ya habíamos pasado la aspiradora.

I. *Ya habíamos hecho muchas cosas.*

1. Cuando Julia vino a buscarnos, nosotros ya habíamos hecho ejercicio.
2. Cuando yo fui a su casa, Virginia ya había dado una vuelta.
3. Cuando Ud. se levantó, sus padres ya se habían desayunado.
4. Cuando volvimos a casa, Juanita ya había escrito su composición.
5. Cuando los bomberos llegaron, Uds. ya habían apagado el incendio en la cocina.
6. Cuando los bisnietos lograron ver a su bisabuelo, el bisabuelo ya se había enfermado.

J. *Nunca habíamos visto …*

1. Laura no había visto una corrida de toros en Madrid.
2. Rodolfo y Eva no habían dado una vuelta en las carreteras gallegas.
3. Yo no había hecho una excursión a El Escorial.
4. Tú y Susana no se habían paseado por el Barrio de Santa Cruz.
5. Mamá, papá y yo no habíamos subido al monte Tibidabo.
6. Jaime no había conocido la Alhambra.
7. Tú no habías pasado Semana Santa en Sevilla.

K. *¿Qué habrá ocurrido?*

1. Elena se habrá graduado para el año próximo.
2. Alfredo y Armando se habrán mejorado antes de regresar al colegio.
3. Nosotros habremos ahorrado dinero antes de las vacaciones de invierno.
4. Yo te habré dado tu regalo antes de tu fiesta de cumpleaños.
5. Ud. y Laura se habrán mudado para mediados del mes.
6. Tú habrás sacado un pasaporte para julio.

L. *Conjeturas.*

1. Su coche le habrá costado un ojo de la cara.
2. Clara habrá escrito la carta.
3. Felipe y Eduardo habrán ganado la regata.
4. Uds. habrán tomado la merienda.
5. Martín y yo no habremos entendido el motivo.
6. Ud. no habrá hecho cola por mucho tiempo.

M. *No lo habríamos hecho.*

1. Patricia y yo no habríamos salido.
2. Sofía no habría roto su compromiso con su novio.
3. Los turistas venezolanos no habrían hecho el viaje a California en autobús. (no lo habrían hecho en autobús)
4. Tú no te habrías cortado el pelo en la peluquería Melenas. (no te lo habrías cortado)
5. Ud. no lo habría creído.
6. Yo no me habría reído.

N. *¡Felicidades!*

1. A Lope Cernuda por haber dirigido "Plátanos y cerezas".
2. A Ernesto del Olmo por haber compuesto la música de "Mosquitos mágicos".
3. A Ela Pantoja y Roberto Campillo por haber escrito el guión de "Agua hervida".
4. A Agustín Domingo por haber cantado en "Después de haber bailado".
5. A Beatriz Perales por haber sido primera actriz en "Salchichas al sol".
6. A Mateo de León y Diana Duque por haber producido "Grapadora en la mesa".
7. A Silvia Siles por haber hecho la escenografía de "Narices al aire".
8. A Memo Morado por haber actuado en "Langostas en el cielo".

9. A Edit Revueltas por haber diseñado el vestuario de "Tijeras de poliéster".
10. A Pepe del Oeste por haberles maquillado a los actores de "Tamales quemados".

O. *Allá en el rancho grande.*

1. El rancho (La estancia) habría sido muy grande.
2. Los granjeros habrían tenido gallinas en un gallinero.
3. Los campesinos habrían recogido cerezas y fresas.
4. El paisaje del campo habría sido hermoso.
5. Mi bisabuelo habría ido de pesca en el lago que quedaba cerca.
6. Mi bisabuela habría cocinado frutas y verduras frescas de la cosecha.
7. Habría habido caballos y vacas en el rancho (la estancia).
8. Los granjeros habrían sembrado semillas en el huerto.
9. Nos habría encantado la vida del rancho.

P. *Diálogos.*

Answers will vary.

Q. *Estructuras en acción*

1. b	5. a
2. c	6. c
3. b	7. b
4. a	8. c

CHAPTER 10
The Gerund and the Progressive Tenses

A. *¡La vecina entremetida!*

1. Sí, yo pasé el día llamando por teléfono.
2. Sí, Carlos y Celeste pasaron el día estudiando en la biblioteca.
3. Sí, el señor Marqués pasó el día durmiendo.
4. Sí, mi hermano y yo pasamos el día leyendo.
5. Sí, pasé el día oyendo las noticias.
6. Sí, la señora Pelayo pasó el día bañándose.

B. *¡Cómo va volando el tiempo!*

1. Yo pasé cuarenta y cinco minutos arreglándome.
2. Estrella y yo pasamos hora y media montando en bicicleta.
3. Yo pasé dos horas escribiendo un informe.

4. Fernando, Chelo y yo pasamos un par de horas comprando cosas en el centro comercial.
5. Mis amigos y yo pasamos una hora y cuarto vistiéndonos.
6. Yo pasé una hora viendo un documental.

C. *En el campamento de verano.*

1. Los niños están acampando en la sierra.
2. Ricardo está nadando en el lago.
3. Lupe y yo estamos llenando la mochila.
4. Ester está desenvolviendo el saco de dormir.
5. Ud. y Andrés están atrapando mariposas para su colección.
6. Pablo está acostándose (se está acostando) en el saco de dormir.
7. Yo estoy observando las hormigas en el hormiguero.
8. Tú estás encendiendo el fuego para asar los perros calientes.
9. Pepe y Lucía están metiendo las pilas en la linterna.
10. Todos nosotros estamos quejándonos (nos estamos quejando) de las picaduras de los mosquitos.
11. Ud. está asustándose (se está asustando) al ver las arañas en la tienda de campaña.
12. Consuelo está gritando al ver una serpiente.

D.

1. Estábamos leyéndolos. / Los estábamos leyendo.
2. Uds. estarán haciéndolas. / Las estarán haciendo.
3. Estoy poniéndomelo. / Me lo estoy poniendo.
4. Ud. estaba lavándosela. / Ud. se la estaba lavando.
5. Estarás diciéndonoslos. / Nos los estarás diciendo.
6. Rita está vistiéndose en el dormitorio. / Rita se está vistiendo en el dormitorio.

E. *¡Cuando estalló el fuego ... !*

1. Los señores Sotomayor estaban registrándose. / Los señores Sotomayor se estaban registrando.
2. La señorita Serrano estaba pidiendo un juego de toallas.
3. El botones estaba subiéndoles el equipaje a unos huéspedes. / El botones les estaba subiendo el equipaje a unos huéspedes.

4. Las camareras estaban arreglando los cuartos.
5. Los mozos estaban sirviéndoles la cena a los clientes. / Los mozos les estaban sirviendo la cena a los clientes.
6. El gerente estaba prendiendo el aire acondicionado.
7. El doctor López estaba afeitándose. / El doctor López se estaba afeitando.
8. La lavandera estaba devolviéndole el lavado a la señora Casona. / La lavandera le estaba devolviendo el lavado a la señora Casona.
9. Los huéspedes del noveno piso bajaban en el ascensor.
10. Los turistas ingleses tocaban el timbre en la recepción.
11. ¡Los cocineros estaban jactándose de los plátanos flameados que habían preparado! / ¡Los cocineros se estaban jactando de los plátanos flameados que habían preparado!

F. *¡Qué va! Siguen haciéndolo.*

1. ¡Qué va! Elena sigue diciéndolos.
2. ¡Qué va! Siguen construyéndola.
3. ¡Qué va! Yo sigo leyéndola.
4. ¡Qué va! Mis padres siguen durmiéndola.
5. ¡Qué va! Yo sigo asistiendo a los conciertos de jazz.
6. ¡Qué va! Seguimos jugándolo en el estadio.

G. *¡Nosotros, los trasnochadores!*

1. Luisa estará viendo televisión a las dos y media.
2. Ud. estará duchándose a medianoche. (Ud. se estará duchando a medianoche.)
3. Mis amigos y yo estaremos muriéndonos de sueño a las cuatro. (Mis amigos y yo nos estaremos muriendo de sueño a las cuatro.)
4. Pablo y Ramón estarán jugando al ajedrez a las doce y media.
5. Yo estaré oyendo música a la una y media.
6. Tú estarás comiéndote unos bocadillos a las tres. (Tú te estarás comiendo unos bocadillos a las tres.)

H. *Una entrevista.*

1. Llevo doce años pintando retratos.
2. Llevo unos meses usando estos pinceles.
3. Llevo varios años dibujando con modelos.
4. Llevo toda la vida dedicándome a la pintura.
5. Llevo un año colgando mis cuadros de paisajes en la galería Olmo.

6. Llevo poco tiempo interesándome en los murales.
7. Llevo nueve años trabajando en cerámica.
8. Llevo cinco años viviendo en París.

I. *Un partido de fútbol.*

1. están animando	6. está regateando
2. está robando	7. están pidiéndoles
3. estamos viendo	8. están entusiasmándose
4. está marcando	9. están oyendo
5. están saliendo	10. está atrayendo

J.

1. ¡Estamos divirtiéndonos mucho! (Nos estamos divirtiendo mucho.)
2. Ud. estuvo corriendo (trotando) hasta que empezó a llover.
3. Siguen sirviendo la cena en el Hotel Palacio.
4. Voy conociendo Madrid.
5. Mateo y Victoria estarán jugando tenis toda la tarde.
6. Pedro y yo seguimos leyendo.

K. *¿Qué están haciendo?*

Answers will vary.

L. *Estructuras en acción*

1. b
2. c
3. a
4. b
5. a
6. c
7. (a) estudiando (b) aprendiendo
8. (a) perdiendo (b) hablando (c) eligiendo (d) pudiendo (e) comunicándose (f) consiguiendo (g) reservando (h) llamándonos (i) viniendo

CHAPTER 11
The Subjunctive in Noun Clauses: Present and Present Perfect Subjunctive

A. *¡Pero yo sí quiero!*

1. Pero yo quiero que Marcos trabaje.
2. Pero yo quiero que consigas empleo.
3. Pero yo quiero que nos escriban.
4. Pero yo quiero que siga nuestros consejos.
5. Pero yo quiero que comamos fuera hoy.
6. Pero yo quiero que tú vuelvas temprano.
7. Pero yo quiero que duerman por la tarde.

8. Pero yo quiero que pidamos taxi.
9. Pero yo quiero que abran la tienda hoy.
10. Pero yo quiero que entienda.
11. Pero yo quiero que piense en nosotros.
12. Pero yo quiero que la oficina envíe el paquete.
13. Pero yo quiero que cierres las ventanas.
14. Pero yo quiero que nos divirtamos.
15. Pero yo quiero que repitamos el vocabulario.

B. *Le parece muy bien.*

1. Sí. Se alegra de que conozca a Pedro.
2. Sí. Se alegra de que tengamos un día libre.
3. Sí. Se alegra de que Alfredo le traiga flores.
4. Sí. Se alegra de que no veas más películas de terror.
5. Sí. Se alegra de que los Ibáñez construyan una casa.
6. Sí. Se alegra de que Marcos y Julia salgan juntos.
7. Sí. Se alegra de que nosotros oigamos mucha música clásica.
8. Sí. Se alegra de que su hermanito obedezca a su profesor.
9. Sí. Se alegra de que Raquel componga música.
10. Sí. Se alegra de que la fiesta sea mañana.
11. Sí. Se alegra de que haya reunión la semana que viene.
12. Sí. Se alegra de que sus primos vayan a España.

C. *Ortografía.*

1. realices	9. entregues
2. se acerquen	10. consiga
3. comience	11. organicen
4. dirija	12. almuerce
5. saquen	13. convenza
6. recojamos	14. apaguemos
7. se dedique	15. venzan
8. explique	

D. *¿Indicativo o subjuntivo?*

1. digamos	9. tiene
2. aprenden	10. podemos
3. se gradúe	11. sea
4. comiencen	12. haya
5. te quejas	13. están
6. me matricule	14. hagas
7. vayan	15. sé
8. sale	16. consigue

E. *¡Viva México!*

1. Laura espera perfeccionar su español.
2. Ricardo y Beti prefieren visitar la catedral del Zócalo.
3. Ud. debe conocer Taxco.
4. Pablo y yo deseamos ir a Puebla.
5. Tú prefieres hacer una excursión a la Ciudad Universitaria.
6. Yo siento no poder quedarme más tiempo en el Bosque de Chapultepec.
7. Uds. insisten en escaparse un par de días a Mérida.
8. Todos nosotros nos alegramos de estar en Oaxaca.

F. *¡Con la palomilla en México!*

1. Laura espera que nosotros perfeccionemos nuestro español.
2. Ricardo y Beti prefieren que Ud. visite la catedral del Zócalo.
3. Ud. necesita que Leo conozca Taxco.
4. Pablo y yo deseamos que Uds. vayan a Puebla.
5. A ti te gusta que yo haga una excursión a la Ciudad Universitaria.
6. Yo siento que nosotros no podamos quedarnos más tiempo en el Bosque de Chapultepec.
7. Uds. insisten en que los cuates se escapen un par de días a Mérida.
8. Todos nosotros nos alegramos de que tú estés en Oaxaca.

G. *Una familia unida.*

1. Elena espera que sus cuñados tengan éxito.
2. El señor Ayala les pide a sus suegros que vengan a verlos los domingos.
3. La madrina se alegra que su ahijado saque buenas notas en el colegio.
4. Los padres quieren que sus hijos se ganen la vida.
5. A la señora Ayala le gusta que los bisabuelos sean felices en la tercera edad.
6. Yo le aconsejo a la nieta que se haga arquitecta.
7. Terencio les prohíbe a las ahijadas que vayan solas al extranjero.
8. Tú sientes que el cuñado no esté contento con el nuevo empleo.
9. La suegra prefiere que los novios se muden con ella.
10. Uds. les ruegan a los padrinos que acepten su regalo.

11. Ricardo y yo necesitamos que los nietos nos den muchos besos y abrazos.
12. Los hijos no dejan que sus padres trabajen demasiado manteniéndolos.

H. *Una carta.*

1. te encuentres
2. estamos
3. puedas
4. voy
5. llegues
6. pasen
7. compren
8. traigan
9. hace
10. está
11. llueve
12. debes
13. sé
14. vas
15. vas
16. hay
17. se despierten
18. puedo
19. tengo
20. escribas
21. viene

I. *¡Qué desorden! ¡Y viene mamá!*

1. Es malo que las mamás vean el desorden.
2. Es necesario que hagamos la limpieza del apartamento.
3. Es importante que Lupe friegue las cacerolas.
4. Es útil que Juan y Antonio barran los pisos.
5. Es probable que Uds. enceren los pisos.
6. Más vale que las mamás traigan trapos y productos para la limpieza.
7. Es dudoso que los papás no se metan en todo esto.
8. Es preciso que yo sacuda el polvo.
9. Ojalá que Leonor guarde los libros en las estanterías.
10. Es posible que Mario y Griselda laven los cristales de las ventanas.
11. Es mejor que tú quites las telarañas del techo.
12. ¡Qué lástima que no nos relajemos en todo el día!

J. *Reacciones.*

1. No estoy seguro que Lorenzo siga enfermo.
2. Es obvio que Teresa y Jesús se quieren mucho.
3. No es cierto que Uds. tengan problemas con el coche.
4. Es que Julia llega el sábado.
5. No es seguro que Alejandro sea de origen ruso.
6. No es evidente que los niños estén aburridos.
7. No es que Carmen lo sepa todo.
8. Es cierto que Martín renuncia a su puesto.

K. *Pereza del fin de año.*

1. Oye, Anita, insisto en que estudies para los exámenes finales.
2. Oye, Miguel, me sorprende que no trabajes en la librería.
3. Oye, Rebeca, más vale que escribas el informe para sociología.
4. Oye, Tomás, es útil que practiques ruso en el laboratorio de lenguas.
5. Oye, Graciela, es importante que tomes apuntes en historia.
6. Oye, Alfredo, te ruego que hagas la tarea.
7. Oye, Carolina, espero que saques buenas notas.
8. Oye, Joaquín, te prohíbo que juegues al béisbol todo el día.

L. *En un coloquio.*

1. Es bueno que haya tantos adelantos tecnológicos.
2. Preferimos usar la energía nuclear aún más.
3. Todo el mundo se alegra (está contento) de tener la computadora.
4. Es una lástima que las guerras sigan estallando.
5. Sentimos que las ciudades tengan tanto crimen.
6. Tengo miedo que las enfermedades nuevas estén matando a muchas personas.
7. Es probable que la contaminación del ambiente no haga tanto daño.
8. Es obvio que la economía del mercado libre es la mejor.
9. Es necesario controlar la inflación y el desempleo.
10. Les aconsejamos a los líderes políticos que gasten el dinero con más responsabilidad.
11. Ojalá que haya elecciones libres en todos los países.
12. Nadie duda que el siglo veintiuno va a traer muchos cambios.

M.

1. Clara siente que Uds. no hayan visto la exposición de arte.
2. Dudamos que Patricia haya escrito las cartas.
3. Me alegro que Carlos se haya hecho ciudadano.
4. Esperan que hayas visto la nueva película policíaca.
5. Es una lástima que haya muerto el bisabuelo de Paco.

6. Es mejor que las chicas no hayan dicho nada.
7. Nos sorprende que haya habido un incendio en el metro.
8. No piensan que Luz se haya puesto brava.
9. Se alegran que me haya encantado el concierto.

N.

1. Me alegro que Julia y Paco se hayan casado.
2. Es bueno que una librería se haya abierto en este barrio.
3. Ellos dudan que los Tigres hayan ganado el campeonato de fútbol.
4. Esperamos que Fernando se haya hecho rico.
5. ¿Está Ud. sorprendido que la familia Núñez se haya mudado?
6. Ana no piensa que los chicos hayan roto la ventana.

CHAPTER 12
The Imperfect Subjunctive and Past Perfect Subjunctive; Conditional Sentences

A.

1. se diera / se diese
2. encontrara / encontrase
3. se pusieran / se pusiesen
4. supiéramos / supiésemos
5. hubiera / hubiese
6. siguieras / siguieses
7. durmiera / durmiese
8. viera / viese
9. se reunieran / se reuniesen
10. oyéramos / oyésemos
11. dijera / dijese
12. fueran / fuesen
13. construyeran / construyesen
14. trajeras / trajeses
15. se fuera / se fuese

B. *Un caso de celos.*

1. Felipe les sugirió que fueran a una discoteca.
2. Felipe esperaba que Angélica bailara con él toda la tarde.
3. Teodoro también deseaba que Angélica pasara la tarde con él.
4. Angélica temía que los chicos tuvieran celos.
5. Era posible que Felipe y Teodoro se pelearan por Angélica.

6. Felipe no creía que fuera una buena idea ir a la discoteca.
7. Felipe le propuso a Angélica que vieran una película.
8. A Angélica le agradaba que Felipe y Teodoro la quisieran, ¡pero ella estaba enamorada de Julio!

C. *Expectativas.*

1. hubiera	5. cayera
2. fuera	6. aprobaran
3. pudiera	7. quisiera
4. se llevara	

D. *¿Qué tal le fue a Timoteo?*

1. fueran	5. jugara
2. colgaran	6. trataran
3. saliera	7. condujera
4. acompañara	

E. *Vida de familia.*

1. me hiciera	6. fuéramos
2. siguiéramos	7. nos dedicáramos
3. tuviéramos	8. nos ayudáramos
4. trabajara	9. vivieran
5. nos casáramos	

F. *¡Me sobra tiempo!*

1. cortaras	6. pusieras
2. descongelaras	7. guardaras
3. regaras	8. sacaras
4. hicieras	9. repararas
5. bañaras	

G. *¡Josefina la muy pesada!*

1. saliera	6. invitaran
2. mintiera	7. tomara
3. rompiera	8. fueran
4. tuviera	9. metiera
5. hiciera	

H. *¡Ojalá!*

1. Ojalá que yo encontrara las llaves del coche.
2. Ojalá que Uds. recibieran el cheque.
3. Ojalá que Diana no se quejara de todo.
4. Ojalá que se sirviera la cena antes de las diez de la noche.
5. Ojalá que Bernardo y Marta no discutieran tanto.
6. Ojalá que Lorenzo se vistiera más rápido.

7. Ojalá que tú y yo nos ocupáramos del congreso.
8. Ojalá que Timoteo mantuviera a sus padres.

I.

1. Era bueno que Jorge hubiera llegado a ser arquitecto.
2. Nos gustó que las hermanas Cela hubieran hecho un viaje a Santo Domingo.
3. Me extrañó que Uds. se hubieran quedado tanto tiempo.
4. Esperaban que tú hubieras comprado una pulsera de oro.
5. Era importante que yo hubiera asistido a la conferencia en Roma.
6. Todos se alegraron que Juan y yo nos hubiéramos comprometido.

J.

1. Tú esperabas que ellos hubieran tenido éxito.
2. Ellos temían que alguien me hubiera dicho.
3. Sentíamos que Ud. no hubiera oído lo que pasó.
4. Sarita dudaba que hubiéramos vuelto del campo.
5. Me alegraba que hubiera hecho calor y sol.
6. Ojalá que Uds. nos hubieran dicho lo antes posible.

K. *Todo está pendiente.*

1. puedo / visitaré
2. ofrecen / aceptará
3. saldremos / tenemos
4. llama / diré
5. pones / harán
6. Habrá / hace
7. tendrás / comes
8. preguntan / sabrán
9. vendremos / hay

L. *Si fuera posible ...*

1. tuviera / haría
2. vendrían / invitáramos
3. vería / hubiera
4. ganara / se compraría
5. hiciera / saldríamos
6. dormiría / se sintiera
7. pudieras / resolverías
8. saldrían / fuera
9. supieran / dirían

M. *Cuentos de hadas.*

1. encontrara / me casaría
2. besara / dejaría / me convertiría
3. hubiera / notaría
4. vinieran / comería
5. mintiera / crecería
6. diera / se despertaría
7. tuviera / tendría
8. soplara / derrumbaría

N. *¡Viajes soñados!*

1. fuera / gustaría
2. hicieran / irían
3. pudieran / se quedarían
4. pasáramos / tomaríamos
5. visitaras / probarías
6. quisiera / conocería

O. *Si hubiera sido posible ...*

1. hubieran preguntado / habríamos dicho
2. habría devuelto / hubiera visto
3. se hubiera hecho médico / habría estado
4. habríamos llamado / hubiéramos sabido
5. hubiera jugado / habría roto

P. *¿Campo o ciudad?*

1. Pablo habría / hubiera asistido al teatro si hubiera vivido en la ciudad.
2. Gregorio habría / hubiera ordeñado las vacas si hubiera nacido en una finca.
3. Pablo se habría / se hubiera puesto más nervioso si hubiera oído tanto ruido todos los días.
4. Gregorio habría / hubiera respirado aire no contaminado si hubiera vivido en el campo.
5. Pablo habría / hubiera tomado el metro y los taxis si hubiera trabajado en la ciudad.
6. Gregorio habría / hubiera aprendido a montar a caballo si hubiera viajado por el campo.
7. Pablo habría / hubiera comprado comida en el supermercado si hubiera ido de compras en la ciudad.
8. Gregorio habría / hubiera comido frutas y legumbres muy frescas si se hubiera criado en el campo.
9. Pablo habría / hubiera llevado un traje, camisa y corbata si se hubiera ganado la vida en una empresa.
10. Gregorio habría / hubiera usado un sombrero de paja si hubiera cultivado la tierra.

Q. *¡Julio el tardón!*

1. hubiera terminado / habría (hubiera) podido
2. hubiera planeado / habría (hubiera) perdido
3. hubiera hecho / habría (hubiera) bailado
4. hubiera gastado / habría (hubiera) disfrutado
5. hubiera manejado / me habría (hubiera) atrasado
6. se hubieran divertido / se habrían (hubieran) quedado
7. se hubiera acostado / habría (hubiera) tenido

R.

1. Si Victoria hubiera tenido la llave habría abierto la maleta.
2. Si Ud. hiciera un viaje este verano, ¿adónde iría?
3. Si ellos hubieran tenido más cuidado, no se les habrían perdido sus cheques de viajero.
4. Si Uds. doblan a la derecha en la esquina, verán el museo.
5. Yo le haría caso a Roberto si diera buenos consejos.

S.

Answers will vary.

T. *Estructuras en acción*

1e. Yo les digo a mis hijos que no se preocupen porque otros saquen un 10.
2j. Le pido a mi madre que me lo pregunte ella.
3h. Me da igual que saquen sobresalientes o aprobados.
4n. Tengo miedo de que me pregunten cosas que no han entrado en el temario.
5i. Procuro entender.
6k. Lo que quiero es que trabajen.
7d. No me gusta memorizar.
8g. Es imposible que puedan aprobar.
9l. Mi madre me dice que me tranquilice.
10c. Intento comprender los temas.
11a. Les dice a nuestros hijos que no se agobien.
12b. Les exijo lo que puedan dar de sí.
13f. Hay que reñirle para que salga.
14m. La verdad es que son un poco vagos.

CHAPTER 13
The Subjunctive: Adverb and Adjective Clauses

A. *No se sabe todavía.*

1. manden
2. aconseje
3. llueva
4. haya
5. quieras
6. sea
7. prefiera
8. digamos
9. vaya

B. *Haciendo las diligencias.*

1. Elena y Mario salieron de la gasolinera antes de que nosotros entráramos en la zapatería.
2. Ud. llevó el lavado a la lavandería antes de que yo volviera a la droguería.
3. Uds. compraron los sellos antes de que Consuelo pudiera ir al correo.
4. Fernando y yo no hablamos con el mecánico antes de que él nos reparara los frenos.
5. Yo saqué la ropa de la tintorería antes de que Juana tuviera su cita en la peluquería.
6. Tú fuiste a la joyería antes de que Arturo y Paco buscaran una librería.

C.

1. sepa
2. vino
3. necesiten
4. pudiera
5. invitemos
6. entramos
7. diera
8. terminó
9. lleguen
10. tuviera
11. me duché
12. hagan

D.

1. Los llamaré cuando llegue al aeropuerto.
2. Vamos a ver el partido de fútbol hasta que empiece a llover.
3. Consuelo puso la mesa una hora antes de que llegaran sus amigos.
4. Hicieron cola en la taquilla después que almorzaron (después de almorzar).
5. Ud. no quería ir de compras sin que nosotros fuéramos también.
6. Háganlo como ellos quieran.
7. Aunque hace frío debemos dar un paseo.
8. Te presto el libro para que no tengas que sacarlo de la biblioteca.
9. Carlos va a estudiar para su examen antes de jugar tenis (antes que juegue tenis).

E. *Se busca apartamento.*

1. Quieres un apartamento que tenga dos baños.
2. Mateo necesita un apartamento donde haya aire acondicionado.
3. Javier y yo buscamos un apartamento que esté cerca de la universidad.
4. Uds. necesitan un apartamento que no cueste un ojo de la cara.
5. Yo quiero un apartamento que no necesite renovación.
6. Pepe y Leo desean un apartamento que sea moderno y fácil de limpiar.
7. Octavio busca un apartamento que dé a una calle poco transitada.
8. Ud. necesita un apartamento donde quepan todos los fiesteros.

F. *¡Mi novia ideal!*

1. sepa
2. pueda
3. comprenda
4. me divierta
5. sea
6. tenga

G. *¡No hay candidatas al puesto!*

1. reúna
2. sea
3. quieras
4. vaya
5. tenga
6. se enamore

H. *¡En la cumbre!*

1. diera
2. se esforzara
3. permitiera
4. compartiera
5. invirtiera
6. fuera
7. pudiera
8. hubiera
9. realizaran

I.

1. Mario y Carmen buscan una casa que tenga nueve cuartos.
2. ¡No hay ninguna comida que le guste!
3. Yo quería un(a) amigo(a) que fuera conmigo a los museos.
4. ¿No conoce Ud. a nadie que llegue antes de las tres?
5. Rosa preparará el plato que escojamos.
6. Necesitaban un(a) secretario(a) que trabajara los sábados.
7. Tomaremos la clase con el (la) profesor(a) que enseñe mejor.

J.

Answers will vary.

K. *Estructuras en acción*

1. Depende de las ganas que tengas de divertirte en Grecia. *It depends on how much you want to enjoy yourself in Greece.*
2. ... para que usted elija cómodamente su programación. *... so that you can choose your programming comfortably.*
3. Este mes, el SEAT Ibiza que tú quieras por sólo 9.900 Ptas. al mes. *This month, the (whichever) SEAT Ibiza you want for only 9,900 pesetas a month.*
4. ... para que se compre un nuevo Olivetti. *... so that you'll buy a new Olivetti.*
5. Para que disfruten, desde 3.250 pesetas, de lugares de ensueño. *So that you'll enjoy the places of your dreams, from 3,250 pesetas.*

CHAPTER 14
Commands

A. *Una receta: La tortilla española.*

1. Añada las patatas y cebollas peladas y picadas.
2. Cocine a fuego lento.
3. No rehogue las patatas y las cebollas.
4. Espolvoree con sal.
5. Bata los huevos.
6. Ponga los huevos en la sartén.
7. Haga dorar los huevos.
8. No deje que se pegue la tortilla.
9. Sirva en una fuente.

B. *Una formación profesional.*

1. Encuéntrense en la oficina del señor Aguilar.
2. Traigan la calculadora.
3. Hagan preguntas.
4. Usen la computadora.
5. Sigan los consejos del gerente.
6. Estudien informática.
7. Lean el manual de telecomunicaciones.
8. Tengan cuidado con la entrada y salida de datos.

C. *Trámites de banco.*

1. Sí, retírelo. No, no lo retire.
2. Sí, acérquese a la ventanilla. No, no se acerque a la ventanilla.
3. Sí, fírmela. No, no la firme.
4. Sí, llénelo. No, no lo llene.
5. Sí, démela en pesos. No, no me la dé en pesos.

6. Sí, pídanoslo. No, no nos lo pida.
7. Sí, calcúlemelos. No, no me los calcule.
8. Sí, ciérrela. No, no la cierre.
9. Sí, cóbremelos. No, no me los cobre.

D. *¡Veámoslo todo en Perú!*

1. Demos un paseo por la zona de la Plaza de Armas. Vamos a dar un paseo …
2. Vamos de compras en el Jirón de la Unión. Vamos de compras …
3. Conozcamos la Universidad de San Marcos. Vamos a conocer …
4. Hagamos una excursión a Machu Picchu. Vamos a hacer …
5. Visitemos la catedral y unas iglesias de Cuzco. Vamos a visitar …
6. Quedémonos en Miraflores. Vamos a quedarnos …
7. Tomemos un colectivo a una playa limeña. Vamos a tomar …
8. Sentémonos en el Malecón. Vamos a sentarnos …

E. *¡Cómo no!*

1. Cómo no. Démosela. Cómo no. Vamos a dársela.
2. Cómo no. Saquémoslas. Cómo no. Vamos a sacarlas.
3. Cómo no. Vamos al museo por la tarde.
4. Cómo no. Caminemos por el parque. Cómo no. Vamos a caminar por el parque.
5. Cómo no. Inscribámonos en la clase de computación. Cómo no. Vamos a inscribirnos en la clase de computación.
6. Cómo no. Juguemos al tenis. Cómo no. Vamos a jugar al tenis.
7. Cómo no. Digámoselo a los chicos. Cómo no. Vamos a decírselo a los chicos.
8. Cómo no. Tumbémonos en la playa. Cómo no. Vamos a tumbarnos en la playa.

F. *¡Venid a la fiesta!*

1. Haced la torta, pero no le pongáis el glaseado todavía.
2. Abrid las botellas de sangría, pero no cortéis las rebanadas de naranja todavía.
3. Sacad los platitos para las tapas, pero no preparéis el chorizo y el pulpo todavía.
4. Poned la mesa, pero no coloquéis los claveles todavía.
5. Salid a comprar aceitunas, pero no vayáis todavía.

6. Destapad el vino, pero no lo serváis en un jarro todavía.
7. Colgad los globos, pero no los dejéis en la entrada.
8. Escoged los discos compactos, pero no pongáis música con palabrotas.

G.

1. Seáis pacientes.
2. Idos.
3. Decid la verdad.
4. Seáis encantadores.
5. Bañaos.
6. Escribid un cuento corto.
7. Asistid a la conferencia.
8. Tocad el piano.
9. Acostaos temprano.

H. *¡Tengo los nervios de punta!*

1. Da un paseo todos los días.
2. Haz ejercicio.
3. Toma una infusión de manzanilla.
4. Tranquilízate escuchando música.
5. No bebas mucha cafeína.
6. Duerme la siesta todas las tardes.
7. Reúnete con los amigos.
8. No te preocupes por tonterías.
9. Búscate otro novio.

I. *¡Paquito, deja de poner el grito en el cielo!*

1. Pórtate bien.
2. No hagas payasadas.
3. No seas terco.
4. Deja al perro en paz.
5. Recoge las migas de las galletas.
6. No derrames el perfume de tu mamá.
7. Hazme caso.
8. No te encierres en el baño.
9. Ven acá inmediatamente.

J. *¡Tito el desgraciado!*

1. Tito, date prisa.
2. Tito, no te lastimes.
3. Tito, no te cortes el dedo.
4. Tito, ten cuidado.
5. Tito, no te rompas el pie.
6. Tito, no enciendas los fósforos.
7. Tito, conduce más lentamente.
8. Tito, ponte una armadura.

K. *El médico aconseja …*

1. déjelo
2. te mojes
3. déle
4. juegues
5. hágale

6. te quites
7. tráigalo
8. ven
9. sal

L. *Sí, hágalo.*

1. Sí, dáselos.
2. Sí, mándenoslas.
3. Sí, entréguenmela.
4. Sí, pónmelo.
5. Sí, prepárenoslos.

6. Sí, sírvannoslo.
7. Sí, explícamela.
8. Sí, dígamelos.
9. Sí, enséñenselos.
   (Enseñémoselos.)

M. *No, no lo haga.*

1. No, no se los des.
2. No, no nos las mande(s).
3. No, no me la entreguen.
4. No, no me lo pongas.
5. No, no nos los prepare(s).
6. No, no nos lo sirvan.
7. No, no me la expliques.
8. No, no me los diga.
9. No, no se los enseñen. (No, no se los enseñemos.)

N. *¡Que lo hagan los otros!*

1. Que los lea Manolo.
2. Que las dibujen Terencio y Elena.
3. Que los observe Paulina.
4. Que los hagan los otros.
5. Que las investigue Samuel.
6. Que se dediquen a ellas mis amigos.
7. Que lo escriba Federico.

O.

1. Que ella se lo dé a Ud.
2. Que se vayan.
3. Que él se las mande.
4. Que no se te pierda la cartera.
5. Que vuelvan por la tarde.
6. Que no se les acaben los refrescos.

P. *Libro de cocina.*

1. Cortarlos a tiritas.
2. Añadir el vino.
3. Dejarlo evaporar.
4. Partirlos en trozos.
5. Tapar las patatas.
6. Secar los tomates.
7. Añadirlas a la salsa.

8. Removerlo.
9. Ponerla en una fuente.

Q. *El primer día de clase.*

1. Hagan el favor de ir al laboratorio de lenguas.
2. Tengan la bondad de aprender los diálogos de memoria.
3. Favor de traer el diccionario.
4. Tengan la bondad de matricularse si no lo han hecho.
5. Háganme el favor de comprar el libro de texto y el cuaderno de trabajo.
6. Favor de apuntarse en esta lista.
7. Hagan el favor de hacer hincapié en los ejercicios de fonética todos los días.
8. Tengan la bondad de no actuar mucho en grupo.
9. Favor de ver películas y leer periódicos en español.

R. *Busque empleo.*

1. llamar
2. enviar
3. escribir
4. presentarse

5. dirigirse
6. adjuntar
7. ponerse en contacto
8. concertar

S. *Escenas de teatro.*

Answers will vary.

T. *Estructuras en acción*

A. 1. No permitas que dejen sin bosques a tu hijo. *Don't let your child grow up without forests.*
   2. Hazle socio del Club del Árbol. *Make him/her a member of the Tree Club.*
   3. Planta un árbol para tu hijo. *Plant a tree for your child.*
   4. Llámanos al (91) 308 23 09 para más información. *Call us at (91) 308 23 09 for more information.*
   5. Regálale un árbol. *Give him/her a tree as a present.*

B. 1. Aproveche los precios de otoño. *Take advantage of fall prices.*
   2. No se pierda esta oportunidad. *Don't miss this opportunity.*
   3. compre ahora su celular *buy your cellular phone now*
   4. pague el equipo en julio a precio contado. *pay for it in July at a discount price.*

5. Exija su casilla de mensajes gratis. *Ask for your free voice mail.*
6. Llame hoy mismo al 339-5050. *Call today: 339-5050.*

C. 1. ¡No se la pierda! *Don't miss out!*
   2. Llame primero a: *Call first:*
   3. Visítenos en el stand 104. *Visit us at stand 104.*

D. 1. APRENDA INGLÉS *Learn English*
   2. ¡Mejore sus oportunidades ... ! *Improve your opportunities ... !*
   3. ... obtenga una vida mejor en Nueva York! *... live a better life in New York!*
   4. ¡Matricúlese ahora ... *Enroll today ... !*
   5. ... y reciba una semana gratis! *and receive a free week!*
   6. ¡Llame hoy! *Call today!*
   7. Pregunte por María. *Ask for Maria.*

CHAPTER 15
The Infinitive

A. *Fiestas y celebraciones.*

1. Los españoles quisieron celebrar el santo del Rey Juan Carlos el 24 de junio.
2. Uds. siempre procuraban ir de vacaciones en Semana Santa.
3. Paco no pudo salir con su novia el Día de los Enamorados.
4. Sueles comer una uva por cada campanada el 31 de diciembre.
5. Raúl y Pepita no consiguieron asistir a la Misa del Gallo este año.
6. Los niñitos esperaban recibir muchos regalos lindos el Día de Reyes.
7. No resuelves gastar bromas el Día de los Inocentes.
8. Debe haber unas fiestas grandes el Día de la Raza.
9. Decidí traerles flores y bombones a los tíos por el Año Nuevo.

B. *Expansión de oraciones.*

1. Sabían nadar muy bien.
2. Ud. mereció ganar más plata.
3. Logré terminar el proyecto.
4. Felipe teme estar solo en la casa.
5. Se prohíbe salir por esa puerta.
6. Han ofrecido tocar un vals.
7. Hacíamos limpiar la casa.
8. No dejaste escuchar los discos compactos.

C. *¿Qué hacen los estudiantes?*

1. para	8. de
2. en	9. con
3. en	10. a
4. a	11. de
5. de	12. con
6. a	13. de
7. en	14. que

D.

1. Solíamos (Estábamos acostumbrados a) cenar a las nueve de la noche.
2. ¿Por qué demoraron tanto en llamarnos?
3. Esteban se negó a prestarle dinero a Diego.
4. Trate de pagar con una tarjeta de crédito.
5. Vuelvan a cantar esa canción.
6. Voy a asistir a la conferencia.
7. Silvia amenazó con irse inmediatamente.
8. ¡Ellos sueñan con hacerse millonarios!

E. *Sinónimos.*

1. Pedro llegó a hacerse presidente de la empresa.
2. Consuelo presume de ser la mejor futbolista del equipo.
3. Los Arcos se dispondrán a recibir a sus tíos.
4. El profesor obligó a cerrar los libros.
5. Uds. se arrepintieron de perderse la boda.
6. Yo no me acordé de recoger los pasteles.
7. ¿Cómo es que comenzaste a hacer la tarea a las dos de la mañana?
8. No se permitía entrar en las salas de escultura.
9. Están vacilando en invertir dinero en la compañía.

F.

1. Te llamaremos antes de salir.
2. Viajaron a Ponce en auto sin parar.
3. Niños, acuéstense después de cepillarse los dientes.
4. Bernardo debe leer un libro en vez de mirar la televisión.
5. Voy a estar en la biblioteca hasta volver a casa.
6. Elena va a patinar con tal que Daniel patine también.
7. Invítales en caso de verlos.
8. Cuando llegamos a la fiesta, empezamos (nos pusimos) a bailar.

G. ¿Qué oyó?

1. Sí, lo oí retumbar.
2. Sí, lo oí maullar.
3. Sí, los oí despegar y aterrizar.
4. Sí, las oí susurrar.
5. Sí, los oí gritar.
6. Sí, la oí roncar.

H. ¿Qué vieron Uds.?

1. Los vimos trotar.
2. Las vimos hacer los bocadillos.
3. Lo vimos entrar en la discoteca.
4. La vimos dictar una conferencia.

I. .

1. que   3. para
2. para   4. que

J.

1. X   3. X
2. de   4. de

CHAPTER 16
Nouns and Articles

A. ¿Masculino o femenino?

1. el   14. el
2. el   15. la
3. el   16. la
4. la   17. el
5. el   18. el
6. la   19. la
7. la   20. el
8. el   21. el
9. la   22. el
10. el   23. la
11. la   24. el
12. el   25. el
13. la

B. Por parejas.

1. la profesora   9. la emperatriz
2. la reina   10. la actriz
3. la artista   11. la estadista
4. la abogada   12. la holandesa
5. la princesa   13. la cliente
6. la gobernadora   14. la atleta
7. la representante   15. la programadora
8. la policía

C.

1. El señor Galíndez se va en viaje de negocios el martes y volverá el jueves.
2. No ponga la sartén en el lavaplatos.
3. El inglés y el francés son las lenguas oficiales de Canadá.
4. Beethoven nació el diez y seis de diciembre de mil setecientos setenta.
5. Mis colores favoritos son el verde y el azul.
6. Vamos a recoger manzanas de ese manzano.
7. El pájaro (ave) oficial de los Estados Unidos es el águila.
8. ¿Les gustó más el crucero en el Mediterráneo o en el Caribe?
9. El leer es tan agradable.
10. Un frente tropical llegará mañana.
11. Vamos a invertir (Invertiremos) nuestro capital en una compañía internacional.
12. ¿Cómo se llaman los personajes de la novela?
13. Al cámara se le perdió su cámara.
14. En la película que vimos, los ángeles salvaron al bebé.
15. Los testigos hablaron con la víctima del accidente.

D. En plural.

1. los guantes   9. las toses
2. los lavaplatos   10. los martes
3. las religiones   11. los irlandeses
4. los orígenes   12. los paréntesis
5. los pizarrones   13. los señores Sánchez
6. los colores   14. las luces
7. las amistades   15. los tés
8. los reyes

E. El arca de Noé.

1. vacas   9. delfines
2. orangutanes   10. gorriones
3. elefantes   11. faisanes
4. avestruces   12. panteras
5. leones   13. tigres
6. castores   14. ovejas
7. loros   15. monos
8. cóndores

F. Sobre gustos no hay nada escrito.

1. Lucía pide guisantes.
2. Yo prefiero los espárragos.
3. Tú ordenas papas fritas.
4. Claudia y Jesús quieren macarrones.

5. Tenemos ganas de comer espinacas.
6. Ud. y Lourdes piden frijoles.
7. Ud. quiere palomitas de maíz.

G. *¡Que toque la orquesta!*

1. los pianos
2. las flautas
3. las violas
4. los clarinetes
5. los violonchelos
6. los violines
7. las trompetas
8. los trombones
9. las arpas
10. los oboes
11. los tambores
12. las tubas

H. *El artículo definido.*

1. la / las / aceitunas
2. el / los / ensayos
3. el / las / aguas
4. el / los / árboles
5. el / los / dulces
6. la / las / demoras
7. la / las / sales
8. el / los / pasaportes
9. el / los / volcanes
10. la / las / actividades
11. el / los / salvavidas
12. el / los / orígenes
13. la / las / fotos
14. el / los / meses
15. la / las / serpientes
16. el / los / sillones
17. la / las / mieles
18. el / los / lápices
19. el / los / franceses
20. la / las / veces
21. el / los / tenedores
22. la / las / pirámides
23. la / las / raíces
24. el / los / sacapuntas
25. la / las / pensiones
26. el / los / pintores
27. el / los / jardines
28. el / los / jugadores
29. el / los / esquíes (esquís)
30. el / los / panes

I. *¡Retrato de la heroína romántica!*

1. los ojos
2. las mejillas
3. las manos
4. los dedos
5. los labios
6. los dientes
7. el pelo
8. el cuello
9. las orejas

J. *¿Artículo definido o no?*

1. X
2. el
3. el
4. X
5. X
6. las
7. X
8. el
9. Las / la
10. El
11. X
12. la
13. Los / la
14. la
15. La / la

K.

1. La familia Sánchez va a la Florida en la primavera.
2. Florencia se puso los calcetines.
3. Denos los libros de latín.
4. A Juli y a Nicolás les encanta nadar.
5. ¿Qué hicieron los turistas en el mar?
6. Los gemelos se lavaron la cara.
7. Elías sabe portugués, habla italiano, lee ruso, y aprende alemán.
8. El baile de disfraz fue el sábado. Comenzó a las nueve y media de la noche.
9. La novela fue escrita en polaco y traducida al griego.

L. *¿Falta el artículo definido?*

1. X / X
2. el
3. X / X
4. los
5. X
6. X
7. X / X

M. *¡Artículos en el museo!*

1. El
2. un (al)
3. X
4. lo
5. del
6. Lo
7. del
8. las
9. X
10. X
11. las
12. el
13. un
14. el
15. los (unos)
16. al
17. las
18. la
19. unas
20. Un
21. lo
22. la
23. el
24. un

N. *El artículo indefinido.*

1. un / unos / mares
2. un *or* una / unos *or* unas / optimistas
3. un *or* una / unos *or* unas / órdenes
4. un / unos / paradores
5. un / unos / olores
6. un / unos / oboes

7. un / unas / áreas
8. una / unas / mochilas
9. un *or* una / unos *or* unas / jóvenes
10. un / unos / nadadores
11. un / unos / papeles
12. un / unos / voliboles
13. un / unos / menús
14. un / unos / cereales
15. un / unos / buzones
16. un / unos / irlandeses
17. un / unas / almas
18. un / unos / paraguas
19. un / unos / camarones
20. un / unos / garajes
21. una / unas / voces
22. un / unos / desfiles
23. una / unas / naciones
24. un / unos / lavaplatos
25. un / unos / lemas
26. una / unas / sucursales
27. un / unos / ascensores
28. un / unas / hablas
29. una / unas / postales
30. un / unas / aguas

O. En el taller.

1. un	6. una
2. un	7. unos
3. unos	8. una
4. un	9. unos
5. unas	

P. ¿Artículo indefinido o no?

1. X	6. un
2. un	7. X
3. X / X	8. X
4. X / X	9. un
5. X	

Q. ¿Dónde están todos?

1. Concepción y Simón fueron al puesto de periódicos.
2. Yo fui al ayuntamiento.
3. Domingo y Brígida fueron al supermercado.
4. Ud. fue al parque de atracciones.
5. Lourdes fue a la iglesia.
6. Mi hermano fue a la bolsa.
7. Nosotros fuimos a la estación de tren.
8. Fuiste al centro comercial.

R. ¿De quién es?

1. ¿De quién es el almacén? Es del señor Acosta.
2. ¿De quién son los peines? Son de Adela y Matilde.
3. ¿De quién es el equipaje? Es de las turistas.
4. ¿De quién son los discos compactos? Son del pianista.
5. ¿De quién es este llavero? Es de la empleada.
6. ¿De quién son las sartenes? Son del cocinero.
7. ¿De quién son las raquetas? Son de estas tenistas.
8. ¿De quién es el reloj? Es del doctor Villanueva.

S.

1. la florería del señor Valle
2. la oficina del presidente
3. los discos del programador
4. las vitrinas (los escaparates) de la tienda
5. la energía de la planta nuclear
6. los cuadernos de los estudiantes
7. las conferencias del profesor Salas

T. Un programa de concursos.

Answers will vary.

U. Estructuras en acción

1. un	12. una
2. X	13. la
3. la	14. La
4. la	15. X
5. la	16. el
6. La	17. Las
7. X	18. el
8. X	19. las
9. X	20. la
10. la	21. X
11. X (los)	

CHAPTER 17
Adjectives

A. ¿Cómo están?

1. Están felices.
2. Estoy contento.
3. Se encuentra nerviosa.
4. Se siente deprimido.
5. Se encuentran tristes.
6. Estamos cansados.

7. Se sienten enfermos.
8. Está preocupada.
9. Está aburrida.

B. *¡Don de gentes!*

1. Paco cree que Jacobo es listo.
2. La señora Alvarado piensa que Luisa es encantadora.
3. El profesor de cálculo encuentra a los hermanos inteligentes y trabajadores.
4. Nieves cree que Jacobo es sincero.
5. El señor Alvarado dice que Luisa es graciosa y generosa.
6. Las profesoras de literatura europea encuentran a Jacobo serio y responsable.
7. Los hijos de los Alvarado creen que Luisa es independiente y simpática.
8. Todo el mundo dice que Jacobo y Luisa son buena gente y corteses.

C. *¿Qué se piensa de ellos?*

1. arrogante
2. molesto
3. tacaños
4. tontos
5. mentirosa
6. desleales
7. engañosos

D. *Pintura mexicana.*

1. azul
2. amarillo
3. morena
4. rosada
5. blancos / azules
6. negros
7. marrón
8. roja
9. verde / marrón

E. *¡El Príncipe Azul!*

1. roja
2. amarillos
3. marrones
4. negros / rojos
5. amarillas / anaranjadas / verdes
6. negro
7. negro
8. morada
9. morados / grises

F. *Adjetivos pre- y pospuestos.*

1. mejor día
2. algunos discos compactos
3. muchos días
4. poemas renacentistas
5. energía nuclear
6. ambas clases
7. ojos castaños
8. suficiente
9. vino tinto
10. cuántas horas
11. peor decisión
12. políticas

G. *¡Qué exclamación!*

1. ¡Qué absurda situación!
2. ¡Qué clima tan perfecto!
3. ¡Qué partido más emocionante!
4. ¡Qué paella tan rica!
5. ¡Qué hermosos zapatos!
6. ¡Qué ideas más estupendas!
7. ¡Qué problemas más complicados!
8. ¡Qué frescas legumbres!
9. ¡Qué cariñosos niños!
10. ¡Qué reunión tan animada!

H. *Adjetivos: ¿forma apócope o no?*

1. primer
2. mala
3. grandes
4. buen
5. tercera
6. algún
7. ningún
8. San
9. buenas
10. gran
11. ninguna
12. algunas
13. Cualquier
14. Santa
15. primeros
16. tercer
17. mal

I. *Adjetivos: antes o después del sustantivo.*

1. mismo dentista
2. ciudad antigua
3. cosa cierta
4. medio portugués / medio mexicano
5. gran soldado
6. funcionario cualquiera
7. dramaturgo propio
8. pura agua
9. persona única
10. Cierta empresa
11. hombres pobres
12. vieja casa
13. muchos libros / mismo tema
14. cualquier regalo
15. únicos pianistas
16. pobre señora

J. *¿De dónde son?*

1. Sí, es ruso.
2. Sí, son canadienses.
3. Sí, es israelí.
4. Sí, es costarricense.
5. Sí, es guatemalteco.
6. Sí, son belgas.
7. Sí, es japonés.
8. Sí, es india.
9. Sí, son egipcias.
10. Sí, es inglesa.
11. Sí, es coreano.
12. Sí, son franceses.

K. *¡De muchos uno solo!*

1. Yo soy de origen neocelandés.
2. Teodoro e Irene son de origen salvadoreño.
3. Uds. son de origen libanés.
4. Gabriel es de origen vietnamita.
5. Adela y Rosa son de origen iraní.
6. Estanislao y Sofía son de origen griego.
7. Tú eres de origen marroquí.
8. Ud. y yo somos de origen taiwanés.
9. Gualterio es de origen húngaro.

L. *Sustantivos en plural.*

1. buenos
2. españoles
3. recogidas
4. ingleses
5. blancos
6. frescos
7. rojas
8. rebajados
9. minerales
10. nuevos
11. magníficas
12. negros

M. *El rodaje de una película.*

1. Federico Felino es el mejor director de cine joven.
2. Es su primer film doblado.
3. Será una gran película extranjera.
4. Tiene algunas escenas románticas.
5. Se oye un diálogo bueno.
6. Hay algunos efectos especiales.
7. Escribieron un guión inteligente.
8. Trabajaron en el film algunos intérpretes principales.
9. Hay algunos subtítulos bien traducidos.
10. La película tiene un argumento interesante.
11. La película ganará un premio cinematográfico importante.

N. *Diálogos.*

1. frita / fritos
2. hecho / hecha
3. muertas / muertos
4. comida / comidas
5. metido / metidos
6. pagada / pagadas
7. dormido / dormido
8. hechas / hecha

O. *¿Qué están haciendo?*

1. está acostada
2. está parado
3. están sentados
4. está asomada
5. están arrodillados
6. están tirados
7. está inclinada

P. *¡Preparados! ¡Listos! ¡Ya!*

1. Ya está bañado.
2. Ya están afeitados.
3. Ya está maquillada.
4. Ya estamos vestidos.
5. Ya estoy peinado.
6. Ya están duchados.
7. Ya estoy pintada.

Q. *¡A comer pues!*

1. Ya están puestos.
2. Ya está servida.
3. Ya está preparado.
4. Ya están rotos.
5. Ya está cortado.
6. Ya está hecha.
7. Ya están batidas.
8. Ya están pelados.

R. *Opciones y preferencias.*

1. Me gusta más la instrumental. Me gusta más la vocal.
2. Prefiero los serios. Prefiero los cómicos.
3. Prefiero uno chino. Prefiero uno francés.
4. Me gustan más los azules. Me gustan más los marrones.
5. Prefiero uno moderno. Prefiero uno viejo.
6. Me gusta más una particular. Me gusta más una estatal.
7. Prefiero las norteamericanas. Prefiero las extranjeras.
8. Quiero vivir en una grande. Quiero vivir en una pequeña.
9. Me interesan más las políticas. Me interesan más las naturales.

S. *En comparación.*

1. Luisa es más astuta que Ana. Ana es menos astuta que Luisa.
2. El museo de historia natural es mejor que el de arte. El museo de arte es peor que el de historia.
3. Yo soy más inteligente que mi novia. Mi novia es menos inteligente que yo.
4. Tu cuarto es más hermoso que el de Elena. El cuarto de Elena es menos hermoso que el tuyo.
5. La película francesa es más aburrida que la inglesa. La película inglesa es menos aburrida que la francesa.
6. Los cantantes son más talentosos que los bailarines. Los bailarines son menos talentosos que los cantantes.
7. Las blusas de seda son más elegantes que las de algodón. Las blusas de algodón son menos elegantes que las de seda.
8. Tu hermana es mayor que tu hermano. Tu hermano es menos grande que tu hermana.

T. *Comparación de adverbios.*

1. más / que // menos / que // tan / como
2. más / que // menos / que // tan / como
3. más / que // menos / que // tan / como

U. *Adjetivos: igualdad.*

1. La obra de teatro es tan divertida como la película.
2. Las clases de física son tan fáciles como las clases de cálculo.
3. Los documentales son tan artísticos como los reportajes.

4. Los platos griegos son tan sabrosos como los platos húngaros.
5. Esta actriz es tan célebre como ese actor.
6. El arroz es tan bueno como el maíz.
7. El príncipe es tan valiente como el rey.
8. Francisca es tan aburrida como su hermana María.
9. La inflación es tan baja como la de hace tres años.

V. *Nuestra clase.*

1. Juan Pablo es el estudiante más aplicado.
2. Fermín y Cosme son los estudiantes menos obedientes.
3. Silvia es la estudiante más simpática.
4. Irene y María son las estudiantes menos trabajadoras.
5. Verónica es la estudiante más inteligente.
6. Íñigo y Esteban son los estudiantes más habladores.
7. Sergio es el estudiante más encantador.
8. Rosa y Jacinto son los estudiantes menos preparados.

W. *¡Qué parque más precioso!*

1. Sí. Es interesantísima.
2. Sí. Es viejísimo.
3. Sí. Son hermosísimas.
4. Sí. Es grandísimo.
5. Sí. Parece ferocísimo.
6. Sí. Son simpatiquísimos.
7. Sí. Son larguísimas.
8. Sí. Es bellísimo.

X. *Visitando la ciudad.*

1. Allí se encuentra la plaza más imponente de la ciudad.
2. Aquí ven la catedral más antigua del estado.
3. En frente hay la universidad más conocida del país.
4. Ésta es la calle más larga de la ciudad.
5. En esta calle hay las tiendas más hermosas de la zona.
6. Allí está la tienda de comestibles más estimada del barrio.
7. Delante de nosotros hay el hotel más internacional del país.
8. En este barrio se encuentran los restaurantes más concurridos de la ciudad.
9. Aquí ven la casa más vieja de la ciudad.
10. Pronto veremos el estadio más grande de la región.

Y. *La clase de literatura.*

1. Es el poema más conocido de la literatura europea.
2. Es la obra de teatro más presentada del año.
3. Es la comedia más aplaudida del teatro nacional.
4. Es la novela más vendida de la literatura moderna.
5. Es la tragedia más estimada de nuestro teatro.
6. Es el poeta más respetado de su siglo.
7. Es el novelista más leído del mundo.
8. Es el dramaturgo más apreciado de nuestra época.

Z.

1. Yo leo más que Ud.
2. Ellos saben menos que nosotros.
3. Ignacio se queja tanto como su mujer.
4. Yo tengo más discos compactos que Federico.
5. Eva ve menos películas que Margarita.
6. Nosotros hacemos tantos viajes como ellos.
7. Nosotros tenemos más de diez mil libros en nuestra biblioteca.
8. El partido de fútbol fue más emocionante que esperaban.
9. ¡Quiero más joyas que me diste!
10. Éste es el abrigo más caro que he comprado.
11. Ruíz es el mejor programador de la compañía.
12. Ésta es la playa más bella del país.

AA.

Answers will vary.

BB. *Estructuras en acción*

1.

1. soleado	8. abundante
2. tormentoso	9. despejado
3. costero	10. matinal
4. occidental	11. débil
5. cubierto	12. ligero
6. nuboso	13. disperso
7. andaluz	14. flojo

2.

1. Estará nublado, lluvia, hasta tormentas.
2. Hará sol por casi toda la región.
3. Estará más y más nublado durante el día, lluvias hasta tormentas en la noche; no hará mucho viento.

4. Muy nublado con tormentas moderadas.
5. Estará nublado, particularmente en Menorca donde habrá lluvia.
6. Estará algo nublado en Ceuta y Melilla.
7. Estará nublado con lluvia ligera.
8. Estará claro por la mayor parte pero algo nublado en la costa.

CHAPTER 18
Demonstratives and Possessives

A. *Útiles de escuela.*

1. Estos libros de texto están bien escritos. / Esos libros de texto están bien escritos. / Aquellos libros de texto están bien escritos.
2. Compré este compás anteayer. / Compré ese compás anteayer. / Compré aquel compás anteayer.
3. Consultaré este atlas. / Consultaré ese atlas. / Consultaré aquel atlas.
4. Prefiero este papel cuadriculado. / Prefiero ese papel cuadriculado. / Prefiero aquel papel cuadriculado.
5. Esta marca de sacapuntas es conocida. / Esa marca de sacapuntas es conocida. / Aquella marca de sacapuntas es conocida.
6. Me gusta este diccionario de español. / Me gusta ese diccionario de español. / Me gusta aquel diccionario de español.
7. Estos bolígrafos no sirven. / Esos bolígrafos no sirven. / Aquellos bolígrafos no sirven.
8. Encontré estas reglas en esta papelería. / Encontré esas reglas en esa papelería. / Encontré aquellas reglas en aquella papelería.
9. Estas enciclopedias no tienen información sobre este tema. / Esas enciclopedias no tienen información sobre ese tema. / Aquellas enciclopedias no tienen información sobre aquel tema.

B. *De compras en El Corte Inglés.*

1. este
2. Ese
3. este
4. aquel
5. estas
6. ese / esas / aquella
7. Esta / ese
8. estas / esos / Este / esta / ese / aquel / esa
9. Esto

C. *Un crítico de restaurantes.*

1. Me gustó ésa más que aquélla.
2. Me gustaron aquéllos más que éstos.
3. Me gustó éste más que ése.
4. Me gustaron ésas más que aquéllas.
5. Me gustó éste más que ése.
6. Me gustaron éstos más que aquéllos.
7. Me gustó ésta más que ésa.

D. *¡En el depósito de artículos perdidos!*

1. No, no es suyo. Será de Martina.
2. No, no son suyas. Serán de nosotros.
3. No, no es suyo. Será de Rosita.
4. No, no son suyos. Serán de Uds.
5. No, no son suyas. Serán tuyas.
6. No, no es suyo. Será de la profesora Márquez.
7. No, no es nuestra. Será de Eduardo.

E. *Viajes.*

1. las maletas tuyas
2. el equipaje de mano nuestro
3. los cheques de viajero suyos
4. la bolsa de viaje suya
5. los maletines nuestros
6. la mochila suya
7. el pasaporte mío
8. las visas suyas
9. los billetes de ida y vuelta tuyos

F. *¡Fernando el fanfarrón!*

1. ¡Pero la mía es más moderna que la tuya!
2. ¡Pero los míos son más nuevos que los tuyos!
3. ¡Pero la mía es más simpática que la tuya!
4. ¡Pero la mía funciona mejor que la tuya!
5. ¡Pero las mías son más interesantes que las tuyas!
6. ¡Pero las mías son mejores que las tuyas!
7. ¡Pero el mío es más inteligente que el tuyo!

G. *¿Dónde está?*

1. Los suyos estarán en el estante.
2. El mío estará en mi cartera.
3. Las suyas estarán en la cómoda.
4. Los nuestros estarán en la gaveta.
5. La nuestra (La suya) estará en el escritorio.
6. Los nuestros estarán en el baño.
7. La mía estará encima del piano.

H. *¡Qué niño más repipí!*

1. No, no se salen con la suya.
2. No, no se sale con la suya.
3. Sí, me salgo con la mía.
4. No, no se sale con la suya.
5. No, no nos salimos con la nuestra.

6. Sí, te sales con la tuya.
7. Sí, os salís con la vuestra.

I.

1. Esto de la compañía es difícil de comprender.
2. Eso de nuestro viaje tiene que resolverse.
3. Vamos a tener que hablar de eso de comprar un coche nuevo.
4. Un viejo amigo mío llega el sábado.
5. ¿Cómo está tu familia?
6. Esperamos que gane nuestro equipo.
7. Lo suyo es traer las flores.
8. Lo mío es fotocopiar.

CHAPTER 19
Personal Pronouns: Subject, Object, Prepositional

A. *Identifique el sujeto de cada oración.*

1. nosotros
2. Ud., él
3. vosotras
4. Uds., ellos, ellas
5. yo
6. Ud., ella
7. vosotros, vosotras
8. tú
9. Uds., ellas
10. ella, Ud.

B. *Yo … pero tú …*

1. Yo trabajo de lunes a viernes, pero tú trabajas los fines de semana.
2. Nosotros estudiamos en una universidad particular, pero Uds. estudian en una universidad estatal.
3. Ellas viven en pleno centro, pero Ud. vive en las afueras.
4. Tú vas de compras el sábado, pero nosotros vamos de compras el jueves.
5. Él es abogado, pero yo soy profesor.
6. Ud. desayuna fuerte, pero ella desayuna poco.
7. Ellos escuchan música clásica, pero vosotros escucháis rock.

C. *Pronombres preposicionales.*

1. para él
2. contigo
3. según tú
4. por nosotros
5. salvo yo
6. sobre Ud.
7. conmigo
8. de vosotros
9. para ellas
10. por ti
11. menos tú
12. como yo
13. en ella
14. entre tú y yo

D. *Pronombres preposicionales.*

1. Sí, vivo cerca de ellas.
2. Sí, trabajaba en ella.
3. Sí, logramos hablar sobre ellos.
4. Sí, pagué un dineral por él.
5. Sí, salí con ellos.
6. Sí, hay mucho trabajo para ella.
7. Sí, se casó con él.
8. Sí, felicité a los jugadores por ella.

E. *¡Te equivocas!*

1. No, con ellas, no.
2. No, con él, no.
3. No, para ella, no.
4. No, por ella, no.
5. No, para ellos, no.
6. No, por él, no.
7. No, con ellos, no.
8. No, para ti, no.

F. *El a personal.*

1. X
2. a
3. X
4. al
5. a
6. A
7. a
8. X
9. X
10. X
11. a
12. X
13. X
14. al
15. a
16. X
17. a
18. al
19. X
20. A

G. *¡Un flechazo!*

1. a
2. a
3. a
4. a
5. a
6. a
7. A / a / a
8. a
9. a
10. a

H. *Verbos.*

1. Pida otra botella de vino.
2. Aprovechemos (Vamos a aprovechar) esta venta (liquidación).
3. Mira el hermoso mar.
4. Voy a esperarlos hasta las tres.
5. Busca a sus hermanos.
6. ¿Pagaron sus padres los muebles?
7. Escuchemos la orquesta.

I. *¡A jugar pues!*

1. Sí, quiero jugarlo. / Sí, lo quiero jugar.
2. Sí, prefiero jugarla. / Sí, la prefiero jugar.
3. No, no quiero hacerlo. / No, no lo quiero hacer.
4. No, no prefiero tirarlos. / No, no los prefiero tirar.

5. Sí, quiero hacerla. / Sí, la quiero hacer.
6. No, no prefiero jugarla. / No, no la prefiero jugar.
7. Sí, quiero verlas. / Sí, las quiero ver.
8. No, no prefiero jugarlo. / No, no lo prefiero jugar.
9. No, no quiero hacerlo. / No, no lo quiero hacer.

J. Mi coche.

1. No, no lo cambié. / Voy a cambiarlo.
2. No, no lo reparé. / Voy a repararlo.
3. No, no las pedí. / Voy a pedirlas.
4. No, no las llevé. / Voy a llevarlas.
5. No, no lo usé. / Voy a usarlo.
6. No, no los puse. / Voy a ponerlos.
7. No, no lo arreglé. / Voy a arreglarlo.
8. No, no lo instalé. / Voy a instalarlo.

K. Bernardo y los coches.

1. Piensa comprarlo. / Lo piensa comprar.
2. Tiene que llenarlo. / Lo tiene que llenar.
3. Trata de leerlas. / Las trata de leer.
4. Prefiere conducirlo. / Lo prefiere conducir.
5. Debe cargarla. / La debe cargar.
6. Teme tenerlo. / Lo teme tener.
7. Procura evitarlas. / Las procura evitar.

L. Lo significa you.

1. la conozco	5. lo llevo
2. los comprendo	6. las conozco
3. la llamo	7. lo ayudo
4. las busco	8. los veo

M. ¡Míralo!

1. Márquelos. / No los marque.
2. Llámalo. / No lo llames.
3. Juéguenlo. / No lo jueguen.
4. Sáltelas. / No las salte.
5. Hazla. / No la hagas.
6. Mírenla. / No la miren.
7. Lánzala. / No la lances.
8. Séalo. / No lo sea.
9. Levántenlas. / No las levanten.

N. ¿Lo ha visto Ud.?

1. Sí, lo he visto.	5. No, no las he visto.
2. No, no los he visto.	6. Sí, las hemos visto.
3. Sí, la hemos visto.	7. Sí, lo he visto.
4. No, no los he visto.	8. No, no la he visto.

O. La catedral de Sevilla.

1. Los arquitectos están empleándolo. / Los arquitectos lo están empleando.
2. Los constructores van destruyéndola. / Los constructores la van destruyendo.
3. Los dibujantes están dibujándolas. / Los dibujantes las están dibujando.
4. Los maestros de obras están echándolos. / Los maestros de obras los están echando.
5. Los frailes y las monjas siguen rezándolas. / Los frailes y las monjas las siguen rezando.
6. Los trabajadores siguen colocándolos. / Los trabajadores los siguen colocando.
7. Los albañiles van trayéndolas. / Los albañiles las van trayendo.
8. Los obreros están poniéndola. / Los obreros la están poniendo.

P. Una criada muy trabajadora.

1. La revista la puse en su mesa de trabajo.
2. A los chicos los llevé al cine.
3. El balón de fútbol lo dejé en el jardín.
4. Al bebé lo acosté.
5. Sus libros los arreglé en su cuarto.
6. Las cartas que escribió las eché al correo.
7. Su camisa amarilla la colgué en su armario.
8. Las galletas que compró las comí.

Q. El complemento indirecto.

1. Te traje los refrescos.
2. Nos dieron flores.
3. Me mandó una tarjeta postal.
4. Le dijeron los precios.
5. Le ofrecimos el escritorio.
6. Le preguntó la hora.
7. Os expliqué mis ideas.
8. Les recordaron el cumpleaños de Leo.

R. Salir ganando o salir perdiendo.

1. A nosotros / a Uds.
2. a mí / a ti
3. a él / a ella
4. A ti / a ellos
5. A vosotros / a nosotros
6. A ellas / a Ud.

S. Un mal día en el barrio.

1. Un joven le arrebató el bolso.
2. Dos hombres enmascarados les robaron treinta mil pesos.

3. Los compradores le pagaron con billetes falsos.
4. Alguien le quitó la bicicleta.
5. Su hijo de cuatro años le escondió las llaves del coche.
6. El juez le suspendió el permiso de manejar.
7. Éste le ocultó sus salidas con Elvira Camacho.
8. Su sobrino le pidió prestado mucho dinero.

T. En plural.

1. Le encantan sus perfumes.
2. Nos interesan estas novelas.
3. Les quedan unos exámenes.
4. Te entusiasman las comedias.
5. Os importan las ideas.
6. Me hacen falta unas guías.
7. Les fascinan estas materias.
8. Le faltan unos cuadernos.

U. En el futuro.

1. Nos van a importar sus problemas.
2. No les va a quedar mucho dinero.
3. Le va a encantar visitar a sus abuelos.
4. No les va a sobrar comida.
5. Os va a convenir viajar en tren.
6. Te van a fascinar esos cuadros.
7. Me van a entusiasmar sus obras.
8. No le van a interesar esos programas.

V.

1. A él.
2. Ellos.
3. A ella no.
4. Yo no.
5. Nosotros sí.
6. A Ud.
7. A mí sí.
8. Yo sí.

W. Los Castellón planean un viaje.

1. (A mí) Me gustaría hacer un viaje a España.
2. (A mí) Me encantaría visitar a mis parientes en Venezuela y Argentina.
3. (A mí) Me interesaría ir de camping en Nuevo México o Arizona.
4. Y (a mí) me fascinaría ver la nueva moda italiana.
5. (A mí) me entusiasmaría seguir a Miguel Induráin en el Tour de Francia.
6. Nos conviene tomar una decisión lo antes posible.
7. Nos sobran sugerencias. ¡Echemos suertes!
8. ¡Me toca a mí primero!

X. Sucesos inesperados.

1. Se nos acabó
2. Se le perdieron
3. Se me olvidó
4. Se os quedó
5. se te rompieron
6. se les ocurrió
7. se les cayeron

Y. Prevenir contra lo inesperado.

1. Que no se les olvide asistir a la conferencia.
2. Que no se le pierdan los anteojos.
3. Que no se le acabe la paciencia.
4. Que no se os queden los cheques de viajero.
5. Que no se le rompan las estatuillas de porcelana.
6. Que no se te ocurran tales cosas.
7. Que no se les caiga la torta de chocolate.

Z.

1. ¿Se le perdió su cartera? / No, se me había quedado en casa.
2. Se les están acabando los pasteles en la pastelería. / ¿No se te ocurrió comprarlos esta mañana?
3. ¡Tengan cuidado! ¡Se les van a caer las tazas! / ¡Se nos rompieron dos ya!
4. Se me olvidó recoger (buscar) a Tere y a Leo. / ¿No se te ocurrió que esperaban toda la noche?

AA. Dos pronombres complementos directo e indirecto.

1. Me los dijeron.
2. Se los hemos puesto.
3. Está explicándosela.
4. Os lo muestro.
5. ¿Te la darían?
6. Se los cuentas.
7. Nos las ha hecho.
8. Devuélvamelo.
9. Me las estaban enseñando.
10. ¿A quién se lo vendiste?
11. Os la había escrito.
12. ¿Nos los prestarás?
13. Apréndanselas.
14. ¿Estáis preguntándoselo?
15. Se la pusieron.
16. Se los preparó.
17. Estará bajándomelo.
18. Vendámosela.
19. Estuvimos trayéndoselos.
20. Te la apagaré.

BB. *Algo pasará. | Algo pasó.*

1. Van a traérmela. / Me la van a traer.
2. Acaba de decírtelo. / Te lo acaba de decir.
3. Vamos a hacérselos. / Se los vamos a hacer.
4. Acabo de ponéroslas. / Os las acabo de poner.
5. Va a mostrárselo. / Se lo va a mostrar.
6. Acabáis de comprárnosla. / Nos la acabáis de comprar.
7. Vas a contármelos. / Me los vas a contar.
8. Acabo de arreglárselas. / Se las acabo de arreglar.
9. Van a subírtela. / Te la van a subir.
10. Acabamos de dároslo. / Os lo acabamos de dar.
11. Vamos a describírselo. / Se lo vamos a describir.
12. Acabas de probársela. / Se la acabas de probar.
13. Va a limpiártelos. / Te los va a limpiar.
14. Acabo de encontrárselas. / Se las acabo de encontrar.
15. Van a pedírmela. / Me la van a pedir.
16. Acabas de buscárnoslo. / Nos lo acabas de buscar.
17. Vamos a llevároslos. / Os los vamos a llevar.
18. Acaba de servírselas. / Se las acaba de servir.
19. Vais a devolvérselo. / Se lo vais a devolver.
20. Acabo de cantártela. / Te la acabo de cantar.

CC. *¡Mami, papi, cómprenmelo!*

1. Papi, dámelos. / Sí, hijita, te los doy.
2. Mami, cómpramelas. / Sí, hijita, te las compro.
3. Juan, préstamela. / Sí, hermanita, te la presto.
4. Amparo, cómpramelos. / Sí, hermanita, te los compro.
5. Abuelo, regálamelo. / Sí, hijita, te lo regalo.
6. Elvira, sírvemelo. / Sí, hermanita, te lo sirvo.
7. Tía, pónmelas. / Sí, hijita, te las pongo.

DD. *¿Las cosas claras?*

1. Fernando gave it to her (him, them, you). / She (He, You) gave it to Fernando.
2. The professors told it to you (her, him, them). / You (They) told it to the professors.
3. The neighbor lent them to you (her, him, them). / He (You, She) lent them to the neighbor.
4. My colleagues asked her (him, them, you) for them. / They (You) asked my colleagues for them.
5. Laura returned it to you (him, her, them). / He (She, You) returned it to Laura.

EE. *¡En español, por favor!*

1. —¿Sabes si las tiendas están abiertas? —No te lo sabría decir. *or* No sabría decírtelo.
2. No sé cómo Raúl se las apaña / arregla / compone. Cree que todo el mundo se la tiene jurada. *or* que todos se la tienen jurada.
3. Cualquier estudiante que se porte mal tendrá que vérselas conmigo.
4. —¿Son estudiantes Ramón y Sergio? —No, no lo son. Son programadores. —Creo que son muy inteligentes. —Sí, lo son.
5. Pedrito no se pudo poner el abrigo, entonces se lo puse yo.
6. —¿Debo pedirles sus apuntes de historia a Alicia y a Pedro? —Pídeselos a él. No se los pidas a ella.

FF.

Answers will vary.

GG. *Estructuras en acción*

I. 1. Se vende una casa.
    2. Huarte le da al comprador una sauna equipada e instalada.
    3. Se le da al cliente dos noches en el Hotel Alcora de Sevilla por conocer el chalet piloto.
    4. Satafi es el lugar donde se vende el chalet.
II. 1. You'll only have to deal with how to decorate it.
    2. Huarte is giving you a luxurious gift.
    3. or if you prefer it
    4. Visit us or call us.
    5. We'll give you (reward you with) two fantastic nights at the Alcora Hotel in Sevilla.

CHAPTER 20
Relative Pronouns

A. *Seamos precisos.*

1. Veo al médico que tiene su consulta en aquel edificio.
2. Quiero ver la película que se rodó en Perú.
3. Me gustan más las revistas que se publican en Asunción.
4. Prefiero el restaurante que sirve comida del Caribe.
5. Voy a la peluquería que está en la calle del Conde.
6. Quiero comprar los libros que nos recomendó el profesor.
7. Llevo el abrigo que me regalaron mis padres para Navidad.
8. Hablábamos con la secretaria que contratamos la semana pasada.
9. El mecánico que conoce el vecino repara mi coche.
10. Estoy leyendo la carta que me mandó Silvia ayer.

B. *Más precisiones.*

1. La profesora que todos los estudiantes admiran. / La profesora que enseña francés y español. / La profesora que acaba de casarse. / La profesora que conocen mis padres.
2. La casa que compraron Juana y Rafael. / La casa que tiene patio y piscina. / La casa que construyeron en 1975. / La casa que es de ladrillos.
3. El regalo que mis hermanos y yo recibimos hace dos días. / El regalo que nos mandaron mis tíos. / El regalo que te enseñé ayer. / El regalo que nos gustó tanto.
4. El restaurante que nuestros amigos abrieron el año pasado. / El restaurante que sirve comida española. / El restaurante que tiene manteles rojos. / El restaurante que frecuentan muchos artistas.
5. El senador que eligió el pueblo el año pasado. / El senador que prometió combatir la inflación. / El senador que está casado con una extranjera. / El senador que los obreros apoyan.

C. *El profesor, quien …*

1. El señor Mora, quien se encarga de los archivos, es secretario general de la universidad.
2. El profesor Uriarte, quien asistió a un congreso en la UNAM, enseña química.
3. Los estudiantes, quienes se gradúan en junio, tienen que entregar una tesis.
4. La doctora Arrieta, quien figura en el tribunal de exámenes, tiene dos ayudantes de laboratorio.
5. Estos decanos, quienes planean el programa, trabajan en la facultad de ingeniería.
6. El rector de la universidad, quien dicta conferencias de ciencias políticas, es abogado.
7. Algunos estudiantes de medicina fueron a hablar con el profesor Quijano, quien estaba ya en el salón de actos.
8. La profesora Arenas, quien hace investigaciones de biología, se jubila el año que viene.

D. *… a quien / … a quienes*

1. Mis primos a quienes vi en Caracas hace dos años están de vacaciones en Estados Unidos.
2. La pintora a quien vieron en la exposición sólo pinta acuarelas.
3. La muchacha a quien le di un regalo ayer me dio las gracias hoy.
4. Los amigos a quienes llamamos a la una de la mañana no quisieron salir.
5. Los vecinos a quienes buscábamos se habían mudado.
6. La dependiente a quien Ud. conoció el año pasado ya no trabaja en esta tienda.
7. El señor a quien encontraste en la calle es mi profesor de cálculo.

E. *¿Sujeto u objeto?*

1. a quien	5. quienes
2. quien	6. a quien
3. quienes	7. a quien
4. a quienes	8. quien

F. *¿El que o lo que?*

1. los que	5. lo que
2. lo que	6. el que
3. la que	7. las que
4. lo que	

G. *¿El cual o lo cual?*

1. los cuales	5. lo cual
2. lo cual	6. el cual
3. la cual	7. las cuales
4. lo cual	

H. *Te enseño mi ciudad.*

1. Éstas son las calles debajo de las cuales / debajo de las que hay varias líneas de metro.
2. Allí ven la facultad cerca de la cual / cerca de la que vivimos.
3. Allí está el cine en frente del cual / en frente del que hay un restaurante.
4. Ven y te presento a los muchachos con quienes / con los cuales / con los que solemos pasar los domingos aquí.
5. Ésta es la plaza en medio de la cual / en medio de la que hay una exposición de arte.
6. Aquéllos son los edificios detrás de los cuales / detrás de los que hay un mercado al aire libre.
7. El barrio hacia el cual / hacia el que caminamos ahora es muy antiguo.
8. Éste es el río al otro lado del cual / al otro lado del que se encuentran unas tiendas elegantes.

I. En *de varios significados.*

1. en que
2. en el que
3. en que
4. en que
5. en el que
6. en los que
7. en que
8. en las que

J.

1. The benefit concert was an event through which the university received a lot of money.
2. A new skyscraper has been built from which there are fabulous views of the city.
3. These are the books according to which Professor Sorolla reached his conclusions.
4. I always remember the Greek ruins we walked through.
5. A bookstore opened next to where an ice cream store will open.
6. Let's get together in front of (opposite) the candy shop where we met.
7. There's the fountain in front of which we fell in love!
8. What's the name of the company Antonio works for?
9. Do you know which are the ideas on which the researchers formulated their theories?

K. *Cuyo.*

1. cuyas
2. cuyos
3. cuyo
4. cuya
5. cuyo
6. cuyas
7. cuya
8. cuyos

L.

1. Now you know the reason why I got angry.
2. We used to live in a neighborhood where there were many shops.
3. There to the right is the door through which the actors enter and leave.
4. I don't understand the reasons why the union declared the strike.
5. The children didn't tell me where they were heading.
6. They're the hours during which Menchu does her homework.
7. Here's the newspaper stand behind which Sergio and Sol agreed to see each other.

CHAPTER 21
Adverbs

A. *Para describir acciones.*

1. alegremente
2. descuidadamente
3. cruelmente
4. artísticamente
5. normalmente
6. abiertamente
7. francamente
8. nerviosamente
9. evidentemente
10. responsablemente
11. débilmente
12. verdaderamente
13. torpemente
14. violentamente
15. perspicazmente
16. burlonamente
17. comercialmente
18. sagazmente
19. honradamente
20. humildemente
21. difícilmente
22. admirablemente
23. estupendamente
24. afectuosamente
25. vulgarmente

B. *¿Cómo hablaron?*

1. Sí, habló nerviosamente.
2. Sí, habló honestamente.
3. Sí, hablaron tristemente.
4. Sí, hablé furiosamente.
5. Sí, habló malhumoradamente.
6. Sí, hablamos incómodamente.
7. Sí, hablé distraídamente.
8. Sí, habló incoherentemente.

C. *Cada adverbio en su lugar.*

1. Pronunciaron las frases mal.
2. Trabajaron muy responsablemente.
3. Las cosas andaban bien.
4. Quiero que mis hijos vivan felizmente.
5. Su última película fue muy interesante.
6. El niño miraba a sus padres inocentemente.

7. Patricia encontró esos problemas sumamente difíciles.
8. Salgan de la casa muy rápidamente.
9. Encontramos el proyecto totalmente ridículo.

D. *En otras palabras.*

1. Martín y Fernando trabajan inteligentemente.
2. Lola canta maravillosamente.
3. Carmen y Pilar escriben hábilmente.
4. El señor Ibáñez conduce prudentemente.
5. Lucas estudia diligentemente.
6. Marcos pinta divinamente.
7. Carla y Pedro viajan frecuentemente.
8. Alfonso juega enérgicamente.

E. Con + *sustantivo* = *adverbio* + -mente.

1. con inteligencia
2. con armonía
3. con elegancia
4. con diligencia
5. con delicadeza
6. con cariño
7. con alegría
8. con ligereza
9. con lealtad
10. con suavidad
11. con fuerza
12. con felicidad
13. con tristeza
14. con calor
15. con claridad

F. *Exprese los siguientes diálogos en español.*

1. ¿Ya fueron al supermercado? / Todavía no.
2. Vuelvo en seguida. / Ven acá ahora mismo.
3. Mariana no puede encontrar a su gato por ningún lado. / ¡Mire en lo alto! El gato está en el árbol.
4. ¿Están los chicos por aquí? / Estarán dentro de la casa. / ¿Sabes si están arriba o abajo? / Estarán escondidos detrás de algún mueble.

G. *Un adverbio más otro.*

1. elegante y cuidadosamente
2. lenta y suavemente
3. cariñosa y calurosamente
4. oportuna y apasionadamente
5. ligera y perezosamente
6. fiel y lealmente
7. sabia y astutamente
8. deprimida y tristemente

CHAPTER 22
Prepositions

A. *¿A o nada?*

1. a	6. X
2. X	7. A
3. a	8. X
4. X	9. a
5. al / a	

B.

1. Escribí el informe a doble espacio.
2. A su llegada a medianoche se acostó.
3. El bebé anda a gatas.
4. Me encanta la ropa que está hecha a mano.
5. Los niños comieron todas las galletas a escondidas.

C. *¿De o nada?*

1. de	5. X
2. X	6. de
3. X	7. de
4. del	8. de

D.

1. Me regalaron una pulsera de oro y pendientes de plata.
2. Bernardo es alto de estatura y ancho de espaldas.
3. ¿Quieres trabajar de día o de noche?
4. La pobre de su tía está de luto.
5. Se pusieron de rodillas.

E.

1. I recognized her (you) by her (your) voice.
2. They sold it to me for $2,000.
3. The value has gone up by 15%.
4. The workers are against the strike.

F.

1. Pensamos ir en avión.
2. Los recogeré en el aeropuerto.
3. Miguel es más alto que Juan en una cabeza.
4. ¿Dices esto en serio o en broma?

G. *¿Con qué?*

1. con leche	4. con una sonrisa
2. con una llave	5. con caramelos
3. con cuerda	6. con esfuerzo

H. *¿Qué falta?*

1. del
2. Con
3. a
4. en
5. en
6. (para) con
7. de
8. a
9. de
10. con
11. con
12. en
13. a
14. a
15. en
16. de
17. a
18. de
19. a
20. de
21. Al
22. Al

I. *¡Pepita la preguntona!*

1. Fui al almacén por un par de zapatos.
2. La felicitamos por su cumpleaños.
3. Me duele (la espalda) por jugar tenis por cuatro horas.
4. No lo terminó por pereza.
5. Los veremos (verán) por la tarde.
6. Salieron por el puente más céntrico.
7. Iremos por salchicha y queso.
8. Tendré que hacerla por escrito.
9. Darán un paseo por el bulevar Alameda.
10. Voy a pasar por Micaela y Angustias.

J. *¿Una película encantadora?*

1. Por la fotografía.
2. Por el argumento.
3. Por la dirección.
4. Por el guión.
5. Por los decorados.
6. Por la banda sonora.
7. Por los efectos especiales.
8. Por el diálogo.

K. *¿Para qué?*

1. Para ganar plata
2. Para aprender mucho.
3. Para ayudar a mamá y a papá.
4. Para demostrarle mi cariño.
5. Para perfeccionarlo.
6. Para ser buen ciudadano.
7. Para llevar una vida moral y feliz.

L. *¡Una semana muy ocupada!*

1. Para pasado mañana.
2. Para la semana entrante.
3. Para el martes.
4. Para finales del mes.
5. Para el mes próximo.
6. Para las cinco de la tarde.
7. Para el fin de semana.

M. *¿Por o para?*

1. para / por / por / por
2. para / por
3. Para / Por
4. por / para / Para / por / para
5. Para / para / por
6. por / Para / por / Para / para / por
7. por / Para
8. por / Por / Por / por
9. por / por

N.

1. I'm an American on both sides.
2. We'll go with you earlier just in case.
3. They praise aunt Natalia to the skies.
4. Ricardo must have called for a reason.
5. Three times eight is twenty-four.
6. Mortadelo and Filemón are two of a kind.
7. "I'll love you forever," don Quijote said to Dulcinea.

O. *¡Vivan los fiesteros!*

1. Beatriz fue por los panecillos. Pagó treinta dólares por ellos.
2. Carlos y Leo fueron por los refrescos. Pagaron cincuenta y cinco dólares por ellos.
3. Paula y yo fuimos por las servilletas. Pagamos siete dólares por ellas.
4. Tú fuiste por los fiambres. Pagaste ciento setenta y nueve dólares por ellos.
5. Yo fui por la torta. Pagué dieciocho dólares por ella.
6. Uds. fueron por el vino. Pagaron cuarenta y tres dólares por él.
7. Ud. fue por la fruta. Pagó veintidós dólares por ella.

P. *En español, por favor.*

1. Mi tarea está (queda) sin terminar.
2. Puse (Coloqué) un libro sobre otro (encima de otro).
3. Lo vi salir hacia atrás.
4. Vivió durante muchos años entre los indios.
5. Hace calor hasta en la sierra (en la montaña).
6. Los inmigrantes sienten amor hacia su nuevo país.
7. Nos siguieron desde la puerta del cine.
8. Estoy leyendo un libro sobre Puerto Rico.

Q. *Ejercicio de conjunto.*

1. c	11. c
2. c	12. c
3. c	13. c
4. a	14. a
5. a	15. a
6. b	16. b
7. a	17. a
8. b	18. c
9. b	19. c
10. a	20. c

R. *Preposiciones: por, para, y mas.*

Answers will vary.

S. *Estructuras en acción*

1. de	6. sobre
2. por	7. a
3. de	8. en
4. de	9. para
5. de	10. en

CHAPTER 23
Interrogative Words and Question Formation

A. *Los detalles, por favor.*

1. ¿De qué se quejaba?
2. ¿En qué se interesan?
3. ¿De qué se jacta?
4. ¿Con quién se casó?
5. ¿En qué se metieron?
6. ¿En qué se fija?
7. ¿De qué se ríe?
8. ¿De quién se enamoró?
9. ¿Con quiénes soñó?

B. *¿Quiénes son?*

A. 1. ¿De dónde es? / ¿De qué nacionalidad es?
   2. ¿Qué es? / ¿Cuál es su profesión?
   3. ¿Dónde trabaja? / ¿Para qué / quiénes trabaja?
   4. ¿Dónde vive?
   5. ¿Con quién está casado?
   6. ¿Cuántos hijos tienen?

B. 7. ¿Dónde nació? / ¿En qué país nació?
   8. ¿De qué origen es? / ¿De dónde son sus abuelos?

9. ¿Cuándo se mudó al Canadá? / ¿Cuántos años tenía cuando se mudó al Canadá? / ¿Adónde se mudó cuando tenía cuatro años?
10. ¿Qué estudia? / ¿Dónde estudia?
11. ¿Para qué estudia?
12. ¿Dónde vive? / ¿Con quiénes vive?

C. 13. ¿Qué ganó?
   14. ¿Qué es? / ¿Dónde es un héroe nacional?
   15. ¿Por quién fue condecorado? / ¿Quién lo condecoró? / ¿Qué le hizo el rey español?
   16. ¿Cuántas bicicletas tiene?
   17. ¿Cuál de sus bicicletas le gusta más? / ¿De dónde es la bicicleta que le gusta más? / ¿De qué color es la bicicleta que le gusta más?
   18. ¿Qué quiere hacer?
   19. ¿Adónde irá de vacaciones? / ¿Para qué irá al Caribe?
   20. ¿A quiénes llevará? / ¿Cuántas hijas tiene?

C. *¿Cómo? ¡Habla más fuerte!*

1. ¿Adónde? / ¿A cuál?
2. ¿Cuántas?
3. ¿Cuántos?
4. ¿Cuántos?
5. ¿A quién?
6. ¿Cuánto?
7. ¿De qué?
8. ¿Cuál?
9. ¿Cómo? / ¿Con qué?
10. ¿Cómo? / ¿En qué?
11. ¿A qué hora? / ¿Adónde?
12. ¿Cuándo? / ¿Antes de qué? / ¿Adónde?

D. *Estudiantes.*

A. 1. ¿Cuántas?
   2. ¿Cuáles?
   3. ¿Quién?
   4. ¿Cómo?
   5. ¿Cuántos?
   6. ¿Por qué?
   7. ¿Cuándo?
   8. ¿Qué?
   9. ¿A qué?

B. 10. ¿De quién?
   11. ¿Qué?
   12. ¿Dónde?
   13. ¿De qué?
   14. ¿Cuál?
   15. ¿Adónde?
   16. ¿quién?
   17. ¿Cómo? / ¿Qué?
   18. ¿Qué / ¿Por qué?
   19. ¿Dónde?

E. Un testigo.

1. ¿Dónde?
2. ¿Qué?
3. ¿Cuándo? / ¿A qué hora?
4. ¿Cuál?
5. ¿Quién?

6. ¿Adónde?
7. ¿De dónde?
8. ¿Cuántos?
9. ¿Cuántos?

F. Una conversación telefónica.

1. ¿De parte de quién?
2. ¿Dónde queda la casa?
3. ¿De quién es el coche?
4. ¿De qué color es?
5. ¿A quién vas a llevar?
6. ¿A qué hora llegarán?
7. ¿Cuántos tienes?
8. ¿A quiénes piensas ver?
9. ¿Cuándo será?
10. ¿Quiénes llegan?
11. ¿Cuánta plata gastaste? / ¿Cuánto gastaste?
12. ¿Qué tiempo hace?
13. ¿Cómo se encuentran?
14. ¿Hasta cuándo te quedas?
15. ¿Cuál quieres?
16. ¿Qué jugaron?

G. Vamos a comprar boletos.

1. ¿Cuándo vamos a comprar los boletos / los billetes (sacar las entradas) para la obra de teatro?
2. ¿Qué te parece si vamos mañana? ¿Dónde queda la taquilla?
3. En la avenida Pamplona. ¿Cuántos boletos necesitamos (nos hacen falta)?
4. Seis. ¿Cuánto cuestan (valen)?
5. Dieciocho dólares cada uno. ¿Quién(es) los paga(n)?
6. Cada persona pagará el billete suyo. ¿Qué día vamos?
7. El jueves. ¿A qué hora empieza la función?
8. A las ocho. ¿A quién invitas?
9. ¡A nadie! ¡El billete es demasiado caro! (¡El billete cuesta demasiado caro!) ¿Cómo llegamos?
10. En coche o en tren (metro).

H. ¡Maravillas naturales de las Américas!: Para expresar la magnitud

1. ¿Cuánto tiene el río Iguazú de largo?
2. ¿Qué longitud tiene el río Amazonas?
3. ¿Cuánto mide el río Mississipi de largo?
4. ¿A qué altura está el lago Titicaca?

5. ¿Cuánto tiene el desierto de Atacama de largo?
6. ¿Qué altura tiene el monte McKinley?
7. ¿Cuánto mide la cumbre Aconcagua de alto?

I.

1. ¿Cuál?
2. ¿Qué?
3. ¿Cómo?
4. ¿Cuál?

5. ¿Cómo?
6. ¿Cuál?
7. ¿Qué?

J.

1. ¿Para quién son estas rosas?
2. ¿Sobre qué hablaron los ingenieros?
3. ¿En qué oficina trabaja Celeste?
4. ¿Con cuántas personas fue Alberto?
5. ¿De quiénes son los disquetes?
6. ¿Hacia dónde caminabas?
7. ¿Por dónde entró Jeremías?
8. ¿Con quién soñó?
9. ¿En qué se metieron?

K. ¿Cuál es la pregunta?

1. ¿Aprenden Gustavo y Melinda francés?
2. ¿Trabaja Pepe en una tienda de videos?
3. ¿Toca Ud. piano?
4. ¿Se han vestido los niños?
5. ¿Jugará Cristóbal tenis?
6. ¿Se matriculó Elena anteayer?
7. ¿Deben Uds. quedarse unos días más?
8. ¿Está Ramona a dieta?

L. ¿Ser/estar + adjetivo + sujeto?

1. ¿Son traviesos estos niños?
2. ¿Son bonitas las margaritas?
3. ¿Estaba descompuesto el televisor?
4. ¿Está abierto el museo?
5. ¿Es italiana la revista?
6. ¿Fueron robadas las joyas?
7. ¿Están rotos los pantalones?
8. ¿Es buena esta marca?
9. ¿Fue impresionante el espectáculo?

M. Para hacer un picnic.

1. No, Pedro no. Los compra Memo.
2. No, Domingo y Toni no. Nos llevan Salvador y Bartolo.
3. No, Dora no. Las va a preparar Leonor.
4. No, Jorge no. Los traerá Miguel.
5. No, Carmen no. Piensa llevarlos Marcos.
6. No, nosotros no. Los harán Olivia y Nacho.

7. No, Jesús y Marta no. Los invitarás tú.
8. No, yo no. Se ocupa de ella Mari.

N. *¡Cuántas preguntas!*

1. Felipe me preguntó qué haría en la tarde.
2. Isabel me preguntó con quiénes había salido (*or* salí).
3. Carlos me preguntó por qué no quería jugar baloncesto.
4. Sol me preguntó a qué hora había vuelto (*or* volví) a casa.
5. Claudio me preguntó para cuándo necesitaba escribir el informe.
6. Mi hermanita me preguntó cuándo la llevaba a una discoteca.
7. Mis primos me preguntaron por qué no les invitaba al parque de atracciones.
8. Mi mamá me preguntó por qué tenía dolor de cabeza.
9. Yo me pregunté a mí mismo por qué me había levantado (*or* me levanté) de la cama.

O. *Una adivinanza.*

Answers will vary.

P. *Estructuras en acción*

1. ¿Dónde tiene lugar (es) la corrida de toros / la novillada? / ¿Qué tiene lugar en Las Ventas / Madrid?
2. ¿Qué día es la Gran novillada? / ¿Cuál es la fecha de la Gran novillada?
3. ¿A qué hora es la gran novillada?
4. ¿Cuántos novillos hay?
5. ¿Qué es un novillo?
6. ¿Quiénes son los toreros? / ¿Cómo se llaman los toreros?
7. ¿Cuánto pagan los niños acompañados? / ¿Quiénes entran gratis / sin pagar?
8. ¿Qué día es la Gran corrida? / ¿Cuál es la fecha de la Gran corrida de toros?
9. ¿A qué hora es la corrida?
10. ¿Cuántos toros hay?
11. ¿Para qué se venden localidades?
12. ¿Para quiénes son las localidades?
13. ¿Qué día se venden?
14. ¿Cuándo se venden las localidades? / ¿Cuáles son las horas de venta?

CHAPTER 24
Negative and Indefinite Words

A. *¡No!*

1. No, no fui nunca / jamás.
2. No, no aprendimos chino tampoco.
3. No, nadie ha llamado.
4. No, no va a tomar álgebra nunca más.
5. No leeré ni la novela ni el guión de la película.
6. No, ninguno (ningún jefe) renunció a su puesto.
7. No, no conoció a nadie.
8. No, no queda ninguno.
9. No, nunca limpio la casa los sábados.
10. No, no he visto a ninguna.

B. *¡Angustias, la aguafiestas!*

1. No queda nada de la comida.
2. No hay refrescos tampoco.
3. No bailan ni los chicos ni las chicas.
4. No se acerca ninguno de los chicos para hablarme.
5. No canta bien ningún cantante.
6. No tiene ganas nadie de quedarse.
7. No dan fiestas divertidas nunca.

C. *¡Qué iluso!*

1. ¡Qué va! Nadie te regaló dos millones de dólares.
2. ¡Qué va! Ninguna chica dice que eres un Adonis.
3. ¡Qué va! Nunca / Jamás sacas un diez en tus exámenes.
4. ¡Qué va! Tú ni nadas ni patinas mejor que nadie.
5. ¡Qué va! Los reyes de España no te mandaron nada.
6. ¡Qué va! Tú tampoco vas a la luna.
7. ¡Qué va! Conchita no va a salir contigo nunca más.
8. ¡Qué va! Tus padres no te van a regalar ni un Jaguar ni un Ferrari.

D. *Hay que ser negativo.*

1. nada / nadie	8. nunca acabar
2. En la vida / Nunca	9. de nada
3. nada / algo	10. nadie
4. nunca	11. no solamente / sino también
5. sino también	12. ninguna
6. de nada	
7. alguien	

E. ¿Cómo se dice eso en inglés?

1. I can't stand her at all!
2. None of that!
3. They're going to see each other at the usual time.
4. They don't call her charming for nothing.
5. Guillermo says he hasn't the slightest idea.
6. All the time and all the plans came to nothing.
7. When all is said and done all the arguing was useless.
8. What you're saying has nothing to do with the present situation.

F. ¿Algo? ¿Nada? ¿Nunca?

1. a
2. b
3. b
4. a
5. b
6. a
7. a
8. b
9. a

G. ¡En español, por favor!

1. No por nada renunció a su puesto.
2. Llamarán en cualquier momento.
3. Caminamos todo el día por toda la ciudad.
4. Cualquiera podría ayudarnos con el trabajo.
5. Toda avenida está embotellada (Todas las avenidas están embotelladas) en las horas punta.
6. Hay ruinas romanas por toda España.

H. ¡Finales dramáticos o "Lo que el viento se llevó"!

1. Aunque te querré para siempre, tengo que decir: "¡hasta nunca!"
2. Más vale algo que nada. / Algo es algo.
3. ¡Nada de ir a Marte antes de graduarte!
4. ¡Y aquí acaba el cuento de nunca acabar!
5. De algo lo / la conozco. Será alguien.
6. ¡Haz lo que quieras! ¡Ve adonde quieras! ¡Yo no te olvidaré nunca jamás!
7. ¿Este final? ¿Ese final? ¡Yo estoy contento(a) con cualquiera de los dos!
8. Nada más. ¡Mañana será otro día!

I.

Answers will vary.

J. Estructuras en acción

1. ¿Have you ever dreamed of being in … ?
2. The Holy Land

3. Travel on the Roads of Faith.
4. Galilee, Tiberias, Nazareth, Bethlehem, Jerusalem
5. audience with the Pope, Rome, Assisi, Florence
6. Hay salidas a Jerusalén todos los meses / cada mes.
7. Los hoteles son de primera clase.
8. Habla español.
9. Se sirven desayunos y cenas.
10. No se incluyen los impuestos aéreos.
11. Aeroméxico es de México y El Al es de Israel.

CHAPTER 25
Numbers; Dates; Time

A. Para hacer un inventario.

1. cien grapadoras
2. mil ochocientos veintiún tacos
3. mil quinientos cuarenta y nueve rotuladores y bolígrafos
4. setecientas cincuenta y una cajas de gomas, grapas y sujetapapeles
5. cuatrocientas sesenta y siete cajas de papel de escribir y sobres
6. novecientas nueve agendas de entrevistas y calendarios
7. mil tubos de pegamento y etiquetas
8. mil trescientos ochenta y un sujetalibros de metal y de plástico

B. El censo: población de países.

1. treinta y dos millones novecientos mil
2. treinta y cuatro millones doscientos noventa y seis mil
3. trece millones quinientos veintiocho mil
4. diez millones novecientos treinta y tres mil
5. treinta y nueve millones ciento dieciocho mil
6. noventa y dos millones trescientos ochenta mil

C. ¡Todos juntos en los Estados Unidos!

1. Silvia y Adela viven en el piso doce.
2. Carlos vive en el quinto piso.
3. Yo vivo en el primer piso.
4. Margarita vive en el noveno piso.
5. Ana María vive en el décimo piso.
6. Patricio vive en el cuarto piso.
7. Lucía vive en el tercer piso.
8. Daniela vive en el piso catorce.

D. *El premio Nobel.*

1. mil novecientos noventa / mil novecientos catorce
2. mil novecientos ochenta y nueve / mil novecientos dieciséis
3. mil novecientos ochenta y dos / mil novecientos veintiocho
4. mil novecientos setenta y siete / mil ochocientos noventa y ocho / mil novecientos ochenta y cuatro
5. mil novecientos setenta y uno / mil novecientos cuatro / mil novecientos setenta y tres

E. *¡Qué desastre!*

1. del treinta de julio al cinco de agosto de mil novecientos setenta / treinta y un muertos
2. del diecinueve al veinte de septiembre de mil novecientos setenta y cuatro / dos mil muertos
3. del diez al diecisiete de septiembre de mil novecientos ochenta y ocho / doscientos sesenta muertos
4. del veinticuatro al veintiséis de agosto de mil novecientos noventa y dos / catorce muertos

F. *En el tren turístico.*

1. El sábado a las siete y treinta (y media).
2. El sábado a las once treinta y seis.
3. El sábado a las veintiuna (horas) treinta.
4. El domingo a las diez y treinta.
5. A las catorce horas.
6. El domingo a las dieciséis treinta.
7. A las dieciocho treinta y nueve.

G. *Operaciones matemáticas.*

1. $174 + 89 = 263$
2. $603 - 281 = 322$
3. $49 \times 5 = 245$
4. $1284 \div 4 = 321$
5. $80 \times 3/4 = 60$
6. $15.000 \times .30 = 4.500$

H. *¿Cuál es la fecha?*

Answers will vary.

CHAPTER 26
Idioms, Expressions, and Proverbs

A. *Tener.*

1. éxito
2. pies ni cabeza
3. en la punta de la lengua
4. pelo de tonto
5. los huesos molidos
6. buena suerte (buena estrella)
7. malas pulgas
8. ojos de lince
9. mala cara / los nervios de punta
10. vergüenza / líos

B. *Tomar.*

1. Amparo se lo tomó con calma.
2. Los García tomaron a pecho la muerte del vecino.
3. Pedro tomó a broma / risa las diabluras de su hijo.
4. La profesora tomó a mal lo que le dijo Marianela.
5. Paco tomó partido por Juan Carlos en la discusión.

C. *Estar.*

1. estar hecho polvo
2. estar calado / mojado hasta los huesos; estar hecho una sopa
3. estar sin blanca
4. estar hecho una fiera
5. estar a sus anchas / estar como el pez en el agua

D. *¿Qué le pasó a don Juan?*

1. de menos
2. flores
3. se las echaba
4. chispas
5. la bronca

E. *Dar. ¿Qué se dio en cada caso?*

1. la lata / guerra
2. por vencidos
3. el golpe de gracia
4. rienda suelta
5. por sentado

F. *¿Qué quieren hacer?*

1. hacer las paces
2. hacer su agosto / hacerse rico
3. hacer un papel
4. hacer la vista gorda
5. hacer de las suyas

G. *Ir, llevar, quedar.*

1. va sobre ruedas
2. Quedamos en
3. Se llevan como el perro y el gato.
4. llevarte un chasco
5. lleva la contraria
6. llevar a cabo
7. quedé boquiabierto
8. se quedó con el día y la noche / se quedó sin blanca

H. *Definiciones.*

1. d
2. e
3. f
4. b
5. i
6. a
7. j
8. g

I. *¿Cuál es?*

1. c
2. a
3. c
4. b
5. b

J. *Sinónimos.*

1. f
2. h
3. c
4. i
5. d
6. e
7. a
8. g

K. *Antónimos.*

1. g
2. e
3. i
4. a
5. j
6. c
7. f
8. b

L. *Sinónimos.*

1. g
2. d
3. a
4. b
5. i
6. c
7. j
8. e

M. *¿Qué se diría?*

1. b
2. a
3. a
4. c
5. c

N. *¡El zoológico de expresiones!*

1. la mona / mona: You can't make a silk purse out of a sow's ear.
2. pájaro: A bird in the hand is worth two in the bush.

3. perro: Nonsense! Don't give me that!
4. gato / liebre: Don't get taken in.
5. El sapo / la sapa: Beauty is in the eye of the beholder.
6. peces: big shots
7. caballo: Never look a gift horse in the mouth.
8. gato: Something's fishy here.

CHAPTER 27
Word Formation and Diminutives

A. *¿Y el verbo original?*

1. formar
2. comprender
3. dominar
4. preparar
5. convertir
6. decidir
7. obligar
8. complicar

B. *El sustantivo que falta.*

1. el comportamiento
2. el encarcelamiento
3. el consentimiento
4. el movimiento
5. el pensamiento
6. el planteamiento
7. el tratamiento
8. el nombramiento
9. el crecimiento

C. *Verbos nuevos.*

1. saborear *to savor, relish*
2. gotear *to drip, leak*
3. golpear *to hit, beat*
4. teclear *to run one's fingers over the keys, to strike the keys repeatedly*
5. hojear *to leaf through*
6. zapatear *to stamp one's feet*
7. patear *to kick*

D.

1. encasillar
2. grease, to grease, engrasamiento
3. ensañar
4. embotellar, embotellamiento
5. emparejamiento
6. enfrentamiento

E. *El detective del diccionario.*

1. e
2. f
3. h
4. g
5. c
6. b
7. d
8. a

F. *Acertijos léxicos.*

1. to flower, bloom
2. to strengthen
3. to moisten
4. to strengthen
5. humidifier

G. *Formación de verbos.*

1. endurecer
2. embellecer
3. enflaquecer
4. ennoblecer
5. enloquecer
6. ennegrecer
7. enrojecer
8. enronquecer
9. ensordecer

H. *¿Qué significa?*

1. pastry chef
2. spoonful
3. hat shop
4. coffee pot
5. salad bowl
6. pencil case
7. silly thing *or* silly remark
8. boatload
9. slam of a door
10. stepdaughter
11. salt-shaker
12. party-lover

I. *Diminutivos.*

1. la vocecita
2. la cartita
3. el trajecito
4. el pececito
5. el cuentecito
6. la piernecita
7. el caballito
8. el bosquecito
9. el dolorcito
10. la cabecita
11. el laguito
12. suavecito
13. el vientecito
14. el juguito
15. el carrito
16. fuertecito
17. chiquito
18. nuevecito
19. fresquito
20. la lucecita

CHAPTER 28
¡Ojo! Common Errors and Pitfalls

A. *¿Cómo se dice?*

1. dejar
2. salir / deje
3. te vayas (te marches) / dejes
4. se marchó (se fue) / dejó
5. salimos
6. deja / salir
7. salió
8. salieron
9. dejan

B. *¿Saber o conocer?*

1. conoce
2. conocen
3. Sabe
4. conozco
5. sabe

C. *¿Oyes?*

1. oídos
2. la oreja
3. buen oído
4. la oreja
5. oído

D. *Quedar.*

1. Nos quedan dos semanas en Puerto Rico.
2. Quédate con el dinero. A mí no me hace falta.
3. Me he quedado sin salidas.
4. Se quedaron con una familia mexicana.
5. Les quedan tres oraciones por traducir.
6. Quedó sordo a causa de / por la explosión.
7. ¿Dónde queda el correo, por favor?
8. Paula y yo quedamos en ir al cine.

E. *¿Cómo se dice eso en español?*

1. ¿Quién rompió mi periódico? / ¿Quién me rompió el periódico?
2. Mi silla está rota.
3. La radio está descompuesta.
4. Tengo el abrigo roto. / Mi abrigo está roto.
5. Espero que no se nos descomponga el coche.
6. No comprendemos por qué rompió a llorar.
7. No te rompas la chaqueta.
8. Elena rompió con su novio.
9. El enemigo rompió el fuego.
10. Quien rompe paga.

F. *Está mal.*

1. Marqué mal. / Marqué un número equivocado.
2. Tomamos un avión equivocado / que no debíamos.
3. ¿Qué le pasa a la grabadora?
4. No es el momento adecuado.
5. Leí mal el título.
6. Tienes los guantes al revés.
7. Tiene un puesto que no le conviene.
8. La definición está mal / es inexacta / es incorrecta.
9. Hice mal en no creerlo.
10. Sumaste mal.

G. ¡A completar!

1. se perdió
2. falta
3. perder
4. erró el tiro / falló el blanco
5. no entendí / no oí / no comprendí
6. falla
7. faltan
8. echo de menos / extraño
9. desaparecidos

Index